PHP and MySQL
by Example

PHP and MySQL by Example

Ellie Quigley

with Marko Gargenta

PRENTICE
HALL

Upper Saddle River, NJ • Boston • Indianapolis • San Francisco
New York • Toronto • Montreal • London • Munich • Paris • Madrid
Capetown • Sydney • Tokyo • Singapore • Mexico City

Many of the designations used by manufacturers and sellers to distinguish their products are claimed as trademarks. Where those designations appear in this book, and the publisher was aware of a trademark claim, the designations have been printed with initial capital letters or in all capitals.

The authors and publisher have taken care in the preparation of this book, but make no expressed or implied warranty of any kind and assume no responsibility for errors or omissions. No liability is assumed for incidental or consequential damages in connection with or arising out of the use of the information or programs contained herein.

The publisher offers excellent discounts on this book when ordered in quantity for bulk purchases or special sales, which may include electronic versions and/or custom covers and content particular to your business, training goals, marketing focus, and branding interests. For more information, please contact:

U.S. Corporate and Government Sales
(800) 382-3419
corpsales@pearsontechgroup.com

For sales outside the United States, please contact:

International Sales
international@pearsoned.com

Visit us on the Web: www.prenhallprofessional.com

 This Book Is Safari Enabled

The Safari® Enabled icon on the cover of your favorite technology book means the book is available through Safari Bookshelf. When you buy this book, you get free access to the online edition for 45 days.

Safari Bookshelf is an electronic reference library that lets you easily search thousands of technical books, find code samples, download chapters, and access technical information whenever and wherever you need it.

To gain 45-day Safari Enabled access to this book:

• Go to http://www.prenhallprofessional.com/safarienabled
• Complete the brief registration form
• Enter the coupon code B1RZ-TMVP-LB3I-QGP5-U6Y5

If you have difficulty registering on Safari Bookshelf or accessing the online edition, please e-mail customer-service@safaribooksonline.com.

Library of Congress Cataloging-in-Publication Data

Quigley, Ellie.
  PHP and MySQL by example / Ellie Quigley with Marko Gargenta.
    p. cm.
  Includes index.
  ISBN 0-13-187508-6 (pbk. : alk. paper) 1. Web site development. 2.
Web databases—Design. 3. PHP (Computer program language) 4. MySQL
(Electronic resource) I. Gargenta, Marko. II. Title.
  TK5105.888.Q54 2006
  006.7'6—dc22

                                               2006030160

ISBN 0-13-187508-6
Text printed in the United States on recycled paper at Courier in Stoughton, Massachusetts.
2nd Printing   May 2007

Contents

12   Regular Expressions and Pattern Matching   497

13   Introduction to MySQL   567

15   PHP and MySQL Integration   647

Preface

Over the past few years, students taking my Perl/CGI course continued to ask me when I would be graduating from CGI to PHP, and whether I would offer a course or write a PHP "by Example" book. I didn't really take the idea of a book seriously until attending a PHP/MySQL class here in San Francisco a few years ago, where I met Marko Gargenta, who was the teacher of that class and the inspiration for this book. We had lunch together and I mentioned to him that the girl sitting next to me in the class was a Web designer, with little programming experience. She was concerned that she couldn't keep up with the class and wondered if I knew where she could find a book that explained PHP for designers, not just programmers. Marko had heard similar concerns from his students. We talked about how to address this issue, and from that conversation, the seeds were sown for *PHP and MySQL by Example*.

Although, theoretically, the Web designer/developer should need no PHP programming experience to change the content of a page, and the programmer should be concerned only with the logic, such as calculations, sending data to a database, and so on, they do not always work in isolation. For example, suppose a page is designed so that when the user enters bank information in an HTML form, a PHP program, after doing some calculations, finds that there are insufficient funds, and sends back an error in a bold red font. In such a case, PHP and HTML are integrated—one to calculate and produce the error message, the other to display it in a bold red font. Keeping the design and program logic separated may be the goal, but it is often impossible with the complexities of today's Web development.

And then there is the issue of the database management system. Where does the processed data get stored? Who designs the database and its tables? Who administers it? How does the information get from the Web page, to the PHP program, and then to the database? Enter MySQL. Is this yet another world in isolation?

Since my first meeting with Marko, I was challenged to bring these technologies together. When Prentice Hall agreed to publish our book, the learning curve was steep, and after the initial draft was done, I began teaching "An Introduction to PHP and MySQL Programming" from the PDF version of that first draft. I noticed that more Web designers were signing up than programmers, and they came in with trepidation that it would be way over their heads. But with the real-world examples and labs we provided, they started to enjoy feelings of success on the first morning. It was wonderful to witness both designers and programmers sharing their experiences without the artificial boundary that has kept them isolated from each other in the workplace.

The mission of *PHP and MySQL by Example* is to create a gentle yet thorough introduction to the shared power of PHP and MySQL, to make static HTML pages dynamic. The labs and exercises have been tested by myself, Marko, and our students. I think you will find this "by Example" book a helpful and complete guide, no matter what side of the Web site you support, or even if you are just starting your own.

Acknowledgments

Many people helped with the creation of this book. I'd like to thank Mark L. Taub, my longtime editor at Prentice Hall; Vanessa Moore, the most gifted compositor on the planet; and Julie Nahil, a great production editor. Matthew Leingang, Sander van Zoest, David Mercer, and Jason Wertz provided extremely helpful manuscript reviews. Any remaining mistakes are my own.

I'd also like to thank the students in my classes who provided valuable input for the labs. These include Rita McCue, Sanjay Shahri, Ryan Belcher, Debra Anderson, and Catherine Nguyen.

The fantastic illustrations in the book were created by Elizabeth Staechelin and Daniel Staechelin. And many thanks to the artists who provided artwork for the art gallery example. They are Elliott Easterling, Laura Blair, Stuart Sheldon, and Todd Brown.

Errata and solutions to the labs can be found on the book's Web site at *www.prenhall-professional.com/title/0131875086*. The Northwind database script, used in the chapters, can be found at *http://marakana.com/download/sql/northwind.sql*.

Ellie Quigley
San Francisco, California
September 2006

1

Introduction

1.1 From Static to Dynamic Web Sites

1.1.1 Static Web Sites

"The dream behind the Web is a common information space in which we communicate by sharing information. . . ."

—Tim Berners-Lee

Sir Tim Berners-Lee

When Tim Berners-Lee invented the World Wide Web in 1989, he unleashed an information revolution unparalleled since Gutenberg invented the printing press in the fifteenth century. Within less than 10 years the world as we knew it would be forever changed by his creation.

A 25-year-old computer consultant, Tim Berners-Lee started his initial work on the Web while working at CERN, a physics lab in Geneva, Switzerland. CERN was a huge scientific research center consisting of thousands of researchers and hundreds of systems. Berners-Lee first attempted to organize the documents on his hard drive by linking them together, which culminated in a hypertext language making it possible to link and distribute related documents, not only on his computer, but on networks of computers. His system kept track of the researchers, their projects and papers, the software they were using, their computers, and so on. To retrieve and send documents, he developed a simple protocol, HTTP (the Hypertext Transfer Protocol), and created HTML (the Hypertext Markup Language) to describe the layout for the text in the documents. The early Web was like an online library, documents connected by links, where the high-energy scientific community could freely read and access information throughout their company and eventually around the world.

The original Web was funded by the government, limited to research and education. The Web sites were made up of a collection of documents written in the HTML language. The pages were text based, simple, and static. Every time the user reloaded a page in his or her browser, it looked exactly the same. It consisted of HTML text, images, and links. It was not the complex commercial Web we know today where you can do anything from online shopping, to trading stocks, booking vacations, or finding a mate. Static Web pages were useful for sending and retrieving reports, pictures, and articles, but they couldn't manage data that changed, remember users' names and preferences, instantly create customized output from a database, or embed streaming video into a page on the fly. As the Web grew and became a virtual shopping mall, competitors needed Web sites that would lure in potential buyers and traders with an interactive and exciting experience, quick response time, and on-the-fly feedback. They needed dynamic Web sites.

1.1.2 Dynamic Web Sites

A dynamic Web site is one with content that is regenerated every time a user visits or reloads the site. Although it can be as simple as displaying the current date and time, in most cases it requires the use of a database, which contains the site's information, and a scripting language that can retrieve the information from the database. Google and Yahoo! are examples of dynamic sites, search engines that create customized pages based on a key word or phrase you type. The resulting page is created on the fly, customized just for you, based on your request. Farms of powerful computers all over the world are constantly taking such requests and processing them. In the early days of the Web, processing was done through the Common Gateway Interface, called CGI, a server-side technology that allowed Web developers to create dynamic sites. Most CGI scripts were written in Perl. A browser would send information from an HTML Web page, such as information from a fillout form, to the server for processing. The server then would create a gateway to an external program called a CGI script or helper program. Although any programming language could be used, the most popular language for CGI was Perl. The Perl script would then parse the data, generate HTML based on certain conditions, send an e-mail, open a file or database, and send information through the gateway back to the server, where it then was relayed onto the browser. (See the top portion of Figure 1.1.)

Although the basic underlying process of creating dynamic Web sites hasn't changed, new languages have evolved, making the process much simpler by allowing the processing to be embedded right in the server.[1] PHP is such a language. A PHP script can be embedded right in the Web page. It can generate HTML and images on the fly, retrieve up-to-date information from a file or database, encrypt data, remember user preferences, and so on. It executes PHP instructions and inserts the results right back into the Web page before the server sends the page back to the browser, thus making the page truly dynamic. (See the bottom portion of Figure 1.1.)

---

1. To imply that Perl is outdated is not the intention here. Perl has Mason and mod_perl to allow Perl and HTML to be embedded in the Apache server.

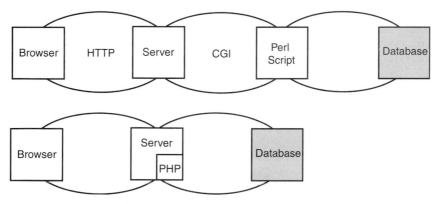

Figure 1.1   The process of creating dynamic Web sites.

Web sites often handle huge amounts of information. A database management system is essential for storing, retrieving, and updating that information. MySQL, the world's most popular open source database, has become the choice for applications that interact with database-enabled Web sites. PHP and MySQL, working together, form a marriage of two powerful technologies used to produce dynamic Web pages. This book will show you how that marriage works.

1.1.3   What Is Open Source?

> "Free software" is a matter of liberty, not price. To understand the concept, you should think of "free" as in "free speech," not as in "free beer."
>
> —The Free Software Foundation, *http://www.gnu.org/philosophy/free-sw.html*

PHP and MySQL represent the latest generation of open source applications. What does that mean? In the beginning Berners-Lee envisioned making information freely accessible to everyone. As the Web evolved, this idea of "free" took on different meanings for different groups. But however "free" is defined, it is safe to say that proprietary[2] (privately owned and controlled) software is not free. (See *http://www.gnu.org/philosophy/free-software-for-freedom.html#relationship.*) The Open Source movement is designed to make software source code freely available with limited restrictions. According to the Open Source Initiative,

> The basic idea behind open source is very simple: When programmers can read, redistribute, and modify the source code for a piece of software, the software evolves. People improve it, people adapt it, people fix bugs. And this can happen at a speed that, if one is used to the slow pace of conventional software development, seems astonishing.

---

2. Microsoft Windows, Adobe Photoshop, and WinZip are examples of proprietary software.

For the complete discussion, see *http://www.opensource.org/docs/definition.php*.

PHP and MySQL are both open source. Simply stated, you can download and use these applications without a credit card or a free trial period.

1.2 About PHP

Rasmus Lerdorf

So what is PHP? PHP is a simple, fast, portable scripting language well suited for development of database-enabled Web sites. It was developed in 1995 and is currently powering tens of millions of Web sites worldwide. The predecessor to PHP was PHP/FI, Personal Home page/Forms Interpreter, developed by Rasmus Lerdorf in 1995 to help him track the number of visitors accessing his online résumé. It was basically a set of Perl/CGI scripts later rewritten by Lerdorf in the C language and open-sourced; that is, made freely available. PHP was very Perl-like in sytnax, but whereas Perl is an all-purpose, jack-of-all-trades scripting language, PHP was designed specifically to master the Web. PHP instructions can be embedded with HTML right in the Web page so that whenever the page is loaded, PHP can execute its code. PHP made processing forms easier by providing automatic interpretation of form variables. It allowed for interaction with databases. It enabled users to create simple dynamic Web sites. The toolset Rasmus Lerdorf developed was so popular that in 1997, PHP/FI 2.0 was released. Due to the popularity of this new release, Lerdorf was soon joined by a core group of developers, who continued to provide improvements and enhancements to the new language. By this time, there where thousands of users and approximately 50,000 Web sites running PHP/FI pages.

Zeev Suraski and Andi Gutmans, two students attending Technion-Israel Institute of Technology, needed a language for their university e-commerce project. They chose PHP/FI for their project. Dissatisfied with its limitations and bugs, they put their project aside, and rewrote PHP almost from scratch. PHP 3.0 was a significant departure from the previous code base. The new language supported add-on modules and had a much more consistent syntax. At this time, the meaning of the acronym changed as well. PHP now stands for PHP: Hypertext Preprocessor. PHP 3.0 was released in 1998 and is the closest version to PHP today.

By May 2000, PHP 4 was released. The core of PHP 4 was entirely rewritten to improve the performance of complex Web applications and improve modularity of the platform. Zeev Suraski and Andi Gutmans, the authors of PHP 3, introduced a new parsing engine, called the Zend engine,[3] which is the scripting language that powers PHP today. Because of their internationally recognized authority, Suraski and Gutmans founded Zend Technologies, the PHP company, and their contributions to PHP have been a major reason for its explosive worldwide growth. See *www.zend.com*.

---

3. The term Zend is a *portmanteau*, a word created by combining the letters in their first names: Zeev and Andrew

Version 4 offered an open Application Programming Interface (API), allowing other programmers to write modules for PHP, modules that would extend its functionality, modules that allowed PHP 4 to support most of the available databases and Web servers available. With this release, PHP became a serious programming language and platform for developing and deploying complex Web applications.

The latest incarnation of PHP was released in July 2004. PHP 5 added a whole new object-oriented model to the language. The new model is based on Zend Engine 2 and greatly improves PHP performance and capabilities. Most of the functionality is backward compatible, allowing programs written in older versions to continue working.

According to a Netcraft survey, as of October 2005, 23,299,550 domains and 1,290,179 IP addresses endorse PHP. See *http://www.php.net/usage.php*.

1.2.1   Where to Get PHP and Documentation

You can get the latest distribution of PHP for Apache and Microsoft servers at the official Web site for PHP, *php.net* (see Figure 1.2). This Web site is also an excellent up-to-date

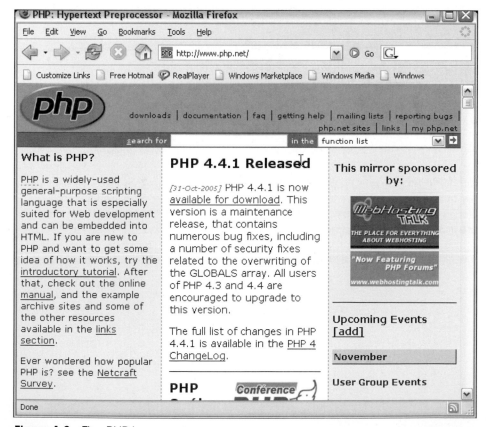

Figure 1.2   The PHP home page.

resource for PHP documentation. You can find a particular function, for example, by typing the search string into the top right corner of the page, and the result returned will be very close to what you were looking for, including links to other functions that perform a similar task. Most of the official documentation pages are annotated with the comments from other users as well as any bugs or revision changes (see Figure 1.3).

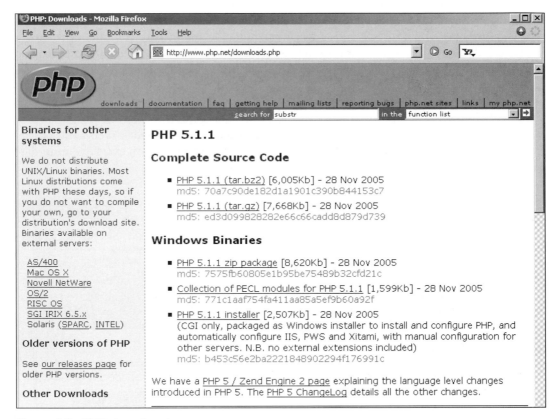

Figure 1.3 PHP download page.

1.3 About MySQL

Monty Widenius

Today many organizations face the double threat of increasing volumes of data and transactions coinciding with a need to reduce spending. Many such organizations are migrating to open source database management systems to keep costs down and minimize change to their existing systems. The world's most popular of these open source database systems (it's free to download, use, and modify) is MySQL. It is distributed and supported by MySQL AB, a Swedish commercial company founded by the original developers, David Axmark and Michael "Monty" Widenius, who wrote MySQL in 1995. MySQL has its roots in mSQL or mini SQL, a lightweight database developed at Bond University in Australia, to provide fast access to stored data with low memory requirements. Its symbol is a dolphin called "Sakila" representing "speed, power, precision and good nature of the MySQL database and community."[4]

1.3.1 Where to Get MySQL and Documentation

MySQL is installed on more than 6 million servers worldwide to power many high-volume and business-critical Web sites. See *http://www.mysql.com/company/factsheet.html*. MySQL was created by MySQL AB and is available for download from their Web site at *http://www.mysql.com/*, where you can also find the latest information about MySQL software and MySQL AB (see Figures 1.4 and 1.5).

1.3.2 Features of MySQL

MySQL is a relational database management system. Whether you're involved with a Web site that processes millions of requests a day like eBay or Yahoo!, or a smaller site such as your own online shop or training course, the data must be stored in an organized and structured way for easy access and processing. This is handled by a database management system such as MySQL where the data is stored in tables rather than in a flat file.

MySQL uses the client/server model; that is, a database server (MySQL) that serves (communicates) with multiple clients (application programs), where the clients may or may not be on the same computer. It also supports SQL, the structured query language, a standardized language used by most modern databases for working with data and administering the database.

---

4. Monty Widenius, MySQL founder and CT0, from a news release: *http://www.mysql.com/news-and-events/news/article_116.html*.

Figure 1.4 The MySQL home page.

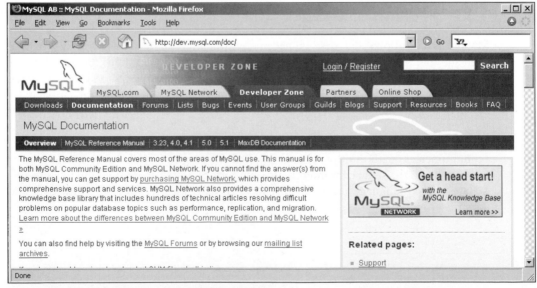

Figure 1.5 The MySQL Documentation page.

MySQL software is open source. As discussed earlier in this chapter, open source means that it is possible for anyone to download MySQL from the Internet, and use and modify the software without paying anything. The MySQL software uses the GPL (GNU General Public License), *http://www.fsf.org/licenses/*, to define what you may and may not do with the software in different situations. If you need to use MySQL code in a commercial application, you can buy a commercially licensed version. See the MySQL Licensing Overview for more information (*http://www.mysql.com/company/legal/licensing/*).

The MySQL Database Server is very fast, reliable, and easy to use. MySQL Server was originally developed to handle large databases much faster than existing solutions and has been successfully used in highly demanding production environments for several years. Its connectivity, speed, and security make MySQL Server highly suited for accessing databases on the Internet.

MySQL serves as a back end for all kinds of information such as e-mail, Web images and content, games, log files, and so on. The server can be embedded in applications such as cell phones, electronic devices, public kiosks, and more.

1.3.3   How to Install MySQL and PHP

Appendix E of this book contains instructions on the installation procedures for Windows, UNIX, Macintosh, and so on. The source code for PHP and MySQL can also be found on the CD included in the back cover of this book.

1.3.4   Advantages of MySQL and PHP

Certain technologies play together better than others. PHP, a simple and powerful scripting language, and MySQL, a solid and reliable database server, make a perfect marriage between two modern technologies for building database-driven, dynamic Web sites. Some of the advantages of both PHP and MySQL are:

- High performance
- Built-in libraries
- Extensibility
- Relatively low cost
- Portability
- Developer community
- Ease of learning

High Performance.   PHP is no longer considered just a grassroots scripting language, but now with PHP 5, and its highly efficient built-in Zend engine, PHP accommodates developers and IT decision makers in the business trend to rapidly release and update software on the Web faster than conventional programming cycles have allowed.

MySQL, a highly optimized database server, provides the response time and throughput to meet the most demanding applications.

With PHP scripts connected to a MySQL database, millions of pages can be served on a single inexpensive server.

Built-In Libraries.   PHP comes with many built-in functions addressing common Web development tasks. Problems encountered by other programmers have been solved and packaged into a library of routines, made available to the PHP community. The official PHP Web site at *http://www.php.net* provides excellent documentation explaining how to use all of the functions currently available.

Extensibility.   PHP and MySQL are both extensible, meaning that developers around the world are contributing add-on modules to extend the functionality and power of the languages to stay current with the growing market needs and standards of the day. You can also obtain the source code for both PHP and MySQL. Source code is the code that a program consists of before the program is compiled; that is, the original building instructions of a program.

Relatively Low Cost.   As a Web developer you can demand a lot more money for your time if you can master PHP and MySQL. Because they are open source projects, there is no license fee associated with using PHP or MySQL. Because both applications run on almost any platform, you also have a wide range of hardware choices lowering the total cost of ownership. With so many qualified PHP developers sharing information on the Web, and excellent online documentation, you can get the most up-to-date, reliable information without paying for it.

Portability.   PHP and MySQL run on almost any platform, including Linux, Windows, Mac OS X, FreeBSD, Solaris, and so on. If well written, you can simply copy the code from one server to another and expect the same results, perhaps with some minor adjustments.

Developer Community.   Both PHP and MySQL have a huge following in the development community. If you run into a problem, you can usually very quickly find support on the Web, where your problem can be posted, identified, and resolved by other users and developers sharing your problem. Developers worldwide are constantly finding and resolving bugs and security holes, while working to keep these languages up-to-date and optimized.

Ease of Learning.   PHP and MySQL are relatively easy to learn. Most of the PHP constructs are similar to other languages, specifically Perl, making it familiar to most developers. MySQL uses the SQL query language and English-like language used by most modern database management systems today. If you have had any experience with SQL, you will find using it with MySQL an easy transition.

1.4   Chapter Summary

1.4.1   What You Should Know

Now that you have been introduced to PHP and MySQL, you should be able to answer the following questions:

1. What is the difference between a *static* and *dynamic* Web site?

2. What is the meaning of *open source* software?

3. Why was PHP developed, what it is used for, and where can you get it?

4. What is MySQL used for and where can you get it?

5. What are the benefits of using PHP and MySQL?

6. Why do PHP and MySQL work well together?

1.4.2   What's Next?

In Chapter 2, "Getting Started," we will review the life cycle of a typical Web page that uses PHP. We will learn how to create and execute simple PHP scripts both from the browser and at the command line. We will talk about built-in functions and how to use them by viewing the PHP documentation Web site.

chapter

2

Getting Started

2.1 The Life Cycle of a Web Page

Before you start learning PHP, it is helpful to understand what makes up a dynamic Web page and how PHP interacts with the other applications involved in the process. Figure 2.1. diagrams the life cycle of a typical Web page.

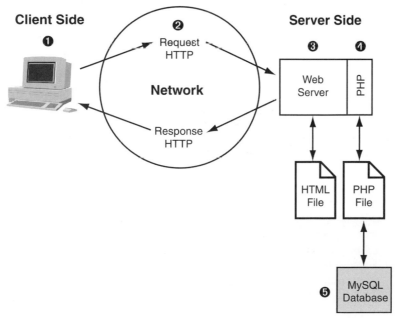

Figure 2.1 The life cycle of a typical Web page.

2.1.1   Analysis of a Web Page

The Players.   The players in Figure 2.1 represent the applications involved in the life cycle of a Web page. When you start using PHP, it is normally not the only player, but part of a team of players, including a browser (Firefox, Netscape, Internet Explorer), a network (HTTP), a server (Apache, Windows IIS, Sambar), a server module (PHP, ASP, ColdFusion), and external files or a database (MySQL, Oracle, Sybase).

The Steps.   Figure 2.1 illustrates the life cycle of a Web page from when the client makes a request until it gets a response. We will explain each of steps by the number shown in the diagram.

1. On the left side of the diagram, we see the client, or browser where the request is made. The browser may be Internet Explorer, Firefox, Netscape, and so on. The user makes a request for a Web site by typing the address of the Web site in the browser's URL location box. The "request" is transmitted to the server via IITTP. The Web server on the other side accepts that request. If the request is for a static HTML file, the Web server responds by simply returning the file to the client's browser. The browser then renders the HTML tags, formats the page for display, and waits for another request. Going back and forth between the browser and the server is known as the Request/Response loop. It is the basis of how the Web works.

2. The circle between the client side and the server side represents the network. This can be a very large network such as the Internet consisting of millions upon millions of computers, an intranet within an organization, or a wireless network on a personal desktop computer. The user doesn't care how big or small the network is—it is totally transparent. The protocol used to transfer documents to and from the server is called HTTP.

3. The server side includes an HTTP Web server such as Apache, Sambar, or Microsoft's Internet Information Services (IIS). Web servers are generic programs capable of accepting Web-based requests and providing the response to them. In most cases, this response is simply retrieving the file from server's local file system. With dynamic Web sites, Web servers turn over the request for a specific file to an appropriate helper application. Web servers, such as Apache and IIS have a list of helper applications that process any specific language. The helper application could be an external program, such as a CGI/Perl script, or one built right into the server, such as ColdFusion, ASP.Net, or a PHP script. For example, if the Web server sees a request for a PHP file, it looks up what helper application is assigned to process PHP requests, turns over the request to the PHP module, and waits until it gets the result back.

4. PHP is a module that resides within the Web server. The server opens the file (script) and reads it line by line. It hands over any PHP instructions to the PHP module for processing and replaces the PHP code with the output it generated back into the page. Because this processing is done first, PHP is called

a hypertext preprocessor. Once the PHP instructions have been processed, the page that travels across the network back to the user's browser consists of just plain HTML and text.

5. If the Web page consists of PHP with MySQL (or any other database) statements, then PHP may make further requests to the database to retrieve, send, or update information on the fly.

2.2 The Anatomy of a PHP Script

A PHP script is a file (ending with a `.php` extension) consisting of text, HTML, and PHP instructions interspersed throughout the file. The PHP instructions are contained within two HTML style tags; `<?php` is the opening tag and `?>` is the closing tag. Everything between these two tags is interpreted by the PHP module (also called interpreter) and converted to regular text and HTML before being sent back to the requesting browser. If, for example, one of the PHP instructions is to get today's date from the server, PHP will get the date and replace the PHP instruction with the current date. When the browser gets the file, it will not see the PHP tags or any of the PHP instructions; it will get only what PHP generated as a result of its processing. Consider the following simple PHP instruction consisting of an echo statement containing the string `"Hello, world.<br />"`, some plain text, and an HTML break tag.

What the PHP interpreter gets:

```
<?php
    echo "Hello, world.<br />";
?>
```

What the Web browser gets:

```
Hello, world.<br />
```

2.2.1 The Steps of Writing a PHP Script

After you have installed PHP successfully (see Appendix E for installation instructions), and the Web server is running, it is time to write your first PHP script.

Finding a Text Editor.   Because PHP is a scripting language designed to be integrated with other text documents, most commonly HTML, you will write your scripts in a text editor. Some popular text editors are BBEdit (Macintosh), Wordpad, Notepad (Windows), pico, vi, emacs (Linux/UNIX), and so on. Also available are third-party editors, TextPad and WinEdit, as well as integrated development environments (IDEs) such as Dreamweaver and Eclipse.

Naming the PHP File—The .php Extension.   When you name the file, be sure to add the PHP extension to its name. Normally the extension is `.php`, but this depends on how your server was configured. The following lines were taken from the Apache server's `httpd.conf` file. This server accepts `.php`, `.php3`, and `.phtml` as valid extensions to PHP script names.

From the Apache `httpd.conf` file:

AddType application/x-httpd-php `.php`
AddType application/x-httpd-php `.php3`
AddType application/x-httpd-php `.phtml`

PHP Tags.   The script file may contain HTML, XHTML, XML, and so on, but PHP will consider the file as just plain text and leave it alone, unless you explicitly embed the PHP statements between its own special tags:

```
<?php
    statement;
    statement;
 ?>
```

Each statement must be terminated with a semicolon (with an exception if it is the last line of the script). PHP will produce an error message if you omit the semicolon, similar to this:

```
Parse error: syntax error, unexpected T_PRINT in
c:\wamp\www\exemples\first.php on line 4
```

EXAMPLE 2.1

```
1   <?php
2       print "It's such a perfect day!";
3   ?>
```

EXPLANATION

1   This is the opening PHP tag. This tag alerts PHP to start processing the text from here until the closing tag on line 3.
2   PHP prints the string of characters enclosed in double quotes, and replaces the output back in the file before sending it to the browser. We will cover strings in detail in Chapter 6, "Strings," but for now, all strings are enclosed in either a set of single or double quotes.
3   This is the closing PHP tag. It tells PHP to stop processing.

Additional PHP Tags.   To promote flexibility, PHP supports three other types of tags, but the full PHP tags just described are really the most reliable, and your particular PHP configuration may not support the ones listed in Table 2.1.

Table 2.1   Additional PHP Tags

Tag	*Description*
PHP tags	`<?php` php code `?>`
HTML style tags	`<script language="php">` php code `</script>`
ASP-style	`<%` php code `%>`
PHP short tags	`<?=` php code `?>`

The special shortcut tags, `<?=` and `?>` are used to evaluate PHP expressions embedded in HTML. These tags are discussed in more depth in Chapter 4, "The Building Blocks." They are used as follows:

```
<html>
This is a line in the html document <?= php code here ?> more html here
</html>
```

To use short tags, you may have to change a setting in the PHP initialialization file, called `php.ini` found in with your server's configuration files. When you find the `php.ini` file, look for "short_open_tag" and change the setting to "On", as follows. From the `php.ini` file:

```
; Allow the <? tag.  Otherwise, only <?php and <script> tags are recognized.
; NOTE: Using short tags should be avoided when developing applications or
; libraries that are meant for redistribution, or deployment on PHP
; servers which are not under your control, because short tags may not
; be supported on the target server. For portable, redistributable code,
; be sure not to use short tags.
short_open_tag = On
```

Where to Save the Script.   When you have completed writing the script, it will normally be saved in a file under the server's document root,[1] the place where your standard Web pages are served; for example, *htdocs* or *C:/wamp/www* or */var/www/html*. In the following examples, the scripts were saved in a folder or directory under the server's root, called "exemples".

The Script Content.   Developers often prefer to seperate the presentation code (HTML, XML) from business logic (program instructions) and PHP offers the best of both worlds. A PHP script can be an independent file consisting of PHP tags and instructions, or it can be embedded in an HTML document. The PHP tags are often inserted between the <body> tags of an HTML document, although they can be inserted anywhere on the page. To format your output, HTML tags can be embedded in PHP statements as well, but cannot stand alone in a PHP script. You can have multiple PHP scripts within the HTML page. Figure 2.2 demonstrates how PHP blocks of instructions are inserted in a Web page.

```
    ... html text ...
    ... html text ...
<?php
  php instructions
?>
    ... html text ...
    ... html text ...
<?php
  php instructions
?>
```

Figure 2.2   PHP and the Web page.

Before sending the page to the browser, the Web server will send any PHP instructions to the PHP module for preprocessing. The PHP module starts interpreting code when it finds the first <?php opening tag, and continues until it reaches the closing tag ?>, executing the code between the tags. Any other text in the file is left as is. If there is output, this output replaces the original PHP code between the tags. PHP tags will be removed. HTML tags will be left alone. The Web server will send the resulting page, consisting of plain HTML and text, back to the browser that requested the page. (To see the source code received by the browser, go to the browser's "View" menu option and select "Page Source" or "Source".)

---

1. Look in the configuration file for your server to find the directory named as your server's Document Root. For Apache, for example, the file is called `httpd.conf`.

EXAMPLE 2.2

(*Filename: first.php*)

```
        <html>
        <head>
            <title>Hello World</title>
        </head>
        <body>
        <h1>Hello World example</h1>

1       <?php
2           print "It's such a perfect day!<br />";
3       ?>

        </body>
        </html>
```

EXPLANATION

1   The `<?php` tag indicates the beginning of a PHP block. (You can also use short open tag `<?` instead of `<?php` if this option is enabled in the PHP initialization file, `php.ini`.

2   Line 2 is the actual PHP code. The `print()` function prints the text enclosed in double quotes. The `<br />` tag will not be touched by the PHP interpreter. It will be sent to the browser for rendering because that's the browser's job. The semicolumn terminates each PHP statement.

3   The `?>` tag is the ending tag. See Figure 2.3.

Quoting in Strings.   Many statements you write in PHP will contain text, called strings, such as `"Have a good day!"`. We have devoted a whole chapter to strings (Chapter 6, "Strings"), but as you start learning PHP, you should be aware of some basic rules concerning strings to write even the simplest PHP statements.

1. All strings must be enclosed in a pair of either single or double quotes. The quotes must be matched:

    `"Hello there"` or `'Hello there'`

2. To join two strings together, use the concatenation operator, a dot:

    `"Hello, " . "world"`

3. If you need a quote to be printed literally, precede it with a backslash or enclose a single quote within double quotes:

    `"\"Ouch\""` or `"I don't care"`

Printing Strings.   You can start printing output with the `echo` and `print` language constructs. `Print` displays a string. Parentheses are not required around the string. To print more than one string with `print`, you can use the dot to concatenate the strings into one string. `Echo` is like `print` but allows you to print more than one string by separating each string with a comma. These constructs are quite simple and do not do any fancy formatting (see Example 2.3). If you need to format the output, PHP provides a number of functions, including the `printf()`, `sprintf()`, and `fprintf()` functions described in Chapter 6, "Strings."

EXAMPLE 2.3

```php
<?php

    echo "Hello, ", "world!", "<br />";          // Don't use parentheses
    echo ("It's such a perfect day!<br />");      // Parens okay
    print "Hello, " . "world!" . "<br />";        // Concatenation
    print "Hello to world again!<br />" ;         // Don't need parens
    print ("It's such a perfect day!<br />") ;    // Parens okay

?>
```

Executing the Script.   To execute the script, go to your browser and in the address bar, type the URL of the PHP script you want to execute. If running locally, for example, it might be *http://localhost/file.php* or *http:127.0.0.1/file.php*; if you are working with an ISP, you will have to upload the file to its site. Ask your ISP for the correct method for uploading your file, and the correct URL to execute it. (If you are running on a UNIX system, you may have permission issues. To turn on execute permission for the script, go to the shell prompt and type `chmod +x` *scriptname*.)

See Figures 2.3 and 2.4 for examples of script output in a browser, and viewing its source code.

Figure 2.3   Output of the PHP script in the browser.

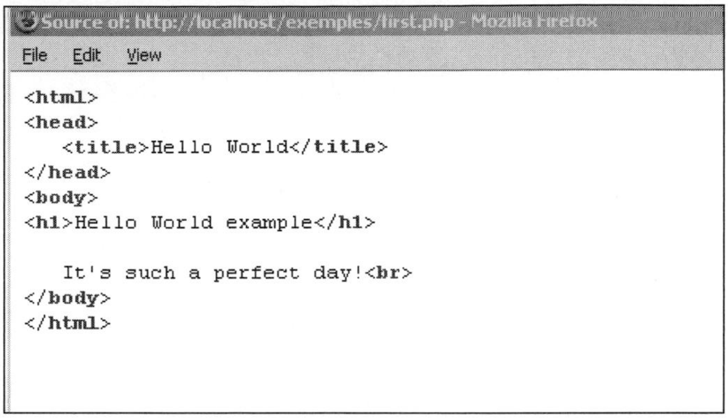

```
<html>
<head>
    <title>Hello World</title>
</head>
<body>
<h1>Hello World example</h1>

    It's such a perfect day!<br>
</body>
</html>
```

Figure 2.4 Viewing the source code of the page that you opened in your Web browser.

2.3 Some Things to Consider

Although PHP statements consist of text, terminated by a semicolon, there are a number of issues to consider before we really get started on specific language constructs, such as numbers, strings, operators, variables, loops, and so on.

2.3.1 PHP and HTML Are Different Languages

It is important to keep in mind that HTML and PHP are two very different languages used for different purposes and executed by totally different processes. HTML is called a markup language, which combines text with tags to define the structure and describe the way a document will be displayed. PHP is a programming language that consists of data and instructions and procedures that tell the computer what operations to perform on the data.

It is a common mistake to place HTML tags *directly* in a PHP block and vice versa. Notice in Example 2.4 the placement of the HTML tags. See the error message in its output in Figure 2.5. See the correct placement of the HTML tags in Example 2.5, and its corresponding output in Figure 2.6.

EXAMPLE 2.4

```
    <html><head><title>Mixing HTML and PHP</title>
    <body>

1   <?php
2       <font size="+2">    // Wrong!!! Cannot place HTML directly
                            // into PHP script
3       print "It's such a perfect day!<br />";  // Okay here within
                                                 // the statement
    ?>

    </body>
```

EXPLANATION

1   The PHP script starts here.
2   This HTML `<font>` tag is placed within the PHP script. This not a legal PHP statement. You could embed the `<font>` tag within a PHP `print` statement as:

    `print "<font size='+2'>";`

    or move the HTML code out of the script back into the HTML document as shown in Example 2.5.
3   This is the only valid PHP statement in this script.

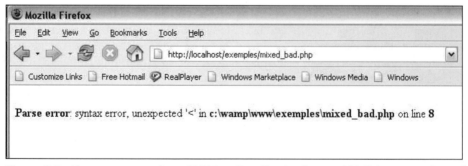

Figure 2.5 Error message from PHP for directly placing an HTML tag on a line of its own in the PHP script. PHP doesn't understand the HTML opening < tag.

EXAMPLE 2.5

```
<html><head><title>Mixing HTML and PHP</title>
<body>
<font size="+2">  <!--OK. Moved font tag here -->
<?php
    print "It's such a perfect day!<br />";
?>
</font>
</body>
</html>
```

Figure 2.6 Output of PHP code after HTML `<font` line was moved outside the PHP script.

2.3.2 Statements, Whitespace, and Line Breaks

A PHP statement is somewhat like an English sentence, but is terminated with a semicolon instead of a period. PHP is called a free form language, meaning you can place statements anywhere on the line, even cross over lines.

Whitespace refers to spaces, tabs, and newlines. Whitespace is used to delimit words and does not have other significance. Any number of blank spaces are allowed between symbols and words. Both of the following PHP statements are correct:

```
print "This is a PHP statement.";

print "This
    is
    also
    a PHP
    statement.";
```

Table 2.2 lists whitespace characters and how they are represented in PHP. Note the characters preceded by a backslash and enclosed in quotes. In Chapter 6, "Strings," we discuss the use of these backslash sequences in your scripts.

Table 2.2 Whitespace Characters

Description		Written As
An ordinary space	ASCII 32 (0x20)	`" "`
A tab	ASCII 9 (0x09)	`"\t"`
A newline (line feed)	ASCII 10 (0x0A)	`"\n"`
A carriage return	ASCII 13 (0x0D)	`"\r"`
The NUL-byte	ASCII 0 (0x00)	`"\0"`
A vertical tab	ASCII 11 (0x0B)	`"\x0B"`

Even though you have a lot of freedom when formatting the script, it is good practice to make the program readable to yourself and others by providing indentation and putting statements on their own line, with comments describing what you are doing. Certainly a clean style makes it easier to read as well as debug programs, especially when they become more complex. The first PHP script in Example 2.6, although correct, is obviously not a very readable style. The entire script could be written on one clean line (see Figure 2.7)!

EXAMPLE 2.6

```
1   <?php
      print "It's
         such    a perfect
      day!  ";
    ?>
    ---------------------------------------------------------------
    <?php
2     print "It's such a perfect day!";
    ?>
```

EXPLANATION

1   Although the statement here is perfectly valid, it demonstrates free form at its worst. This style would be almost impossible to read in a longer program!
2   This PHP code outputs exactly the same text as in the previous statement, but it is easy to read. Note that the line is indented, making the PHP tags easier to find.

Figure 2.7
Output from Example 2.6
showing free form.

2.3.3 Comments

You may write a very clever PHP script this afternoon, and in two weeks have no idea what your script was supposed to do. If you pass the script on to someone else, the confusion magnifies. Hence, comments. Comments are plain English text inserted within a script to explain what is going on; they are annotations written for anyone who reads your script, including you. They are extremely important when working with a team of people to help communicate your intentions.

Comments are ignored by the PHP interpreter. If the user views the source file in his or her browser, the comments will not be there, because once the PHP code is preprocessed, the comments are removed from the output.

PHP comments can be written on a single line or cover multiple lines. The style PHP uses comes from other languages such as C, C++, and UNIX shells, and Perl. The style you use depends on how much you want to say. A single-line comment starts with either a hash mark # (like Shell and Perl comments) or double slashes // (like C++ comments). The /* */ (C style) comment can be used as a single-line comment as well, but it is also useful if you want your comments to cover multiple lines.

Examples:

```
<?
    // This is a single-line comment.
    #  This is also a single-line comment
    print 5 + 2;  // Another single-line comment
    /*  This style of comment allows you to write comments to span
        over multiple lines
    */
?>
```

(Note that HTML has a different syntax for the comments. HTML comments consist of text inserted between <!-- open tag and --> close tag. These comments are visible by viewing the source of the page.)

EXAMPLE 2.7

```
    <?php
1   /*
    Author: Marko Gargenta
    Date: 12/11/2006
    Description:
    This is a simple PHP script that output Hello World text
2   */
    ?>
    <html>
    <head>
    <title>Hello World</title>
    <body>
    <h1>Hello World example</h1>
```

EXAMPLE 2.7 (CONTINUED)

```php
    <?php
3      // This is a comment line (C++ style)
4      print "It's such a perfect day!";    # Another comment here
    ?>

5   <!--this is an HTML comment -->
    </body>
    </html>
```

EXPLANATION

1, 2   Lines 1 and 2 represent the long-style, C-style comment, using the opening tag /*
       and the closing tag */. Everything between these tags is ignored by PHP. Make
       sure that for each opening tag you have the corresponding closing tag. You cannot
       nest the comment tags (i.e., enclose comment tags within other comment tags).

3   Line 3 is an inline comment. Everything after the // characters is ignored up to
       the end of the line. Use this style to write short notes in your code.

4   The hash mark # is a UNIX shell style comment that is exactly like the // com-
       ment. It spans a line.

5   This is an HTML comment, not recognized by PHP, and not part of the PHP code.
       See the source code shown in Figure 2.8 and the output in Figure 2.9.

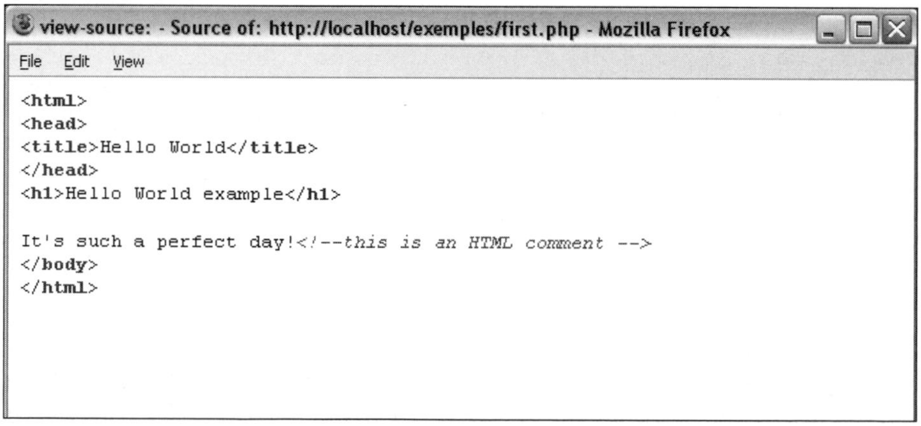

Figure 2.8 Viewing the source. PHP comments are not visible; HTML comments
are in italics.

Figure 2.9   All comments are invisible in the page.

2.3.4   Using PHP Functions

A big part of any programming language is the set of functions that are built into the language or packaged in special libraries. In Chapter 9, "User-Defined Functions," you will learn how create your own functions, but for now, we concentrate on the ones that are part of the PHP language, called built-in functions (see Figure 2.10).

So what is a function? A function is an independent piece of program code that is created to make your life easier. You don't see what's going on inside the function. You just have to know what it is supposed to do, and then when you need it, call it by its name. You can send a value (or values) to a function and the function can send back a result. Perhaps the function just performs some operation such as getting today's date or printing a formatted string of text. For a simple example, if you want to round a number such as 4.5, you can call the built-in `round()` function. For example, `round(4.5)` will return `5` and `round(4.2)` will return `4`. The values you send to the function are called arguments, a comma-separated list of words enclosed in the parentheses after the function name. Different functions have different numbers of arguments and some have none at all. What the function sends back is called the return value. If you wanted to save the return value, you would ordinarily print it or save it in a variable; for example, `$rounded_number = round(4.5)`. We discuss variables in Chapter 4, "The Building Blocks."

PHP comes with many useful functions, all of which are well documented at the PHP Web site, *http://www.php.net/*. For example, if you didn't know how to get get the current date, go to *php.net* and type "date" in the top right corner search box (see Figure 2.11). Make sure you select to search in the "function list" and the following page will be displayed. You will find the PHP Web site an invaluable reference for everything that has to do with PHP.

Although it is customary to see function names in lowercase, the names are not case sensitive; `date()` and `DAte()` and `DATE()` are all valid.

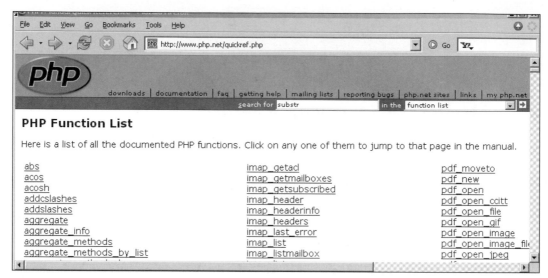

Figure 2.10   The PHP Web page for a complete list of built-in functions.

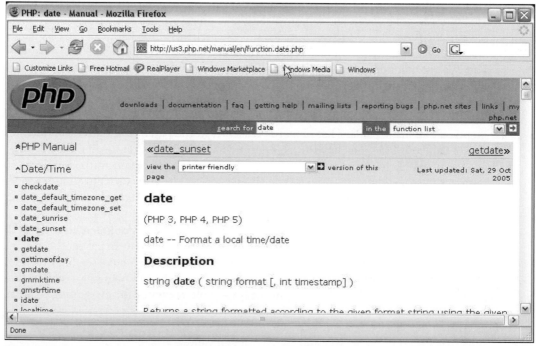

Figure 2.11   How to get documentation for a specific PHP built-in function.

We discuss functions in more detail in Chapter 9, "User Defined Functions," where you will learn how to create your own, but for now, just think of a function as a black box. You can send data to it, the function statements will be executed, and then it will return, and maybe send something back to you. You must know what it does, but how it was written and designed is hidden in the black box.

Example 2.8 demonstrates how to use the `date()` function to print out the current date. This function is built into the PHP language.

EXAMPLE 2.8

```
        <html>
        <head><title>Current Date and Time</title></head>

        <body>
        <h1>Current Date and Time</h1>

        <?php
1           print "Today is ";
2           print date("D M j G:i:s T Y");   // Function names are NOT case
                                             // sensitive
3           print "<br />";
4           print "Current time is ";
5           print Date( "g:i a" );  // Function names are not case
                                    // sensitive
        ?>

        </body>
        </html>
```

EXPLANATION

1   All the PHP is within `<?php` and `?>` tags. Line 1 will be replaced by `"Today is "` when PHP has finished processing it.

2   The built-in `date()` function is called here. It will return the current date and time to be printed. The letters within the parentheses (called arguments) are passed to the `date()` function to specify how to display the date. For a list of arguments, see the `date` function in Appendix C or *www.php.net/quickref.php*.

3   This HTML `<br />` tag will create a line break when the page is displayed in the browser.

4   When PHP has processed this line, it will be `"Current time is "`.

5   The `date()` function will return the current time to be inserted into the page that is generated. Once PHP is preprocessed, the corresponding HTML becomes what you see in the source of the page. See Figure 2.12 for the source, and the output is shown in Figure 2.13.

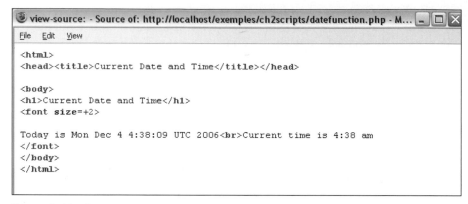

Figure 2.12   Source page—what our browser gets after PHP processing.

Figure 2.13   The output of the PHP `date()` function in the Web browser.

EXAMPLE 2.9

```
<html>
    <head><title>short tags and functions</title></head>
    <body bgcolor="lightgreen">
    <h1>Current Date and Time</h1>
    <font size="+2">
1   You are looking at this page on <strong><?=date("l")?></strong>
    and life is good!<br />
    </font>
    </body>
</html>
```

EXPLANATION

1 The `date()` function is embedded within PHP short tags right in the HTML document. Its output, `"Monday"`, is inserted into the text and sent to the browser. See Figure 2.14.

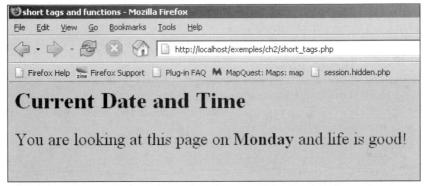

Figure 2.14 The output of a function embedded within PHP short tags in the HTML document.

For more information on the `date()` function, see Appendix C.

2.4 Review

To review once again the life cycle of a PHP file, let's look at the steps involved.

1. The user on the browser (client) requests a Web page over the network (Internet or local area network). An HTTP connection allows the browser to transfer the page to the server listed in the URL.
2. The Web server receives the request. Because the file being requested is a PHP file (a filename ending with a `.php` extension), the Web server hands over the request to the PHP module residing in the server.
3. The PHP module opens the PHP file and ignores everything until it reaches a PHP opening tag. PHP then starts processing the instructions until it reaches the closing PHP tag. The text/HTML that results from the processing is inserted back into the file and the PHP tags and statements are removed.
4. The server sends the processed document back to the browser. After rendering any HTML tags, the browser displays the document on the user's browser.

2.4.1   PHP on the Command Line

UNIX and Linux users are normally more familiar with working at the command line than Windows or Mac users. Executing PHP at the command line requires that you know where PHP is installed and that the PHP executable is included in your search path. On some operating systems, such as Linux and MacOS, PHP comes preloaded, but on Windows, after you have installed PHP, you might have to set the PATH environment variable to execute PHP at the command line. See installation instructions in Appendix E of this book.

2.4.2   Finding the Version of PHP

As we discussed in Chapter 1, "Introduction," there are a number of versions of PHP, the latest being Version 5. Each version brought changes to the language, so you might want to check that you have the correct version installed if some of the newer features are not working for you, and if not, go to the PHP Web site and download the most current version. To find what version of PHP you are currently running (see Figure 2.15), go to the command line and type:

```
php -v
```

Figure 2.15   This is PHP Version 5.0.3 for Windows.

2.4.3   Script Execution at the Command Line

Although PHP is best suited for Web development, it can also be used for developing command-line applications. Command-line applications are scripts that run from the command-line prompt and work well with plain text and files. They typically don't have a graphical interface. Consider that everything you learn to do in PHP for the Web can be executed as a command-line script as well. Testing your script at the command line is often helpful for testing and debugging.

Let's look at our date example executed on the command line. First we create the script.

```php
<?php
   print date( "D M j G:i:s T Y" );
?>
```

This script is saved as `ShowDate.php`. To execute this script from the command line, you will need to open window where you can execute commands. For Windows users, click Start, then Run, and type in "cmd" to bring up the MS-DOS shell. See Figure 2.16.

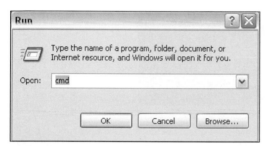

Figure 2.16 Windows: Click Start, then Run.

For Macintosh users, start the Terminal application located under the Applications/Utilities folder.

For UNIX/Linux users, start up a Shell terminal if you aren't already using one.

On the command line, specify the path to your PHP executable (`php.exe` for Windows). This is located in the folder/directory where PHP was installed. Give the php executable the `-f` switch and the name of your script. The `-f` switch tells PHP to treat the file as a script.

Type this at the prompt: `php -f ShowDate.php`. You will get output similar to that shown in Figure 2.17.

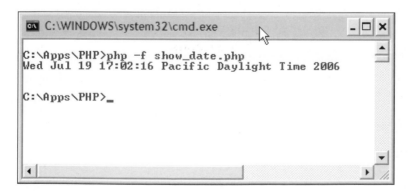

Figure 2.17 PHP at the command line.

2.4.4   Running PHP Interactively

You can also run PHP interactively, that is, write the PHP on the fly and see what it does. This is helpful when you want to check syntax before actually writing a script. Be sure to start your interactive session with the opening PHP tag as shown in Figure 2.18. You can press Control-C to exit.

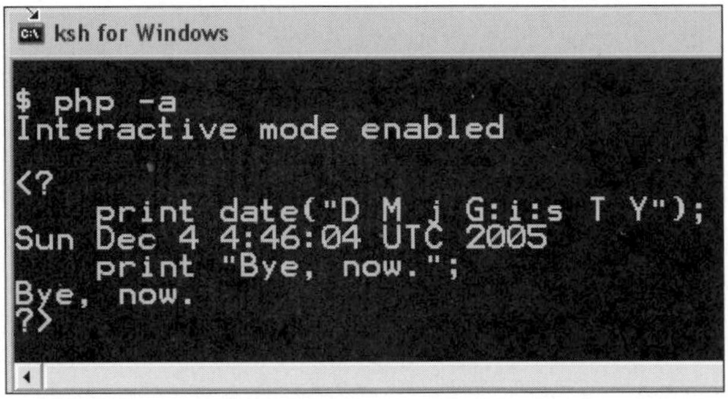

```
ksh for Windows

$ php -a
Interactive mode enabled

<?
     print date("D M j G:i:s T Y");
Sun Dec 4 4:46:04 UTC 2005
     print "Bye, now.";
Bye, now.
?>
```

Figure 2.18   Using PHP interactively.

2.4.5   PHP Command-Line Options

Table 2.3 specifies some of the options that we can use for running PHP on the command line.

Table 2.3   PHP Options on the Command Line

Option	What It Does
-a	Run interactively.
-B <begin_code>	Run PHP <begin_code> before processing input lines.
-c <path>|<file>	Look for php.ini file in this directory.
-d foo[=bar]	Define INI entry foo with value 'bar'.
-E <end_code>	Run PHP <end_code> after processing all input lines.
-e	Generate extended information for debugger/profiler.
-F <file>	Parse and execute <file> for every input line.
-f <file>	Parse <file>.
-H	Hide any passed arguments from external tools.
-h	This helps.

Table 2.3 PHP Options on the Command Line (continued)

Option	What It Does
-i	PHP information.
-l	Syntax check only (lint).
-m	Show compiled in modules.
-n	No php.ini file will be used.
-R *<code>*	Run PHP *<code>* for every input line.
-r *<code>*	Run PHP *<code>* without using script tags <?..?>.
-s	Display colour syntax highlighted source.
-v	Version number.
-w	Display source with stripped comments and whitespace.
-z *<file>*	Load Zend extension *<file>*.
args...	Arguments passed to script. Use -- args when first argument starts with - or script is read from stdin.

2.4.6 The php.ini File

Many of the operations you perform will depend on how the PHP initialization directives have been set in the php.ini file. For the most part, you should go with the default configuration, because the PHP developers selected default settings they determined to be the best for security, performance, and so on. Occasionally you might want to change a setting, especially if you are developing PHP scripts for your own use, not part of a Web project that will be used on the Internet. Because the php.ini file is a text file, it is easy to modify it. You might have to restart your Web server once you have changed the php.ini file.

You might have several copies of the php.ini file. If making a change doesn't seem to work, look in the following locations. This is typically where the Web server will look for the php.ini file:

1. The directory from which the PHP script was called.
2. The server's document root; for example, *public_html*, *htdocs*, and so on.
3. The Web server's default php.ini.

You can use the phpinfo() function in a script to find the path to your php.ini file. Look at the sixth line in Figure 2.19.

| PHP Version 5.0.3 | |

System	Windows NT PRE-J7Z6MKEQ0GY 5.1 build 2600
Build Date	Dec 15 2004 08:06:41
Configure Command	cscript /nologo configure.js "--enable-snapshot-build" "--with-gd=shared"
Server API	Apache
Virtual Directory Support	enabled
Configuration File (php.ini) Path	c:\wamp\apache\php.ini
PHP API	20031224
PHP Extension	20041030
Zend Extension	220040412
Debug Build	no
Thread Safety	enabled
IPv6 Support	enabled
Registered PHP Streams	php, file, http, ftp, compress.zlib
Registered Stream Socket Transports	tcp, udp

This program makes use of the Zend Scripting Language Engine:
Zend Engine v2.0.3, Copyright (c) 1998-2004 Zend Technologies

Powered By

Figure 2.19 Finding the path to your `php.ini` file (see line 6).

Common settings you might want to change are:

```
register_globals
display_errors
error_reporting
magic_quotes_gpc
```

This is an excerpt from the `php.ini` file:

```
;;;;;;;;;;;
; WARNING ;
;;;;;;;;;;;
; This is the default settings file for new PHP installations.
; By default, PHP installs itself with a configuration suitable for
; development purposes, and *NOT* for production purposes.
; For several security-oriented considerations that should be taken
; before going online with your site, please consult php.ini-recommended
; and http://php.net/manual/en/security.php.
```

```
;;;;;;;;;;;;;;;;;;;;;
; About this file ;
;;;;;;;;;;;;;;;;;;;;;
; This file controls many aspects of PHP's behavior.  In order for PHP to
; read it, it must be named 'php.ini'.  PHP looks for it in the current
; working directory, in the path designated by the environment variable
; PHPRC, and in the path that was defined in compile time (in that order).
; Under Windows, the compile-time path is the Windows directory.  The
; path in which the php.ini file is looked for can be overridden using
; the -c argument in command line mode.
;
; The syntax of the file is extremely simple.  Whitespace and Lines
; beginning with a semicolon are silently ignored (as you probably guessed).
; Section headers (e.g. [Foo]) are also silently ignored, even though
; they might mean something in the future.
;
; Directives are specified using the following syntax:
; directive = value
; Directive names are *case sensitive* - foo=bar is different from FOO=bar.
;
```

Again, make these changes to this file with caution.

2.5   Chapter Summary

2.5.1   What You Should Know

Now that you have been introduced to PHP and MySQL, you should be able to answer the following questions:

1. What is the life cycle of a Web page?

2. Describe the anatomy of a PHP script.

3. What are PHP tags?

4. How do you define whitespace?

5. What is meant by "free form"?

6. What types of comments does PHP support?

7. How are statements terminated?

8. How does PHP deal with HTML?

9. Where do you get PHP documentation?

10. What are PHP functions and where can you get information about them?

11. How do you find out what version of PHP you are using?

12. How do you run PHP at the command line?

2.5.2   What's Next?

Chapter 3, "PHP Quick Start," is intended for programmers who have some experience in other languages and want to get a sneak peek at how PHP compares. Because most of the programming concepts are very similar between languages, the chapter describes only those features specific to the PHP language.

The next chapter also serves as quick reference after learning PHP. Each section references the chapter and page number where a particular construct is described in detail.

CHAPTER 2 LAB

1. At the command line, find the version of PHP you are using. Now write a simple PHP script that prints out today's date and time. Use the `date()` function. Now print the time the sun will set today. See the `date_sunset()` function from the PHP manual. Run the program at the command line.

2. Write and execute the following script:

```
<?php
   phpinfo();
?>
```

On the sixth line down, do you see "Configuration File (php.ini) Path"? That is the path to the `php.ini` file being used by your server. Find that file and change `turn on error_reporting` to show all errors and notices. What are some of the arguments you can pass to the `phpinfo()` function? (See the PHP manual.)

3. Combine HTML and PHP using your last example to produce a "Twilight Time" message:

Between the dark and the daylight,
When the night is beginning to lower,
Comes a pause in the day's occupation,
That is known as the children's hour.
                    — Henry Wordsworth Longfellow

Place an image of the sun setting under the line that tells when the sun will set. View the output in your browser.

1. Write a PHP script containing both HTML and PHP code. Use an Arial font and increase the point size by 1. The background color of the page will be light blue. Use three styles of comments in your PHP program to include your name, the date, and the number of the lab exercise.

   The PHP portion of the program will print the incoming costs for a book store, shown below. You do not need to do any calculations at this point, just print the text shown. View the output in your browser.

```
================================================
                   Book Store
================================================

Sales:            $190000

Expenses:
    Rent:         $25000
    Salary:       $37500
    Supplies:     $410

Total:
    Operating income:
    Income after taxes:


================================================
```

5. Use PHP interactively. Write PHP statements with both the `print` and `echo` constructs. How are they different? (Don't forget to use the PHP opening and closing tags after you get into the interactive mode.)

chapter
3

PHP Quick Start

3.1 Quick Start, Quick Reference

3.1.1 A Note to Programmers

If you have had previous programming experience in another language, such as Visual Basic, C/C++, Java, ASP, or Perl, and you are familiar with basic concepts such as variables, loops, conditional statements and functions, Table 3.1 gives you a quick overview of the constructs and syntax of the PHP language.

At the end of each section, you are given the chapter number that describes the particular construct and a short, fully functional PHP example designed to illustrate how that constuct is used.

3.1.2 A Note to Nonprogrammers

If you are not familiar with programming, skip this chapter and go to Chapter 4, "The Building Blocks." You might want to refer to this chapter later for a quick reference.

3.1.3   PHP Syntax and Constructs

Table 3.1   PHP Syntax and Constructs

The tags	The PHP script is placed between the PHP open tag `<?php` and the PHP close tag `?>`. The code between these two tags is what the PHP module processes. The HTML code is just left as is (see Chapter 2, "Getting Started").

EXAMPLE

```
<?php
    print "Hello, world";
?>
```

Comments	There are three styles of PHP comments: C, C++, and Shell (see Chapter 2, "Getting Started").

EXAMPLE

```
<?php
    print "Hello, world";    // This is the C++ style comment
    /* This is a  C style comment and it can span
       multiple lines */
    #  And this is a Shell style comment
?>
```

Printing output	The `echo` and `print` are language constructs used to display output. Technically, `print` and `echo` are not functions and do not require parentheses around the data passed as arguments. `Print` displays a string and returns an integer value. Parentheses are not required around the string.

Echo prints comma-separated strings and does not return anything. If `echo` gets more than one string, parentheses cannot be used unless each string is enclosed in a set of parentheses (see Chapter 6, "Strings").

If you need to format the output, the `printf()`, `sprintf()`, and `fprintf()` functions are available (see Chapter 6, "Strings").

EXAMPLE

```
echo string [ , string[ , string] ... ];
int print (string);
int printf ( string format [, mixed args [, mixed ...]] );

<?php
    echo "Hello ", "world", "<br />";          // Don't use parens
    echo ("It's such a perfect day!<br /><br />"); // Parens okay
    print "Hello to world again!<br />" ;      // Don't need parens
    print ("It's such a perfect day!<br />") ; // Parens okay
    printf("Meet %s%:Age 5d%:Salary \$10.2f\n", "John",
           40, 55000);
?>
```

Table 3.1   PHP Syntax and Constructs (continued)

Data types	PHP supports four core data types and another four special types: • Core: integer, float, string, and boolean. • Special: null, array, object, and resource (see Chapter 4, "The Building Blocks").
Variables	Variable names start with a dollar sign ($), followed by a letter and any number of alphanumeric characters, including the underscore.

EXAMPLE

```php
<?php
   $first_name = "Ellie";
   $last_name = "Quigley";
   $salary = 125000.00;
   echo $first_name, $last_name, $salary;
?>
```

Predefined variables	PHP provides a large number of predefined variables, called superglobals, meaning they are available anywhere in the script. The following is a list of the most common predefined variables:

```
$_GLOBALS          $_FILES
$_SERVER           $_ENV
$_GET              $_REQUEST
$_POST             $_SESSION
$_COOKIE
```

Constants	A constant value, once set, cannot be modified. An example of a constant is pi or the number of feet in a mile. It does not change. Constants are defined with the define() function. They are global in scope.

EXAMPLE

```php
define("PI", 3.141592);
PI=6;  // Cannot modify PI; produces an error
```

Numbers	PHP supports both integers (decimal, octal, hexadecimal) as well as floating-point numbers, scientific notation, booleans, and null.

EXAMPLE

```php
<?php
   $year = 2006;                    // integer
   $product_price = 29.95;          // floating-point number in base 10
   $favorite_color = 0x33CC99;      // integer in base 16 (hexadecimal)
   $distance_to_moon=3.844e+5;      // floating-point in sci. notation
?>
```

Table 3.1 PHP Syntax and Constructs (continued)

Strings and quotes	A string is a sequence of bytes (characters) enclosed in quotes. Although a string consists of plain text, PHP allows binary data to be placed in a string as well. When quoting strings, make sure the quotes are matched; for example, `"string"` or `'string'`. Variables (`$x`, `$name`, etc.) and backslash sequences (`\n`, `\t`, `\"`, etc.) are interpreted within double quotes; a backslash will escape a quotation mark, a single quote can be embedded in a set of double quotes, and a double quote can be embedded in a set of single quotes. A *here document* (here-doc) is a block of text embedded between user-defined tags, the first tag preceded by `<<<`.

The following shows three ways to quote a string:

1. Single quotes: `'It rains in Spain'`

2. Double quotes: `"It rains in Spain"`

3. Here document method:
```
<<<END
    It
    rains in
    Spain
END;
```

EXAMPLE

```php
<?php
    $question = 'He asked her if she wouldn\'t mind going to
        Spain'; // Single quotes
    $answer = 'She said: "No, but it rains in Spain."';
        // Single quotes
    $question = "\tHe said he wouldn't take her to Spain\n";
    $temperature = "78";
    print "It is currently $temperature degrees"; /* Prints: "It
        is currently 78 degrees." Variables are interpreted when
        enclosed in double quotes, but not single quotes */
?>
```

Boolean values	A boolean value is exactly one bit with two possible values: true or false.

EXAMPLE

```php
<?php
    $answer = 1;
    if ( $answer == true ){
        print "Yes, it's true.<br />";
    }
    $answer = 0;
    if ( $answer == FALSE ){   // Booleans are not case sensitive
        print "The answer is false.<br />";
    }
?>
```

Table 3.1 PHP Syntax and Constructs (continued)

Null	Null value means that there is no value assigned, that the value NULL was assigned, or the value has been unset with the unset() function. Null means "nothing"—not a blank space, not an empty string, and not zero.

EXAMPLE

```php
<?php
   $string = Null;   // Null
   $string = " ";    // Not Null
   $n = 0;           // Not Null
   unset($n);        // Now $n is Null
?>
```

Operators	PHP offers many types of operators, but for the most part they are the same as C, C++, Java, or Perl operators. Types of operators are: Assignment: = += -= *- %= ^= &= |= .- Equality: == != Identical: = = = != = = Relational: > >= < <= Logical: && (AND) || (OR) ! (XOR) Auto increment/auto decrement: ++ -- Bitwise: ~ & | ^ << >> String concatenation: . Arithmetic: * / - + % Casting: (int), (float), (string), (bool), (array), (object)

EXAMPLE

```php
<pre>
<?php
   print "\nArithmetic Operators\n";
   print (3+2) * (5-3)/2;

   print "\nString Operators\n"; // Concatenation
   print "\tMarko" . ' ' . "Gargenta";

   print "\nComparison Operators\n";
   print 5>=3 . "\n";
   print 47==23 . "\n";

   print "\nLogical Operators\n";
   print ( (5<3) && (47>23) || 'hello' != "HELLO");
   print "\nTypecasting\n";
   print (int) 23.87;

   print "\nCombined Assignment Operators\n";
   $a = 47;
   $a += 3;   // short for $a = $a + 3
   $a++;      // autoincrement
   print $a;
?>
</pre>
```

Table 3.1 PHP Syntax and Constructs (continued)

Arrays	An array is an indexed collection of data. PHP supports two types of arrays: traditional arrays and associative arrays. Traditional arrays are indexed by integers starting at 0; associative arrays are indexed by strings.

EXAMPLES

```php
<?php
// Traditional array
    $names = array( "Jessica", "Michelle", "Linda" );
    print "$names[0] and $names[2]"; // Prints "Jessica"
                                     // and "Linda"
    $names[3]="Nicole";  // Assign a new value to the 4th element
>
```

```php
<php
// Associative array
    $address_book = array (
        "Jessica"  => "(415) 555-2946",
        "Michelle" => "(925) 555-1274",
        "Linda"    => "(707) 555-3349"
    );

    print $address_book["Jessica"];  // prints (415) 555-2946
    $address_book["Jody"] = "(530) 343-6555";

    var_dump( $address_book );       // prints out the whole array

?>
```

Conditionals	The `if` statement construct:

```php
if ( expression ){
    statements;
}
```

The basic `if` construct evaluates an expression enclosed in parentheses, and if the condition evaluates to true, the block following the expression is executed.

EXAMPLE

```php
<?php
    if ( $a = = = $b ){ print "$a is identical to $b"; }
?>
```

The `if/else` statement construct:

```php
if ( expression ){
    statements;
}
else{
    statements;
}
```

Table 3.1   PHP Syntax and Constructs (continued)

Conditionals *(continued)*	The `if/else` block is a two-way decision. If the expression after the `if` condition is true, the block of statements are executed; if false, the `else` block of statements is executed.

EXAMPLE

```php
<?php
   $coin_toss = rand( 1, 2 );   // Generate a random number
                                // between 1 and 2
   if( $coin_toss == 1 ) {
      echo "You tossed HEAD";
   }
   else {
      echo "You tossed TAIL";
   }
?>
```

The `if/elseif` statement construct:

```
if ( expression ){
   statements;
}
elseif ( expression ){
   statements;
}
elseif (expression){
   statements;
else{
   statements;
}
```

The `if/else if/else` offers a multiway branch; if the expression following the `if` is not true, each of the `elseif` expressions are evaluated until one is true; otherwise, the optional `else` statements are executed.

EXAMPLE

```php
<?php
   // Let's say 1 is Monday, 7 Sunday
   $day_of_week = rand( 1, 7 );
   echo "Today is: $day_of_week<br />";
   if ( $day_of_week >=1 && $day_of_week <=4 ) {
      echo "Business hours are from 9 am to 9 pm";
   }
   elseif ( $day_of_week == 5) {
      echo "Business hours are from 9 am to 6 pm";
   }
   else {
      echo "We are closed on weekends";
   endif
   }
?>
```

Table 3.1   PHP Syntax and Constructs (continued)

Conditionals *(continued)*	The switch statement construct:

```
switch ( $variable_name  ) {
case valueA:
   statements;
   break;  // optional
case valueB:
   statements;
   break;  // optional
default:
   statements;
}
```

The switch construct is an alternative to if/else if/else. The expression after the switch keyword is evaluated and matched against a series of case values until one matches; if there is a matching case, then the block of statements following the colon are executed; otherwise, if there is not a valid case, the statements after the default are executed. The break is optional, but is used to exit the switch construct.

EXAMPLE

```php
<?php

// Let's say 1 is Monday, 7 Sunday
$day_of_week = rand( 1, 7 );

echo "Today is: $day_of_week<br />";

switch( $day_of_week ) {
case 1:
case 2:
case 3:
case 4:
   echo "Business hours are from 9 am to 9 pm";
   break;
case 5:
   echo "Business hours are from 9 am to 6 pm";
   break;
default:
   echo "We are closed on weekends";
   break;
}

?>
```

Table 3.1   PHP Syntax and Constructs (continued)

Conditional operator	Like C, C++, PHP also offers a short form of the `if/else` syntax, which uses three operands and two operators (also called the ternary operator). The question mark is followed by a statement that is executed if the condition being tested is true, and the colon is followed by a statement that is executed if the condition is false:

```
(condition) ? statement_if_true : statement_if_false;
```

EXAMPLE

```
<?php
$coin_toss = rand( 1, 2 );
echo ($coin_toss == 1 ? "You tossed HEAD" : "You tossed TAIL" );
?>
```

Loops	A loop is a way to specify a piece of code that repeats many times. PHP supports several types of loops: the `while` loop, `do-while` loop, `for` loop, and `foreach` loop.

The `while` loop construct:

```
while ( conditional expression ) {
    code block A
}
```

The `while` is followed by an expression enclosed in parentheses, and a block of statements. As long as the expression tests true, the loop continues to iterate.

EXAMPLE

```
<?php
    $count=0;       // Initial value
    while ($count < 10 ){  // Test
        echo $n;
        $count++;  // Increment value
    }
?>
```

The `do-while` loop construct:

```
do   {
    code block A
} while (expression);
```

The `do-while` loop is similar to the `while` loop except it checks its looping expresssion at the end of the loop block, rather than at the beginning, guaranteeing that the loop block is executed at least once.

Table 3.1   PHP Syntax and Constructs (continued)

Loops *(continued)*	**EXAMPLE**

```php
<?php
   $count=0;        // Initial value
   do {
       echo $n;
       $count++;  // Increment value
   while ($count < 10 );  // Test
   }
?>
```

The for loop construct:

```
for( initialization; conditional expression; increment/decrement ) {
   block of code
}
```

The for loop has three expressions to evaluate, each separated by a semicolon. The first inititializes a variable and is only evaluated once; the second tests whether the value is true, and if it is true, the block is entered; if not, the loop exits. After the block of statements is executed, control returns to the third expression, which changes the value of the variable being tested. The second expression is tested again, and so on.

EXAMPLE

```php
<?php
for( $count = 0; $count < 10; $count = $count + 1 ) {
   echo "$count";            # Prints the values 0 1 2 3 4 5 6 7 8 9
}
?>
```

There are two constructs for using a foreach loop:

```
foreach( $array_name as $value ) {
   block of code
}

foreach( $array_name as $name=>$value ) {
   lock of code
}
```

The foreach loop is used only to iterate through an array, and issues an error if you try to use it on any other data type or uninitialized variable.

Table 3.1   PHP Syntax and Constructs (continued)

Loops *(continued)*	**EXAMPLES**

```php
<?php
// Initialize the array
$dessert= array ( "ice cream", "cake", "pudding", "fruit");
foreach ($dessert as $value){  // Iterates through array elements
    echo "Dessert choice is: $value<br />";
}
?>
```

```php
<?php
// Initialize the array
$address_book = array (
"Jessica"  => "(415) 555-2946",
"Michelle" => "(925) 555-1274",
"Linda"    => "(707) 555-3349" );

foreach( $address_book as $name=>$phone ) {
    echo "$name, $phone<br />"; // Iterates through each key-value
                                // pair in the array
}
?>
```

Loop control	The break statement is used to break out of a loop from within the loop block. The continue statement is used to skip over the remaining statements within the loop block and start back at the top of the loop.

EXAMPLES

```php
<?php
   $n=0;
   while( $n < 10 ){
      print $n;
      if ($n == 3){
         break;  // Break out of loop
      }
      $n++;
   }
   print "Out of the loop.<br />";
?>
```

```php
<?php
for($n=0; $n<10; $n++){
   if ($n == 3){
      continue;  // Start at top of loop; skip remaining
                 // statements in block
   }
   echo "\$n = $n<br />";
}
   print "Out of the loop.<br />";
?>
```

Table 3.1 PHP Syntax and Constructs (continued)

Functions	The `function` construct is:

```
function function_name( argument1, argument2, argument3, ... ) {
   block of code
}
```

A function is a block of code that peforms a task and can be invoked from another part of the program. Data can be passed to the function via arguments. A function might or might not return a value. Any valid PHP code can make up the definition block of a function. Variables outside the function are not available inside the function.

The `global` command will make the specified variables available (see Chapter 9, "User-Defined Functions").

EXAMPLES

```
<?php
   function greetings() {
      print "Welcome to PHP!<br />";   // Function definition
   }
   greetings;      // Function call
?>
```

```
<?php
$my_year = 2000;

if ( is_leap_year( $my_year ) ) { // Call function with argument
   print "$my_year is a leap year";
}
else {
   print "$my_year is not a leap year";
}

function is_leap_year( $year ) {    // Function definition
   return ((($year % 4 == 0) && ($year % 100 != 0)) ||
   ($year % 400 == 0)) ? 1 : 0;     // Returned from the function
}
?>
```

Classes and objects	PHP supports objects, a special type of variable. A class is a collection of variables and functions, called properties and methods. The properties (also called attributes) are variables used to describe the object. Properties can be defined as public, private, or protected.

Objects and methods are functions that allow you to create and manipulate the object. Objects are created with the new operator. $this is a special pseudo variable that references the current object (see Chapter 17, "Objects").

Table 3.1   PHP Syntax and Constructs (continued)

| Classes and objects *(continued)* | **EXAMPLES** |

Creating a class:

```php
<?php
class Pet
{
    public $pet_name;
        function set_name($string_of_text){  // Accessor methods
            $this->name = $string_of_text;
        }
        function get_name(){
            return $this->name
        }
}
```

Instantiating a class:

```php
$cat = new Pet;   // Create object with a constructor method
$cat->set_name("Sneaky"); // Access object with an instance method
echo "Your cat is rightly named ",$cat->get_name(), ".<br";
?>
```

PHP also supports inheritance. A new class can be created from an existing class, a parent–child relationship where the child class inherits properties and methods of the parent class and extends or defines the functionality of its parent. PHP also has special constructor and desctructor methods for creating and destroying objects, as well as special setter and getter methods (also called access or instance methods) for assigning and retrieving the object's properties.

An example that creates a new Laptop class from a Computer class is shown here.

EXAMPLE

```php
<?php
class computer {
    private $password; // Visible only within this class
    protected $userId; // Visible within this class and subclass
    public $printer;   // Visible anywhere in the script

    function __construct() {  // Parent's constructor
        print "In the parent constructor.\n<br />";
        $this->userId = "willie";     // protected
        $this->password = "urAok5";   // private
    }
    function setUserId($userId){
        $this->userId=$userId;
    }
    function getUserId() {
        return $this->userId;
    }
```

Table 3.1 PHP Syntax and Constructs (continued)

| Classes and objects (*continued*) | ```php
    private function setPassword($password){   // private method
        $this->password-$password;
    }
    private function getPassword(){
        return $this->password;
    }
}
class Laptop extends Computer{     // Child/derived/subclass
    public $brand;
    public $weight;
    private $password="LetMeIn2";

    function __construct($brand,$weight){ // Subclass constructor
        parent::__construct();     // Call to parent's constructor
        echo "Child constructor just called.\n<br />";
        $this->brand=$brand;        // new properties for the child
        $this->weight=$weight;
    }
    function __destruct(){
        echo "$this being destroyed\n";
    }
    function setPassword($password){
        $this->password=$password;
    }
    function getPassword(){
        return $this->password;
    }
}

// Class user
$pc=new Computer();   // Create two new objects
$portable = new Laptop();
$portable->setPassword("letmein2");
    .....
``` |
| Files | PHP comes with a set of built-in functions that allow you to work with files. You can include external files with the `require` and `include` statements. The included files can consist of PHP, HTML, XML, text, and so on. The requested file's contents replace the line containing the word `require` or `include`.

EXAMPLE

To include a file:
```php
// replaces instances of require with the contents of file
require("copyright.inc");
// replaces only first instance of require with contents of file
require_once("header.inc");
// same as replace but happens only during program execution
include("disclaimer.inc");
// happens only once during program execution
include_once("title.inc");
``` |
```

Table 3.1   PHP Syntax and Constructs (continued)

Files *(continued)*	To open a file for reading, writing, appending, and so on, the filename must be assigned to a filehandle. The following is a list of some of the basic functions for opening, closing, reading, and writing to a file.

> **EXAMPLES**
>
> **To open a file:**
> ```
> // Opens "filename" for reading
> $filehandle = fopen("filename", "r");
> // Opens "filename" for writing
> $filehandle = fopen("filename", "w");
> // Opens "filename" for binary writing
> $filehandle = fopen("filename", "wb");
> ```
>
> **To close a file:**
> ```
> fclose($filehandle);
> ```
>
> **To read from a file:**
> ```
> // Reads a line from file attached to $filehandle
> $string = fgets($filehandle);
> // Reads a character from file attached to $filehandle
> $char = fgetc($filehandle);
> // Reads chunk of bytes from file attached to $filehandle
> $text = fread($filehandle, $bytes );
> // Reads entire contents from "filename"
> $text = file_get_contents("filename");
> ```
>
> **To write to a file:**
> ```
> // Writes $string to $filehandle
> fwrite($filehandle, $string);
> // Writes $string to "filename"
> file_put_contents("filename", $string);
> ```

Regular expressions	PHP supports pattern matching with regular expressions and regular expression metacharacters (see Table 3.2). The pcre (Perl style) functions are used to test whether a text string matches a pattern.

> **EXAMPLES**
>
> ```
> // $result is 1, $matches contains needle
> $result  =  preg_match("/needle/", "looking for a needle in a
>                          haystack", $matches);
>
> // Regular expression metacharacters
> if ( preg_match("/^[Nn]..dle/", "Needle in a haystack" )){
>    echo "Found match.\n";
> }
> // $new_array contains: normal, mama, man
> $new_array = preg_grep("/ma/", array("normal", "mama",
>                          "man","plan"));
> ```

Table 3.1 PHP Syntax and Constructs (continued)

| Regular expressions (*continued*) | ```php
// $new_array contains: plan
$new_array = preg_grep("/ma/",array("normal","mama","man",
                                    "plan"),PREG_GREP_INVERT);


// $new_string: "I am feeling upbeat, upbeat, upbeat."
$new_string = preg_replace("/blue/", "upbeat", "I am feeling
                            blue, blue, blue.");


// $new_string: "I am feeling upbeat, blue, blue"
$new_string = preg_replace("/blue/", "upbeat", "I am feeling
                            blue, blue, blue.",1);


// $new_string: "I am feeling upbeat, upbeat.
$new_string = preg_replace("/blue/i", "upbeat", "I am feeling
                            BLue, BLUE.");


// $new_string: "War and Peace"
$new_string = preg_replace("/(Peace) and (War)/i", "$2 and $1",
                            "Peace and War");


// $new_string: "He gave me 42 dollars."
$new_string = preg_replace("/5/e", "6*7", "He gave me 5
                            dollars.")e;
``` |

Table 3.2 Some Regular Expression Metacharacters

Metacharacter	What It Does
^	Matches at the beginning of a line
$	Matches at the end of a line
a.c	Matches an a, any single character, and a c
[abc]	Matches an a or b or c
[^abc]	Matches a character that is not an a, or b, or c
[0-9]	Matches one digit between 0 and 9
ab*c	Matches an a, followed by zero or more of the letter b, and a c
ab+c	Matches an a, followed by one or more of the letter b, and a c
ab?c	Matches an a, followed by zero or one b, and a c
```

3.2   Chapter Summary

This chapter was provided for programmers who need a quick peek at what PHP looks like, its general syntax, and programming constructs. Later, this chapter can serve as a tutorial to refresh your memory without having to search through the index to find what you are looking for.

3.2.1   What's Next?

In Chapter 4, "The Building Blocks," we discuss the basic building blocks of all languages: data types. You learn how to work with different types of numbers, strings, booleans, and more.

You also learn how to define and display variables, how to use variables, how PHP deals with data coming in from HTML forms, and how to define constants.

4

The Building Blocks: Data Types, Literals, Variables, and Constants

"One man's constant is another man's variable."
—Alan Perlis

4.1 Data Types

A program can do many things, including perform calculations, sort names, prepare phone lists, display images, play chess, ad infinitum. To do anything, however, the program works with the data that is given to it. Data types specify what kind of data, such as numbers and characters, can be stored and manipulated within a program. PHP supports a number of fundamental basic data types, such as integers, floats, and strings. Basic data types are the simplest building blocks of a program. They are called scalars and can be assigned a single literal value such as a number, 5.7, or a string of characters, such as "hello", a date and time, or a boolean (true/false). See Figure 4.1.

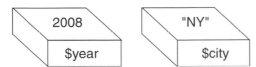

Figure 4.1 Scalars hold one value.

PHP also supports composite data types, such as arrays and objects. Composite data types represent a collection of data, rather than a single value (see Figure 4.2). The composite data types are discussed in Chapter 8, "Arrays," and Chapter 17, "Objects."

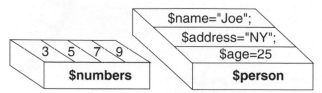

Figure 4.2   Arrays and objects hold multiple values.

The different types of data are commonly stored in variables. Examples of PHP variables are `$num = 5` or `$name = "John"` where variables `$num` and `$name` are assigned an integer and a string, respectively. Variables hold values that can change throughout the program, whereas once a constant is defined, its value does not change. `PHP_VERSION` and `PHP_OS` are examples of predefined PHP constants. The use of PHP variables and constants is addressed in "Variables" on page 70 and "Constants" on page 99 of this chapter.

PHP supports four core data types:

- Integer
- Float (also called double)
- String
- Boolean

In addition to the four core data types, there are four other special types:

- Null
- Array
- Object
- Resources

4.1.1 Numeric Literals

PHP supports both integers and floating-point numbers. See Example 4.1.

- **Integers**—Integers are whole numbers and do not contain a decimal point; for example, 123 and –6. Integers can be expressed in decimal (base 10), octal (base 8), and hexadecimal (base 16), and are either positive or negative values.
- **Floating-point numbers**—Floating-point numbers, also called doubles or reals, are fractional numbers such as 123.56 or –2.5. They must contain a decimal point or an exponent specifier, such as 1.3e–2. The letter "e" can be either upper or lowercase.

PHP numbers can be very large (the size depends on your platform), but a precision of 14 decimal digits is a common value or ($\sim 1.8e^{308}$).

EXAMPLE 4.1

```
12345        integer
23.45        float
.234E-2      float in scientific notation
.234e+3      float in scientific notation
0x456fff     integer in base 16, hexadecimal
0x456FFF     integer in base 16, hexadecimal
0777         integer in base 8, octal
```

EXAMPLE 4.2

```php
<html>
<head><title>Printing Numbers</title>
</head>
<body bgcolor="lightblue">
<font face = "arial" size = '+1'>
<?php
   print "The positive integer is <em><b>" . 5623 . "
      .</b></em><br />";
   print "The negative integer is <em><b>" . -22 . ".</b></em><br />";
   print "The floating point number is <em><b>" . 15.3 . "
      .</b></em><br />";
   print "The number in scientfic notation is <em><b> " . 5e3 . "
      . </b></em><br />";
   print "\tThe string is: <em><b>I can't help you!</em>
      </b><br />";
?>
</body>
</html>
```

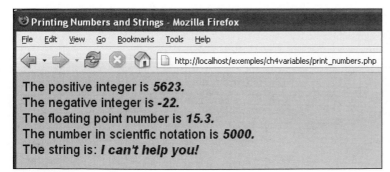

Figure 4.3   Output from Example 4.2.

4.1.2   String Literals and Quoting

We introduce strings in this chapter but Chapter 6, "Strings," provides a more comprehensive coverage. String literals are a row of characters enclosed in either double or single quotes.[1] **The quotes must be matched**. If the string starts with a single quote, it must end with a matching single quote; likewise if it starts with a double quote, it must end with a double quote. If a string of characters is enclosed in single quotes, the characters are treated literally (each of the characters represents itself). We can say the single quotes are the democratic quotes: All characters are treated equally.

Double quotes do not treat all characters equally. If a string is enclosed in double quotes, most of the characters represent themselves, but dollar signs and backslashes have a special meaning as shown in the following examples.

Single quotes can hide double quotes, and double quotes can hide single quotes:[2]

```
"This is a string"
'This is another string'
"This is also 'a string'"
'This is "a string"'
```

An empty set of quotes is called the null string. If a number is enclosed in quotes, it is considered a string; for example, `"5"` is a string, whereas 5 is a number.

Strings are called constants or literals. The string value `"hello"` is called a string constant or literal. To change a string requires replacing it with another string.

Strings can contain escape sequences (a single character preceded with a backslash). Escape sequences cause a character to behave in a certain way; for example, a `"\t"` represents a tab and `"\n"` represents a newline. The backslash is also used for quoting a single character so that it will not be interpreted; for example, `\$5.00` where the dollar sign in PHP is used to represent variables rather than money. `\$5.00` could also be written as `'$5'` because single quotes protect all characters from interpretation.

Here documents, also called *here-docs*, provide a way to create a block of text that simplifies writing strings containing lots of single quotes, double quotes, and variables (see Example 4.4).

EXAMPLE   4.3

```
    <html>
        <head><title>Quotes</title></head>
        <body bgcolor="lightblue"><font size='+1'>
1       <?php
2           $name = "Nancy";   // Setting a PHP variable
            print "<ol>";
```

---

1. PHP always null-terminates strings internally and keeps track of the length of the string.

2. PHP recognizes editors that use straight quotes, such as vi or Notepad, but not editors that automatically transform straight quotes into curly quotes.

EXAMPLE 4.3 (CONTINUED)

```
3          print "<li> $name is my friend.</li>";     // Double quotes
4          print '<li> $name is my neighbor.</li>';  // Single quotes
5          print "<li> I can't go with you.</li>";   // Nested quotes
6          print "<li> She cried, \"Help!\"</li>";   // Escaping quotes
7          print "<li> I need \$5.00.</li>";     // The backslash
                                                 // quotes one character
8          print "<li> $name needs ". '$5.00 </li>'; // Nested quotes
           print "</ol>";
       ?>
       </body>
     </html>
```

EXPLANATION

1 PHP program starts here.
2 $name is a PHP variable. It is assigned the string "Nancy". You will learn all about variables in the section "Variables" on page 70.
3 When a string is enclosed within double quotes, the PHP interpreter will substitue the variable with its value; for example, $name will be replaced with "Nancy".
4 When a string is enclosed in single quotes, all characters are treated as literals. Variable substitution will not occur.
5 Single quotes can be nested within double quotes and vice versa.
6 Quotes can be escaped with a backslash to make them literal characters within a string.
7 The dollar sign is escaped from PHP interpretation, that is, is treated as a literal character.
8 A string in double quotes is concatenated to a string in single quotes. Just as the backslash protects the dollar sign from interpretaion, so do the single quotes. Remember, characters in single quotes are all treated as literals; that is, PHP does not consider any of the enclosed characters as special. See the output in Figure 4.4.

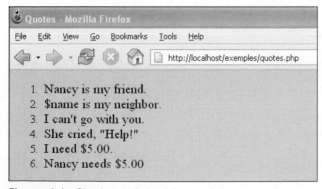

Figure 4.4 Single and double quotes.

The Here Document—A Special Kind of Quoting.   Here documents are a kind of quoting popular in a number of languages, such as JavaScript, Perl, Shell scripts, and so on. Here documents, also called *here-docs*, allow you to quote a large block of text within your script without using multiple print statements and quotes. The entire block of text is treated as though it is surrounded by double quotes. This can be useful if you have a large block of HTML within your PHP script interspersed with variables, quotes, and escape sequences.

Rules for a Here Document:

1. The user-defined delimiter word starts and terminates the here document. Text is inserted between the delimiters. The delimiter can contain letters, numbers, and the underscore character. The first letter must be a letter or an underscore. By convention, the delimiter should be in all uppercase letters to make it stand out from other words in your script. The delimeter is preceded by three < characters; for example, `<<<DELIMITER`

    ```
    print <<<HERE_DOC_DELIMITER
       <text here>
       ...
       < more text>
       ...

    HERE_DOC_DELIMITER
    ```

2. The delimiter cannot be surrounded by any spaces, comments, or other text. The final delimiter can optionally be terminated with a semicolon and must be on a line by itself.
3. All variable and escape sequences will be interpreted within the here document.

EXAMPLE 4.4

```
1   <?php
2       $bgcolor="darkblue";
        $tablecolor = "yellow";
3       print <<<MY_BOUNDARY
4       <html><head><title>heredoc</title></head>
5       <body bgcolor="$bgcolor">
6       <table border="1" bgcolor=$tablecolor>
            <tr><th>Author</th><th>Book</th></tr>
            <tr>
                <td>Marcel Proust</td>
                <td>Remembrance of Things Past</td>
            </tr>
```

EXAMPLE 4.4 (CONTINUED)

```
          <tr>
             <td>Charles Dickens</td>
             <td>Tale of Two Cities</td>
          </tr>
          </table>
        </body>
7       </html>
8       MY_BOUNDARY;
     ?>
```

EXPLANATION

1 PHP starts here.
2 Two scalar variables are defined.
3 This is the *here-doc*. The user-defined terminator, MY_BOUNDARY, is prepended with <<<. There can be no space after the terminator; otherwise an error like this will be displayed: *Parse error: syntax error, unexpected T_SL in c:\wamp\www\exemples\ch4variables\heredoc.php on line 4*
4 All of the HTML document is embedded in the here document. The HTML will be sent to the browser as is. Any PHP code embedded withing the HTML tags will be handled by the PHP interpreter.
5 The value of the variable, $bgcolor, will be assigned as the background color of the page.
6 An HTML table is started here. The value of the variable, $tablecolor, will be assigned as the background color of the table cells.
7 The HTML document ends here, inside the *here-doc*.
8 The user-defined terminator, MY_BOUNDARY, marks the end of the here document. There can be no spaces surrounding the terminator. The semicolon is optional.

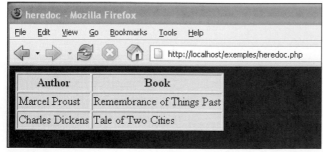

Figure 4.5 Here document output.

Escape Sequences.   Escape sequences consist of a backslash followed by a single character. When enclosed in double quotes, the backslash causes the interpretation of the next character to "escape" from its normal ASCII code and to represent something else (see Table 4.1). To display the escape sequences in your browser, the HTML <pre> tag can be used (see Example 4.5); otherwise, the escape sequences placed within your PHP script will not be interpreted.

Table 4.1   Escape Sequences

Escape Sequence	What It Represents
\'	Single quotation mark
\"	Double quotation
\t	Tab
\n	Newline
\r	Return/line feed
\$	A literal dollar sign
\\	Backslash
\70	Represents the octal value
\x05	Represents the hexadecimal character

EXAMPLE 4.5

```
      <html><head><title>Escape Sequences</title></head>
      <body bgcolor="orange">
      <b>
1     <pre>
2     <?php
3        print "\t\tTwo tabs are \\t\\t, and two newlines are
             \\n\\n.\n\n";
4        print "\tThe escaped octal numbers represent ASCII
             \101\102\103.\n";
         print "\tThe escaped hexadecimal numbers represent ASCII
             \x25\x26.\n";
5        print '\tWith single quotes, backslash sequences are not
             interpreted.\n';
         ?>
      </pre>
      </b>
      </body>
      </html>
```

EXPLANATION

1 Because this file will be displayed in a browser window, the HTML `<pre>` tags are used to retain spaces and tabs. If you run PHP at the command line, the escape sequences will be interpreted.

2 The PHP program starts here with its opening tag.

3 The escape sequences must be enclosed in double quotes. The sequences for tab (`\t`) and newline (`\n`) characters produce tabs and newlines. If a backslash is prepended with another backslash, then the backslash is treated as a literal.

4 In this example, by preceding an octal or hexadecimal number with a backslash, its ASCII equivalent is displayed.

5 If a string is enclosed in single quotes, escape sequences are ignored. See the output in Figure 4.6.

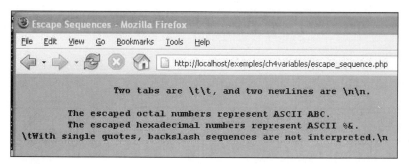

Figure 4.6 Escape sequences and the `<pre>` tag.

```
$ php escape_sequence.php
<html><head><title>Escape Sequences</title></head>
<body bgcolor="orange">
<b>
<pre>
            Two tabs are \t\t, and two newlines are \n\n.

      The escaped octal numbers represent ASCII ABC.
      The escaped hexadecimal numbers represent ASCII %&.
\tWith single quotes, backslash sequences are not interpreted.\n</pre>
</b>
</body>
</html>
```

Figure 4.7 Escape sequences at the command line.

4.1.3   Boolean Literals

Boolean literals (introduced in PHP 4) are logical values that have only one of two values, *true* or *false*, both **case insensitive**. You can think of the values as *yes* or *no*, *on* or *off*, or *1* or *0*. They are used to test whether a condition is true or false. When using numeric comparison and equality operators, the value *true* evaluates to 1 and *false* evaluates to the empty string (see Figure 4.8).

```
$answer1 = true;
   or
if ($answer2 == false) { do something; }
```

EXAMPLE 4.6

```php
<?php
if ( 0 == False  && "" == FALSE) {
    print "zero and null are <em>false.</em><br /> ";}
if ( 1 == True && "abc" == true) {
    print "1 and \"abc\" are both <em>true.</em><br /> "; }
?>
```

Figure 4.8   True and false.

4.1.4   Special Data Types

Null.   NULL represents "no value," meaning "nothing," not even an empty string or zero. It is a type of NULL. An uninitialized variable contains the value NULL. A variable can be assigned the value NULL, and if a variable has been unset, it is considered to be NULL.

Resource.   A resource is a special variable, holding a reference to an external resource such as a database object or file handler. Resources are created and used by special functions. File and database resources are defined by the PHP interpreter and are only accessible by functions provided by the interpreter (see Chapter 11, "Files and Directories," and Chapter 15, "PHP and MySQL Integration).

The gettype() Function.   The `gettype()` built-in function returns a string to identify the data type of its argument. The argument might be a variable, string, keyword,
and so on. You can use the `gettype()` function to check whether or not a variable has
been defined because if there is no value associated with the variable, the `gettype()`
function returns NULL (see Figure 4.9).

Strings returned from the `gettype()` function include the following:

`"boolean"` (since PHP 4)
`"integer"`
`"double"` (for historical reasons `"double"` is returned in case of a float,
and not simply `"float"`)
`"string"`
`"array"`
`"object"`
`"resource"` (since PHP 4)
`"NULL"` (since PHP 4)

FORMAT

```
string gettype ( mixed var )
```

Examples:
```
$type=gettype(54.6);  // Returns "float"
print gettype("yes"); // Returns and prints "string"
```

EXAMPLE 4.7

```
<html>
<head><title>Getting the Data Type with gettype()</title>
</head><body bgcolor="lightblue">
<font face = "arial" size = '+1'>
<pre>
<?php
    print "Type <b>5623</b> is: " . gettype(5623) . ".\n";
    print "Type <b>-22</b> is: " . gettype(-22) . ".\n";
    print "Type <b>15.3</b> is: " . gettype(15.3) . ".\n";
    print "Type <b>5e3</b> is: " . gettype(5e3) . ".\n";
    print "Type <b>\"Hi\"</b> is: " . gettype("Hi") . ".\n";
    print "Type <b>true</b> is: " . gettype(true) . ".\n";
    print "Type <b>false</b> is: " . gettype(false) . ".\n";
    print "Type <b>null</b> is: " . gettype(null) . ".\n";
    print "Type <b>\$nothing</b> is: " . gettype($nothing) . ".\n";
?>
</body>
</html>
```

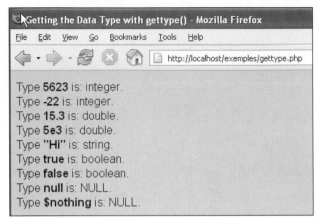

Figure 4.9   PHP data types. Output from Example 4.7.

4.2   Variables

4.2.1   Definition and Assignment

Variables are fundamental to all programming languages. They are data items that represent a memory storage location in the computer. Variables are containers that hold data such as numbers and strings. In PHP programs there are three types of variables:

1. Predefined variables
2. User-defined variables
3. Form variables related to names in an HTML form

Variables have a *name*, a *type*, and a *value*.

```
$num = 5;             // name: "$num", value: 5, type: numeric
$friend = "Peter";    // name: "$friend", value: "Peter", type: string
$x = true;            // name: "$x", value: true, type: boolean
```

The values assigned to variables can change throughout the run of a program whereas constants, also called literals, remain fixed.

PHP variables can be assigned different types of data, including:

- Numeric
- String
- Boolean
- Objects
- Arrays

Computer programming languages like C++ and Java require that you specify the type of data you are going to store in a variable when you declare it. For example, if you are going to assign an integer to a variable, you would have to say something like:

```
int n = 5;
```

and if you were assigning a floating-point number:

```
float x = 44.5;
```

Languages that require that you specify a data type are called "strongly typed" languages. PHP, conversely, is a dynamically, or loosely typed, language, meaning that you do not have to specify the data type of a variable. In fact, doing so will produce an error. With PHP you would simply say:

```
$n = 5;
$x = 44.5;
```

and PHP will figure out what type of data is being stored in $n and $x.

4.2.2 Valid Names

Variable names consist of any number of letters (an underscore counts as a letter) and digits. The first letter must be a letter or an underscore (see Table 4.2). Variable names are case sensitive, so Name, name, and NAme are all different variable names.

Table 4.2   Valid and Invalid Variable Name Examples

Valid Variable Names	*Invalid Variable Names*
$name1	$10names
$price_tag	box.front
$_abc	$name#last
$Abc_22	A-23
$A23	$5

4.2.3 Declaring and Initializing Variables

Variables are normally declared before they are used. PHP variables can be declared in a script, come from an HTML form, from the query string attached to the script's URL, from cookies, from the server, or from the server's environment. Variable names are explicitly preceded by a $. You can assign a value to the variable (or initialize a variable) when you declare it, but it is not mandatory.

FORMAT

```
$variable_name = value;      initialized
$variable_name;        uninitialized, value is null
```

To declare a variable called `firstname`, you could say:

```
$first_name="Ellie";
```

You can declare multiple variables on the same line by separating each declaration with a semicolon. For example, you could say:

```
$first_name; $middle_name; $last_name;
```

Double, Single, and Backquotes in Assignment Statements.   When assigning a value to a variable, if the value is a string, then the string can be enclosed in either single or double quotes; if the value is returned from a function, then the function is not enclosed in quotes; and if the value is returned from a system command (see "Execution Operators" on page 143), then the command is enclosed in backquotes:

```
$name = "Marko";         // Assign a string
$city = 'San Francisco';   // Assign a string
$now = date("m/d/Y");  // Assign output of a function
$dirlist = `ls -l`;    // Assign output of a UNIX/Linux system command
$dirlist = `dir /D/L`  // Assign a Windows system command
```

EXAMPLE 4.8

```
      <html>
      <head><title>Variables</title></head>
      <body bgcolor="lightblue">
      <font face = "arial" size='+1'>
      <?php
1         $name="Joe Shmoe";
2         $age=25.4;
3         $now=date("m/d/Y");
4         $nothing;
5         echo "$name is $age years old.<br />";
6         echo '$nothing contains the value of ',gettype($nothing),
                ".<br />";
7         echo "Today is $now<br />";
      ?>
      </font>
      </body>
      </html>
```

EXPLANATION

1 The variable called $name is defined and initialized within the string value "Joe Shmoe". The string can be enclosed in either single or double quotes.

2 The variable called $age is assigned the floating-point value, 25.4. When assigning a number, the value is not quoted.

3 The variable called $now is assigned the return value of the built-in date() function. The function is not enclosed in quotes or it will not be executed. Its arguments, "m/d/Y", must be a string value, and are enclosed in quotes.

4 The variable $nothing is not assigned an initial value; it will have the value NULL.

5 The string is enclosed in double quotes. The floating-point value of $age is evaluated within the string.

6 The gettype() function tells us that the type of $nothing is NULL; that is, it has no value.

7 The output of the PHP built-in date() function was assigned to $now and is printed (see Figure 4.10).

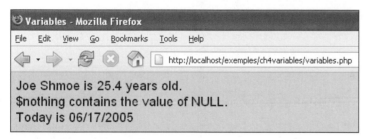

Figure 4.10 With or without quotes. Output from Example 4.8.

EXAMPLE 4.9

```
<html><head><title>Backticks</title></head>
<body bgcolor="lightgreen">
<b>
<pre>
<?php
1      $month=`cal 7 2005`; // UNIX command
2      echo "$month<br />";
?>
</b>
</pre>
</body>
</html>
```

EXPLANATION

1   The UNIX/Linux `cal` command and its arguments are enclosed in backquotes (also called backticks). In PHP the backquotes are actually operators (see "Execution Operators" on page 143). The command is executed by the operating system. Its output will be assigned to the variable, $month.

2   The PHP code is embedded within HTML `<pre>` tags to allow the calendar, $month, to be displayed in its natural format (see Figure 4.11).

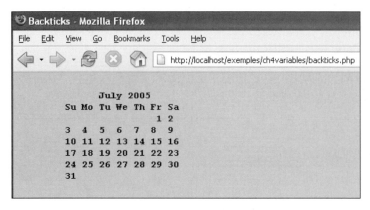

Figure 4.11
Backquotes and UNIX.
Output from Example 4.9.

EXAMPLE 4.10

```
<html><head><title>Backticks for Windows Command</title></head>
<body bgcolor="66cccc">
<b>
<pre>
<?php
1    $today =`date /T`;   // Windows command
2    echo "Today is $today<br />";
?>
</b>
</pre>
</body>
</html>
```

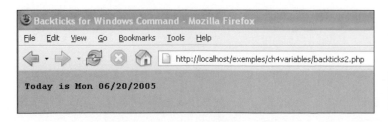

Figure 4.12
Backquotes and Windows.
Output from Example 4.10.

4.2.4 Displaying Variables

The print and echo Constructs.   So far, we have seen examples using both `print` and `echo` to display data. These language constructs can be used interchangeably. The only essential difference between `echo()` and `print()` is that `echo` allows multiple, comma-separated arguments, and `print` doesn't. Neither require parentheses around their arguments because technically they are not functions, but special built-in constructs. (In fact, arguments given to `echo` must not be enclosed within parentheses.) To print formatted strings, see `printf` and `sprintf` in Chapter 6, "Strings."

Consider the following. Three variables are declared:

```
$name - "Tom";
$state = "New York";
$salary = 80000;
```

`echo()` can take a comma-separated list of string arguments:

```
echo $name, $state, $salary;
```

`print()` takes one string argument:

```
print $name;
```

However, the concatenation operator can be used to print mutliple strings or strings containing multiple variables:

```
print  $name . $state . $salary;
   echo $name . $state . $salary;
```

or all of the variables can be enclosed in double quotes:

```
print "$name $state $salary<br />";
   echo "$name $state $salary<br />";
```

If a variable is enclosed in double quotes, it will be evaluated and its value displayed. If enclosed in single quotes, variables will not be evaluated. With single quotes, what you see is what you get. Like all other characters enclosed within single quotes, the $ is treated as a literal character.

The following strings are enclosed in single quotes:

```
echo '$name lives in  $state and earns $salary.';
```
$name lives in $state and earns $salary.

```
print '$name lives in  $state and earns $salary.';
```
$name lives in $state and earns $salary.

The same strings are enclosed in double quotes:

```
echo "$name lives in  $state and earns \$salary.";
```
Tom lives in New York and earns $80000.

```
print "$name lives in  $state and earns \$salary.";
```
Tom lives in New York and earns $80000.

Shortcut Tags.   There are several shortcuts you can use to embed PHP within the HTML portion of your file, but to use these shortcuts, you must make a change in the `php.ini` file. (If you don't know where to find the `php.ini` file you are using, look at the output of the built-in `phpinfo()` function where you will find the correct path to the file.) Use caution: The PHP developers set this directive to "off" for security reasons.

From the `php.ini` file:

```
; Allow the <? tag. Otherwise, only <?php and <script> tags are recognized.
; NOTE: Using short tags should be avoided when developing applications or
; libraries that are meant for redistribution, or deployment on PHP
; servers which are not under your control, because short tags may not
; be supported on the target server. For portable, redistributable code,
; be sure not to use short tags.
short_open_tag = Off              <-- Turn this "On" to make short tags work
```

Instead of using the `print()` or `echo()` functions to ouput the value of variables, they can be nested within HTML code by using `<?=` and `?>` shortcut tags where they will automatically be evaluated and printed. (Note: There can be no space between the question mark and the equal sign.) All of the following formats are acceptable:

FORMAT

```
<?= expression ?>
<?= $color ?>


<? echo statement; ?>
<? echo $color; ?>


You have chosen  a <?= $color ?> paint for your canvas.
```

EXAMPLE 4.11

```
      <html>
      <head><title>Variables</title></head>
      <body bgcolor="lightblue">
      <?php
1         $name = "Marko";
2         $city = "San Francisco";
      ?>
      <font face = "verdana" size='+1'>
      <p>
3     Today is <?=date("l")?>.   // same as <?php echo date("l"); ?>
      <br />
4     His name is <?=$name?> and he works in <?=$city?>.
      </font>
      </body>
      </html>
```

EXPLANATION

1, 2   Two variables are assigned the string values, "Marko" and "San Francisco".
3, 4   The PHP shortcut tag is embedded within the HTML tags. PHP will evaluate the
       expression within the shortcut tags and print their values. The resulting HTML
       code contains the result of the evaluation as shown when viewing the browser's
       source (see Figure 4.13). In this example, the built-in date() function with a "l"
       option will return the day of the week. The variables, $name and $city are eval-
       uated and placed within the HTML code.

```
<html>
<head><title>Variables</title>
</head>
<body bgcolor="lightblue">
<font face =" verdana" size='+1'>
<p>
Today is Thursday.
<br>
His name is Marko and he works in San Francisco.
</font>
</body>
</html>
```

Figure 4.13 HTML source page viewed in the browser.

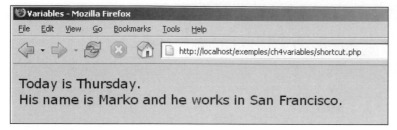

Figure 4.14   Using shortcut tags. The output from Example 4.11.

4.2.5   Variables and Mixed Data Types

Remember, strongly typed languages like C++ and Java require that you specify the type of data you are going to store in a variable when you declare it, but PHP is loosely typed. It doesn't expect or allow you to specify the data type when declaring a variable. You can assign a string to a variable and later assign a numeric value. PHP doesn't care and at runtime, the PHP interpreter will convert the data to the correct type. In Example 4.12, consider the following variable, initialized to the floating-point value of 5.5. In each successive statement, PHP will convert the type to the proper data type (see Table 4.3).

Table 4.3   How PHP Converts Data Types

Variable Assignment	Conversion
`$item = 5.5;`	Assigned a float
`$item = 44;`	Converted to integer
`$item = "Today was bummer";`	Converted to string
`$item = true;`	Converted to boolean
`$item = NULL;`	Converted to the null value

Example 4.12 demonstrates data type conversion. The gettype built-in function is used to display the data types after PHP has converted the data to the correct type. See Figure 4.15 for the output.

EXAMPLE 4.12

```
      <html><head><title>Type Conversion</title></head>
      <body bgcolor="pink"><font size="+1">
      <?php
1     $item = 5.5;
          print "$item is a " . gettype($item) . "<br />";
2     $item = 44;
          print "$item is a " . gettype($item) . "<br />";
```

EXAMPLE 4.12 (CONTINUED)

```
3   $item = "Today was a bummer!";
        print "\"$item\" is a " . gettype($item) . "<br />";
4   $item = true;
        print "$item is a " . gettype($item) . "<br />";
5   $item = NULL;
        print "$item is a " . gettype($item) . "<br />";
    ?>
    </body>
    </html>
```

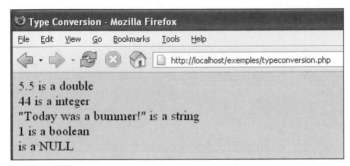

Figure 4.15 Mixing data types. Output from Example 4.12.

Type Casting.   Like C and Java, PHP provides a method to force the conversion of one type of value to another using the cast operator (see Chapter 5, "Operators").

4.2.6 Concatenation and Variables

To concatenate variables and strings together on the same line, the dot (.) is used. The dot is an operator because it operates on the expression on either side of it (each called an operand). In expressions involving numeric and string values with the dot operator, PHP converts numeric values to strings. For example, consider the following statements:

```
// returns "The temperature is 87"
$temp  = "The temperature is  " .  87;
// returns "25 days till Christmas"
$message =  25  . " days till Christmas";
```

EXAMPLE 4.13

```
<html>
<head><title>Concatenation</title></head>
<body bgcolor="ccff66">
<b>
<?php
    $n = 5 . " cats";
    $years = 9;
    print "The $n " . "lived ". $years * 5 .
    " years. <br />";
    echo "He owns ", $years. $n , ".<br />";
?>
</b>
</body>
</html>
```

Line numbers in the code: 1 (`$n = 5 . " cats";`), 2 (`$years = 9;`), 3 (`" years. <br />";`), 4 (`echo "He owns ", $years. $n , ".<br />";`)

EXPLANATION

1   Variable $n is assigned a number concatenated to a string. The number is converted to a string and the two strings are joined together as one string by using the concatenation operator, resulting in the string `"5 cats"`.
2   Variable $years is assigned the number 9.
3   The concatenation operator joins all the expressions into one string to be displayed. The `print()` function can only take one argument.
4   The `echo` statement takes a list of comma-separated arguments, which causes the values of $years and $n to be displayed just as with the concatenation operator. See Figure 4.16 for the output.

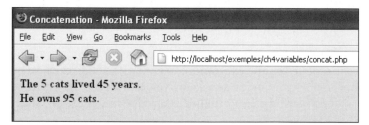

Figure 4.16   Concatenation.

4.2.7   References

Another way to assign a value to a variable is to create a reference (PHP 4). A reference is when one variable is an alias or pointer to another variable; that is, they point to the same underlying data. Changing one variable automatically changes the other. This might be useful in speeding things up when using large arrays and objects, but for now, we will not need to use references.

To assign by reference, prepend an ampersand (&) to the beginning of the old variable that will be assigned to the new variable; for example, $ref = & $old;. See Example 4.14 and it's output in Figure 4.17.

EXAMPLE 4.14

```
    <html><head><title>References</title></head>
    <body bgcolor="yellow"><font size="+1">
    <?php
1   $husband = "Honey"; // Assign the value "Honey" to $husband
2   $son = & $husband;   // Assign a reference to $son.
                         // Now $husband is a reference or alias
                         // for $husband. They reference the same data.
3   print "His wife calls him $husband, and his Mom calls him $son.
    <br />";
4   $son = "Lazy";       // Assign a new value to $son;
                         // $husband gets the same value
5   print "Now his wife and mother call him $son, $husband man.<br />";
    ?>
    <body>
    </html>
```

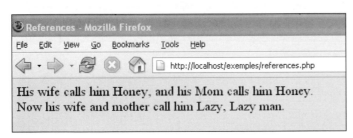

Figure 4.17 References. Output from Example 4.14.

One important thing to note is that only named variables can be assigned by reference, as shown in Example 4.15.

EXAMPLE 4.15

```
    <?php
    $age = 26;
    $old = &$age;        // This is a valid assignment.
    $old = &(26 + 7);    // Invalid; references an unnamed expression.
    ?>
```

4.2.8 Variable Variables (Dynamic Variables)

A variable variable is also called a dynamic variable. It is a variable whose name is stored in another variable. By using two dollar signs, the variable variable can access the value of the original variable. Consider the following example:

```
$pet ="Bozo";
$clown = "pet";    // A variable is assigned the name of another variable
echo $clown;       // prints "pet"
echo ${$clown};    // prints Bozo
```

Dynamic variables are useful when you are dealing with variables that all contain a similar name such as form variables. Curly braces are used to ensure that the PHP parser will evaluate the dollar signs properly; that is, `$clown` will be evaluated first, and the first dollar sign removed, resulting in `${pet}`, and finally `$pet` will be evaulated to `"Bozo"`. Example 4.16 demonstrates how variable variables can be used dynamically to change the color of a font. Output is shown in Figure 4.18.

EXAMPLE 4.16

```
     <html>
     <head><title>Variable Variables</title></head>
     <body bgcolor="669966">
     <font face = "arial" size="+1">
     <?php
1        $color1 = "red";
         $color2 = "blue";
         $color3 = "yellow";
2        for($count = 1; $count <= 3; $count++){
3            $primary = "color" . $count;   // Variable variable
4            print "<font color=${$primary}>";
             echo "The value stored in $primary: ${$primary}<br />";
5        }
     ?>
     </font>
     </body>
     </html>
```

EXPLANATION

1 Three variables are defined and assigned colors. Notice the variable names only differ by the number appended to the name, 1, 2, and 3.

2 Although we haven't yet discussed loops, this is the best way to illustrate the use of variable variables (or dynamic variables). The initial value in the loop, $count, is set to 1. If the value of $count is less than 3 ($count < 3), then control goes to line 3. After the closing curly brace is reached on line 5, control will go back to the top of the loop and the value of $count will be incremented by 1. If $count is less than 3, the process repeats, and when $count reaches 3, the loop terminates.

3 The first time through the loop, the value of $count is appended to the string "color" resulting in color1. The value, "color1", is then assigned to the variable, $primary, so that $primary = color1;.

4 PHP expands ${$primary}[a] as follows:

${color1}   First evaluate $primary within the curly braces.

$color1   Remove the braces and now evaluate $color1 resulting in "red".

The color of the font and the text will be red. Next time through the loop, the count will go up by one ($count = 2) and the $color2 will be "blue", and finally $color3 will be "yellow".

5 See "The for Loop" on page 235 for an example of how to make use of dynamic variables with forms.

a. The curly braces are required. If you omit them, the variable $$primary will be evaluated as $color1 but not "red".

Figure 4.18 Dynamic variables. Output from Example 4.16.

4.2.9 Scope of Variables

Scope refers to where a variable is available within a script. Scope is important because it prevents important variables from being accidentally modified in some other part of the program and thus changing the way the program behaves. PHP has specific rules to control the visibility of variables. A local variable is one that exists only within a function. A global variable is available anywhere in the script other than from within functions. (See Chapter 9, "User-Defined Functions," for creating global variables within functions.) For the most part all PHP variables have a single scope, global.

Local Variables. Variables created within a function are not available to the rest of the script. They are local to the function and disappear (go out of scope) when the function exits. If you have the same name for a variable within a function as in the main program, modifying the variable in the function will not affect the one outside the function (see Chapter 9, "User-Defined Functions"). Likewise, the function does not have access to variables created outside of the function. Most of the variables we create will be visible in the script or function in which they are declared. See Chapter 9, "User-Defined Functions," to get a full understanding of scope, including local variables, globals, superglobals, and static.

Global and Environment Variables. Superglobal variables (see Table 4.4) are accessible everywhere within a script and within functions. They are special variables provided by PHP to help you manage HTML forms, cookies, sessions, and files, and to get information about your environment and server.

Table 4.4 Some Superglobal Variables

Name	Meaning
$GLOBALS	An array of all global variables
$_SERVER	Contains server variables (e.g., REMOTE_ADDR)
$_GET	Contains form variables sent through GET method
$_POST	Contains form variables sent through POST method
$_COOKIE	Contains HTTP cookie variables
$_FILES	Contains variables provided to the script via HTTP post file uploads
$_ENV	Contains the environment variables
$_REQUEST	A merge of the GET variables, POST variables, and cookie variables
$_SESSION	Contains HTTP variables registered by the session module

4.2.10   Managing Variables

You might want to find out if a variable has been declared, you might want to delete one that has been set, or check to see if one that is set is not empty or is a string, number, scalar, and so on. PHP provides a number of functions (see Table 4.5) to help you manage variables.

Table 4.5   Functions for Managing Variables

Function	*What It Returns*
isset()	True if variable has been set.
empty()	True if variable is empty: `" "` (an empty string) `"0"` (a string) 0 (an integer)
is_bool()	True if variable is boolean; that is, contains TRUE or FALSE.
is_callable()	True if variable is assigned the name of a function or an object.
is_double(), is_float(), is_real()	True if variable is a floating-point number (e.g., 5.67 or .45).
is_int, is_integer, is_long	True if a variable is assigned a whole number.
is_null()	True if a variable was assigned the NULL value.
is_numeric()	True if the variable was assigned a numeric string value or a number.
is_object()	True if the variable is an object.
is_resource()	True if the variable is a resource.
is_scalar()	True if the value was assigned a single value, such as a number (e.g., `"555"` a string, or a boolean, but not an array or object).
is_string()	True if a variable is a string of text (e.g., `"hello"`).
unset()	Unsets or destroys a list of values.

The isset() Function.   The isset() function returns true if a variable has been set and false if it hasn't. If the variable has been set to NULL or has no value, it returns false. If you want to see if a variable has been set to NULL, use the is_null() function. To ensure that a variable has an initial value, the isset() function can be used to set a default value. See Examples 4.17 and 4.18.

FORMAT

```
bool isset ( variable, variable, variable .... );
```

Example:
```
$set = isset( $name );      // returns true or false
print isset($a, $b, $c);    // prints 1 or nothing
```

EXAMPLE 4.17

```
      <html><head><title>Testing Variables</title></head>
      <body bgcolor="#66CC66">
      The <b>isset()</b> function returns a boolean value. <br />
      If one or more variables exist and have a value, true is returned;
          otherwise false.
      <font face="verdana" size="+1">
      <p />
      <?php
1         $first_name="John"; $middle_name=" "; $last_name="Doe";
2         $age;
3         $state=NULL;
4         print 'isset($first_name,$middle_name,$last_name) : ' .
                  isset($first_name,$last_name) ."<br />";
5         print 'isset($age) : '. isset($age) ."<br />";
          print 'isset($city ) : '. isset($city) ."<br />";
          print 'isset($state ) : '. isset($state) ."<br />";
      ?>
      </body>
      </html>
```

EXPLANATION

1   Three variables are assigned string values; $middle_name is assigned the empty string, a set of double quotes containing no text.

2   $age is declared but has not been assigned any value yet, which evaluates to NULL.

3   $state is declared and assigned the value NULL, which means it has no value.

4   The isset() function returns true if a variable has been set and given a non-null value. In this case, all three variables have a value, even the variable assigned an empty string. If true, 1 is displayed; if false, 0 or nothing is displayed.

5   Because $age was not given any value, it is implied to be null, and isset() returns false. $city was never even declared, and $state was assigned NULL; isset() returns false. If you want to check explicitly for the NULL value (case insensitive), use the built-in is_null() function (see Figure 4.19).

Testing Variables - Mozilla Firefox

File   Edit   View   Go   Bookmarks   Tools   Help

http://localhost/exemples/ch4variables/isset.php

The **isset()** function returns a boolean value.
If one or more variables exist and have a value, true is returned; otherwise false.

isset($first_name,$middle_name,$last_name) : 1
isset($age) :
isset($city) :
isset($state) :

Figure 4.19 Is the variable set? Output from Example 4.17.

EXAMPLE 4.18

```
      <html><head><title>Give a Variable a Default Value</title></head>
      <body bgcolor="66C68">
      <font face="verdana" size="+1">
      <p>
      <?php
1        if ( ! isset($temp)) { $temp = 68 ; }   // Sets a default value
2        echo "The default temperature is $temp degrees.<br />";
      ?>
      </p>
      </body>
      </html>
```

EXPLANATION

1   The `isset()` function returns true if `$temp` has been set. The `!` operator, the unary "not" operator, reverses the boolean result. The expression reads, "if `$temp` is not set, define it with a value of 68."

2   The `echo` statement displays the default value in the browser (see Figure 4.20).

Give a Variable a Default Value - Mozilla Firefox

File   Edit   View   Go   Bookmarks   Tools   Help

http://localhost/exemples/ch4variables/isset_def

The default temperature is 68 degrees.

Figure 4.20 Setting a default value. Output from Example 4.18.

The empty() Function.   The empty() function returns true if a variable does not exist, or exists and has been assigned one of the following: an empty string " ", 0 as a number, "0" as a string, NULL, or no value at all. Example 4.19 demonstrates the use of the empty() function.

FORMAT

```
boolean empty ( variable );
```

Example:
```
if ( empty($result) ){
print "\$result either doesn't exist or is empty\n";
```

EXAMPLE 4.19

```
    <html><head><title>Testing Variables</title></head>
    <body bgcolor="66C66">
    The <b>empty()</b> function returns a boolean value. <br />
    If a variable doesn't exist or is assigned the empty string,
    0, <br />or "0", NULL, or hasn't been assigned any value;
    returns true, otherwise false.
    <font face="verdana" size="+1">
    <p>

    <?php
1       $first_name=""; $last_name=" ";
2       $age=0;
3       $salary="0";
4       $state=NULL;
        print 'empty($first_name) : ' . empty($first_name) ."<br />";
        print 'empty($last_name) : ' . empty($last_name) ."<br />";
        print 'empty($age) : '. empty($age) ."<br />";
        print 'empty($salary) : '. empty($salary) ."<br />";
        print 'empty($state ) : '. empty($state) ."<br />";
    ?>

    </p>
    </body>
    </html>
```

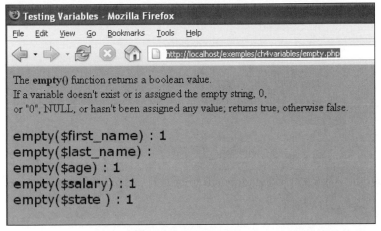

Figure 4.21   Is the variable empty? Output from Example 4.19.

The unset() Function.   The unset() function (technically a language construct) unsets or destroys a given variable. It can take a varied number of arguments and behaves a little differently within functions (see Chapter 9, "User-Defined Functions"). As of PHP 4, it has no return value and is considered a statement.

FORMAT

```
void unset ( mixed var [, mixed var [, mixed ...]] )
```

Example:
```
unset($a, $b); // unsets the variables
```

EXAMPLE 4.20

```
      <html><head><title>Testing Variables</title></head>
      <body bgcolor="66C66">
      The <b>unset()</b> function destroys a variable. <br />
      <font face="verdana" size="+1">
      <p>
      <?php
1         $first_name="John";
          $last_name="Doe";
          $age=35;
2         unset($first_name, $last_name);
          print 'After unset() was used, isset($first_name,$last_name) '.
3             isset($first_name,$last_name). "returns false.<br />";
      ?>
      </p>
      </body>
      </html>
```

Figure 4.22   Destroying variables.

4.2.11   Introduction to Form Variables

Now we are starting to get into what makes PHP so popular. As we mentioned in the introduction to this book, PHP was designed as a Web-based programming language to create dynamic Web content, to gather and manipulate information submitted by HTML forms. For now, because we are talking about variables, we will examine a simple form and how PHP collects and stores the form information in variables. Chapter 10, "More on PHP Forms," provides a comprehensive discussion on HTML forms and introduces the special global arrays used to process them in your PHP scripts.

The php.ini File and register_globals.   Before getting started, there are some issues to be aware of based on the version of PHP you are using. The PHP initialization file, called php.ini, contains a directive called register_globals. Older versions of PHP (prior to 4.2.0) had this directive turned to "On" as the default, allowing PHP to create simple variables from form data. Since then, register_globals has been set to "Off" to avoid potential security breaches. If using PHP 5, you will have to turn this feature on before PHP can directly assign form input to simple global variables, or the data must be extracted programatically. We discuss both ways to do this in the following section. The next excerpt is taken from the PHP 5 php.ini file, showing the line where register_globals is set. The default is "Off" and you should really try to adhere to this setting.

From the `php.ini` file:

```
; You should do your best to write your scripts so that they do not require
; register_globals to be on; Using form variables as globals can easily lead
; to possible security problems, if the code is not very well thought of.
register_globals = Off
```

If you do not set `register_globals` to "On," add the following line to your PHP program:

```
extract($_REQUEST);
```

The `$_REQUEST` superglobal array contains the information submitted to the server from the HTML form. After extracting this information, PHP will create simple variables corresponding to the form data as shown in Example 4.24. In Chapter 10, "More on PHP Forms," all aspects of extracting form data are discussed in detail. For now, assume `register_globals` is set to "On."

How PHP Handles Form Input.   For each HTML form parameter, PHP creates a global variable by the same name and makes it available to your script. For example, consider this HTML input type for two text fields:

```
<input type="text" name="your_name">
<input type="text" name ="your_phone">
```

If you have a text field named `"your_name"`, PHP will create a variable called `$your_name`. And if you have another text field named `"your_phone"`, PHP will in turn, create a variable called `$your_phone`. The values assigned to the PHP variables are the same values the user entered in the HTML text fields when filling out the form.

Example 4.21 illustrates a simple HTML form consisting of two fields. The form starts with the opening `<form>` tag. The ACTION attribute of the form tag is assigned the name of the PHP script that will handle the form input: `<form ACTION="php script">`.

After the user fills out the form (see Figure 4.25) and presses the submit button, the values that he or she typed in the text boxes will be sent to the PHP script (see Example 4.22). The browser knows *where* to send the data based on the ACTION attribute of the `<form>` tag, but it also needs to know *how* to send the form data to the server. The *how,* or method, is also an attribute of the `<form>` tag, called the METHOD atribute. There are two popular HTTP methods used to send the form information to the server—the GET method (default) and the POST method. Because the GET method is the default, you don't have to explicitly assign it as an attribute. The browser just assumes that is the method you are using. The GET method tells the browser to send a URL-encoded string, called the query string, to the server. It attaches this encoded query string to the end of the URL in the browser's location box, prepended with a ?. It is the method used when doing searches or handling static pages and GET query strings are limited in size (see Figure 4.23).

If using the POST method, the METHOD attribute must be added to the HTML <form> tag METHOD="POST" (case insensitive). With the POST method, the browser sends an encoded message body in the HTTP header to the server so that it doesn't appear in the URL. It is not limited in size, but it can't be bookmarked or reloaded, and does not appear in the browser's history (see Figure 4.24).

When PHP gets the form input from the server, it takes care of decoding the query string or message body and assigning the respective input values to PHP variables as shown in Example 4.21. (For a complete discussion of the differences between the GET and POST methods, see *http://www.cs.tut.fi/~jkorpela/forms/methods.html*.)

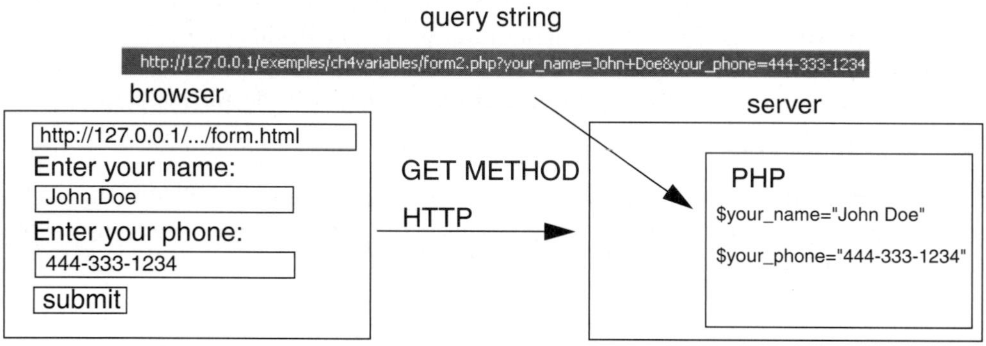

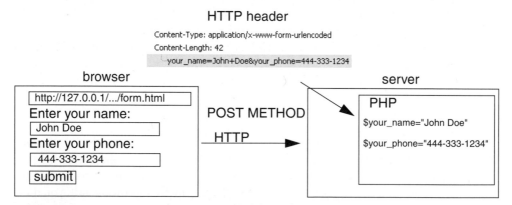

Figure 4.23 The GET method sends form input in the URL.

Figure 4.24 The POST method sends form input in an HTTP header.

EXAMPLE 4.21

```
         <html>
         <head>
         <title>Simple HTML Form</title>
         </head>
         <body bgcolor="lightblue"><font size="+1">
1            <form action="http://localhost/exemples/ch4variables/
                           form_example.php" />
             <p>
             please enter your name: <br />
2            <input type="text" size=30 name="your_name" />
             <br />
3            please enter your phone number: <br />
             <input type="text" size=30 name="your_phone" />
             <br />
4            <input type=submit value="submit" />
5            </form>
         </body>
         </html>
```

EXPLANATION

1   The HTML <form> tag starts the form. The URL of the script that will handle the form data is assigned to the action attribute. The "method" on *how* the data will be transmitted is assigned to the method attribute. Because the GET method is the default method for transmitting data to the server, you do not have to explicitly assign it as an attribute. This example is using the GET method.

2, 3   The HTML input type is a text box that is set to hold 50 characters. One is named "your_name" and the other is named "your_phone".

4   After the user enters his or her name and phone number in the respective text boxes, and presses the submit button (see Figure 4.25), the browser will collect and URL encode the input data, then send it to the server. The server will hand it to the PHP script listed (see Example 4.22) in the action attribute on line 1. When PHP gets the input data, it will decode it, and create a variable called $your_name (the name of the first text box) and a variable called $your_phone (the name of the second text box) and give it the values that were entered in the form by the user.

5   This </form> tag ends the HTML form.

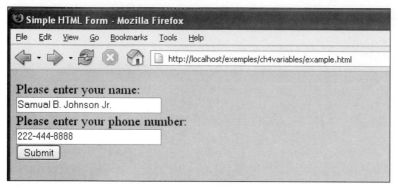

Figure 4.25   The HTML form has been filled out by a user.

EXAMPLE 4.22

(The PHP Script)

```
    <?php
    extract($_REQUEST);
1   print "Your phone number is $your_name. <br />";
    print "Your phone number is $your_phone.";
    ?>
```

or in the HTML document use the PHP shortcut tags:

```
    <html><head><title>Testing Variables</title></head>
    <body>
2   Your phone number is <?=$your_name?> and your phone number is
              <?=$your_phone?>
    </body></html>
```

EXPLANATION

1   The browser bundles up the input data, encodes it, and attaches it as a query string to the URL as:

```
?http://localhost/exemples/ch4variables/form_example.php?
your_name=Samual+B.+Johnson+Jr.&your_phone=222-444-8888
```

PHP decodes the query string; that is, it removes the + signs and & and any other encoding characters, and then creates global variables, called $your_name and $your_phone, and assigns values based on the user input. In this example, the values of the variables are printed as part of the PHP script.

2   You can also use the shortcut tags within the HTML document to display the value of the PHP variables. The output is displayed in the browser, as shown in Figure 4.26.

Figure 4.26 Output from the PHP script in Example 4.22. The input data is appended to the URL after the ?.

Extracting the Data by Request.   In the previous example, we used the default GET method to send form input to the server. We also assumed the register_globals in the php.ini file was turned "On," allowing PHP to create simple global variables with the form data. In the following example, we assume that register_globals is turned "Off" (the recommended and default setting) and that the method is POST, the more commonly used method when working with form input, as shown in Figure 4.24. This method sends the form input as a message body in the HTTP header to the server and does not append the data to the URL in the browser. Even though the input data is sent using a different method, it is received in the same URL-encoded format. When register_globals is turned off, PHP provides special variables, called arrays, to store the form information. Because we do not cover arrays until Chapter 8, "Arrays," we will create simple variables to hold input data from the form, but first must explicitly extract the data from a special global array called $_REQUEST. This special array contains all of the input data for both GET and POST methods, and once it is extracted will be assigned to PHP variables with the same name as was given to the corresponding input devices in the HTML form.

EXAMPLE 4.23

(The HTML Form Source)
```
        <html>
        <head>
        <title>First HTML Form</title>
        </head>
        <body bgcolor="lightblue"><font size="+1">
1       <form action="/phpforms/form1.php" method="POST">
        <p>
        Please enter your name: <br />
2       <input type="text" size=50 name="your_name">
        <p>
        Please enter your phone: <br />
3       <input type="text" size=50 name="your_phone">
        <p>
        Please enter your email address:<br />
4       <input type="text" size=50 name="your_email_addr">
        <p>
```

EXAMPLE 4.23 (CONTINUED)

```
5        <input type=submit value="submit">
         <input type=reset value="clear">
6        </form>
     <hr>
     </body>
     </html>
```

EXPLANATION

1   The HTML `<form>` tag starts the form. The URL of the script that will handle the form data is assigned to the `action` attribute. The "method" on how the data will be transmitted is assigned to the `method` attribute. The POST method is used here. This is the most common method for processing forms. The form input is sent in an HTTP header to the server.

2, 3, 4   The input devices are three text boxes for accepting user input. The name attribute is assigned the names of the respective boxes, `your_name`, `your_phone`, and `your_email` (see Figure 4.27). These same names will be used as variable names in the PHP program, `/phpforms/form1.php`, listed in the forms action attribute.

5   When the user presses the submit button, the form input is encoded and sent to the server. The form input will not be visible in the URL as it is with the GET method.

6   This marks the end of the form.

Figure 4.27   Data has been entered into the HTML form.

EXAMPLE 4.24

(The PHP program)
```
<html><head><title>Processing First Form</title>
</head>
<body bgcolor = "lightgreen"><font size="+1">
<h2>Here is the form input:</h2>
<?php
1       extract($_REQUEST, EXTR_SKIP);   // Extracting the form input
        print "Welcome to PHP $your_name<br />"; // register_globals
                                                 // is off
        print "Can I call you at $your_phone<br />";
        print "Is it ok to send you email at $your_email_addr<br />";
?>
</body>
</html>
```

EXPLANATION

1   If the register_globals directive in the php.ini file is set to "Off," the built-in PHP extract() function can be used to get the form input stored in $_REQUEST, an array that contains input recieved from both GET and POST methods. The extract() function will convert the input into variables of the same name as the input devices in the HTML file. The EXTR_SKIP flag ensures that if there is a collision, that is, you have already defined a variable with the that name somewhere in your PHP program, it won't be overwritten.

2   The variables $your_name, $your_phone, and $your_email_addr were created by the extract() function and named after the text boxes originally named in the HTML form. The output is displayed in the browser, as in Figure 4.28.

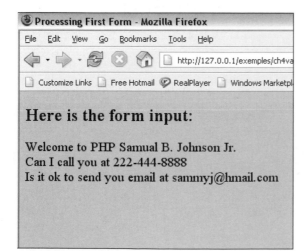

Figure 4.28
After PHP processes the input
data from the form.

Predefined Variables. PHP provides a number of predefined variables (see Table 4.6 and Figure 4.29), some that are not fully documented because they depend on which server is running, its configuration, and so on. Some are defined in the php.ini file. These variables describe the environment, server, browser, version number, configuration file, and so on.

Table 4.6 Predefined Variables[a]

Variable	What It Does
AUTH_TYPE	If running the Apache server as a module, this is set to the authentication type.
DOCUMENT_ROOT	The full path of the Web's document root, normally where HTML pages are stored and defined in the server's configuration file.
HTTP_USER_AGENT	Identifies the type of Web browser to the server when it requests a file.
HTTP_REFERER	The full URL of the page that contained the link to this page. Of course if there isn't a referring page, this variable would not exist.
REMOTE ADDRESS	The remote IP address of the client machine that requested the page.

a. See the full list of predefined variables at
    http://www.phpfreaks.com/PHP_Reference/Predefined-Variables/8.php

There many more predefined variables; which ones are set depends on your PHP configuration. The function phpinfo() can be used to retrieve built-in variables that have been set.

```
<?php
phpinfo(INFO_VARIABLES);
?>
```

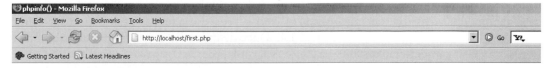

PHP Variables

Variable	Value
_SERVER["COMSPEC"]	C:\WINDOWS\system32\cmd.exe
_SERVER["DOCUMENT_ROOT"]	c:/wamp/www
_SERVER["HTTP_ACCEPT"]	text/xml,application/xml,application/xhtml+xml,text/html;q=0.9,text/plain;q=0.8,image/png,*/*;q=0.5
_SERVER["HTTP_ACCEPT_CHARSET"]	ISO-8859-1,utf-8;q=0.7,*;q=0.7
_SERVER["HTTP_ACCEPT_ENCODING"]	gzip,deflate
_SERVER["HTTP_ACCEPT_LANGUAGE"]	en-us,en;q=0.5
_SERVER["HTTP_CONNECTION"]	keep-alive
_SERVER["HTTP_HOST"]	localhost
_SERVER["HTTP_KEEP_ALIVE"]	300
_SERVER["HTTP_USER_AGENT"]	Mozilla/5.0 (Windows; U; Windows NT 5.1; en-US; rv:1.7.5) Gecko/20041107 Firefox/1.0 (ax)
_SERVER["PATH"]	C:\Perl\bin\;C:\WINDOWS\system32;C:\WINDOWS;C:\WINDOWS\system32\WBEM;C:\WINDOWS\System32;C:\Program Files\Common Files\Adaptec Shared\System;C:\Program Files\QuickTime\QTSystem\
_SERVER["REMOTE_ADDR"]	127.0.0.1
_SERVER["REMOTE_PORT"]	4061
_SERVER["SCRIPT_FILENAME"]	c:/wamp/www/first.php
_SERVER["SERVER_ADDR"]	127.0.0.1
_SERVER["SERVER_ADMIN"]	webmaster@localhost
_SERVER["SERVER_NAME"]	localhost
_SERVER["SERVER_PORT"]	80
_SERVER["SERVER_SIGNATURE"]	<ADDRESS>Apache/1.3.33 Server at localhost Port 80</ADDRESS>
_SERVER["SERVER_SOFTWARE"]	Apache/1.3.33 (Win32) PHP/5.0.3
_SERVER["SystemRoot"]	C:\WINDOWS
_SERVER["WINDIR"]	C:\WINDOWS
_SERVER["GATEWAY_INTERFACE"]	CGI/1.1
_SERVER["SERVER_PROTOCOL"]	HTTP/1.1

Figure 4.29   PHP variables (partial output from the `phpinfo()` function).

4.3   **Constants**

> "The only thing constant in life is change."
> —Francois de la Rouchefoucauld, French classical author

Some real-world constants, such as pi, the speed of light, the number of inches in a foot, and the value of midnight, are values that don't change. PHP not only provides its own predefined constants but lets you create your own. Using constants makes it easy to write and maintain your programs.

4.3.1   What Is a Constant?

Unlike variables, a constant is a value that, once set, cannot be changed or unset during the execution of your script. An example of a constant is the value of pi or the version of PHP you are using. Constants are very useful because they are visible throughout a program (global in scope) and their values don't change; for example, a constant might be defined for the document root of your server, the name of your site, or the title, author, and copyright year of this book. Once defined, those values are fixed.

You can define constants at the top of your program or in another file that can be included in your script. (See the `require()` and `include()` functions discussed in "Managing Content with Include Files" on page 487.) Later if a constant value needs to be modified, once you change its value in the program, then when the program is executed, the new value will be reflected wherever the constant is used throughout the program, thus facilitating program maintenance.

4.3.2 Creating Constants with the define() Function

PHP constants are defined as words, and by convention, capitalized. Like variables, they are case sensitive and consist of uppercase and lowercase letters, numbers, and the underscore. Like variables, they cannot start with a number.

Unlike variables, constants are *not* preceded by a dollar sign and are *not* interpreted when placed within quotes.

Constants are global in scope, meaning they are available for use anywhere in a PHP script.

The only way that you can create a constant is with he PHP built-in `define()` function. Only a single, scalar value can be assigned to a constant, including strings, integers, floats, and booleans.

The `define()` function creates a named constant. The first argument is the name of the constant and the second argument is the value that will be assigned to it. Constants are normally case sensitive, but you can use an optional third argument of TRUE to turn off case sensitivity.

FORMAT

```
bool define ( string name, mixed value [, bool case_insensitive] )
```

Example:
```
// defines document root
define( 'DOC_ROOT', '/http://artemis/~ellie/public_html' );
// defines the include folder
define( 'INCLUDES', DOC_ROOT.'/../includes' );
```

EXAMPLE 4.25

```php
<?php
1   define('ISBN', "0-13-140162-9");
2   define('TITLE', "JavaScript by Example" );
3   if ( defined('ISBN') and defined('TITLE')){
4         print ISBN . "<br />";
          print TITLE . "<br />";
    }
5   define('TITLE', "PHP by Example");   // Can't change TITLE, and
                                         // can't redefine it.
6   print TITLE;
?>
```

EXPLANATION

1, 2   Two constants are defined, ISBN and TITLE, the first argument to the function. The second argument is the value being assigned to each of the constants. Once set, the only way to change a constant is to redefine it with the define() function.

3   The define() function returns TRUE if the named constant has been defined. The expression reads, "if the constant ISBN and the constant TITLE have both been defined, proceed to line 3."

4   Notice that the constants are not quoted. If they are quoted, their values will not be printed, but just the words ISBN and TITLE.

5   You cannot redefine a constant like this. If you want to modify the value, you must go back into the program and change the original definition on line 2.

6   The constant TITLE was unaffected by line 5. By definition, a constant cannot be changed or unset. The output of this program is shown in Figure 4.30.

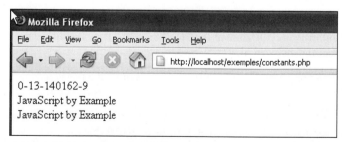

Figure 4.30   User-defined constants. Output from Example 4.25.

The defined() function checks whether a constant has been set. It returns TRUE if the constant has been defined; otherwise, FALSE.

4.3.3 The constant() Function

The `constant()` function returns that value of a constant. This function can be helpful if you don't know the name of the constant because its name was stored in a variable or was returned from a function.

FORMAT

```
mixed constant ( string name )
```

Example:
```
define (ISBN, "0-13-140162-9");
$value=constant(ISBN);  // Returns 0-13-140162-9
```

4.3.4 Predefined and "Magic" Constants

PHP comes with a number of predefined constants shown in Table 4.6. They provide information that doesn't change such as the name of the script file, the version of PHP and the operating system, and so on.

There are five predefined constants called magic constants (see Table 4.7). These are constants that change depending on how they are used in a program. They cannot be enclosed in quotes and are not case sensitive. The name of the contant is enclosed in *two* underscores on both sides.

Table 4.7 Magic Constants

Name	Description
__LINE__	The current line number of the file.
__FILE__	The full path and filename of the file. If used inside an include, the name of the included file is returned.
__FUNCTION__	The function name (added in PHP 4.3.0). As of PHP 5 this constant returns the function name as it was declared (case sensitive). In PHP 4 its value is always lowercased.
__CLASS__	The class name (added in PHP 4.3.0). As of PHP 5 this constant returns the class name as it was declared (case sensitive). In PHP 4 its value is always lowercased.
__METHOD__	The class method name (added in PHP 5.0.0). The method name is returned as it was declared (case sensitive).

PHP has several special built-in constants described in Table 4.8.

Table 4.8   Built-In Constants

Name	Description
PHP_VERSION	The version of the PHP parser currently running
PHP_OS	The operating system of the server on which the PHP parser is running
PHP_OS	The name of the operating system on which the PHP parser is executing; e.g., Linux
TRUE	A true value.
FALSE	A false value.

The script in Example 4.26 shows how the predefined constants can be used to give information to the browser. It's output is displayed in Figure 4.31.

EXAMPLE   4.26

```php
<?php
    // Using PHP built-in constants
    echo "PHP version = " . PHP_VERSION . "<br />";
    echo "Server operating system = " . PHP_OS . "<br />";
    echo "Current file name= " . __FILE__ . "<br />";
    echo "Current line number= " . __LINE__ . "<br />";
    echo "TRUE = ". TRUE . "<br />";
    echo "false = ". FALSE . "<br />";
?>
```

Figure 4.31   Predefined constants. Output from Example 4.26.

4.4 Chapter Summary

4.4.1 What You Should Know

Now that you have finished this chapter you should be able to answer the following questions:

1. What are the PHP basic data types?

2. What is the `gettype()` function?

3. What is the difference between a *scalar* and a *composite* data type?

4. What is the difference between a *variable* and a *constant*?

5. When do you need double quotes? Single quotes?

6. How can you see a backslash interpreted in the browser?

7. How do you concatenate two strings?

8. Why would you use a *here-doc*?

9. What data type is represented by true or false? Are true and false case sensitive?

10. What is NULL?

11. Is `"$_over-out"` a valid variable name? Why or why not?

12. Is it mandatory to initialize a variable?

13. What function can you use to tell if a variable exists?

14. How do you get rid of a variable?

15. What is meant by *scope*?

16. What is the function of the `register_globals` directive? In what file is it located? Is it on or off in your version of PHP?

17. What are *form* variables?

18. What is the difference between the GET and POST methods?

19. What is the value of `$_REQUEST`?

20. How do you create a constant?

21. Why are constants useful?

22. What is a "magic constant"?

4.4.2 What's Next?

Another important chapter basic to all programming languages, Chapter 5, "Operators," covers PHP's rich set of operators and how to use them to manipulate data; for example, how to perform arithmetic on numbers, compare strings and numbers, test equality, combine expressions, and test them with logical operators, bitwise operations, and more.

CHAPTER 4 LAB

1. Create a string variable to contain *one* string that will be printed in bold text on two lines as:

   "Ouch! That's not nice," snickered Mrs. O'Connell.
   "You mustn't do that, Mr. O'Connell."

2. What does the following code print?

```
print ("What a <b>perfect</b> day.");
print ("3" + 2);
print ("5 dogs" + "6 cats" . "10 birds");
print ("<pre>\t\tIt's been real!\n</pre>");
print ("\t\tLater, dude.\n");
```

3. Create four variables that contain an integer, float, string, and boolean value. Print the value of each variable and its data type in an HTML table. Use `gettype()`.

4. In Exercise 1 you created the following PHP output. Now we will rewrite this script to include user-defined variables. Where you see < > in the example, input your variable values.

   Print the output in the browser. Can you format the output so that a dollar sign appears before the money values and format the numbers with a precision of two places to the right of the decimal point (e.g., $410.00)? Hint: See *http://www.htmlite.com/php011.php*.

   Check to see if the variables are set (`isset()`) before displaying them.

Set variables as follows;

```
$sales     =   190000;
$rent      =    25000;
$salary    =    37500;
$supplies  =      410;
$total     =    $rent + $salary + $supplies;   // Addition
$operating_income = $sales - $exp_total;       // Subtraction
$net_income = $operating_income * 0.60;        // Multiplication

          Book Store Operating Costs
===========================================
Sales:   <print variable values here>

Expenses:
   Rent:  < >
   Salary:
   Supplies:

Total:  < >
   Operating income:  < >
   Income after taxes (net):  < >
===========================================
```

5. Use the shortcut PHP tags, `<?= ?>`, within the HTML document to display the variables in the previous exercise. (Check the `php.ini` file to see if shortcut tags are allowed and if set to "Off", turn them "On".)

6. Create an HTML form that contains three text boxes, one for the user's name, one for his cell phone number, and one for his e-mail address. Write a PHP script to display the output.

7. Rewrite Exercise 4 so that the user enters input into an HTML form, and write a PHP script to process the form and display the output as it did in Exercise 4.

8. Write a PHP script that displays the values entered into the form fields. Add a constant to the following script that will define a COPY_RIGHT constant containing your SITE_NAME with the copyright symbol appended (concatenated) to it. Display the constants and their corresponding values in an HTML table. Hint: See *http://www.desilva.biz/php/constants.html*.

```php
<?php>
// Define your site name, since it does NOT change
// anywhere within your script.
define( 'SITE_NAME', 'Your site' );

// Define the current year, possibly to use in your copyright
// statement or for 'date' calculations.
define( 'THIS_YEAR', date('Y') );
?>
```

chapter

5

Operators

> "Operator, give me the number for 911."
> —Dan Castellaneta

5.1 About PHP Operators and Expressions

Data objects can be manipulated in a number of ways by the large number of operators provided by PHP. Operators are symbols, such as +, -, =, >, and <, that produce a result based on some rules. An operator manipulates data objects called operands; for example, 5 and 4 are operands in the expression 5 + 4. Operators and operands are found in expressions. An expression combines a group of values to make a new value, n = 5 + 4. When you terminate an expression with a semicolon, you have a complete statement; for example, n = 5 + 4;

	Expression			
sum	=	5	+	4
new value	operator	operand	operator	operand

In the numeric *expression* 5 + 4 - 2, three numbers are combined. The *operators* are the + and - signs. The *operands* for the + sign are 5 and 4. After that part of the expression is evaluated to 9, the expression becomes 9 - 2. After evaluating the complete expression, the result is 7. Because the plus and minus operators each manipulate two operands, they are called a binary operators. If there is only one operand, the operator is called a unary operator, and if there are three operands, it is called a ternary operator. We'll see examples of these operators later in the chapter.

The operands can be either strings, numbers, booleans, or a combination of these. Some of the operators we have already used are the concatenation operator to join two strings together, the reference operator to create an alias for a variable, and the assignment operator to assign a value to a variable. Now let's look at a whole plethora of additional PHP operators and see how they manipulate their operands.

5.1.1 Assignment

An assignment statement evaluates the expression on the right side of the equal sign and assigns the result to the variable on the left side of the equal sign. The equal sign is the assignment operator.

```
$total = 5 + 4;
$name = "Tony";
```

5.1.2 Precedence and Associativity

When an expression contains a number of operators and operands, such as 5 * 4 + 3 / -2.2, and the order of evaluation is ambiguous, then PHP must determine what to do. This is where the precedence and associative rules come in. They tell PHP how to evaluate such an expression. *Precedence* refers to the way in which the operator binds to its operand; that is, should addition be done before division or should assignment come before multiplication. The precedence of one operator over another determines what operation is done first. As shown in the precedence table (see Table 5.1), the operators are organized as a hierarchy, with the operators of highest precedence at the top, similar to a social system where those with the most power (or money) are at the top. In the rules of precedence, the multiplication operator is of higher precedence than the addition operator, technically meaning the operator of higher precedence binds more tightly to its operands. The assignment operators are low in precedence and thus bind loosely to their operand. In the expression sum = 5 + 4, the equal sign is of low precedence so the expression 5 + 4 is evaluated first and then the result is assigned to sum. Parentheses are of the highest precedence. An expression placed within parentheses is evaluated first; for example, in the expression 2 * (10 - 4), the expression within the parentheses is evaluated first and that result is multiplied by 2. When parentheses are nested, the expression contained within the innermost set of parentheses is evaluated first.

Associativity refers to the order in which an operator evaluates its operands: left to right, in no specified order, or right to left. When all of the operators in an expression are of equal precedence (see Table 5.1), normally the association is left to right; for example, in the expression 5 + 4 + 3, the evaluation is from left to right. In the following statement, how is the expression evaluated? Is addition, multiplication, or division done first? In what order, right to left or left to right?

EXAMPLE 5.1

```
        <html>
        <head><title>Precedence and Associativity()</title>
        </head>
        <body bgcolor="lightgreen">
        <font face = "arial" size = '+1'>
        <?php
1           $result = 5 + 4 * 12 / 4;
            print "$result = 5 + 4 * 12 / 4";
2           $result = (5 + 4) * 12 / (4 - 2);
            print "<br />$result = ( 5 + 4 ) * 12 / (4 - 2) ";
        ?>
        </body>
```

EXPLANATION

1   The order of associativity is from left to right. Multiplication and division are of a higher precedence than addition and subtraction, and addition and subtraction are of a higher precedence than assignment. To illustrate this, we'll use parentheses to group the operands as they are grouped by PHP. In fact, if you want to force precedence, use the parentheses around the expression to group the operands in the way you want them evaluated. The following two examples produce the same result.

```
var result = 5 + 4 * 12 / 4;
```

could be written

```
result = (5 + ( ( 4 * 12 ) / 4));
```

2   In this example, the expressions enclosed within parentheses are evaluated first. The * and / are evaluated left to right because they are of the same precedence. Output of this example is shown in Figure 5.1.

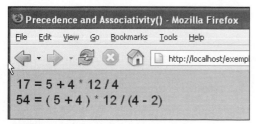

Figure 5.1   Output from Example 5.1.

Table 5.1 summarizes the rules of precedence and associativity for the PHP operators. The operators on the same line are of equal precedence. The rows are in order of highest to lowest precedence.

Table 5.1   Precedence and Associativity (Highest to Lowest)

Operator	Description	Associativity
`()`	Parentheses	Left to right[a]
`new`	Creates an object	Nonassociative
`[`	Array subscript	Right to left
`++   --`	Auto increment, decrement	Nonassociative
`!   ~   -`	Logical not, bitwise not, negation	Nonassociative
`(int) (float)` `(string) (array) (object)`	Cast	
`@`	Inhibit errors	
`*   /   %`	Multiply, divide, modulus	Left to right
`+   -   .`	Add, subtract, string concatenation	Left to right
`<<   >>`	Bitwise left shift, right shift	Left to right
`<   <=`	Less than, less than or equal to	Left to right
`>   >=`	Greater than, greater than or equal to	
`= =   !=`	Equal to, not equal to	Nonassociative
`= = =   != =`	Identical to (same type), not identical to	
`&`	Bitwise AND	Left to right
`^`	Bitwise XOR	
`|`	Bitwise OR	
`&&`	Logical and	Left to right
`||`	Logical or	Left to right
`?  :`	Ternary, conditional	Left to right
`=  +=  -=  *=  /=  %=  <<=  >>=`	Assignment	Right to left
`and`	Logical AND	Left to right
`xor`	Logical XOR	Left to right
`or`	Logical OR	Left to right
`,  (comma)`	List separator, etc.	Left to right

a. Not listed in the PHP manual, but seems to behave the same as in other languages.

EXAMPLE 5.2

```
<html>
<head><title>Precedence and Associativity()</title>
</head>
<body bgcolor="lightgreen">
<font face = "arial" size = '+1'>
<?php
1     $result = 5 + 4 * 12 / 4;
2     print "$result = 5 + 4 * 12 / 4";
3     $result = (5 + 4) * (12 / 4) ;
4     print "<br />$result = ( 5 + 4 ) * (12 / 4) ";
?>
</body>
</html>
```

EXPLANATION

1 The variable, called `$result`, is assigned the result of the expression.

```
$result = 5 + 4 * 12 / 4;
    produces:
$result = 5 + 48 / 4
    produces:
$result = 5 + 12
   and finally the sum:
17
```

Because multiplication and division are higher on the precedence table than addition, those expressions will be evaluated first, associating from left to right.

2 The result of the previous evaluation, the value of `$result`, is sent to the browser.

3 The expressions enclosed in parentheses are evaluated first and then multiplied.

```
$result = ( 5 + 4 )  * ( 12 / 4 );
   produces: 9 * 3
$result = 9 * 3
   results in: 27
```

4 The result of the previous evaluation, the value of `$result`, is sent to the browser. See Figure 5.2.

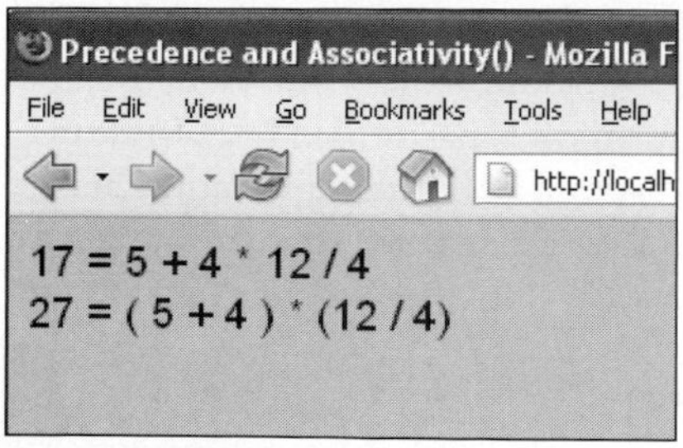

Figure 5.2
Output from Example 5.2.

5.1.3   Arithmetic Operators

Arithmetic operators take numerical values (either literals or variables) as their operands and return a single numerical value. The standard arithmetic operators are addition (+), subtraction (–), multiplication (*), and division (/). See Table 5.2.

Table 5.2   Arithmetic Operators

Operator/Operands	*Function*
x + y	Addition
x – y	Subtraction
x * y	Multiplication
x / y	Division
x % y	Modulus

EXAMPLE 5.3

```
        <html>
        <head><title>Arithmetic Operators</title></head>
        <body bgcolor="#ccccff" text="000033">
        <h2>Arithmetic operators</h2>
        <p>
1       <?php>
2           $num1 = 5;
            $num2 = 7;
3           $result = $num1 + $num2;
            print "<h3>$result =  $num1 + $num2 <br />";
4           $result = $result + (10 / 2 + 5) % 7;
            print "$result =  12 + (10 / 2 + 5) %7<br /></h3>" ;
        ?>
        </body></html>
```

EXPLANATION

1   This is the start of a PHP program.
2   Variables $num1 and $num2 are declared and assigned values 5 and 7, respectively.
3   The sum of $num1 and $num2 is assigned to $result and printed on line 3.
4   This arithmetic operation illustrates precedence and associativity. The expression in parentheses is evaluated first, then the module operator (the % sign) will divide that result by 7 and return the remainder, and addition is performed last. To show the order of evaluation, we can put parentheses around all of the expressions. Start evaluating with the innermost set of parentheses first (10/2 + 5), then the next set, and so on:

```
(12 +( (10 / 2 + 5)  %7))
```

See Figure 5.3 for output of this example.

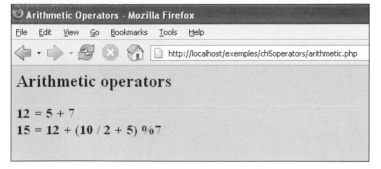

Figure 5.3   Output from Example 5.3.

5.1.4   Short Circuit Assignment Operators

The short circuit assignment operators allow you to perform an arithmetic or string operation by combining an assignment operator with an arithmetic or string operator. For example, $x = $x + 1 can be written $x+=1.

Table 5.3   Assignment Operators

Operator	Example	Meaning
=	$x = 5;	Assign 5 to variable $x.
+=	$x += 3;	Add 3 to $x and assign result to $x.
-=	$x -= 2;	Subtract 2 from $x and assign result to $x.
*=	$x *= 4;	Multiply $x by 4 and assign result to $x.
/=	$x /= 2;	Divide $x by 2 and assign result to $x.
%=	$x %= 2;	Divide $x by 2 and assign remainder to $x.

EXAMPLE 5.4

```
     <html>
     <head><title>Arithmetic Operators</title></head>
     <body bgcolor="#99ff66">
     <h2>Shortcut Operators</h2>
     <font size="+1" >
1    <?php>
         //Using shortcuts
2        $num=10;
         print "10 is assigned to \$num.<br />";
```

EXAMPLE 5.4 (CONTINUED)

```
3        $num += 2;
         print "\$num += 2; \$num is $num. <br />";

4        $num -= 1;
         print"\$num -= 1; \$num is $num. <br />";

5        $num *= 3;
         print "\$num *= 3; \$num is $num. <br />";

6        $num %= 5;
         print "\$num %= 5; \$num is $num.<br />";
     ?>
     </body>
     </html>
```

EXPLANATION

1   The PHP program starts here.
2   10 is assigned to the variable $num.
3   The shortcut assignment operator, +=, adds 2 to the variable, $num. This is equiv-
    alent to: $num = $num + 1;
4   The shortcut assignment operator, -=, subtracts 1 from the variable, $num. This is
    equivalent to: $num = $num - 1;
5   The shortcut assignment operator, *, multiplies the variable $num by 3. This is
    equivalent to: $num = $num * 3;
6   The shortcut assignment modulus operator, %, yields the integer amount that re-
    mains after the scalar $num is divided by 5. The operator is called the modulus op-
    erator or remainder operator. The expression $num %=5 is equivalent to: $num =
    $num % 5;. See Figure 5.4 for output of this example.

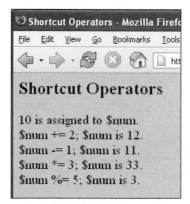

Figure 5.4   Output from Example 5.4.

5.1.5 Autoincrement and Autodecrement Operators

To make programs easier to read, to simplify typing, and, at the machine level, to produce more efficient code, the autoincrement (++) and autodecrement (--) operators are provided.

The autoincrement operator performs the simple task of incrementing the value of its operand by 1, and the autodecrement operator decrements the value of its operand by 1. The operator has two forms: The first form *prefixes* the variable with either ++ or -- (e.g., ++$x or --$x); the second form *postfixes* (places the operator after) the variable name with either ++ or -- (e.g., $x++, x--). For simple operations, such as $x++ or $x--, ++$x or --$x, the effect is the same; both ++$x and $x++ add 1 to the value of $x, and both --$x and $x-- subtract one from the value of $x. See Table 5.4 for examples.

Now you have four ways to add 1 to the value of a variable:

```
$x = $x + 1;
$x += 1;
$x++;
++$x ;
```

You also have four ways to subtract 1 from the value of a variable:

```
$x = $x - 1;
$x -= 1;
$x--;
--$x;
```

In Chapter 6, "Strings," these operators are commonly used to increment or decrement loop counters.

Table 5.4 Autoincrement and Autodecrement Operators

Operator	Function	What It Does	Example	
++$x	Preincrement	Adds 1 to $x	$x = 3; $x++;	$x is now 4
$x++	Postincrement	Adds 1 to $x	$x = 3; ++$x;	$x is now 4
--$x	Predecrement	Subtracts 1 from $x	$x = 3; $x--;	$x is now 2
$x--	Postdecrement	Subtracts 1 from $x	$x = 3; --$x;	$x is now 2

The Autoincrement/Autodecrement and Assignment. The placement of the operators does make a difference in more complex expressions especially when part of an assignment; for example, $y = $x++ is not the same as $y = ++$x. See Figure 5.5.

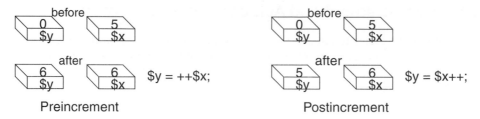

Figure 5.5 Start with: $y = 0 ; $x = 5;. See Example 5.5.

EXAMPLE 5.5

```
    <html>
    <head><title>Autoincrement and Autodecrement</title></head>
    <body bgcolor="6699ff">
    <?php
1       $x=5; $y=0;
2       $y = ++$x;          // add 1 to $x first; then assign to $y
        print "<h3>Preincrement:<br />";
3       print "\$y is $y.<br />";
        print "\$x is $x.<br />";
        print "<hr>";
4       $x=5; $y=0;
5       $y = $x++;
        print "Postincrement:<br />";
6       print "\$y is $y. <br />";
        print "\$x is $x. <br />";
    ?>
    </body>
    </html>
```

1   The variables, $x and $y, are initialized to 5 and 0, respectively. See Figure 5.5.
2   The preincrement operator is applied to $x. This means that $x will be increment-ed *before* the assignment is made. The value of $x was 5, now it is 6. The variable $y is assigned 6. $x is 6, $y is 6.
3   The new values of $y and $x are displayed in the browser window.
4   The variables, $x and $y, are assigned values of 5 and 0, respectively.
5   This time the postincrement operator is applied to $x. This means that $x will be incremented *after* the assignment is made. 5 is assigned to the variable $y, and then $x is incremented by 1. $x is 5, $y is 6.
6   The new values of $y and $x are displayed in the browser window. See Figure 5.6.

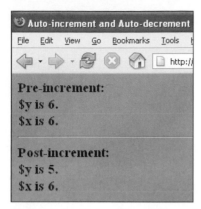

Figure 5.6   Output from Example 5.5.

5.1.6   Some Useful Math Functions

Table 5.5 lists some of the math functions provided by PHP. The complete list can be found at the PHP Web site.

Table 5.5   Math Functions

Function	Meaning	Example
abs()	Absolute value	echo abs(-5); // 5 echo abs(5.3); // 5

base_convert()	Convert a number between arbitrary bases	echo base_convert("ff",16,10); // 255
		echo base_convert("a",16,2); // 1010
		echo base_convert(11,10,8); // 13

bindec()	Binary to decimal	echo bindec('1010'); // 10 echo bindec('110010'); // 50
ceil()	Round fractions up	echo ceil(6.2); // 7 echo ceil(6.8); // 7
decbin()	Decimal to binary	echo decbin(5); // 101 echo decbin(20); // 10100

dechex()	Decimal to hexadecimal	echo dechex(15); // f
		echo dechex(124); // 7c

decoct()	Decimal to octal	echo decoct(8); // 10 echo decoct(20); // 24
floor()	Round fractions down	echo floor(6.2); // 6 echo floor(6.8); // 6
getrandmax()	Show largest possible random value	echo getrandmax(); // returns 32767

Table 5.5   Math Functions (continued)

Function	Meaning	Example

hexdec()	Hexadecimal to decimal	echo hexdec("ff"); // returns 255
		echo hexdec("a"); // returns 10

is_finite()	Finds whether a value is a legal finite number, returns boolean	echo is_finite(pi()); // returns 1 true
is_infinite()	Finds whether a value is infinite	echo is_infinite(pow(10, 1000000)); // returns 1 true
is_nan()	Finds whether a value is not a number	echo is_nan(5.2) // returns false
max()	Find highest value	echo max(1,3,5,12,8); // 12
min()	Find lowest value	echo min(5,3.2, 8, 4); // 3.2
octdec()	Octal to decimal	echo octdec(10); // returns 8
pi()	Get value of pi	echo pi(); // 3.1415926535898
pow()	Exponential expression	echo pow(3,2); // 9 echo pow(10,3); // 1000

rand(start,finish)	Generate a random integer between start and finish	echo rand(1,10); // 5
		echo rand(1,10); // 7
		echo rand(1,10); // 10

round()	Rounds a float	echo round(6.4); // 6 echo round(6.5); // 7
sqrt()	Square root	echo sqrt(81); // 9
srand()	Seed the random number generator	

5.1.7   Casting Operators

As defined earlier, PHP is a loosely typed language, which really means that you don't have to be concerned about what kind of data is stored in a variable. You can assign a number to $x on one line and on the next line assign a string to $x; you can compare numbers and strings, strings and booleans, and so on. PHP automatically converts values when it assigns values to a variable or evaluates an expression. If data types are mixed, that is, a number is compared to a string, a boolean is compared to a number, a string is compared to a boolean, PHP must decide how to handle the expression. Most of the time, letting PHP handle the data works fine, but there are times when you want to force a conversion of one type to another. This is done by using the casting operators listed in Table 5.6. Casting doesn't change the value in a variable; it affects the way other operators interpret the value. Casting can be useful when casting strings to integers, arrays to objects, and so on.

Table 5.6 Casting Operators

Operator	Synonym	Changes Data Type To
(int)	(integer)	Integer
(float)	(real)	Floating point
(string)		String
(bool)	(boolean)	Boolean
(array)		Array (see Chapter 8, "Arrays")

FORMAT

```
variable = (cast operator) value;
```

Example:
```
$salary = "52000";        // Variable is assigned a string value
$salary = (float) $salary; // Value is forced to float and reassigned
```

EXAMPLE 5.6

```
       <html><head><title>Type Casting</title></head>
       <body bgcolor="aqua">
       <font face="verdana" size="+1">
       <?php
1          $string = "500 dogs";
2          $number = (int) $string;
           echo "The value in \$string has been cast to an int:
               ", $number, "<br />";
       ?>
       <hr>
       <?php
           $total_seconds = 1132; //Total running time in seconds
3          $minutes = (int)($total_seconds / 60); /* Result of expression
                                               is cast to an integer */
           $seconds_left = $total_seconds % 60; // Modulus returns
                                               // seconds left
         print "You ran for $minutes minutes and $seconds_left
             seconds\n.";
       ?>
       <hr>
       <?php
         $total = 5;
         $total = (float) $total;
         echo "\$total has been cast to float: ", $total + 2.3, "<br />";
         if( "2"> "100 dogs") {print "true";}
       ?>
       </body>
       </html>
```

EXPLANATION

1   The variable, `$string`, is assigned a string containing some leading numbers.
2   The new type is placed within parentheses, causing the variable, `$string`, to be temporarily cast from a string data type to an integer. The original `$string` will not be changed. It is still a string type, but `$number` will be an integer. PHP retains only the leading numbers in `$string`, thus removing `dogs` during the type cast.
3   (`$total_seconds / 60`) is cast to an integer before assigning the result to `$minutes`. See Figure 5.7 for output of this example.

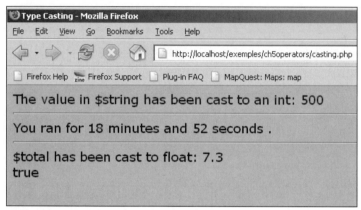

Figure 5.7   Type casting. Output from Example 5.6.

5.1.8 Concatention Operator

> Concatenation is from Late Latin *concatenatio*, from *concatenare*,
> "to chain together," from Latin con-, "with, together" + catena,
> "a chain, a series."[1]

The process of joining strings together is called concatenation. The PHP string concatenation operator is a dot (`.`). Its operands are two strings. It returns the concatenation of its right and left operands. If either operand is a number and the other is a string, PHP still concatenates them as strings.

```
"pop" . "corn"      // results in "popcorn"
"Route " . 66       // results in "Route 66"
```

There is also a shortcut concatenation assignment operator used like the shortcut operators (`.=`).

---

1. *http://dictionary.reference.com/search?r=10&q=concatenation*

EXAMPLE 5.7

```
    <html><head><title>Concatenation</title></head>
    <body bgcolor="#33ff99">
    <font face="verdana" size="+1">
    <?php
1      $string1 = "My dog";
       $string2 = "has fleas";
2      $string3 = $string1 . $string2 . "<br />";
       // $string1 .= $string2
       echo "First string: $string1<br />";
       echo "Second string: $string2<br />";
       echo "After concatenation: $string3";
       echo "Whoops! Let's add a space: ";
3      $string3 = "$string1". " " . "$string2";
       echo "After adding a space: $string3";
    ?>
    </body>
    </html>
```

EXPLANATION

1   $string1 is assigned the string, "My dog"; $string2 is assigned the string, "has fleas". These two strings will be linked together with the concatenation operator.

2   $string3 is created by concatenating $string1 and $string2 together. The comment shows another way to use the concatenation operator: $string1 .= $string2. When combined with the assignment operator, .=, $string1 will be assigned its value concatenated to the value of $string2, same as: $string1 = $string1 . $string2.

3   A space, represented as " ", is concatenated to $string1 to provide a space between $string1 and $string2. See Figure 5.8.

Figure 5.8 Output from Example 5.7.

5.1.9 Comparison Operators

When operands are compared, relational and equality operators are used. The operands can be numbers or strings. The result of the comparison is either *true* or *false*, a Boolean value. Comparisons are based on the type of the operands being compared. If, for example, two numbers are compared, the comparison is numeric, such as 5 > 4. When comparing two strings, they are compared letter by letter (lexographically) using ASCII values to represent the numeric value of each letter; for example, "A" is less than "B" and when comparing "Daniel" to "Dan", "Daniel" is greater than "Dan". What if a string contains only numbers and is compared to another string that contains only numbers? Then the strings are converted to numbers and compared numerically. See Table 5.7 for examples.

If you want to make sure you are always comparing strings, rather than using comparison operators, you should use string comparison functions. (See Chapter 6, "Strings.")

Table 5.7 Comparison Operators

Operator/Operands	*Function*
$x == $y	$x is equal to $y
$x != $y	$x is not equal to $y
$x > $y	$x is greater than $y
$x >= $y	$x is greater than or equal to $y
$x < $y	$x is less than $y
$x <= $y	$x is less than or equal to $y
$x === $y	$x is identical to $y in value and type
$x !== $y	$x is not identical to $y

What Is Equal?   Men are equal, but they are not identical. Clones are identical. In PHP, operators determine the equality or inequality of their operands, based on specific rules. When using the == or != equality operators, the operands may be of any given data type (e.g., numbers, strings, booleans, objects, arrays, or a combination of these), and there are rules that govern whether or not they are equal. For example, two strings are equal when they have the same sequence of characters, same length, and same characters in corresponding positions. Two numbers are equal when they have the same numeric value. If a string is compared to a number, they are equal if their values are the same (e.g., "500" is equal to 500). Positive and negative zeros are equal. Two objects are equal if they refer to the same object (objects are discussed in Chapter 17, "Objects"). Two Boolean operands are equal if they are both *true* or both *false*. Two strings are equal if all the characters are the same: Is "William" equal to "william"? No. The case of the letters makes the difference. See Table 5.8.

Table 5.8   Equality Test with Strings and Numbers

Test	Are They Equal?
`"William" == "William"`	True
`"william" == "William"`	False
`5 == 5.0`	True
`"54" == 54`	True
`"5.4" == 5.4`	True
`null == null`	True
`-0 == +0`	True
`false == false`	True
`true == 1`	True
`null == ""`	True

What Is Identical?   The `===` and `!==` operators test that their operands are not only of the same value, but also of the *same data type*. String `"54"` is equal to number `54`, but *not identical* because one is a string and the other is a number, even though their values are equal. See Table 5.9.

Table 5.9   Identity Test with Strings and Numbers

Test	Are They Identical?
`"William" === "William"`	True
`"william" === "William"`	False
`5 === 5.0`	False
`"54" === 54`	False
`null === null`	True
`-0 == +0`	True
`false === false`	True
`true === 1`	False
`null === ""`	False

5.1.10 Comparing Numbers

When the comparison operators are used to compare numbers, numeric values are compared; for example, is 50 > 45? A boolean value of either true or false is returned. PHP compares its operands numerically if:

1. Both operands are numbers: 4 > 5
2. One operand is a number and the other is a string consisting of all numbers: "54" > 6
3. Both operands are strings containing all numbers: "56" < "57"

For example:

$x > $y	$x is greater than $y
$x >= $y	$x is greater than or equal to $y
$x < $y	$x is less than $y
$x <= $y	$x is less than or equal to $y

EXAMPLE 5.8

```
        <html><head><title>Comparing Numbers</title></head>
        <body bgcolor="#00ff99">
        <?php
1           $x = 5;
            $y = 4;
2           $result = $x > $y;
3           echo "<h3>Is \$x > \$y? The result is $result, true.<br />";
4           $result = $x < $y;
5           echo "Is \$x < \$y? The result is ", (int) $result,",
                false.<br />";
        ?>
        </body>
        </html>
```

EXPLANATION

1   The variables $x and $y are assigned values, to be compared later in the program.
2   If the value of $x is greater than the value of $y, a boolean value of either 1 or "" is returned and assigned to the variable result.
3   The boolean result of the comparison is displayed by the browser. It is true or 1; $x is greater than y.
4   If $x is less than $y, 1 is assigned to the variable, result; otherwise it is assigned the null string.
5   The boolean result of the comparison is displayed by the browser. It is cast to an integer so that you can see the value 0, representing false; $x is not greater than $y. See Figure 5.9.

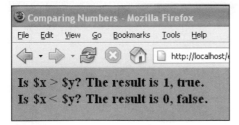

Figure 5.9   Comparison operators. Output from Example 5.8.

5.1.11   Comparing Strings

Because PHP doesn't have different operators for comparing strings and numbers (e.g., like Perl), you must be sure that the values you are comparing are expressed as either numbers or strings. For example, consider the following statements:

```
"php" > 100          "php" will be converted to number 0
2 > "100"            "100" will be converted to number 100
"3" > "100 dogs"     The operands are compared as strings
```

If you want to compare strings, rather than using comparison operators, it is better to use you the string comparison functions discussed in Chapter 6, "Strings." They ensure that all arguments are cast to strings before comparing them and allow you to control the method in which the comparison occurs.

The difference between comparing strings and numbers is that numbers are compared numerically and strings are compared alphabetically, based on the ASCII character set. The strings are compared letter by letter, from left to right, and if they are exactly the same all the way to end, they are equal. Once a letter in one string differs from the corresponding letter in the second string, the comparison stops and each of the differing letters is evaluated. For example, if the string "Dan" is compared to "dan", the comparison stops at the first letter D and d. "Dan" is smaller than "dan", because the letter D has a lower ASCII value than the letter d. D has an ASCII decimal value of 68, and d has an ASCII value of 100.

```
"string1" > "string2"      "string1" is greater than "string2"
"string1" >= "string2"     "string1" is greater than or equal to "string2"
"string1" < "string2"      "string1" is less than "string2"
"string1" <= "string2"     "string1" is less than or equal to "string2"
```

EXAMPLE 5.9

```
      <html><head><title>Comparing Strings</title></head>
      <body bgcolor="#00ff99">
      <font face="verdana" size="+1">
      <?php
1         $fruit1 = "pear";
2         $fruit2 = "peaR";
3         if($fruit1 > $fruit2){print "True: pear is greater than
              peaR.<br />";}
      ?>
      </body>
      </html>
```

EXPLANATION

1   The variables, $fruit1 and $fruit2, are assigned to string values, differing by only one letter, r and R.

2   The string values are compared. "pear" is greater than "peaR" because the r has an ASCII value of 114 and the R has an ASCII value of 82.

3   The result of the comparison is true and the statement enclosed in curly braces is sent to the browser. See Figure 5.10.

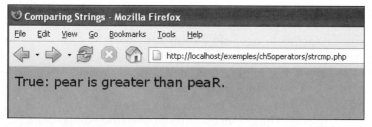

Figure 5.10   Comparing strings. Output from Example 5.9.

5.1.12   Logical Operators

Logical operators let you test combinations of expressions resulting in boolean value, true and false. See Table 5.10.

Table 5.10   Testing Expressions with Logical Operators

Example	Name	Result
$a && $b	And	TRUE if both $a and $b are TRUE.
$a || $b	Or	TRUE if either $a or $b is TRUE.
$a and $b	And	TRUE if both $a and $b are TRUE.

Table 5.10   Testing Expressions with Logical Operators (continued)

Example	Name	Result
$a or $b	Or	TRUE if either $a or $b is TRUE.
$a xor $b	Xor	TRUE if either $a or $b is TRUE, but not both.
! $a	Not	TRUE if $a is not TRUE.

They allow you combine the relational operators into more powerful expressions for testing conditions and are most often used in conditional `if` statements. They evaluate their operands, from left to right, testing the boolean value of each operand in turn, that is, does the operand evaluate to `true` or `false`? In the expression,

```
if ( $x > 5 && $x < 10 )
```

the `&&` is a logical operator. The expression simplified means, "if $x is greater than 5 and x is also less than 10, then do something." In the case of the logical AND (`&&`), if the first expression returns `true` and the second expression also returns `true`, then the whole expression is `true`.

A numeric operand is true if it evaluates to any number that is not zero. 5, -2, and 74 are all true. 0 is false. For example, when using the `&&` (AND) operator, both operands must be true for the whole expression to be true. The value returned from an expression such as 5 `&&` 6 is 1, the last value evaluated by the operator. 5 is not zero (true) and 6 is not zero (true), therefore, the expression is true. 5 `&&` 0, 0 `&&` 0, and 0 `&&` 5 all yield 0, which is false. See Table 5.11.

The three logical operators are the logical AND, logical OR, and logical NOT. The symbol for AND is `&&`, the symbol for OR is `||`. The English version for `&&` is *and* and for `||` is *or*. The only difference is that of precedence, the English version being of lower precedence.

The && (and) Operator, the Logical AND.   We all know the meaning of the English statement, "If you have the money *and* I have the time . . ." Whatever is supposed to happen is based on two conditions, and both conditions must be met. You must have the money *and* I must have the time. PHP uses the symbol `&&`[2] to represent the word AND. This operator is called the logical AND operator. If the expression on the left side of the `&&` evaluates to zero, null, or the empty string " ", the expression is false. If the expression on the left side of the operator evaluates to true (nonzero), then the right side is evaluated, and if that expression is also true, then the whole expression is true. If the left side evaluates to true, and the right side is false, the expression is false. If evaluated as booleans, the same rules apply, except the returned value will be either boolean `true` or `false`. See Table 5.11.

---

2. The single & is a bitwise AND and evaluates both of its operands even if the first one is false. The | is the bitwise OR and evaluates both operands as well. See "Bitwise Operators" on page 140 for bitwise operators and how they work.

Table 5.11   Logical AND Examples

Expression	What It Evaluates To
true && false	False
true && true	True
"honest" && true	True
true && ""	False
true && "honest"	True
5 && 0	False
5 && -6	True
5 && false	False
null && 0	False
null && ""	False
null && false	False
"hello" && true && 50	True
"this" && "that"	True

EXAMPLE   5.10

```
    (The HTML Form)
    <html><head><title>Logical Operators</title>
    </head>
    <body bgcolor="yellow"><font face="arial" size="+1">
1       <form action="logical.php">
        <p> Dude, what is your name:
2       <input type="text" size=25 name="name" />
        <p>
        Like how old are you?
3       <input type="text" size=5 name="age" />
        <p>
4       <input type=submit value="Submit">
        </form>
    </body>
    </html>
```

EXAMPLE 5.10 (CONTINUED)

```
(The PHP Script -- logical.php)
<html><head><title>Logical Operators</title></head>
<body bgcolor="330033" text="white"><font face="arial" size="+1">
<?php
    extract($_REQUEST);  // Get the form input
5   // if( $age > 12 and $age < 20 and $age != ""  )
6   if( $age > 12 && $age < 20 && $age != ""  ){
    print "Hey $name, teenagers rock, dude!";
    }
?>
<img src="teenager.jpg" border="1">
</body></html>
```

EXPLANATION

1   The HTML form starts here. The action attribute names the PHP script that will handle the form, shown in Figure 5.11.

2   This input device is a text box, named "name". PHP will create a variable, called "$name" and assign it whatever the user types in the box.

3   This input device is another text box, named "age". PHP will create a variable, called "$age" and assign it whatever the user typed in the text box.

4   When the user presses the submit button, the browser will collect the form input, encode it, and send it to the server where PHP resides.

5, 6   The && and the alternative word and require that both of its operands are true for the expression to be true. In this example, all of the expressions must be true for line 6 to be executed; that is, if the value of $age is greater than 12 and less than 20 and not an empty string, then "Hey dude, (name of teenager), teenagers rock!" is displayed. If the user enters any other value, nothing happens. Note: The word and instead of && is fine in this example, but it is not exactly the same as && because it is of lower precedence. See Table 5.1 on page 110 for precedence rules. See Figure 5.12 for output of this example.

Figure 5.11
The HTML form from Example 5.10.

Figure 5.12
After PHP processing.
Output from Example 5.10.

The || (or) Operator.   In the English statement, "If you have some cash *or* I have a credit card . . ." the word *or* is used in the condition. With the *or,* only one of the conditions must be met (hopefully you have the cash!). PHP uses the || symbol or the word or to represent the logical inclusive OR. If the expression on the left side of the || operator is evaluated as true (nonzero), the value of the expression is true, and no further checking is done. If the value on the left side of the || operator is false, the value of the expression on the right side of the operator is evaluated, and if true, the expression is true; that is, only one expression must be true.

Table 5.12   Logical OR Examples

Expression	*What It Evaluates To*
true || false	True
true || true	True
"honest" || true	True
true || ""	True
5 || 0	True
5 || -6	True

Table 5.12   Logical OR Examples (continued)

Expression	What It Evaluates To
5 || false	True
null || 0	False
null || ""	False
null || false	False
"hello" || true || 50	True
"this" || "that"	True

EXAMPLE 5.11

```
(The HTML File)
<html><head><title>Logical OR Operators</title></head>
<body bgcolor="yellow"><font face="arial" size="+1">
<form action="logicalor.php" method=get>
<p> Where should we eat:
<br />
<input type="checkbox" name="place1" value="Wendy" />Wendy's
<br />
<input type="checkbox" name="place2" value="Taco" />Taco Bell
<br />
<input type="checkbox" name="place3" value="CliffHouse" /> Cliff House
<br />
<input type="checkbox" name="place4" value="OliveGarden" /> Olive
Garden
<br />
<input type="checkbox" name="place5" value="McDonald" /> McDonald's
<p>
<input type=submit value="submit now!">
</p>
</form>
</body></html>

(The PHP Script)
    <html><head><title>Logical OR Operator</title></head>
    <body bgcolor=CCFF66><font face="arial" size="+1">
    <?php
       extract($_REQUEST);
1      if ( $place1 || $place2 || $place5 ){
2          print "No fast food joints today, thanks!<br />";
       }
    ?>
    </body></html>
```

EXPLANATION

1   If any one of the variables $place1 or $place2 or $place5 evaluates to true, the
expression is true, and the block of statements on line 2 is executed. With the logical OR, only one of the expressions must be true for the expression to be evaluated as true, but any others can be true as well.

2   The statements within the curly braces are called a block. This line will be executed only if line 1 evaluates to be true. See Figures 5.13 and 5.14 for output of this
example.

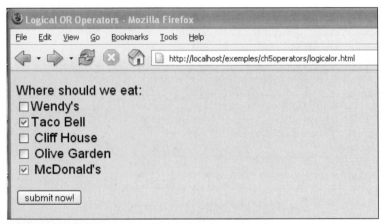

Figure 5.13   The HTML form from Example 5.11.

Figure 5.14   The PHP script output from Example 5.11.

The Difference Between &&/|| and the Words and/or.   You can use the words
and and or to replace && and ||, respectively, but they are not exactly the same because
they have a different precedence. Look at the precedence table (Table 5.1 on page 110)
and notice that the and and or operators are lower on the table than the corresponding
&& and ||. In fact, they're lower than even the equal sign. Normally this won't make a
difference, but consider Example 5.12.

EXAMPLE 5.12

```
        <html>
        <head>
        <title>Logical Word Operators</title>
        </head>
        <body bgcolor="330066" text="white"><font face="arial" size="+1">
        <h3>Dealing with Precedence</h3>
        <hr>
        <?php
1           $x = 5;
            $y = 6;
            $z = 0;
2           $result = $x && $y && $z;
            echo "$x && $y && $z <em>yields</em> " .
                (int)$result .".\n<br />";

3           $result = $x and $y and $z;
            echo "$x and $y and $z <em>yields</em> " .
                (int)$result .".\n<br />";

4           $result = ($x and $y and $z);
            echo "($x and $y and $z) <em>yields</em> " .
                (int)$result .".\n<br />";

        ?>
        <hr>
        </body>
        </html>
```

EXPLANATION

1   Three variables are intialized and assigned values.

2   The `&&` is higher in precedence than the equal sign, so its operands are evaluated left to right. The value of `$x` is logically "anded" to `$y` and both values yield true, but when "anded" to `$z`, because `$z` is 0 (false), the whole expression will be false. Finally, the value of the expression is assigned to `$result`, and, when cast to an integer will print 0, what you would expect.

3   By using the word `and` instead of `&&`, the situation changes. The equal sign is now higher in precedence and will force the value on its immediate right to be assigned to `$result`. The rest of the expression will be discarded. `5` is assigned to `$result`.

4   By placing the whole expression in parentheses, now the expression takes precedence over the equal sign and the behavior is as it should be. The result is the same as line 2. See Figure 5.15.

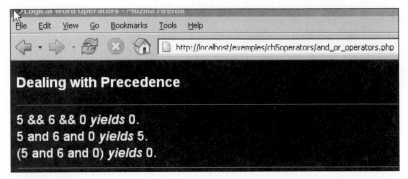

Figure 5.15   Logical and is lower in precedence than logical &&.

The Logical XOR Operator.   You can have either a bagel or a scone, but *not both*. The result of the logical XOR operator, known as the exclusive OR operator, is true if either operand, but not both, are true; otherwise, the result is false. In contrast, an inclusive OR operator returns a value of `true` if either or both of its operands are true. See Table 5.13.

Table 5.13   Logical XOR Examples

Expression	*What It Evaluates To*
`true xor false`	True
`true xor true`	False
`false xor false`	False
`true xor ""`	True
`5 xor 0`	True
`5 xor -6`	False
`5 xor false`	True
`null xor 0`	False
`null xor ""`	False
`null xor false`	False
`"this" xor "that"`	False

EXAMPLE 5.13

```html
<html>
<head><title>Logical XOR/title></head>
<body bgcolor="CC99CC"><font face="arial" size="+1">
<h3>Logical XOR</h3>
<?php
```
```php
1     $married = true;
      $single = true;
2     if($married xor $single){ print "Status O.K.<br />"; }
3     else{
          echo "Sorry, you can't have the best of both worlds. <br />
          You are either married or single. <br />
          Only one can be true. <br />";
      }
?>
</body>
</html>
```

EXPLANATION

1   Two variables are assigned boolean `true` value.
2   The exclusive `xor` operator evaluates both its operands. Only one, not both, of the operands can result in true for the expression to be true. Because both the `$married` and `$single` evaluate to true, the expression is false.
3   The `else` condition block is executed because the `xor` evaluated to false. See Figure 5.16 for output of this example.

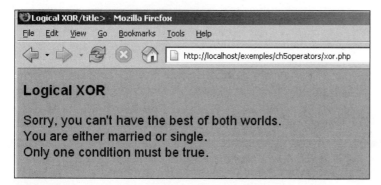

Figure 5.16   The Logical `xor` operator. Output from Example 5.13.

The ! Operator.   In the English statement, "*Not* true!" the word *not* is used for negation; that is, not true is false, and not false is true. PHP provides the NOT (`!`) operator for negation. The `!` operator is called a unary operator because it has only one operand, for example, `! true` or `! 5`. It returns `true` if the expression evaluates to false, and returns `false` if the expression evaluates to true. See Table 5.14 for examples.

Table 5.14   NOT Operator Examples

Expression	What It Evaluates To
! "this"	False
! 0	True
! 2	False
! false	True
! null	True

EXAMPLE 5.14

```
<html><head><title>Logical Not Operator</title>
</head>
<body bgcolor="CC99CC"><font face="arial" size="+1">

<?php
1       $answer = true;
2       print "\$answer is $answer, true. Now ! \$answer is "
            . ! $answer;
    ?>

</body>
</html>
```

EXPLANATION

1   The boolean value, true, is assigned to the variable, $answer.
2   The ! operator caused true to become false.

In summary, Example 5.15 illustrates the logical operators and the values they return.

EXAMPLE 5.15

```
(The PHP Program)
<html><head><title>Logical Operators</title></head>
<body bgcolor="330066" text="white"><font face="arial" size="+1">
<hr />
<?php
1       $num1 = 50;
        $num2 = 100;
        $num3 = 0;
2       print "50 && 100 is " . (int)($num1 && $num2) ;
3       print "<br /> 0 && 100 is " . (int)($num3 && $num2) ;
4       print "<br /> 50 || 100 is " . (int)($num1 || $num2) ;
        print "<br /> 0 || 100 is " . (int)($num3 || $num2) ;
```

EXAMPLE 5.15 (CONTINUED)

```
        print "<br /> 100 || 0 is " . (int)($num2 || $num3) ;
5       print "<br /> 50 xor 100 is " . (int)($num2 xor $num3);
        print "<br /> ! 100 is " . ! $num3 ;
6       print "<br /> !(100 && 0) is " . !($num3 && $num2);
    ?>
    <hr />
    </body>
    </html>
```

EXPLANATION

1   Three variables, $num1, $num2, and $num3, are initialized.

2   The && operator expects both of its operands to be true, if the expression is to be true. A true value is any number that is not zero. In the expression, 50 && 100, both operands are true. Boolean true, 1, is returned. The cast operator (int) is used to force a 1 value to be returned. There is no output otherwise.

3   Because 0 represents a false value, the whole expression is false when using &&, the logical AND.

4   The || operator expects only one of its operands to be true if the whole expression is to be true. 50 || 100 is true because the first operand evaluates to a nonzero value. Because 50 is true and only one operand must be true, the evaluation stops here and 1 is returned.

5   The xor operator expects one operand to be true, but not both. Otherwise, the expression evaluates to false. Because in this example 50 and 100 are both true, the expression evaluates to false.

6   Because the expression $num1 && $num2 is enclosed in parentheses, it is evaluated first, resulting in 50 && 100, true. Then the ! (NOT) operator evaluates ! (true), resulting in boolean false.

7   The expression, $num1 && $num3, enclosed in parentheses, is evaluated first. Because num3 is 0, the expression evaluates to false. ! (false) is true. See Figure 5.17.

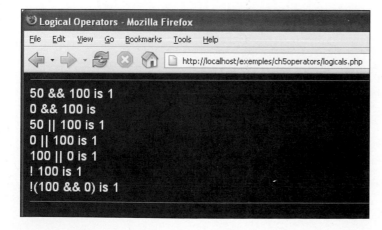

Figure 5.17
Logical operators. Output from Example 5.15.

5.1.13 The Conditional Operator

The conditional operator is called a ternary operator because it requires three operands. It is often used as a shorthand method for *if/else* conditional statements. (See Chapter 6, "Strings.")

FORMAT

```
conditional expression ? expression : expression
```

Examples:

$x ? $y : $z   If $x evaluates to true, the value of the expression becomes $y, else the value of the expression becomes $z.

$big = ($x > $y) ? $x : $y   If x is greater than $y, $x is assigned to variable $big, else $y is assigned to variable $big.

EXAMPLE 5.16

```
    (The HTML Form)
    <html><head><title>HTML Form</title></head>
    <body bgcolor="lightblue"><font size="+1">
1   <form action="conditional.php" method="get">
        <p> Please enter your name: <br />
2       <input type="text" size=50 name="name" />
        <p>
        Please enter your age: <br />
3       <input type="text" size=50 name="age">
        <p>
4       <input type=submit value="Submit" />
    </form>
    </body>
    </html>
    ---------------------------------------------------------------
    (The PHP Script)
    <html><head><title>Conditional Statement</title></head>
    <body bgcolor="lightgreen"><font size="+1">
    <?php
        extract($_REQUEST);
5       $price = ($age > 55)? 3.00: 8.50;
6       print "$name, age $age pays \$$price for the Happy Meal
            Special! <br />";
    ?>
    </body>
    </html>
    </body>
    </html>
```

1   The HTML form starts here.

2   The input type is a text field. The user will type his or her name here. It will be assigned to the `"name"` attribute of the text field.

3   The input type is a text field. The user will type his or her age here. It will be assigned to the `"age"` attribute of the text field.

4   When the user presses the submit button, the PHP script named in the `action` attribute will be executed.

5   If the value of `$age` is greater than `55`, the value to the right of the `?` is assigned to the variable `$price`; if not, the value after the `:` is assigned to the variable `$price`.

6   The browser displays the value of the variable `price`.
    In Figures 5.18 and 5.19 see what happens when the user enters 60. This value is assigned to variable `$age` in the program. Because the value of `$age` is greater than `55`, `$price` is assigned `3.00`. Otherwise, `$price` is assigned `8.50`.

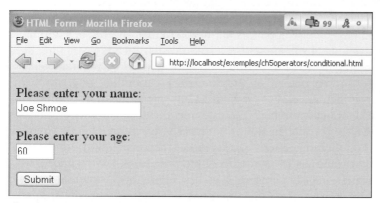

Figure 5.18   The HTML form output from Example 5.16.

Figure 5.19   The PHP script output from Example 5.16.

5.1.14 Bitwise Operators

A Little Bit About Bits.   People represent numbers in decimal or base 10, a numbering system based on 10 values starting from 0 to 9; for example, $100,000 or 1955. The HTML color codes are represented in hexadecimal, base 16, values ranging from 0 to 15; for example, #00FFFF is cyan and #FF00FF is fuschia. Computers store everything in binary or base 2. A binary numbering system represents numbers in two values, 0 or 1. Each of the the individual ones and zeros are called bits. All the data you use is stored in your computer using bits. A byte is made up of eight bits, a word is two bytes, or 16 bits, and finally, two words together are called a double word or dword, which is a 32-bit value. A computer only uses zeros and ones for everything because a binary digit is represented by the presence of an electric current. If the level of electricity reaches a certain level, the digit is 1. Otherwise, the digit is a 0. Using just two numbers makes building hardware less difficult and cheaper than if electrical levels were represented by a bigger combination of bits, like base 10 (decimal) or base 16 (hexadecimal). Hence, computers store everything in binary.

Using Bitwise Operators.   Most processors today are built to operate on 32-bit numbers. For example, the term Win 32 is derived from the fact that an integer on a Win 32 compiler defaults to 32 bits. Bitwise operators allow you to turn specific bits within an integer on or off. For example, if you are setting a readonly flag on a file, you only need two values, on or off, represented as 1 or 0. And if both the left and right parameters are strings, the bitwise operator will operate on the characters within the string.

Bitwise operators treat their operands as a set of 32 bits (zeros and ones), rather than as decimal, hexadecimal, or octal numbers. For example, the decimal number nine has a binary representation of 1001 (only the significant bits are represented here). Although bitwise operators perform their operations on bits rather than expressions, they return standard PHP numerical values as shown in Example 5.17. If you are working with graphics, games, encryption, registers, setting switches, or any operation that requires "twiddling bits," then the bitwise operators might become useful. Generally speaking, those types of operations are more fitting for higher level languages like C or Java.

Table 5.15 Bitwise Operators

Operator	Function	Example	What It Means
&	Bitwise AND	x & y	Returns a 1 in each bit position if both corresponding bits are 1.
|	Bitwise OR	x | y	Returns a 1 in each bit position if one or both corresponding bits are 1.
^	Bitwise XOR	x ^ y	Returns a 1 in each bit position if one, but not both, of the corresponding bits are 1.

Table 5.15 Bitwise Operators (continued)

Operator	Function	Example	What It Means
~	Bitwise NOT	~x	Inverts the bits of its operands. 1 becomes 0; 0 becomes 1.
<<	Left shift	x << y	Shifts x in binary representation y bits to left, shifting in zeros from the right.
>>	Right shift	x >> y	Shifts x in binary representation y bits to right, discarding bits shifted off.
>>>	Zero-fill right shift	x >>> b	Shifts x in binary representation y bits to the right, discarding bits shifted off, and shifting in zeros from the left.

When performing bitwise operations with &, |, ^, and ~, each bit in the first operand is paired with the corresponding bit in the second operand: first bit to first bit, second bit to second bit, and so on. For example, the binary representation for 5 & 4 is 101 & 100.

```
    101      101      101
& 100    | 100    ^100
-----    -----    ----
    100      101      001
```

Bitwise Shift Operators. The bitwise shift operators take two operands: The first is a quantity to be shifted, and the second specifies the number of bit positions by which the first operand is to be shifted. The direction of the shift operation is controlled by the operator used.

The << (left shift) operator shifts the first operand the specified number of bits to the left. Excess bits shifted off to the left are discarded. Zero bits are shifted in from the right.

The >> (sign-propagating right shift) operator shifts the first operand the specified number of bits to the right. Excess bits shifted off to the right are discarded. Copies of the leftmost bit are shifted in from the left.

Consider the following example:

```
$y = $x >> 4;
// Before shift: $x == 0110 1111 1001 0001
// After shift:  $y == 0000 0110 1111 1001
```

The >>> (zero-fill right shift) operator shifts the first operand the specified number of bits to the right. Excess bits shifted off to the right are discarded. Zero bits are shifted in from the left. For example, 19 >>> 2 yields 4, because 10011 shifted two bits to the right becomes 100, which is 4. For nonnegative numbers, zero-fill right shift and sign-propagating right shift yield the same result.

Shift operators convert their operands to 32-bit integers and return a result of the same type as the left shift operator.

EXAMPLE 5.17

```
<html>
<head>
<title>Bitwise Operators</title>
</head>
<body bgcolor="lightblue">
<font size="+1" face="arial">
<h3> Testing Bitwise Operators</h3>
<?php
1      $result = 15 & 9;
       echo "15 & 9  yields: " . $result;
2      $result = 15 | 9;
       echo "<br /> 15 | 9  yields: " . $result;
3      $result = 15 ^ 9;
       echo "<br /> 15 ^ 9  yields: " . $result;
4      $result = 9 << 2;
       echo "<br /> 9 << 2 yields: " . $result;
5      $result = 9 >> 2;
       echo "<br /> 9 >> 2 yields: " . $result;
6      $result = -9 >> 2;
       echo "<br /> -9 >> 2 yields: " . $result;
7      $result = 15 >>> 2;
       echo "<br /> 15 >>> 2 yields: " . $result;
?>
</body>
</html>
```

EXPLANATION

1   The binary representation of 9 is 1001, and the binary representation of 15 is 1111. When the bitwise & (AND) operator is applied to 1111 & 1001, the result is binary 1001 or decimal 9.

2   When the bitwise | (OR) operator is applied to 1111 | 1001, the result is binary 1111 or decimal 15.

3   When the bitwise ^ (Exclusive OR) is applied to 1111 ^ 1001, the result is binary 0110 or decimal 6.

4   9 << 2 yields 36, because 1001 shifted two bits to the left becomes 100100, which is 36.

5   9 >> 2 yields 2, because 1001 shifted two bits to the right becomes 10, which is 2.

6   -9 >> 2 yields -3, because the sign is preserved.

7   15 >>> 2 yields 3, because 1111 shifted two bits to the right becomes 0011, which is 3. For nonnegative numbers, zero-fill right shift and sign-propagating right shift yield the same result. See the output in Figure 5.20.

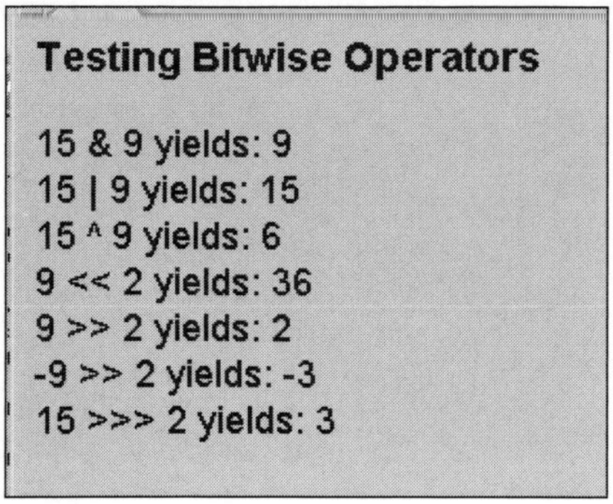

Testing Bitwise Operators

15 & 9 yields: 9
15 | 9 yields: 15
15 ^ 9 yields: 6
9 << 2 yields: 36
9 >> 2 yields: 2
-9 >> 2 yields: -3
15 >>> 2 yields: 3

Figure 5.20 Output from Example 5.17.

5.1.15 Execution Operators

PHP supports one execution operator: backquotes or backticks (` `` `). Note that these are not single quotes! PHP will attempt to execute the contents of the backticks as an operating system command; the output will be returned and can be assigned to a variable. The built-in function `shell_exec()` does the same thing as backquotes.[3] Keep in mind that what you place between the backquotes is operating-system dependent. In the following example, the command is for UNIX or Linux. For Windows, the command would be `dir`.

EXAMPLE 5.18

```
<?php
$output = `ls -al`;
echo "<pre>$output</pre>";
?>
```

5.1.16 Error Control Operator

PHP supports one error control operator: the at sign (@). When prepended to an expression, any error messages that would normally be generated by PHP will be silenced. The operator suppresses errors that happen when your script is executing, not errors that are caused when the program is first parsed, such as syntax errors (see "Debugging" on page 841). The @ operator works only on expressions that represent a value such as variables, functions and `include()` calls, constants, and so forth, but not constructs like `if`, `switch`, `foreach`, or function definitions.

Generally speaking it's a bad idea to use this operator unless you have created an error-handling function of your own to take care of a potential error in your program. If

---

3. The execution operator, backquotes, is disabled if safe mode is enabled or `shell_exec()` is disabled.

the `track_errors` feature is enabled, any error message generated by the expression will be saved in the variable `$php_errormsg`. This variable will be overwritten each time a new error occurs.

EXAMPLE 5.19

```
    <html><head><title>The Error Operator</title></head>
    <body bgcolor="lightblue" ><font face="arial">
    <?php
1       $num1 = 0;
        $num2 = 2;
        echo "Error coming. Watch out!<br />";\
        // Illegal division by zero will generate an error
2       $div = $num2 / $num1;
    ?>
    </body>
    </html>
```

EXPLANATION

1   Two variables are declared and assigned numbers.
2   It is illegal to divide a number by zero, and doing so will cause an error to be displayed. See Figure 5.21 for the output.

Figure 5.21   Without the error operator.

Adding the @ Operator.   In Example 5.19, if we had prepended the @ error operator to the statement in line 2, such as

`@$div = $num2 / $num1;`

the error message would have been suppressed. Figure 5.22 shows the output after adding the @ operator to this line.

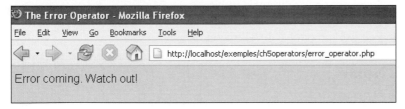

Figure 5.22   With the @ operator, the PHP error message is suppressed.

See also `error_reporting()` and the manual section for error handling and logging functions.

5.1.17   Type Operators

PHP 5 has a single type operator: `instanceof`. `instanceof` is used to determine whether a given object is of a specified object class (see Chapter 17, "Objects").

5.2 Chapter Summary

5.2.1   What You Should Know

Now that you have finished this chapter you should be able to answer the following questions:

1. What is an *operator*?

2. What are *operands*?

3. What is an *expression*?

4. How do you use operators in expressions?

5. What is the importance of operator *precedence* and *associativity*?

6. What is *equal* and what is *identical*?

7. What is the difference between logical `&&` and logical `||` and bitwise `&` and bitwise `|`?

8. How do you compare numbers and strings?

9. What is *concatenation*?

10. What is *casting*?

11. What is the purpose of a conditional operator?

12. Why would you use the error-control operator?

5.2.2 What's Next?

In Chapter 6, "Strings," we discuss strings, one of the most essential data types when processing text. You will learn how to use many of the PHP built-in functions to manipulate strings, change their case, find strings within strings, split them, trim them, reverse them, format them, and more.

CHAPTER 5 LAB

1. Print the average of three floating-point numbers with a precision of two decimal places.

2. a. What are two other ways that you could write $x = $x + 1;?
   b. Write the following expression using a shortcut: $y = $y + 5;.

3. Calculate the volume of a room that is 12.5 feet long, 9.8 feet wide, and 10.5 feet high.

4. Square the number 15 and print the result. Find the square root of 89 and print the result.

5. What would the following program print? Write your answer before you print the output.

```
$a = 15;
$b = 4;
$c = 25.0;
$d = 3.0;
echo   4 + $c / 4 * $d, "\n";
echo $a / $d * $a + $c, "\n";
echo $b + $c, $b, $c, "\n";
echo   $c = = $d, "\n";
echo   $a = = = 15, "\n";
```

6. Given the values of $a=10, $b=3, $c=7, and $d=20, print the value of $result:

```
$result = ( $a >= $b ) && ( $c < $d );
$result = ( $a < $b) || ( $c <= $d );
$result = $a % $b;
```

7. Write a program called `area.php` that finds and prints the area of a circle.

8. The following formula is used to calculate the fixed monthly payment (*P*) required to fully amortize a loan of *L* dollars over a term of *n* months at a monthly interest rate of *c*. (If the quoted rate is 6%, for example, *c* is .06/12 or .005). Write a PHP expression to represent the following formula. (Hint: See *http://en.wikipedia.org/wiki/Amortization_%28business%29.*)

    $$P = L[c(1 + c)]n / [(1 + c) n - 1]$$

9. Write a script that creates a random background color for a Web page every time it is loaded (see the hexadecimal color charts at *webmonkey.com*).

    Pick a range of hexadecimal colors. Give the `rand()` function a starting number and an ending number from a range of colors. The random number returned will be a decimal number. You will need to convert it back to hexadecimal in order to use it as a background color. (Hint: See the `hexdec()` function.)

    ```
    <body bgcolor = #$hexadecimal_color >
    ```

chapter

6

Strings

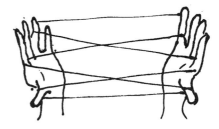

6.1 What Is a String?

Because PHP is a hypertext preprocessor, and most textual data is represented as strings, strings are an essential part of the language and probably more used than any other data type. For example, data read in from a file, database, e-mail, or Web page is represented as string data.

By definition, a PHP string is a piece of text, a series of characters (called bytes) enclosed in quotes. Because PHP puts no boundaries on the length of a string, it can consist of one character, a word, or an entire novel. See Example 6.1.

In Chapter 4, "The Building Blocks," we discussed strings as a basic data type, how to create strings, quote strings, assign them to variables, and print them. In Chapter 5, "Operators," we covered the operators used to concatenate strings, compare them, and test whether or not strings are equal or identical. PHP, in addition to basic operators, provides a huge collection of useful string functions to help you manipulate actions such as comparing strings, searching for strings, extracting substrings, copying strings, trimming strings, and translating characters in strings to uppercase or lowercase. This chapter introduces some of the most useful of these built-in functions.

EXAMPLE 6.1

```
<?php
// Two simple strings
1    $name = 'John Doe';
2    print "$name is my mentor\n";
?>
```

EXPLANATION

1 The first line defines a string 'John Doe' and stores it in a variable called $name.
2 The second line prints out the value of that variable, the string 'John Doe' and the text that follows it.

6.1.1   Quotes

In Chapter 4, you were introduced to strings as a data type and how quotes are used to delimit a string. We provide a review here because strings and quotes are so intrinsically part of each other.

There are two types of quotes and thus two types of strings: singly quoted strings and doubly quoted strings. For example:

```
'I am a string.'
```

and

```
"I am also a string."
```

Single Quotes.   All characters enclosed within single quotes are treated as literals, so what you see is what you get, with the exception of a single quote embedded within a set of single quotes, and the backslash character. The quotes must be matched, a single quote to start the string and a single quote to terminate it. Example 6.2 demonstrates how single quotes are used. The output is shown in Figure 6.1.

EXAMPLE   6.2

```
    <?php
1       print 'His salary is  $50,000';
        $salary=50000 * 1.1;
2       print 'After his raise his salary is $salary\n';
    ?>
```

EXPLANATION

1   The characters within the single quoted string are treated as themselves, literally.
2   Because all characters are treated literally within single quotes, the dollar sign in salary is not interpreted as a variable. The \n to represent the newline is also treated literally. When these characters are inserted between double quotes, they will be interpreted; that is, the value of the variable, $salary, will be extracted, and the backslash sequence \n will be converted into a newline. See Figure 6.1.

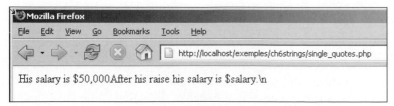

Figure 6.1   The output from Example 6.2. Characters within single quotes are treated literally.

Quoting Errors.   Because quotes are matched from left to right, embedding a single quote in a string, such as `'I don't care'`, would produce an error because PHP would treat the quote in the contraction `don't` as the terminating single quote for the string. The solution is to either place the whole string in double quotes or precede the apostrophe in `don't` with a backslash (e.g., `don\'t`). Example 6.3 demonstrates this problem. The error is shown in Figure 6.2.

EXAMPLE   6.3

```
      <?php
1         $business = 'Joe's Pizza';
          print $business;
      ?>
```

EXPLANATION

1   The first single quote opens the string and is matched by the next single quote. The problem: PHP sees the apostrophe in `Joe's` as the string's closing quote because it is the next quote it encounters after the initial single quote. The rest of the string is syntactically invalid and PHP reports an error, shown in the output of this example in Figure 6.2.

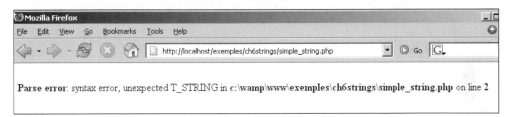

Figure 6.2   The error output from Example 6.3.

To solve the problem, the inner quote must be escaped with the backslash character as shown here:

```
$business = 'Joe\'s Pizza';
```

The backslash character takes away the special meaning of the inner quote. PHP will treat it as any other character in the string and continue looking for the closing single quote to terminate the string. See Figure 6.3.

Figure 6.3   Corrected quoting problem.

Double Quotes.   Another way to denote a string is to enclose it within double quotes:

```
$business = "Joe's Pizza";
```

When PHP encounters the first double quote in the string `"Joe's Pizza"` it considers all the enclosed text as part of a string until it reaches the closing double quote. The inner quote is ignored and treated as just another character.

Double quotes are like single quotes, but with three important exceptions:

1. They interpret escape sequences, which consist of a backslash followed by a single character. For a complete list, see Table 4.1 on page 66. When enclosed in double quotes, the backslash causes the interpretation of the next character to "escape" from its normal ASCII code and to represent something else. For example, `"\t"` is interpreted as a tab character and `"\n"` as a newline character. (If the ouput from PHP will be displayed in a browser, the HTML `<pre>` tag should be used or the escape sequences will not be interpreted.) Escape sequences will not be displayed in your browser unless you use the HTML `<pre>` tag. See "Escape Sequences" on page 66.
2. Single quotes are ignored within double quotes, such as in `"Joe's Pizza"`.
3. Variables are replaced with their values when placed between double quotes. More on this topic is given in "Formatting and Printing Strings" on page 155.

6.1.2   String Operators

Operators that can be used with strings were discussed in Chapter 5, "Operators." But just as we reviewed quotes in this chapter, we revisit the operators used to manipulate strings. It seems only fitting in a chapter devoted to strings to refresh your memory here on how to use PHP operators with strings.

Concatenation.   String concatenation is the merging of one or more strings into one string. You might recall the string concatenation operator is a dot (`.`). It concatenates its left and right operand. For more, see Chapter 5, "Operators." Example 6.4 demonstrates how to use the string concatenation operator.

EXAMPLE 6.4

```
<html>
<head><title>String Concatenation</title></head>
<body bgcolor="silver">
<h3>String Concatenation</h3>
<pre>
<?php
```

EXAMPLE 6.4 (CONTINUED)

```
1       $name      = 'Ellie Quigley';
        $street    = '123 Main Street';
        $city      = 'San Francisco';
        $state     = 'CA';
        $zip       = '94107';

2       $address="Name: " . "$name\n" . "Address: " . "$street\n" .
           "Zip: ". $zip ."\n";
3       print $address;
4       print "............................\n";
    ?>
    </pre>
    </body>
    </html>
```

EXPLANATION

1   String values are assigned to a set of variables.
2   In this example we use the dot (.) operator, the PHP concatenation operator, to "glue" together multiple strings into one long string. You use the concatenation operator to merge any two strings, whether they are single-quoted, double-quoted, or assigned to variables.
3   The variable, `$address`, contains the concatenated string values. Figure 6.4 shows the output.
4   If you put the dot within a string, it is just the literal dot character with no special meaning.

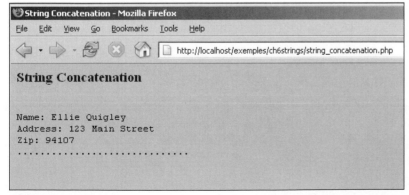

Figure 6.4   String concatenation with the dot operator. Output from Example 6.4.

Equal and Identical.   The equality operator, ==, can be used to see if two strings are equal, and the === operator can be used to check that the strings are identical. If you are using these operators for string comparison, make sure that both of the operands are strings, because if you are comparing a string to a number, PHP will first cast the string to a number. This means that all strings that don't begin with a numeric value will be cast to zero. For instance, if ("total" > 5) will actually be compared as if (0 > 5). See Chapter 5, "Operators," for further discussion on mixing data types. Example 6.5 demonstrates how to use the equal and identical operators. The output is shown in Figure 6.5.

EXAMPLE 6.5

```
        <html><head><title>Equal and Identical Strings</title>
        </head>
        <body bgcolor="lavender">
        <font size="+1">
        <h3>The -- and --- Operator</h3>
        <?php
1           $str1="hello";
            $str2="hello";
            $str3=0;

2           if ( $str1 == $str2 ){
                // They are equal
                print "\"$str1\" and \"$str2\" are equal.<br />";
            }
            else{
                print "\"$str1\" and \"$str2\" are not equal.<br />";
            }

3           if ( $str2 == $str3  ){
                print "\"$str2\" and $str3 are equal.<br />";
            }
             else{
                print "\"$str2\" and $str3 are not equal.<br />";
            }

4           if ($str2 === $str3){
                print "\"$str2\" and $str3 are identical.<br />";
            }
            else{
                print "\"$str2\" and $str3 are not identical.<br />";
            }
        ?>
        </body>
        </html>
```

EXPLANATION

1   Three variables are defined. The first two are assigned string values, and the third is assigned a number.

2   Because both strings contain the same value, `"hello"`, they are considered equal; that is, all the characters are the same.

3   Here a string, `"hello"`, is being compared to a number, `0`. PHP will convert the string to `0` and compare. They are now equal numeric values.

4   This time, the identity operator compares the string by both data type and value. One is a string and the other a number, so they are not identical.

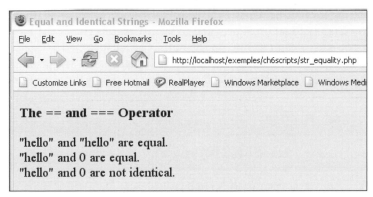

Figure 6.5   Testing with the equality and identity operators.

6.2 String Functions

Now it is time to talk about some of the useful built-in string functions provided by PHP. These functions allow you to manipulate the entire string or parts of the string such as the individual characters or words within it, and because you will spend so much of your time working with text in PHP, it's more practical to use these functions than trying to write your own. If you want to do more sophisticated pattern matching, PHP offers regular expressions, which are covered in Chapter 12, "Regular Expressions and Pattern Matching."

The following functions are broken down into categories to help you find the one that best fits your needs.

6.2.1 Formatting and Printing Strings

There are a number of built-in functions that allow you to output the string or number in a specified format. See Table 6.1 for a list of the functions described in this section.

Table 6.1 Formatting Strings

Function	What It Does
printf()	Displays a formatted string
sprintf()	Saves a formatted string in a variable
fprintf()	Prints a formatted string to a file
number_format()	Formats numbers as strings

The printf() Function.   Like C/C++ and most modern languages, PHP supports the printf() function for string formatting. Unlike the print or echo constructs that just print a string as is, the printf() function allows you to format text to give it the look you want; for example, you might want to line up the output in left-justified 30-space columns or print numbers representing money with only two places after the decimal point. The printf() function has a number of format specifiers to control the appearance of strings.

FORMAT

```
int printf ( string format [, mixed args [, mixed ...]] )
```

Example:
```
// prints "The number is 152.00\n"
printf("The number is %.2f\n", 152);
```

The first argument to printf() is called the control string. It is enclosed in quotes and consists of text and formatting conversion specifiers. The formatting conversion specifier starts with a percent sign followed by a character, which represents the type of data you want to format; for example, %s says a string will be formatted and %d says a whole decimal number will be formatted. In the preceding example, the control string is "The number is %.2f\n". The format specifier is %.2f, which represents a floating-point number with two significant digits to the right of the decimal point. Any other text within the control string is printed as is. There are a number of format specifiers listed in Table 6.2. The control string is followed by a comma and an argument list, each argument also separated by a comma. For each format conversion specifier in the control string, there is a corrsponding value in the argument list. In the following example, %.2f specifies the value 152 will be printed as 152.00.

```
printf("The number is %.2f\n", 152);
```

If the format specifier character is preceded by a number, the number can be used to specify the width of a field; for example, %10s specifies a string with a width of 10 characters, %5d a field to hold a 5-digit number, and %10.1f a floating-point number consisting of 10 digits, including the decimal point and one significant digit.

Consider Example 6.6.

EXAMPLE 6.6

```
    <?php
1       printf( "Value of Pi to 2 decimals is %.2f <br />\n", M_PI );
2       printf( "Value of Pi to 4 decimals is %.4f <br />\n", M_PI );
    ?>
```

EXPLANATION

1   In the control string, %.2f specifies the format we will use to represent pi. The value corresponding to %.2f is the first argument after the control string, M_PI, a predefined PHP constant. %.2f says that pi will be printed as a floating-point number with a precision of two digits. See Figure 6.6.

2   This printf() control string is identical to the first except the precision of the floating-point number is 4 now, instead of 2. Notice how this changes the way the number is displayed. See Figure 6.6.

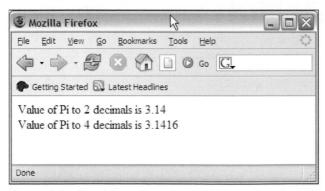

Figure 6.6   Precision of numbers. Output from Example 6.6.

In the next example, printf() will format a string and a number.

EXAMPLE 6.7

```
    <?php
        $product_name = "Black shoes";
        $product_price= 249.95;
1       printf( "Product %s will cost %6.2f dollars",
                $product_name, $product_price );
    ?>
```

EXPLANATION

1   The control string contains two format specifiers, `%s` and `%6.2d`. The variable `$product_name`, the first argument, will be printed according to the first format specifier, `%s`, a string. The second argument, `$product_price`, will be printed according to the second format specifier, `%6.2f`. In this case, 6 refers to total number of digits that this number can occupy and `.2` specfiies a precision of 2 places to the right of the decimal point. If the number is larger than 6, `printf()` will not truncate it. It just might not look the way you had envisioned it. See Figure 6.7.

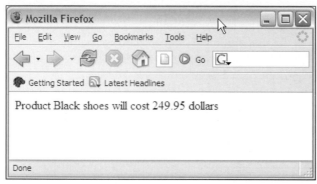

Figure 6.7   Output from Example 6.7.

Table 6.2 shows the most common format specifiers.

Table 6.2   Format Specifiers

Specifier	Format
b	Integer in binary format
c	ASCII character value for that integer
d	Signed integer
e	Scientific notation (`%1.5e+1`)
f	Floating-point number
o	Integer presented in octal representation
s	String of characters
u	Unsigned integer
x	Integer presented in hexadecimal representation in lowercase
X	Integer presented in hexadecimal representation in uppercase

The format specifier can be modified by placing specifying a precision, left or right justification, padding characters, and so on, as shown in Table 6.3.

Table 6.3 Modifiers for the `printf()` Format Specifier

Modifier	Example	Format
.	%.2f	Specifies a precision of two digits to the right of the decimal point in a floating-point number
integer	%8d	Specifies number of characters for this argument to be displayed; e.g., field width of 8 digits
–	%-8.2f %-30s	Causes the formatting to be left justified; e.g., left-justified floating-point number with a field width of 8, or left-justified 30-space string
0	%08d	Pads the number with 0s

There are some other formatting functions similar to the `printf` function differing primarily in how the output is displayed.

The sprintf() Function.   This function is identical to `printf()` except that instead of displaying the formatted string, `sprintf()` returns the formatted string so that you can assign it to a variable. See Example 6.8.

FORMAT

```
string sprintf ( string format [, mixed args [, mixed ...]] )
```

Example:
```
$formatted_string=sprintf("%s owes me %.2f dollars\n",
                          $name, $amount);
```

EXAMPLE 6.8

```
    <?php
    $product_name = "Purple Dress";
    $product_price = 199.95;
1   $output = sprintf( "Product <b>%s</b> will cost <u>$%6.2f</u> +
                    tax", $product_name, $product_price );
    ?>
    <html><title>The sprintf() Function</title></head>
    <body bgcolor="#EBF4F3">
    <h1>Shopping Cart Checkout</h1>
    <font face="Arial">
2   <?= $output ?>
    </font></body>
```

EXPLANATION

1   The first parameter to the `sprintf()` function is the control string specifying how
    to print the string. The two arguments following the control string are the actual
    variables, `$product_name` and `$product_price`, that correspond to each of the
    format conversion specifiers, `%s` and `%6.2f`, in turn. The `sprintf()` function will
    format the string and assign it to the variable, called `$output variable`.

2   Here we use the short form to print out a value of the variable `$output` into the
    HTML browser, as shown in Figure 6.8.

Figure 6.8   The `sprintf()` function. Output from Example 6.8.

The fprintf() Function.   Whereas the `printf()` function writes the output to the
standard output stream (the browser), the `fprintf()` function sends the output to any
output stream specified, usually a file.

FORMAT

```
int fprintf ( resource handle, string format [, mixed args
            [, mixed ...]] )
```

Example:
```
sprintf($filehandle, "%04d-%02d-%02d", $year, $month, $day);
```

For more information on streams and files, see Chapter 11, "Files and Directories."

6.2.2 Formatting Numbers and Money

Putting commas or spaces in numbers or printing out the dollar value of money causes
a number to become a string and can be handled with `printf()`. PHP also provides two
special functions, the `number_format()` function and the `money_format()` function.

The number_format() Function. PHP provides the `number_format()` function to format a number with grouped thousands. There are three ways to use this function. You can specify no arguments, two arguments, or four arguments, but not three arguments.

When only one number is specified, the number returned will be a whole number. It will include commas for every group of thousands, but the fractional part will be truncated along with the decimal point. If the first number after the decimal point is 5 or higher, the new number will be rounded up.

If two numbers are specified, the second number will indicate the number of decimal places to format, such as two places after the decimal point for a dollar and cents amount. Groups of thousands will still be comma-separated.

The third way to use this function is to specify the number to format, number of decimal places, as well as the characters to use for separating groups of thousands, as well as the decimal point. This is useful for locales that use number formats different than North American formats.

Example 6.9 illustrates how to use the `number_format()` function. Figure 6.9 shows the output, three formatted numbers.

FORMAT

```
string number_format ( float number [, int decimals
                    [, string dec_point, string thousands_sep]] )
```

Example:
```
$number=123456.5456
$new_string =  number_format($number);    // Returns: 123,457
$new_string = number_format($number, 2); // Returns: 123,456.55
$num_francais = number_format($number, 2, ',', ' '); // Returns 1 234,56
```

EXAMPLE 6.9

```
    <?php
    $number = 7634.887;
    // American format is the default: 7,643.89
1   $us_format = number_format($number, 2);
    print "$us_format<br />";


    // French format: 7 634,89
2   $french_format = number_format($number, 2, ',', ' ');
    print "$french_format<br />";


    // American format without thousands separator: 7634.89
3   $us_format2 = number_format($number, 2, '.', '');
    print "$us_format2<br />";


    ?>
```

EXPLANATION

1   This is the default format for the U.S. numbers. The second parameter specifies the number of decimal places, in this case two. `number_format()` automatically rounds to two decimals in this case.

2   This line shows how to use the `number_format()` function with four arguments. The first two arguments are the same as in the previous line: the number to be formatted and the number of decimal places. The third argument specifies the separator character to be used for decimal places. In France, a comma is used rather than a decimal point. The fourth argument is the separator for the thousands and here we use a single space, rather than a comma, the thousands separator commonly used in most European countries.

3   This example is very similar to the previous one. The main difference is that the fourth argument is empty, specifying no character for the thousands separator.

Figure 6.9 The `number_format()` function. The output from Example 6.9.

The money_format() Function.   The `money_format()` function formats a number as a string representing currency. Because this function depends on a C library function called `strfmon()`, it cannot be implemented on your system if you are using Windows. This function can format money for any number of locales and comes with a large array of formatting specifications. It works with negative numbers, deals with left and right precision, padding, and so on, similar to the `printf()` function. For a complete discussion on how to use this function, see the PHP manual.

FORMAT

```
string money_format ( string format, float number )
```

Example:
```
setlocale(LC_MONETARY, 'en_US');
echo money_format('%i', $number) . "\n";  // USD 1,234.56
```

6.2.3 Finding the Length of a String

The strlen() Function.   To find the length of a string (how many characters there are in the string), PHP provides the `strlen()` function. See Example 6.10.

FORMAT

```
int strlen ( string string )
```

Example:
```
$length = strlen("Hello, world\n");
```

EXAMPLE 6.10

```
        <html><head><title>Finding the Length of a String</title>
        </head>
        <body bgcolor="lightgreen">
        <font size="+1">
        <?php
1           $string="\t\tHello, world.";
2           $length=strlen($string);
            print nl2br("There are $length characters in \"$string\"");
        ?>
        </body>
        </html>
```

EXPLANATION

1   The variable, `$string`, contains a string of characters including the tab character.
2   The `strlen()` function returns the number of characters in `$string`. The tab character doesn't show up in the browser, but by viewing the source code, you can see it, as shown in Figure 6.10.

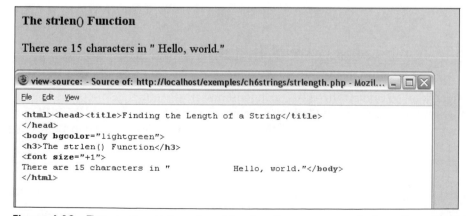

Figure 6.10   The `strlen()` function. Viewing the source code from Example 6.10.

6.2.4   Finding the Number of Words in a String

The str_word_count() Function.   The `str_word_count()` function returns information about the words that make up a string. A *word* is defined as a locale-dependent (Germany, U.S., etc.) string containing alphabetic characters, which also can contain, but not start with ' and – characters. By default, the `str_word_count()` function counts the number of words in a string. An optional third argument can be one of the three values shown in Table 6.4.

Table 6.4   Optional Third Arguments to the `str_word_count()` Function

Argument	What It Returns
0	Returns the number of words found.
1	Returns an array containing all the words found inside the string.
2	Returns an associative array, where the key is the numeric position of the word inside the string and the value is the actual word itself.

An optional fourth argument, `charlist`, allows you to add characters that will be accepted as part of a word, such as foreign accent marks, ellipses, long dashes, or hyphens.

FORMAT

```
mixed str_word_count(string string [, int format [, string charlist]] )
```

Example:
```
$num_words  = str_word_count("Happy New Year, to you!");
print_r(str_word_count("Solstickan säljes till förmån för barn och
                        gamla",1, "åÅö");
```

6.2.5   Changing the Case of Strings

If you are validating an e-mail address or the abbreviation for a state, such as CA or MD, you might want to convert the entire string into lowercase letters before proceding, or you might want to convert just the first character in a string, as in Mrs. or Dr. PHP provides functions for changing the case of the characters in a string, as shown in Table 6.5.

Table 6.5   Functions That Change the Case of Strings

Function	What It Does
strtoupper()	Converts a string to uppercase letters
strtolower()	Converts a string to lowercase letters
ucfirst()	Converts the first letter in a string to uppercase
ucwords()	Converts the first letter in each word of a string to uppercase
mb_convert_case()	Converts case of a string based on Unicode character properties

The strtoupper() and strtolower() Functions.   The functions strtoupper() and strtolower() are used to convert the case of characters in a string from upper- to lowercase or vice versa. strtoupper() takes a string and returns a new string with every single letter capitalized. strtolower() returns a new string with every character converted to lowercase.

FORMAT

```
string strtoupper ( string  )
string strtolower ( string  )
```

Example:
```
$newstring=strtoupper("merry christmas"); // returns "MERRY CHRISTMAS"
$newstring=strtolower("HAPPY NEW YEAR");  // returns "happy new year"
```

EXAMPLE 6.11

```
    <?php
    $text = "Marko@Marakana.Com";
1   print strtolower( $text . "<br />" ); //prints: marko@marakana.com
2   print strtoupper( $text . "<br />" ); //prints: MARKO@MARAKANA.COM
    ?>
```

EXPLANATION

1   This line will just output the text converted all in lowercase.
2   strtoupper() does the opposite, converting the text into uppercase letters.

The ucfirst() and ucwords() Functions.   If you want to change just the first character in a string to uppercase, PHP provides the ucfirst() and ucwords() functions. The ucfirst() function converts the first character of a string to uppercase. The ucwords() function capitalizes first letters of all the words in the string.

FORMAT

```
string ucfirst ( string str )
string ucword( string str)
```

Example:
```
// Returns "San jose, california"
$newstring=ucfirst("san jose, california");
// Returns "San Jose, California"
$newstring=ucwords("san jose, california");
```

EXAMPLE 6.12

```
  <?php
  $text = "it rains in spain";
1 print ucfirst( $text . "<br />" );   // prints: It rains in spain
2 print ucwords( $text . "<br />" );   // prints: It Rains In Spain
  ?>
```

EXPLANATION

1   This line outputs It rains in spain. The ucfirst() function returns the string
     with the first letter capitialized. See Figure 6.11.
2   The ucwords() function capitalizes the first letter in each word of the string, like
     the title in a book, for example. The output will be It Rains In Spain, as shown
     in Figure 6.11.

Figure 6.11   The ucfirst() and ucwords() functions.

The mb_convert_case() Function.   The mb_convert_case() function is like
strtolower() and strtoupper() but is not locale dependent; that is, it bases its conversion on Unicode characters rather than just ASCII, which means letters containing

the German umlaut, the Swedish ring, or French accent marks are folded (included) into case conversion. To specify the case, this function provides three modes: `MB_CASE_UPPER`, `MB_CASE_LOWER`, or `MB_CASE_TITLE`. You can also specify a supported character set to establish how the string will be encoded.

Table 6.6 Supported Character Sets

Charset	Aliases	Description
ISO-8859-1	ISO8859-1	Western European, Latin-1
ISO-8859-15	ISO8859-15	Western European, Latin-9. Adds the Euro sign, French and Finnish letters missing in Latin 1(ISO 8859 1)
UTF-8		ASCII compatible multibyte 8-bit Unicode
cp866	ibm866, 866	DOS-specific Cyrillic charset; supported in 4.3.2

FORMAT

```
string mb_convert_case ( string str, int mode [, string encoding] )
```

Example:
```
$string = "exit here!!";
echo mb_convert_case($string, MB_CASE_UPPER,"UTF-8");
// Returns: EXIT HERE!!

$string = "förvaras oåtkomligt för barn";
echo mb_convert_case($string, MB_CASE_TITLE,"ISO-8859-15");
// Returns: Förvaras Oåtkomligt För Barn
```

6.2.6   Comparing Strings

Does the password a user entered match the one on file? Does the user's response compare to the expected answer? PHP provides a number of functions to make comparing strings relatively easy.

To ensure you are always comparing strings, you should use string comparison functions rather than comparison operators because the functions always cast their arguments to strings before comparing them. Also keep in mind when comparing strings, that " hello"[1] is not the same as "hello" or "Hello", for example. PHP provides several functions to compare two strings, listed in Table 6.7.

---

1. You can use the `trim()` function to remove unwanted whitespace (See "The trim() Functions—trim(), ltrim(), chop, rtrim()" on page 182).

All string comparisons take at least two arguments and return a value based on comparing those arguments. The return value is always an integer that can be interpreted as shown in Table 6.7.

Table 6.7 Return Value from Comparison

Value	What It Means
0 (zero)	The two values are equal
> 0 (greater than zero)	Value two is greater than value one
< 0 (less than zero)	Value one is greater than value two

Table 6.8 lists string comparison functions and how they compare two strings.

Table 6.8 String Comparison

Function	What It Does
strcmp()	Compares two strings (case sensitive)
strcasecmp()	Compares two strings (not case sensitive)
strnatcmp(str1, str2);	Compares two strings in ASCII order, but any numbers are compared numerically
strnatcasecmp(str1, str2);	Compares two strings in ASCII order, case insensitive, numbers as numbers
strncasecomp()	Compares two strings (not case sensitive) and allows you to specify how many characters to compare
strspn()	Compares a string against characters represented by a mask
strcspn()	Compares a string that contains characters not in the mask

The strcmp() Function (Case Sensitive). The strcmp() function is most often used to compare two strings.

FORMAT

```
int strcmp ( string str1, string str2 )
```

Example:
```
$number = strcmp( "apples", "oranges");
```

The strcmp() function uses a lexicographical comparison algorithm to compare two strings, meaning it compares each character in the string alphabetically based on the system's collating sequence. Because PHP uses the ASCII collating sequence, an uppercase "A" is represented as decimal 65 and an uppercase "B" as decimal 66, and so on. On the other hand, a lowercase "a" is 97 and a lowercase "b" is 98, and so on. If you compare "A" to "a," you can say that "A" is less than "a" because of their numeric representation in the ASCII table; that is, 65 is less than 97.

The strcmp() function returns a number less than 0 if the first string is less than second string, a number greater than 0 if the first string is greater than the second string, and 0 if they are equal.

The strcmp() function is case sensitive meaning that "Dan" and "dan" are not the same. If you want to ignore the case of the letters, use the strcasecmp() function discussed next. See Example 6.13 to see how the strcmp() function works and its output in Figure 6.12.

EXAMPLE 6.13

```
<html>
<head><title>The strcmp() Function</title></head>
<body bgcolor="lavendar">
<font face="verdana">
<pre>
<h3>Comparing Strings</h3>
<?php
    $string1 = "Dan";
    $string2 = "Daniel";
1   print "strcmp( '$string1', '$string2' ) outputs " . strcmp(
        $string1, $string2 );
2   print "\nstrcmp( '$string2', '$string2' ) outputs " . strcmp(
        $string2,$string2 );
3   print "\nstrcmp( '$string2', '$string1' ) outputs " . strcmp(
        $string2, $string1 );
4   print "\nstrcmp( 'dan', 'Dan' ) outputs " . strcmp(
        'dan', 'Dan');
    print "\nstrcmp( 'Dan', 'dan' ) outputs " . strcmp(
        'Dan', 'dan');
?>
<pre>
</body>
</html>
```

EXPLANATION

1   Dan is lexiographically smaller then Daniel, resulting in a negative number.
2   Daniel and Daniel are identical, thus we get zero as the result of comparison.
3   Daniel is larger then Dan, resulting in a positive number.
4   The d in dan is greater than the D in Dan, a positive number. See Figure 6.12.

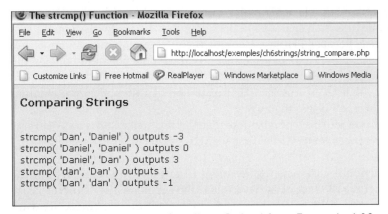

Figure 6.12 The `strcmp()` function. Output from Example 6.13.

The strcasecmp() Function (Case Insensitive). The `strcasecmp()` function works like the `strcmp()` function, but ignores the case of characters in strings; that is, an uppercase "A" and a lowercase "a" are treated as equals when comparing characters.

The `strcasecmp()` function returns a number less than 0 if the first string is less than the second string, a number greater than 0 if the first string is greater than the second string, and 0 if they are equal. Example 6.14 demonstrates how the function works.

FORMAT

```
int strcasecmp ( string str1, string str2 )
```

Example:
```
$number=strcasecmp("apples", "APples"); // Case-insensitive comparison
```

EXAMPLE 6.14

```
    <html><head><title>The strcasecmp() Function</title></head>
      <body bgcolor="lightblue">
      <h3>Comparing Strings--Case-Insensitive</h3>
      <?php
1        $str1 = "new york";
         $str2 = "New York";
2        if (strcasecmp($str1, $str2) == 0) {
             print "<em>$str1</em> is equal to <em>$str2</em>.<br />";
         }
      ?>
      </body></html>
```

EXPLANATION

1   Two string variables are assigned the same string, only differing in case.

2   The `strcasecmp()` function ignores the difference in case and compares the characters. The strings are equal. Remember that if the returned value == 0, the strings are equal. See Figure 6.13.

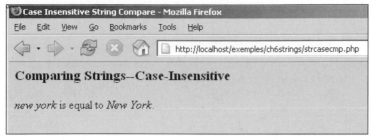

Figure 6.13 Case-insensitive string comparison.

The strncasecmp() Function (Limits Character Length). This `strncasecmp()` function is similar to `strcasecmp()` in that it also ignores the case of characters when doing the comparison, but in addition, it lets you specify the (upper limit of the) number of characters (length) from each string to be used in the comparison.

The `strncasecmp()` function returns a number less than 0 if the first string is less than the second string, a number greater than 0 if the first string is greater than the second string, and 0 if they are equal. Example 6.15 demonstrates how this function works.

FORMAT

```
int strncasecmp ( string str1, string str2, int length )
```

Example:
```
// compares first 4 characters in each string
$number = strncasecmp("Homeland", "homeland", 4);
```

EXAMPLE 6.15

```
        <html><head><title>The strncasecmp() Function</title></head>
        <body>
        <h3>Comparing Strings by Limit of Characters</h3>
        <?php
1           $str1="chronometer";
            $str2="Chronology";
2           if ( strncasecmp($str1,$str2, 5)==0){
                print "The first 5 characters of <em>$str1</em> are the
                same as the first 5 characters in <em>$str2 </em><br />";
            }
            else{
                print "They do not compare.<br />";
            }
        ?>
        </body>
        </html>
```

1   Two string variables are assigned the same string, differing only in case.
2   The `strncasecmp()` function ignores the difference in case and compares only the first 5 characters. The third argument, `5`, specifies how many characters you want to compare starting at the beginning of the string. The strings are equal. See Figure 6.14.

Figure 6.14   The `strncasecmp()` function.

The strnatcmp() Function (Natural Order Comparison).   If you compare numeric strings, the expression `'2' > '100'` will evaluate to true because in the first position 2 is greater than 1 when using the ASCII collating sequence. The other character positions are irrelevant because the first string only has one character. The string comparison functions we have seen so far always cast their arguments to strings before doing the comparison. The `strnatcmp()` function takes into consideration strings that contain numbers. This function compares characters in two strings using the ASCII collating sequence, but if there are any numbers within the string they are compared in natural order; that is, as numbers the way we think of numbers, where 100 is greater than 2. This is true even if the numbers occur in the middle of the string. Thus `'January 2'` will evaluate to less than `'January 10'`, whereas in a normal string comparison it would be greater since 2 is greater than 1.

The `strnatcasecmp()` function is just like the `strnatcmp()` function except that it is not case insensitive when comparing strings.

FORMAT

```
int strnatcmp ( string str1, string str2 )
```

Example:
```
// Returns 1 -- string 2 > string 1
echo strnatcmp('January 2, 2006', 'January 10, 2006');
// Returns -1 -- string 1 > string 2
echo  strcmp( 'January 2, 2006', 'January 10, 2006' );
```

The strspn() Function (Using a Mask for Comparison).   The strspn() function
compares two strings and returns the number of characters that are contained in the initial part of the first string that match a set of characters provided in the second string,
called the *mask*. For example, if you want to check that a password contains both digits
and letters or if a zip code consists of only numbers, this function can be used to check
that specified characters are included in the string.

   The two optional arguments allow you define where you want to start looking for the
characters in the string and the length of the string to compare. Example 6.16 demonstrates how to use the strspn() function.

FORMAT

```
int strspn ( string str1, string str2 [, int start [, int length]] )
```

Example:
```
$year = "1953 was a very good year!";
$mask="0123456789"
$count=strspn($year,$mask,0,4); // The string must start with 4 digits
```

EXAMPLE   6.16

```
     <html><head><title>The strspn() Function</title>
     </head>
     <body bgcolor="lavender">
     <font size="+1">
     <h3>Finding the Length of a String by a Mask</h3>
     <?php
1        $mask = "0123456789";
2        $zip = "95926";
3        $count=strspn($zip,$mask);
4        if ($count == strlen($zip)){
             print "The zip code consists of $count numbers.<br />";
         }
     ?>
     </body>
     </html
```

EXPLANATION

1   $mask consists of a string of numbers that will serve as the mask.
2   The variable, $zip, contains numbers.
3   The strspn() function returns the number of characters in $zip that match the
    characters in the mask. The strspn() function should return a count of 5, be-
    cause there are 5 numbers in $zip and they are all found in the mask variable.
4   This line checks if the value of $count is equal to the number of characters in
    $zip, the string length, and if so, prints "The zip code consists of 5 numbers."

The strcspn() Function (Comparison Not Matching a Mask).   The strcspn()
function is just like the strspn() function, but finds length of initial segment *not*
matching the mask; that is, it returns the length of the initial segment of the first string
not containing any of the characters in the second string. The strcspn() function
accepts two optional integer parameters that can be used to define the start position and
the length of the string being compared.

FORMAT

```
int strcspn ( string str1, string str2 [, int start [, int length]] )
```

Example:
```
$filename = "test3";
$length=strcspn("$filename", "1234567890", 0, 4);
// Returns 4; first 4 characters should not be numbers
```

6.2.7   Finding Similarities in Strings

The string comparison functions previously discussed perform alphanumeric string
comparisons, but what if we want to see if one string sounds or is pronounced like
another or how and where the text differs in two strings? PHP provides a set of functions
to find similarities or differences in strings. These functions might be useful for programs that check spelling, perform database searches, or any advanced text processing.

The soundex() and metaphone() Functions (Phonic Similarity).   Phonic similarity bases its comparison on whether or not two strings are homophones, that is, they
sound alike. Words such as "genes" and "jeans" or "morning" and "mourning" are
homophones.

The soundex() and metaphone() functions take a string as an argument, and return
a key. Soundex keys are short alphanumeric representations of a word's English pronounciation that can be used to compare the sound in strings. If the keys are the same,
then the words sound the same in English. After testing different words, you will see that
these functions base their comparison on American English pronounciation rather than
British English. For example, "father" and "farther" do not sound the same in America,
nor do "source" and "sauce," or "tuba" and "tuber."

The only obvious difference between the two functions is that metaphone() is more
precise in determining which words have the same pronunciation. Example 6.17 demonstrates how to use the soundex() and metaphone() functions. The output is diplayed
in Figure 6.15.

FORMAT

```
string soundex ( string str )
string metaphone ( string str [, int phones] )
```

Example:
```
$key1=soundex("bored");
$key2=soundex("board");
if ( $key1 == $key2 ){ echo "The strings sound alike<br />";}
```

EXAMPLE 6.17

```
        <html><head><title>Words that Sound the Same</title>
        </head>
        <body bgcolor="silver">
        <font size="+1">
        <?php
1           $sound1 = "bald";
            $sound2 = "bawled";
2           $key1=soundex("$sound1");
            $key2=soundex("$sound2");
3           if ($key1 == $key2){
                print "The key values are: $key1 and $key2.\n<br />";
                print "\"$sound1\" and \"$sound2\" are homophones.\n<br />";
            }
4           $sound1 = "tuba";
            $sound2 - "tuber";
5           if (metaphone($sound1) == metaphone($sound2)){
                print "\"$sound1\" and \"$sound2\" are homonyms.\n";
            }
            else{
                print "\"$sound1\" and \"$sound2\" do not sound the
                same.\n";
            }
        ?>
        </font>
        </body>
        </html>
```

EXPLANATION

1   The two variables, $string1 and $string2, are assigned strings whose values sound the same, called homophones.
2   The keys produced by the soundex() function are shown in Figure 6.15. They are four character strings, which can be compared.
3   If the keys are the same, the words are homophones.
4   Two more homophones are assigned to $sound1 and $sound2, respectively.
5   The keys returned from the metaphone() function are more precise in dealing with English pronunciation.

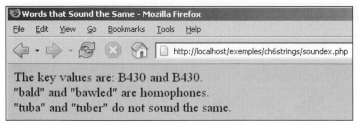

Figure 6.15 Homophones—words that sound the same.

The similar_text() and levenshtein() Functions (Textual Similarity). PHP provides two functions to test the similarity between the text in two strings. They are the similar_text() and the levenshtein() functions.

The similar_text() function calculates the similarity of two strings and returns the number of characters that are the same, allowing for additions, subtraction, and repetition. It also takes an optional third parameter, containing a value that represents the percentage of similarity between the strings. Example 6.18 demonstrates how the similar_text() function is used.

FORMAT

```
int similar_text ( string first, string second [, float percent] )
```

Example:
```
$number_same = similar_text($a, $b, $percent);
```

EXAMPLE 6.18

```
      <html><head><title>Text that is Similar</title>
      </head><body bgcolor="silver">
      <font size="+1">
      <?php
1        $string1 = "Once upon a time, there were three little pigs...";
2        $string2 = "Once upon a time, there were three bears...";
         print "First string: $string1\n<br />";
         print "Second string: $string2\n<br />";
3        $number=similar_text("$string1", "$string2", $percent);
         print "There are $number of the same characters in the two
            strings.\n";
4        echo "The strings are similar by " . number_format($percent,
            0). "%.<br />";
      ?>
      </font>
      </body>
      </html>
```

1, 2   Two similar strings are assigned to variables.

3, 4   The similar_text() function returns the number of characters that are the same and a value indicating the percentage of the alikeness of the two strings. They are 87% similar. See Figure 6.16.

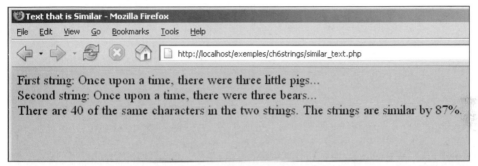

Figure 6.16   The `similar_text()` function.

The `levenshtein()` function is used to find the Levenshtein[2] distance (also called the edit distance) between two strings (strings cannot be longer than 255 characters). What's that? Suppose you have two strings and you want to know how you could edit one of the strings to make it just like the other string. (If you have ever used the UNIX `diff` command, it will give you this kind of information.) The Levenshtein distance is defined as the fewest number of insertions, substitutions, and deletions required to transform one string into another string. (The function is not case sensitive.) The greater the Levenshtein distance, the more different the strings are. If the distance is 0, the strings are the same. (For full discussion see *http://www.merriampark.com/ld.htm*.) Example 6.19 demonstrates how to use the `levenshtein()` function.

```
int levenshtein ( string str1, string str2 [, int cost_ins
                 [, int cost_rep, int cost_del]] )
```

Example:
```
$diff = levenshtein($string1, $string2);
$diff = levenshtein($string1, $string2, 100, 5, 1);
```

---

2. Levenshtein distance is named after the Russian scientist Vladimir Levenshtein, who wrote the algorithm in 1965.

EXAMPLE 6.19

```
<html><head><title>Text that is Similar</title>
</head>
<body bgcolor="silver">
<font size="+1">
<?php
1      $string1 = "I attended a funeral.";
       $string2 = "He attended a fun rally.";
       print "First string: $string1\n<br />";
       print "Second string: $string2\n<br />";
2      $distance=levenshtein("$string1", "$string2");
       print "It would take $distance changes to transform string1
           into string2.<br />";
?>
</font>
</body>
</html>
```

EXPLANATION

1   Two strings are assigned. They have some characters in common. What would it take to transform the first string into the second?

2   The `levenshtein()` function will figure out the minimum number of insertions, deletions, or substitutions it would take to transform the first string into the second. In this example, the first change would be I. It would take two substitutions to change it to He. The next change would be to replace the e in funeral with a space (three changes so far), then to add the `ly` in `rally`, two more changes, making a total of five. See Figure 6.17 for output.

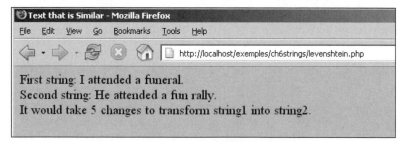

Figure 6.17   The `levenshtein()` function.

The `levenshtein()` function includes the first two strings and three additional parameters that define the cost of insert, substitute, and delete operations. This allows you to specify how you want scores weighted with numeric values. Otherwise, all scores are given equal weight. The weight or cost indicates what steps should be taken to make the strings similar; that is, should insertions or deletions be made to transform the string?

6.2.8 Splitting a String

PHP provides a number of functions to split strings. The `split()` and `spliti()` functions split up a string and return an array. The `explode()` function splits up a string by a specified delimiter and returns an array. The `implode()` function takes an array and joins the elements together to form a string. Because these functions require that you understand PHP arrays and regular expressions, they are covered in Chapter 8, "Arrays," and Chapter 12, "Regular Expressions and Pattern Matching." Table 6.9 provides the names of these functions, what they do, and where to find a complete discussion and examples.

Table 6.9 PHP Functions for Splitting Strings

Function	*What It Does*
`split()`	Splits up a string into words using a regular expression (see Chapter 12)
`spliti()`	Same as the `split()` function, but case-insensitive regular expression (see Chapter 12)
`str_split()`	Converts a string into an array where the size of the elements can be specified (see Chapter 8)
`preg_split()`	Splits up a string by a Perl-compatible regular expression and returns an array of substrings (see Chapter 12)
`explode()`	Splits up a string by another string (not a regular expression) and returns an array (see Chapter 8)
`implode()`	Joins array elements together by a string and returns a string

The strtok() Function.   The `strtok()` function splits a string into smaller strings called tokens. Tokens are created by choosing a character(s) that will be used as a string delimiter. Most tokens are words delimited by spaces, as in any typical sentence. For example, "I love you." is a space-delimited string consisting of three tokens.

The first time you call `strtok()`, you use two arguments: the string (the `str` argument) that will be tokenized, and the delimiters you will use as separators (the `token` argument). The first tokenized string will be returned. The next time you call the function, you don't use the string argument because `strtok()` keeps track of where it is in the string, token by token until it reaches the end of the string. If you want to start tokenizing over again, then you will use both the string and its delimiters to initialize the process.

This function might return boolean FALSE, but might also return a non-boolean value that evaluates to FALSE, such as `0` or `""`. Example 6.20 demonstrates how to use the `strtok()` function to split up a string. The results are displayed in Figure 6.18.

FORMAT

```
string strtok ( string str, string token )
```

Example:
```
$piece1 = strtok("/usr/local/bin", "/");  // Returns: usr
$piece2 = strtok ("/"); // Returns: local
$piece3 = strtok ("/"); // Returns: bin
```

EXAMPLE 6.20

```
       <html><head><title>The str_tok() Function</title></head>
       <body bgcolor="lavender">
       <font size="+1">
       <h3>Splitting a String into Tokens</h3>
       <pre>
       <?php
1          $string = "Joe Shome:3/15/56:Boston, MA.";
2          $delimiters=":,/ ";
3          $token = strtok($string,$delimiters);
           $n=1;
4          while($token){
               echo "Token $n: <b>$token</b><br />";
5              $token=strtok($delimiters);
               $n++;
           }
       ?>
       </body>
       </html>
```

EXPLANATION

1   A string is created containing some characters that will be used as delimiters; that is, where we will divide the string into words or tokens.

2   A variable is assigned a string containing four characters: the colon, comma, slash, and space.

3   The strtok() function will split up the string based on the delimiters it is given. It will return the first word (token) it finds, in this case, Joe.

4   Because the strtok() function keeps track of where it is in the string as it parses it, and finds one word at a time, the while loop will call the function until there are no more words in the string.

5   This time the strtok() function only has one argument, the list of delimiters it uses to mark each word. The $string argument is only used the first time the function is called, or when you want to start over.

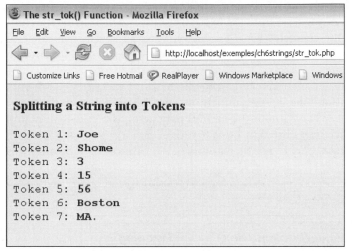

Figure 6.18 Splitting up a string with the `strtok()` function.

6.2.9 Repeating a String

Suppose you want to separate two blocks of text by a row of dashes. PHP provides the `str_repeat()` function to repeat a string a specified number of times. The first argument is the string that will be repeated and the second argument, called the multiplier, is the number of times you want to repeat it. The multiplier must be greater than or equal to zero and if it is zero, an empty string will be returned.

FORMAT

```
string str_repeat( string input, int multiplier)
```

Example:
```
print str_repeat("-", 30);   // prints 30 dashes
```

6.2.10 Trimming and Padding Strings

PHP provides a set of functions that trim and pad strings. Trimming means to remove excess or to prune, as in trimming your hair, your hedges, or your budget. You might want to clean up a string by getting rid of excess whitespace (or some other character) from the beginning or end of the string.

Padding a string is the opposite of trimming it. If you pad your wallet or your shirt, you add more to it. To pad a string means to add surrounding characters to either or both sides of the string.

The trim() Functions—trim(), ltrim(), chop(), rtrim(). The `trim()` function strips whitespace (or other characters) from the beginning and end of a string. If a third argument is given, called the character list (`charlist`), you can specify the range of characters you want to remove from the string. You can also use the `trim()` function to trim array values (see Chapter 8, "Arrays").

The `ltrim()` and `rtrim()` functions work just like `trim()`, except `ltrim()` only trims the left side of a string and the `rtrim()` function trims the right side of the string. The alias for `rtrim()` is `chop()`. Without the second parameter, the `trim()` function will strip the whitespace characters listed in Table 6.10.

Example 6.21 demonstrates how to use the various `trim()` functions. The output is shown in Figure 6.19.

Table 6.10   Whitespace Characters

Whitespace Character	ASCII Value(Decimal/Hex)	Meaning
" "	32 (0x20))	An ordinary space
"\t"	9 (0x0)	A tab
"\n"	10 (0x0A)	A newline (line feed)
"\r"	13 (0x0D))	A carriage return
"\0"	0 (0x00))	The NULL-byte
"\x0B"	11 (0x0B))	A vertical tab

FORMAT

```
string trim ( string str [, string charlist] )
string ltrim ( string str [, string charlist] )
string rtrim ( string str [, string charlist] )
```

Example:
```
$trimmed_string= trim( "\t\tHello\n"); // Removes tabs and newline
$trimmed_string=ltrim("\t\tHello\n");  // Removes two tabs on the left
$trimmed_string=rtrim("\t\tHello\n");  // Removes newline on the right
```

If you want to specify characters other than whitespace, you can list all characters in the second optional argument, `charlist`. With `..` you can specify a range of characters.

Example:
```
// Removes all asterisks
$trimmed_string = trim("****Hello*****", "*");
// Removes asterisks on the left
$trimmed_string = ltrim("****Hello*****", "*");
// Removes asterisks on the right
$trimmed_string = rtrim("****Hello*****", "*");
```

EXAMPLE 6.21

```
        <html><head><title>The trim() Function</title>
        </head>
        <body bgcolor="lavender">
        <font size="+1">
        <h3>Trimming a String</h3>
1       <pre>
        <b>
        <?php
2           $text = "\x20\x0a\t\tCutting away the excess whitespace!\n\n";
            echo "Original: $text<br />";
3           echo "Modified: ", trim($text), "<br />";
            echo "<hr>";
4           $text = "Cutting away the excess dots!...";
            echo "Original: $text<br />";
5           echo "Modified: ", rtrim($text, ".");
        ?>
        </pre>
        </b>
        </body>
        </html>
```

1 The `<pre>` tag is use here so that the whitespace characters will be displayed.
2 A string is created with leading whitespace represented by hexadecimal characters for a space, a newline, and two tabs. It ends with two newlines.
3 Whitespace (tabs, newlines, spaces) is trimmed from both ends of a string, called `$text`.
4 The right portion of the string contains an ellipsis (three dots).
5 The `rtrim()` function removes the dots from the right side of the string.

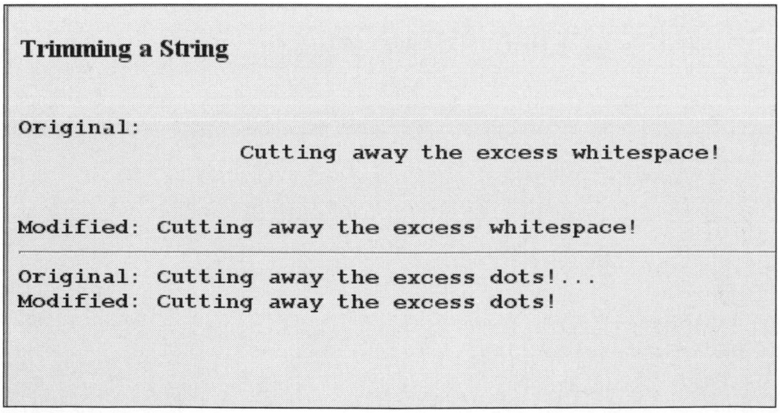

Trimming a String

```
Original:
               Cutting away the excess whitespace!


Modified: Cutting away the excess whitespace!
```
```
Original: Cutting away the excess dots!...
Modified: Cutting away the excess dots!
```

Figure 6.19 Trimming a string of excess characters. Output from Example 6.21.

The str_pad() Function.   You can pad a wallet or pad a cell. Similarly, to pad a string means to lengthen it by adding a specified number of characters to the string. PHP provides the str_pad() function to pad strings; the default is to pad with spaces on the right side of the string. The first argument is the string to be padded, the second argument, pad_length, is the width of the string with the padding characters. If a third argument is provided, you can specify whether the padding will occur on the left, right, or both sides of the string. The fourth argument, pad_type, represents the character that will be used for padding (see Table 6.11).

Table 6.11 Padding Types

Function	What It Does
STR_PAD_RIGHT	Pad to the right, the default.
STR_PAD_LEFT	Pad to the left.
STR_PAD_BOTH	Pad both ends of the string.

Example 6.22 demonstrates how to use the str_pad() function.

FORMAT

```
string str_pad ( string input, int pad_length [, string pad_string [,
             int pad_type]] )
```

Example:
```
$string = "Testing";
echo str_pad($string, 15);
echo str_pad ($string, 15, STR_PAD_BOTH);
echo str_pad($string, 15, STR_PAD_BOTH, "=_");
```

EXAMPLE 6.22

```
    <html><head><title>The trim() Function</title>
    </head>
    <body bgcolor="lavender">
    <font size="+1">
    <h3>Padding a String</h3>
    <b>
    <pre>
    <?php
1       $name="Elvis Presley";
2       $prof="Singer";
3       echo str_pad("Name:",15).$name,"<br />" ;
4       echo str_pad("Profession:",15). $prof,"<br />" ;
        echo "<br />";
```

EXAMPLE 6.22 (CONTINUED)

```
        $string="Table of Contents";
5       echo str_pad($string, 25, "-=",STR_PAD_BOTH), "<br />";
    ?>
    </b>
    </body>
    </html
```

EXPLANATION

1, 2   String values are assigned to $name and $prof.
3, 4   The str_pad() function, by default, pads the string (its first argument) by spaces
        to the right, thus creating a 15-space field. In this example, $name and $prof are
        concatenated to the padded strings, Name: and Profession:, in turn, as shown
        in Figure 6.20.

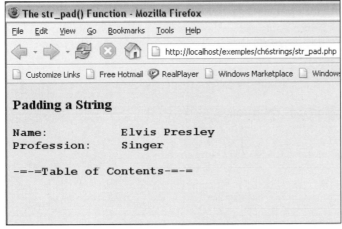

Figure 6.20   Padding a string. Output from Example 6.22.

6.2.11 Search and Replace

Searching and replacing text is a function you use commonly in a text editor.

PHP provides a set of functions to search for a string and replace it with a new one.
If you are trying to fine-tune your search pattern (e.g., search for all strings starting with
a number or a lowercase letter), you have the option to use regular expressions, covered
in Chapter 12, "Regular Expressions and Pattern Matching." The str_replace() function discussed here can be summarized as "Search for a string within some text and
replace it with another string."

The str_replace() and stri_replace() Functions. The `str_replace()` function replaces all occurrences of the search string with the replacement string. It returns a string (or an array) with the replacements wherever the search string was found. If the third argument is specified, then `str_replace` will return the number of times it found the searched for string. The only difference between `str_replace()` and `stri_replace()` is that `stri_replace()` is not case sensitive. See Chapter 8, "Arrays," to see how these functions work with arrays.

Example 6.23 demonstrates how to use the `str_replace()` function. The output is shown in Figure 6.21.

FORMAT

```
mixed str_replace( mixed search, mixed replace, mixed subject [,
                   int &count] )
mixed str_ireplace ( mixed search, mixed replace, mixed subject [,
                     int &count] )

Example:
// Returns: "Better to have loved once..."
$newstring=str_replace("hate", "love", "Better to have hated once..."
$newstring=str_replace("no", "yes", "No, no, no, a million times no.",
                  $howmany);
$newstring=str_ireplace("no", "yes", "No, no, no, a million times
                      no.", $howmany);
```

EXAMPLE 6.23

```
    <html>
    <head><title>Search and Replace</title></head>
    <body>
    <?php
        $text = "Icecream is good for you. You should eat icecream
            daily.";
1       $modified_text = str_replace( "icecream", "broccoli", $text );
        print "original: $text";
        print "<br />";
2       print "modified: $modified_text";
    ?>
    </body>
    </html>
```

EXPLANATION

1   The `str_replace()` function replaces the first argument, `"icecream"`, with `"broccoli"` in the string, `$text`.

2   The first occurrence of `Icecream` wasn't replaced because the `str_replace()` function is case sensitive. To perform a case-insensitive search and replace, use `str_ireplace()`.

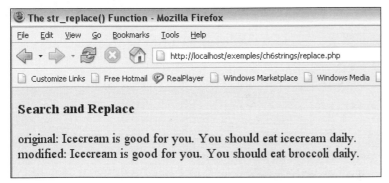

Figure 6.21 Search and replace—case sensitive.

The str_ireplace() function is just like the str_replace() function except that it is not case sensitive when searching for a string. Example 6.24 demonstrates how to use the str_ireplace() function. The output is shown in Figure 6.22.

EXAMPLE 6.24

```
    <html><head><title>The str_ireplace() Function</title>
    </head>
    <body bgcolor="lavender">
    <font size="+1">
    <h3>Case Insensitive Search and Replace</h3>
    <?php
        $text = "Icecream is good for you. You should eat icecream
            daily.";
1       $modified_text = str_ireplace( "icecream", "broccoli", $text );
2       print "original: $text<br />";
        // Not exactly what we want
3       print "modified: $modified_text<br />";
        // Capitalize the first character
4       print ucfirst($modified_text)."<br />";
    ?>
    </body></html>
```

EXPLANATION

1 The str_ireplace() function is case insensitive. It searches in the string assigned to $text, for icecream or Icecream or ICECReam, and so on, and replaces it with broccoli.
2 The original string is displayed.
3 In the modified string, we see that both Icecream and icecream will become broccoli. Problem: The first letter in the first occurrence of broccoli should be a capital B.
4 To correct this problem, we need to use the ucfirst() function to uppercase the first letter in broccoli at the beginning of the string.

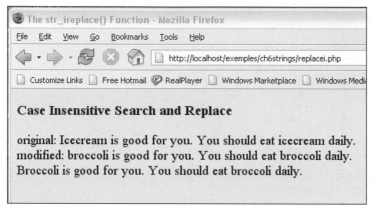

Figure 6.22 The `str_ireplace()` function.

Another way to use `str_replace()` is to replace multiple strings all at the same time. Since 4.0.5 all parameters of `str_replace()` can also be strings. Example 6.25 demonstrates how to use the `str_replace()` function with arrays or multiple strings. The output is displayed in Figure 6.23.

EXAMPLE 6.25

```
      <html>
      <head><title>Search and Replace with Arrays</title></head>
      <body>
      <?php
          $text = "I love pizza and beer!";
1         $search  = array( "love", "pizza", "beer" );
          $replace = array( "hate", "fruits", "vegetables" );
2         $modified_text = str_ireplace( $search, $replace, $text );
          print "original: $text";
          print "<br />";
          print "modified: $modified_text";
      ?>
      </body>
      </html>
```

EXPLANATION

1 Two array variables are intialized. They will be used in the search and replace.
2 The `str_replace()` function matches elements of the `$search` array and replaces them with corresponding elements of the `$replace` array. See Figure 6.23.

Figure 6.23 The `str_replace()` function.

6.2.12 Finding a Position in a String

Finding a position of a character in a string is often an auxiliary task. For example, if we wanted to find out the user name and the domain name of a user based on his or her e-mail address, we would look for the position of the @ character in the e-mail address. The left of it would be the user name, and the right of it would be the domain name.

The strpos() Function.   The `strpos()` function returns the position of the first case-sensitive occurrence of a character or substring within a string. This can also be called the index position of the substring starting at offset 0, meaning you start counting characters from the left side of the string, starting at character 0, until you reach the beginning of the target character or string. If nothing is found, boolean `false` is returned.

If the third, optional argument (a number) is used, the `strpos()` function will start searching from that character position, but counts characters from the beginning of the string.

Example 6.26 demonstrates how to use the `strpos()` function to find the occurrence of a character or substring in a string. The output is shown in Figure 6.24.

FORMAT

```
int strpos ( string , substring [, int offset] )
```

Example:
```
// $offset is 2
$offset = ("a needle in a haystack", "needle");
// start looking after character 1, returns 5
$offset=("big, bigger, biggest", "big", 1);
```

EXAMPLE 6.26

```
         <html>
         <head><title>The strpos() Function</title></head>
         <body bgcolor="lightgreen">
         <h>Finding the Index Position of a Substring</h3>
         <font size="+1">
         <?php
1            $email = "joe@yahoo.com";
2            $position_of_at_symbol = strpos($email,'@');
             print "The starting position of the '@' symbol in
             <em>$email</em>: $position_of_at_symbol";
3            $position_of_dot_symbol = strpos($email,'.com');
             print "<br />The starting position of '.com' in <em>$email</em>:
                 $position_of_dot_symbol";
         ?>
         </font>
         </body>
         </html>
```

EXPLANATION

1 The variable, $email, is assigned a string. We will be searching for the position of the @ symbol and for the substring .com.

2 The strpos() function returns the index position of the @ sybmol in the $email string. The first position at the beginning of the string starts at the index of 0. Counting from 0, the @ symbol is at position 3. See Figure 6.24.

3 The strpos() function returns the index position of the substring .com. Starting a position 0, and counting to the beginning of the substring (i.e., to the dot in .com), the position retuned is 9. See Figure 6.24.

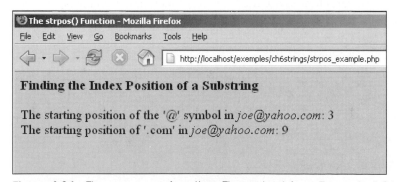

Figure 6.24 The strpos() function. The output from Example 6.26.

The strrpos() and strripos() Functions. The strrpos() function returns the position of the last occurrence of a character in a string. You can think of the second "r" in the function name, as meaning "rightmost" position. The strripos() function does the same thing, but is not case sensitive. The "i" in the function name means "insensitive" to case.

> ### FORMAT
>
> ```
> int strrpos ( string , character [, int offset] )
> int strripos ( string , character [, int offset] )
> ```
>
> Example:
> ```
> // finds the position of the last slash
> $offset=sttrpos( "/usr/local/bin", "/");
> // finds the position of "beans"
> $offset=sttrpos( "Boston baked beans", 'B')
> ```

6.2.13   Extracting Pieces of a String—Substrings

A substring is a portion of another string; for example, pie is a substring of piece and spiel, and arch is a substring of hierarchy and architect. If a user were to enter an e-mail address, perhaps you really only wanted to know the the domain name, a substring of the e-mail address; or perhaps you only want the country code for an entered telephone number.

PHP provides a set of functions specifically designed to extract smaller strings from larger strings. Table 6.12 lists the substring functions discussed in this chapter.

Table 6.12   Substring Functions

Function	What It Does
strchr()	Alias of strstr(). Finds the first occurrence of a character in a string and returns it and all characters to the end of the string.
strichr()	Case-insensitive form of strstr().
strrchr()	Finds last occurrence of a character in a string and returns it and all characters to the end of the string.
substr()	Returns part of a string, specified by a start position and length.
substr_replace()	Returns a string, replaced with part of another string.
substr_count()	Counts the number of times a substring is found in a string.

The strchr(), strrchr(), and strichr() Functions. The strchr() function searches for a character starting at the left side of the string and returns all the characters from that character to the end of the string. The first argument is the original string (called the *haystack*) and the second argument (called the *needle*) is the starting character of the substring within the string. All the characters after the needle including the needle, will be returned. If the needle is not found, the function returns FALSE.

FORMAT

```
string strchr ( string haystack, string needle )
```

Example:
```
echo strchr("debbiejean@somewhere.edu, ".");  // Returns: .edu
```

The strrchr() function searches for a character at the rightmost position in the string, and returns all of the characters from that character to the end of the string. It returns FALSE if the target character is not found.

The strichr() function is the same as strchr() but ignores case when searching for a character.

Example 6.27 demonstrates how to use the strrchr() function to find the rightmost substring within a string.

FORMAT

```
string strrchr ( string haystack, character neele)
```

Example:
```
$substring = ( "/usr/local/bin", "/"); // Returns "/bin"
```

EXAMPLE 6.27

```
<html><head><title>The strchr Function</title>
</head>
<body bgcolor="lavender">
<font size="+1">
<h3>Searching for a Character</h3>
<?php
  $address="15 Sleepy Hollow Rd, Boston, Massachusetts";
  print "$address<br />";
1  $state=strrchr($address, "M");
  print "$state<br />";

  $path="C:\\Documents and Settings\\Ellie Quigley\\My Documents";
  print "$path<br />";
2  print strrchr($path, "\\");
?>
</body></html>
```

EXPLANATION

1   The strrchr() function looks for the character M in the address at the rightmost position at which it occurs in the string and returns all the characters from M to the end of the string. Massachusetts is printed. See Figure 6.25.

2   The strrchr() function looks for \\ in the string at its rightmost position and prints everything to the end of the string. In this example, it finds the base name of the path. (Two backslashes are used, one to protect the other from special interpretation.) See Figure 6.25.

Figure 6.25   The strrchr() function. Output of Example 6.27.

The substr() Function.   The substr() function returns a part of a string, called a substring. It takes up to three aruguments. The first argument is the original string, the second arugument is the offset or starting position of the substring, and the third, optional argument specifies how many characters are to be extracted.

If the second argument, starting position, is a positive number, the search for the substring starts from the beginning of the string, position 0. If the starting position is a negative number, the search starts at the end of the string at position –1.

If the third argument is not specified, the substring will consist of all the characters found from where it started until the end of the string. If length specified is negative, then that many characters will be omitted from the end of string.

If length is given and is positive, the string returned will contain at most length characters beginning from start (depending on the length of string). If the string is less than or equal to start characters long, FALSE will be returned.

Example 6.28 demonstrates how to use the substr() function to retrieve part of a string. The output is displayed in Figure 6.26.

FORMAT

```
string substr ( string string, int start [, int length]
```

Example:
```
$newstring = substr("Happy New Year", 6);   // Returns "New Year"
$newstring = substr("Happy New Year", 6, 3) // Returns "New"
$newstring = substr("Happy New Year", -4)   // Returns "Year"
```

EXAMPLE 6.28

```
    <html><head><title>The substr() Function</title>
    </head>
    <body bgcolor="lavender">
    <font size="+1">
    <h3>Extracting Substrings</h3>
    <?php
        print '<b>substr("Happy New Year", 6)</b>  produces: <em>';
1       print substr("Happy New Year", 6) . "</em><br />";

        print '<b>substr("Happy New Year", 6, 3)</b> produces: <em>';
2       print substr("Happy New Year", 6, 3) . "</em><br />";

        print '<b>substr("Happy New Year", -4)</b> produces: <em>';
3       print substr("Happy New Year", -4) . "</em><br />";

        print '<b>substr("Happy New Year", -4, -1)</b> produces: <em>';
4       print substr("Happy New Year", -4, -1) . "</em><br />";

        print '<b>substr("Happy New Year", 6, -2)</b> produces: <em>';
5       print substr("Happy New Year", 6, -2) . "</em><br />";
    ?>
    </body>
    </html>
```

EXPLANATION

1   Starting from the beginning of the string, at offset 0, the `substr()` function counts over 6 characters, which starts the substring at the N in the string Happy New Year. The rest of the string is printed.

2   Starting at the beginning of the string, at offset 0, the `substr()` function counts over 6 characters, a length of 3, returning the substring New. The first argument is the starting position and the second argument specifies the length of the substring.

3   Starting at the end of the string, with -4 offset, the `substr()` function starts at the end of the string and backs up to the Y in Year, and starting there takes characters up to the end of the string.

4   Starting at the end of the string, with -4 as the offset, the substr() function starts at the end of the string and backs up to the Y in Year. The second argument, -1, tells the function to go to the end of the string and back up by 1 character. The substring is Yea.

5   Starting at the beginning of the string, the substr() function takes the first 6 characters, New Year. The second argument, -2, tells the function to back up 2 characters from the end of the substring, producing New Ye.

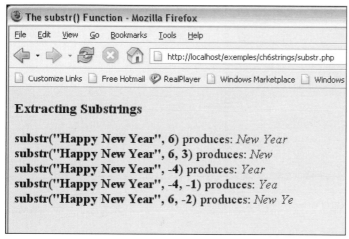

Figure 6.26   The substr() function gets part of a string. Output from Example 6.28.

Example 6.29 uses both the substr() and strpos() functions to extract parts of a string.

EXAMPLE 6.29

```
    <html>
    <head><title>Extract Email</title></head>
    <body>
    <?php
        $email = "joe@yahoo.com";
1       $user_name = substr( $email, 0, strpos($email,'@') );
2       $domain    = substr( $email, strpos($email,'@')+1 );
        print "user name: $user_name";
        print "<br />";
        print "domain:    $domain";
    ?>
    </body>
    </html>
```

EXPLANATION

1   To extract the user name part of an e-mail address, we start at location 0 (in PHP all indicies start at 0 and go to maximum –1). The end of the user name is where the @ symbol is. We use `strpos` to determine at what index that symbol is in that string. That's how we get the user name. See Figure 6.27.

2   To extract the domain name, we only need to specify the start location. In this case that location is just the location of @ symbol plus 1 (this is because we don't want to include @ in the returned substring). See Figure 6.27.

Figure 6.27   Using the `substr()` and `strpos()` functions. Output from Example 6.29.

The substr_replace() Function.   The `substr_replace()` function is similar to the `substr()` function, but instead of returning a portion of a string, it returns a copy of the original string replaced with a substring. The substring portion is inserted in the string at a given offset and optional length value. (If the first argument is an array, then an array is returned.)

The `substr_replace()` function takes up to four arguments. The first argument is the original string, the second argument is the replacement string, the third argument is the offset or starting position of where the replacement string will be inserted, and the fourth, optional argument can be either a positive or negative number.

If the third argument, starting position, is a positive number, the search for the substring starts from the beginning of the string, position 0. If the starting position is a negative number, the search starts at the end of the string at position –1.

If the fourth, length, argument is a positive number, it specifies how many characters to overwrite when the substring is inserted in the string. For example, if the starting position is 0 and the length is 4, then the first four characters will be replaced. A negative length specifies how many characters to exclude when inserting the new substring. For example, –2 says to not replace the last two characters in the string. If the length is not given, then the default is the length (`strlen`) of the string. Default is to `strlen(string)`; that is, it will replace the entire string with the value of the second argument, the substring.

Example 6.30 demonstrates how to use the `substr_replace()` function to insert a new string into an existing string at a designated position. The output is displayed in Figure 6.28.

FORMAT

```
mixed substr_replace ( mixed string, string replacement, int start
                       [, int length] )
```

Example:

```
// Returns: two jars of jam
echo substr_replace("three jars of jam", "two", 0, 5);
// Returns: three jars of jelly
echo substr_replace("three jars of jam", "jelly", -3);
// Returns: I  made three jars of          jam
echo substr_replace("three jars of jam", "I made ", 0,0);
// Returns: three jars of plum jam
echo substr_replace("three jars of jam", " plum", -4, -4);
```

EXAMPLE 6.30

```
        <html><head><title>The substr_replace() Function</title>
        </head>
        <body bgcolor="lavender">
        <font size="+1">
        <h3>Replace a Portion of a String</h3>
        <?php
1           $text = "Tom used a teaspoon of sugar.";
            print "Original string: $text<br />";
            // Find the starting position of the substring
            $start=strpos($text, "teaspoon");
2           $modified_text = substr_replace( "$text", "table", $start, 3 );
            print "1. Modified: $modified_text\n<br />";

            $text = "Tom used a teaspoon of sugar.";
3           $modified_text = substr_replace( "$text", "Peter", 0, 3 );
            print "2. Modified: $modified_text\n<br />";

            $text = "Tom used a teaspoon of sugar.";
4           $modified_text = substr_replace( "$text", "Yesterday ", 0, 0 );
            print "3. Modified: $modified_text\n<br />";

            $text = "Tom used a teaspoon of sugar.";
5           $modified_text = substr_replace( "$text", "vanilla", -6, -1 );
            print "4. Modified: $modified_text\n<br />";
        ?>
        </body>
        </html>
```

EXPLANATION

1 This is the original string that will be modified by the substr_replace() function.
2 The substring is teaspoon starting at position $start. The first 3 characters in teaspoon will be replaced with table, making the new substring tablespoon. Simply put, the substring teaspoon is replaced in the string with tablespoon.
3 Starting at position 0, that is, the beginning of the string, replace the first 3 characters, Tom, with Peter.
4 Starting at position 0, insert at the beginning of the string, the substring Yesterday.
5 Starting 6 characters from the end of the string, -6, replace sugar with vanilla, but don't overwrite the period. –1 backs off 1 character.

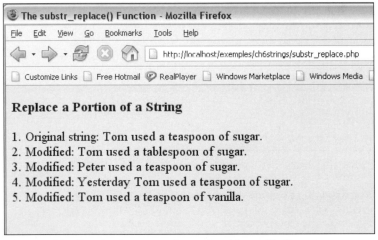

Figure 6.28 Replacing a portion of a string with the substr_replace() function. Output of Example 6.30.

The substr_count() Function. The substr_count() function counts and returns the number of times a substring occurs within string. It is case sensitive. The first argument, called the haystack, specifies the string that contains the substrings. The second string is the substring that we are looking for. The third, optional argument is the offset where to start counting, and the last, optional argument is the maximum length after the specified offset to search in the substring.

Example 6.31 demonstrates the use of the substr_count() function.

FORMAT

```
int substr_count ( string , substring [, int offset [, int length]] )
```

Example:
```
$count = ("\t\tCounting tabs\tis fun\t", "\t"); // Returns 4
```

EXAMPLE 6.31

```
       <html><head><title>The substr_count() Function</title>
       </head>
       <body bgcolor="lavender">
       <font size="+1">
       <h3>Counting Substrings</h3>
       <?php
1          $text = "One little, two little, three, little Indians...";
           echo '$text= '. "$text<br />";
           echo '<b>substr_count("$text","little") </b>counts: ' ;
2          echo substr_count("$text","little");
           echo '<br /><b>substr_count("$text","little", 5) </b>counts: ' ;
3          echo substr_count("$text","little", 5);
       ?>
       </body>
       </html>
```

EXPLANATION

1 This string will contain the substrings being searched for.
2 The substr_count() function will find the number of times the substring little appears in the string One little, two little, three, little Indians.... See Figure 6.29.
3 The third argument to the substr_count() function specifies the offset, the position where the function will start counting substrings. Instead of starting the count at the beginning of the string, the count will start at position 5, which is the character "i" in the string "little". The next occurrence of little will start the count. The substring little appears twice after position 5. See Figure 6.29.

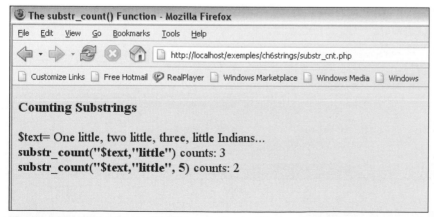

Figure 6.29 Counting substrings. Output of Example 6.31.

6.2.14 Special Characters and Strings

Individual Characters and the Curly Brace Syntax.   Until PHP 5, if you wanted
to extract a character from a string, you could treat the string as an array and use square
brackets to extract a particular character. Arrays are discussed in Chapter 8, "Arrays."
Consider the following example:

```php
<?php
    $car = "Honda";
    echo $car[0];    // Prints the "H" in "Honda"
    echo $car[1];    // Prints the "o" in "Honda"
    echo $car[2];    // Prints the "n" in "Honda"
?>
```

The problem with using square brackets is that it's impossible to tell whether
$car[0] references an array or a string. As of PHP 5, using the square brackets to extract
a character has been replaced with a curly brace syntax as follows:

```php
<?php
    $car = "Honda";
    echo $car{0};    // Prints the "H" in "Honda"
    echo $car{1};    // Prints the "o" in "Honda"
    echo $car{2};    // Prints the "n" in "Honda"
?>
```

Line Breaks with the nl2br() and wordwrap() Functions.   To insert line breaks in
the browser, you can use the HTML <pre> tag with the \n escape sequence, use the HTML

 tag within your PHP strings, or use the built-in nl2br() and wordwrap() functions.
    The nl2br() is a simple PHP function that inserts a <BR> tag in front of every newline
in the text. We can use this function to quickly format plain text into HTML code.
    Example 6.32 demonstrates how to use the nl2br() function to insert HTML line
breaks.

FORMAT

```
new_string = nl2br( old_string );
```

Example:
```
print nl2br("Break this string here\n and here
                and here");
```

EXAMPLE 6.32

```
<html>
<head><title>Breaking Lines</title></head>
<body bgcolor="silver">
<h2>Breaking Lines</h2>
<h3>Using Escape Sequences</h3>
```

EXAMPLE 6.32 (CONTINUED)

```
1   <pre>
    <?php
        // Backslash sequences within the <pre> tag
2       print "Goofy Rufus\n";
        print "123 Fantasia Street\n";
        print "San Francisco, CA 94111\n";
    ?>
3   </pre>
    <h3>Using the HTML &lt;br&gt; Tag</h3>
    <?php
4       print "Goofy Rufus\n<br />"; // The <br> tag within the strings
        print "123 Fantasia Street\n<br />";
        print "San Francisco, CA 94111\n<br />";
    ?>
    <h3>Using the PHP <em>nl2br()</em> Function</h3>
    <?php
        $address="Goofy Rufus
        123 Fantasia Street
        San Francisco, CA 94111
        ";
        // the nl2br() function replaces newlines with <br />
5       print nl2br("$address");
    ?>
    </body>
    </html>
```

EXPLANATION

1   The HTML <pre> tags are often useful for debugging and quick page layout. When viewing the source in the browser, the output is exactly the same as the page viewed in the browser.

2   Each of the lines is terminated with \n to represent a newline. Normally, PHP will output a newline, but HTML will ignore it. When enclosed within <pre> tags, the \n will produce a newline.

3   The </pre> tag is closed here. If at this point, the \n is used for a line break, HTML will ignore it.

4   The HTML <br> tag is used here to create line breaks. We also included the \n. Although \n will not affect the output displayed in the browser, it is a good idea to include it in case you want to view the source of the page in your browser to find bugs, or if you execute the script at the command line. We will discuss more about fixing common bugs in Appendix D.

5   The nl2br() function will add a <br> tag in front of every \n character or break in the line, so that HTML can display the line breaks in the browser (see Figure 6.30). Notice in Figure 6.31 that the <br> tags were inserted. nl2br() actually inserts <br /> to be XHTML.

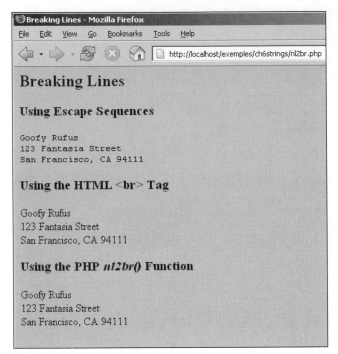

Figure 6.30 Creating `<br>` tags with `nl2br()`. Output from Example 6.32.

Figure 6.31 Page source.

The `wordwrap()` function wraps a string to a given number of characters using a string break character such as `<br>` or `\n`. Without specifying any arguments `wordwrap()` inserts a `\n` at the 75 column (i.e., the 75th character in the string starting from the beginning of the string). If a width is given, then the line will be broken at that column and even if the word is too large, it will be preserved on that line before the break. By default, the break character is `\n` unless specified as something else. You can use the HTML `<br>` character if viewing the output in the browser.

Examples 6.33 and 6.34 demonstrate how to use the wordwrap() function for determining the width of a string.

FORMAT

```
string wordwrap (string str [, int width [, string break [,
                bool cut]]] )
```

Example:
```
// Words are 5 or more characters; line break is "\n"
$wrapped_string = wordwrap("Today is Christmas", 5);
// Each character is on a line by itself; line break is "<br />"
$wrapped_string = wordwrap("Today is Christmas",1,"<br />",1);
```

EXAMPLE 6.33

```
      </head>
      <body bgcolor="lavender">
      <font size="+1">
      <h3>Word Wrap</h3>
      <?php
1         $text = "The snow is falling in Stockholm on Christmas day
                  and I am absolutely mesmerized by its beauty.";
2         $new_text = wordwrap($text,9,"<br />");
      ?>
      Original text: <?=$text?>
      <br />
      Wrapped text:<br />
      <font color="red">
3     <?=$new_text?>
      </font></body></html>
```

EXPLANATION

1   The original string will be displayed as a single string in the browser and will not be broken until it reaches the rightmost border of the window.
2   The `wordwrap()` function will insert a break at every ninth character. The words "absolutely" and "mesmerized" will not be broken even though they are longer than nine characters. See Figure 6.32.
3   After inserting line breaks, the string is broken as close as possible to the ninth character without corrupting a word by breaking it somewhere other than at spaces, tabs, or newlines.

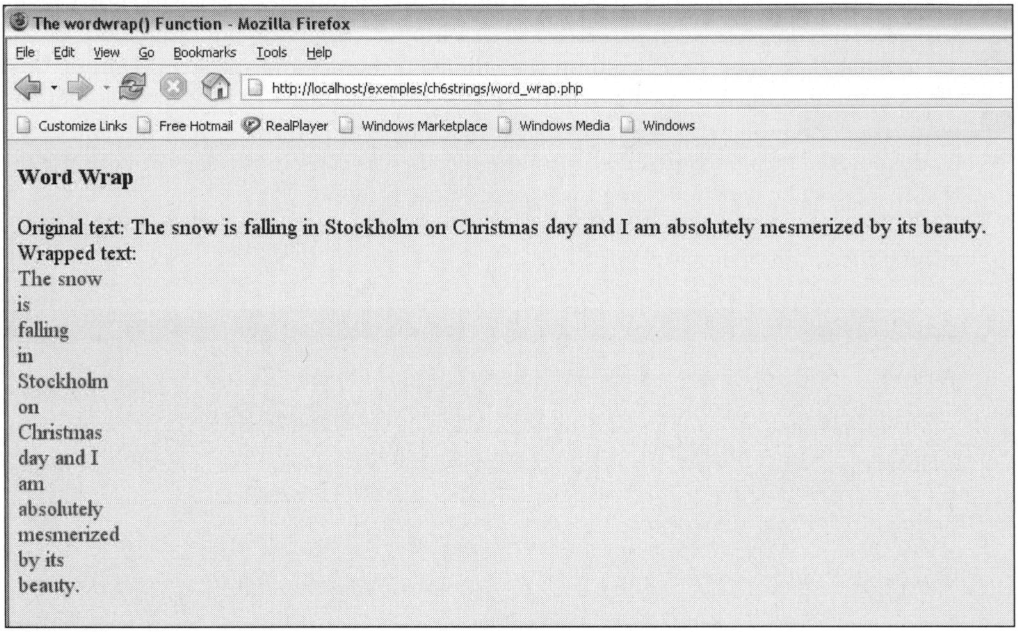

Figure 6.32 The `wordwrap()` function with a specified width and line break character. Output of Example 6.33.

If the boolean cut argument is set to 1, the string is always wrapped at the specified width. So if the word is larger than the given width, it is broken apart, which is not always what you want (see Example 6.34).

EXAMPLE 6.34

```
      <html><head><title>The wordwrap() Function</title>
      </head>
      <body bgcolor="lavender">
      <font size="+1">
      <h3>Word Wrap</h3>
      <?php
1        $text = "The snow is falling in Stockholm on Christmas day and
                  I am absolutely mesmerized by its beauty.";
2        $new_text = wordwrap( $text,9, "<br />\n", 1);
      ?>
      Original text: <?=$text?><br />
      Wrapped text:<br />
      <font color="red">
      <?=$new_text?>
      </font>
      </body>
      </html>
```

EXPLANATION

1 The original string is assigned to `$text`.
2 The `wordwrap()` function breaks the string at every ninth character, and because the third argument is set to 1, the word will be broken at the ninth character even if it means putting part of the word on the next line. See Figure 6.33.

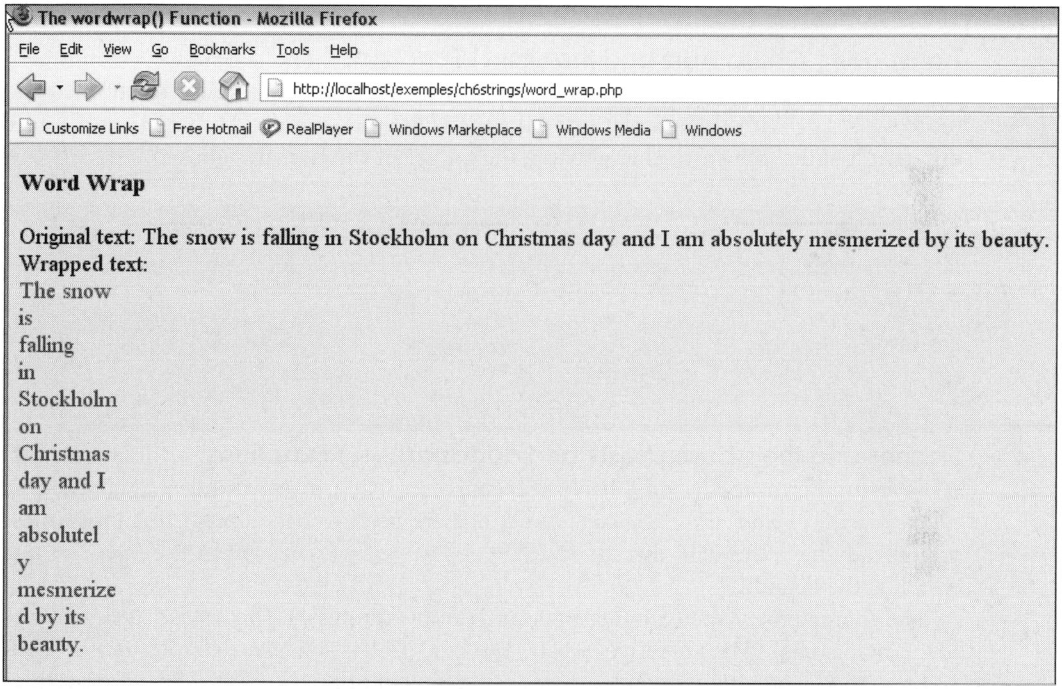

Figure 6.33 The `wordwrap()` function with the optional boolean argument. Output from Example 6.34.

ASCII Character Values and the chr() Function. The `chr()` function takes the numeric ASCII value of a character and returns the character.

FORMAT

```
string chr ( int ascii )
```

Example:
```
echo chr(66), "<br />";  // Returns: "B"
```

ASCII Character Values and the ord() Function. The `ord()` function returns the numeric ASCII value for a character.

FORMAT

```
int ord (string string)
```

Example:
```
echo ord("B"), "<br />";   // Returns: 66
```

Transposing Characters and the strstr() Function. The `strstr()` function translates characters on a one-to-one correspondence from one string to another and returns a string with the translations (like the UNIX `tr` command). If `from` and `to` are different lengths, the extra characters in the longer of the two are ignored.

FORMAT

```
string strtr ( string str, string from, string to )
string strtr ( string str, array replace_pairs )
```

Example:
```
echo strtr("aaacaa", "a", "b")   // Returns: bbbcbb
```

Slashes and the addslashes() and addcslashes() Functions. Certain characters need to be escaped with a backslash character when inserted into a database. The `addcslashes()` and `addslashes()` functions are used to accomplish this task unless you already have the PHP directive `magic_quotes_gpc` turned on in the `php.ini` file, which is the default.

The characters escaped are the single and double quotes, the backslash itself, and the NULL byte. The PHP directive `magic_quotes_gpc` is on by default, and it runs `addslashes()` on all GET, POST, and COOKIE data. Do not use `addslashes()` on strings that have already been escaped with `magic_quotes_gpc`, as you'll then do double escaping. You can use the `get_magic_quotes_gpc()` function to see if `magic_quotes_gpc` is on.

Example 6.35 demonstrates how to check for the `get_magic_quotes_gpc()` directive and how `addslashes()` is used. Output is displayed in Figure 6.35.

Table 6.13   Adding Slashes to Special Characters

Function	What It Returns
addcslashes()	Quotes a string with slashes in a C style
addslashes()	Quotes a string with slashes

FORMAT

```
string addslashes ( string str )
```

Example:
```
echo addslashes( "I can't help you.") // Returns: I can\'t help you.
```

EXAMPLE 6.35

```
<html><head><title>Adding Slashes to Characters</title>
</head>
<body bgcolor="lightgreen">
<h3>The addslashes() Function</h3>
<font size="+1">
<?php
1       $last_name=$_GET[last_name];
2       if (get_magic_quotes_gpc() == 1){
            echo "get_magic_quotes_gpc() is on<br />";
3           $query=("SELECT first_name, last_name from Persons WHERE
                    last_name='$last_name'");
4           echo $query;
        }
        else{
5           $query=addslashes("SELECT first_name,
            last_name from Persons WHERE last_name='$last_name'");
        }
?>
</body>
</html>
```

EXPLANATION

1   The HTML form uses the GET method to retrieve the data from the form. It is assigned to the PHP $_GET array. See Figure 6.34.

2   The get_magic_quotes_gpc() function returns 1 if the magic_quotes_gpc directive is turned on, and if it is, the backslashes will automatically be added to the quote character.

3   An SQL query string is created. Any quote marks should be backslashed before executing the query.

4   By viewing the value of $query, you can see that the single quote in the query string value of the last name, O\'Conner, is preceded by a backslash. This is the default behavior when magic_quotes_gpc is set to "On". See Figure 6.35.

5   If the magic_quotes_gpc directive has not been set, this line is executed to assure that backslashes are added before the single quote for the database query. If get_magic_quotes_gpc() returns true, then you shouldn't use the addslashes() function, because it is already the default. If you do, the string will be escaped twice as shown here:

```
SELECT first_name, last_name from Persons WHERE
lastname=\'O\\\'Conner\'
```

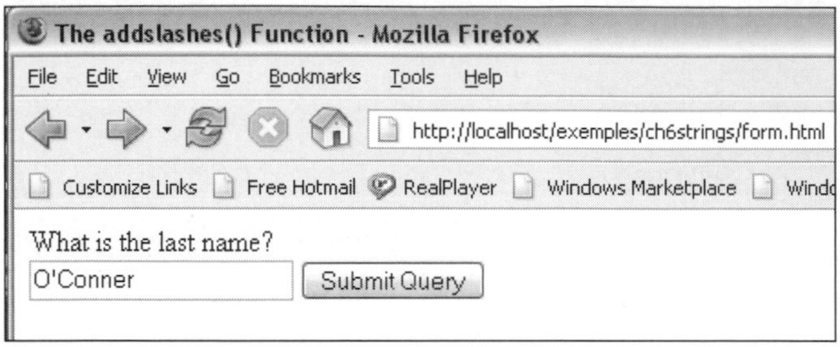

Figure 6.34   The HTML form from Example 6.35.

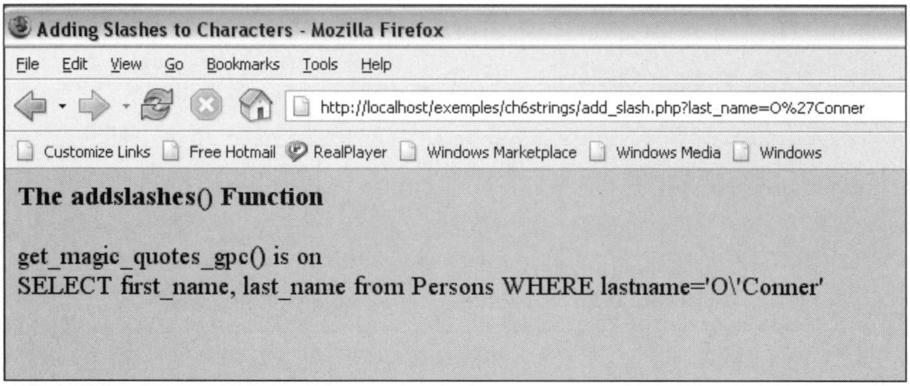

Figure 6.35   The PHP script and the `addslashes()` function. Output from Example 6.35.

Slashes and the stripslashes() Function.   The `stripslashes()` function removes backslashes that precede quotation marks and if there are double slashes \\, they become a single slash \. This function is useful if you are displaying data directly from a form rather than sending it to a database where backslashes are often required. (See the PHP directive `magic_quotes_gpc` in the `php.ini` file.)

Example 6.36 demonstrates how `stripslashes()` works. The output is shown in Figure 6.37.

FORMAT

```
string stripslashes ( string str )
```

Example:
```
$string = "She said, \"Don\'t do that.\"";
echo stripslashes($string);  // Output: She said, "Don't do that."
```

EXAMPLE 6.36

```
        <html><head><title>The stripslashes() Function</title>
        </head>
        <body>
1       <form action="form.php" method="post">
        <textarea rows=3 cols=30 name="story" </textarea>
        <br />
        <input type=submit name="submit">
        <input type=reset>
        </form>
2       <?php
3          if (isset($_POST['submit'])){
4              $input=$_POST["story"];
5              print stripslashes($input);
           }
        ?>
        </body></html>
```

EXPLANATION

1   The HTML form is started here. Its action calls the script `form.php`.
2   The PHP script is started here. It will process the form input.
3   If the form has been submitted, the value `$_POST['submit']` will be set.
4   The `$_POST` array contains the text that the user typed in the text area box, named `story`. (See Chapter 10, "More on PHP Forms," for more information on the `$_POST` array.) For now, `$input` contains the input typed by the user. See Figure 6.36.
5   The `stripslashes()` function removes the slashes that were added by `addslashes()`, the default behavior when the `magic_quotes_gpc` directive has been turned on in the `php.ini` file.

Figure 6.36   The user fills in a form.

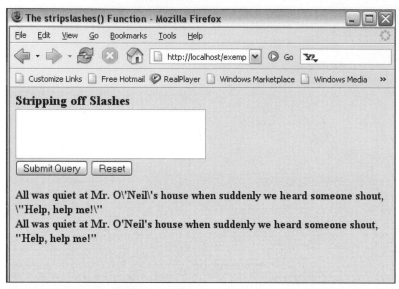

Figure 6.37   After the form in Figure 6.36 is submitted. Output of Example 6.36.

6.2.15   Working with HTML Special Characters

Like all languages, HTML has certain characters that have special significance and those characters are represented by HTML entities, special symbols starting with an ampersand and terminated with a semicolon; for example, the < and > symbols are written as < and >. If the user enters text that contains these HTML characters (see Table 6.14) when filling out a form, you can use the htmlspecialchars() function to convert the most common special characters to their respective HTML entities. If you require all HTML character entities to be translated, use htmlentities() shown in the next section.

Table 6.14   HTML Special Character Functions

Function	What It Does
htmlspecialchars_decode()	Converts special HTML entities back to characters
htmlspecialchars()	Converts special characters to HTML entities

The htmlspecialchars() Function. The `htmlspecialchars()` function converts special characters (shown in Table 6.15) to HTML entities.

Table 6.15 Conversion of Special Characters

Character Before	The HTML Entity
& (ampersand)	`&amp;`
" (double quote)	`&quot;` when `ENT_NOQUOTES` is not set
' (single quote)	`&#039;` only when `ENT_QUOTES` is set
< (less than)	`&lt;`
> (greater than)	`&gt;`

FORMAT

```
string htmlspecialchars (string string [, int quote_style [,
                         string charset]])
```

Example:
```
$text = "Isn't the << symbol is used in here-docs?";
echo htmlspecialchars($text, ENT_QUOTES), "<br />";
```

You can define how to handle single or double quotes using the `quote_style` optional third argument, and define the character set for your locale by using the optional fourth argument, called `charset`. Quote constants are shown in Table 6.16.

Example 6.37 demonstrates how to use the `htmlspecialchars()` function. The output can be viewed in Figure 6.38.

Table 6.16 Quote Constants

Constant Name	Description
`ENT_COMPAT`	Converts double quotes and leaves single quotes alone, the default mode
`ENT_QUOTES`	Converts both double and single quotes
`ENT_NOQUOTES`	Leaves both double and single quotes unconverted

EXAMPLE 6.37

```
    <html><head><title>The htmlspecialchars() Function</title>
    </head>
    <body bgcolor="lavender">
    <font size="+1">
    <h3>Creating HTML Entities</h3>
    <b>
    <?php
1       $text = "<<Johnson&Son's Tobacco Store>>";
2       echo "Original: $text<br /><br />";
3       echo "Modified: ", htmlspecialchars($text), "<br />";
    ?>
    </b>
    </body>
    </html>
```

EXPLANATION

1   The variable, $text, is assigned a string containing some characters considered special when rendered by the HTML interpreter; they are the < and & characters.
2   When this string is viewed in the browser, the HTML interpreter sees the < as an opening tag symbol followed by an irrelevant HTML element. Nothing is displayed other than the next opening < and the closing >.
3   The htmlspecialchars() function creates HTML entities out of the < and & so that the browser can display text. Note that the source page (see Figure 6.39) for the Web page shows that these entitities are now part of the page.

Figure 6.38   Converting special characters to HTML entities. Output from Example 6.37.

Figure 6.39 Viewing the source page in the browser.

The htmlentities() Function.
The htmlentities() function converts all applicable characters to their HTML entities equivalents.

FORMAT

```
string htmlentities (string string [, int quote_style [,
                     string charset]])
```

Example:
```
$string = "5¢ won't get you much at the café Française!";
echo htmlentities($string, ENT_COMPAT);
// Returns: 5&#162 won't get you much at the caf&egrave;
Fran&ccedil;aise!
```

Table 6.17 Supported Character Sets

Charset	Aliases	Description
ISO-8859-1	ISO8859-1	Western European, Latin-1.
ISO-8859-15	ISO8859-15	Western European, Latin-9. Adds the Euro sign, French and Finnish letters missing in Latin-1 (ISO-8859-1).
UTF-8		ASCII-compatible multibyte 8-bit Unicode.
cp866	ibm866, 866	DOS-specific Cyrillic charset. This charset is supported in 4.3.2.
cp1251	Windows-1251, win-1251, 1251	Windows-specific Cyrillic charset. This charset is supported in 4.3.2.

Table 6.17 Supported Character Sets (continued)

Charset	Aliases	Description
cp1252	Windows-1252, 1252	Windows-specific charset for Western Europe.
KOI8-R	koi8-ru, koi8r	Russian. This charset is supported in 4.3.2.
BIG5	950	Traditional Chinese, mainly used in Taiwan.
GB2312	936	Simplified Chinese, national standard character set.
BIG5-HKSCS		Big5 with Hong Kong extensions, Traditional Chinese.
Shift_JIS	SJIS, 932	Japanese.
EUC-JP	EUCJP	Japanese.

6.3   Other String Functions

This chapter focused on some of the most useful string functions, but PHP provides other useful string functions, as shown in Table 6.18.

Table 6.18 PHP Functions

Function	What It Does
addcslashes	Quotes string with slashes in a C style.
addslashes	Quotes string with slashes.
bin2hex	Converts binary data into hexadecimal representation.
chop	Alias of `rtrim()`.
chr	Returns a specific character.
chunk_split	Splits a string into smaller chunks.
convert_cyr_string	Converts from one Cyrillic character set to another.
convert_uudecode	Decodes a uuencoded string.
convert_uuencode	Uuencodes a string.
count_chars	Returns information about characters used in a string.
crc32	Calculates the crc32 polynomial of a string.
crypt	One-way string encryption (hashing).

Table 6.18 PHP Functions (continued)

Function	What It Does
echo	Outputs one or more strings.
explode	Splits a string by string.
fprintf	Writes a formatted string to a stream.
get_html_translation_table	Returns the translation table used by `htmlspecialchars()` and `htmlentities()`.
hebrev	Converts logical Hebrew text to visual text.
hebrevc	Converts logical Hebrew text to visual text with newline conversion.
html_entity_decode	Converts all HTML entities to their applicable characters.
htmlentities	Converts all applicable characters to HTML entities.
htmlspecialchars_decode	Converts special HTML entities back to characters.
htmlspecialchars	Converts special characters to HTML entities.
implode	Joins array elements with a string.
join	Alias of `implode()`.
levenshtein	Calculates Levenshtein distance between two strings.
localeconv	Gets numeric formatting information.
ltrim	Strips whitespace (or other characters) from the beginning of a string.
md5_file	Calculates the `md5` hash of a given file.
md5	Calculates the `md5` hash of a string.
metaphone	Calculates the metaphone key of a string.
money_format	Formats a number as a currency string.
nl_langinfo	Query language and locale information.
nl2br	Inserts HTML line breaks before all newlines in a string.
number_format	Formats a number with grouped thousands.
ord	Returns ASCII value of character.
parse_str	Parses the string into variables.

Table 6.18   PHP Functions (continued)

Function	What It Does
print	Outputs a string.
printf	Outputs a formatted string.
quoted_printable_decode	Converts a quoted-printable string to an 8-bit string.
quotemeta	Quotes metacharacters.
rtrim	Strips whitespace (or other characters) from the end of a string.
setlocale	Sets locale information.
sha1_file	Calculates the sha1 hash of a file.
sha1	Calculates the sha1 hash of a string.
similar_text	Calculates the similarity between two strings.
soundex	Calculates the soundex key of a string.
sprintf	Returns a formatted string.
sscanf	Parses input from a string according to a format.
str_ireplace	Case-insensitive version of str_replace().
str_pad	Pads a string to a certain length with another string.
str_repeat	Repeats a string.
str_replace	Replaces all occurrences of the search string with the replacement string.
str_rot13	Performs the rot13 transform on a string.
str_shuffle	Randomly shuffles a string.
str_split	Converts a string to an array.
str_word_count	Returns information about words used in a string.
strcasecmp	Binary-safe case-insensitive string comparison.
strchr	Alias of strstr().
strcmp	Binary-safe string comparison.
strcoll	Locale-based string comparison.
strcspn	Finds length of initial segment not matching mask.
strip_tags	Strips HTML and PHP tags from a string.

Table 6.18 PHP Functions (continued)

Function	What It Does
stripcslashes	Unquotes string quoted with addcslashes().
stripos	Finds position of first occurrence of a case-insensitive string.
stripslashes	Unquotes string quoted with addslashes().
stristr	Case-insensitive strstr().
strlen	Gets string length.
strnatcasecmp	Case-insensitive string comparisons using a "natural order" algorithm.
strnatcmp	String comparisons using a "natural order" algorithm.
strncasecmp	Binary-safe case-insensitive string comparison of the first n characters.
strncmp	Binary-safe string comparison of the first n characters.
strpbrk	Searches a string for any of a set of characters.
strpos	Finds position of first occurrence of a string.
strrchr	Finds the last occurrence of a character in a string.
strrev	Reverses a string.
strripos	Finds position of last occurrence of a case-insensitive string in a string.
strrpos	Finds position of last occurrence of a character in a string.
strspn	Finds length of initial segment matching mask.
strstr	Finds first occurrence of a string.
strtok	Tokenizes string.
strtolower	Makes a string lowercase.
strtoupper	Makes a string uppercase.
strtr	Translates certain characters.
substr_compare	Binary-safe optionally case-insensitive comparison of two strings from an offset, up to length characters.
substr_count	Counts the number of substring occurrences.
substr_replace	Replaces text within a portion of a string.

Table 6.18   PHP Functions (continued)

Function	What It Does
substr	Returns part of a string.
trim	Strips whitespace (or other characters) from the beginning and end of a string.
ucfirst	Makes a string's first character uppercase.
ucwords	Uppercases the first character of each word in a string.
vfprintf	Writes a formatted string to a stream.
vprintf	Outputs a formatted string.
vsprintf	Returns a formatted string.
wordwrap	Wraps a string to a given number of characters using a string break character.

6.4   Chapter Summary

6.4.1   What You Should Know

Now that you have finished this chapter you should be able to answer the following questions:

1. What is a string?

2. When do you use double quotes or single quotes?

3. What are escape characters?

4. Define whitespace.

5. What functions let you format strings?

6. How can you get the length of a string and count the characters in a substring?

7. What functions compare strings? Are strings case sensitive when they are compared?

8. What functions find similarities in strings?

9. How do you find a position in a string? What functions let you find a specified position in a string?

10. What is a substring? What functions extract parts of a string?

11. What is meant by "trimming" and "padding"?

12. What functions are used for searching and replacing within strings?

13. What are special characters?

14. What are HTML entities?

15. How do you force breaks in a string?

16. What functions deal with homophones?

6.4.2 What's Next?

Chapter 7, "Conditionals and Loops," covers PHP conditional statements (if/else/elseif, switch) and loops (while, for, foreach).

CHAPTER 6 LAB

1. Assign your e-mail address to a string. Use PHP string functions to get the user name and the domain name.

2. Create the following string:

```
$string = "   mary jones lives in santa cruz, california at 22 ocean drive."
```

   a. Find the number of characters in the string.
   b. Capitalize all the letters in the string.
   c. Now make all the characters lowercase.
   d. Use the substr() function to print Santa Cruz, California. The first letter in each word will be in uppercase.
   e. Use the substr() function to print Mary's street address.
   f. Trim out the whitespace at the beginning of the string.
   g. Find the index position of California.
   h. Replace Santa Cruz with Los Altos (case insensitive).
   i. Find the number of words in the string.

3. Use the `strcmp()` function to compare the following two strings, first comparing `$str1` and `$str2`, then comparing `$str2` and `$str1`. Explain the value that is returned from the function.

   ```
   $str1="Pear";
   $str2="Pearson";
   ```

   What value is returned from `strcmp()` if you compare `$str1` to `$str1`?

4. Write a script to generate a 4-letter random password with uppercase, lowercase, and numeric characters. Store the password as a variable and display it. Start with:

```
$str = "abcdefghijklmnopqrlsuvwxyzABCDEFGHIJKLMNOPQRSTUVWXYZ0123456789";
```

   Hint: Try `str_shuffle()`.

5. Create a scalar variable to contain a money amount of 155000000. Use the `number_format()` function to display the number as U.S. dollars with a comma separator and decimal point. Now display the same number in Euros as it would be formatted in Western Europe and place the Euro symbol before the number (&#8364).

chapter
7

Conditionals and Loops

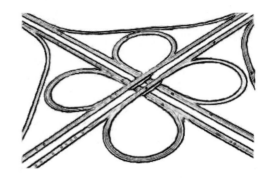

7.1 Control Structures, Blocks, and Compound Statements

Figure 7.1 shows a flow chart. A flow chart is defined as a pictorial representation of how to plan the stages of a project. It helps to visualize what decisions need to be made to accomplish a task. People control their lives by making decisions, and so do programs. In fact, acccording to computer science books, a good language allows you to control the flow of your program in three ways:

- Execute a sequence of statements.
- Based on a test, branch to an alternative sequence of statements.
- Repeat a sequence of statements until some condition is met.

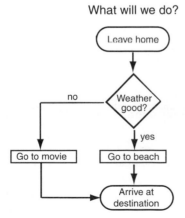

Figure 7.1 A flow chart.

Well, then, PHP must be a good language.

We've already used programs that execute a sequence of statements, one after another. Now we examine the branching and looping control structures that allow the flow of the program's control to change depending on some conditional expression.

The decision-making constructs (`if`, `if/else`, `if/else if`) contain a control expression that determines whether a block of statements will be executed. The looping constructs (`while`, `for`) allow the program to repetitively execute a statement block until some condition is satisfied.

A compound statement or *block* consists of a statement or a group of statements surrounded by curly braces. The block is syntactically equivalent to a single statement and usually follows an `if`, `else`, `while`, or `for` construct. This is a block:

```
{ statement; statement; statement }
```

7.1.1 Conditionals

Conditional constructs control the flow of a program. If a condition is true, the program will execute a block of statements and if the condition is false, flow will go to an alternate block of statements. Decision-making constructs (`if`, `else`, `switch`) contain a control expression that determines whether or not a block of expressions will be executed. If the condition after the `if` is met, the result is true, and the following block of statements is executed; otherwise, the result is false and the block is not executed.

FORMAT

```
if (condition){
    statements;
}
```

Example:
```
if ( $age > 21 ){
    print "Let's Party!";
}
```

The block of statements (or single statement) is enclosed in curly braces. Normally statements are executed sequentially. If there is only one statement after the conditional expression, the curly braces are optional.

if/else. "You better pay me now, or else . . ." Have you heard that kind of English statement before? PHP statements can be handled the same way with the `if/else` branching construct. This construct allows for a two-way decision. The `if` evaluates the first conditional expression in parentheses, and if the expression evaluates to true, the block after the opening curly braces is executed; otherwise, the block after the `else` is executed. The `else` is optional. See Example 7.1.

FORMAT

```
if (condition){
    statements1;
}
else{
    statements2;
}
```

Example:
```
if ( $x > $y ){
    print "$x is larger";
}
else{
    print "y is larger";
}
```

EXAMPLE 7.1

```
(The HTML Form)
<html><head><title>Your Fare</title></head>
    <body bgcolor="lightgreen">
    <font face="arial" size="+1">
    <form method="get" action="iffare.php">
    <p>How old are you?
    <input type="text" name="age" size=2>
    <p>
    <input type="submit" name="submit_age" value="Get Fare" >
    </form>
    </body>
</html>
---------------------------------------------------------------------
(The PHP Script)
<html><head><title>Your Fare</title></head>
<body bgcolor="lightgreen">
<font face="arial" size="+1">
<p>
<?php
extract($_REQUEST);
```
```
1       if ( ! isset ( $submit_age )){  // Simple conditional
            exit;
        }
    ?>
    <table border="1" cellpadding="10"><tr bgcolor="yellow">
    <?php
2       if ( $age >= 55 ){
3           $price = 8.25;
4           print "<td><b>You pay \$$price, the senior fare!</td>";
5       }
```

EXAMPLE 7.1 (CONTINUED)

```
6        else{
7            $price = 10.00;
8            print "<td><b>You pay \$$price regular adult fare.</td>";
         }
    ?>
```

EXPLANATION

1   If the variable has not been set, the program will exit.

2–4 If the value of the variable `$age` is greater than or equal to `55`, lines 3 and 4 are executed. See Figures 7.2 and 7.3.

5   This closing curly brace closes the block of statements following the `if` expression. Because there is only one statement in the block, the curly braces are not required.

6–8 The `else` statements, lines 7 and 8, are executed if the expression in line 2 is false.

Figure 7.2 The HTML form from Example 7.1.

Figure 7.3 After the user presses the "Get Fare" button to submit the form. Output of the PHP script from Example 7.1.

if/elseif.   If you've got $1, we can go to the Dollar Store, else if you've got $10, we could get a couple of movies, else if you've got $20 we could buy a CD . . . or else forget it!" PHP provides yet another form of branching, the `if/elseif` construct. This construct provides a multiway decision structure.

```
if (condition) {
    statements1;
}
elseif (condition)  {
    statements2;
}
elseif (condition)  {
    statements3;
}
else{
    statements4;
        }
```

If the first conditional expression following the `if` keyword is true, the statement or block of statements following the expression are executed and control starts after the `else` block. Otherwise, if the conditional expression following the `if` keyword is false, control branches to the first `elseif` and the expression following it is evaluated. If that expression is true, the statement or block of statements following it are executed, and if false, the next `elseif` is tested. All `else ifs` are tested and if none of their expressions are true, control goes to the `else` statement. Although the `else` is not required, it normally serves as a default action if all previous conditions were false. See Example 7.2 for `if/elseif` construct.

EXAMPLE 7.2

```
    (The HTML Form)
    <html>
    <head><title>Your Movie Fare</title></head>
    <body bgcolor="azure">
1   <form method="get" action="iffare2.php">
        <p>How old are you?<br />
2       <input type="text" name="age" size=3 />
        <p>
3       <input type="submit" name="submit_fare" value="Get Fare" />
    </form>
    </body>
    </html>
```

EXAMPLE 7.2 (CONTINUED)

```
     (The PHP Script)
     <html><head><title>Your Fare</title></head>
     <body bgcolor="chartreuse">
     <font face="arial" size="+1">

4    <?php
         extract($_REQUEST);  // Get form input data
5        if ( ! isset ($submit_fare) || $age == "" ){
             print "You must enter your age..<br />";
             exit;
         }
     ?>
     <table border="1" cellpadding="10">
         <tr bgcolor="azure">
     <?php
6        if ($age > 0 && $age < 13) {
             $price = 5.00;
             print "<td><b>You pay \$$price, the child's fare!</td>";
         }
7        elseif ($age >= 13 && $age < 55 ){
             $price = 8.25;
             print "<td><b>You pay \$$price regular adult fare.</td>";
         }
8        elseif ( $age >= 55 && $age <= 120){
             $price = 10.00;
             print "<td><b>You pay \$$price, the senior fare.</td>";
         }
9        else {
             print "<td><b>You are not a human!</td>";
         }
10   ?>
     </tr>
     </table>
     </font>
     </body>
     </html>
```

EXPLANATION

1 The HTML form starts here. The `action` attribute is assigned the name of the PHP script that will be executed after the form is submitted.
2 The text box is named `"age"` and will be sized to hold three characters.
3 The HTML submit input type is given a name, `submit_fare`, that will be used in the following PHP script.
4 The opening PHP tag tells PHP to start processing.

EXPLANATION (CONTINUED)

5   Now we are looking at the PHP instructions. If the user pressed the submit but-
    ton, this file will execute. PHP will store the names of the input devices in vari-
    ables, `$age` and `$submit_fare`. This conditional expression tests to see if those
    variables were set. If they weren't set, then the form was either not submitted or
    the user left it empty, or both.

6   If is true that the user's age is greater than 0 and also less than 13, the block that
    follows the expression will be executed. As soon as the block is executed, the pro-
    gram will start execution on line 10. If the expression evaluates to false, then the
    program will go to line 7.

7   If the condition on line 6 is false, the program checks the conditional expression
    after the `elseif`, and if it is true (i.e., the age is greater than or equal to 13 and
    less than 55), the block of statements will be executed. Otherwise, the program
    will go to line 8.

8   If the conditional test in line 7 is false, this `elseif` condition will be checked, and
    if true, the block of statements following it will be executed. If false, the block of
    statements after the `else` on line 9 are executed.

9   If none of the preceding conditions are met, control goes to the `else` block, often
    called the default condition, and the statements in its block are executed.

Figure 7.4   The HTML form from Example 7.2.

Figure 7.5   The PHP output from Example 7.2.

The switch Statement. The `switch` statement is an alternative to the `if/elseif` conditional construct, commonly called a a *case statement*, and often makes the program more readable when handling multiple options.

FORMAT

```
switch (expression){
    case label :
        statement(s);
        break;
    case label :
        statement(s);
        break;
        ...
    default : statement;
}
```

Example:
```
switch ($color){
    case "red":
        print "Hot!";
        break;
    case "blue":
        print "Cold.";
        break;
    default:
        print "Not a good choice.";
        break;
}
```

The value of the `switch` expression is matched against the expressions, called *labels*, following the `case` keyword. The `case` labels are constants, either string or numeric. Each label is terminated with a colon. The default label is optional, but its action is taken if none of the other cases match the `switch` expression. After a match is found, the statements after the matched label are executed for that case. If none of the cases are matched, the control drops to the `default` case. The default is optional. If a `break` statement is omitted, all statements below the matched label are executed until either a `break` is reached or the entire `switch` block exits.

EXAMPLE 7.3

```
(The HTML File)
<html>
<head>
<title>Pick a Font Color</title>
</head>
<body bgcolor="9BCD93">
<font face="arial" >
<b>
<form method="get" action="switch.php">
<br />Choose a font color:
    <br /><input type="radio" name="color" value="red"  /> red
    <br /><input type="radio" name="color" value="blue"/> blue
    <br /><input type="radio" name="color" value="purple" /> purple
    <br /><input type="radio" name="color" value="green" /> green
    <p>
    <input type="submit" name="submit_color" value="Submit color" />
</form>
</b>
</body>
</html>
```

```
(The PHP Script)
<html>
<html><head><title>Font Color</title></head>
<body bgcolor-"lightgreen">
<font face="arial" size="+1">
<p>
```
```
1    <?php
         extract($_REQUEST);
2        if ( ! isset ($submit_color)) { // check that variables were set
             exit;
         }
     ?>
     <table border="2" cellpadding="10">
     <tr bgcolor="white">
3    <?php
4        switch ( $color ) {
5        case "red":
             print "<td><b><font color=".$color.">Font is red</td>";
6            break;
7        case "blue":
             print "<td><b><font color=".$color.">Font is blue</td>";
             break;
         case "purple":
             print "<td><b><font color=".$color.">Font is purple</td>";
             break;
         case "green":
             print "<td><b><font color=".$color.">Font is green</td>";
             break;
```

EXAMPLE 7.3 (CONTINUED)

```
8        default:
            print "<td><b><font color=".'black'.">Font is black</td>";
            break;
9        }
     ?>
     </tr>
     </table>
     </font>
     </body>
     </html>
```

EXPLANATION

1   The PHP script starts here.
2   If $submit_color has not been set, then the form was not submitted.
3   The PHP program starts here.
4   In the switch expression, the value of $color is matched against the values of
    each of the following case labels. (PHP names the variable, $color, by the same
    name assigned to the radio button and assigns to the variable the value that was
    selected by the user when he or she clicked the button. If the user clicked red,
    then $color will evaluate to red.) See Figures 7.6 and 7.7.
5   The first case that is tested is "red". If the user clicked the "red" radio button,
    then the font color of the text will be assigned red and the message "Font is red"
    will be displayed in the table cell.
6   The break statement causes program control to continue after line 9. Without it,
    the program would continue executing statements into the next case, "blue",
    and continue doing so until a break is reached or the switch ends, and we don't
    want that.
7   The first case that is tested is "red". If the user picked blue as his or her choice,
    then the PHP interpreter will skip the "red" case and test the next one, which is
    "blue". Because that value is matched successfully against the value of the color
    variable, the font is displayed in blue and the message "Font is blue" will appear
    in the table cell.
       The break statement sends control of the program to line 9.
       If "red" and "blue" are not matched successfully against the value of the color
    variable, then "purple" is tested, and if there is a match, then its block of state-
    ments is executed.
       The break statement sends control of the program to line 9.
       If "red", "blue", or "purple" are not matched successfully against the value
    of the color variable, then "green" is tested, and if there is a match, its block of
    statements is executed.
       The break statement sends control of the program to line 9.

8 The `default` statement block is executed if none of the preceding cases is matched.

This final `default` statement is not necessary, but is good practice in case you should decide to replace the `default` with an additional `case` label later on.

9 The final curly brace ends the `switch` statement block.

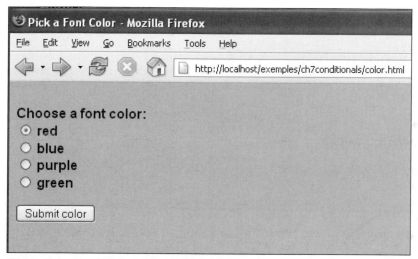

Figure 7.6 The HTML form from Example 7.3.

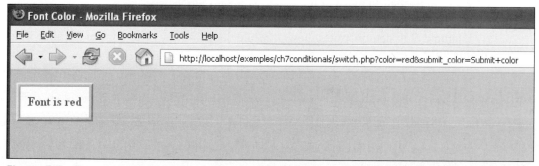

Figure 7.7 The user selected the button labeled "red". The PHP output from Example 7.3.

7.2 Loops

Loops are used to execute a segment of code repeatedly until some condition is met. Suppose you have a program that prints 10, 9, 8, . . . down to 1 and then prints "Blast off!". To get from 10 to 1, you could write 10 print statements or you could write one if you use a loop.

PHP's basic looping constructs are the following:

- `while`
- `for`
- `foreach`
- `do/while`

Loops work differently than `if` statements. A block of statements after an `if` are executed once, whereas a block of statements after a loop expression can be executed repeatedly.

7.2.1 The while Loop

The `while` statement keeps executing its statement block as long as the expression after the `while` evaluates to true; that is, nonnull, nonzero, nonfalse. If the `while` expression evaluates to true, the block of statements that follow are executed. After the last statement in the block is executed, the program jumps back to the `while` expression again and checks if the expression is still true. If the condition never changes and is true, the loop will iterate forever (infinite loop). The programmer determines how many times he or she wants the loop to iterate by changing the test condition or by breaking out of the loop with a `break` statement. If the condition is false, control goes to the statement right after the closing curly brace of the loop's statement block.

The `break` and `continue` functions are used for loop control.

Example 7.4 demonstrates how a while loop works. The output is shown in Figure 7.8.

FORMAT

```
while (condition) {
    statements;
    increment/decrement counter;
}
```

EXAMPLE 7.4

```
        <html>
        <head>
        <title>Looping Constructs</title>
        </head>
        <body>
        <h3>While Loop</h3>
        <font face=arial size='+1'>

1   <?php
2      $i=10;                   // Initialize loop counter
3      while ($i > 0 ){         // Test the condition
4         echo "$i  ";
5         $i--;                 // Decrement the counter
6      }                        // End of loop block

7   ?>
        <font size="+3" color="red">
8   ...Blast Off!
        </font>
        </body></html>
```

EXPLANATION

1   The PHP program starts here.
2   The variable `$i` is initialized to `10`.
3   The expression after the `while` is tested. If `$i` is greater than 0, the block in curly braces is entered and its statements are executed. If the expression evaluates to false (i.e., `$i` is not greater than 0), the loop block exits and control goes to line 8.
4   The value of `$i` is displayed in the browser window.
5   The value of `$i` is decremented by 1. This step is crucial because if the value of `$i` never changes, the loop will never end.
6   This curly brace marks the end of the `while` loop's block of statements. Program control will follow the arrow in the example, as long as the `while` expression tests true.
7   The PHP program ends here.
8   This HTML text is displayed after the loop exits.

Figure 7.8
The `while` loop. Output from Example 7.4.

7.2.2   The do/while Loop

The `do/while` statement executes a block of statements repeatedly until a condition becomes false. Due to its structure, this loop necessarily executes the statements in the body of the loop at least once before testing its expression, which is found at the bottom of the block. Example 7.5 demonstrates how the `do/while` loop works. The output is shown in Figure 7.9.

FORMAT

```
do
    { statements;}
while (condition);
```

EXAMPLE 7.5

```
      <html>
      <head>
      <title>Looping Constructs</title>
      <body bgcolor='f0f8ff'>
      <h3>Do... While Loop</h3>
      <font face='arial' size='+1'>
      <?php
1         $i=10;
2         do{
3             echo "$i ";
4             $i--;
5         }while ( $i > 0 );
      ?>
      </body>
      </html>
```

EXPLANATION

1   The variable `$i` is initialized to `10`.
2   The `do` block is entered. This block of statements will be executed before the `while` expression is tested. Even if the `while` expression proves to be false, this block will be executed the first time around.
3   The value of `$i` is displayed in the browser window. See Figure 7.9.
4   The value of `$i` is decremented by 1.
5   Now, the `while` expression is tested to see if it evaluates to true; that is, if `$i` is greater than 0. If so control goes back to line 2 and the block is reentered.

Figure 7.9
The do/while loop.

7.2.3 The for Loop

The for loop functions essentially just like the while loop. It is just more compact. The for loop consists of the for keyword followed by three expressions separated by semicolons and enclosed within parentheses. Any or all of the expressions can be omitted, but the two semicolons cannot. The first expression is used to set the initial value of variables and is executed just once, the second expression is used to test whether the loop should continue or stop, and the third expression updates the loop variables, i.e., it increments or decrements a counter that will usually determine how many times the loop is repeated.

The for loop is demonstrated in Example 7.6. The output is displayed in Figure 7.10.

FORMAT

```
for(Expression1;Expression2;Expression3)
    {statement(s);}
for (initialize; test; increment/decrement)
    {statement(s);}
```

This format is equivalent to the following while statement:

```
Expression1;
while( Expression2 )
    { Block; Expression3};
```

EXAMPLE 7.6

```
       <html>
       <head>
       <title>Looping Constructs</title>
       <body bgcolor="lightblue">
       <h3>For Loop</h3>
       <font face='arial' size='+1'>
       <?php

1          for( $i = 0; $i < 10; $i++ ){

2              echo "$i  ";
3          }
       ?>
       </head>
       <body></body>
       </html>
```

EXPLANATION

1   The `for` loop is entered. The expression starts with step ❶, the initialization of the variable `i` to zero. This is the only time this step is executed. The second expression, step ❷, tests to see if `$i` is less than 10, and if it is, the statements after the opening curly brace are executed, step ❸. When all statements in the block have been executed and the closing curly brace is reached, control goes back into the `for` expression to the last expression of the three, step ❹. `$i` is now incremented by 1 and the expression in step ❷ is retested, which now becomes step ❺. If it tests false, the loop ends. If true, the block of statements is entered and executed.

2   The value of `$i` is displayed in the browser window.

3   The closing curly brace marks the end of the `for` loop.

Figure 7.10   The `for` loop.

The for Loop and Repetitive Form Fields.   The HTML form in Example 7.7 consists of a set of five check boxes with repetitive names. The only part of the name that differs is the number value fixed to the end of the name. By using a `for` loop and variable variables[1], you can dynamically create the names of the fields and access their respective values.

EXAMPLE 7.7

```
(The HTML Form)
<html><head><title>Multiple Choice</title></head>
<body bgcolor="aqua">
<form action="checkbox2.php" method="post">
<b>Choose a vacation spot:</b>
    <br />
    <input type="checkbox" name="place1" value="New York">New York
    <br />
    <input type="checkbox" name="place2" value="Chicago">Chicago
    <br />
```

---

1. Variable variables are discussed in Chapter 4, "The Building Blocks."

EXAMPLE 7.7 (CONTINUED)

```
        <input type="checkbox" name="place3" value="London">London
        <br />
        <input type="checkbox" name="place4" value="Tokyo">Tokyo
        <br />
        <input type="checkbox" name="place5" value="San Francisco"
           Checked>San Francisco
        <p>
        <input type="submit" value="submit">
        <input type="reset" value="clear">
        </p>
    </form>
    </body>
    </html>
```

```
    (The PHP Script)
    <html><head><title><For Loop and Variable Variables>
    </title></head>
    <body bgcolor="000099">
    <font face="arial" size="+1">
    <table border="1" bordercolor="white" cellpadding="3">
    <tr>
        <td bgcolor="00ff66" align="center">Checkbox Item</td>
        <td bgcolor="00ff66" align="center">Checked Values</td>
    </tr>

    <?php
    extract($_REQUEST);
1       for( $i=1; $i <= 5; $i++){
2           $temp = "place$i";
3           echo "<tr><td bgcolor='00ff99'>$temp</td>";
4           echo "<td bgcolor='00ffcc'>${$temp}</td></tr>";
        }
    ?>
    </table>
    </font>
    </body>
    </html>
```

EXPLANATION

1   After extracting the user input sent in the form shown in Figure 7.11, the `for` loop is executed for each one of the five check box items that may have been selected.

2   The variable, `$temp`, is assigned the string `"place$i"` the first time in the loop because `$i` starts at 1.

3   The value of `$temp` is inserted into a table cell.

4   The variable $temp (i.e., "place$i") is now evaluated as a "variable variable," where place1 becomes $place 1, the value that was checked for that check box. If the user didn't check the box, the value is null. The value of the selected check box is inserted into a table cell to the right of its name. The for loop executes five times, incrementing the value of $i each time it goes through the loop, resulting in the output shown in Figure 7.12.

Figure 7.11   The HTML form from Example 7.7 with checked boxes.

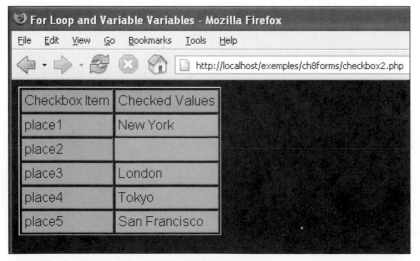

Figure 7.12   Output from the PHP program.

7.2.4 The foreach Loop

The `foreach` loop is designed to work with arrays and works only with arrays. Arrays are covered in Chapter 8, "Arrays," but because we are talking about looping constructs, the `foreach` loop should be mentioned here.

An array is a list of items, like an array of numbers or strings. The loop expression consists of the array name, followed by the `as` keyword, and a user-defined variable that will hold each successive value of the array as the loop iterates. The `foreach` loop, as the name implies, works on each element of the array, in turn, moving from left to right, until all of the elements of the array have been processed. The loop expression is followed by a block of statements that will be executed for each item in the expression.

FORMAT

```
$array_name=array( item1, item2, item3, ...);
foreach ($array_name as $value){
    do-something with the element's value;
}
```

Example:
```
$suit=array("diamond", "spade", "club", "heart");   // An array
foreach ( $suit as $card_type){
    echo $card_type . "<br />";        // displays: diamond
                                                      spade
                                                      club
                                                      heart

}
```

7.2.5 Loop Control with break and continue

The control statements, `break` and `continue`, are used to either break out of a loop early or return to the testing condition early; that is, before reaching the closing curly brace of the block following the looping construct (see Table 7.1).

Example 7.8 demonstrates the `break` control statement used to exit a loop based on some condition. The output is shown in Figure 7.13.

Table 7.1 The break and continue Statements

Statement	What It Does
break	Exits the for, foreach, while, do/while loop to the next statement after the closing curly brace. break accepts an optional numeric argument that tells it how many nested enclosing structures are to be broken out of.

Table 7.1   The `break` and `continue` Statements (continued)

Statement	What It Does
continue	Sends loop control directly to the top of the loop and reevaluates the loop condition. If the condition is true, enter the loop block. `continue` accepts an optional numeric argument that tells it how many levels of enclosing loops it should skip to the end of.

EXAMPLE 7.8

```
<html><head><title>Breaking out of Loops</title></head>
<body bgcolor="indigo">
<p>
<table border="1" bordercolor="white" cellpadding="3">
<bgcolor='thistle'>
<caption><font color="white">Freezing Cold!</font></caption>
<tr><th>Celsius</th><th>Farenheit</th><tr>

<?php
1      $C=-10;
2      while($C < 100){
3          $F = (  $C * 1.8) + 32;
4          print "<tr><td><b>$C</td><td><b>$F</td>";
5           if ( $F == 32 ){    //Break out of loop
6              break;
           }
7          $C+=2;
8      }
9   ?>

</tr>
</table>
</body>
</html>
```

EXPLANATION

1   The variable, `$C`, is initialized with a value of –10.
2   The `while` loop expression is tested. Is the value of `$C` less than 100? If so, enter the loop block on line 3.
3   This formula converts Celsius to Farenheit.
4   The value of `$F` is printed into an HTML table cell.
5   If the value of the Farenheit temperature is equal to 32, control goes to line 6.
6   The `break` statement causes the program to stop executing statements in the block and jump out to after line 9.
7   The variable `$C` is incremented by 2 each time through the loop.
8   This marks the end of the loop block. Until the looping condition on line 1 is false or a `break` statement is executed, the program will continue to loop.

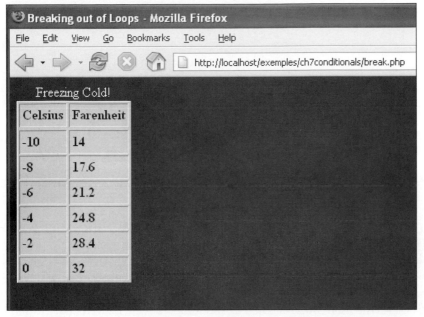

Figure 7.13   Loop control. Output from Example 7.8.

Nested Loops.   A loop within a loop is a nested loop. A common use for nested loops is to display data in rows and columns where one loop handles the rows and the other handles the columns. The outside loop is initialized and tested; the inside loop then iterates completely through all of its cycles; and the outside loop starts again where it left off. The inside loop moves faster than the outside loop. Loops can be nested as deeply as you wish, but there are times when it is necessary to terminate the loop due to some condition.

Example 7.9 demonstrates a loop nested within a loop. The output is displayed in Figure 7.14.

EXAMPLE 7.9

```
        <html><head><title>Looping</title></head>
        <body bgcolor="lightgreen">
        <font face="arial" size="+1">
        <div align="center">
        <b>

        <?php
1          $character = "**";
2          echo "*";
3              for ($row=0; $row < 10; $row++){
4                  for ($col=0; $col < $row; $col++){
                        echo $character;
                }
```

EXAMPLE   7.9 (CONTINUED)

```
5              echo "<br />";
           }
       echo "|   |<br />";
    ?>

    <font color='red'>Merry Christmas!</font></font><br />
    </div>
    </body>
    </html>
```

EXPLANATION

1   The variable, character, is assigned a string "**".
2   A single * is printed.
3   The outer for loop is entered. The variable $row is initialized to 0. If the value of row is less than 10, the loop block (in curly braces) is entered; that is, go to line 4.
4   The inner for loop is entered. The varibale $col is initialized to 0. If the value of $col is less than the value of $row, the loop block is entered and an * is printed. Next the value of $col will be incremented by 1, tested, and if still less than the value of $row, the loop block is entered, and another ** displayed. When this loop has completed, a row of * symbols will be displayed, and the statements in the outer loop will start up again.
5   When the inner loop has completed looping, this line is executed producing a break in the rows.

Figure 7.14   Nested loops: Rows and columns. Output from Example 7.9.

Normally, if you use loop-control statements such as `break` and `continue`, the control is directed to the innermost loop. There are times when it might be necessary to switch control to some outer loop. To do this you have an optional second argument for `break` and `continue` to allow you choose what loop you to break (or continue) from. This argument represents the loop where control will go; for example, break 2 would break you out of the current loop, loop 1, and the next outer loop, loop 2.

EXAMPLE   7.10

```
(A Demo Script)
    <?php
1   while(1){
2       < Program continues here >
3       while(1){
4           if ( <expression is true> ) { break 2;}
            < Program continues here >
5           while(1){
6               if ( <expression is true> ){ continue 3;}
                <Program continues here>
            }
        }
    }
7   print "Out of all loops.<br />";
    ?>
```

7.3   Chapter Summary

7.3.1   What You Should Know

Now that you have finished this chapter you should be able to answer the following questions:

1. What is a block? How are statements nested in blocks?

2. How do control structures, such as `if`, `else`, and `elseif`, work?

3. How do you use a `switch` statement?

4. How do you use `while`, `do/while`, `for`, and `foreach` loops?

5. What causes an infinite loop?

6. How do you control the `break` and `continue` loops?

7. How do you nest loops?

7.3.2 What's Next?

In Chapter 8, "Arrays," you will learn about numeric and associative arrays, and the many useful built-in functions available to manipulate them. You will also learn about the superglobal built-in arrays and how they are used.

CHAPTER 7 LAB

1. Conditional statements with `if/else`.

   a. Write an HTML form that asks a user's age. If he is not at least 21, tell him he's too young to drink, and if he's 21 or older, tell him he's too old to drink and drive.

   b. Write an HTML form that prompts the user for his or her grade on three different tests. Grades range from 0 to 100.
      Write a PHP program that tests that the user typed in a numeric grade (see `is_numeric()`). Average the three grades using the following scale. Use the `if/elseif` conditional construct to determine the student's letter grade.

      90–100 = A
      80–89 = B
      70–79 = C
      60–69 = D
      0–59 = F

      Display the average and the letter grade in the browser. If the student got an A, print the output using an HTML heading level 1 <H1>. If he or she got a B, do the same, but decrease the heading level to <H2> and continue this for each lower grade. If he or she received an F score, send a message such as, "You need to concentrate!" in a red <H5> tag.

   c. Create a form that asks a user to select a destination from a list of radio buttons. The choices are: San Francisco, New York, London, Paris, Honolulu, and Tokyo.
      Write a PHP script that uses a switch statement to evaluate each of the cities, and based on the city selected by the user, sends back a message such as, "Welcome to San Francisco. Be sure to bring your heart and a jacket!" or "Bonjour, let's take a stroll on the left bank!".

d. Create the following form that uses radio buttons:

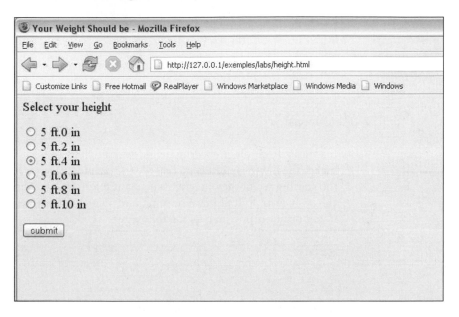

Create a PHP script that will use case statements to produce output based on the radio button selected. Select any image you like. The PHP output should be as follows:

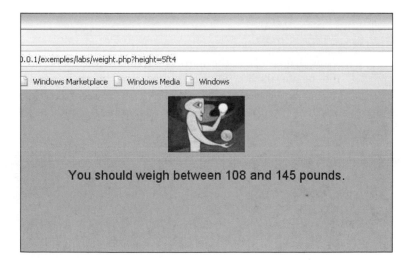

Use the following chart to create your conditions based on the button the user selected:

Height	Healthy Weight Range
5 ft. 0 in.	95–128
5 ft. 2 in.	101–136
5 ft. 4 in.	108–145
5 ft. 6 in.	115–154
5 ft. 8 in.	122–164
5 ft. 10 in.	129–174

2. Using loops.

   a. It appears from the preceding height/weight chart that for every additional 2 inches the lower weight is increased by 7 pounds. Write a loop that will print the starting weight for heights starting at 6 ft. 0 in. all the way to 6 ft. 10 in. (i.e., 6 ft. 0 in., 6 ft. 2 in., 6 ft. 4 in., and so on). Each time through the loop it will print output such as the following:

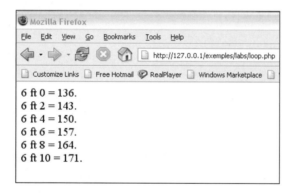

   b. Now that you have the starting weights, create an HTML table that includes the height, the starting weight, and the ending weight. Let's just say that at 6 ft. 0 in. the ending weight is 184, and for every 2 additional inches, add 10 (so that at 6 ft. 2 in., the ending weight is 194, and so on).

chapter

8

Arrays

8.1 What Is an Array?

An array of products, an array of pills, an array of shoes, an array of problems . . . When we speak of an array of things, we think of not just one, but a list or a lineup of more than one thing. PHP thinks the same way about data.

A variable that stores one value is called a *scalar* variable, whereas an *array* is a variable that can store a collection of scalars, such as an array of numbers, an array of strings, an array of images, colors, and so on (see Figure 8.1). If you want to define one number you would store it in a simple scalar variable, but if you want to store a whole list of numbers, it would be more practical to use an array, and give the array a name to represent all of the numbers. Otherwise, you would have to create individual scalars for each number. It would be hard to come up with individual names for, let's say, 100 numbers, or even for 10 numbers, but with an array you can use one name to reference all of them.

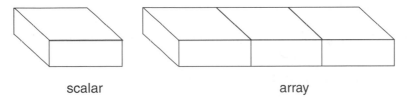

scalar   array

Figure 8.1 A scalar variable holds one value, and an array holds many scalars.

An array is described in the PHP manual as "an ordered map" where a map is a type that maps values to keys. Simply stated, an array is collection of key–value pairs. The key, called an index, can be a number or a string, or a combination of both, used to identify a corresponding value in the array. The value in an array is called an element and can be of any data type, even mixed types.

Although PHP internally treats both numeric and associative arrays in the same way, there are two ways to visualize an array: an array indexed by a number and an array indexed by a string (see Figure 8.2). If the key is a number, it represents the position of the value (or element) in the array (usually starting at position 0 and incrementing by 1 for each successive value). If the key is a string, the string is associated with a corresponding value. Arrays indexed by numbers are called numeric arrays and those indexed by strings are called associative arrays.

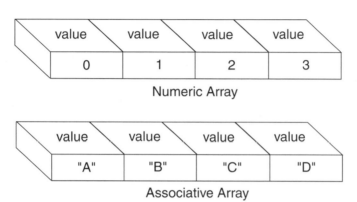

Figure 8.2 A numeric array indexed by number, and an associative array indexed by string.

When you access elements with an array, PHP keeps track of the current position with an internal pointer, and provides built-in functions to move the array pointer; for example, if you want to go to the end of the array you can use the end() function and if you want to go back to the beginning of the array, you can use the reset() function.

Let's look at Example 8.1, which shows a numeric array, an array indexed by number.

EXAMPLE 8.1

```
    <html>
    <head><title>Array of Products</title></head>
    <body bgcolor="lightgreen">
    <?php
1       $products=array('floral talc','body mist',
                        'perfumed powder','bath gel');
        echo "<b>\$products is $products.<br />\n";
2       echo "\$products[0] is $products[0].<br />\n";
        echo "\$products[1] is $products[1].<br />\n";
        echo "\$products[2] is $products[2].<br />\n";
        echo "\$products[3] is $products[3].<br />\n";
    ?>
```

EXAMPLE   8.1 (CONTINUED)

```
            <br /><em>Let's add another element to the array.</em><br />
            $products[]='gentle soap';<br />
            <?php
3              $products[]='gentle soap';
4              echo "\$products[4] is $products[4].<br />\n";
            ?>
            </body>
            </html>
```

EXPLANATION

1   The numeric array called $products is defined with a string of four values, called elements.
2   The array is indexed by numbers, starting at 0. The value of the first element of the array, $products[0], is 'floral talc'.
3   A new element is added to the end of the array. PHP figures out the value of the new index by adding 1 to the index value of the last element in the original array. The new element is $products[4], which is assigned the value 'gentle soap'.
4   The new array element is displayed in the browser (see Figure 8.3).

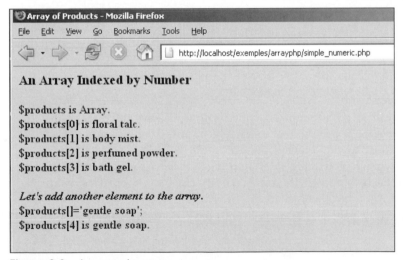

Figure 8.3   A numeric array.

Now let's look at Example 8.2, which shows an associative array, an array indexed by a string.

EXAMPLE 8.2

```
       <html>
       <head><title>Array of Key/Value Pairs</title></head>
       <body bgcolor="lavender">
       <h3>An Array Indexed by String</h3>
       <b>
       <?php
1          $show=array( 'Title'=>'Aga-Boom',
                          'Author'=> 'Dmitri Bogatirev',
                          'Genre'=> 'Physical comedy',
                          );
2          echo "\$show is $show.<br />\n";
       ?>

3          $show['Title'] is <?=$show['Title']?>.<br />
           $show['Author'] is <?=$show['Author']?>.<br />
           $show['Genre'] is <?=$show['Genre']?>.<br />

           <br /><em>Let's add another element to the array.</em><br />
           $show['Theater']='Alcazar';<br />

       <?php
4          $show['Theater'] = "Alcazar";
           echo $show['Theater']. "<br />\n";
       ?>
       </b>
       </body>
       </html>
```

EXPLANATION

1   An associative array called $show is defined with three keys and three values.
2   The value of $show displays only the data type of this variable. It is an array. (Use
    print_r() to display the contents of the array.)
3   This HTML segment contains a PHP short tag and the associative array with its
    index, a key. Each value associated with the key enclosed in brackets will be ex-
    tracted and printed. See Figure 8.4.
4   A new key–value pair is created for the $show associative array, the key is
    'Theater' and the value associated with it, "Alcazar".

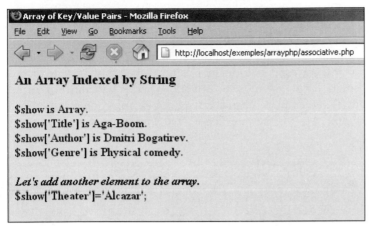

Figure 8.4 An associative array. Output from Example 8.2.

8.1.1 Creating and Naming an Array

Like PHP scalar variables, the array's name starts with a dollar sign and the first character is a letter or a number, followed by any number of letters, numbers, and/or an underscore. Scalar variables and array variables cannot have the same name. If you have a variable called $menu and then create an array called $menu, the first $menu will be overwritten. Names are case sensitive; for example, $foods is not the same as $Foods. Table 8.1 describes a number of PHP functions that can be used to create an array. The most common of them is the array() function.

Table 8.1 Functions to Create an Array

Function	What It Does
array()	Creates an array
array_combine()	Creates an array by using one array for keys and another for its values
array_fill()	Fills an array with values
array_pad()	Pads an array to the specified length with a value
compact()	Creates array containing variables and their values
range()	Creates an array containing a range of elements

The array() Function.   One way to create a PHP array is with a special built-in function called `array()`.[1] The arguments to the `array()` function are the key–value pairs
that will make up the elements of the array variable. If you do not specify a key, PHP
automatically assigns it a number, starting at 0 and incrementing by 1 for each successive value. The number 0 will correspond to the first value in the array, 1 to the second
value in the array, and so on. If you assign your own key, whether a number or string,
the key is separated from its value by two characters, `=>`; for example, `"Name"=>"Tom"`,
where `"Name"` is the key, and `"Tom"` is the value associated with it.

FORMAT

```
$array_name = array(value1, value2, value3 ...);
$array_name = array(key=>value, key=>value, ...);
```

Example:
(Array indexed by number, starting at 0, no key specified, the default)
```
$colors = array('red', 'green', 'blue');
```

(Array indexed by number, key specified)
```
$colors = array(1 => 'red', 2 => 'green', 3 => 'blue');
```

(Array indexed by string)
```
                 key          value          key          value
$book = array ('Title' => 'War and Peace', 'Author' => 'Leo Tolstoy');
```

The Array Identifier ().   Another way to create PHP arrays is with the array identifier,
`[]`. If you assign a value to an array and do not include an index between the square
brackets, PHP automatically creates a numeric array, with an index starting at 0, and
increments the index for each value added to the array. If you provide a starting index
value or ending index value, PHP creates an array consisting of the named elements and
does not attempt to fill the array with the missing elements; for example, `$names[4] =
"Tommy"` creates a one-element array where the size of the array is 1, and indexes 0, 1,
2, and 3 do not exist.

---

1. A constructor is a special kind of function that allows you to create an object, in this case an array object.

FORMAT

```
$array_name[] = value1;
$array_name[] = value2;
```

Example:
```
$colors[] = "red";     // Will become $colors[0]
$colors[] = "green";   // Will become $colors[1]
$colors[] = "blue";    // Will become $colors[2]
```

Example:
```
// A one-element array, starting at index 10
$names[10] = "Tommy";
// A two-element array
$cars[0]="Ford"; $cars[5]="Honda";
// A two-element array, first index is 0
$cars[ ] = "Ford"; $cars[5]="Honda";
// A two-element array, second index is 6
$cars[5]="Ford"; $cars[ ] = "Honda";
// A two-element array, second index is 0
$cars[-1]="Ford"; $cars[ ] = "Honda";
```

The range() Function.   Starting from a low value and going to a high value, the range() function creates an array of consecutive integer or character values. It takes up to three arguments: a starting value, an ending value, and an increment value. If only two arguments are given, the increment value defaults to 1.

Example 8.3 demonstrates the range() function. The output is shown in Figure 8.5.

FORMAT

```
array range ( mixed low, mixed high [, number step] )
```

Example:
```
range(1,10);       // Returns 1,2,3,4,5,6,7,8,9,10
range(1,10,2);     // Returns 1,3,5,7,9
range(15,0, -5);   // Returns 15,10,5,0
range(10,1);       // Returns 10,9,8,7,6,5,4,3,2,1
range(-2,-8);      // Returns -2,-3,-4,-5,-6,-7,-8
range('a','c');    // a,b,c
```

EXAMPLE 8.3

```
<html>
<head><title>Setting a Range of Values</title></head>
<body bgcolor="azure">
<font face="arial" size='+1'>
<?php
    echo "Range of numbers incrementing by 1<br />";
1   $years=range(2000, 2010);
2   foreach( $years as $value){
        echo "$value ";
    }
    echo "<hr>";
    echo "Range of numbers incrementing by 10<br />";
3   $decades=range(2000,2050,10);
4   foreach( $decades as $value){
        echo "$value ";
    }
    echo "<hr>";
    echo "Range of numbers decrementing by 5<br />";
5   $decades=range(2000,1980,-5);
6   foreach( $decades as $value){
        echo "$value ";
    }
    echo "<hr>";
    echo "Range of characters incrementing by 1(ASCII value)<br />";
7   $alpha=range('A', 'Z');
8   foreach( $alpha as $value){
        echo "$value ";
    }
?>
</font></body></html>
```

EXPLANATION

1   The array, $years, is assigned a range of numbers starting at 2000 and increment-
    ing by 1 until the end of the range, 2010, is reached.
2   The foreach loop iterates through each element in the $years array displaying
    its value, one number at a time.
3   The array, $decades, is assigned a range of values starting at 2000, incrementing
    in steps of 10, up to and including 2050.
4   The foreach loop iterates through each element in the $decades array displaying
    its value, one number at a time, in increments of 10.
5   The array, $decades, is assigned a range of values, starting at 2000, in decremental
    steps of 5, ending at 1980.
7   The array, $alpha, is assigned a range of uppercase letters, 'A', 'B', 'C' ... 'Z'.
8   The foreach loop iterates through each element in the array displaying its value,
    one letter at a time. Each letter corresponds to its ASCII value.

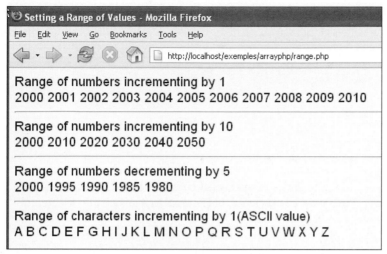

Figure 8.5   The `range()` function. Output from Example 8.3.

The array_fill() Function.   PHP provides the `array_fill()` function to declare and populate an array at the same time. (Populating an array means giving it values.) The function takes three arguments: the starting index value, the number of elements to put into the array (must be greater than 0), and the default value to be assigned to each element.

Example 8.4 demonstrates the `array_fill()` function. The output is displayed in Figure 8.6.

FORMAT

```
array array_fill ( int start_index, int num, mixed value )
```

Example:
```
// A 5-element array, starting at index 0, each value given
// the string "to be defined".
$names=array_fill(0, 5, "to be defined");

// A 10-element array, starting at index 5, each element given
// a value of 0.
$nums=array_fill(5, 10, 0);
```

EXAMPLE 8.4

```
<html>
<head><title>The array_fill() Function</title></head>
<b>
The arrays are displayed as: index value => element value<br />
<pre>
<body bgcolor="lightgreen">
<?php
```

EXAMPLE 8.4 (CONTINUED)

```
1        $numbers=array_fill(0,10, 0);
2        print_r($numbers);
3        $methods=array_fill(1,3, "To be defined");
         print_r( $methods);
      ?>
      </pre>
      </body>
      </html>
```

EXPLANATION

1   The `array_fill()` function creates an array called $numbers. The index starts at 0 (first argument). There will be 10 elements (second argument), and the default value for each element will be 0.

2   The `print_r()` function prints out the keys and value of the new array.

3   The `array_fill()` function creates an array called $methods, starting with an index value of 1, containing three elements, with the string `"To be defined"` as its default value.

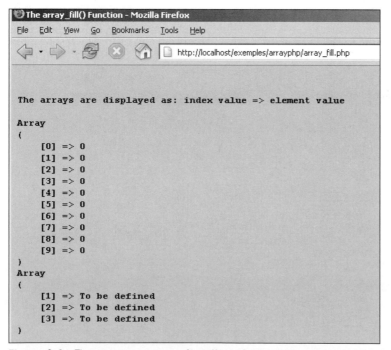

Figure 8.6   The `array_fill()` function. Output from Example 8.4.

8.1.2   Accessing an Array's Elements (Values)

A particular element of an array can be selected by appending the array operator `[]`, square brackets, to the array name. The key/index is placed within the brackets, such as `$name[0]` or `$book['Author']`. If a key is not specified when the array is created, the array is automatically indexed by a number starting at 0. If an array is assigned a new element, PHP automatically increments numeric keys by 1. The index of the last element of the array will be one less than the size of the array; for example, if an array has five values, its last index value would be four. See Example 8.5. If the array has been assigned both a key and a value, and the key is a string, then the index is the key enclosed in either single or double quotes.

Elements of a Numeric Array.   At the beginning of this chapter, our first example was a numeric array. To reiterate, a numeric array is indexed by numbers, by default, starting at 0 and incrementing by 1 as each element is added to the array, although you can start the array at a different number, as shown in Figure 8.7.

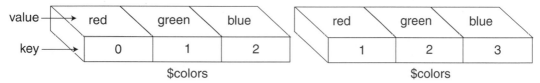

Figure 8.7   The default index starts at 0 (left), but you can change it (right).

```
EXAMPLE 8.5

      <html>
      <html>
      <head><title>Array of Colors</title></head>
      <body bgcolor="lightgreen">
      <?php
          // PHP assigns keys starting at 0
1         $colors=array('red','green', 'blue');
2         echo "<b>\$colors is $colors.<br />";
          // Accessing array elements
3         echo "\$colors[0] is $colors[0].<br />";
          echo "\$colors[1] is $colors[1].<br />";
          echo "\$colors[2] is $colors[2].<br />";
4         $colors[ ]='yellow';   // Let's add another element
          echo "\$colors[3] is $colors[3].<br />";
          echo "<hr>";
          // Start a new $colors  array
5         $colors=array(1=>'purple', 2=>'orange');
```

EXAMPLE 8.5 (CONTINUED)

```
6        $colors[ ] = 'yellow';
         echo "\$colors[1] is $colors[1].<br />";
         echo "\$colors[2] is $colors[2].<br />";
         echo "\$colors[3] is $colors[3].<br />";
     ?>
     </body>
     </html>
```

EXPLANATION

1   The `array()` function creates a numeric array called `$colors`, consisting of three elements, `'red'`, `'green'`, and `'blue'`. By default, the index starts at 0.
2   The data type of `$colors` is displayed as an array.
3   The first element of the array is printed by appending to the name of the array the index value enclosed in the `[]` operator; that is, `$colors[0]`.
4   A new element is added to the array. PHP will figure out what number to use for the index by adding 1 to the last index number in the existing array. Because the last index value was 3, the value `'yellow'` will be assigned to `$colors[4]`.
5   A new array is created with the `array()` function. Because this array is also called `$colors`, the original `$colors` array will be overwritten. This array starts with an index of 1.
6   A new element is added to the array. PHP will figure out what number to use for the index by adding 1 to the last index number in the existing array. Because the last index value was 2, the value `'yellow'` will be assigned to `$colors[3]`. See Figure 8.8.

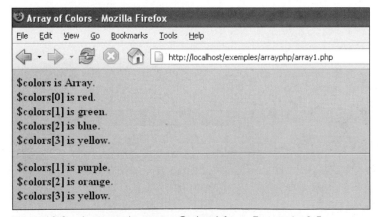

Figure 8.8   A numeric array. Output from Example 8.5.

Elements of an Associative Array. The second example we showed you was an associative array, an array indexed by strings. An associative array consists of both keys and values separated by the => symbol; for example, $key => $value. The key is a string that will be used to key into the value associated with it. The key will be inserted within the [] operator, just as a number was used in the numeric arrays. Be sure that you quote a string index with either single or double quotes. Otherwise, the bare string may be interpreted as a predefined constant value. Figure 8.9 depicts an associative array called $book, its keys, and its values.

Example 8.6 demonstrates an associative array. The output is shown in Figure 8.10.

Figure 8.9 An associative array called $book.

EXAMPLE 8.6

```
<html>
<head><title>Array of Books</title></head>
<body bgcolor="lightblue">
<?php
1      $book=array('Title' => 'War and Peace',
                   'Author' => 'Tolstoy';
                   'Publisher' => "Oxford University Press"
                   );
2      $book['ISBN'] = "0192833987";  // Add a new element
       echo "<b>\$book is $book.<br />";
3      echo "\$book['Title'] ". $book['Title'] ."<br />";
       echo "\$book['Author'] is ". $book['Author'] ."<br />";
       echo "\$book['Publisher'] is ". $book['Publisher'] ."<br />";
       echo "\$book['Pages'] is ". $book['ISBN'] ."<br />";
?>
</body>
</html>
```

EXPLANATION

1 An associative array called $book is created consisting of key–value pairs. The keys are on the left side of the => operator. The associated values are on the right side of the => operator.
2 A new value, "0192833987", is assigned to the $book array. The key is 'ISBN'.
3 The value of the $book array is accessed via the key, 'Title', enclosed in square brackets. Now, instead of using a number to access the array, a string is used.

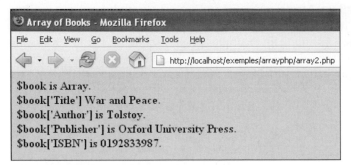

Figure 8.10   An associative array.

Watch Those Quotes!   When quotes are embedded within other quotes, you can run into problems. Look at the following example:

```
echo "$book['Title']<br />";
Parse error: syntax error, unexpected T_ENCAPSED_AND_WHITESPACE,
expecting T_STRNG  or TVARIABLE orT_NUM_STRING inC:\\wamp\php- on line
11
```

A parse error occurred because single quotes were embedded within double quotes. This can be fixed by concatenating the strings as follows:

```
echo  $book['Title'] .  "<br />";
```

or by surrounding the array element with curly braces:

```
echo "{$book['Title']}<br />"
```

Do not eliminate the quotes around the key as shown here:

```
echo $book[Title];
```

as PHP will treat the key `Title` as a constant, not as a string. You might inadvertently use a key value that has been defined somewhere else as a constant to produce the error message "E_NOTICE (undefined constant)."

Mixing Elements in an Array.   The index/key value in an array can be a positive or negative number or a string, and the value associated with it can be a string, a number, another array, and so on. If an index value is not given, PHP provides a numeric index, incrementing the index of the next position in the array by 1.

Example 8.7 demonstrates how the index and the value of the elements can be mixed. The output is shown in Figure 8.11.

EXAMPLE 8.7

```
       <html>
       <head><title>Using a Negative Index</title></head>
       <body bgcolor="lightgreen">
       <b>
       <?php
1          $colors=array(-1 =>'purple','orange',"brown"=>"burnt sienna");
2          $colors[]=255;
3          echo "\$colors[-1] is ". $colors[-1] . ".<br />";
4          echo "\$colors[0] is $colors[0].<br />";
           echo "\$colors[1] is $colors[1].<br />";
5          echo "\$colors['brown'] is " . $colors['brown'] . ".<br />";
6      //  echo "\$color['brown'] is {$colors['brown']}<br />";
       ?>
       </b>
       </body>
       </html>
```

EXPLANATION

1 The array $colors starts with a negative index, -1. PHP will add 1 to each con-
   secutive index in the array, so that element 'orange' will be associated with index 0. The third element is a string, "brown", associated with "burnt sienna".
   If another element is added later on, the index will be numeric and incremented
   by 1 from the last numeric index.

2 A new element is added to the array. Because the last numeric index was 0, the
   index of this element will be 1.

3 The value of the array element at index –1 is extracted and printed.

4 Although the value 'orange' was not explicitly assigned an index, PHP will add
   1 to the previous numeric index value. Because that index was –1, the index for
   'orange' will be assigned 0.

5 Here the index is a string, "brown", associated with a value, "burnt sienna". Using a string will have no effect on the numeric indexes.

6 This line is commented out, but provided to demonstrate the use of curly braces
   when using arrays and nested quotes; that is, quotes within quotes. When an array
   element is enclosed within a string in double quotes, the curly braces allow the
   key to be surrounded by single quotes, without causing a PHP error. Without the
   curly braces the error is:

   Parse error: syntax error, unexpected T_ENCAPSED_AND_WHITESPACE, expecting T_STRNG or TVARIABLE orT_NUM_STRING inC:\\wamp\php- on line
   18

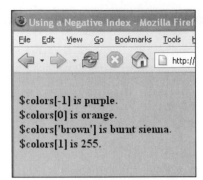

Figure 8.11
Mixed array elements. Output from Example 8.7.

8.1.3 Printing an Array

There are a number of ways to print the contents of an array. PHP provides built-in functions to display all of the keys and values, or you can use loops. We discuss the built-in functions first.

The print_r() Function.   The print_r() built-in function displays detailed information about a variable, such as its type, length, and contents. It displays the value of a string, integer, or float. In the case of arrays, print_r() displays all of the elements of an array; that is, the key–value pairs. (Use the HTML <pre> tag, to display each element on a separate line; otherwise, the output is displayed on one line.) If you would like to capture the output of print_r() in a variable, set the return parameter to boolean TRUE. The print_r() function can also be useful when debugging a program.

Remember that print_r() will move the internal array pointer to the end of the array. Use reset() to bring it back to the beginning. PHP 5 appears to reset the pointer automatically after using print_r().

Example 8.8 demonstrates the print_r() function. The output is shown in Figure 8.12.

FORMAT

```
bool print_r ( mixed expression [, bool return] )
```

Example:
```
print_r($colors);  // Display the contents of the array
$list=print_r( $colors, true);  // Save the return value in $list
reset($colors);  // Move internal array pointer to array beginning
```

EXAMPLE 8.8

```html
<html>
<head><title>The print_r() Function</title></head>
<body bgcolor="yellow">
<b>
<pre>
<?php
1      $colors=array('red','green', 'blue','yellow');
2      $book=array('Title' => 'War and Peace',
                   'Author' => 'Tolstoy',
                   'Publisher' => "Oxford University Press",
               );
3      print_r($colors);
       echo "<hr>";
4      print_r($book);
?>
</b>
</pre>
</body>
</html>
```

EXPLANATION

1 A numeric array called `$colors` is created with four elements.
2 An associative array called `$book` is created with key–value pairs.
3 The `print_r()` function displays the array in a humanly readable format, numeric indexes on the left of the => operator and the value of the elements on the right side. Use the HTML <pre> tag to present the array on separate lines; otherwise it will be displayed as one long line.
4 The `print_r()` function displays the associative array, key–value pairs in an easy-to-read format.

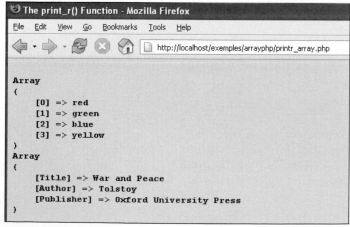

Figure 8.12   Printing an array with the `print_r()` function. Output from Example 8.8.

EXAMPLE 8.9

```
<html>
<head><title>The print_r() Function</title></head>
<body bgcolor="CCFF66">
<pre>
<b>
<?php
    $colors=array('red','green', 'blue','yellow');
    $book=array('Title' => 'War and Peace',
                'Author' => 'Tolstoy',
                'Publisher' => 'Oxford University Press',
            );
1   $display= print_r($colors,true);  // Assign output to $display
2   echo $display;
3   reset($colors);
?>
</b>
</pre>
</body>
</html>
```

EXPLANATION

1 By giving `print_r()` an additional boolean argument of TRUE, you can capture the output of `print_r()` in a variable.

2 The `$display` variable contains the output of the `print_r()` function; that is, the contents of the array. See Figure 8.13.

3 The `reset()` function puts the internal array pointer back at the beginning of the array. The PHP manual suggests using this function to reset the array pointer, but in PHP 5 it is not necessary.

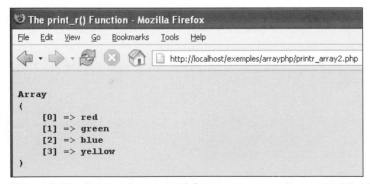

Figure 8.13   Saving the output from `print_r()` in a variable. Output from Example 8.9.

The var_dump() Function.   The `var_dump()` function displays the array (or object), the number of elements, and the lengths of each of the string values. It also provides output with indentation to show the structure of the array or object. (See Chapter 17, "Objects," for more on objects.)

Example 8.10 demonstrates the `var_dump()` function. The output is shown in Figure 8.14.

FORMAT

```
void var_dump ( mixed expression [, mixed expression [, ...]] )
```

Example:
```
$states=array('CA' => 'California','MT'=>'Montana','NY'=>'New York');
var_dump($states); // Dumps output in a structured format
```

EXAMPLE 8.10

```
      <html>
      <head><title>The var_dump() Function</title></head>
      <body bgcolor="CCFF99">
      <pre>
      <b>
      <?php
1         $colors=array('red','green', 'blue','yellow');
2         $book=array('Title' => 'War and Peace',
                      'Author' => 'Tolstoy',
                      'Publisher' => "Oxford University Press",
                     );
3         var_dump($colors);
          var_dump($book);
      ?>
      </b>
      </pre>
      </body>
      </html>
```

EXPLANATION

1 The numeric array, `$colors`, is assigned a list of colors.
2 The associative array, `$book`, is assigned key–value pairs.
3 The `var_dump()` function takes the name of the array as its argument, and displays the output by first printing the number of elements in the array, index value, and then the number of characters in each of the assigned string values and its value. See Figure 8.14.

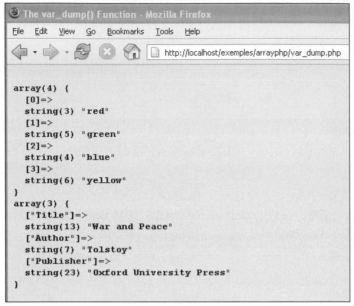

Figure 8.14 Printing an array with the `var_dump()` function. Output Example 8.10.

8.1.4 Using Loops to Access Array Elements

Loops make it easy to step through an array. The `for` and `while` loops are useful for numeric arrays where you can determine the size, and starting point of the array is usually 0, incremented by 1 for each element. The best way to loop through an associative array is with the `foreach` loop, although you can use this loop for numerically indexed arrays as well.

The for Loop.   The `for` loop can be used to iterate through a numeric array. The initial value of the `for` loop will be the first index value of the array, which will be incremented each time through the loop until the end of the array is reached.

Example 8.11 demonstrates how the `for` loop is used to view each element of an array. The output is displayed in Figure 8.15.

EXAMPLE 8.11

```
        <html>
        <head><title>The for Loop</title></head>
        <body bgcolor="lightgreen">
        <table border="1" bordercolor="black" bgcolor="yellow">
            <caption>Elements</caption>
        <?php
  1         $colors=array('red','green', 'blue','yellow');
```

EXAMPLE 8.11 (CONTINUED)

```
2        for($i = 0; $i < count($colors); $i++){
3            echo "<tr><td><b>$colors[$i]</b></td></tr>";
        }
    ?>
    </table>
    </body>
    </html>
```

EXPLANATION

1   The numeric array, $colors, is assigned a list of colors.
2   The first argument to the for loop, $i = 0, sets the initial value of $i to 0, which represents the first index in the array. If the index value, $i, is less than the size of the array (returned from the count() function), the loop body is entered, after displaying the color, the third argument of the for loop is executed; that is, increment the value of $i by 1.
3   Each time through the loop, the next element in the $colors array is displayed in a table cell.

Figure 8.15   Using the for loop to loop through an array. Output from Example 8.11.

The while Loop.   The while loop can be used to iterate through a numeric array as shown in Examples 8.12 and 8.13.

By setting the initial value to 0, the loop will iterate from the first element of the array (assuming that the array starts at element zero) until it reaches the end of the array. The count() or sizeof() functions can be used to find the length of the array.

EXAMPLE 8.12

```
        <html>
        <head><title>The while Loop</title></head>
        <body bgcolor="lightgreen">
        <table border='1' bordercolor='black' bgcolor='yellow'>
        <caption>Elements</caption>
        <?php
1           $colors=array('red','white', 'aqua','yellow');
2           $i = 0;
3           while( $i < count($colors)){
4               echo "<tr bgcolor=$colors[$i]><td><b>$colors[$i]
                </b></td></tr>";
5               $i++;
            }
        ?>
        </table>
        </body>
        </html>
```

EXPLANATION

1   A numeric array called $colors is created and assigned string values.
2   Variable, $i, set to 0, will be the initial value in the loop, and will used as the array's index.
3   The count() function returns the number of elements in the array. The while expression tests that the value of $i is less than the size of the array.
4   The value of $i will be used as the index value of the array, $colors. Each time through the loop, the value will be incremented by 1. In this example, the value of the element, a color, will be used as the background color for the current row, and as the text printed within the table's data cell. See Figure 8.16.
5   The value of $i is incremented by 1. If you forget to increment $i, the loop will go forever because $i will always be less than the size of the array.

Figure 8.16   Using the while loop to iterate through an array. Output from Example 8.12.

EXAMPLE 8.13

```
<html><head><title>Table Colors</table></head>
<body bgcolor="blue">
<table border=1 bordercolor="white" align="center"
                    cellpadding="2">
<caption><b><font size="+2" color="yellow">Colored Rows</font></b>
</caption>
<?php
1       $colors=array("orange","lightgreen", "lightblue","yellow");
2       $i=0;
3       while ( $i< 8 ){
            // Each time through the loop the index value in the array
            // will be changed, with values 0, 1, 2, 3, 0, 1, 2, 3, etc.
4           $color=$colors[$i%4];
        ?>
<tr bgcolor="<?=$color?>">
5       <td><?=$color?></td>
        <td><?=$color?></td>
        <td><?=$color?></td>
        <td><?=$color?></td>
        <td><?=$color?></td>
</tr>
<?php
6       $i++;       // Increment the value of the loop counter
7   }
    ?>
</body>
</html>
```

EXPLANATION

1   An array called $colors is assigned four color values.
2   The variable, $i, is initialized to 0.
3   The while loop evaluates the expression in parentheses. Is the value of $i less than 8? If it is, the loop body is entered.
4   The index value of the $colors array is divided by 4 and the remainder (modulus) is replaced as the new index value.
5   The first time in the loop the index is 0. The value $color[0] is "orange" and will be filled in the table for a row of 5 table cells. See Figure 8.17.
6   The value of $i is incremented by 1. Next time through the loop, $color[1] is "lightgreen" and that color will fill a row of table cells.
7   This is the closing brace for the while loop.

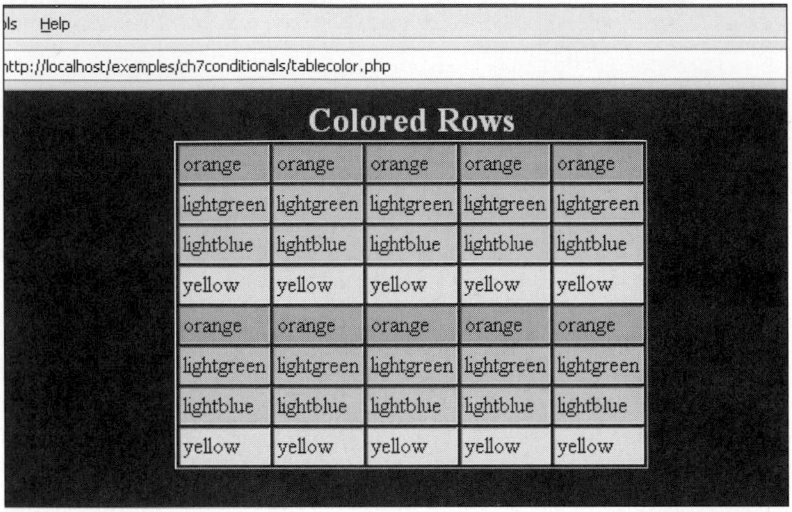

Figure 8.17 The `while` loop and arrays. Output from Example 8.13.

The foreach Loop.   The `foreach` statement is designed to work with both numeric and associative arrays (works only on arrays). The loop expression consists of the array name, followed by the `as` keyword, and a user-defined variable that will hold each successive value of the array as the loop iterates. The expression in the `foreach` statement can include both the key and value as shown in Example 8.14. The `foreach` loop operates on a copy of the original array. If you change the value of an element of the array, it will only change the copy, not the value in the original.

FORMAT

```
(Numeric Array)
foreach ($array_name as $value){
   do-something with the element's value;
}
foreach($array_name as $index=>$value){
   do-something with the element's index and value
}
```

Example:
```
$suit=("diamond", "spade", "club", "heart");
foreach ( $suit as $card_type){
   echo $card_type . "<br />";          // displays: diamond
}                                        //           spade
                                         //           club
                                         //           heart
```

FORMAT (CONTINUED)

```
(Associative Array)
foreach ($array_name as $key => $variable){
   do-something $key and/or $variable;
}
```

Example:
```
$courses=("101A"=>"Intro to CS",
               "200B"=>"Data Structures",
               "130A"=>"Visual Basic"
);
foreach ( $courses as $number=>$class_name){
   echo $number . '=>' . $class_name . "<br />"; // displays keys
                                                 // and values

}
```

EXAMPLE 8.14

```
    <html>
    <head><title>The foreach Loop</title></head>
    <body bgcolor="lightgreen">
    <b>
    <?php
1       $colors=array('red','green', 'blue', 'yellow');
2       $employee=array('Name' => 'Jon Doe',
                        'ID'  => '23d4',
                        'Job Title'=> 'Designer',
                        'Department'=>'Web Development',
                        );
3       foreach ($colors as $value){  // Each value is stored in $value
            echo "$value <br />";
        }
        echo "<hr>";
4       foreach ($employee as $key => $value){  // Associative array
            echo "employee[$key] => $value<br />";
        }
    ?>
    </b>
    </body>
    </html>
```

EXPLANATION

1   A numeric array of four colors is defined.
2   An associative array of four key–value pairs is defined.
3   The foreach loop is used to iterate through each element of the $colors array.
    The expression $colors as $value, means: In the $colors array assign the value of each element to the variable $value, one at a time, until the array ends. Each value will be displayed in turn. See Figure 8.18.

EXPLANATION (CONTINUED)

4   This `foreach` loop iterates through each key–value pair of an associative array, called `employee`. The array name is followed by the `as` keyword and a variable to represent the key, called `$key`, followed by the `=>` operator, and a variable to represent the value, called `$value`.

Figure 8.18   Looping through an array with the `foreach` loop. Output from Example 8.14.

Modifying a Value by Reference with a foreach Loop.   As of PHP 5, you can easily modify an array's elements by preceding the value after the `as` keyword with `&`. This will assign by reference instead of copying the value; that is, whatever you do to the array while in the loop will change the original array, not a copy of it.

EXAMPLE 8.15

```
    <html>
    <head><title>The foreach Loop--Changing Values by Reference
    </title></head>
    <body bgcolor="lightblue">
    <b>
    <pre>
    Original array
    <?php
1      $val="hello";
2      $years=array(44, 53, 64, 77);
3      print_r($years);
4         foreach ($years as &$val){  // $val is a reference
5            $val += 1900;
              echo "$val<br />";  // $val is global in scope
          }
```

EXAMPLE 8.15 (CONTINUED)

```
6        echo "After foreach: \$val=$val<br />";
    ?>
    <hr>
    Array has been changed
    <?php
7        print_r($years);
    ?>
    </pre>
    </b>
    </body>
    </html>
```

EXPLANATION

1   A variable, $val, is assigned the string,"hello".
2   A numeric array, called $years, is assigned four numbers.
3   The print_r() function prints the original array. See Figure 8.19.
4   In the foreach expression the variable $val is used as a reference to each element of the $years array. The & preceding the variable name makes it a reference. Any changes made to the value that $val references will change the original array.
5   1900 is added to each value in the array via the reference, $val.
6   Because $val is a global variable (i.e., visible throughout the program), its original value is changed in the foreach loop, and the last value assigned to it remains after the loop exits.
7   The print_r() function prints the modified array. See Figure 8.19.

```
Original array
Array
(
    [0] => 44
    [1] => 53
    [2] => 64
    [3] => 77
)
After foreach: $val=1977


Array has been changed
Array
(
    [0] => 1944
    [1] => 1953
    [2] => 1964
    [3] => 1977
)
```

Figure 8.19   Modifying values by reference. Output from Example 8.15.

8.1.5 Checking If an Array Exists

PHP makes it possible to check to see if an array exists, and to check for the existence of keys, values, or both. See Table 8.2.

Table 8.2 Functions to Check for Existence of an Array

Function	What It Does
array_key_exists()	Checks if the given key or index exists in the array
in_array()	Checks if a value exists in an array
is_array()	Checks if the variable is an array; returns TRUE or FALSE

Example 8.16 demonstrates how to perform array checks using the functions in Table 8.2. The output is displayed in Figure 8.20.

EXAMPLE 8.16

```
        <html>
        <head><title>Checking for Existence of an Array or Element
        </title></head>
        <body bgcolor="lightblue">
        <h3>Does it Exist?</h3>
        <pre>
        <?php
1       $country="USA";    // $country is a scalar
2       $states=array('CA'=>"California",
                       'MT'=>"Montana",
                       'VA'=>"Virginia");
3       if ( is_array($country)){
            print '$country is an array'."<br />";
        }
        else{
            print '$country is not an array'."<br />";
        }
4       if (array_key_exists("VA", $states)){
            print 'Array key "VA" exists'."<br />";
        }
5       if (in_array("Montana", $states)){
            print 'Array value "Montana" exists'."<br />";
        }
        ?>
        <pre>
        </body>
        </html>
```

EXPLANATION

1 A simple scalar variable called $country is assigned the string "USA".
2 An associative array called $states is assigned key–value pairs.
3 The is_array() built-in function returns true if its argument is an array, and false if it is not. $states is not an array.
4 The array_key_exists() built-in function returns true if its argument is the key or index in an array.
5 The in_array() built-in function returns true if its argument is a value that exists in an array. The array value "Montana" does exist in the $states associative array.

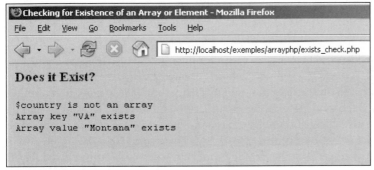

Figure 8.20 Checking an array's existence.

8.1.6 Creating Strings from Arrays and Arrays from Strings

In Chapter 6, "Strings," we discussed strings and their many functions. Now that we have learned about arrays, PHP provides functions that serve the dual purpose of creating arrays from strings and strings from arrays (see Table 8.3).

Table 8.3 Arrays and Strings

Function	What It Does
explode()	Splits up a string by a specified delimiter and creates an array of strings
implode()	Creates a string by gluing together array elements by a specific separator
join()	Alias for implode()
split()	Splits up a string into an array by a regular expression (see Chapter 12, "Regular Expressions and Pattern Matching")

The implode() Function.   The `implode()` function creates a string by joining together the elements of an array with a string delimiter, called the *glue string*. As of PHP 4.3.0, the glue parameter of `implode()` is optional and defaults to the empty string(`""`). Another name for `implode()` is its alias, `join()`.

The `implode()` function returns a string containing a string representation of all the array elements in the same order, with the glue string between each element.

FORMAT

```
string implode ( string glue, array elements )
```

Example:
```
$stats_array = array('name', 'ssn', 'phone');
// implode() creates a string from an array
$stats_string = implode(",", $array);
```

The explode() Function.   The `explode()` function splits up a string and creates an array, the opposite of `implode()`. The new array is created by splitting up the original string into substrings based on the delimiter given. The delimiter is what you determine is the word separator, such as a space or comma. If given a limit, the new array will be limited to that many substrings, and the last one will contain the rest of the string. See also "The preg_split() Function—Splitting Up Strings" on page 510.

Example 8.17 demonstrates how the explode function works. Its output is displayed in Figure 8.21.

FORMAT

```
array explode(string separator, string string [, int limit])
```

Example:
```
$fruit  =   explode(" ", "apples pears peaches plums")
// Creates a 4-element array

$fruit  =   explode("|", "apples|pears|peaches|plums" , 3)
echo $fruit[0], $fruit[1], $fruit[2];
// Creates a 3-element array
```

EXAMPLE 8.17

```
        <head><title>explode() Array</title></head>
        <body bgcolor="black">
        <font size="+1" color="white">
        <pre>
        <?php
1           $colors="red green orange blue";  // Create a string
2           echo "<b>\$colors is a ". gettype($colors)."\n";
3           $colors=explode(" ",$colors);  // Split up the string by spaces
            echo "<img src='explosion.jpg'>","\n";
```

EXAMPLE 8.17 (CONTINUED)

```
4        echo "<b>After explode():\$colors is an ".
            gettype($colors)."\n";
         print_r($colors);
         // Let's give explode() second parameter limiting
         // array size to 3 elements
5        $colors=explode(" ","red green orange blue",3);
         echo "\n";
6        print_r($colors);
     ?>
     </pre>
     </body>
     </html>
```

EXPLANATION

1   A variable called $colors is created and assigned a string.
2   The gettype() function returns the data type of the variable, a string.
3   The explode() function splits up the string with whitespace as the separator and creates an array called $colors.
4   After explode(), the the gettype() function returns the data type of $colors, an array.
5   This time the explode() function is given an optional second parameter, which will limit the new array created to a length of three elements.
6   The new array consists of three elements, the last element contains both "orange blue", the remainder of the string after it was divided into three array elements.

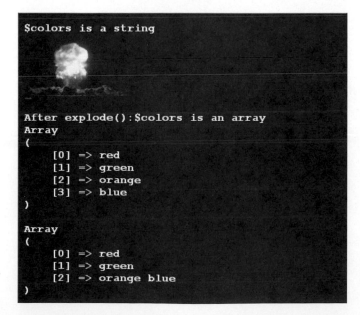

```
$colors is a string


After explode():$colors is an array
Array
(
    [0] => red
    [1] => green
    [2] => orange
    [3] => blue
)

Array
(
    [0] => red
    [1] => green
    [2] => orange blue
)
```

Figure 8.21
Converting a string to an array with the explode() function. Output from Example 8.17.

8.1.7 Finding the Size of an Array

PHP provides built-in functions to count the number of elements in an array. They are count(), sizeof(), and array_count_values(). Example 8.18 demonstrates how to find the size of a multidimensional array.

Table 8.4 Functions to Find the Size of an Array

Function	What It Does
array_count_values()	Returns an array consisting of the values of an array and the number of times each value occurs in an array
count()	Returns the number of elements in an array or properties of an object
sizeof()	Returns the size of the array, same as count()

The count() and sizeof() Functions.   The count()[2] and sizeof() functions do the same thing: They both return the number of elements in an array (or properties in an object). To find the number of elements in a multidimensional array, the count() function has an optional mode argument that recursively counts the elements.

FORMAT

```
$number_of_elements =count(array_name);
$number_of_elements=count(array_name, 1);
$number_of_elements=count(array_name, COUNT_RECURSIVE)
```

Example:
```
$bytes=range('a','z');
$size = count( $bytes);   //  26 elements
$size = sizeof( $bytes);  //  26 elements
```

---

2. The sizeof() function is simply an alias for the count() function.

EXAMPLE 8.18

```
        <html>
        <head><title>The count() function</title></head>
        <body bgcolor="lightgreen">
        <?php
1           $colors=array('red','green', 'blue');
2           $colors[]='yellow';
3           $size = count($colors);
4           echo "The size of the array is $size.<br />";
            echo "<hr>";
        ?>
        </body>
        </html>
```

EXPLANATION

1   The array called $colors is assigned three values.
2   A new element is added to the $colors array.
3   The count() function returns the number of elements in the array.
4   See Figure 8.22 for the return from the count() function.

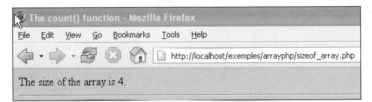

Figure 8.22   Finding the size of an array. Output from Example 8.18.

The array_count_values() Function.   The   array_count_values()   function counts how many times a unique value is found in an array. It returns an associative array with the keys representing the unique element of the array, and the value containing the number of times that unique element occurred within the array.

FORMAT

```
array array_count_values ( array input )
```

Example:
```
$hash_count = array_count_values( array("a","b", "a","a"));
// Creates an associative array with "a" and "b" as the two keys and
// the number of times each occurs in the array (the associated value)
```

EXAMPLE 8.19

```
      <html><head><title>Array of Colors</title></head>
      <body bgcolor="lightgreen">
      <pre>
      <?php
1         $colors=array("red", "blue", "green", "red", "yellow",
                          "red","blue");
2         $unique_count = array_count_values($colors);
3         print_r($unique_count)."<br />";
      ?>
      </pre>
      </body>
      </html>
```

EXPLANATION

1   The arrray called $colors is created with some duplicate colors.
2   The built-in array_count_values() function creates an associative array with
    the key being a unique value from the original array and the value of the number
    of times that element occurs in the array. In the example, the color "red" appears
    three times, the color "blue" twice, and the colors "green" and "yellow" once.
    The associative array, $unique_count, will contain keys representing the color el-
    ement ("red", "blue", "green", "yellow") and the value associated with each
    color will be the number of times the color occurred in the array.
3   The print_r() function displays the contents of the associated array created by
    array_count_values(). See Figure 8.23.

Figure 8.23   The array_count_values() function. Outpuf from Example 8.19.

8.1.8 Extracting Keys and Values from Arrays

PHP provides functions that allow you to extract elements from an array and assign the keys and values to variables. The `array_keys()` function returns all the keys in an array, the `array_values()` function returns all the values of the elements in an array, and the `each()` function can be used to extract both keys and values.

The array_keys() Function.   The `array_keys()` function returns all the keys of an array. If the optional `search_value` argument is specified, you can get the keys for that particular value. See Example 8.20.

FORMAT

```
array array_keys ( array input [, mixed search_value [, bool strict]] )
```

Example:
```
$array_of_keys = array_keys("apples", "pears", "peaches", "plums");
// Returns 0,1,2,3

$array_of_keys = array_keys("Title"=>"King", "Name"=>"Barbar");
// Returns "Title", "Name"
```

EXAMPLE 8.20

```
    <html><head><title>The array_keys() Function</title>
    </head>
    <body bgcolor="silver">
    <b>
    <pre>
    <?php
        $colors=array("red", "green", "blue", "yellow");
        print"The original array:<br />";
1       $keys=array_keys($colors);
2       print_r($colors);
        print"The keys:<br />";
3       print_r($keys);
        echo "Key for \"blue\"<br />";
4       $keys=array_keys($colors,"blue");
        print_r($keys);
    ?>
    <hr>
    <?php
5       $poem=array("Title"=>"The Raven", "Author"=>"Edgar Allen Poe");
6       $keys=array_keys($poem);
        print"The original array:<br />";
        print_r($poem);
        print"The keys:<br />";
        print_r($keys);
    ?>
    </pre>
    </b>
    </body>
    </html>
```

1 The array_keys() function returns an array of keys; in this example the keys are numeric index values starting at 0.
2 The print_r() function displays the array. See Figure 8.24.
3 The array of keys is printed. See Figure 8.24.
4 The array_keys() function returns an array of keys only for the value "blue" in the array $colors; the key or index is 2.
5 An associative array called $poem is assigned key–value pairs.
6 The array_keys() function returns the keys in the associative array $poems; that is, "Title" and "Author" are assigned to the $keys array. See Figure 8.24.

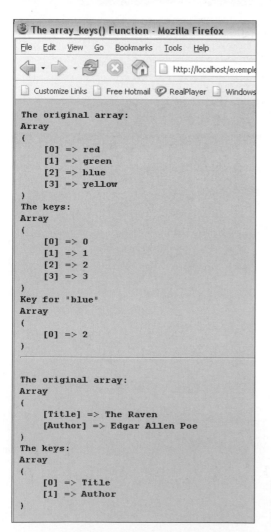

Figure 8.24
Getting the keys from an array. Output from Example 8.20.

The array_values() Function.   The array_values() function returns an array with all the values of the original array. The new array is indexed by numbers. See Example 8.21 and Figure 8.25 for its output.

FORMAT

```
array array_values ( array input )
```

Example:
```
$animals=array("tiger", "lion", "camel","elephant");

$array_of_values=array_values($animals);
// Returns:"tiger","lion","camel","elephant"
```

EXAMPLE 8.21

```
        <html><head><title>The array_values() Function</title>
        </head>
        <body bgcolor="silver">
        <b>
        <pre>
        <?php
1           $colors=array("red", "green", "blue", "yellow");
            print"The original array:<br />";
2           $values=array_values($colors);
            print_r($colors);
            print"The values:<br />";
            print_r($values);
        ?>
        <hr>
        <?php
3           $poem=array("Title"=>"The Raven", "Author"=>"Edgar Allen Poe");
4           $values=array_values( $poem );
            print"The original array:<br />";
            print_r($poem);
            print"The values:<br />";
            print_r($values);
        ?>
        </pre>
        </b>
        </body>
        </html>
```

EXPLANATION

1   The numeric array called $colors is assigned values.
2   The array_values() function returns an array of the values in an array, numerically indexed.

EXPLANATION (CONTINUED)

3   An associative array called $poem is defined with key–value pairs.
4   The array_values() function returns an array of the values in the array, $poem, numerically indexed.

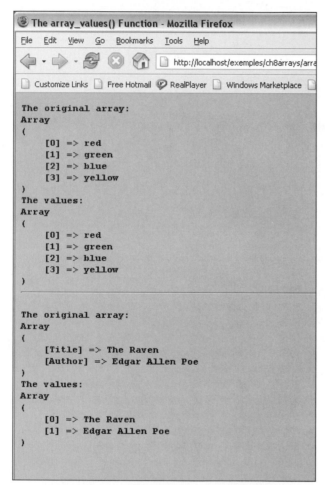

Figure 8.25
Getting the values from an array.
Output from Example 8.21.

The each() Function.   The each() function returns the current key–value pair in an array, and moves to the next element, making that the current element. The returned value is an array of two alternating values to represent each key and its corresponding value. To access the array elements, you can use either 0 and 1 to represent each key and value, or the keywords key and value to do the same thing. Used with a looping construct, each element of the array can be accessed until the array has reached its end. The reset() function sets the internal array pointer back to the beginning of the array if you want to access the array elements again. See Example 8.22.

FORMAT

```
array each ( array &array )
```

Example:
```
$keyval_array = each ( $employee );
```

EXAMPLE 8.22

```
    <html>
    <head><title>The each() Function</title></head>
    <body bgcolor="CCFFCC">
    <pre>
    <b>
    <?php
1       $colors=array('red','green', 'blue','yellow');
        echo "<u>Numeric Array</u><br />";
2       while($array = each($colors)){
        //  echo $array[0]." => " . $array[1]. "<br />";
3           echo $array['key']." => " . $array['value']. "<br />";
        }
4       $book=array('Title' => 'War and Peace',
                    'Author' => 'Tolstoy',
                    'Publisher' => "Oxford University Press",
                    );

        echo "<p><u>Associative Array</u> <br />";
5       while($novel = each($book)){
6           echo $novel[0]." => " . $novel[1]. "<br />";
        //  echo $novel['key']." => " . $novel['value']. "<br />";
        }
7       reset($book);   // Move the internal array pointer to beginning
                        // of the array
    ?>
    </b>
    </pre>
    </body>
    </html>
```

EXPLANATION

1   A numeric array called $colors is defined with values.

2   The while loop evaluates the expression in parentheses. The each() function returns two values: the array element's first numeric index value and its value. These two values are assigned to $array. The internal array pointer will then move to the next element in the array.

3   The each() function allows you to index the array it returned either by using a number, 0 or 1, or by using the reserved strings key and value. Both ways are shown here.

EXPLANATION (CONTINUED)

4   The associative array, `$book`, is assigned key–value pairs.

5   The `while` loop evaluates the expression in parentheses. The `each()` function returns two values: the array element's first string index value and its associated
string value. These two values are assigned to an array called `$novel`. The internal
array pointer will then move to the next element in the associative array.

6   The index values are printed. See Figure 8.26.

7   The `reset()` function sets the internal array pointer back to the beginning of the
array:

```
'Title' => 'War and Peace',
'Author' => 'Tolstoy',
'Publisher' => "Oxford University Press"
```

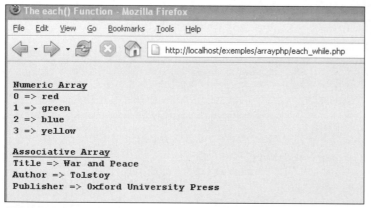

Figure 8.26   Getting both keys and values from an array. Output from Example 8.22.

8.1.9   Creating Variables from Array Elements

The `list()` and `extract()` functions create variables from numeric and associative
arrays, respectively.

The list() Function and Numeric Arrays.   The `list()` function[3] extracts elements
from a numeric array (with index starting at 0) and assigns them to individual variables.
The `list()` function is on the left side of the assignment operator. Its arguments are a
comma-separated list of variable names. The variables created by `list()` correspond to
the array elements on the right side of the assignment operator. If there are less variables
than array elements, the extra elements are ignored.

---

3. Technically, although `list()` acts like a function, it is a language construct with no return value.

The list() and each() functions work nicely together when iterating through an associative array (see Example 8.23).

FORMAT

```
void list ( mixed varname, mixed ... )
```

Example:
```
$swatch = array('blue', '#33A1C9', 'peacock');
list($color, $code, $name) = $swatch;   // Create variables from array
list($color, $code) = $swatch;          // Ignore 'peacock'
list($color, , $name)=$swatch;          // Skip '#33A1C9'
```

EXAMPLE 8.23

```
    <html>
    <head><title>The each and list Functions</title></head>
    <body bgcolor="CCFFCC">
    <pre>
    <b>
    <?php
        echo "Using the list() and each() Functions<p>";
        echo "<hr /><br />";
1       $colors=array("red", "green", "blue");
2       list($a,$b)=$colors;  // Create two variables, $a and $b
        echo "The list() function assigns array elements to
            variables: ";
        echo 'list($a,$b)=$colors'. ".<br />";
3       echo "\$a == '$a' and \$b == '$b'.";
        echo "<p>";
4       $book=array('Title' => 'War and Peace',
                    'Author' => 'Tolstoy',
                    'Publisher' => "Oxford University Press",
                    );
5       while(list($key, $val) = each($book)){
            echo "$key => $val<br />";
        }
6       reset($book);
    ?>
    </b>
    </pre>
    </body>
    </html>
```

EXPLANATION

1   A new numeric array called $colors is created and assigned three string values.
2   The list() function will create two variables from the first two array elements.
    "red" will be assigned to $a, and "green" will be assigned to $b.
3   The values of the new variables are displayed. See Figure 8.27.
4   An associative array, called $book, is assigned key–value pairs.
5   The each() function returns the first key and value in the $book array. Those val-
    ues are assigned to $key and $val, two variables created by the list() function.
    Because the each() function only returns the first key–value pair, the while loop
    is used to iteratate through the rest of the associative array. See Figure 8.27.
6   After the loop exits, $key and $val are empty. To reset the array's internal pointer
    to the beginning of the array, use the reset() function.

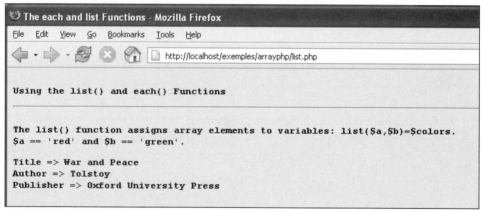

Figure 8.27   Creating variables from arrays with list(). Output from Example 8.23.

The extract() Function and Associative Arrays.   We used the extract() function in previous chapters to extract variables from the $_REQUEST array. You might
remember that the $_REQUEST array contains name–value pairs. The name represents
the name of the HTML input device and its value, whatever the user typed as a value.
For example, Figure 8.28 displays the output of print_r($_REQUEST) after a form has
been filled out.

```
[name] => Marko Marakana
[cellphone] => 999-000-8888
[email] => mm@mm.com
[submit] => Send
```

Figure 8.28
Contents of the $_REQUEST array.

The PHP statement `extract($_REQUEST)` creates variables named after the keys of this array—`$name`, `$cellphone`, `$email`, and `$submit`—with the values representing what the user typed into each of the corresponding form fields.

The `extract()` function creates variables from any associative array, not just the `$_REQUEST` array. The variables are named after the keys, and the values assigned to them are the same as the correspnding values in the associative array. For example, if the array has a key–value pair consisting of `"first_name" => "John"`, the `extract()` function would create a variable called `$first_name` and assign it the value `"John"`. (To be more precise in computer parlance, `extract()` imports variables from an array into the current symbol table.)

If a local variable has the same name as one of the keys in the associative array, a collision can occur, the default being to overwrite the existing variable, and if a value in the associative array is not a valid variable name, the `extract()` function will not import it. The behavior of this function can be changed based on the `extract_type` and prefix parameters, shown in Table 8.5.[4]

It is not wise to use this function when extracting values from superglobal arrays such as `$_GET`, `$_POST`, `$_REQUEST`, and so on (arrays that contain user input) unless you use one of the flags that prevents overwriting existing variables.

FORMAT

```
int extract ( array var_array [, int extract_type [, string prefix]] )
```

Example:
```
$dimensions = array("height"=>"65 in",
                    "weight"=>"50 lb.",
                    "width" => "65" in"
                   );
extract($dimensions);
extract($dimensions, EXTR_PREFIX_SAME,"my");
```

Table 8.5   Extract Arguments

Extract Type	What It Does
EXTR_IF_EXISTS	Only overwrite the variable if it already exists; otherwise do nothing
EXTR_OVERWRITE	If there is a collision, overwrite the existing variable
EXTR_PREFIX_ALL	Prefix all variable names with a prefix
EXTR_PREFIX_IF_EXISTS	Only create prefixed variable names if the nonprefixed version of the same variable exists

---

4. As of PHP 4.0.5, `extract()` returns the number of variables extracted.

Table 8.5   Extract Arguments (continued)

Extract Type	What It Does
EXTR_PREFIX_INVALID	Only prefix invalid or numeric variable names with a prefix
EXTR_PREFIX_SAME	If there is a collision, prefix the variable name with a prefix
EXTR_REFS	Extract variables as references
EXTR_SKIP	If there is a collision, do not overwrite the existing variable

Example 8.24 demonstrates how to use the `extract()` function to create variables. Its output is shown in Figure 8.29.

EXAMPLE 8.24

```
    <html><head><title>Extracting Values</title></head>
    <body bgcolor="CCCFFF">
    <font style="arial" size="+1">
    <b>
    <?php
1       $model="Pan TH-33XYZXYTV";
        print "Original model number: <em>$model</em><br />";
2       $television = array("model"=>"Pan PX-44BBCCSTV",
                            "type"=>"plasma",
                            "color"=>"charcoal bezel",
                            "size"=>"42 in. widescreen",
                            );
3       extract($television);    // Create variables from keys
4       print " Model number after <em>extract(): $model</em><p>";
        print "Values of variables created by <em>extract():<br /> ";
5       print "$model, $type, $color, $size</em><br />";
    ?>
    </b>
    </font>
    </body></html>
```

EXPLANATION

1   A variable, called $model, is defined and assigned the value Pan TH-33XYZXYTV.
2   An array, called $television, is defined. Note that one of the keys is called "model". It is assigned a different model number than the one on line 1.
3   The extract() function takes an array, $television, as its argument and returns a list of variables, named after the keys in the $television array. Each variable is assigned the value associated with the corresponding key of the associative array. The original variable, $model, is overwritten by the new variable of the same name created by extract().
4   The value of $model is displayed showing that the original variable, called $model, has been overwritten.
5   All of the values of the variables created by the extract() function are displayed.

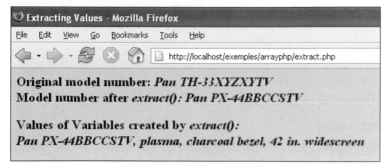

Figure 8.29 Extracting values and overwriting existing variables. Output from Example 8.24.

Example 8.25 demonstrates how to use the `extract()` function with the `EXTR_SKIP` argument. The output is shown in Figure 8.30.

EXAMPLE 8.25

```
<html><head><title>Extracting Values</title></head>
<body bgcolor="CCCFFF">
<font style="arial" size="+1">
<b>
<?php
1     $model="Pan TH-33XYZXYTV";
      print "Original model number: <em>$model</em><br />";
2     $television = array("model"=>"Pan PX-44BBCCSTV",
                          "type"=>"plasma",
                          "color"=>"charcoal bezel",
                          "size"=>"42 in. widescreen",
                          );
      // Don't overwrite existing variables
3     extract($television, EXTR_SKIP);
      print " Model number after <em>extract(): $model</em><p>";
      print "Values of variables created by <em>extract():<br /> ";
      print "$model, $type, $color, $size</em><br />";
?>
</b>
</font></body></html>
```

EXPLANATION

1   A variable, called $model, is defined and assigned the value Pan TH-33XYZXYTV.
2   An array, called $television, is defined. Note that one of the keys is called "model". It is assigned a different model number than the one on line 1.
3   The extract() function takes an array, $television, as its argument, and returns a list of variables, named after the keys in the $television array. The EXTR_SKIP flag prevents the function from overwriting any existing variables with the same name. The original variable, $model, will not be overwritten by the new variable of the same name in the $television array.

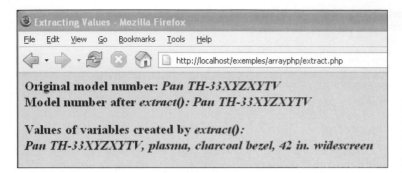

Figure 8.30
Extracting values and
skipping existing
variables. Output from
Example 8.25.

Example 8.26 demonstrates how to use the `extract()` function with the `EXTR_PREFIX_ALL` argument to create prefixes for any variables it creates. The output is shown in Figure 8.31.

EXAMPLE 8.26

```
      <html><head><title>Extracting Values and Adding Prefixes
      </title></head>
      <body bgcolor="CCCFFF">
      <font style="arial" size="+1">
      <b>
      <?php
1         $model="Pan TH-33XYZXYTV";
          print "Original model number: <em>$model</em><br />";
2         $television = array("model"=>"Pan PX-44BBCCSTV",
                              "type"=>"plasma",
                              "color"=>"charcoal bezel",
                              "size"=>"42 in. widescreen",
                             );
          // Adding a prefix
3         extract($television,EXTR_PREFIX_ALL, "myvar" );
          print "Variables created by <em>extract()</em> all have
              prefixes. Here are the values:<br /> ";
4         print "$myvar_model, $myvar_type, $myvar_color, $myvar_size
              </em><br />";
      ?>
      </body></html>
```

EXPLANATION

1   A variable, called `$model`, is defined and assigned the value `Pan TH-33XYZXYTV`.
2   An array, called `$television`, is defined. Note that one of the keys is called `"model"`. It is assigned a different model number than the one on line 1.
3   The `extract()` function takes an array, `$television`, as its argument and returns a list of variables, named after the keys in the `$television` array. The `EXTR_PREFIX_ALL` flag causes the function to prepend all the variable names with with the prefix, `myvar`.
4   Using the new prefix prepended to the variable names, the values are printed.

Figure 8.31   Creating variable using a user-defined prefix. Output from Example 8.26.

8.1.10   Multidimensional Arrays

To this point, we have been talking about one-dimensional arrays; that is, arrays in which each key or index has one value. A multidimensional array is an array that contains another array. Instead of having a single set of key–value pairs, the key–value pairs can be nested, allowing you to create more complex data structures. For example, you might have numbers stored in a matrix consisting of rows and columns, or an array of teachers each teaching multiple subjects, or an array of employees each with a set of his or her own keys and values, and so on. See Example 8.27.

EXAMPLE 8.27

```
      <html>
      <head><title>Array of Arrays</title></head>
      <body>
      <font face="arial">
      <?php
1         $numbers=array(array(10,12,14,16),
                         array(15,18,21,24),
                         array(20,25,30,35),
                        );
2         echo "<table border='1'><caption><font size='-2'>Rows and
             Columns</font></caption>";
3         for($i=0; $i < 3; $i++){      // 3 rows
             echo "<tr bgcolor='999FFF'>";
4            for($j=0; $j<4; $j++){     // 4 columns
5                echo "<td><b>".$numbers[$i][$j] ;
             }
             echo "</td></tr>";
          }
          echo "</table>";
      ?>
      </body>
      </html>
```

EXPLANATION

1   An array of arrays is created. This is a two-dimensional array consisting of rows and columns. Each of the rows in declared as an array within the array `$numbers`.

2   An HTML table is started here. It will hold the rows and columns.

3   The outer `for` loop is used to cycle through each of the rows, starting at the first row, `$numbers[0]`.

4   The inner `for` loop is used to cycle through each of the columns, starting at column 0, `$numbers[0][0]`. This inner loop will execute faster than the outer loop, the value of `$j` increasing by 1 until `$j` is 4, producing `$numbers[0][[0]`, `$numbers[0][1]`, `$numbers[0][2]`, `$numbers[0][3]`.

5   Each row and column value is printed. After the inner loop has completed, the value of `$i` in the outer `for` loop is incremented by 1 and the process starts again. See Figure 8.32.

Figure 8.32
A two-dimensional array of rows and columns. Output from Example 8.27.

Example 8.28 demonstrates how to create an array of associative arrays. The output is shown in Figure 8.33.

EXAMPLE 8.28

```
    <html>
    <head><title>Array of Associative Arrays</title></head>
    <body bgcolor="9999CC"><font face="arial">
    <b>
    <?php
1       $teachers=array(
2           array('Name' => "John Doe",
                    'Subjects' =>array('Government','English'),
                    'Salary'=> 56000,
                    ),
3           array('Name' => "Steven Lee",
4                   'Subjects' => array("Math", "Science", "PE"),
                    'Salary'=> 65000,
                    ),
```

EXAMPLE   8.28 (CONTINUED)

```
5                array('Name' => "Jean Perot",
                      'Subjects' => array("French", "Literature"),
                      'Salary'=> 57000,
                     ),
                 );
6        foreach( $teachers as $value){
            echo "<hr>";
7            foreach( $value as $key=>$val){
8                if ( $key == "Subjects"){
                    echo "$key: ";
9                    foreach( $val as $subjects){
                        echo "$subjects ";
                     }
                 }
                 else{
10                   echo "<br />$key: $val<br />";
                 }
             }
         }
    ?>
    </b>
    </body>
    </html>
```

EXPLANATION

1   The array called `$teachers` consists of three nested associative arrays, and each of the associative arrays contains an array with a like key: `'Subjects'`.

2   This is the first associative array contained within the array called `$teachers`.

3   This is the second nested associative array.

4   Notice that each of the associative arrays nested within the `$teacher` array contains a set of key–value pairs, where the value corresponding to the `"Subject"` key is an array of subjects.

5   This is the third nested associative array.

6   The outer `foreach` loop will start cycling through each of the associative arrays contained within the `$teacher` array. Each of the associative arrays is a value of the `$teachers` array.

7   This inner `foreach` loop will cycle through the keys and values of each associative array.

8   If the key for the associative array is `"Subject"`, then another `foreach` loop will be started to get the array of values associated with that key.

9   This inner `foreach` loop is used to cycle through all the subjects in the array assigned the to `"Subject"` key. Each subject in the array will be printed.

10 If the key in the associative array is not `"Subject"`, its single value will be printed.

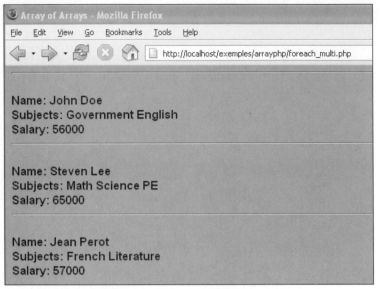

Figure 8.33   An array of arrays. Output from Example 8.28.

Finding the Size of a Mutidimensional Array.   To find the size of an array, we used the built-in `count()` function. To find the size of a multidimensional array, the `count()` function can be given the `COUNT_RECURSIVE` argument, which causes the `count()` function to go into each nested array and count its elements. *Recursion* is when a function, to accomplish a task, calls itself with some part of the task until it has applied the task to all of its targets, in the case with the `count()` function, counting the elements of all of the nested arrays, not just the outer one.

Example 8.29 demonstrates how to get the size of a multidimensional array and how to count all of its elements. See Figure 8.34 for its output.

EXAMPLE   8.29

```
<html><head><title>Counting Elements in a Multidimensional Array
</title>
</head>
<body bgcolor="blue">
<div align="center">
<table border="2">
<tr><td bgcolor="cornflowerblue">
<img src="cosmos.jpg" align="right"><br />
<?php
```

EXAMPLE   8.29 (CONTINUED)

```
1          $plants= array('perennials' => array('Day Lilies',
                                                 'Coral Bells',
                                                 'Goldenrod',
                                                 'Russian Sage'),
                           'annuals' => array('Begonia',
                                              'Sweet Alyssum',
                                              'Cosmos',
                                              'Helioptrope')
                          );
           // Recursive count
           echo "The number of elements: ",
2          count($plants, COUNT_RECURSIVE), "\n<br />"; // output 10
3          echo "The number of arrays: ", count($plants),
               "\n<br />"; // output 2
        ?>
        </td></tr>
        </table>
        </body>
        </html>
```

EXPLANATION

1   An array called $plants is assigned to associative arrays.
2   The count() function, with the COUNT_RECURSIVE flag argument, will recursively count all the elements in all of the arrays.
3   The count() function, without COUNT_RECURSIVE, counts just the two outer arrays.

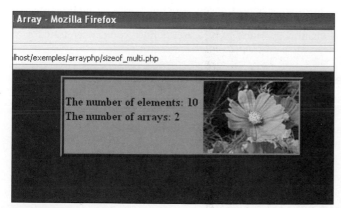

Figure 8.34   Counting elements in a multidimensional array. Output from Example 8.29.

8.1.11 Sorting Arrays

PHP provides numerous built-in functions to sort an array, listed in Table 8.6. The following examples select the more common array sorting functions and examples of how to use them.

Table 8.6 Sorting an Array

Function	*What It Does*
array_multisort()	Sorts multiple or multidimensional arrays
arsort()	Sorts an array in reverse order and maintains index association
asort()	Sorts an array and maintains index association
krsort()	Sorts an array by key in reverse order
ksort()	Sorts an array by key
natcasesort()	Sorts an array using a case-insensitive "natural order" algorithm
natsort()	Sorts an array using a "natural order" algorithm
rsort()	Sorts an array in reverse order
shuffle()	Shuffles an array
sort()	Sorts an array
uasort()	Sorts an array with a user-defined comparison function and maintains index association
uksort()	Sorts an array by keys using a user-defined comparison function
usort()	Sorts an array by values using a user-defined comparison function

Alphabetic Sort of Numerically Indexed Arrays.   The sort() function sorts an array alphabetically, and given specific flags, can also sort numerically. An alphabetic, also called a lexicographic sort, is performed according to the traditional "dictionary order," using the ASCII collating sequence. Uppercase letters come before lowercase letters, with numbers and punctuation interspersed. The built-in PHP sort() function sorts an array in ascending order by the value of the elements in the array. The index values are reset after the array is sorted. This function should be used on arrays with numeric indexes, and the asort() function used on associative arrays. The value returned is TRUE for success or FALSE for failure.

Table 8.7 lists the `sort_flags` (an optional parameter) used to modify the sorting behavior.

Table 8.7   Sort Flags

Flag	What It Does
SORT_LOCALE_STRING	Compares items as strings, based on the current locale[a]
SORT_NUMERIC	Compares items numerically
SORT_REGULAR	Compares items normally (does not change types)
SORT_STRING	Compares items as strings

a.   Added in PHP 4.3.12 and 5.0.2.

Alphabetic Sort.   The `sort()` function sorts the elements of an array alphabetically (ASCII sort). See Example 8.30.

EXAMPLE 8.30

```
          <html><head><title>Sorting an Array</title></head>
          <body bgcolor="CCFFFF">
          <font size="+1">
          <pre>
          <b>
          Sorting an Array Alphabetically
          <br />
          <?php
1             $animals = array("dog", "cat", "horse", "monkey",
                              "gorilla","zebra");
2             sort($animals);
3             print_r($animals);
          ?>
          </pre>
          </b>
          </body>
          </html>
```

EXPLANATION

1   The array called `$animals` is assigned a list of string values.
2   The `sort()` function sorts the values in the array alphabetically and resets the index values.
3   The `print_r()` prints the new assorted array. All of the index values have been reset. See Figure 8.35.

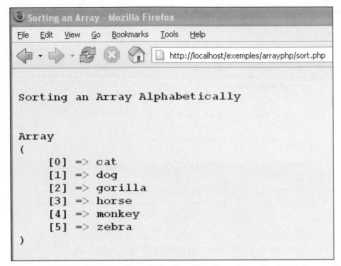

Figure 8.35 Sorting in alphabetical order. Output from Example 8.30.

Numeric Sort.   When the `sort()` function is given the `SORT_NUMERIC` argument, the values in the array are sorted numerically. See Example 8.31.

EXAMPLE 8.31

```
<html><head><title>Sorting an Array</title></head>
<body bgcolor="CCFFFF">
<font size="+1">
<pre>
<b>
Sorting an Array Numerically
<br />
<?php
1     $animals = array("5 dogs", "15 cats", "10 horses", "1 monkey",
                       "1 gorilla", "2 zebras");
2     sort($animals, SORT_NUMERIC);
3     print_r($animals);
?>
</pre>
</b>
</body>
</html>
```

1   The $animals array is assigned a list of strings beginning with numbers. If the array is sorted alphabetically, that is, without the SORT_NUMERIC argument, the output would be as shown in Figure 8.36.

2   The sort() function with the SORT_NUMERIC argument sorts the array numerically; that is, the numbers in the strings are sorted as numbers, alphabetic characters.

3   The print_r() function prints the numerically sorted array. The index values have been reset. See Figure 8.37

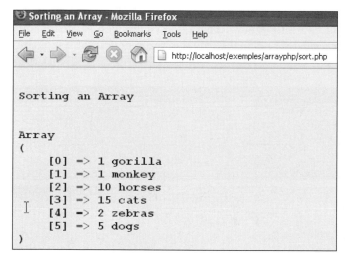

Figure 8.36
Before numeric sort.

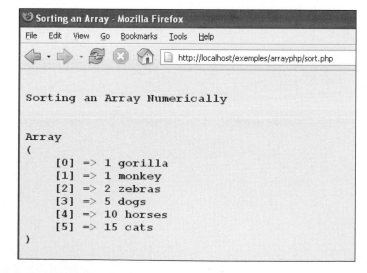

Figure 8.37
After numeric sort.

Reversed Sort.   The `rsort()` function sorts an array in reverse order. This function assigns new keys for the elements in the array. It will remove any existing keys you might have assigned, rather than just reordering the keys. This function sorts an array in reverse order (highest to lowest). It returns TRUE on success or FALSE on failure.

FORMAT

```
bool rsort ( array &array [, int sort_flags] )
```

Sort an Associative Array by Values.   The `asort()` function sorts an associative array so that the relation between the key and value is maintained. The function returns boolean TRUE for success, and FALSE for failure. The `asort()` function is used mainly when sorting associative arrays where the actual element order is significant. See Example 8.32.

FORMAT

```
asort( associative_array_name);
```

Example:
```
asort($states );   // Sorts by value
```

EXAMPLE 8.32

```
      <html><head><title>Sorting an Array</title></head>
      <body bgcolor="CCCFFF">
      <font style="arial" size="+1">
      <table border="2" cellspacing="3">
      <caption>Sorting by Values</caption>
      <tr><td>
      <?php
1     $states = array("HI"=>"Hawaii",
                       "ME"=>"Maine",
                       "MT"=>"Montana",
                       "CA"=>"California",
                       "AZ"=>"Arizona",
                       "MD"=>"Maryland",
                     );
2     asort($states);   // Sort by value
3     while (list($key, $val) = each($states)) {
4        echo "states[" . $key . "] => ". "<b>$val</b>\n<br />";
      }
      ?>
      </td></tr>
      </table>
      </body>
      </html>
```

EXPLANATION

1   An associative array called $states is defined consisting of keys and values.
2   The asort() function sorts the values of an associative array, alphabetically.
3   The while loop evaluates its expression and cycles through each of the key–value pairs of the $states array.
4   When the array key–values are printed, the values have been sorted alphabetically and the keys reordered to match their original corresponding values. See Figure 8.38.

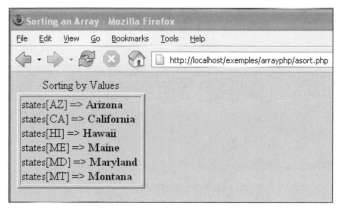

Figure 8.38   Sorting an associative array by values. Output from Example 8.32.

Sort by Value in Reverse Order.   The arsort() function sorts an array in reverse order and maintains index association with keys and values associated with them. It is used mainly with associative arrays where the association is significant. The function returns a boolean TRUE for success and FALSE for failure. See Example 8.33.

FORMAT

```
arsort ( array_name );
arsort (array_name, flags); // See sort() function for flag arguments
```

Example:
```
arsort ($states);    // Sorts in reverse order by value
```

EXAMPLE 8.33

```
          <html><head><title>Sorting an Array</title></head>
          <body bgcolor="CCFFFF">
          <font style="arial" size="+1">
          <table border="2" cellspacing="3">
          <caption>Reverse Sort by Values</caption>
          <tr><td>
          <?php
1             $states = array("HI"=>"Hawaii",
                              "ME"=>"Maine",
                              "MT"=>"Montana",
                              "CA"=>"California",
                              "AZ"=>"Arizona",
                              "MD"=>"Maryland",
                             );
2             arsort($states);
3             while (list($key, $val) = each($states)) {
4                 echo "states[" . $key . "] => ". "<b>$val</b>\n<br />";
              }
          ?>
          </td></tr>
          </table>
          </body>
          </html>
```

EXPLANATION

1   An associative array called $states is defined consisting of keys and values.
2   The arsort() function sorts the values of an associative array, alphabetically and in reverse order.
3   The while loop evaluates its expression and cycles through each of the key–value pairs of the $states array.
4   When the array key–values are printed, the values have been sorted in reverse, alphabetically, and the keys reordered to match their original corresponding values. See Figure 8.39.

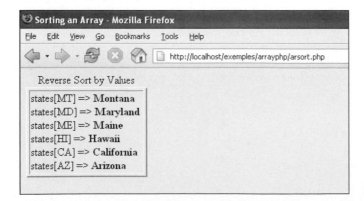

Figure 8.39
Sorting by value in reverse order. Output from Example 8.33.

Sort an Associative Array by Key. The `ksort()` function sorts an array by keys, maintaining the relation between the key and its corresponding value. This is used mainly for associative arrays. This returns TRUE on success or FALSE on failure. See Example 8.34.

EXAMPLE 8.34

```
       <html><head><title>Sorting an Array</title></head>
       <body bgcolor="CCFFFF">
       <font style="arial" size="+1">
       <table border="2" cellspacing="3">
       <caption>Sorting by Keys</caption>
       <tr><td>
       <?php
1          $states = array("HI"->"Hawaii",
                           "ME"=>"Maine",
                           "MT"=>"Montana",
                           "CA"=>"California",
                           "AZ"=>"Arizona",
                           "MD"=>"Maryland",
                          );
2          ksort($states);
3          while (list($key, $val) = each($states)) {
4              echo "states[<b>" . $key . "</b>] => ". "$val\n<br />";
           }
       ?>
       </td></tr>
       </table>
       </body>
       </html>
```

EXPLANATION

1   An associative array called `$states` is defined consisting of keys and values.
2   The `ksort()` function sorts the keys of an array alphabetically.
3   The `while` loop evaluates its expression and cycles through each of the key–value pairs of the `$states` array.
4   When the array key–values are printed, the keys have been sorted alphabetically, and the values reordered to match the original keys that correspond to them. See Figure 8.40.

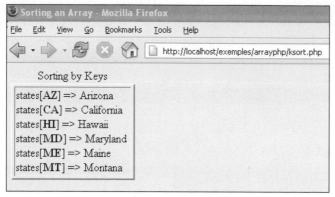

Figure 8.40 Sorting by keys. Output from Example 8.34.

8.1.12 Randomizing an Array

Randomizing an array means that you can select the keys or the values in random order.

Randomizing the Keys.   The `array_rand()` function lets you select one or more random entries from an array.

It takes an array as its argument and by default returns one random key or index value. If a second optional numeric argument is given, you can specify how many random keys to pick from the array, and an array of that number of random keys will be returned.[5] See Examples 8.35 and 8.36.

FORMAT

```
random_key= array_rand ( array_name );
array_of_keys = array_rand( array_name, integer);
```

Example:
```
$colors=array("red","green","blue","yellow");
$random= array_rand($colors);      // Returns a random color
$random= array_rand($colors, 2); // Returns two random colors
print $colors[$random_keys[0]];
print $colors[$random_keys[1]];
```

---

5. As of PHP 4.2.0, there is no need to seed (give it a starting random point) the random number as it is now done automatically.

EXAMPLE 8.35

```html
<html>
<head><title>Getting a Random Array Element</title></head>
<body bgcolor="lightgreen">
<font face="verdana" size="+1">
<?php
1       $sayings=array("An apple a day keeps the doctor away",
                    "Too many cooks spoil the broth",
                    "A stitch in time saves 9",
                    "Don't put the cart before the horse",
                    );
2       $selection = array_rand($sayings);
3       print $selection;  // Prints the index value
?>
4   <b><?=$sayings[$selection]?></b>.  // Prints the random value
    </body>
    </html>
```

EXPLANATION

1   The array called $sayings is assigned a list of strings.
2   The array_rand() function will return a random item from the list of strings in
    the $sayings array.
3   The index value of the random selection is printed.
4   The random saying selection is printed. See Figures 8.41 and 8.42.

Figure 8.41   Getting a random element from an array. Output from Example 8.35.

Figure 8.42   Refreshing the screen for another random element. Output from Example 8.35.

EXAMPLE 8.36

```
        <html>
        <head><title>Random Array of Two Strings</title></head>
        <body bgcolor="lightgreen">
        <font face="verdana" size="+1">
        <?php
1           $sayings=array("An apple a day keeps the doctor away",
                           "Too many cooks spoil the broth",
                           "A stitch in time saves 9",
                           "Don't put the cart before the horse",
                    );
2           $selection = array_rand($sayings,2);
3           print "${sayings[$selection[0]]}.<br />";
            print "${sayings[$selection[1]]}.<br />";
        ?>
        </body>
        </html>
```

EXPLANATION

1   The array called $sayings is assigned a list of strings.
2   The array_rand() function is given a second argument, the number 2, which is
    the number of random items to return. The array called $selection will contain
    another array of two random key/index values.
3   The first and second randomly selected strings are printed. The value of $selec-
    tion[0] is a random index number. So is the value of $selection[1]. By using
    those array elements as indexes for the $sayings array, a randomized string will
    be returned. Notice the curly braces surrounding the $sayings array. The curly
    braces block the array elements so that the first $ applies to the whole array. If you
    remove the curly braces, you will get an error. The other way to print this would
    be to remove the quotes:

    print $sayings[$selection[1]] . ".
";

    See Figures 8.43 and 8.44.

Figure 8.43   Selecting two random elements from an array. Output from Example 8.36.

Figure 8.44 Refreshing the screen for two more random elements.

Shuffling a Numeric Array (Randomizing the Values). The `shuffle()` function causes the elements of a numerically indexed array to be randomized. It randomizes the values of an associative array, but destroys the keys. The function returns boolean TRUE or FALSE. See Example 8.37.

Prior to PHP 4.2.0, it was necessary to seed the random number generator (give it a different starting point) with `srand()`, but now that is done automatically. To randomize a selected number of elements of an array, see the `array_rand()` function.

FORMAT

```
boolean_value = shuffle( array_name );
```

Example:
```
$numbers = ( 1, 2, 3, 4, 5, 6, 7, 8, 9, 10);
shuffle($numbers);
```

Output:
```
9 4 6 5 1 3 2 8 7 10
```

EXAMPLE 8.37

```
    <html><head><title>Shuffle the Array</title></head>
    <body bgcolor="33FF66">
    <div align="center">
    <font size="+1">
    <h3>
    Shuffle the Array
    </h3>
    <?php
1       $months=range(1,12);
2       // srand(time());
        echo "<b>Before:</b> ", implode(", ", $months), "<br /><br />";
3       shuffle($months);
        echo "<b>After: </b>", implode(", ", $months), "<br />";
    ?>
    </font>
    </div>
    </body>
    </html>
```

EXPLANATION

1   An array called $months is created. A range of 1 to 12 months is created with the
    range() function.
2   It is no longer necessary to seed the random number generator with srand(); that
    is, give it a random starting point.
3   The shuffle() function shuffles or randomizes the elements of the array,
    $months. See Figure 8.45 for before and after the shuffle.

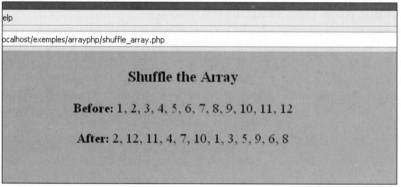

Figure 8.45   Shuffling an array of months. Output from Example 8.37.

8.2   Modifying Arrays (Unsetting, Deleting, Adding, and Changing Elements)

PHP makes it easy to modify both numeric and associative arrays by providing a number
of built-in functions to add new elements, remove existing elements and/or replace
those elements with new ones, copy elements from one array to another, to rearrange
elements, and so on.

8.2.1   Removing an Array and Its Elements

There are a number of built-in functions to remove elements from an array (see
Table 8.8).

Table 8.8 Functions That Remove Elements

Function	What It Does
array_pop()	Removes and returns the last element of an array
array_shift()	Removes and returns the first element of an array
array_splice()	Removes and/or replaces elements in an array
array_unique()	Removes duplicates from an array

Removing an Entire Array.   The unset() function completely removes an array, as though it never existed. Setting the element's value to zero or the null string assumes the element is still there.

FORMAT

```
void unset ( mixed var [, mixed var [, mixed ...]] )
```

Example:
```
$colors=array("red","green","blue");
unset($colors);   // Removes the array
```

Removing the Last Element of an Array.   The array_pop() function removes the last elment of an array and returns it, shortening the array by one element. If the array is empty (or is not an array), NULL will be returned. This function resets the array pointer after it is used.

FORMAT

```
mixed array_pop ( array &array )
```

Example:
```
$animals = ("dog", "cat", "pig", "cow");
$strayed = array_pop($animals);   // The "cow" is removed from the
                                  // array, and assigned to $strayed
```

EXAMPLE 8.38

```
        <html><head><title>array_pop()</title></head>
        <body bgcolor="cccc99">
        <font face="verdana" size="+1">
        <?php
            echo "Before pop(): ";
1           $names=array("Tom", "Dan", "Steve", "Christian", "Jerry");
2           foreach($names as $val){
                echo "<em>$val </em>";
            }
3           $popped = array_pop($names);    // Remove last element
            echo "<br />After pop(): ";
4           foreach($names as $val){
                echo "<em>$val </em>";
            }
            echo "<p>$popped was removed from the end of the array.</p>";
        ?>
        </pre>
        </body>
        </html>
```

EXPLANATION

1   The numeric array $names is created and assigned a list of values.
2   The foreach loop is used to iterate through the array and display its values.
3   The array_pop() function removes the last element of the array, "Jerry". The
    popped off value is returned and assigned to a variable, called $popped.
4   The $names array is displayed after the last element was removed with the
    array_pop() function. See Figure 8.46.

Figure 8.46 The last element from an array is removed with pop(). Output from
Example 8.38.

Removing the First Element of an Array. The array_shift() function removes the first element from an array and returns it, decreasing the size of the array by one element. All numerical array keys start at zero and literal keys will not be touched. If an array is empty (or is not an array), NULL will be returned. See Example 8.39.

FORMAT

```
mixed array_shift ( array &array )
```

Example:
```
$colors=array("red", "blue","green", "yellow");
// First element, "red", removed and assigned to $shifted_off_color
$shifted_off_color = array_shift( $colors);
```

EXAMPLE 8.39

```
    <html><head><title>array_shift()</title></head>
    <body bgcolor="lightblue">
    <font face="verdana" size="+1">
    <?php
        echo "Before the shift: ";
1       $names=array("Tom", "Dan", "Steve", "Christian", "Jerry");
2       foreach($names as $val){
            echo "<em>$val </em>";
        }
3       $shifted=array_shift($names);   // Remove first element
        echo "<br />After the shift: ";
4       foreach($names as $val){
            echo "<em>$val </em>";
        }
5       echo "<p>$shifted was removed.</p>";
    ?>
    </pre>
    </body>
    </html>
```

EXPLANATION

1 A numeric array called $names is defined.

2 The foreach loop is used to iterate through the array and get the individual values, each one in turn, assigned to $val.

3 The array_shift() function removes and returns the first element of the array, "Tom", assigned to $shifted.

4 The foreach loop is used again to iterate through the array showing that the array has been shortened by one element. See Figure 8.47.

5 The value returned from the array_shift() function is "Tom", the first element in the array. This value is printed. See Figure 8.47.

Figure 8.47   Removing the first element of an array with `shift()`. Output from Example 8.39.

Removing Duplicate Values from an Array.   The   `array_unique()`   function removes duplicate values from an array and returns a new array without the duplicates. The `array_unique()` function first sorts the values treated as strings, then keeps the first key encountered for every value, and thereafter, ignores any duplicate keys. Two elements are considered equal only if they are identical (same data type, same value); that is, the `===` operator applies. See Example 8.40.

FORMAT

```
array array_unique ( array array )
```

Example:

```
unique_values = array_unique(array("apples", "pears",
                                    "apples", "Apples"));
// Removes duplicates and returns an array with unique values.
```

EXAMPLE   8.40

```
        <html><head><title>array_unique()</title></head>
        <body bgcolor="cccc99">
        <font face="verdana" size="+1">
        <?php
            echo "Before: ";
    1       $numbers=array(1, 3, 5, 7, 7, 7, 9, 9, 8);
    2       foreach($numbers as $val){
                echo "<em>$val </em>";
            }
            echo "<br />After: ";
    3       $numbers=array_unique($numbers);  // Remove duplicates
            echo '$numbers=<b>array_unique($numbers)i</b><br />';
            foreach($numbers as $val){
                echo "<em>$val </em>";
            }
        ?>
        </pre>
        </body>
        </html>
```

1   A numerically indexed array called $numbers is assigned a list of integers.
2   The foreach loop is used to loop through the array, $numbers. The value of each of the elements is printed.
3   Notice that there are a number of duplicate values in the array $numbers. The array_unique function returns an array with duplicates removed; that is, an array of unique values. See Figure 8.48.

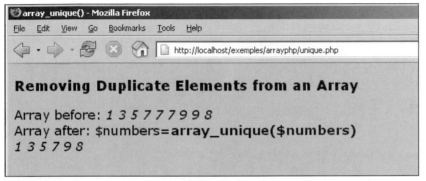

Figure 8.48   The array_unique() function. Output from Example 8.40.

8.2.2   Adding Elements to an Array

PHP provides built-in functions to increase the size of an array by allowing you to add elements.(see Table 8.9).

Table 8.9   Array Functions to Add Elements to an Array

Function	What It Does
array_push()	Pushes a new element(s) onto the end of the array
array_splice()	Removes and/or adds elements to an array at any position
array_unshift()	Adds a new element(s) to the beginning of the array

Adding Elements to the Beginning of an Array.   The array_unshift() function prepends one or more elements onto the beginning of an array, increasing the size of the array by the number of elements that were added. It returns the number of elements that were added. See Example 8.41.

FORMAT

```
int array_unshift ( array &array, mixed var [, mixed ...] )
```

Example:
```
$colors=("yellow", "blue", "white");
$added=array_unshift($colors,"red","green");
// "red", "green", "yellow", "blue", "white"
```

EXAMPLE 8.41

```
     <html><head><title>array_unshift()</title></head>
     <body bgcolor="yellow">
     <font face="verdana" size="+1">
     <?php
         echo "Before unshift(): ";
1        $names=array("Tom", "Dan", "Steve", "Christian", "Jerry");
2        foreach($names as $val){
             echo "<em>$val </em>";
         }
         // Add new element to the beginning
3        array_unshift($names, "Willie", "Liz");
         echo "<br />After unshift(): ";
         foreach($names as $val){
             echo "<em>$val </em>";
         }
4        echo "<p>Willie and Liz were added to the beginning of the
             array.</p>";
     ?>
     </pre>
     </body>
     </html>
```

EXPLANATION

1   The numeric array called $names is assigned five string values.
2   The foreach loop is used to iterate through the array $names. Each value is print-
    ed as the loop cycles through the array.
3   The array_unshift() function is used to append new elements to the beginning
    of an array. In this example, "Willie" and "Liz" are prepended to the array
    $names. "Willie" will be assigned the index of 0, and all the rest of the index val-
    ues will be incremented accordingly.
4   Figure 8.49 displays the array after "Willie" and "Liz" are prepended with the
    array_unshift() function.

Figure 8.49 Adding elements to the beginning of an array with `unshift()`. Output from Example 8.41.

Adding Elements to the End of an Array. The `array_push()` function pushes one or more elements onto the end of array, increasing the size of the array by the number of elements that were added. It returns the number of elements that were added. See Example 8.42.

FORMAT

```
int array_push ( array &array, mixed var [, mixed ...] )
```

Example:
```
$colors=("yellow", "blue", "white");
$added = array_push($colors, "red", "green");
// "yellow", "blue", "white", "red", "green"
```

EXAMPLE 8.42

```
        <html><head><title>array push()</title></head>
        <body bgcolor="lightblue">
        <font face="verdana" size="+1">
        <?php
            echo "Before push(): ";
1           $names=array("Tom", "Dan", "Christian", "Jerry");
2           foreach($names as $val){
                echo "<em>$val </em>";
            }
3           array_push($names, "Tina", "Donna");   // Add two elements
            echo "<br />After push(): ";
            foreach($names as $val){
                echo "<em>$val </em>";
            }
4           echo "<p>Tina and Donna were added to the end of the
                array.</p>";
        ?>
        </pre>
        </body>
        </html>
```

EXPLANATION

1   The numeric array called $names is assigned four string values.
2   The foreach loop is used to iterate through the array $names. Each value is print-
    ed as the loop cycles through the array.
3   The array_push() function is used to append new elements to the end of an ar-
    ray. In this example, "Tina" and "Donna" are appended to the array $names.
    "Tom" will be assigned the index of 0, and all the rest of the index values are in-
    cremented accordingly.
4   Figure 8.50 displays the array after "Tina" and "Donna" are appended to it with
    the array_push() function.

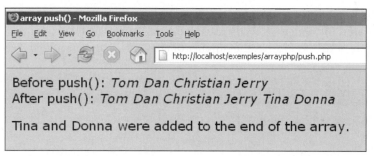

Figure 8.50   The array_push() function. Output from Example 8.42.

Splicing an Array—Removing and Adding Elements.   The word *splice* is often
associated with splicing two pieces of rope, film, or DNA strands. It means to join. Array
elements can be removed and then what is left can be joined back together. The
array_splice() function removes a portion of the array and joins it back together, pos-
sibly replacing the removed values with new ones. The first argument is the array, and
the second argument is the place in the array (called the *offset*) where you want the function to start removing elements. Offset 0 is the first position in the array. If you are taking
elements from the end of the array, the offset starts at a negative number. An offset of
–1 indicates the end of the array. The third, optional argument tells the function how
many elements you want to remove. If you do not specify a length, splice() removes
everything from the offset to the end of the array. A fourth optional argument allows you
to list the replacement values. (Use the built-in count() function to get the length of
the array.) The returned values are the elements that were removed.

Simply put, splice() removes any number of elements from an array, starting at
some position, and lets you replace those elements with new ones if you want to.

The next set of examples demonstrate how array_splice() is used to remove and
replace elements in an array. Figure 8.51 displays the resulting spliced array.

FORMAT

```
array array_splice ( array &input, int offset [, int length [,
                     array replacement]] )
```

Examples:
1. `$foods=array("bread","milk", "eggs", "fruit", "meat");`
   `array_splice($foods, 4);` `// Removes "meat"`
2. `$foods=array("bread","milk", "eggs", "fruit", "meat");`
   `array_splice($foods,0,3);` `// Removes "bread", "milk", and "eggs"`
3. `$foods=array("bread","milk", "eggs", "fruit", "meat");`
   `array_splice($foods, -2);` `// Removes "fruit" and "meat"`
4. `$foods=array("bread","milk", "eggs", "fruit", "meat");`
   `array_splice($foods, 0,0, array("fish", "cheese"));`
   `// Prepends the array with "fish" and "cheese"`
5. `$foods=array("bread","milk", "eggs", "fruit", "meat");`
   `array_splice($foods, -3, 2, "veggies");`
   `// Backs up three from the end, removes "eggs" and "fruit",`
   `// and replaces them with "veggies"`
6. `$foods=array("bread","milk", "eggs", "fruit", "meat");`
   `array_splice($foods,2 ,count($foods),array("beer","peanuts"));`
   `// Removes "eggs", "fruit", and "meat" and replaces them with`
   `// "beer" and "peanuts"`

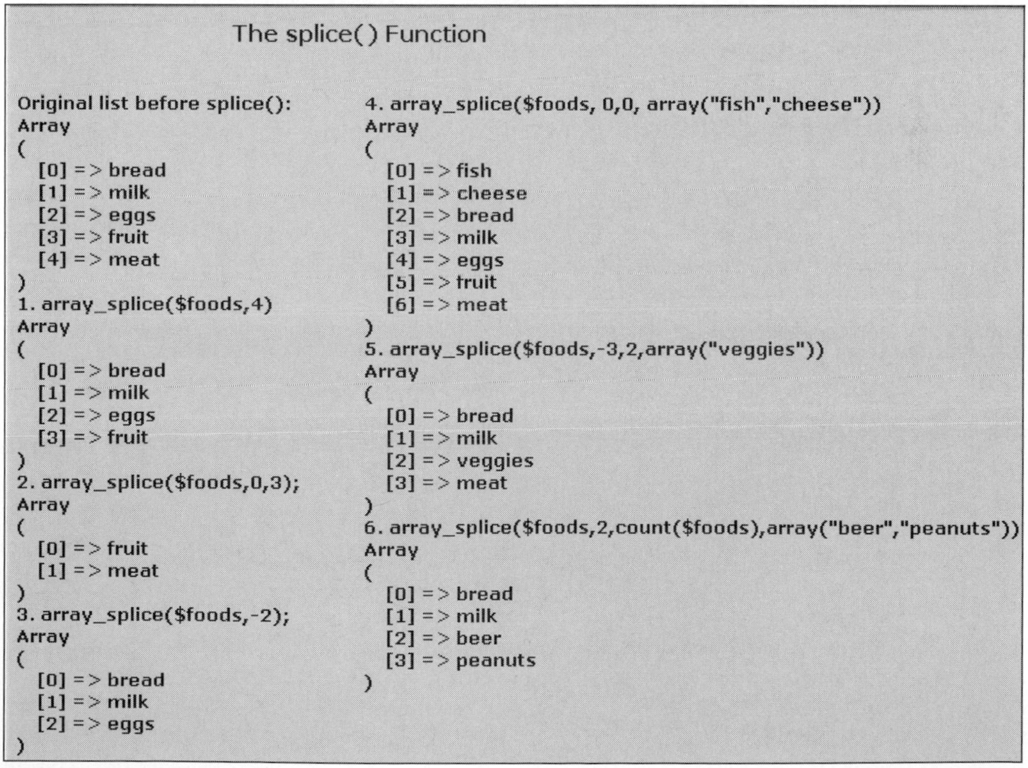

Figure 8.51   The `splice()` function. Each numbered example is applied to the original array.

8.2.3 Copying Elements of an Array

The array_slice() Function.   In case you get the terms *splice* and *slice* confused, think of a splice as joining two pieces of tape or rope together and think of slice as in a slice of bread or a slice of apple pie. The array_slice() function extracts a slice (some specified elements) of an array, specified by an offset and the number of elements to extract. It returns the specified sequence of elements from the array and resets the key/index values. If the boolean argument is set to TRUE, then the index values will not be adjusted.

To simplify, the array_slice() function copies elements from one array, and assigns them to another array. The array that is being sliced is not changed. See Example 8.43

FORMAT

```
array array_slice ( array array, int offset [, int length [,
                bool preserve_keys]] )
array  = array_slice ( array_name, integer offset);
array  = array_slice ( array_name, integer offset,  length);
array  = array_slice ( array_name, integer offset,  length, boolean
value);
```

Example:
```
foods = array("bread", "milk", "eggs", "fruit");
$slice = array_slice ( $foods, 2);
// $slice contains "eggs"

$slice = array_slice ( $foods, 0, 2);
// $slice contains "bread" and "milk"

$slice = array_slice ( $foods, -2, 1);
// $slice contains "milk"

$slice = array_slice ( $foods, 0, 3, TRUE);
// $slice contains "bread", "milk", and "eggs"; the order of the
// keys/index values are preserved
```

EXAMPLE 8.43

```
    <html><head><title>array_slice()</title></head>
    <body bgcolor="cccc99">
    <font face="verdana">
    <pre>
    <b>
    <?php
1       $names=array("Tom", "Dan", "Steve", "Christian", "Jerry");
        echo "Original array before slice(): <br />";
        print_r($names);
2       $good_guys=array_slice($names, 0, 3);
        echo "<br />New array from array_slice(0,3):<br /> ";
        print_r($good_guys);
```

EXAMPLE 8.43 (CONTINUED)

```
3       $chosen_ones=array_slice($names, -2);
        echo "New array from array_slice(-2):<br />";
        print_r($chosen_ones);
        echo "Original array after the slice(): <br />";
4       print_r($names);
    ?>
    </pre>
    <b>
    </body>
    </html>
```

EXPLANATION

1 $names is a numeric array intialized with a list of strings.
2 The first argument to the `array_slice()` function is the offset position, where to start selecting elements, and the second argument is the length or number of elements to copy. In this example, `"Tom"`, `"Dan"`, and `"Steve"` are copied into an array called $good_guys.
3 In this example, the offset starts from the end of the array. An offset of –2 means back up two positions from the end of the array. Because a length is not specified, the `array_splice()` function will copy the last two elements, `"Christian"` and `"Jerry"`, from the array and assign them to $good_guys.
4 For output of this example, see Figure 8.52.

```
Original array before slice():
Array
(
  [0] => Tom
  [1] => Dan
  [2] => Steve
  [3] => Christian
  [4] => Jerry
)

New array from array_slice(0,3):
 Array
(
  [0] => Tom
  [1] => Dan
  [2] => Steve
)
New array from array_slice(-2):
Array
(
  [0] => Christian
  [1] => Jerry
)
Original array after the slice():
Array
(
  [0] => Tom
  [1] => Dan
  [2] => Steve
  [3] => Christian
  [4] => Jerry
)
```

Figure 8.52

The `array_slice()` function.
Output from Example 8.43.

8.2.4   Combining and Merging Arrays

The array_combine() Function.   The `array_combine()` function returns an array made up of keys and values. The keys of the new array are the made up of the values from the first array and the values associated with the new keys are made up of the values from the second array (PHP 5). The function returns FALSE if there are an unequal number of values in either of the arrays used as arguments.

FORMAT

```
array array_combine ( array keys, array values )
```

Example:
```
$titles=array("President", "Programmer", "Accountant");
$names=array("Bill McClintock", "Pearl White", "Barry Buck");
$new_array = array_combine( $titles, $names);
// Returns: "President =>"Bill McClintock, "Programmer"=>"Pearl
// White", "Accountant"=>"Barry Buck"
```

EXAMPLE 8.44

```
      <html>
      <head><title>Combining Arrays</title></head>
      <body bgcolor="lightblue">
      <h3>Combining Arrays</h3>
      <pre>
      <?php
1         $abbrev=array('CA', 'MT', 'VA');
2         $states=array('California','Montana','Virginia');
          echo 'After combining $abbrev and $states',"<br />";
3         $combined=array_combine($abbrev, $states);
4         print_r($combined);
      ?>
      <pre>
      </body>
      </html>
```

EXPLANATION

1   An numeric array called $abbrev is assigned three string values.
2   An numeric array called $states is assigned three string values.
3   The `array_combine()` function combines the two arrays so that the values in the first array $abbrev become the keys corresponding to the values in the second array, $states. A new array called $combined, an associative array of key–value pairs, is returned.
4   The combined array is printed. The keys are made up of the first array, $abbrev, and the values from the second array, $states. See Figure 8.53 for the output.

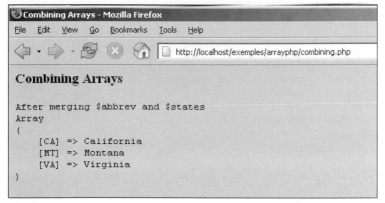

Figure 8.53 Combining arrays with keys and values. Output from Example 8.44.

The array_merge() Function. The `array_merge()` function joins two or more arrays together to return a single array. The values of one array are appended to the end of the previous array.

FORMAT

```
array array_merge ( array array1 [, array array2 [, array ...]] )
```

Example:
```
$newarray=array_merge($array1, $array2);  // Returns one array
```

If array elements have the same keys, then the key of the first array will be overwritten by the key of the next one. If, however, the arrays contain numeric keys, the later value will not overwrite the original value, but will be appended.

If only one array is given and the array is numerically indexed, the keys get reindexed in order.

Merging Numerically Indexed Arrays. Example 8.45 demonstrates the merging of numerically indexed arrays using the `array_merge()` function.

EXAMPLE 8.45

```
<html>
<head><title>Merging Arrays</title></head>
<body bgcolor="lightblue">
<h3>Merging Arrays</h3>
<pre>
```

EXAMPLE 8.45 (CONTINUED)

```php
        <?php
1           $primary=array('red', 'blue', 'yellow');
            echo '$primary=array("red", "blue", "yellow")',"<br />";
2           $secondary=array('orange','purple','green');
            echo '$secondary=array("orange","purple","green")',"<br />";
            echo 'After merging $primary and $secondary',"<br />";
3           $merged=array_merge($primary, $secondary);
            print_r($merged);
        ?>
        <pre>
        </body>
        </html>
```

EXPLANATION

1   A numeric array, called $primary, is initialized.
2   A second numeric array, called $secondary, is initialized with three values.
3   The array_merge() function appends the second array to the first one. The index values of the second array are incremented in the order in which they appear in the new merged array.
4   The merged arrays are shown in Figure 8.54.

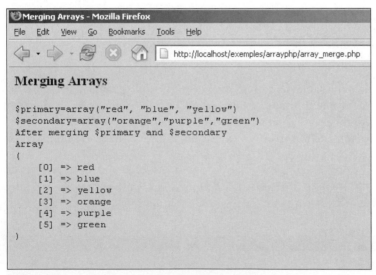

Figure 8.54   Merging two arrays. Output from Example 8.45.

Merging Associative Arrays.   Example 8.46 demonstrates merging associative arrays and removing duplicate keys.

EXAMPLE 8.46

```
<body bgcolor="lightblue">
<h3>Merging Associative Arrays</h3>
<pre>
<?php
1       $cyclewear1=array('item'=>'jersey', 'color'=>'blue',
                          'type'=> 'hooded');
2       $cyclewear2=array('size'=>'large','color'=>'white',
                          'cost'=>'145');
        echo 'After merging $cyclewear1 and $cyclewear2',"<br />";
3       $merged=array_merge($cyclewear1, $cyclewear2);
4       print_r($merged);
?>
</pre>
</body>
</html>
```

EXPLANATION

1   An associative array is initialized with key–value pairs.
2   This associative array has a `'color'` key, and so does the first one. When they are merged, the value of the `'color'` key in the first array will be overwritten by the value in the second array.
3   The second array, `$cyclewear2`, is appended to the first array, `$cyclewear1`. If the first array and the second array have duplicate keys, the duplicate keys in the first array are overwritten.
4   The output is printed as shown in Figure 8.55.

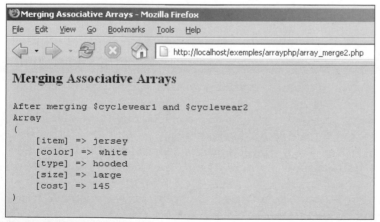

Figure 8.55   Merging associative arrays. Output from Example 8.46.

The array_merge_recursive() Function. The array_merge_recursive() function merges two or more arrays recursively. array_merge_recursive() merges the elements of one or more arrays together so that the values of one are appended to the end of the previous one. It returns the resulting array.

FORMAT

```
array array_merge_recursive ( array array1 [, array ...] )
```

If you have two associative arrays being merged and their keys are the same but their values are different, the array_merge_recursive() function will combine the values of both arrays into another array as shown in Example 8.47.

If the arrays have the same numeric key, the later value will not overwrite the original value, but it will be appended.

EXAMPLE 8.47

```
      <head><title>Merging Associative Arrays</title></head>
      <body bgcolor="lightblue">
      <h3>Merging Associative Arrays</h3>
      <pre>
      <?php
1         $cyclewear1=array('item'=>'jersey', 'color'=>'blue',
                            'type'=> 'hooded');
2         $cyclewear2=array('size'=>'large','color'=>'white',
                            'cost'=>'145');
          echo 'After merging $cyclewear1 and $cyclewear2',"<br />";
3         $merged=array_merge_recursive($cyclewear1, $cyclewear2);
4         print_r($merged);
      ?>
      </pre>
      </body>
      </html>
```

EXPLANATION

1 The associative array, $cyclewear1, contains key–value pairs describing an item called "jersey".
2 The associative array, $cyclewear2, contains more descriptive key–value pairs, and also has a 'color' key, but with a different value.
3 The array_merge_recursive() function merges the two arrays and where the key is the same, creates an array of values. The 'color' key now consists of an array of colors, 'blue' and 'white'.
4 After merging two arrays recursively, the new array returned from array_merge_recursive() is printed. See Figure 8.56.

The Equality and Identical Operators.   When using the equality operator to compare two arrays, if both keys and values have the same value, they are equal, but the order and data type does not matter. To be identical, both the keys and values must be of the same data type, same value, and in the same order. See Example 8.49.

EXAMPLE   8.49

```
         <html>
         <head><title>Equality and Identity</title></head>
         <body bgcolor="lightgreen">
         <font face="arial" size='+1'>
         <?php
1            $pets=array('dog', 'cat', 'bird');
2            $animals=array(1=>'cat',0 =>'dog', "2" => 'bird');
3            if ($pets == $animals){    // key-value pairs are equal
                 echo "\$pets and \$animals are equal.<br />";
             }
             else{
                 echo "\$pets and \$animals are not equal.<br />";
             }
4            if ($pets === $animals){ /*key-value pairs must be in the same
                                        order and keys are of the same type */
                 echo "\$pets and \$animals are identical.<br />";
             }
             else{
5                echo "\$pets and \$animals are not identical.<br />";
             }
6            $pets=array('dog','cat', 'bird');
             // Reorder key-values
7            $animals=array(0=>'dog', 1=>'cat', 2=> 'bird');
8            if ($pets === $animals){
                 echo "Now \$pets and \$animals are identical.<br />";
             }
         ?>
         </body>
         </html>
```

EXPLANATION

1   The array called $pets is assigned three values. The index values of 0, 1, and 2 are assigned automatically if not specified.

2, 3   The array called $animals is assigned three values. The index values of 0, 1, and 2 are assigned to each of the elements, but the elements are arranged in a different order. When checking for equality, as long as the keys and values are equal, then the arrays are equal.

4   When testing for "identical," the keys and values not only have to be equal, but they must be in the same order.

5   This line is executed because the "identical" test failed on line 4.

EXPLANATION (CONTINUED)

6   The array called $pets is assigned three values. The index values of 0, 1, and 2 are assigned automatically if not specified.

7   The $animals array is assigned numeric indexes and values that are in the same order and contain the same values as the $pets array on line 6. Even though they look different, the array elements in the $pets array are set to start at index 0 by default.

8   The $pets array is identical to the $animals array; that is, the keys and values are the same and they are in the same order, then the expression is true and the output in Figure 8.58 will be printed.

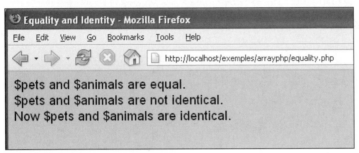

Figure 8.58   Equal or identical? Output from Example 8.49.

8.2.6 More Array Functions

PHP 4 introduced more than 30 functions that allow you to manipulate an array in numerous ways. Table 8.11 lists of most of the built-in array functions, many of which we described in detail in this chapter. See the PHP manual for a complete list.

Table 8.11   The Most Common Array Functions

Function	*What It Does*
Creating Arrays	
array()	Creates an array (see page 252).
array_fill()	Declares and populates an array (see page 255).
range()	Creates an array starting from a low to high value (see page 253).
Printing Arrays	
print_r()	Displays both keys/indexes and values of an array (see page 262).
var_dump()	Displays an array's size, keys/indexes, values, and length (see page 265).

Table 8.11   The Most Common Array Functions (continued)

Function	What It Does
Merging or Combining Arrays	
array_combine()	Combines two arrays. The first array consists of elements that will serve as keys, and elements of the second array will serve as values for the returned associative array (see page 322).
array_merge()	Merges one or more arrays (see page 323).
array_merge_recursive()	Merges two or more arrays recursively (see page 326).
Arrays and Strings	
explode()	Splits up a string by a specified delimiter and creates and array of strings (see page 276).
implode()	Glues the elements of an array together by some delimiter and creates a string (see page 276).
join()	Same as implode().
split()	Splits a string into an array by a delimiter expressed as a regular expression (see also preg_split on page 510).
spliti()	Same as split, but case insensitive.
Checking for Existence of an Array, Key, or Value	
array_key_exists()	Checks if a given key or index exists in an array (see page 274).
in_array()	Checks if a value exists in an array (see page 274).
is_array()	Checks if the variable is an array (see page 274).
Extracting Array Keys and Values	
array_keys()	Returns all the keys of an array (see page 281).
array_key_exists()	Checks if the given key or index exists in the array (see page 274).
array_sum()	Calculates the sum of values in an array.
array_values()	Returns all the values of an array (see page 283).
each()	Returns the current key and value pair from an array and advances the array cursor (see page 284).
extract()	Extracts values from an array and creates variables of the same name (see page 288).
key()	Fetches a key from an associative array.
list()	Extracts values from an array and creates user-defined variables (see page 286).

Table 8.11 The Most Common Array Functions (continued)

Function	What It Does
Modifying, Adding, and Deleting Array Elements	
array_chunk()	Splits an array into chunks.
array_filter()	Filters elements of an array using a callback function.
array_map()	Applies the callback function to the elements of the given arrays (see page 359).
array_pop()	Pops the element off the end of an array (see page 311).
array_product()	Calculates the value of the product of the values in an array.
array_push()	Pushes one or more elements onto the end of an array (see page 317).
array_reduce()	Iteratively reduces the array to a single value using a callback function.
array_shift()	Shifts an element off the beginning of an array (see page 313).
array_slice()	Extracts a slice of the array (see page 320).
array_splice()	Removes a portion of the array and replaces it with something else (see page 318).
array_unique()	Removes duplicate values from an array (see page 314).
array_unshift()	Prepends one or more elements to the beginning of an array (see page 315).
array_walk()	Applies a user function to every member of an array.
array_walk_recursive()	Applies a user function recursively to every member of an array (see page 360).
unset()	Completely removes an array, as if it never existed (see page 311).
Randomizing an Array	
array_rand()	Picks one or more random entries from an array (see page 306).
shuffle()	Randomizes all the elements of a numeric array (see page 309).
Reversing an Array	
array_flip()	Exchanges all keys with their associated values in an array.
array_reverse()	Returns an array with elements in reverse order.

Table 8.11 The Most Common Array Functions (continued)

Function	What It Does
Searching for Elements in an Array	
array_search()	Searches the array for a given value and returns the corresponding key if successful.
array_values()	Returns all the values of an array (see page 283)
current()	Returns the current element in an array.
pos()	Alias of current().
Dealing with Uppercase and Lowercase	
array_change_key_case()	Returns an array with all string keys in lower- or uppercase.
Finding Differences in Arrays	
array_diff()	Computes the difference of arrays.
array_diff_assoc()	Computes the difference of arrays with additional index check.
array_diff_key()	Computes the difference of arrays using keys for comparison.
array_diff_uassoc()	Computes the difference of arrays with additional index check that is performed by a user-supplied callback function.
array_diff_ukey()	Computes the difference of arrays using a callback function on the keys for comparison.
array_udiff()	Computes the difference of arrays by using a callback function for data comparison.
array_udiff_assoc()	Computes the difference of arrays with additional index check; compares data by a callback function.
array_udiff_uassoc()	Computes the difference of arrays with additional index check; compares data and indexes by a callback function.
Counting the Elements in an Array	
array_count_values()	Counts all the values of an array (see page 279).
count()	Counts elements in an array, or properties in an object (see page 278 and page 296).
sizeof()	Alias of count() (see page 278).

Table 8.11   The Most Common Array Functions (continued)

Function	What It Does
Moving the Array Pointer	
next()	Advances the internal array pointer of an array.
prev()	Rewinds the internal array pointer.
reset()	Sets the internal pointer of an array to its first element.
end()	Sets the internal pointer of an array to its last element.
Intersecting an Array	
array_intersect()	Computes the intersection of arrays.
array_intersect_assoc()	Computes the intersection of arrays with additional index check.
array_intersect_key()	Computes the intersection of arrays using keys for comparison.
array_intersect_uassoc()	Computes the intersection of arrays with additional index check; compares indexes by a callback function.
array_intersect_ukey()	Computes the intersection of arrays using a callback function on the keys for comparison.
array_uintersect()	Computes the intersection of arrays; compares data by a callback function.
array_uintersect_assoc()	Computes the intersection of arrays with additional index check; compares data by a callback function.
array_uintersect_uassoc()	Computes the intersection of arrays with additional index check; compares data and indexes by a callback function.
Sorting an Array	
array_multisort()	Sorts multiple or multidimensional arrays.
arsort()	Sorts an array in reverse order and maintains index association (see page 303).
asort()	Sorts an array and maintains index association (see page 302).
krsort()	Sorts an array by key in reverse order.
ksort()	Sorts an array by key (see page 305).
natcasesort()	Sorts an array using a case-insensitive "natural order" algorithm.
natsort()	Sorts an array using a "natural order" algorithm.
rsort()	Sorts an array in reverse order (see page 302).

Table 8.11   The Most Common Array Functions (continued)

Function	*What It Does*
Sorting an Array (***continued***)	
shuffle()	Shuffles an array (see page 309).
sort()	Sorts an array (see page 298).
uasort()	Sorts an array with a user-defined comparison function and maintains index association
uksort()	Sorts an array by keys using a user-defined comparison function
usort()	Sorts an array by values using a user-defined comparison function

8.3   Chapter Summary

8.3.1   What You Should Know

Now that you have finished this chapter you should be able to answer the following questions:

1. How do you create an array and assign values to it?

2. What is the difference between numerically indexed and string indexed arrays?

3. How do you print an array with print_r() and var_dump()?

4. How do you get the size of an array?

5. How do you loop through array elements with the while, for, and foreach looping constructs?

6. How do you create arrays of arrays?

7. How do you use PHP functions to manipulate an array to add or decrease its size?

8. How do you delete an array?

9. How do you create variables from arrays?

10. What is the difference between extract() and list()?

11. How do you sort arrays?

12. How do you combine arrays?

13. How do you use array operators?

8.3.2 What's Next?

You have been exposed now to a multitude of PHP's built-in functions. Chapter 9, "User-Defined Functions," shows you how to define and call your own functions.

CHAPTER 8 LAB

1. Create a string of names consisting of `"John, Jerry, Ann, Sanji, Wen, Paul, Louise, Peter"`.

   a. Create an array out of the string. (Hint: See `explode()`).
   b. Sort the array.
   c. Reverse the array.
   d. Remove the first element from the array.
   e. Add `"Willie"` and `"Daniel"` to the end of the array.
   f. Replace `"Paul"` with `"Andre"`.
   g. Add `"Alisha"` to the beginning of the array.
   h. Create another array of names.
   i. Merge both of your arrays together and display them in sorted order.

2. Create a PHP associative array called `"student"` of key–value pairs. The keys are `"Name"`, `"ID"`, `"Address"`, `"Major"`, `"Email"`, and `"Phone"`. The values will be entered by the user in an HTML form. Check that each field was filled out. Assign the values extracted from the form to correspond to the keys in the `$student` array.

   a. Sort the array by keys.
   b. Print the array as an HTML table.
   c. Print just the values.
   d. Print the student's name, e-mail address, and phone number.

3. Create an array of six images. One of the images will be a 2006 BMW. The rest of the images will be small items. The images will represent prizes for a drawing. Ask the user to pick a number between 1 and 6. Shuffle the array and use the user's number to index into the array. In an HTML page, display the image of the user' prize. Congratulate the winner of the 2006 BMW.

chapter
9

User-Defined Functions

9.1 What Is a Function?

We have already seen a number of PHP built-in functions to manipulate arrays and strings, perform tests on variables, display output, and more. PHP provides you with a large array of built-in functions to perform common tasks to save you the trouble of writing your own functions. As your programs become more sophisticated, you might find that the particular task you need is not handled by PHP or that you want to break your program into smaller units to make it more manageable. Then it is time to write your own functions, and this chapter will show you how. But first things first—let's define a function now.

Functions are self-contained units of a program designed to accomplish a specified task such as calculating a mortgage payment, retrieving data from a database, or checking for valid input. When a function is called in a program, it is like taking a detour from the main part of the program. PHP starts executing the instructions in the function, and when finished, returns to the main program and picks up where it left off. Functions can be used over and over again and thus save you from repetitious programming. They are also used to break up a program into smaller modules to keep it better organized and easier to maintain.

By definition, a function is a block of statements that not only performs some task, but can also return a value. A function is independent of your program and not executed until called. A function, often referred to as a "black box," is like the pocket calculator or remote control. Information goes into the black box as input (like the calculator or remote control when you push buttons), and the action or value returned from the box is its output (such as a calculation or a different channel). What goes on inside the box is transparent to the user. The programmer who writes the function is the only one who cares about those details. When you use PHP's built-in functions such as print() or rand(), you send a string of text or a number to the function, and it sends something back. You do not care how it does its job, you just expect it to work. If you send bad input, you get back bad output or maybe nothing, hence the expression "Garbage in, garbage out."

Functions are like miniscripts. They contain PHP statements that behave as a single command and can be called repeatedly throughout a program without rewriting the code.

The terms *function* and *method* are often used interchangeably. The term *method* refers to a function that is used with PHP objects (covered in Chapter 17, "Objects"). The term *function* as used in this chapter is a stand-alone block of statements, independent of the program until invoked by a caller.

9.1.1   Function Declaration, Definition, and Invocation

The terms *declaration* and *definition* are often used interchangeably, but they are really different terms. To declare a function is to give it a name followed by the keyword `function`, and a set of parentheses that might or might not contain parameters (messages) that the function will accept.

```
function do_something()     // Declaration
```

The function definition is the declaration and the body of statements found within the curly braces after the function's name.

```
function do_something(){
   statements;            // Definition
}
```

By itself, a function does not do anything. *Invocation* refers to calling a function; that is, telling PHP to start executing the statements within the curly braces. Typically, a function is called from a statement in another part of the program by its name, followed by a set of parentheses that might or might not be empty.

```
 do_something();
```

Now we are ready to put all of these peices together to create a function and call it.

Where to Put Functions.   User-defined functions can be declared anywhere within a file. They are placed within the `<?php` and `?>` tags and are available only to the script where they are defined. The function can be called before or after its definition because PHP internally compiles all function definitions before it executes any of the statements in the script.

Commonly used functions are often stored in separate files to reuse them as needed (see "Function Libraries—Requiring and Including" on page 373).

How to Define a Function.   To define a function, the `function` keyword is followed by the name of the function, and a set of parentheses. The parentheses are used to hold parameters, values that are received by the function. The function's statements are enclosed in curly braces.

```php
<?php
   function bye() {
      print "Bye, adios, adieu, au revoir...");
   }
?>
```

Within the curly braces, any legal PHP code is accepted, including other function calls, HTML, declaration of new variables, even calls to itself. Think of a function as a mini PHP script.

The function, like variables, has naming conventions:

1. It must consist of letters, digits, or the underscore and cannot begin with a digit.
2. The function name must be unique for each function. You can have a variable with the same name, but it is not recommended.
3. A function should be given a name that indicates its purpose with an action word, a verb, such as `updateEmail()`, `getList()`, or `calculateTax()`. The name of your function should indicate what the function is supposed to do; for example, a function used to display form output might be named `display-Form()` rather than `showit()`.
4. Unlike variable names, function names are *not* case sensitive. Convention uses lowercase names.

Table 9.1   Naming Functions

Valid Names Examples	*Invalid Names Examples*	
`do_work()`	`5printout()`	`// Can't start with a number`
`Addemup()`	`show-form()`	`// Can't contain a dash`
`calculate2()`	`$moveover()`	`// Can't contain nonalphanumeric`
`_name_that_tune()`		`characters other than an`
		`underscore`

How to Call a Function.   Once you define a function, you can use it. PHP functions are invoked by calling the function; for example, `bye()` or `show_me($a, $b)`. Calling a function is similar to taking a detour from the main highway you are driving on, and then later returning to the main road again. The main highway is analogous to the PHP program, and a function call is analogous to the detour in the road. After you call the function, the statements within the function are executed. When the function ends, control returns to the statement following the function call (i.e., where it left off in the main program), and program execution continues. When called, the function's name is followed by a set of parentheses that might contain messages that will go to the function. These messages are called *arguments*. When the function returns, it might send back information to the main program. To continue the detour analogy, if before you detour, you buy a digital camera and some water to take along with you, these items would be like arguments are to the function. When you return to the main road again, you might bring back some pictures and an empty water bottle. This would be analogous to a return statement in a function. If, for example, the function is sent a list of numbers, and its task is get the average of the numbers, then it might return the average to the caller of the function.

To check whether the function has been defined or if it is truly a function, use the built-in `isset()` function discussed in Chapter 4, "The Building Blocks."

FORMAT

Function definition:
```
function function_name() {statement; statement;}
function function_name (parameter, parameter, ...){statement;
statement;}
```

Function call:
```
function_name();
function_name(argument, argument, ...)
```

EXAMPLE 9.1

```
    <html>
    <html><head><title>A Simple Function</title></head>
    <body bgcolor="009900">
    <font size="+1">
    <center>
    <?php
1       function welcome(){  // Function definition
2           $place="San Francisco Zoo";   // Local variable
            print ("<b>Welcome to the $place!<br />");
3       }
4       welcome();  // Function call
    ?>
5   <img src="zoo.jpg" width="340" height="200">
    </body>
    </html>
```

EXPLANATION

1 A function can be defined before or after the place in the program where it is called. Functions are placed between the PHP tags. In this example, the function is defined, but it will not do anything until it is called from somewhere in the script. The `function` keyword is followed by the user-defined name of the function called `welcome` and a set of parentheses. The name of the function is case insensitive. The parentheses are used to hold parameters, information being received by the function. What the function actually does is handled by the set of statements enclosed within curly braces.

2 The statements enclosed in curly braces are the function definition. They are executed whenever the function is called. When this function is called, the string `"San Francisco Zoo"` will be assigned to the variable called `$place`.

Variables declared within a function are local in scope. They are not visible outside of the function, whereas variables defined outside of the function are not visible within the function unless they are made global. (See "Global Scope" on page 363.)

3   This is the final closing curly brace that ends the function definition.

4   This is where the function is invoked or called. When the function, `welcome()`, is called, the program will jump to line 1 and execute the statements within the function definition. After the function exits, program control goes to line 5, the line right after the function call.

5   The image is part of the HTML page and will be displayed after the function call. See Figure 9.1.

Figure 9.1   The `welcome()` function. Output from Example 9.1.

9.1.2   Passing Arguments

What Are Arguments and Parameters?   If a user wants to send values to a function, he or she calls the function with a comma-separated list of arguments enclosed in parentheses. In the "detour in the road" analogy, this would be like picking up some food or a disposable camera to take along when you temporarily leave the main road.

The following `feed_me()` function takes three arguments when called:

```
feed_me("fruit", $veggies, 5);   <---arguments
```

The arguments can be a combination of numbers, strings, references, variables, and so on. They are received by the function in a list of corresponding values called parameters.

```
function feed_me( $fr, $veg, $num) {   };   <---parameters
```

The names of the arguments are not necessarily the same names in the parameter list, but they correspond to the same values. These values can be assigned to local variables within the function. They disappear when the function exits. PHP does not keep track of the number of arguments sent to the function to make sure they match up with the number of parameters specified in the function definition at the other end. If you send three arguments, and there are only two parameters defined within the function, the third argument is ignored. If you send only two arguments, and the parameter list expects three, then PHP will send a warning such as the following, and the parameter remains unset:

Warning: Missing argument 3 for calc_mileage() in c:\wamp\www\exemples\ch9functions\calc_mileage.php on line 5

```
(Caller)
function_name(argument1, argument2);        // Function call (caller)

(Receiver)
function_name(parameter1, parameter2){      // Function definition (receiver)
   result= parameter1 + parameter2;
   .....
}          // Curly braces required
```

In the analogy of the pocket calculator, you are the caller when you press the buttons, and the internal functions inside the calculator are the receiver.

Passing by Value. When you pass arguments by value, PHP makes a copy of the variable, so that if you change it in the function, you are only changing the copy. When the function exits, the copy is destroyed. In Example 9.2 the parameters, `$m` and `$g`, are copies of the original values of `$miles` and `$gallons`. If you give yourself 10 more gallons of gas in the function (`$m + 10`), then when the function exits, the original value will be unchanged. To prevent inadvertently altering the values of variables declared outside of a function, sending a copy is considered a safe way to pass arguments, and is designed to be the default.

EXAMPLE 9.2

```
     (The HTML File)
     <html><head><title>Passing Arguments</title></head>
     <body bgcolor="lavender">
1    <form  action="volume.php">
     <p>
        Find the volume (in feet) of a rectangular room with sides
2       <input type="text" size=6 name="s1">
        by
        <input type="text" size=6 name="s2">
        by
        <input type="text" size=6 name="s3">
        <p>
        <input type="submit" name="submit" value="Get Volume" >
     </form>
-------------------------------------------------------------------
```

EXAMPLE 9.2 (CONTINUED)

```
      (The PHP Script)
      <html><head><title>Passing Arguments</title></head>
      <body bgcolor = "#ffffcc">
      <font face="verdana" size="+1">
      <?php
3         extract($_REQUEST);
4         volume($s1, $s2, $s3);   // Passing 3 arguments


5         function volume($side1,$side2,$side3){
6            print "The volume of the room is: "
                . $side1 * $side2 * $side3."cubic ft.<br />";
             }
      ?>
      </body></html>
```

EXPLANATION

1   The HTML form starts here. When the user presses the submit button, the PHP script listed in the `action` attribute will be started by the server. The method being used here is the `GET` method, the default method for sending data from the browser to the server.

2   The user will be asked to fill in three text boxes that will contain the dimensions of a room (in feet).

3   In the PHP script, the values (i.e., the user input) are extracted from the `$_REQUEST` array. The values are stored in variables named after the input devices in the HTML form: `$s1`, `$s2`, and `$s3`.

4   The function, `volume()`, is called (invoked) with three arguments, `$s1`, `$s2`, and `$s3`. Copies of these values will be sent to the function.

5   This line defines what the function does. It will multiply the three values passed to get the volume of a room and print the result.

6   After the form in Figure 9.2 is filled out and the user presses the button labeled "Get Volume," the PHP script will be processed. The `volume()` function will calculate the volume of the room and display the results in the browser (see Figure 9.3).

Figure 9.2   The HTML page from Example 9.2.

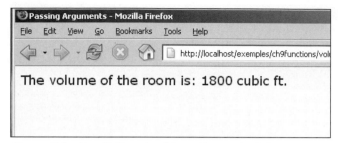

Figure 9.3   The PHP output from Example 9.2.

Missing Arguments.   If you expect a function to take arguments, then you must send that number of arguments to the function or you will get a warning message from the PHP interpreter. To guarantee that a parameter will be set even if the calling function does not provide one, you can set default parameter values in the function declaration as shown in "Setting Default Parameters" on page 347.

EXAMPLE 9.3

```
        <html><head><title>Passing Arguments</title></head>
        <body bgcolor = "#ffffcc">
        <font face="verdana" size="+1">
        <?php
            extract($_REQUEST);
1           volume($s1, $s2);   // Need three arguments, have only two
2           function volume($side1,$side2,$side3){
                print "The volume of the room is: "
                . $side1 * $side2 * $side3." cubic ft.<br />";
            }
        ?>
        </body>
        </html>
```

EXPLANATION

1   The `volume()` function is called with two arguments, but the function expects three.

2   The function is defined to take three arguments, one for each side in the room:

```
volume($s1, $s2);



function volume($side1,$side2,$side3){
```

Because the third argument is missing, the function will multiply `$side1` and `$side2` by zero, which is the value of the missing `$side3`. The warning message is shown in Figure 9.5.

Figure 9.4 The HTML page from Example 9.3. The same form was also used in Example 9.2.

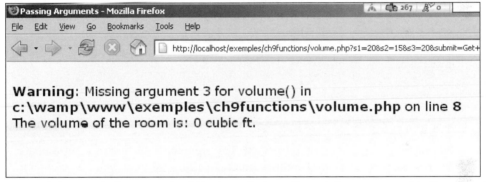

Figure 9.5 The PHP error output that results from the missing argument in Example 9.3.

Variable Number of Arguments. If the function is to take a variable number of arguments, there are three built-in PHP functions that will help you determine how many arguments were passed and what they were. These functions are: `func_num_args`, `func_get_args`, and `func_get_arg` (see Table 9.2).

Table 9.2 Built-In Functions to Handle Variable Arguments

Function	What It Does
`func_num_args()`	Returns the number of arguments passed to the function
`func_get_arg($arg_num)`	Returns a specific argument, based on its index position
`func_get_args()`	Returns an array containing all the arguments

Example 9.4 demonstrates the use of the built-in functions listed in Table 9.2.

EXAMPLE 9.4

```
        <html><head><title>Variable Arguments</title></head>
        <body bgcolor = "#ffffcc">
        <font face="verdana" size="+1">
        <pre>
        <?php
1           average(40,90,89,93,75);   // Arguments must be literals

2           function average(){
                $sum = 0;
3               $all_args = func_get_args();
                print_r($all_args);
4               $size = func_num_args();
                for($i = 0; $i < $size; $i++){
5                   $sum += func_get_arg($i);
                }
6               print "The average is:" . $sum/$size ."<br />";
            }
        ?>
        </pre>
        </body>
        </html>
```

EXPLANATION

1 The function, get_average(), is called. The arguments are an array of numbers.
   When using the special PHP built-in functions, the argument list must be literal;
   that is, a string, a number, and so on. It cannot be a variable.

2 The function, get_average(), is defined here.

3 The built-in function, func_all_args(), returns an array of all the parameters
   received in the function.

4 The built-in function, func_num_args(), returns the number of parameters received in the function.

5 The built-in function, func_get_arg(), takes the index number from an element
   of the array of arguments and returns its value. In this example, the index starts
   at 0, and each time through the loop will be incremented by 1 until the array ends.
   Each time through the loop the value of the element is added to the sum. The sum
   of all the grades is totaled by the time the loop exits.

6 See Figure 9.6 for the output of this script.

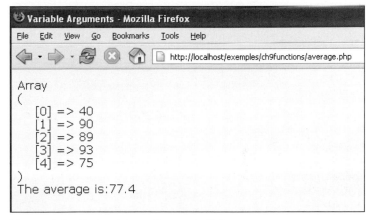

Figure 9.6 Output from Example 9.4.

Setting Default Parameters. If the caller of a function does not pass an argument and the function expects one, you can set a default parameter. Here are some rules for using default parameters:

1. Parameters without defaults must be placed before parameters where defaults are assigned.
2. The value assigned as a default must be a constant such as a string or number, but not a variable.
3. If the caller of the function passes the expected argument, the value of the default parameter will be ignored.

EXAMPLE 9.5

```
    <html><head><title>Default Arguments</title><head>
    <bgcolor="#fffed9">
    <font face="verdana" size="+1">
    <?php
1       function print_table($border, $color="#669966"){
2           print<<<TABLE_BLOCK
        <table border="$border">
        <caption><b>Lincoln High Events</b></caption>
        <tr bgcolor="$color">
            <th>Date</th>
            <th>Event</th>
            <th>Time</th>
            <th>Location</th>
        </tr>
        <tr>
            <td>June 8</td>
            <td>Graduation</td>
            <td>8:00 PM</td>
            <td>Gymnasium</td>
        </tr>
```

EXAMPLE 9.5 (CONTINUED)

```
            <tr>
                <td>June 21</td>
                <td>Piano Recital</td>
                <td>8:00 PM</td>
                <td>Theatre</td>
            </tr>
            <tr>
                <td>July 4</td>
                <td>Fireworks</td>
                <td>9:00 PM</td>
                <td>Football Field</td>
            </tr>
            </table>
            <hr>
3           TABLE_BLOCK;
    }
4       print_table("1");   // One argument passed; default color used
5       print_table("10", "gray"); /* Two arguments passed; second
                                      argument overrides the default */
    ?>
    </body>
    </html>
```

EXPLANATION

1   The function, `print_table()`, has two parameters. The first must be sent from the caller and the second is the default. If the caller doesn't send the color value, it will get a default value of green, `#669966`.

2, 3 This is a *heredoc*. All the text between `<<TABLE_BLOCK` and the ending `TABLE_BLOCK` on line 3 will be printed to the browser. This is an easy way to send a whole section of HTML with only one PHP `print` statement.

4   The `print_table()` function is called with one argument, the border width for the table. The color argument is missing. The function will use the default parameter to set the table row. The value of the default parameter must be a constant. See the top table in Figure 9.7.

5   This time the `print_table()` function is called with two arguments, the border width (`"10"`) and the color (`"gray"`). Both of these values will be assigned to `$border` and `$color`, the default value ignored. See the bottom table in Figure 9.7.

Figure 9.7   Calling a function that is assigned a default parameter. Output from Example 9.5.

Passing by Reference.   When passing a variable by reference (only variables can be passed by reference), the value being passed can be changed directly, because instead of passing a copy of the value, you are passing a reference to the orginial variable. Any changes you make to the variable in the function will change the value in the original variable. When passing large strings, arrays, or objects, this is a less expensive operation for PHP than copying all the values onto the parameter list. When passing by reference, you will not have to send a return value back and assign it to a variable in the main program. However, it is dangerous as it allows modifications of the variable within the function that might later cause harmful side effects to program code outside the function.

EXAMPLE   9.6

```
      <html><head><title>Pass by Reference</title></head>
      <body bgcolor="yellow"><font face="arial">
      <b>
      <?php
          $colors = array('red','green','blue');
1         $list=print_r ($colors,true);
2         html_tags($list);
3         echo "$list";
4         $string = "Hello, world!";
5         html_tags($string,"p");
          echo "$string";
          echo "$string";
```

EXAMPLE   9.6 (CONTINUED)

```
6       function html_tags(&$text, $tags="pre"){
7           switch($tags){
                case 'br':
                    $text = "$text</$tags>";
                    break;
                case 'p':
                    $text = "<$tags>$text";
                    break;
                default:
8                   $text = "<$tags>$text</$tags>";
                    break;
            }
        }
    ?>
    </body>
    </html>
```

EXPLANATION

1   The output from the built-in `print_r()` function is a variable, `$list`. It is a formatted list of the contents of the `$colors` array.

2   The `html_tags()` function is called with one argument, `$list` (the contents of the `$colors` array). The default is to print the text with `<pre>` tags.

3   Because the argument, `$list`, was passed to the function by reference, it was modified in the function. In this example, the HTML `<pre>` tags were added so that the output would appear on separate lines. See Figure 9.8.

4, 5   A string is assigned to `$string`, which will be passed as an argument to the function, `html_tags()`. Another argument, `"p"`, is also passed to the function, causing the string to be printed as a paragraph by prepending the `<p>` tag. The string is printed twice to show that the paragraph tag was added. See Figure 9.8.

6   The function `html_tags()` is defined. It has two parameters: a reference to the text that is being passed, and a default parameter that will set the default tag to a `<pre>` tag, if the user does not provide a second argument when calling the function. Because the first parameter is a reference, PHP will not make a copy of the value coming into the function, but will create a reference, or alias, so that the original value can be modified within the function. A return statement will not be necessary, because the function has access to the original variable.

7   The `switch` statement will evaluate the value of `$tags` and test it against the cases listed below it. The original text passed as the first parameter will be surrounded by the tags selected in the second parameter.

8   The default is to provide an opening and closing tag for the text passed to the function. When the function exits, the original text will have changed to include the selected tags.

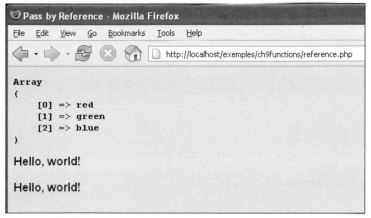

Figure 9.8   Passing by reference. Output from Example 9.6.

Dynamic Function Calls.   In Chapter 4, "The Building Blocks," we discussed dynamic variables, also called variable variables, where a variable could be aliased by giving it the name of another variable. You can also assign a function name as a string to a variable and then use the variable exactly as you would the function name itself.

FORMAT

```
function function_name() { statements... ; }
$variable = function_name;
$variable();
```

Example:
```
function sayGoodbye(){
    echo "So long.<br />";
}
$bye = "sayGoodbye";   // Assign the function's name to a variable
$bye();  // Call the function using the variable variable
// prints "So long."
```

9.1.3   Return Values

After taking a detour from the main road, it is now time to return. The return statement in a function allows you to send a value back to the caller or to exit the function before it reaches the end. Normally if a return call happens before a function ends, it is based on some condition that was met or not met. Single or multiple values, as well as references, can be returned from a function.

Returning a Single Value.   In the following example, the value of a simple scalar variable is returned from a function and assigned to a variable on the receiving end. The function is called on the right side of the equal sign, and the value returned is stored in the variable on the left side.

EXAMPLE 9.7

```
        <?php
1       $grades=array(40,90,89,93,75);
2       $result = average($grades);    // Pass an array
3       print "The average grade is $result.<br />";

4       function average($scores){
            $sum = 0;
5           $size = count($scores);    // Find the size of the array
            if ( $size == 0 ){
                echo "Empty parameter list<br />";
6               exit(); }      // Exit the script here
            for($i = 0; $i < $size; $i++){
7               $sum += $scores[$i];
            }
8           return $sum/$size;    // Return the average
        }
        ?>
```

EXPLANATION

1   A numeric array, $grades, is assigned five numbers.

2, 3   The user-defined function, average(), is on the right side of the equal sign, causing it to be called before an assignment can be made to $result. The function has one argument, the array, $grades. Whatever is returned from the function will be assigned to $result. On the next line that result is displayed in the browser. See the output in Figure 9.9.

4   The function called average is defined with one parameter, a copy of the array passed on line 2.

5   The built-in count() function determines the number of elements in the array that was passed to the function.

6   If the function received no parameters, the return statement will cause the function to quit here and exit the script. This statement prevents further execution of the remaining statements in the function. PHP would throw an error message on line 7, with illegal division of zero, if the program continued at this point.

7   The for loop is used to iterate through the array of scores accumulating the sum of the scores. The size of the array determines when the loop ends.

8   The expression $sum/$size is evaluated and its result is returned to the place where the function was called on line 2 and that value will be assigned to $result.

Figure 9.9   Returning from a function. Output from Example 9.7.

Conditional Returns.   If what is returned from a function is based on some condition, you can have multiple return statements in a function. The return value can be a boolean TRUE or FALSE as we have already seen in a number of the PHP's built-in functions, or a value returned based on a test condition. Consider Example 9.8, where there are three return values.

EXAMPLE 9.8

```
        (The HTML File)
        <html><head><title>What time is it?</title></head>
        <body bgcolor="silver">
        <div align="center">
1       <form action="clock.php" method="post">
            Enter the number of hours since midnight<br />
            <input type="text" size='3' name="time">
            <br /><br />
2           <input type="submit" value="Get the time!">
            <p>
            <input type="reset">
        </form>
        </div>
        </html>
        ----------------------------------------------------------------
        (The PHP file)
        <html><head><title>Conditional Return</title></head>
        <body bgcolor="silver">
        <div align="center">
        <font size="+1">
        <?php
3           function clock_time($total_hours){
                if($total_hours < 0 || $total_hours > 23){
4                   return "Invalid input.<br />";
                }
5               $hours = (($total_hours - 1)  % 12) + 1;
                if ( $total_hours >= 12) {
6                   return "The time is $hours PM.\n<br />";
                }
```

EXAMPLE 9.8 (CONTINUED)

```
        else{
7           return "The time is $hours AM.\n<br />";
        }
    }
    // If the user filled in the text field, enter the block
    if ($_REQUEST['time']){
        $num_hours=trim($_REQUEST['time']);  /* Remove any
                                leading/trail whitespace */
8       print  clock_time($num_hours); // Call clock_time
    }
?>
</font>
</div>
</body>
</html>
```

EXPLANATION

1   This is the HTML file that will display the form, a text box, named `time`. When the user presses the submit button, the form data will be sent to the PHP script assigned to the `action` attribute of the form. The method being used to send the form is `post`.

2   When the user presses this button, the form will be submitted to the PHP script, called `clock.php`. See the HTML form in Figure 9.10.

3   The function, `clock_time()`, is declared. It will take one argument. Its function is to return a string containing the current time in AM/PM notation.

4   If the condition on line 3 is true, then this string returned and printed on line 8.

5   When using modulus, `$total_hours % 12` returns a value in the range of 0 to 11. This formula should adjust the result so that the range is between 1 and 12.

6   If the condition on the previous line is true, then this string returned and printed on line 8.

7   If the time is not PM, then this string is returned to line 8.

8   The function, `clock_time()`, is called. A string is returned and received as an argument to the built-in `print()` function. It will print out the time in AM/PM notation. See the output in Figure 9.11.

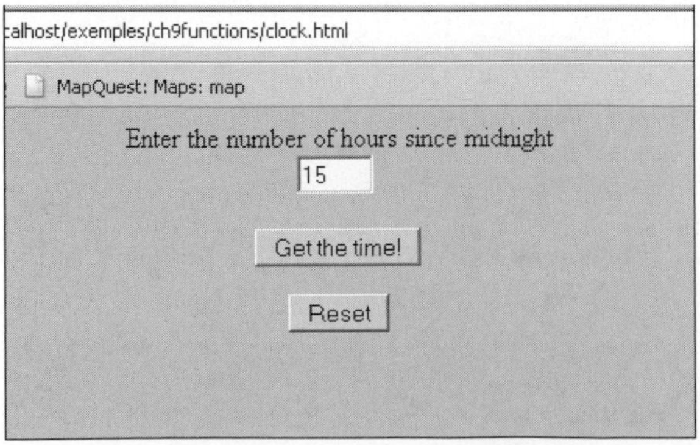

Figure 9.10
The HTML file from Example 9.8.

/localhost/exemples/ch9functions/clock.php

AQ   MapQuest: Maps: map

The time is 3 PM.

Figure 9.11   The PHP file output from Example 9.8.

Returning Multiple Values.   Sometimes you might want to return multiple values from a function. For example, you have opened a file or database, and want to define a function to retrieve information by reading lines from a file or fetching rows from a database. The function will return a list of the items that were retrieved, such as a product, unit number, price, quantity, and so on. PHP allows you to return not only single values, but arrays and associative arrays. Example 9.9 uses a simple function to square all the values in an array and return the modified array. Note: You must return the array, not its individual elements; for example, `return($n[0], $n[1], $n[2], $n[3])` would be wrong.

EXAMPLE   9.9

```
    <?php
1       $numbers=array(1,2,3,4,5,6);
        print "<pre>Before: ";
        print_r($numbers);
2       $new_numbers = square($numbers);
        print "<br />After: ";
        print_r($new_numbers);
        print "</pre><br />";
3       function square($n){
            for($i=0; $i<count($n); $i++){
4               $n[$i] =  $n[$i] * $n[$i];
            }
5           return $n; // Return an array
        }
    ?>
```

EXPLANATION

1   A numeric array of integers is defined.
2   The function, `square()`, is called. The array of integers is passed as a list of arguments to the function.
3   The function `square()` takes one parameter, the array on integers passed on line 2.
4   This is where the function performs its task of squaring each of the numbers passed in the parameter list.
5   The array, `$n`, consisting of a list of numbers, is returned to the caller of this function and then displayed. See Figure 9.12, the array before and after its values were squared.

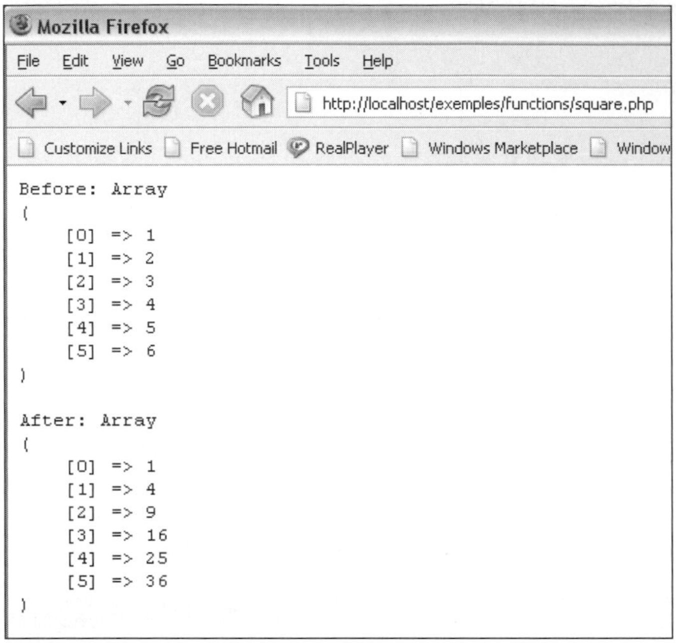

```
Mozilla Firefox
File   Edit   View   Go   Bookmarks   Tools   Help

        http://localhost/exemples/functions/square.php

  Customize Links    Free Hotmail    RealPlayer    Windows Marketplace    Window

Before: Array
(
    [0] => 1
    [1] => 2
    [2] => 3
    [3] => 4
    [4] => 5
    [5] => 6
)

After: Array
(
    [0] => 1
    [1] => 4
    [2] => 9
    [3] => 16
    [4] => 25
    [5] => 36
)
```

Figure 9.12   Returning an array. Output from Example 9.9.

Consider the next example. We have not discussed PHP and how it interacts with MYSQL database, but you can overlook the details and see that the function, `get_info()`, returns a multidimensional array resulting from a database query. The explanation section should clarify how this function works.

EXAMPLE 9.10

```
    <html><head><title>Returning a List</title>
    </head>
    <body bgcolor="lavender">
    <font size="+1">
    <h2>Function Returns an Array of Hashes</h2>
    <?php
        print "Opening a connection<br />";
1       $connection=mysql_connect("localhost","root","") or
            die ("Couldn't open connection");
2       $result=mysql_select_db("northwind");
        if($result){echo "Database \"northwind\" selected<br />";}
3       function get_info(){
            $record=array();
4           $result_set=mysql_query("SELECT * FROM Shippers");
5           while($row=mysql_fetch_assoc($result_set)){
                array_push($record, $row);
            }
```

EXAMPLE 9.10 (CONTINUED)

```
6          return($record);
        }
    ?>
    <br /><br />
    <b>
    <?php
7       $company_records=get_info();
8       foreach ( $company_records as $key=>$value){
9           foreach( $value as $field_key=>$val){
                print "$field_key => $val<br />";
            }
            print "<hr>";
        }
    ?>
    </b>
    </font>
    </body>
    </html>
```

EXPLANATION

1   The PHP `mysql_connect()` function opens up a connection to the MYSQL server and returns a link to the server so that now we can access a database.

2   This is where the database is selected. A popular database called `northwind` is opened and a resource handle is returned to give access to it. A resource type holds a special handler to the database connection created when the database connection was made.

3   The function, `get_info()`, is defined. It will retrieve all the records from the `Shippers` table and return them to the caller.

4   The `mysql_query()` function sends a query to the currently active `northwind` database and returns a reference to the data it selected; that is, all of the records in `Shippers`.

5   The `mysql_fetch_assoc()` function returns an associative array that corresponds to the fetched row and moves the internal data pointer ahead to the next row.

6   A set of records from the `Shippers` table are returned to the caller as an array of associative arrays.

7   The `get_info()` function is called. An array of records (associative arrays) is returned and assigned to `$company_list`.

8   The `foreach` loop is used to iterate through the keys and values of the three arrays, each of which contains an associative array.

9   This inner `foreach` loop retrieves the keys and values from each of the associative arrays returned from the function, which is each record in the `Shippers` table. The output is shown in Figure 9.13.

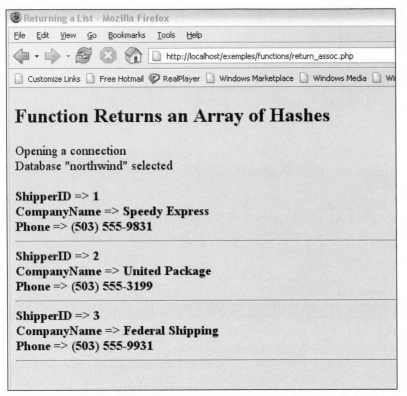

Figure 9.13   A function that returns an associative array. Output from Example 9.10.

9.1.4   Using Callback Functions

A callback function is one that is not directly invoked in the program; instead it is invoked by another function. What that means is that one function takes another function, called the callback function, as its argument. Callback functions are often used to perform some arbitrary task on each item in a list of items. One function traverses the list, and the other provides the code to represent the task that will be performed on each item. PHP provides a number of array functions that utilize "callbacks." Some of these functions are `preg_replace()`, `array_filter()`, `array_map()`, and so on. (Callback functions cannot only be simple functions, but also object methods including static class methods. See Chapter 17, "Objects.")

A PHP function is simply passed by its name as a string. You can pass any built-in or user-defined function with the exception of `array()`, `echo()`, `empty()`, `eval()`, `exit()`, `isset()`, `list()`, `print()`, and `unset()`.

The array_map() Function.   The following example uses PHP's `array_map()` function to demonstrate the use of a callback function. The `array_map()` function returns an array containing all the elements of the original array after applying the callback function to each element. The number of parameters that the callback function accepts should match the number of arrays passed to `array_map()`.

FORMAT

```
array array_map ( callback callback, array arr1 [, array ...] )
```

Example:
```
function square($n){  // User-defined callback function
    return $n * $n;
}
$numbers=array(1,4,6,8);
$squared_list =  array_map("square", "$numbers");
```

EXAMPLE 9.11

```
    <?php
1       function salestax($price){    // Callback function
            $tax = 1.15;
2           return($price * $tax);
        }
3       $before_prices=array(1.50, 3.55, 4.75, 6.00);
4       // array_map
        $after_prices=array_map("salestax", $before_prices);
        print "<b>Before map: ";
        foreach ($before_prices as $value){
5           printf("\$%.2f  ",$value);
        }
        echo "\n<br /><br />";
        print "After map: ";
        foreach ($after_prices as $value){
6           printf("\$%.2f  ",$value);
        }
    ?>
```

EXPLANATION

1   This is a user-defined callback function. It will be called for each element, `$price`, in an array of values that it receives from another function, called `array_map()`.

2   The value of each element of an array will be returned after the sales tax has been applied to it.

3   An array called `$after_prices` is returned by the callback function after it has performed a calculation on each element of `$before_prices`.

EXPLANATION (CONTINUED)

4   The array_map() function applies a specific task to each element of an array by using a callback function to perform the task. In this example, the array_map() function takes two arguments: $salesprice, the name of the callback function (passed as a string) that will be called for each element in an array; and $before_prices, the name of the array on which the callback function will perform the same task for each of the elements. Simply, each price in the list will have a sales tax applied to it. The new array, $after_prices, will reflect the price after the sales tax was added in.

5   The original prices are printed.

6   The new prices, after the sales tax is calculated, are printed. See Figure 9.14.

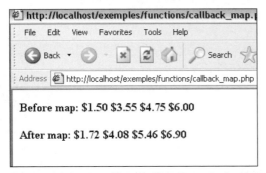

Figure 9.14   A callback function. Output from Example 9.11.

The array_walk_recursive() Function.   The array_walk_recursive() applies a user-defined callback function to every element of an array and will recurse into nested arrays. Normally the array_walk_recursive() function takes two arguments: the first one the array being walked over, and the second one the value of the key or index of the array. A third, optional argument is an additional value that you can send to the callback function. The functon returns true on success and false on failure.

If your callback function needs to be working with the actual values of the array, specify the first parameter of the callback as a *reference*. Then, any changes made to those elements will be made in the original array itself.

FORMAT

```
bool array_walk_recursive ( array &input, callback funcname
                            [, mixed userdata] )
```

Example:
```
$employee=array("Name"=>"Bob", "Title"=>"President");
array_walk_recursive($employee, 'callback_function');
```

EXAMPLE 9.12

```
<html><head><title>Walking Through a Multidimensional Array
</title>
</head><body>
<div align="center">
<h3>Using a Callback Function with a Multidimensional Array</h3>
<?php
```
1
```
    $numbers=array(array(1,2,3,4),
                   array(4,8,10,12),
                   array(20,25,30,35),
                  );
```

2
```
    function cube(&$element,$index){
        print $index;    // prints 012301230123
        $element=$element*$element*$element;
    }
?>
<table border='1'><caption><font size='-1'>The <em>
    array_walk_recursive()</em> function</font></caption>
<?php
```
3
```
    array_walk_recursive($numbers,'cube');
    for($i=0; $i < 3; $i++){
        echo "<tr bgcolor='999FFF'>";
        for($j=0; $j<4; $j++){
            echo "<td><b>".$numbers[$i][$j] ;
        }
        echo "</td></tr>";
    }
    echo "</table>";
?>
</div>
</body>
</html>
```

EXPLANATION

1 $numbers is a numeric array containing three arrays.
2 This callback function takes a reference to the array being walked over as its first argument and $key, which is the index of each element of the array. Its function is to walk through the array cubing each of its elements.
3 The array_walk_recursive() function takes the array as its first argument, and the name of the function, 'cube', as a string value for its second argument. The cube() function is the callback function that will be applied to each element of the two-dimensional array, $numbers. See Figure 9.15.

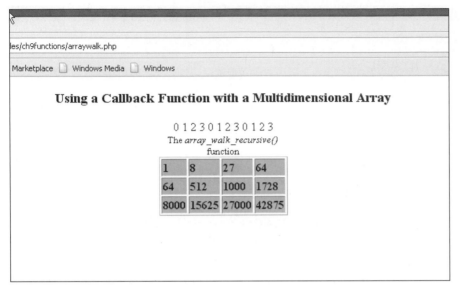

Figure 9.15   Using a callback function. Output from Example 9.12.

9.1.5 Scope

Scope refers to the parts of a program that can see or access a variable; that is, where the variable is visible. *Lifetime* is how long the variable exists. There are three types of scope for PHP variables: *local*, *global*, and *static*.

Local variables are visible within a function and their life ends when the function ends. Global variables are visible to a script, but not normally to a function. They live throughout the run of the script, and die when the script ends. Static variables are local to a function but retain their value from one function call to another. They die when the script ends. Let's look at some examples to see how scope and lifetime work.

Local Scope.   By default, all variables declared within functions are local to the function; that is, they are not visible outside the function and die when the function exits. In computer jargon, these variables are pushed onto a stack when the function starts and popped off when the function ends.

EXAMPLE 9.13

```
<?php
1      $friend = "Sam";   // Global variable, visible outside functions
2      function who(){
3          $friend = "Joe"; // Local variable; disappears when
                            // function ends
           print "In the function $friend is your local friend.<br />";
       }
4      who();  // Function call
5      print "Out of the function, your friend is $friend.<br.>";
?>
```

EXPLANATION

1   $friend is a global variable in that it is visible to the main script, and will disappear when the script ends. It will not be visible within functions.

2   The function called who() is defined.

3   Even though this variable is also called $friend, it is a different variable. It is local to the function and will disappear when the function ends. If this variable had not been defined, the original $friend would still not be visible here.

4   The function, who(), is called. Once in the function the $friend value Sam is out of scope until the function ends. Joe is the friend.

5   Outside the function, global variable $friend is now in scope and Sam is the friend. See Figure 9.16.

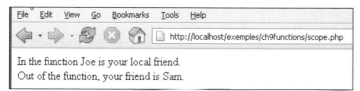

Figure 9.16 Local scope. Output from Example 9.13.

Global Scope. From within a function you cannot access variables that were declared outside the function unless you pass the variable to the function as an argument, by reference. If you need to access an external variable within a function without passing it by reference, then you can use the global statement. By placing the global keyword in front of a variable name, the variable that was defined outside the function can now be accessed.

FORMAT

```
global variable_name1, variable_name2, variable_name3.....;
```

Example:
```
global $salary;
```

EXAMPLE 9.14

```
    <html><head><title>Function Arguments</title></head>
    <body bgcolor="lightgreen"><font size="+1" face="arial">
    <?php
1   function raise_sal(){
2       global $salary;
3       $salary *= 1.1;    //10 percent raise
    }
4   $salary = 50000;
5   raise_sal();
    ?>
6   Congratulations! Your new salary is $<?=$salary?>.<br />";
    </body>
    </html>
```

EXPLANATION

1   The function `raise_sal()` is defined.
2   The keyword, `global`, allows this function to have access to the variable, `$salary`, defined outside this function.
3   The global `$salary` is being modified in the function.
4   The variable, `$salary`, is defined outside the function and is not available to the function, unless it is passed by reference or is made global within the function.
5   The `raise_sal()` function is called.
6   The HTML output shows that the salary was changed in the function. See Figure 9.17.

Figure 9.17   Global scope. Output from Example 9.14.

The $GLOBALS() Array. The other way to access a global variable within a function is with the $GLOBALS[] array. It contains all the variables that have global scope in the script (i.e., any variables declared outside of functions).

EXAMPLE 9.15

```
        <html><head><title>Function Arguments</title></head>
        <body bgcolor="lightgreen"><font size="+1" face="arial">
        <?php
            function raise_sal(){
1               $GLOBALS['salary'] *= 1.1;
            }
            $salary = 50000;
            raise_sal();
        ?>
2       Congratulations! Your new salary is $<?=$salary?>.<br />
        </body>
        </html>
```

EXPLANATION

1   The $_GLOBALS[] array gives the function access to variables defined from out-side the function; in this case, $salary. The name of the variable becomes the key in the $_GLOBALS[] associative array. This example is exactly like Example 9.14 ex-cept, in that example, the global keyword was used to make the variable $salary available to the function.

2   The HTML output shows that the salary was changed in the function. See Figure 9.18.

Figure 9.18   Using the $GLOBALS array. Output from Example 9.15.

Static Variables. The variables declared within functions normally disappear when the function ends. They are *local* to the function. They are created when the function is called and die when it ends. A *static* variable is local to the function, meaning it is not visible outside of the function, but it does not die when the function ends. Once initial-ized a static variable will not lose its value between function calls. It "remembers" the value it held from one call to the next.

EXAMPLE 9.16

```php
    <?php
      function trackme(){
1         static $count=0;
2         $count++;
          echo "You have been here $count times.\n<br />";
      }
3     trackme();
      trackme();
      trackme();
    ?>
```

EXPLANATION

1   By making the variable static, it will retain its value even after the function exits.
    Each time `trackme()` is called, the count will be incremented by 1. The variable,
    $count, is only initialized to zero the first time the function is called.
2   The value of $count is incremented by 1.
3   The function `trackme()` is called three times. Each time it is called, the value of
    the counter is incremented and displayed. See Figure 9.19.

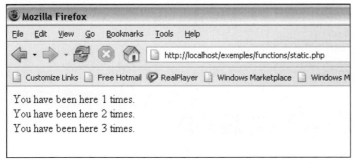

Figure 9.19   Static variables. Output from Example 9.16.

EXAMPLE 9.17

```php
    <html><head><title>Function Arguments</title></head>
    <body bgcolor="lightgreen"><font face="verdana">
    <?php
1     function increase_font($size){
2         static $total=0;   // The value of $total will persist
                             // between calls
3         $newfont= $size++ ;
4         $total += $newfont;    // Keep a running total
    ?>
```

EXAMPLE   9.17 (CONTINUED)

```
5        <font size='<?=+$newfont?>'>bigger<br />
     <?php
6            if ($total > 10){
                 print "+$total: Too big.<br />";
                 exit;
             }
         }
7        for ($n=0; $n<=10; $n++){
             increase_font($n);
         }
     ?>
     </body>
     </html>
```

EXPLANATION

1   The function `increase_font()` is defined. It has parameter, `$size`, which repre-
    sents the font size for the verdana font listed above.
2   The `static` variable `$total` is defined and is assigned an initial value of 0. This
    variable will not forget its value after the function exits. Static variables retain
    their value from function call to function call.
3   The variable, `$newfont`, is increased by 1 when the function is called.
4   The value of variable, `$newfont`, is added to `$total`. `$total` is static; that is, it
    retains its value from the last function call. Otherwise, it would be set back to zero
    each time the function is called.
5   The value of the new font size is assigned.
6   When the accumulated total reaches a value greater than 10, the script exits.
7   Each time through the `for` loop, the function, `increase_font()` is called, caus-
    ing the font to be increased by 1 point size. See Figure 9.20.

Figure 9.20   Static variables. Output from Example 9.17.

9.1.6 Nesting Functions

PHP supports nesting functions. A *nested* function is defined and called from within another function. The outer function, also called the *parent* function, has to be invoked for the nested function to become available to the program. Nested functions are rarely used.

FORMAT

```
function OuterFunction(){
    function NestedFunction(){
            /*OuterFunction() must be called before NestedFunction()
             is available.*/
        statements;
    }
}
```

PHP functions can also be nested inside other statement blocks, such as conditional statements. As with nested functions, such functions will only be defined when that block of code has been executed.

EXAMPLE 9.18

```
    <?php
1       function outer ($a, $b){
            print "Greetings from outer()\n<br />";
2           function square($x) {    // Nested function
                print "Greetings from square()\n<br />";
3               return $x * $x;
                }
4           return square($a) + square($b);
            }
5       $sum=outer(5,8);  // Call to outer()
        echo "The sum of the squares is: $sum\n<br";
6       $squared=square(5);
        print "5 squared is: $squared.\n<br />";
    ?>
```

EXPLANATION

1 The function `outer()` will be the parent function for the function nested within it.
2 This is the declaration for the nested function `square()`. Because it is nested in the `outer()` function, it will not be defined until `outer()` has been called.
3 The return value from this nested function is the square of its parameters.
4 The value returned will be the sum of `$a` and `$b` after the nested `square()` function has squared them both.
5 The parent function, called `outer()`, is called, the two numbers are passed, and the sum of their squared values is returned. Once `outer()` is called the nested function will be defined. See Figure 9.21.
6 Just like any other function, the nested function, `square()`, is available once it is defined. It is not available until the `outer()` function has been called. See Figure 9.22.

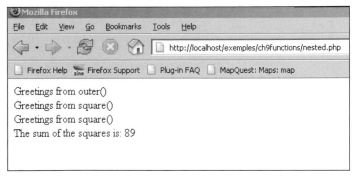

Figure 9.21   Using nested functions.

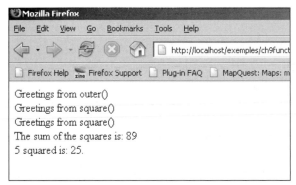

Figure 9.22   Output from Example 9.18.

Once the outer or parent function has been executed, the nested function is defined and accessible from anywhere within the current program just like any other function. You can only execute the parent function once if it contains nested functions; otherwise, PHP will generate a fatal error as shown in Figure 9.23.

EXAMPLE 9.19

```php
<?php
    function outer ($a, $b){
    print "Greetings from outer()\n<br />";
    function square($x){     // Nested function
        print "Greetings from square()\n<br />";
        return $x * $x;
}
return square($a) + square($b);
}
$sum=outer(5,8);
echo "The sum of the squares is: $sum\n<br";
$sum=outer(10,2);   // Wrong! Will cause square() to be redeclared
?>
```

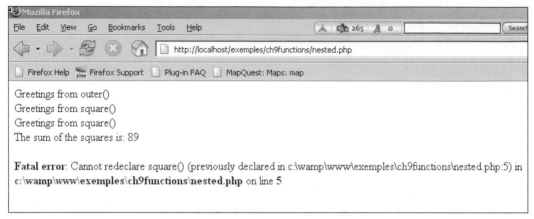

Figure 9.23 Output from Example 9.19.

9.1.7 Recursive Functions

A *recursive* function is a function that calls itself. Recursive functions are often used to handle certain types of mathematical problems; traverse directories, linked lists, and binary trees; crack passwords; create anagrams, and magic squares; and so on. If a task is a smaller version of an original base task, then the problem can be solved by writing a recursive function. When you first encounter recursion, it might seem a little confusing, like being in a house of mirrors. When a function calls itself, the program starts up the same function again, executes the function statements, and when it returns, picks up where it left off in the function that called it. The recursion can go on indefinitely, so you must be careful to create a condition that, at some point, stops it.

An example often used to describe recursion can be demonstrated with a function to produce a Fibonacci number (see Example 9.20). What is that? Well before getting started, read this little bit of history, if you have the time or interest.

In the beginnning of the 13th century an Italian mathemetician, Leonardo Fibonacci, came up with a formula, called the Fibonacci sequence, to solve the following problem presented at a mathematical competition in Pisa: How many rabbits would be produced in a year if, beginning with a single pair of rabbits, every month each pair reproduces a new pair of rabbits, which become productive when they are one month old, and none of them die, and so on?

Fibonacci came up with a formula, named after himself, to answer the rabbit question. The Fibonacci sequence normally starts with 0 and 1, and then produces the next Fibonacci number by adding the two previous Fibonacci numbers together: 0, 1, 1, 2, 3, 5, 8, 13, 21, 34, 55, 89, 144, 233, 377, 610, 987, 1597, 2584, 4181, 6765, 10946 . . .

Thus, to get the next value after 21, add 13 to 21 resulting in the next Fibonacci number, which is 34. So the number of pairs of rabbits at the start of each month is 1, 1, 2, 3, 5, 8, 13, 21, 34, and so on.

EXAMPLE 9.20

```
      <html><head><title>Fibonacci Series</title></head>
      <body>
      <div align="center">
      <?php
1         $count=0;
2         function fib($num){
          /* Find the Fibonacci value of a number */
             global $count;
3             $count++;
4             switch($num) {
             case 0:
                 return(0);
                 break;
             case 1:
                 return(1);
                 break;
             default:  // Including recursive calls
5                 return(fib($num - 1) + fib($num - 2));
                 break;
             }
          }
      ?>
      <table border="1" cellspacing="2" cellpadding="5">
      <caption>Fibonacci Sequence</caption>
      <tr>
      <?php
6         for($num=0; $num < 10; $num++){
7             value=fib($num);
             // The Fibonacci sequence of 9 numbers starting at 0
             echo "<td bgcolor='#33FF66'>$value</td>";
          }
      ?>
      <tr>
      <br />
      </table>
      <br />
8     The function called itself <?php echo $n; ?> times.<br />
      </div>
      </body>
      </html>
```

EXPLANATION

1   The variable, $count, is set outside the function. It will keep track of the number of times the function, fib(), is called.

2   This is the function, called fib(), that will introduce the concept of recursion, a function that calls itself. This function starts the initial task and in itself is not recursive. When the same task needs to be repeated, that is when fib() will call itself.

3   Each time the function is called, the value of $count is incremented by 1.

4   The switch statement is used to check for the incoming values of a number, $num. If $num is 0, the value returned will be 0, and if it is 1 the value returned is 0 + 1, or 1. Because these cases are so simple there is no need for recursion. If the number is greater than 1, then the default case is entered.

5   This is the heart of the recursive program. The result of the first call to the fib() function is added to the result of another call to fib(). The function will continue to call itself until it reaches a point where it either returns 0 or 1. If the $num is 4, then fib() is called 9 times.

The sequence goes something like this:

```
call 1  fib(4)
             3                              Returns 3
call 2  fib(3) + call 7  fib(2)
             2    +         1    Returns 3
call 8  fib(1) + call 9  fib(0)
            ·1    +         0    Returns 1
call 3  fib(2) + call 6 fib(1)
             1    +         1    Returns 2
call 4  fib(1) + call 5 fib(0)
             1    +         0    Returns 1
```

6   The for loop will iterate through 10 numbers, starting at 0. Each number will be sent, in turn, to the fib() function for evaluation.

7   This is the first call to the fib() function. The next value in the Fibonacci series will be returned by adding the current value and its previous value. For example, if 5 is passed to fib(), the number returned will be 5 + 3, or 8. See Figure 9.24.

8   This number shows you how many times the function fib() was called to produce the sequence shown in the table in Figure 9.24.

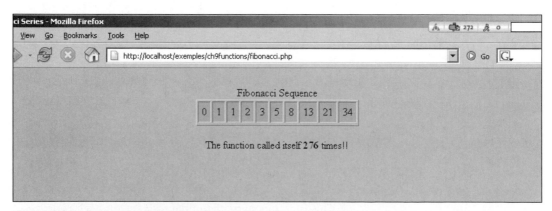

Figure 9.24   Recursive function. Output from Example 9.20.

9.1.8   Function Libraries—Requiring and Including

If you have a function or set of functions that you will reuse in other PHP programs, then you can save the functions in a file, called a library. When you are ready to use the functions, just include the library in the current script with the `include()` or `require()` built-in functions. Suppose, for example, you have two functions: one called `total()` to calculate the total of a set of numbers, and another called `ave()` to calculate the average of a set of numbers. We will store these user-defined functions in a library file called `mylibrary.php` shown in Figure 9.25:

```
<?php
function total(){
    function statements;
}

function ave(){
    function statements;
}
?>
```

Figure 9.25   The library file.

The require() and Include() Constructs.   PHP provides the `require()` and `include()` constructs to allow you to use the functions from the library file in a PHP script as shown here:

```
FORMAT
<?php
    require("mylibrary.php");   // Now functions in the library can be called
    echo "The average  is ", ave(array(11,3,5,7,34));
>?
-----------------------------------------------------------------------------
<?php
    include("mylibrary.php");
    echo "The average is ", ave(array(11,3,5,7,34));
>?
```

The `include()` and `require()` constructs cause a specified file to be included and evaluated in your script, similar to pasting the contents of a file in your script at the line where they were requested. When you place a function within an external file that will later be included, be sure to enclose the function within PHP tags, because, when a file is included, if the PHP tags are missing, PHP automatically starts processing the included file as an HTML document.

The only difference between include() and require() is how they deal with failure. The include() produces a warning and allows the script to continue executing while require() produces a fatal error. For PHP to find the file you want to include, it searches an include_path defined in the php.ini file[1], and if the file is not in the path, this would cause an error. (Files for including are first looked for in the include_path relative to the current working directory and then in the include_path relative to the directory of current script. If a filename begins with ./ or ../, it is looked for only in include_path relative to the current working directory.)

With require() the missing file would cause the script to exit, whereas with include(), the program will continue to run. You can also use an absolute path such as require('C:\pub\library\file.php') or include('/usr/htdocs/file.php').

Just like require() and include(), the require_once() and include_once() statements, respectively, include and evaluate the specified file during the execution of the script, but require_once() and include_once() will only include a file once, even if you have more require or include statements throughout the script.

Include files are often used to help manage the content of a Web site. The files are external to the program and included as needed. For a discussion on content management, see "Managing Content with Include Files" on page 487.

EXAMPLE 9.21

```
    <html><head><title>Including a file</title></head>
    <body>
    <font size="+1">
    <?php
1       $color="red";
2       require_once("test.library");   // Could say:
                                        // include_once("test.library");
3       welcome();
    ?>
    <hr>
    <?php
4       $color="blue";
5       welcome();
        echo $mood, $color,"<br />";
    ?>
    </font>
    </body>
    </html>
-------------------------------------------------------------------
```

---

1. To change include_path from your program, use the built-in ini_set function described in the PHP manual: *http://www.php.net/manual/en/function.ini-set.php*.

EXAMPLE 9.21 (CONTINUED)

```
     (file: test.library)
6    <?php
7        $color="purple";
8        function welcome(){
9            global $color;
10           $mood="marvelous";
             echo "Welcome to you!\n<br />";
11           echo "<font color=$color>"."What a $mood $color
                 sky!\n</font><br />";
         }
     ?>
```

EXPLANATION

1 The variable, $color, is assigned the color "red".

2 The require_once() function includes a file given as its argument. At the point this file is loaded, all variables and functions within it are available to this program. The require_once() function only loads the file once, so that if in the future another require() function is executed, it will not be included again. The value of the variable, $color, in the required file, is purple.

3 The user-defined function, welcome(), is called. Its definition is in the included file. The color of the font will be purple because the variable, $color, is assigned "purple" in the required file on line 7. See Figure 9.26.

4 The variable $color is a global variable. It is assigned the value "blue" on line 4.

5 The user-defined function, welcome(), is called again. This time the color of the text will be "blue". The function defined a global variable, $color. It gets the value of the color defined outside the function.

6 The included file contains PHP code. Remember, if you do not enclose the code of the included file with PHP tags, when PHP starts processing, it will treat the code as though it were an HTML document, causing an error.

7 When a file is required, the variables defined within it become part of the current PHP script. Notice that when the welcome() function is called, the color of the text is purple, not red, because the required file redefined $color, overwriting the $color="red" with $color="purple".

8 This is where the user-defined function is defined within the external file.

9 To make variables from outside the function available to the function, the keyword global is used.

10 The variable, $mood, is defined as a local variable.

11 It is not seen outside the function. The color of the font changes as the value of $color changes. See Figure 9.26.

Figure 9.26 Storing functions in an external file. Output from Example 9.21.

9.2   Chapter Summary

9.2.1   What You Should Know

Now that you have finished this chapter you should be able to answer the following questions:

1. What is the definition of a function?

2. How do you invoke a function?

3. How do you pass arguments to a function by:

    a. Reference?

    b. Value?

4. How do you return values from a function?

5. What are default arguments?

6. What is the difference between local, global, and static scope?

7. How do you make a variable that is defined outside of a function available to that function?

8. What is recursion?

9. What is a callback function?

10. How do you nest a function within other functions?

11. How do you include a function defined in another file?

12. What is the difference between `require()` and `include()`?

9.2.2 What's Next?

Now that you have a good handle on functions, it is time to talk about how PHP and HTML work together when producing forms. In Chapter 10, "More on PHP Forms," you will see a number of functions to handle incoming data, most of them user defined.

CHAPTER 9 LAB

1. Ask the user how many Euros he or she spent in Germany? Write a function to convert the Euros to U.S. dollars based on today's exchange rate.

2. Create a function called `converter()` that will take two arguments. The first argument will be `upper`, `lower`, or `title`. The second argument will be a string. The function should display the string in all uppercase, all lowercase, or as a title (that is, where the first letter in each word is uppercase as in, "Having Fun With Dick and Jane"). The function will be called like this:

```
print converter("title", $string);
```

Output should look similar to the following:

3. Can you create a function for calculating the monthly payments by using the mortgage formula? (Hint: See the Chapter 5 Lab, Question 8.)

$$P = L[c(1 + c)]n / [(1 + c)\,n - 1]$$

chapter
10

More on PHP Forms

10.1 Introduction

We discussed forms briefly in Chapter 3, "PHP Quick Start," and now we are ready to delve into a more thorough discussion about how PHP handles form information. The first part of this chapter is a review of how to set up HTML forms, the HTTP (HyperText Transmission Protocol) methods, and how form information is transmitted from the browser to the server and back. If you browse through the following HTML review section and feel comfortable with the information provided there, then you might want to skip this section and go directly to "PHP and Forms" on page 390.

10.2 Review of HTML Forms

Forms are essential to any Web page that communicates with users. When you order a book or a pillow, register for a course, sign up for a cruise, pay bills online, get directions to a street address, you fill out a form. Once you have filled out the form, you push an Order now! or Submit type button, and the form is submitted. The information you entered is collected by the browser, URL encoded, and sent to a server. The server might then send the encoded information to a program for processing. Traditionally the server would start up a CGI program to process the information, but PHP makes this processing much easier. PHP will decode and process the information according to the instructions in the PHP program that gets it. It might send an e-mail back to the user, store or update the information in a database, save preferences in a cookie, session, and so on.

Working with forms is a two-step process:

1. Create the HTML form.
2. Process the information entered into the form.

379

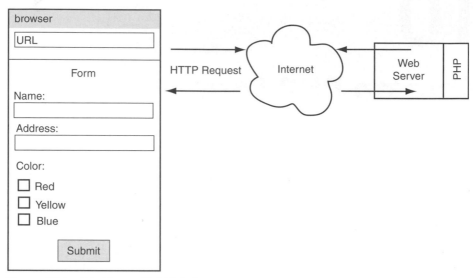

Figure 10.1 Working with HTML forms.

10.2.1 The Browser's Role

HTML forms are created in a text file and displayed in a browser window. They consist of fields or buttons that request user interaction (see Figure 10.1). After the user fills out the form, the form data is URL encoded[1] by the browser and submitted to a server for further processing. Example 10.1 shows a really simple HTML form consisting of two input fields, a text box, and a submit button. Figures 10.2 and 10.3 are screen shots of the form before and after it is filled out.

EXAMPLE 10.1

```
<html><title><Simple Form></title>
<body>
<form>
   What is your name?
   <input type=text name="myname"><br />
   <input type=submit>
</form>
</body>
</html>
```

---

1. For a complete discussion on URL encoding, see Chapter 9, "User-Defined Functions," or go to *http://www.blooberry.com/indexdot/html/topics/urlencoding.htm*.

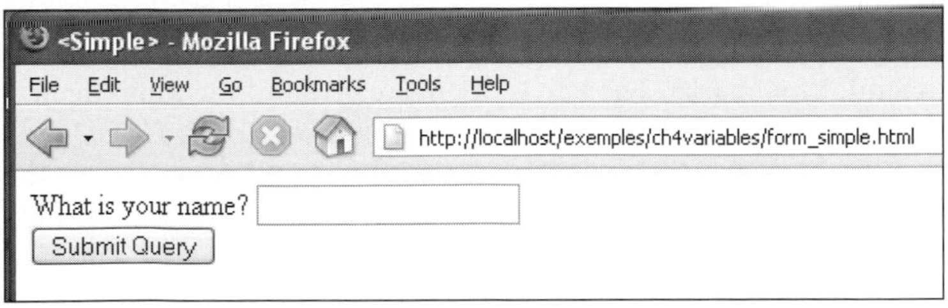

Figure 10.2   A simple HTML form.

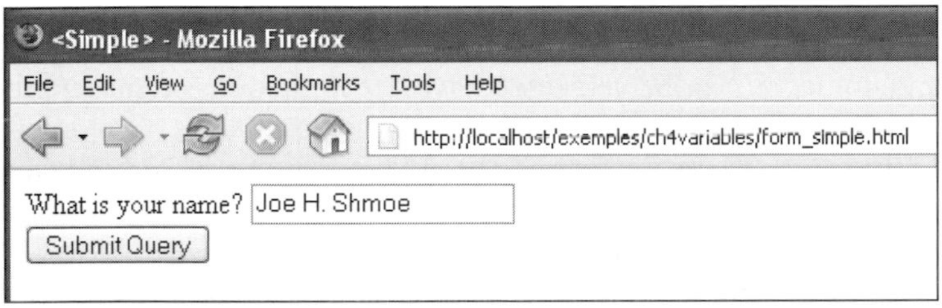

Figure 10.3   The user fills out the form.

There are different ways of sending this data to the server called HTTP request methods. (HTTP is the standard way of sending documents over the Web.[2]) The GET and POST methods are the two most common request types. Essentially these methods perform the same function but how they handle the input data is different.

The GET Method.   If the processing of a form has no lasting observable effect on the state of the world, then the form method should be GET[3] (i.e., it handles requests where the response page will never change). The GET method is the simplest type of method and is used mainly for the simple retrieval of static HTML documents, images, or results of a database query as shown in the URL of Google's search engine in Figure 10.4..

If a method is not supplied as an attribute of the <form> tag, the GET method is the default. The GET method sends submitted data to the server by attaching it to the end of

Figure 10.4   URL using the GET method. The query string is encoded, visible, and can be bookmarked.

---

2. To learn more about HTTP, go to *http://www.w3.org/Protocols/rfc2616/rfc2616-sec1.html#sec1*.

3. Quoted from *http://www.cs.tut.fi/~jkorpela/forms/methods.html#fund*.

the URL in what is called the *query string*. After the user presses the submit button, the browser encodes the content, and appends it to the current URL as a set of key–value pairs (prepended with a question mark). The key is the name given to the input device, and the value (URL encoded) is whatever the user typed in that field. In the URL shown next, the form information has been highlighted; that is, the string appended to the question mark. The name of the text field is "myname" and the value typed into the field by the user is "Joe H. Shmoe". The browser, Mozilla Firefox in this example, encoded the spaces in Joe's name with + signs. See Figure 10.5.

http://localhost/exemples/ch4variables/form_simple.html?**myname=Joe+H.+Shmoe**

Disadvantages of the GET method are that all the form data is sent via the URL, which is visible to the user and limited in size. Servers often have size limitations on the length of the URL. For example, UNIX servers limit the size to 1240 bytes. If a lot of information is being passed to the server, the POST method should be used. Another disadvantage is that the input data might be cached, and the browser might pull previous request results from its cache instead of the most recent one.

Figure 10.5 The GET method and the URL.

The POST Method.   The POST method is used if the processing of a form causes side effects, like the modification of a database, updating a shopping cart, or sending an e-mail message. When the POST method is used, the browser does not put the encoded data in a query string, but rather bundles up the data and puts it into an HTTP header message body. Unlike the query string created by the GET method, the message body does not have size restrictions, is not visible in the Location box of the browser, and cannot be bookmarked. Because the POST method does not append input to the URL, it is often used in processing forms where there is a lot of data being transferred and will send data to a database, send e-mail, or change something. The form data is URL encoded but not limited in size as it was with the GET method. It cannot be bookmarked and is not visible in the URL.

The POST is invoked by adding a METHOD attribute to the <FORM> tag in your HTML document as shown in Example 10.2. The variables sent are sorted and available to the PHP script in the same way as with GET, but the query string is not set. The form is shown in the browser in Figure 10.6.

EXAMPLE   10.2

```
<html><title><Simple Form></title>
<body>
<form METHOD="POST">
   What is your name?
   <input type=text name="myname"><br />
   <input type=submit>
</form>
</body>
</html>
```

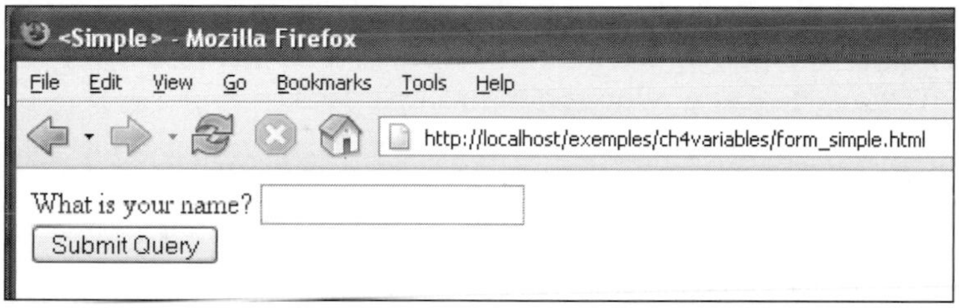

Figure 10.6   A simple HTML form created using the POST method. Output from Example 10.2.

10.2.2   The Server's Role

When the browser requests a Web page from the server, it establishes a TCP/IP connection and sends a request in an HTTP format. The server examines the request and responds. The first line of the HTTP request might look like this:

```
GET /file.php HTTP/1.1
```

This line specifies that the method to handle the incoming data is GET, that the file to retrieve is file.php, and that the version of HTTP is 1.1. PHP runs as part of the server and has access to the form data passed from the browser to the server. After the server gets the file, it sends it to PHP to be processed. PHP knows how the form was sent and provides special variables to hold both GET and POST data as well as variables containing information about the environment, such as server, browser, and so on. PHP automatically converts the names of the form elements into PHP variables and executes any PHP statements, substituting the output within the HTML document (discussed in Chapter 9, "User-Defined Functions"). After PHP has finished handling the form data, the server will send back a response header and send the processed information back to the browser.

A server response looks like this:

```
HTTP/1.1 200 OK
Content-type: text/html

<Contents of HTML Document>
```

When the browser receives the page, it renders the HTML code and then displays the page in the browser.

10.2.3   Creating HTML Forms

Before getting PHP to process the form, you might need a short refresher course on how to create forms, the types of forms, how the information is passed from the browser to the server, and so on. This section reviews basic HTML form creation. To create an HTML form, you start in an editor with a filename ending in *.html* or *.htm*. A form starts with a `<form>` tag and its attributes, followed by the input devices you will need, such as text fields, buttons, check boxes, and so on, a submission button, and ends with the closing `</form>` tag.[4] (The HTML file is normally stored under the server's root in a directory called *htdocs*.) Let's start by displaying an HTML form that contains text fields, radio buttons, check boxes, and pop-up menus (see Figure 10.7). After displaying the form, we look at the HTML code that produced it in Example 10.3.

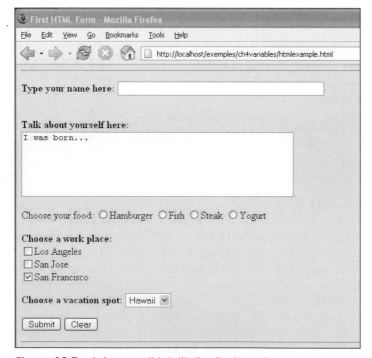

Figure 10.7   A form as it is initially displayed.

---

4. For a complete introduction to forms, see *http://www.w3.org/TR/REC-html40/interact/forms.html#h-17.2*.

The Steps to Produce a Form.   The following steps are essential in producing a form. The next example illustrates how each of these steps is applied.

1. START: Start the form with the HTML `<form>` tag.
2. ACTION: The `action` attribute of the `<form>` tag is the URL of the PHP script that will process the data input from the form.
3. METHOD: Provide an HTTP method on how to process the data input. The default is the `GET` method, but the `POST` method is most commonly used with forms.
4. CREATE: Create the form with buttons, boxes, and whatever looks attractive using HTML tags and fields.
5. SUBMIT: Create a submit button so that the form can be processed. This will launch the program listed in the `action` attribute.
6. END. End the form with the `</form>` tag. End the HTML document with the `</html>` tag.

EXAMPLE 10.3

```
1    <html>
     <head>
2    <title>first html form</title>
     </head>
        <body bgcolor=yellow>
        <hr />
3       <form action="/phpforms/form1.php" method="GET">
4           <b>Type your name here: </b>
5           <input type="text" name="namestring" size=50>

6           <p/><b>Talk about yourself here: </b><br />
7           <textarea name="comments" rows=5
                    cols=50>i was born... </textarea>

8           <p/><b> Choose your food: </b>
9           <input type="radio" name="choice" value="burger"
                    />Hamburger
            <input type="radio" name="choice" value="fish" />Fish
            <input type="radio" name="choice" value="steak" />Steak
            <input type="radio" name="choice" value="yogurt" />Yogurt

            <p /> <b>Choose a work place:</b> <br />
10          <input type="checkbox" name="place1" value="LA"
                    />Los Angeles
            <br />
            <input type="checkbox" name="place2" value="SJ" />San Jose
            <br />
            <input type="checkbox" name="place3"
                    value="SF" Checked>San Francisco
```

EXAMPLE 10.3 (CONTINUED)

```
11          <p/><b>Choose a vacation spot: </b>
12          <select name="location"> <option selected value="hawaii"
                       /> Hawaii
               <option value="bali" />Bali
               <option value="maine" />Maine
               <option value="paris" />Paris
            </select>

            <p/>
13          <input type="submit" value="submit">
            </p>
            <input type="reset" value="clear">
14          </form>
            <hr />
         </body>
         </html>
```

EXPLANATION

1   This tag says that this is the start of an HTML document.

2   The <title> tag; the title appears outside of the browser's main window.

3   This is the beginning of a <form> tag that specifies where the browser will send the input data and the method that will be used to process it. The default method is the GET method. When the data is submitted, the PHP script (or some other program, such as CGI script) will be executed by the server. In this example, the PHP script is stored in a directory called *formstuff* below the server's document root directory, in this case the *www* directory.

4   The <p> tag starts a new paragraph. The <b> tag says the text that follows will be in bold type. The user is asked for input.

5   The input type is a text box that will hold up to 50 characters. When the user types text into the text box, that text will be stored in the user-defined name value, namestring. For example, if the user types *Stefan Lundstom*, the browser will assign to the query string, namestring=Stefan Lundstrom. If assigned a value attribute, the text field can take a default; that is, text that appears in the text box when it is initially displayed by the browser.

6   The user is asked for input.

7   The text area is similar to the text field, but will allow input that scans multiple lines. The textarea tag will produce a rectangle (name comments) with dimensions in rows and columns (5 rows by 50 columns) and an optional default value (I was born...).

8   The user is asked to pick from a series of menu items.

EXPLANATION (CONTINUED)

9   The first input type is a list of radio buttons. Only one button can be selected. The
input type has two attributes: a `type` and a `name`. The value of the `name` attribute
`"choice"`, for example, will be assigned `"burger"` if the user clicks on the Ham-
burger option, `choice=burger` is passed onto the PHP program. If the user selects Fish, `choice=fish` will be assigned to the query string, and so on. These
key–value pairs are used to build a query string to pass onto the PHP program
after the Submit button is pressed.

10 The input type this time is in the form of check boxes. More than one check box
might be selected. The optional default box is already checked. When the user selects one of the check boxes, the value of the `name` attribute will be assigned one
of the values from the `value` attribute; for example, `place1=LA` if Los Angeles is
checked.

11 The user is asked for input.

12 The `select` tag is used to produce a pop-up menu (also called a drop-down list)
or a scrollable list. The `name` option is required. It is used to define the name for
the set of options. For a pop-up menu, the `size` attribute is not necessary; it defaults to 1. The pop-up menu initially displays one option and expands to a menu
when that option is clicked. Only one selection can be made from the menu. If a
`size` attribute is given, that many items will be displayed. If the `multiple` attribute is given (e.g., `SELECT MULTIPLE NAME=whatever`), the menu appears as a
scrollable list, displaying all of the options.

13 If the user clicks the Submit button, the PHP script listed in the form's `action` attribute will be launched. In this example, the script was not programmed to do
anything. An error message is sent to the server's error log and to the browser.

14 If the Clear button is pressed, all input boxes are reset back to their defaults.

After the user fills out the form in Figure 10.8, he or she will click the Submit button.
This causes submission of the form. The browser will collect all the input that was
entered, URL encode it, package it up, and send it to the server listed in the `action`
attribute of the `<form>` tag. The server sends the encoded information to the program
listed in the URL of the `action` attribute. (The input in this example will not be processed, thus causing an error to be sent to the server's error log when the Submit button
is selected. Nothing will be displayed by the browser.)

Table 10.1 describes a list of form input types and their possible attributes.

Figure 10.8   A form filled with user input.

Table 10.1   Form Input Types

Input Type	Attributes	Description
text	name size maxlength	Creates a text box for user input. size specifies the size of the text box. maxlength specifies the maximum number of characters allowed.
textarea	name size rows size cols	Creates a text area that can take input spanning multiple lines. size rows and size cols specify the size of the box.
password	name value	Like a text box but input is hidden. Asterisks appear in the box to replace characters typed.
checkbox	name value	Displays a square box that can be checked. Creates name–value pairs from user input. Multiple boxes can be checked.

Table 10.1   Form Input Types (continued)

Input Type	Attributes	Description
radio	name value	Like check boxes, except only one box (or circle) can be checked.
select	name option size multiple	Provides pop-up menus and scrollable lists. Only one can be selected. Attribute `multiple` creates a visibly scrollable list. A `size` of 1 creates a pop-up menu with only one visible box.
file	name	Specifies files to be uploaded to the server. MIME type must be *multipart/form-data*.
hidden	name value	Provides name–value pair without displaying an object on the screen.
submit	name value	When pressed, executes the form; launches CGI.
image	src value align	Same as submit button, but displays an image instead of text. The image is in a file found at SRC.
reset	name value	Resets the form to its original position; clears all input fields.

The method Attribute.   In an HTML document, the `<form>` tag starts the form. The `method` attribute of the `<form>` tag tells the browser *how* to send the input data collected from the user, and the `action` attribute tells the browser *where* to send the data. The most commonly used methods are GET and POST, discussed earlier in this chapter. In processing forms, use the POST method as a general rule. With the POST method, the variables and their values are sent in the body of the URL request, not the header, thus allowing the transfer of large amounts of data to the server, whereas with the GET method, the default, the variables and their values are sent in the header of the URL request appended as part of the URL itself in a query string. You can see these values in the browser's Navigation bar, a string appended to the question mark following the Web address. (If the GET method is used, the `method` attribute can be left out, as GET is the default.) The following line illustrates the use of the `method` attribute (case insensitive):

```
<form action="/phpforms/form1.php" method="POST">
```

The action Attribute.   The `action` attribute is *where* the form data is going. This is the URL of a program on the server that will process the data by decoding the URL-encoded query string or message body; that is, replacing + signs with spaces, hexadecimal characters with their ASCII equivalent, removing ampersands, and so on. Once decoded, the program can do whatever needs to be done with it, such as sending the data to a database, updating a file, sending an e-mail message to the user, setting preferences, and so on. The `action` listed here sends the form date to a PHP script under the document root of the server. The method is POST.

```
<form action="/phpforms/form1.php" method="POST">
```

10.3 PHP and Forms

There are number of ways that a PHP script can accept user input. As you might recall, in an HTML form, the form elements are given names. For example, in the following simple text box, the name is an attribute of the input device:

(The HTML Form)
```
What is your zip code?
<input type="text" name="zipcode" maxlength = 20>
```

(In the Browser)
The user sees this text box:

and enters his or her zip code:

(The PHP script)
```
echo "You entered ", $zipcode , "<br />";    // Short style
echo "You entered ", $_GET["zipcode"] , "<br />";  // Medium style
echo "You entered ", $HTTP_GET_VARS["zipcode" , "<br />"; // Long style
```

   In this example, when PHP collects form information from the server, it decodes it, and assigns it to variables, making them automatically available to PHP scripts. PHP has three styles for storing form information: the short style, the medium style, and the long, old style.

In Chapter 4, "The Building Blocks," we used the short style where PHP creates a variable with the same name as its respective HTML input device. If, for example, a text field is named zipcode, then the resulting PHP variable will be named $zipcode and its value is whatever the user entered in that field. (See "The register_globals Directive" next.) Another better approach is to use the superglobal associative arrays such as $_POST and $_GET. PHP assigns the names of the input devices as keys to these special arrays, and the value is what the user typed into the input device.

The three ways that PHP creates variables to hold form information are:

1. The simple short style, for example, $name, $id (discussed in Chapter 4, "The Building Blocks").
2. The medium style, for example, $_GET['name'], $_POST['id'].
3. The long style, for example, $HTTP_GET_VARS['name'], $HTTP_POST_VARS['id'].

10.3.1 The register_globals Directive

The method you use to create variables to hold form information depends on your version of PHP. If you are using a version of PHP earlier than 4.2.0, register_globals in the php.ini file is set to "On," allowing you to use the short style described in Chapter 4, "The Building Blocks." The problem with using the short style is that a simple variable like $zipcode could refer to input coming from the URL, cookies or session data, the environment, file uploads, and so on, and not necessarily just from a form. Not knowing where the data came from could present a security risk. To circumvent this problem, the PHP designers decided that using simple variables with the short style should be disabled and register_globals should be set to "Off" in the php.ini file. Using the recommended middle style (e.g., $_POST['zipcode']) more precisely states that the data was posted to the server using a specified method attribute, in this example, the POST method. PHP superglobal arrays were introduced to help you determine where the data came from.

To use the short style, you have to either enable the register_globals directive in the php.ini file (not recommended) or extract the form parameters from the superglobal $_REQUEST array (see "Form Parameters the $_REQUEST Array" on page 396); otherwise, use the middle, recommended style. The more explicit, old style is discussed here for completeness, but it too, is no longer normally used. The following shows the current setting (PHP 5) for register_globals in the php.ini file:

```
; You should do your best to write your scripts so that they do not require
; register_globals to be on;  Using form variables as globals can easily lead
; to possible security problems, if the code is not very well thought of.
register_globals = Off
```

10.3.2   PHP Superglobals for Retrieving Form Data

If you are not using the short style to retrieve information from an HTML form, PHP provides the superglobal arrays. The superglobal arrays allow you to specify where the input data came from; that is, what method was used. These superglobals are listed in Table 10.2 by their older long name, and the newer one (called the alias[5]), which is the middle recommended style, followed by a description of what each array contains. The older predefined variables in the first column of Table 10.2 still exist, but as of PHP 5.0.0, you can disable them by setting the register_long_arrays directive to "Off" in the php.ini file as shown next. In fact, the PHP manual recommends that, for performance reasons, you do set this directive to off. Instead, use the aliases (medium style); for example, use $_POST rather than $_HTTP_POST_VARS, or $_GET rather than $_HTTP_POST_VARS. From the php.ini file:

```
; Whether or not to register the old-style input arrays, HTTP_GET_VARS
; and friends.  If you're not using them, it's recommended to turn them off,
; for performance reasons.
register_long_arrays = Off
```

Table 10.2   PHP Superglobal Arrays[a]

Array Name (Deprecated)	Alias	What It Contains
	$GLOBALS	Contains a reference to every variable currently available within the global scope of the script. The keys of this array are the names of the global variables.
$_HTTP_COOKIE_VARS	$_COOKIE	Values provided to the script with cookies. (See Chapter 16, "Cookies and Sessions.")
$_HTTP_GET_VARS	$_GET	A global associative array of variables passed to the script via the HTTP GET method.
$_HTTP_POST_VARS	$_POST	A global associative array of variables passed to the current script via the HTTP GET method.
$_HTTP_POST_FILES	$_FILES	Variables provided to the script via HTTP POST file uploads.
$_HTTP_SERVER_VARS	$_SERVER	Variables set by the Web server.
$_HTTP_ENV_VARS	$_ENV	Variables provided to the script via the environment.
	$_REQUEST	Variables provided to the script via the GET, POST, and COOKIE input types (not considered safe).
	$_SESSION	Variables currently registered to a script's session.

a. See *http://us2.php.net/manual/en/language.variables.predefined.php#language.variables.superglobals*.

---

5. Although the older style and the medium style represent the same data, they are different variables, so that if you use an older style and its alias in the same program, changing one does not change the other.

10.3.3   The Request Method

As discussed in Chapter 4, "The Building Blocks," the two most commonly used HTTP methods for passing form information from the browser to the server are GET and POST. PHP assigns input submitted in a form or passed in the URL to some superglobal arrays containing the same name as its respective method. If, for example, the GET method was used, the $_GET array contains the URL and form information, and if the POST method is used the $_POST array holds the input data. PHP also has access to the type of request being used in the $_SERVER['REQUEST_METHOD'] special superglobal array. To check which method is used, the following conditional can be included in your PHP script:

```
if ( $_SERVER['REQUEST_METHOD'] == 'GET'){ do something;}
if ( $_SERVER['REQUEST_METHOD'] == 'POST'){do something;}
```

10.3.4   Strange Characters in Form Field Names and User Input

Because the HTML form fields and the user input are so closely linked with your PHP script, what you name your HTML fields and what the user types into them must be dealt with when PHP receives the data from the browser. Did the field names translate nicely into PHP variables or did the user enter weird characters when he or she filled out the fields?

Dots and Spaces in HTML Input Device Names.   A valid PHP variable name starts with a letter or underscore, followed by any number of letters, numbers, or underscores. Recall that when PHP gets information from a form, the name of the HTML input device becomes a variable if using the simple short style or a key to an array if using the medium or long style. What the user types into the form field is assigned to the variable or key. Typically, PHP does not alter these names when they are passed into a script. However, if dots or spaces are used in the names of the HTML input devices, PHP will replace them with an underscore to make them valid PHP variable names. When creating an HTML form, keep this in mind when naming fields. Consider the next example in which the field names contains dots and spaces.

EXAMPLE 10.4

```
      (The HTML File)
      <html><head><title>textbox</title></head>
      <body bgcolor="lightgreen">
         <form action="formdots.php" method="get">
            Please enter your first name:<br />
1           <input type="text" name="first.name" size="20" />
            <br />
            Please enter your last name:<br />
2           <input type="text" name="last.name" size="20" />
            <br />
            Please enter your birth date:<br />
3           <input type="text" name="birth date" size="20" />
            <br />
            <input type="submit">
         </form>
      </body>
      </html>
      ----------------------------------------------------------------
      (The PHP Script)
      <?php
         foreach ($_REQUEST as $key => $value){
4           echo "Input device name=<b>$key</b><br />";
         }
      ?>
```

EXPLANATION

1, 2   This input device name contains a dot. When PHP tries to create a variable from this name, the dot is an illegal character, so it will be replaced with an underscore in your PHP script.

3   This text box name has a space in it. PHP variables cannot contain spaces.

4   The foreach loop is used to cycle through the $_REQUEST array and for each iteration, get the key and value. Notice that where there were spaces and dots in the input device name, PHP has replaced them with the underscore to make them valid variable names. See Figure 10.9.

Figure 10.9
PHP replaced spaces and dots with an underscore.

Stripping out Slashes.   If the `magic_quotes_gpc` directive is enabled in the `php.ini` file (and it is by default), most functions that return data from any external source such as databases and text files will have quotes escaped with a backslash. From the `php.ini` file:

```
; Magic quotes
;

; Magic quotes for incoming GET/POST/Cookie data.
magic_quotes_gpc = On
```

The PHP `stripslashes()` function removes backslashes from the raw data passed from the form. If the user enters quotation marks in his or her input, PHP will escape those quote marks using the backslash character. So, if the user typed `"Help me!"`, PHP will convert the string to `\"Help me!\"`. If the user enters a backslash character, PHP will add another slash to escape it. The `stripslashes()` function removes the backslashes and returns the string as it was originally typed by the user when he or she filled out the form.

FORMAT

```
string stripslashes ( string str )
```

Example:
```
echo stripslashes("O\'Neil")   // Becomes O'Neil
```

Double backslashes (\\) are made into a single backslash (\).

In Figure 10.10, a user has filled out an HTML form with input containing quotes and backslashes. The PHP script in Example 10.5 demonstrates how the `stripslashes()` function handles this input.

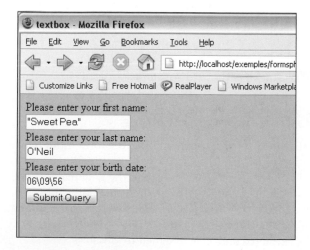

Figure 10.10
The user enters quotes and backslashes.

EXAMPLE 10.5

```
(The PHP Script)
<?php
1   foreach ($_REQUEST as $key => $value){
        echo "User input= <b>$value</b><br />";
    }
?>
-------------------------------------------------------------------
<?php
2   foreach ($_REQUEST as $key => $value){
        echo "User input= <b>".stripslashes($value)."</b><br />";
    }
?>
```

EXPLANATION

1. After the form in Figure 10.10 has been submitted, this PHP script extracts the input data from the `$_REQUEST` array. Each key–value pair is displayed in the browser shown in Figure 10.11 (left). Note the backslashes preceding the quotes and the other backslash character.

2. This time the `stripslashes()` function has removed the backslashes. See Figure 10.11 (right).

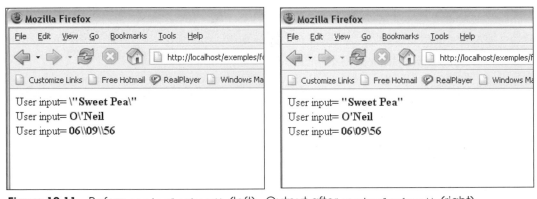

Figure 10.11   Before `stripslashes()` (left). Output after `stripslashes()` (right).

10.3.5 Form Parameters the $_REQUEST Array

The `$_REQUEST` superglobal associative array can be used to collect the form input data. Because it merges the form information found in either `$_GET` or `$_POST` and `$_COOKIE` arrays, you do not have to know what method was used or where the data really came from; it could come form the URL, a link, a cookie, and so on, and therefore, although easy to use, getting the values from `$_REQUEST` is not secure. (See "The POST Method" on page 382 to lessen the vulnerability of input parameters.)

The values from this array can be extracted and then assigned to variables.

EXAMPLE 10.6

```
(HTML File)
<html><head><title>HTML Form</title></head>
    <body bgcolor="#9999CC">
    <font face="verdana" size="+1">
        <form action="get.php" >
        <p>
        Enter your name:
        <br />
        <input type="text" size=50 name="your_name" />
        <p>
        Enter your phone:
        <br />
        <input type="text" size=50 name="your_phone" />
        <p>
        Enter your email address:
        <br />
        <input type="text" size=50 name="your_email_addr" />
        <p>
        <input type=submit name="send" value="submit" />
        <input type=reset value="clear" />
        </form>
    <hr>
    </body>
</html>
```

EXPLANATION

After the user has filled out the form (see Figure 10.12) and pressed the Submit button, the action in the `<form>` tag's `action` attribute is triggered, sending the data to the server and then to the PHP program listed in the URL. The superglobal `$_REQUEST` array receives the form data. Example 10.7 is the PHP program used to process the form input.

Figure 10.12 The HTML form (left). Data has been entered into the HTML form (right).

EXAMPLE 10.7

```
       <html><head><title>Processing First Form</title></head>
       <body bgcolor = "lightgreen"><font size="+1">
       <p>
       <b>The Contents of the $_REQUEST Array</b>

       <?php
1          foreach ($_REQUEST as $key=>$val){
2              echo "$key => $val <br />";
           }
       ?>

       </p>
       </body>
       </html>
```

EXPLANATION

1   The `foreach` loop is used to iterate through the `$_REQUEST` array, retrieving both keys and values.
2   The keys of the `$_REQUEST` array are the names of the input devices, and the values are what the user entered as input when he or she filled out the form. See Figure 10.13.

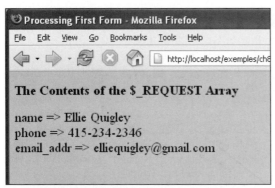

Figure 10.13   The `$_REQUEST` array and forms. Output from Example 10.7.

Using the extract() Function.   You can use the built-in `extract()` function, discussed in Chapter 8, "Arrays," to create variables from an associative array. The variables are named after the keys in the `$_REQUEST` array, and the values assigned to them are the corresponding values in the associative array. For example, if the array has a key–value pair consisting of `"first_name" => "John"`, the `extract()` function would create a variable called `$first_name` and assign it the value `"John"`.

EXAMPLE 10.8

```
       (The PHP program)
       <html><head><title>Processing First Form</title>
       </head>
       <body bgcolor = "lightgreen"><font size="+1">
       <h2>Here is the form input:</h2>
       <?php
1          extract($_REQUEST);   // Get the form input
2          print "Welcome to PHP $name<br />";
           print "Can I call you at $phone<br />";
           print "Is it ok to send you email at $email<br />";
       ?>
       </body>
       </html>
```

EXPLANATION

1   The extract() function will create variables from the $_REQUEST associative array. The variables will be named after keys in the array, and their values will be what the user typed into the form field. The form is shown in Figure 10.12.

2   Now we can use the new variables created by the extract() function. See Figure 10.14 and the program output in Figure 10.15.

keys   values

name	Ellie Quigley
phone	415-234-2346
email	elliequigley@gmail.com

Figure 10.14
The $_REQUEST array from Example 10.8 creates variables named after its keys (first column) and assigns values to each key from the second column.

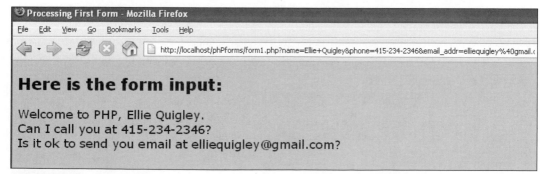

Figure 10.15   After PHP has processed the form from Example 10.8.

10.3.6   Form Parameters and the Medium Style

The medium style is recommended for processing form input and does not require that `register_globals` is turned on. You can retrieve form variables from the superglobal `$_GET` and `$_POST` arrays, depending on what HTTP method was specified in the `action` attribute of the HTML form, GET or POST. Remember, if no `action` is specified, the GET method is the default. (The superglobal arrays, like `$_GET` and `$_POST`, became available in PHP 4.1.0.) When creating the HTML `<form>` tag, the `action` attribute looks something like this:

```
<form action="/phpforms/form1.php" method="GET">
<form action="/phpforms/form1.php">     // No method specified, default is GET
<form action="/phpforms/form1.php" method="POST">
```

When data is submitted in the form, it will be transmitted to the server by one of the methods. PHP will receive the data in one of its superglobal arrays, depending on the method that was used.

The $_GET Array.   The `$_GET` superglobal associative array contains all the values entered into the HTML form fields when the GET method is used. As you know, each form element has attributes such as its `type`, `name`, and so on. PHP uses the value given to `name` attribute of the HTML element to identify that element. The name of the element will become the key to the `$_GET` array and its value whatever the user types into the form field.

The following form is displayed in the browser as shown in Figure 10.16.

EXAMPLE   10.9

```
(The HTML form)
<html><head><title>HTML Form</title></head>
<body bgcolor="#9999CC">
<font face="verdana" size="+1">
<form action="get.php" method="GET">
   <p>
   Enter your name:
   <br />
   <input type="text" size=50 name="your_name" />
   <p>
   Enter your phone:
   <br />
   <input type="text" size=50 name="your_phone" />
   <p>
   Enter your email address:
   <br />
   <input type="text" size=50 name="your_email_addr" />
   <p>
   <input type=submit value="submit" />
   <input type=reset value="clear" />
</form>
<hr />
</body></html>
```

EXAMPLE 10.9 (CONTINUED)

```
--------------------------------------------------------------------
    (The PHP Script to Handle the Form)
    <html><head><title>Processing Form</title>
    </head>
    <body>

    <?php
        // Medium style; use superglobal array
1       $name = $_GET['your_name'];
2       $phone = $_GET['your_phone'];
3       $email = $_GET['your_email_addr'];
    ?>

    <div align="center">
        <table>
            <tr><td><font face="verdana" size="+1" color="#000066">
4               Welcome to PHP, <em><?= $name ?>.</em>
            </td></tr>
            <tr><td><font face="verdana" size="+1" color="#000066">
5               Can I call you at <em><?=$phone ?>? </em>
            </td></tr>
            <tr><td><font face="verdana" size="+1" color="#000066">
6           Is it ok to send you email at <em><?=$email ?>?</em>
            </td></tr>
        </table>
    </div>
    </body>
    </html>
```

EXPLANATION

1 PHP gets the form data from the superglobal $_GET array. The key "your_name" is the name assigned to the input device in the HTML form and the value is what the user typed into the text box, in this example "Jack Sprat" (see Figure 10.16). This value is assigned to the PHP variable, $name.

2 The name assigned to this text box was "your_phone". The value associated with it is the user's phone number. That value is assigned to the PHP variable, $phone.

3 The name assigned to this text box was "your_email_addr". The value associated with it is the user's e-mail address. That value is assigned to the PHP variable, $email.

4–6 The PHP variables are embedded in shortcut tags to be displayed within an HTML table (without a border). (The HTML table was used to center and align the output on the page.) See Figure 10.17.

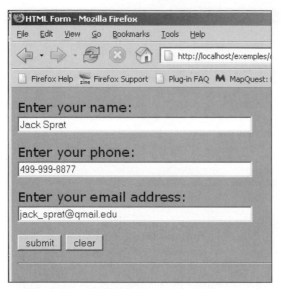

Figure 10.16   The HTML form and the GET method from Example 10.9.

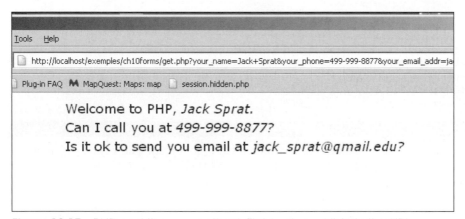

Figure 10.17   PHP and the GET method. Field values visible in the URL.

Security.   A rule of caution would be to use the GET method for passing form information that is not a security risk, such as passwords or login IDs, and if you need to use the GET method, then your program should take additional measures to ensure the safety of the incoming data. Anyone can see what was typed into the form fields simply by looking at the URL in his browser where the key–value pairs are appended to a question mark. And anyone can manually change the parameters right in the URL by typing information that can then easily be passed and stored in the $_GET superglobal. In Figure 10.18, the URL is modified by assigning a different name to "your_name". To help solve this problem, the POST method can be used with some extra checking within the PHP script.

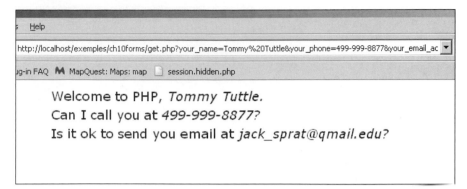

Figure 10.18 The user can easily change the URL. The name was changed in the URL, sent to the server, and then to PHP where it was assigned to the `$_GET[]` array.

The $_POST Array. The `$_POST` superglobal array contains all the names the values entered into the HTML form fields when the POST method is used. With the POST method, the value of parameters is not visible in browser's URL, but POST data is not invulnerable and be can be intercepted. You will need to perform checks in your program to assure that your input data is being retrieved as expected.

EXAMPLE 10.10

```
(The HTML form)
<html><head><title>HTML Form</title></head>
<body bgcolor="#9999CC">
<font face="verdana" size="+1">
<form action="post.php" method="POST">
    <p>
    Enter your name:
    <br />
    <input type="text" size=50 name="your_name" />
    <p>
    Enter your phone:
    <br />
    <input type="text" size=50 name="your_phone" />
    <p>
    Enter your email address:
    <br />
    <input type="text" size=50 name="your_email_addr" />
    <p>
    <input type=submit name="send" value="submit" />
    <input type=reset value="clear" />
</form>
<hr />
</body>
</html>
---------------------------------------------------------------------
```

EXAMPLE 10.10 (CONTINUED)

```
        (The PHP Script)
        <html><head><title>Processing Form</title>
        </head>
        <body>
        <?php
1           if(! empty ($_GET) ){
                die("Parameter wrong. Try again<br />");
            }
2           if( $_POST['send'] == "submit"){
                // Medium style; use superglobal array
3               $name = $_POST['your_name'];
                $phone = $_POST['your_phone'];
                $email = $_POST['your_email_addr'];
            }
            ?>
        <div align="center"
        <table>
            <tr><td><font face="verdana" size="+1" color="#000066">
4               Welcome PHP, <em><?= $name ?>.</em>
            </td></tr>
            <tr><td><font face="verdana" size="+1" color="#000066">
5               Can I call you at <em><?=$phone ?>? </em>
            </td></tr>
            <tr><td><font face="verdana" size="+1" color="#000066">
6               Is it ok to send you email at <em><?=$email ?>?</em>
            </td></tr>
        </table>
        </div></body></html>
```

EXPLANATION

1   The HTML form fields are filled in, as shown in Figure 10.19. If data is entered through the GET method (e.g., by adding it to the URL), the program will die and the die construct will send the error message, as displayed in Figure 10.21. Even though the program is using the POST method, if the user were to assign parameters to the URL, the superglobal $_GET would be assigned the unwanted information. This prevents a user from being able to send unwarranted information via the GET method.

2   If the POST method was used in the HTML form, then PHP will check to see if the submit button was pressed, but testing the value assigned to the name of the submit button. If $_POST['name'] evaluates to "submit", then the form was submitted, and the if block is entered.

3   The key–value pairs of the $_POST array are the names and values of the input devices in the HTML form. The keys are: 'send', 'your_name', 'your_phone', and 'email_addr'. Their values (i.e., what the user typed into the form fields) are stored in PHP variables, $name, $phone, and $email, respectively.

4–6 The values of the PHP variables are displayed in the browser. See Figure 10.20.

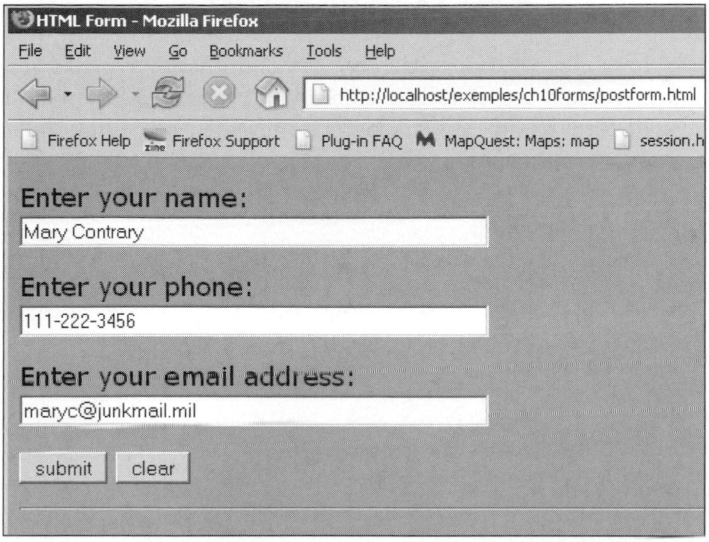

Figure 10.19 The HTML form and the POST method.

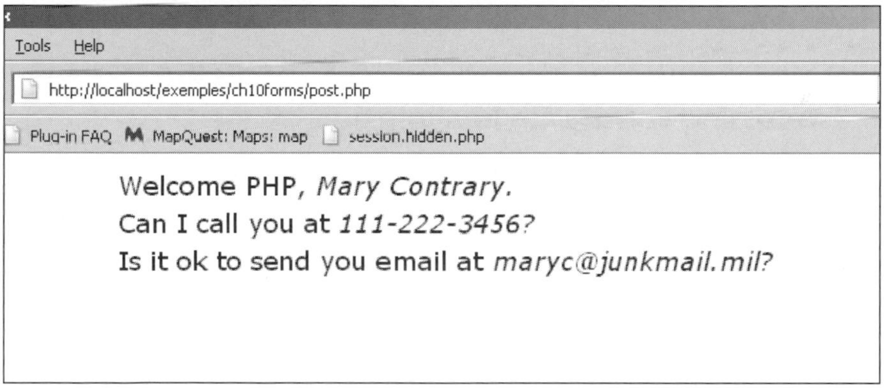

Figure 10.20 PHP and the POST method. Field values not visible in the URL.

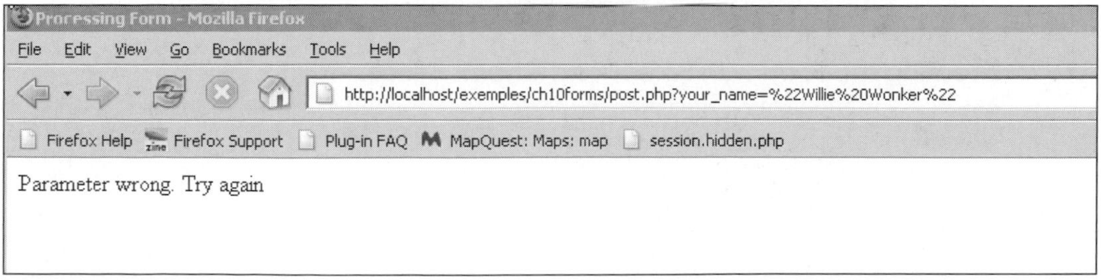

Figure 10.21 User tries to append data to the URL and fails.

10.3.7   Form Parameters and the Long (Old) Style

As of PHP 5.0.0, these long predefined variables can be disabled with the `register_long_arrays` directive and are no longer commonly used. The only reason for including the old long style form parameters here is that they still show up in older scripts that you might be reading or editing.

EXAMPLE 10.11

```
<html><head><title>Processing First Form</title>
</head>
<body bgcolor = "lightgreen"><font size="+1">
<h2>Here is the form input:</h2>
<?php
    $name = $HTTP_GET_VARS['name'];   // Long style with GET method
    $phone = $HTTP_GET_VARS['phone'];
    $email = $HTTP_GET_VARS['email_addr'];
    print "Welcome to PHP $name<br />";
    print "Can I call you at $phone<br />";
    print "Is it ok to send you email at $email<br />";
?>
</body>
</html>
```

10.3.8   Processing Forms with Multiple Selections

HTML forms that allow the user to pick more than one selection in a list or a check box are created with select tags (when the `"multiple"` attribute is set) and `checkbox` input types. Instead of PHP generating a single variable for multiple choices, an array is better suited for that task. To create the array, you simply add a set of square brackets to the name of the input device in your HTML document:

```
<select name="movies[]">
<input type=checkbox name="colors[]" value="red">
```

When the user submits the form, if using the simple form, PHP will create an array of choices with each element of the array assigned the value selected by the user.

Creating the Form with Select and Check Boxes.   With   the   `select`   and `checkbox` input devices, the name of the device is appended with a set of array brackets when multiple choices can be selected.

EXAMPLE 10.12

```
    (The HTML form)
    <html><head><title>Multiple Choice</title></head>
    <body bgcolor="aqua">
1   <form action="checkbox.php" method="POST">
    <b>Choose a vacation spot:</b>
    br />
2   <select name="location[]" multiple="multiple">
        <option>Maui
        <option>Bali
        <option>Miami
        <option>Riviera
    </select> <p>
    <b>Select a city:</b>
    <br />
3   <input type="checkbox" name="place[]" value="New York" />New York
    <br />
    <input type="checkbox" name="place[]" value="Chicago" />Chicago
    <br />
    <input type="checkbox" name="place[]" value="London" />London
    <br />
    <input type="checkbox" name="place[]" value="Tokyo" />Tokyo
    <br />
4   <input type="checkbox" name="place[]" value="San Francisco"
        Checked />San Francisco
    <p>
    <input type="submit" value="submit" />
    <input type="reset" value="clear" />
    </form>
    </body>
    </html>
```

EXPLANATION

1 The HTTP method selected for this form is the POST method. The form is displayed in Figure 10.22.

2 A select drop-down menu starts here and it will allow for the user to select more than one option when "multiple" is specified as an attribute. (Press the Control key at the same time you click the mouse to get multiple options highlighted.) The name of the select menu is appended with [] so that when PHP recieves the input, it will be accepted as an array.

3 This input type is a select menu that is designed to accept multiple checks. Its name is also appended with the [] to indicate that an array will be created when PHP gets the form input.

4 This value has been checked as the default.

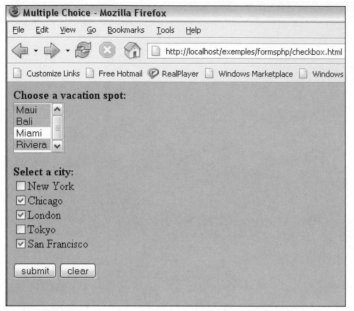

Figure 10.22   An HTML form with multiple selections. Output from Example 10.12.

Processing the Form with Multiple Selections.   With the medium style, we use an associative array, $_POST, $_GET, or $_REQUEST, to receive the input values, the name of the input device.

EXAMPLE 10.13

```
        <html><head><title><Forms and User-defined Arrays>
        </title></head>
        <body bgcolor="8CCCCA">
        <br />
        <fieldset><legend><b>Vacation Choices</b></legend>

        <?php
            // Medium style
1           if (is_array($_POST['location'])){
                print "<ul>";
2               foreach ( $_POST['location'] as $key=>$value ){
                    print "<li>$key=>$value</li>";
                }
                print "</ul>";
            }
        ?>
        </fieldset>
        <fieldset><legend><b>City Choices</b></legend>
```

EXAMPLE 10.13 (CONTINUED)

```php
    <?php
3      extract($_POST);
       if (is_array($place)){
           print "<ul>";
4          foreach ( $place as $key=>$value ){
               print "<li>$key=>$value</li>";
           }
           print "</ul>";
       }
    ?>
    </fieldset></body></html>
```

EXPLANATION

1   The is_array() function will return true if the form was submitted and the
    $_POST superglobal array has a value.
2   The foreach loop will iterate through each element of the $POST['location']
    array, listing both keys and values. The key is the index of the location array,
    where the option was selected, and the value is text after the option attribute. See
    Figure 10.22, Vacation Choices.
3   The extract() function is used to get the keys and values from the $_POST asso-
    ciative array. The name of the array that is returned is $place. It consists of the
    key–value pairs representing the check boxes that were selected.
4   The foreach loop will iterate through each element of the $place array indicating
    where check boxes were selected. See Figure 10.22, City Choices.

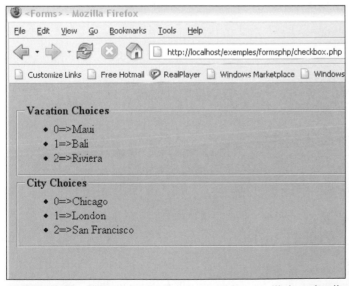

Figure 10.23 PHP output after processing multiple selections.

10.3.9   Forms Using an Image Button

If a Web page has a form for ordering some special item, such as a gift item, it might be cute to use a picture of the item for submitting the order rather than the standard boring submit button.[6] This is done by using a clickable image, also called an image map. Instead of an input type of `"submit"`, you will use the input type of `"image"`, the src, location of the .gif or .jpg file, and a name for the input type:

```
<input type="image" src="toy_car.gif" name="toy" />
```

Even though there is only one image, when the user clicks somewhere on it, the accompanying form will be sent to the server with the location of where the user clicked his or her mouse on the picture; that is, the pixel coordinates represented as *two* variables in the PHP script, image_name_x and image_name_y (image_name is the name assigned to the name attribute of the image input type; that is, toy_x and toy_y). The actual variable names sent by the browser contain a period rather than an underscore (toy.x and toy.y) but, as we discussed earlier in this chapter, PHP will automatically convert a period (or space) to an underscore because periods (and spaces) are not legal characters in PHP variable names. In the following example, after the user clicks on any of the check boxes, he or she will then click on the picture of the pizza man. This causes the form to be submitted with an array of values selected from the check boxes, as well as the x/y coordinates of where the user clicked on the image button.

EXAMPLE 10.14

```
        (The HTML File)
        <html> <head><title>Image Button</title> </head>
        <body bgColor="#CCFF33">
        <font face="verdana"><b>
1       <form method="post" action="image_button.php" >
                Pick your pizza:<p>
2         <input type="checkbox"
                name="topping[]"
                value="tomatoes" />Tomato and Cheese<br />
          <input type="checkbox"
                name="topping[]"
                value="salami" />Salami<br />
          <input type=checkbox
                name="topping[]"
                value="pineapple" />Pineapple and Ham<br />
          <input type=checkbox
                name="topping[]"
                value="Canadian bacon" />Canadian bacon<br />
```

---

6. Some designers warn against changing the standard submit button for the sake of consistency across the board and so as not to confuse users with unfamiliar widgets. Others change the look of the standard button with style sheets.

EXAMPLE 10.14 (CONTINUED)

```
            <input type=checkbox
                name="topping[]"
                value="extra cheese" />Plain Cheese<br />
            <p><font size="-1">
            Press the pizza man to order!
            <br />
3           <input type="image" name='pizzas' src="Pizza_chef.jpg" />
            <br /><br />
            <input type=reset value="Clear the form" />
        </form>
        </body>
        </html>

    ------------------------------------------    --------------------

        (The PHP Script)
        <html><head><title>Finding Pixel Coordinates</title></head>
        <body bgcolor="8CCCCA">
        <br />
        <fieldset><legend><b>Pizza Choices</b></legend>
        <?php
4           if ($_POST['topping']){
                print "<ul>";
5               foreach ( $_POST['topping'] as $value ){
                    print "<li>$value</li>";
                }
                print "</ul>";
            }
            print "The pixel coordinates of the image are: <br />";
6           $coord1 = $_POST['pizzas_x'];
            $coord2 = $_POST['pizzas_y'];
            print "$coord1, $coord2<br />";
        ?>
        </fieldset>
        </body>
        </html>
```

EXPLANATION

1   The form, shown in Figure 10.23, is being submitted to a PHP script using the POST method.

2   The form consists of a set of check boxes that will be passed to PHP as an array called "topping".

3   Here is where we create the image button to be used to submit the form. It is given a name of 'pizzas' and the image src is "Pizza_chef.jpg" located in the current working directory or folder. When the user clicks on this picture, the form will be submitted.

4   If the user has posted the form, there will be a value in the $_POST array, the expression will test true, and the block will be entered.

5   For each of the toppings in the $_POST array, the values will be printed. See Figure 10.24.

6   The x/y coordinates represent the place in the image (pixel position) where the user clicked his or her mouse button. To check whether or not the form was submitted, you can test if these variables are not empty with the empty() function:

```
if ( ! empty($coord1 )
```

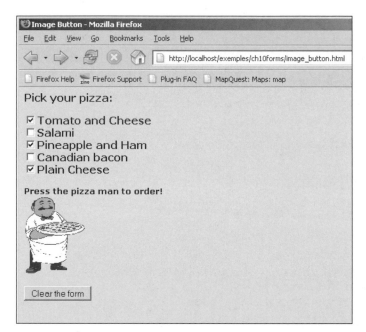

Figure 10.24
Using an image to submit a form.

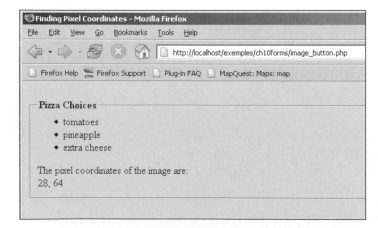

Figure 10.25
After the form input has been processed, the user's choices are listed as well as the pixel positions of the image button (the pizza man).

10.3.10   Self-Processing HTML Forms

Rather than creating a separate HTML document to display a form and another PHP script to process the user input, you might want to combine the HTML document containing the form and the PHP script that processess it all into one script. This is done by assigning the `$_SERVER['PHP_SELF']` array to the `action` attribute of the HTML `<form>` tag as shown in Example 10.15. When the user submits the form information by pressing the submit button, the `action` attribute of the form references the URL of the same page that displayed the form. Because both the HTML form data and the PHP processing code are in the same script, you will need a conditional check in your PHP program to see if the form has been submitted. For example, you can check to see if a field has a value, the submit button has been clicked, or check the request method used. The following examples demonstrate how this is done.

Checking If the Form Was Submitted.   Example 10.15 shows the script that checks whether a form was submitted.

EXAMPLE   10.15

```php
      <?php
1     if ( isset($_POST['submit'])){  // Was the form submitted?
2           $your_name=$_POST[your_name];
            $your_phone=$_POST[your_phone];
            print "<b>Your name is $your_name<br />";
            print "Your phone is $your_phone<br />";
3           print "The path to this file is: ".
                  $_SERVER['PHP_SELF']."<br />";
      }
4     else{  ?>
          <html><head><title>First HTML Form</title></head>
          <body bgcolor="lightblue"><font size="+1">
5         <form action="<?php echo $_SERVER['PHP_SELF']; ?>"
            method="POST">
            <p />
6         Please enter your name: <br />
          <input type="text" size=50 name="your_name">
            <p />
          Please enter your phone: <br />
          <input type="text" size=50 name="your_phone">
            <p />
          <input type="submit" name="submit" value="Send Now">
          <input type=reset value="Clear">
        </form>
        <hr>
        </html>
      <?php } ?>
```

EXPLANATION

1 The PHP `isset()` function checks to see if the form has been submitted using the POST method. If it has, the program continues at line 2; if not, then program control goes to line 4, and the form will be displayed in the browser.

2 Because the form has already been submitted, the values that were entered into the fields can be displayed as variables. See Figure 10.27.

3 The superglobal `$_SERVER['SELF']` array contains information about the path where this script is found starting at the document root of the server, not the root of the file system.

4 If the form has not been submitted, the script jumps into this block where we switch from PHP into the HTML mode to produce the form. See Figure 10.26.

5 The `action` attribute is assigned the address of the current script. The program temporarily switches back into PHP mode to get the path of the script from the `$_SERVER['PHP_SELF']` variable. When the user presses the submit button, this same script will be reexecuted, this time to process the form data.

6 The user is presented with two text boxes, as shown in Figure 10.26.

Figure 10.26
The script displays the form.

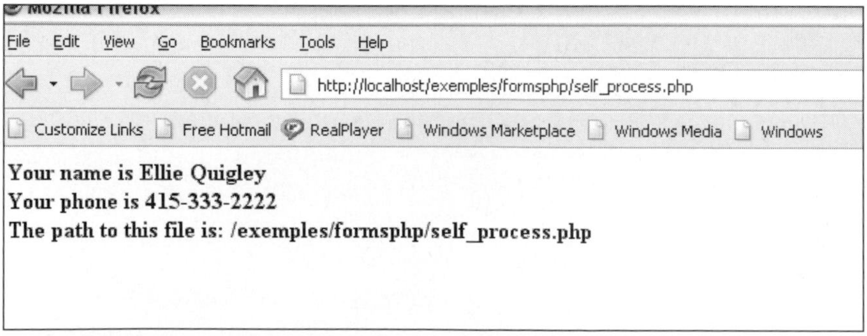

Figure 10.27   The same script processes the form.

10.3.11   Using Hidden Fields

If your Web page contains multiple forms, you can use hidden fields to help identify what form needs to be processed by giving each form its own name. By checking the existence and value of the hidden field, you can determine which form should be displayed and when it should be processed.

You can also use hidden fields to include information that can be used when processing the form but is not something that you do not care to display, such as the date the form was created, your name, and so on.

EXAMPLE 10.16

```
      <html
      <html><head><title>Hidden Fields</title></head>
      <body bgcolor="#ff66ff">
      <font face="verdana">
      <div align="center">
      <b>
      <?php
1         if (isset($_POST['feedback1']) && ($_POST['feedback1'] ==
                  'process_form1')){
              process_form1();
          }
2         else{
              display_form1();
          }

3         function display_form1(){
4             echo <<<EOF
5             <form action="$_SERVER[PHP_SELF]" method="post">
              Rate this page
               <br /><b /r>
              <input type="radio" name="rating" value="excellent"
                      />Really kewl
              <input type="radio" name="rating" value="average" />OK
              <input type="radio" name="rating" value="poor" />Boring
              <input type="radio" name="rating" value="hopeless"
                      />Totally hopeless
6             <input type="hidden" name="feedback1"
                      value="process_form1">
7             <input type="hidden" name="creation_date"
                      value="Feb. 2006" />
              <p>
              <input type="submit" value="submit rating" />
              <input type="reset" value="clear" />
              </form>
```

EXAMPLE 10.16 (CONTINUED)

```
8       EOF;
        }

9       function process_form1(){
            echo "So you think this page is $_POST[rating]!";
        }
    ?>
    </b>
    </div>
    </body>
    </html>
```

EXPLANATION

1   The isset() function will check to see if the variable $_POST['feedback1'] has been set and if it contains the value assigned to the hidden field. If both conditions are true, then the form has already been displayed on the browser and sent back to this PHP script. Because the page has already been displayed and submitted, it is now time to process the form. The user-defined function, process_form(), is called.

2   If the test on line 1 fails, then the form has not been previously displayed. The user-defined function, display_form(), is called.

3   The function display_form() will be responsible for creating the form and displaying it in the browser.

4   This is the start of a here-doc used to print out the HTML form and interpolate any variables. Remember that when in a here-doc you are essentially in a quoted block of text. Adding additional quotes to the array elements will produce an error.

5   The $_SERVER['PHP_SELF'] is a reference to the current script. When the user presses the submit button, the action is specified to call this same script again.

6   The hidden field is set as an input type of the <form> tag. Although it will not be visible when the form is displayed, its name and value will be sent to the PHP script, along with the name and value of the radio button selected by the user.

7   The hidden field is assigned the month and year when this form was created. No one needs to see this information, except maybe you if you are trying to keep track of the development of this page.

8   The user-defined terminator, EOF, for marking the end of the here-doc, cannot have spaces on either side; that is, it must be butted up against the left margin, immediately followed by a newline.

9   After the user has filled out the form, this function processes the input received from the server.

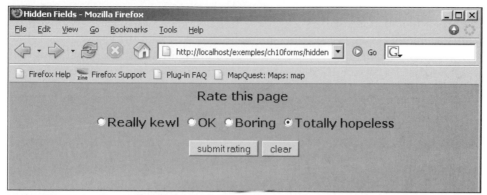

Figure 10.28   Using hidden fields to determine when to process this form. Output from Example 10.16.

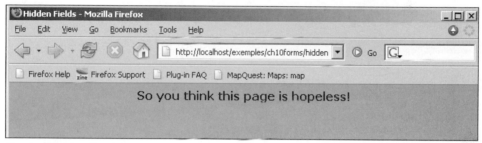

Figure 10.29   Output based on what radio button was selected in Figure 10.28.

10.3.12   Redirecting the User

What if your Web site has moved to a new location? Now when your users go to the old site, you want to redirect them to the new one. What if you want to send the user to a different page depending on some condition: Is the user logged on? Did he or she forget his or her password? What language does he or she speak? Is it a holiday?

The Location Header.   Redirecting a user to another page is easy and quick with PHP. It is done with the built-in `header()` function to modify the HTTP response header sent by the server. The location header can be changed by sending an HTTP `Location` followed by the URL of the new location.

```
<?php
   header( 'Location: http://www.mysite.com/new_page.html' ) ;
?>
```

The header information must be sent to the browser before any HTML and text; therefore, it is important that the `header()` function is executed first. The following example would be wrong because the program is trying to send the `echo` output before the header information. The warning is displayed in Figure 10.30. (See "Buffering and HTTP Headers" on page 689 if you want to move the header after other output lines.)

EXAMPLE 10.17

```php
<?php
   echo "You are going to be redirected to a new page!<br />"; // Wrong!
   header("Location: /www/ellieq.com");
?>
```

EXPLANATION

After being redirected, a user's Back button will take the user where he or she was before the redirection page, not back to the redirection page itself.

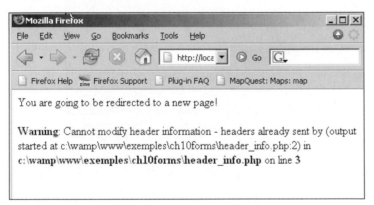

Figure 10.30 The header must be sent first.

Using the Correct URI for Redirection.   The `Location` can be assigned the absolute URI of the redirection page such as the scheme, host name, and absolute path. Then the server will return a "redirect" header to the browser to retrieve the specified page directly.

```
Location: http://marakana.com/company.html
```

If you want to reference another file on your own server, you can output a partial URL, such as the following:

```
Location: /tutorial/PHP/index.html
```

You can make use of PHP's $_SERVER array variables to specify an absoute path. For example, the $_SERVER['HTTP_HOST'], the $_SERVER['PHP_SELF'], and the path of the the current script returned by the dirname() function can be concatenated together to make an absolute URL from a relative one. The following PHP code defines a header described in the PHP manual:

```php
<?php
   header("Location: http://" . $_SERVER['HTTP_HOST']) .
        dirname($_SERVER['PHP_SELF']) . "/my_newpage.php");
?>
```

If you are redirecting a user to a new Web site, it is also a good idea to let him or her know what is happening by adding a line such as "Our site has moved. You will automatically be redirected there."

EXAMPLE 10.18

```
     (The HTML File)
     <html><head><title>Redirecting the User</title></head>
     <body bgcolor="#33ff33">
1    <form action="http://localhost/exemples/ch10forms/redirect.php"
            method="post">
        <b>
        Select a search engine<br />
        </b>
2       <select name="new_url">
            <option value="http://www.google.com" />Google
            <option value="http://www.yahoo.com" /> Yahoo!
            <option value="http://www.lycos.com" /> Lycos
               <option value="/index.php" /> PHP Index
        </select>
3       <input type="submit" value=" Get the Web Page!" />
     </form>
     </body>
     </html>
     ------------------------------------------------------------------
     (The PHP Script)
     <?
4       if($_POST[new_url] == ""){
            exit;
        }
        else {
5           header("Location: $_POST[new_url]");
            exit;
        }
     ?>
```

EXPLANATION

1 The form's `action` attribute is assigned the path to the PHP script that will handle the redirect once the form is submitted. The HTML form is shown in Figure 10.31.

2 The HTML `select` menu will give the user options to choose from.

3 As soon as the user clicks the submit button, the form information will be sent to the server and handled by the PHP script listed in the form's `action` attribute.

4 If the user did not select anything, the value of `$_POST[new_url]` will be empty, and the script will exit.

5 If the user selected one of the search engines in the menu (Figure 10.32), he or she will be directed to that Web site with the PHP `header()` function. The value of `$_POST[new_url]` is the address of the selected Web site; for example, http://www.lycos.com. Once the user is redirected, he or she can use the brower's Back button to go back to the page where the selection was made.

Figure 10.31 The HTML Web page before viewing the menu and selecting an option.

Figure 10.32 The user selects "PHP Index" from the drop-down menu and presses "Get the Web Page!" to redirect to that site.

10.3.13   Uploading Files

In an HTML form, users can upload files from a browser to a Web server. The files might be text files, binary files (such as images or compressed files), spreadsheets, or other data (see *http://www.faqs.org/rfcs/rfc1867.html*). Being able to upload files is also useful if the information is easier to handle from a separate file, such as a registration form or a résumé. To upload files, you will need to create a form using the `"file"` type.

Attributes for the \<Form\> Tag and the file Type.   To upload files the `<form>` tag has three attributes:

1. The `action` attribute of the `<form>` tag specifies the PHP script that will process the form.
2. The `enctype` attribute determines how the form data is encoded by the browser. The default value is `application/x-www-form-urlencoded`, which is the default for almost any kind of form data. However, if you are going to upload files then you must specify that the data is of enctype `multi-part/form-data`. The browser encodes form data differently for `application/x-www-form-urlencoded` and `multipart/form-data`.
3. The `method` attribute should be `"POST"`.

EXAMPLE 10.19

```
     (Sample File Upload Form Values)
1    <form enctype="multipart/form-data"
2         action="PHPscript.php"
3         method="POST">
<!--MAX_FILE_SIZE is optional and must precede the file input field-->
4    <input type="hidden" name="MAX_FILE_SIZE" value="30000" />
5    Choose a file to upload: <input name="uploadfile" type="file" />
     <input type="submit" value="Send File" />
     </form>
```

In addition to the three attributes, the form's input type is `"file"`; for example:

```
<input type="file" name="uploadfile"
```

With an input type of type `"file"`, the browser might show a display of (previously selected) file names, and a Browse button or selection method. Selecting the Browse button would cause the browser to enter into a file selection mode, allowing you to select from a list of files from different directories or folders. See Figure 10.34.

You can also specify the `MAX_FILE_SIZE` field size, the maximum number of bytes that will be accepted, but this only advises what size the file should be. This cannot be larger than `upload_max_filesize` defined in the `php.ini` file (default 2MB). Note also that this hidden field must precede the file input field in the HTML.

Files will, by default, be stored in the server's default temporary directory, unless another location has been given with the upload_tmp_dir directive in php.ini. You can use the built-in move_uploaded_file() function to store an uploaded file somewhere permanently (see Example 10.21).

From the php.ini file:

```
; File Uploads ;
;;;;;;;;;;;;;;;;

; Whether to allow HTTP file uploads.
file_uploads = On

; Temporary directory for HTTP uploaded files (will use system default if not
; specified).
upload_tmp_dir = "c:/wamp/tmp"

; Maximum allowed size for uploaded files.
upload_max_filesize = 2M
```

PHP's $_FILES Array.   When the file is sent to the server, PHP stores all the uploaded file information in the $_FILES superglobal array (see Table 10.3), a two-dimensional array that contains the name of the file input device as the first index and one of the attributes of the file type as the second index.

Table 10.3 The $_FILES Superglobal Array

Array	*Description*
$_FILES['userfile']['name']	The original name of the file on the client machine.
$_FILES['userfile']['type']	The MIME type of the file, if the browser provided this information. An example would be "image/gif".
$_FILES['userfile']['size']	The size, in bytes, of the uploaded file.
$_FILES['userfile']['tmp_name']	The temporary filename of the file in which the uploaded file was stored on the server.
$_FILES['userfile']['error']	The error code associated with this file upload. ['error'] was added in PHP 4.2.0.

EXAMPLE 10.20

```
        (The HTML File)
        <html><head><title>Uploading Files</title></head>
        <body bgcolor="lavender">
        <h3>Uploading Files</h3>
1       <form
2           enctype="multipart/form-data"
3           action="upload_file.php"
4           method="post">
            Type the name of the file to upload: <br />
5           <input name="user_file"
                    type="file"/>
            <br />
            <input type=submit value="Get File"/>
        </form>
        </body>
        </html>
        --------------------------------------------------
        (The PHP Script--upload_file.php)
        <?php
6           $handle=fopen($_FILES['user_file']['tmp_name'], "r");
7           while(!feof($handle)){
8               $text=fgets($handle);
                echo $text,"<br />";
            }
        ?>
```

EXPLANATION

1   The form starts here and is displayed in Figure 10.33.
2   The attribute to the form type is `enctype` and assigned `"multipart/form-data"`. This encoding type is used to send data from files.
3   The `action` attribute specifies the PHP script that will process the uploaded files.
4   Uploaded files must be sent via the `POST` method.
5   The input device is of type `"file"` and will be assigned the name `"user_file"`. The name is how the uploaded file will be identified in the PHP file, not the real name of the file. See Figure 10.35.
6   The `$_FILES['user_file']['tmp_name']` array holds the name of the temporary file that PHP gave to the uploaded file. The `fopen()` function will open that file for reading and return a filehandle that allows access to the file. (See "The fopen() Function" on page 448.)

Figure 10.33   The file upload form from Example 10.20 in the browser.

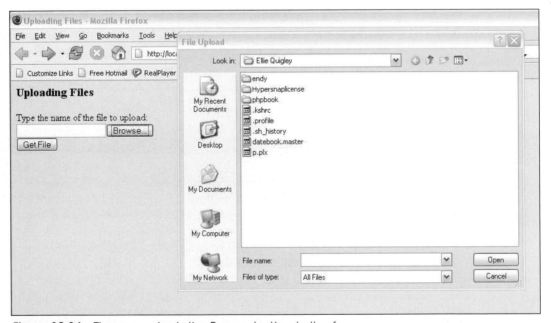

Figure 10.34   The user selects the Browse button in the form.

Figure 10.35   The user then selects a file.

Moving the Uploaded File.   PHP provides the `move_uploaded_file()` function to move an uploaded file to a new location.

FORMAT

```
bool move_uploaded_file ( string filename, string destination )
```

This function checks to ensure that the file designated by filename is a valid upload file (meaning that it was uploaded using the POST method). If the file is valid, it will be moved to the filename given as a destination.

If the filename is not a valid upload file, then no action will occur, and `move_uploaded_file()` function will return FALSE with a warning.

EXAMPLE   10.21

```
      (The HTML Form)
      <html><head><title>Uploading Pictures</title></head>
      <body bgcolor="lavender">
      <h3>Uploading Files</h3>
      <form
1         enctype="multipart/form-data"
          action="upload_move_file.php"
          method="post">

      Browse and select the picture you want to upload: <br />
```

EXAMPLE 10.21 (CONTINUED)

```
2        <input name="picture_file"  type="file" />
         <br />
         <input type=submit value="Get File"/>
    </form>
    </body>
    </html>
--------------------------------------------------------------
    (The PHP Script)
    <html><head><title>File Uploads</title></head>
    <body bgcolor="#33ff33">
    <font face="verdana" size="+1">
    <?php
        echo "The uploaded file is: ", $_FILES['picture_file']
             ['tmp_name'], "<br />";
        $filename=$_FILES['picture_file']['name'];
        $filesize=$_FILES['picture_file']['size'];
        $directory='c:/wamp/www/exemples/formsphp/
             picture_uploads/';
3       $uploadFile = $directory . $filename;
        echo "The moved file is: $uploadFile<br />";
4       if (move_uploaded_file($_FILES['picture_file']['tmp_name'],
                $uploadFile)){
            echo "The file is valid and was successfully uploaded.
                <br /> ";
            echo "The image file, $filename, is $filesize bytes.<br />";
        }
    ?>
    <center>
    <br />
    <img src=<?php
        echo "/exemples/formsphp/picture_uploads/$filename";?>
    width="250" height="175" border="3">
    </center>
    </font>
    </body>
    </html>
```

EXPLANATION

1   To upload files the encoding type must be `"multipart/form-data"` and the method, POST.

2   The uploaded file must be of type `"file"`. Its name is `"picture_file"`, the name used to identify the file in the `$_FILES[]` associative array. The file being upload-ed is shown in Figure 10.36.

3   The variable, `$uploadFile`, contains the directory and filename to where the pic-ture will be moved.

4   The `move_uploaded_file()` function moves the uploaded file to its new location. Its first argument is the original file and its second argument is the destination.

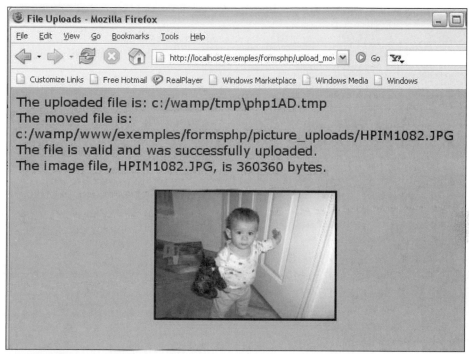

Figure 10.36 Uploading and moving Images.

10.3.14 Sticky Forms

A *sticky form* is a form that remembers the values you typed in the input fields. A typical example is when you fill out a form to purchase some products or fill out a registration form and you left out a field or typed the credit card information wrong. When you submit the order, the page comes back with the form and tells you what you did wrong and asks you to resubmit the order. If the order form is long and contains lots of boxes, how many times will you resubmit it, if you have to start all over again? With a sticky form, the input data can be saved so that when the form is redisplayed, the data is still there. The following example checks if the user left any fields empty and if he or she did, redisplays the form with an error showing what fields need to filled. The fields that had data in them still contain the data. (For a complete discussion on form validation, see Chapter 12, "Regular Expressions and Pattern Matching.")

EXAMPLE   10.22

```
      <html><head><title>Empty Fields</title>
      <body><div align="center">
      <h2>Validating Input</h2>
      <?php
1        $errors=array();
2        if(isset($_REQUEST['submit'])){ // If the form was submitted
3           validate_input();  // Check for empty fields
4           if(count($errors) != 0){  //  If there are errors,
                                      //   redisplay the form
                display_form();
             }
5           else{ echo "<b>OK! Go ahead and Process the form!</b>
                <br />"; }
          }
6        else{display_form();}  // Display the form for the first time
7        function validate_input(){
8           global $errors;
             if($_POST["name"] == ""){
9               $errors['name']="<font color='red'>
                ***Your name?***</font>";
             }
             if($_POST["phone"] == ""){
                $errors['phone']="<font color='red'>
                ***Your phone?***</font>";
             }
          }
10       function display_form(){
             global $errors;
             ?>
             <b>
11           <form method="post"
                   action="<?php echo $_SERVER['PHP_SELF'];
             ?>">
             What is your name? <br />
12           <input type="text" name="name"
                   value="<?php echo $_POST[name]; ?>">
             <br />
13           <?php echo $errors['name']; ?>
             <br />
             What is your phone number?<br />
             <input type="text" name="phone"
                   value="<?php echo $_POST[phone]; ?>">
             <br />
14           <?php echo $errors['phone']; ?>
             <br />
             <input type="reset">
```

EXAMPLE 10.22 (CONTINUED)

```
            <input type="submit" name="submit">
            <br />
            <form>
      <?php
      }
   ?>
   </b>
   </div>
   </body>
   </html>
```

EXPLANATION

1 The $errors array is initialized. It will be used to build a string error message.

2 If the isset() function returns true, the user has already submitted the form and program control will go to line 3.

3 The user-defined function, validate_input(), is called.

4 If the PHP count() function finds that the $errors array is not empty, the display_form() function is called and the same form is displayed again with the error messages displayed in red. See Figures 10.38 and 10.39.

5 If there are no errors, then the form will be processed. We do not do any real processing here, but if we did, this is where the code would go.

6 If line 1 is false (i.e., the form has not yet been displayed), the form will be shown in the browser for the first time.

7 This is a user-defined function that will determine whether or not the user filled in the required fields.

8 The global keyword makes this array available within the function.

9 If the user did not fill the "name" field, the $errors array will be assigned a string of text as its value. The key 'name' is the name of the text box.

10 This function displays the form, as displayed in Figure 10.37.

11 The form is a self-processing form when the action attribute $_SERVER[PHP_SELF] is assigned this value.

12 When the input type is named, the value given to it will be empty the first time it is displayed because PHP has not yet processed the input. If the form has already been displayed and there was an error, then the value of the field, if there was one, will be assigned by switching over to PHP mode and using the value of $_POST[name]. This is what makes the form "sticky." If the user had typed his or her name, PHP would have put the value back in the text box, but if the user did not type his or her name, the value of $_POST[name] will be empty and nothing will be restored to the text box. Instead the user will see an error in red text as shown on line 13.

13 If the user did not enter his or her name in the text box field, this error will be printed right below it. If the user did enter his or her name, the value in this array element will be empty and nothing will be printed.

14 If the user did not enter his or her phone number in the text field box, an error will be printed, as shown in Figure 10.38.

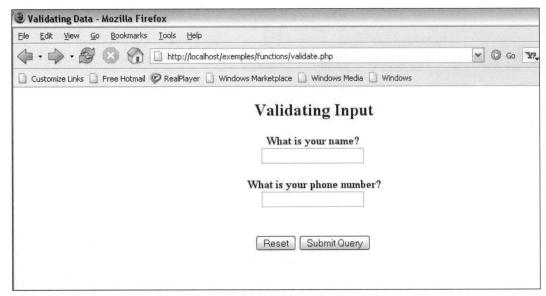

Figure 10.37 The initial HTML form from Example 10.22.

Figure 10.38 The user left one field empty.

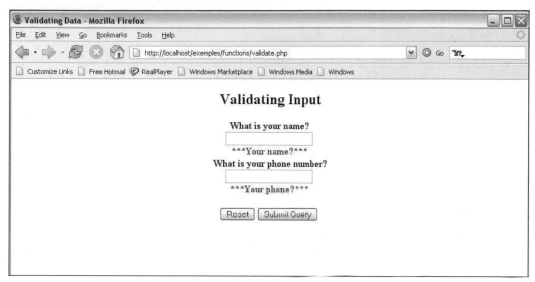

Figure 10.39 The user left both fields empty.

10.3.15 Where to Get Information About Superglobal Arrays

As we have seen throughout this chapter, PHP superglobal arrays (also called autoglobal), such as _GET and _POST are defined as part of the global namespace of your PHP script and used to store the user input coming from HTML forms. Other superglobals, such as the server's configuration, cookies, or information about the environment are also accessible in your PHP script in superglobal arrays. These predefined arrays are referred collectively as EGPCS (**E**nvironment, **G**ET, **P**OST, **C**ookie, and **S**erver information). They are called superglobals because they are available in every part of your program. (Cookies are discussed in Chapter 16, "Cookies and Sessions.")

The phpinfo() Function.   To see the available predefined variables on your system, you can use the phpinfo() function that includes not only all of the EGPCS information, but a huge amount of information about PHP, such as version, operating system, environment, compilation options, server information, HTTP headers, and so on. Table 10.4 lists arguments used to customize the output of the phpinfo() function. You can use either the constant value in column 1 or the number value in column 2. Column 3 describes the output. In the following example phpinfo() displays the EGPCS predefined variables.

```
<?php
    phpinfo(INFO_VARIABLES);    // phpinfo(32) does the same thing
?>
```

Table 10.4 `phpinfo()` Options[a]

Name (Constant)	Value	Description
INFO_GENERAL	1	The configuration line, `php.ini` location, build date, Web server, system, and more.
INFO_CREDITS	2	PHP credits. See also `phpcredits()`.
INFO_CONFIGURATION	4	Current local and master values for PHP directives. See also `ini_get()`.
INFO_MODULES	8	Loaded modules and their respective settings. See also `get_loaded_extensions()`.
INFO_ENVIRONMENT	16	Environment variable information that is also available in $_ENV.
INFO_VARIABLES	32	Shows all predefined variables from EGPCS (Environment, GET, POST, Cookie, Server).
INFO_LICENSE	64	PHP License information. See also the license FAQ.
INFO_ALL	−1	Shows all of the above. This is the default value.

a. From *http://us2.php.net/phpinfo*. For a complete list and definitions see *http://us3.php.net/manual/en/reserved.variables.php*.

10.3.16 How to Get Server Information

We have been working with HTML forms and PHP, going back and forth between the server and browser. PHP makes information about your server available to your scripts. The Web server assigns values to the PHP superglobal $_SERVER array such as header, path, script locations, and version information. All servers are not consistent in the information they provide. Table 10.5 defines some of the superglobals (from the PHP manual) you will encounter in the following chapters. See Figure 10.40 for a partial output.

Table 10.5 Retrieving Server Information

$_SERVER Key	Description of Value
PHP_SELF	The filename of the currently executing script, relative to the document root. For instance, $_SERVER['PHP_SELF'] in a script at the address `http://example.com/test.php/foo.bar` would be `/test.php/foo.bar`. The __FILE__ constant contains the full path and filename of the current (i.e., included) file.
GATEWAY_INTERFACE	The CGI specification the server is using (i.e., `CGI/1.1`).

Table 10.5   Retrieving Server Information (continued)

$_SERVER Key	Description of Value
SERVER_NAME	The name of the server host under which the current script is executing. If the script is running on a virtual host, this will be the value defined for that virtual host.
SERVER_SOFTWARE	Server identification string, given in the headers when responding to requests.
SERVER_PROTOCOL	Name and revision of the information protocol via which the page was requested (i.e., HTTP/1.0).
REQUEST_METHOD	Which request method was used to access the page (i.e., GET, HEAD, POST, PUT).
REQUEST_TIME	The timestamp of the start of the request. Available since PHP 5.1.0.
QUERY_STRING	The query string, if any, via which the page was accessed.
DOCUMENT_ROOT	The document root directory under which the current script is executing, as defined in the server's configuration file.
HTTP_ACCEPT	Contents of the Accept: header from the current request, if there is one.
HTTP_CONNECTION	Contents of the Connection: header from the current request, if there is one. Example: Keep-Alive.
HTTP_HOST	Contents of the Host: header from the current request, if there is one.
HTTP_REFERER	The address of the page (if any) that referred the user agent to the current page. This is set by the user agent. Not all user agents will set this, and some provide the ability to modify HTTP_REFERER as a feature. In short, it cannot really be trusted.
HTTP_USER_AGENT	Contents of the User-Agent: header from the current request, if there is one. A typical example is: Mozilla/4.5 [en] (X11; U; Linux 2.2.9 i586) See also the get_browser() function.
REMOTE_ADDR	The IP address from which the user is viewing the current page.
REMOTE_HOST	The host name from which the user is viewing the current page. The reverse DNS lookup is based off the REMOTE_ADDR of the user.
REMOTE_PORT	The port being used on the user's machine to communicate with the Web server.

Table 10.5   Retrieving Server Information (continued)

$_SERVER *Key*	*Description of Value*
SCRIPT_FILENAME	The absolute pathname of the currently executing script. Note: If a script is executed with the CLI, as a relative path, such as file.php or ../file.php, $_SERVER['SCRIPT_FILENAME'] will contain the relative path specified by the user.
SERVER_PORT	The port on the server machine being used by the Web server for communication, default is port 80; using SSL is your defined secure HTTP port.
SERVER_SIGNATURE	String containing the server version and virtual host name that are added to server-generated pages, if enabled.
PATH_TRANSLATED	The path of the file system (not document root) related to the current script.
SCRIPT_NAME	Contains the current script's path. This is useful for self-processing pages. The __FILE__ constant contains the full path and filename of the current (i.e., included) file.
REQUEST_URI	The URI that was given to access this page; for instance, /index.html.

EXAMPLE 10.23

```
<html><head><title>Server Information</title></head>
<body bgcolor="yellow">
<table border="1">
<?php
    foreach($_SERVER as $key=>$value){
        echo "<tr>";
        echo "<td><b>$key</td><td>$value</td>";
        echo "</tr>";
    }
?>
</table>
</body>
</html>
```

EXPLANATION

A partial output of the $_SERVER array is displayed in Figure 10.40.

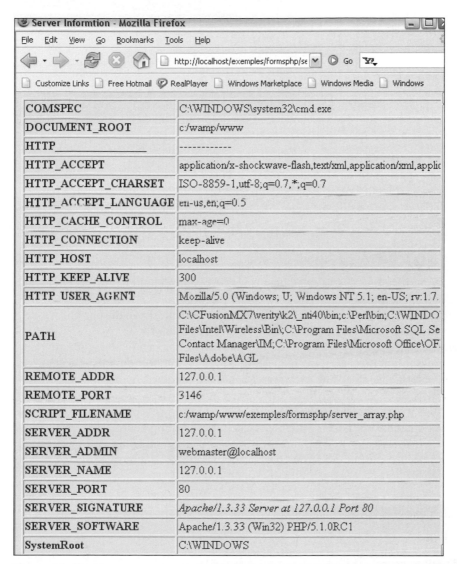

Figure 10.40 The $_SERVER array (partial output).

EXAMPLE 10.24

```
<html><head><title>Server Info</title></head>
<body bgcolor="silver">
<font face="verdana" size="+1">
<?php
1     echo "My server is \"", $_SERVER["SERVER_NAME"], "\".\n<br />";
2     echo "The server's IP address is \"", $_SERVER["REMOTE_ADDR"],
          "\".\n<br />";
3     echo "My browser is \"", $_SERVER["HTTP_USER_AGENT"], "\".
          \n<br />";
4     echo "The PHP script being executed is \"",
          $_SERVER["PHP_SELF"], "\".\n<br />";
?>
</body>
</html>
```

EXPLANATION

1   The server handling this page is called "localhost", the default name for the server
    on the local computer.
2   This is the IP address for the server referred to as "localhost" on the currently used
    computer. This address can be used by TCP/IP applications.
3   The HTTP_USER_AGENT refers to the browser ID or user-agent string identifying
    the browser that is sending the request. In an HTTP transaction, this information
    is sent by the server to the browser as a header followed by a blank line. The
    browser is Firefox.
4   $_SERVER["PHP_SELF"] is the filename of the currently executing script, relative
    to the document root. This variable is useful in creating self-processing forms.
    (See "Self-Processing HTML Forms" on page 413 for more on self-processing
    forms.) See the output in Figure 10.41.

Figure 10.41 Server variables.

10.3.17 How to Get Information About the Environment

The environment variables are predefined variables containing information about the operating system, shell, path, CGI variables,[7] and computer under which PHP is running (see Figure 10.42).

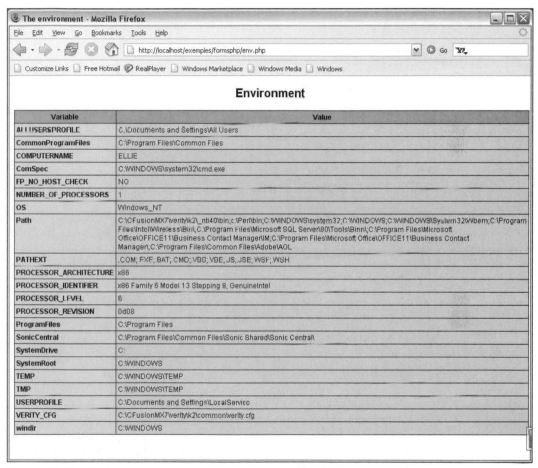

Figure 10.42 Environment variables.

The $_ENV array contains the environment variables that can also be displayed with phpinfo() built-in function. To access the name of the remote host, you would use the following syntax:

```
echo  $_ENV['REMOTE_HOST'];
```

---

7. If PHP is running as a CGI program, then the environment variables are used to pass data about the information request from the server to the script. The environment variables are set when the server executes the gateway program.

or you can use the PHP `getenv()` function to get the value of an environment variable:

```
echo getenv('REMOTE_HOST');
```

The output will vary from one system to another because there are a number of shells, different servers, and so on. For example, you might be running PHP in the Apache server on a Solaris operating system using the Bash shell while I'm using Redhat Linux and the TCshell. The variations can be enormous, resulting in enormous variations in output.

```
<?php
    phpinfo(16);   // Display information about PHP environment
?>
```

10.4 Chapter Summary

10.4.1   What You Should Know

We have yet to discuss how to validate form input, how to send form data to files and databases, how to track users and their preferences, security issues, and so on. All of that is yet to come, but by now you should be able to answer the following questions:

1. What are the attributes of an HTML `<form>` tag?

2. How does the form information get from the browser to the server?

3. What is the difference between the GET and POST methods?

4. How does PHP handle form information?

5. What are the three styles that PHP uses to assign form input to a variable? Which of these is the recommended style and why?

6. What is the `register_globals` directive? What is the recommended setting?

7. What are superglobals?

8. What is a self-processing script?

9. How does PHP handle forms with multiple selections?

10. What is the purpose of the `$_REQUEST` array?

11. What are hidden fields used for?

12. What are the attributes and input type needed to upload a file?

13. What is a redirection header?

14. What are the rules for uploading a file?

15. What is meant by a "sticky" form?

16. How can you get information about your server from PHP?

10.4.2 What's Next?

Much of what you do in PHP will deal with files. In Chapter 11, "Files and Directories," we talk about files and how to open and close them, read from them and write to them, copy them, lock them, upload them, compress them, and more, all from within a PHP script.

CHAPTER 10 LAB

1. Open the `datebook` file and print its contents back to the file with line numbers. Now display the names, phone numbers, and birthdates of everyone born in November or December.

2. From the `datebook` file, display all entries with a salary greater than $45,000. Output should look as follows:

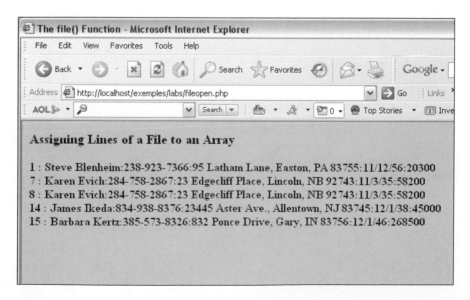

3. Write a self-processing PHP script. It will produce a form to ask for a name, phone, address, birthday, and salary. This information will be appended to the `datebook` file. Sort the file and display it with the new entry. If the user enters input such as `Joe O'Donald`, PHP will precede any quotes with backslashes. Make sure the backslashes are removed. If any of the fields are empty, exit.

4. Create a form with a select menu to accept multiple selections of artists. Based on the user's selection, write a PHP script that will process the selections and display an image(s) for each selected artist. The submit button in the form will be an image. The select menu should look similar to the following:

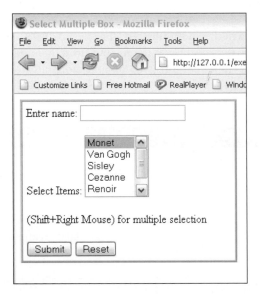

5. Create a form that uploads a file from Google images and displays the image file.

6. Write a PHP program that will ask for a user's name and password. The program will generate an MD5-encrypted password. Store the username and the new password in a file called `db.passwords`. Now create a PHP program that will ask for the username and password and admit the user only if his username and password match. If they match, show him the contents of the `datebook` file.

   The `md5()` function is a one-way encryption program, meaning you cannot unencrypt the password. You can verify the password by comparing it to the password initially created by `md5()`:

```
$password=md5($password);
```

chapter

11

Files and Directories

11.1 Files

After the browser sends data to the server and PHP processes the information, a database management system such as MySQL or Oracle will normally store or retrieve the data. But PHP might also exchange data from simple text files (also called flat files), such as HTML templates, spreadsheet (csv) data, the contents of remote Web pages, or files that contain text that does not need to be stored in a database. This chapter focuses on creating directories and text files for storing and retrieving data, whereas Chapter 13, "Introduction to MySQL," introduces to the power of using a relational database system.

11.1.1   File Permissions and Ownership

To open an external file in a PHP program, you first need to determine where the file is, who owns it, and whether or not you have the proper permission to open it. If you are opening the file simply to view it, you will need read permission and if you want to modify it in any way, you will need write permission. Granting permissions to directories gives users access to the files stored there, and granting permission to files allows users to read, write, or execute the individual files. For obvious security reasons, it is important to be able to control who has permission to access the files and directories on your Web site. Because operating systems differ in how they handle permissions, we look at UNIX/Linux and Windows in the following sections.

11.1.2   UNIX/Linux Permissions

Ownership and Groups.   Users are categorized into three classes of users: (1) you, the owner; (2) the group, a special group of users who can share files without making them public to everyone; and (3) the others (also called "the world"), everyone who has an account on the system. When you create a file, it is automatically owned by you and the group to which you belong. You can change the owner of a file with the `chown` command; that is, if you own it or you are root, the superuser. (Check your version of UNIX/Linux). Changing the group to which a file belongs is done with the `chgrp` command. PHP provides built-in functions of the same name as the UNIX/Linux commands allowing you to mimic these operating system commands from a PHP script (see "PHP Built-In Functions" on page 447).

Permissions.   Permissions are assigned to three classes of users discussed in the last section. Each class can be assigned a combination of three types of permissions:

1. Read
2. Write
3. Execute

The three groups of permissions are set for each of the three classes of users:

1. You, the **user**.
2. The **group** (the group to which you belong).
3. The **others** (anyone else on the system).

Because a directory is simply a place where files are stored (similar to drawers in a file cabinet), and a plain file contains the actual text (similar to the files in the cabinet), the permissions affect directories and plain files somewhat differently. For example, if a directory has execute permission, it means you can enter the directory with the `cd` command, but if a file has execute permission, the file can be executed as a script or program. A directory needs read permission so that you can view the contents of the directory with `ls`, whereas read permission on a file allows you to view it or copy it. Write permission on a directory allows you to create, move, or remove files from within the directory (whether or not you own the files), whereas on a file it means that you can modify it or remove it.

Table 11.1 provides a list of how permissions affect files and directories.

Table 11.1   Permissions on Files and Directories

Permission	What It Allows on a Directory	What It Allows on a File
read	View its contents (`ls`).	View, copy, print it, and so on.
write	Create or remove files in it.	Modify, rename, or remove it.
execute	`cd` into it.	Execute the file as script or program.

Changing Permissions at the Command Line.   Changing permissions of files and directories can be done at the command line or from within a PHP script. We start with the `chmod` command at the command line. (Keep in mind that if the PHP script is being executed by the server, the permissions are limited to what a server can do, whereas if you are running the script at the command line, the program, permissions will apply to what you, the user, can do. Because ownership and permissions are different for the server than for the user, chmod and chgrp might behave differently depending on what process is running the script.

There are two different ways to assign permissions to a file at the command line—one is text-based and the other numeric-based. Because PHP does not provide functions to mimic the behavior of the text-based method, we use the numeric-based method in the following examples.

The UNIX/Linux chmod command takes two arguments: the mode (a number between 0 and 7) for each permission level (owner, group, others) followed by the name of the directory or files that will have their permissions changed.

FORMAT

```
chmod mode file(s)
chmod mode directory
```

Example:
```
chmod 755 filex
```

The three sets of permissions for all classes of users (owner, group, others) can be represented by different numeric values. The three numeric values combined represent the complete numeric permission mode. If a user is assigned 7, a group is assigned 5, and the others are assigned 5, the combined value is 755. Table 11.2 displays the numeric values that will represent each class of users. By adding the values for the owner, group, and others, the resulting number is the permission mode. Read is represented by 4, write by 2, execute by 1, and none of the permissions is 0. If you want the user to have read, write, and execute, add up the first column in Table 11.2, and you get 700. Now if you only want the group to have read and execute, then add up 040 + 010 in the second column, and you get 050, and if you want the same for everybody else, add up the numbers in the third column, 004 + 001, to get 005.

Now combine all three sets of permissions: 700 + 050 + 005 and, presto! you get 755 as your permission mode.

Table 11.2 Numeric Values for File Permissions for a Class of Users

	Owner	*Group*	*Others*
Read	400	040	004
Write	200	020	002
Execute	100	010	001

Some common permission modes are:

777   Owner, group, and others have read, write, or execute (`-rwxrwxrwx`)[1]

755   Owner has read, write, and execute; others have only read and execute
      (`-rwxr-xr-x`)

711   Owner has read, write, and execute; others have only execute (`-rwx--x--x`)

700   Owner has read, write, and execute; others have nothing (`-rwx------`)

644   Owner has read and write; others have only read (`-rw-r--r--`)

EXAMPLE 11.1

```
1   $ chmod 755 myfolder

2   $ chmod 777 *

3   $ chmod 644 `filex
```

EXPLANATION

1   Grant read, write, and execute to the owner, read and execute to the group and
    the others (world).
2   Set all to read, write, and execute on all files and in the current working directory.
3   User gets read and write, group and others get read.

11.1.3   Windows Permissions

Originally, DOS was not intended to be a multiuser, networked operating system,
whereas UNIX was. Consequently, the way that file permissions are handled is quite different between UNIX and Windows. To see the permissions on a Windows file, you can
right-click the file and choose the Properties menu item as shown in Figure 11.1.

Windows has four attributes to describe a file (see Table 11.3):

1. Read-only
2. System
3. Hidden
4. Archive

There is no attribute to specify that a file is executable. DOS and Windows NT file
systems identify executable files by giving them the extensions .exe, .com, .cmd, or .bat.

---

1. If you type `ls -l` at the UNIX prompt, file permissions are represented as three groups. A leading dash
   means you are looking at a file, any other dashes between the `rwx` means the permission is turned off; for
   example, `r-x` means w is turned off.

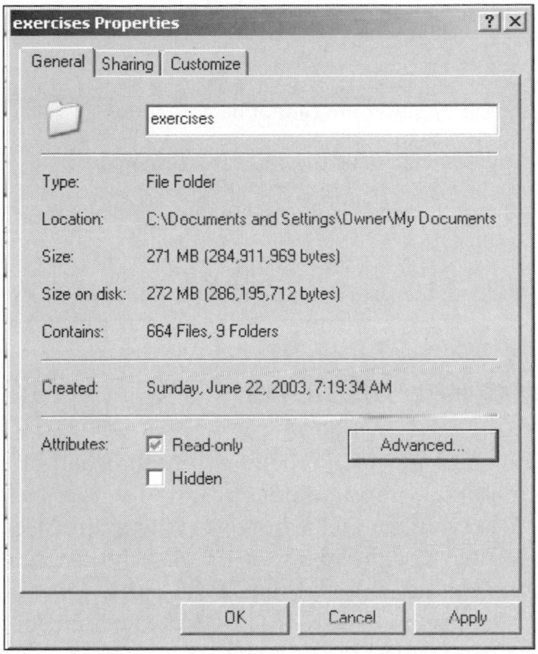
exercises Properties
General
Sharing
Customize
exercises
Type: File Folder
Location: C:\Documents and Settings\Owner\My Documents
Size: 271 MB (284,911,969 bytes)
Size on disk: 272 MB (286,195,712 bytes)
Contains: 664 Files, 9 Folders
Created: Sunday, June 22, 2003, 7:19:34 AM
Attributes:
Read-only
Hidden
Advanced...
OK
Cancel
Apply

Figure 11.1 Permissions and file attributes (Windows).

You can also display and change the attributes of a file from the command line with the DOS `attrib` command by going to the Start menu and clicking Run. In the cmd.exe window type the following and you will see a window similar to that shown in Figure 11.2.

```
help attrib
```

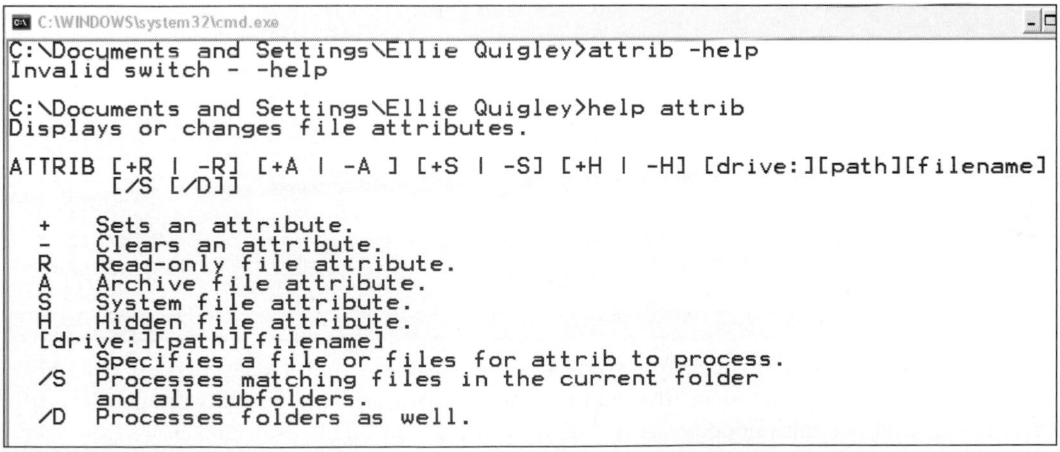
C:\WINDOWS\system32\cmd.exe
C:\Documents and Settings\Ellie Quigley>attrib -help
Invalid switch - -help
C:\Documents and Settings\Ellie Quigley>help attrib
Displays or changes file attributes.
ATTRIB [+R | -R] [+A | -A] [+S | -S] [+H | -H] [drive:][path][filename]
[/S [/D]]
+ Sets an attribute.
- Clears an attribute.
R Read-only file attribute.
A Archive file attribute.
S System file attribute.
H Hidden file attribute.
[drive:][path][filename]
Specifies a file or files for attrib to process.
/S Processes matching files in the current folder
and all subfolders.
/D Processes folders as well.

Figure 11.2 Viewing file attributes at the command line with the `attrib` command.

Table 11.3 File Attributes for Windows

Attribute	What It Means
Read-only	The file's contents can be read by a user but cannot be written to.
System	This file has a specific purpose required by the operating system.
Hidden	This file has been marked to be invisible to the user, unless the operating system is explicitly set to show it.
Archive	This file has been touched since the last DOS backup was performed on it.

11.2 The Web Server, PHP, and Permissions

Like all processes running in a UNIX environment, PHP programs run on behalf of a particular user. If you run a PHP script from the command line (for instance, as a shell script), it will run with the permissions set for you, the user, who started the script. More typically, however, PHP scripts will be executed by your Web server. Under most system configurations, Web servers run as a user (such as nobody) that, for security reasons, has minimal permissions to access the file system (usually read and execute, but not write permission). The reason for limiting access is to keep potential hackers from using your server as a gateway to write whatever they please into an open directory. Because PHP is being executed by the server, it too will have the same limited permissions, thereby restricting its ability to work with files and directories. The solution is to create directories outside the Web directory and put the files PHP will be working with there. If the directory has the same group permissions as the locally running PHP program, others will not have access to those files.

EXAMPLE 11.2

```
1. $ ps -ef | grep apache
   nobody 27874   352  0   Aug 12 ?        0:00 /usr/apache/bin/httpd
   root      352    1  0   Jun 07 ?        0:02 /usr/apache/bin/httpd
   nobody 29038   352  0   Aug 12 ?        0:00 /usr/apache/bin/httpd
   nobody 28987   352  0   Aug 12 ?        0:00 /usr/apache/bin/httpd
   nobody 27877   352  0   Aug 12 ?        0:00 /usr/apache/bin/httpd
   nobody 27876   352  0   Aug 12 ?        0:00 /usr/apache/bin/httpd
   nobody 27873   352  0   Aug 12 ?        0:00 /usr/apache/bin/httpd
   nobody 27875   352  0   Aug 12 ?        0:00 /usr/apache/bin/httpd
```

EXPLANATION

1   When Apache (httpd) is started as root, it opens the privileged ports (80, 443 (SSL)), opens the log files, and then stops acting as the potentially dangerous root and becomes nobody (as specified in httpd.conf). This example shows that user nobody is running the Apache server daemon. (The system is a UNIX system.)

11.2.1 PHP Built-In Functions

PHP provides three functions that correspond to the UNIX commands discussed in the previous section. They are the `chown()`, `chgrp()`, and `chmod()` functions.

The chown() Function. Just like the `chown` command, the `chown()` function changes the ownership of a file, provided the PHP script performing this operation is run by the owner or by a superuser (known as `root`).

FORMAT

```
bool chown(filename, newuser);
```

Example:
```
$success = chown ("myfile", "john");
```

`filename` refers to the file that is being modified, and `newuser` is the username of the new owner. When executed, this function returns a boolean value, true or false, which indicates whether PHP was successful in changing the owner of the file.

The chgrp() Function. The PHP `chgrp()` function, like the `chgrp` command, is used to change group membership. To change the group to which a file belongs, the user must be a member of the new group and the file must reside locally. The function takes two arguments: the name of a file, and the group to which it will be assigned. The group can be represented either by its name or by its group ID, a numeric value.

FORMAT

```
bool chgrp(filename, newgroup);
```

Example:
```
$result=chgrp("myfile", admin);
$result=chgrp("myfile", 0502);
```

The chmod() Function. PHP scripts are often embedded in HTML documents and these files are placed on the Web server and executed by the serverside software. The `chmod()` function changes file permissions to allow the serverside software to read, write, and execute data in the file. The owner of the currently running PHP process must also be the owner of the file to change permissions and the file cannot be on a remote system.

The `chmod()` function takes the filename or full path and filename as its first argument and the octal value for the permission mode as its second value. It returns TRUE if successful in making the change; otherwise, it returns FALSE.

FORMAT

```
bool chmod("file", octal_mode );
```

Example:
```
bool chmod("/dir/filex", 0755);
```

Notice that the mode is set as an octal value, a number with a leading zero. If you are prone to forgetting the leading zero, you can use the PHP built-in function octdec() to assure the number you select is converted from octal to decimal as shown here:

```
chmod("some_filename.ext", octdec($mode));
chmod("filex", octdec(644));
```

11.2.2 The Filehandle

In a PHP script, you cannot access a file directly by the name it was given when it was created (i.e., the name that your operating system uses to identify it). Instead you have to use a filehandle. A filehandle, also called a file pointer, binds the named file to a "stream." Streams were introduced with PHP 4.3.0 to represent a way in which to abstractly deal with all kinds of files (local, compressed, and remote) and the functions they all share, such as reading, writing, appending, or seeking to a certain location within the file.[2] Once the file is opened, the filehandle is used to perform a number of operations on the file. Of course, to access a file, the PHP program must have permission to do so.

11.2.3 Opening a File

The fopen() Function. To create the filehandle, PHP provides the fopen() function. This function opens a file and returns a filehandle, and if it fails, returns false. It normally takes two arguments: a filename and a mode, the mode being how you want to deal with the file; that is, do you want to open it for reading, writing, appending, and so on? A third optional argument, if set to TRUE, tells PHP to check the PHP include path (a list of directories where the require() and include() functions look for files, defined in the php.ini file).

The name of the file is a file or a URL and can be referenced by a full path name, a relative path name, or simply by the name of the file if it resides in the same directory or folder as the PHP script that is trying to open it. If specifying a path, forward slashes can be used as the separator between path elements with both UNIX and Windows. If, however, you are using Windows and want to use backslashes in the path, then the backslash must be escaped, such as \\dir\\file.txt. It is also possible to bind the filehandle to a URL by prefixing the name of the file with either http:// or ftp://.[3]

---

2. For a complete discussion on streams, see: *http://us3.php.net/streams*.
3. You might experience problems using PHP with URLs on some versions of Red Hat Linux.

FORMAT

```
filehandle=fopen("filename", mode, [ 1 or TRUE]));
```

Example:
```
$fh=fopen("../myfile", 'a');              // Open for append
$fh=fopen("http://www.index.php/, 'r');   // Open for read
$handle=fopen("/Documents and Setting/Owner/Desktop/stuff/myfile", "r");
$handle=fopen("myfile", "r+");            // Read and write
$handle=fopen("myfile", "w");             // Write
$handle=fopen("../myfile", "rb");         // Read binary
$handle=fopen("http://www.hostname.com/" );
$handle=fopen("ftp://www.hostname.com/" );
```

The Mode and Permissions. The mode specifies what kind of operation you want to perform on the file; for example, do you want to read its contents, write to it, read and write, and so on, and this depends on who owns the file and what permissions are assigned to the file. The modes are shown in Table 11.4.

Table 11.4 Modes for `fopen()`

Mode	Name	Description
r	Read	Opens only for reading; starts at the beginning of the file.
r+	Read	Opens for reading and writing; starts from the beginning of the file.
w	Write	Opens only for writing; starts at the beginning of the file. If the file exists, truncates it; if not, creates it.
w+	Write	Opens for reading and writing; starts at the beginning of the file. If the file exists, truncates it. If the file does not exist, attempts to create it.
a	Append	Opens for writing only; appends at the end of the file. If the file does not exist, attempts to create it.
a+	Append	Opens for reading and writing; appends at the end of the file. If the file does not exist, attempts to create it.
x	Cautious write	Creates and opens a local file for writing only; starts at the beginning of the file. If the file already exists, `fopen()` returns false, and PHP sends a warning. If the file does not exist, attempts to create it (PHP 4.3.2+).
x+	Cautious write	Creates and opens local files for both reading and writing; starts at the beginning of the file. If the file already exists, `fopen()` returns false and PHP sends a warning. If the file does not exist, attempts to create it.

Table 11.4   Modes for `fopen()` (continued)

Mode	Name	Description
b		The default mode, used with one of the other modes for file systems that differentiate between binary and text files. Necessary with Windows, but not with UNIX or Macintosh.
t		Used with one of the other modes to represent Windows text files. Translates end of line character \n to \r\n. Used with the b mode for portability.

Table 11.5 lists some of the most useful PHP built-in functions provided to work with files. We cover most of these functions in this chapter.

Table 11.5   Some Useful File Functions

Function Name	What It Does	Description
fclose()	Closes a file or URL	fclose(fh);
feof()	Tests for end-of-file on a file pointer	bool feof(fh);
fflush()	Flushes output to a file	fflush(fh);
fgetc()	Gets a character from a file	string fgetc(fh);
fgets()	Gets a line from a file	string fgets(fh);
fgetscsv()	Gets a line from a file, parses for CSV fields (comma-separated value file format)	array fgetscsv(fh);
fgetss()	Gets a line from a file, strips out HTML and PHP tags	
file()	Reads entire file into an array	array file(filename);
file_exists()	Checks if a file (or directory) exists	bool file_exists(filename);
file_get_contents()	Reads an entire file into a string	string file_get_contents(fh)
fopen()	Opens a file or URL	fh=fopen(mode, filename);

11.2.4 Opening a File for Reading

Four PHP functions are used for reading text from a file: `fgets()`, `fgetc()`, `fread()`, and `file_get_contents()`. Before opening a file you need to determine whether or not the file exists and is accessible for reading. The `file_exists()` function checks to see if the file exists, and the `is_readable()` function will return true if a file exists and has read permission.

When a file is initially opened for reading, the internal file pointer is placed at the beginning of the file. When a read operation is performed on a file, the program keeps track of where it is in the file, by repositioning the file pointer to the next byte after the last read; for example, if using the `fgets()` function, after a line is read from the file, the file pointer positioned at the beginning of the next line, unless the end-of-file has already been reached.

The `feof()` function can be used to determine when the end of the file has been reached. If the file does not have read permission, you will get an error as shown in the output in Figure 11.3.

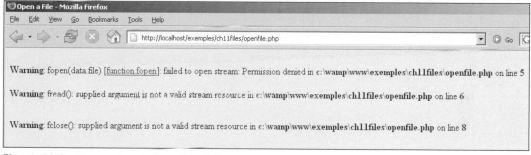

Figure 11.3 The `fopen()` function fails—incorrect permissions.

The fgets() Function—Reading Lines from a File. The `fgets()` function takes a filehandle as its argument and returns a line of text from the file. It can take a third optional argument, the length that will read up to length −1 bytes (characters) from the file, the default being 1042 bytes. As of PHP 4.3, omitting the length will cause the function to keep reading from the file stream until it reaches the end of the line.[4] Remember, the end of line is different on Windows and UNIX.

---

4. If the majority of the lines in the file are all larger than 8 KB, it is more resource efficient for your script to specify the maximum line length (PHP manual).

FORMAT

```
string = fgets(filehandle, [ length ] );
```

Example:
```
$line = fgets("myfile");
$line = fgets("myfile", 4096);
```

EXAMPLE 11.3

```
    <html><head><title>Open a File</title></head>
    <body bgcolor="lavender">
    <pre>
    <?php
        //$filename="c:/wamp/www/exemples/data.file";
1       $filename="$_SERVER[DOCUMENT_ROOT]/exemples/data.file";
2       if (!file_exists($filename)){  // Check for file existence
            print "No such file or directory";
3           exit();
        }
4       $fh=fopen($filename,"r");    // Open the file for reading
5       while( !feof($fh)){
6           $line_of_text=fgets($fh);  // Get text line from the file
            print "$line_of_text";
        }
7       fclose($fh);  // Close the file
    ?>
    </pre>
    </body>
    </html>
```

EXPLANATION

1   The variable, `$filename`, is assigned the path to the file `data.file` starting the server's document root (`$_SERVER[DOCUMENT]`).

2   The `file_exists()` function will return true if `$filename` exists. The `! file_exists` says, "if the file does not exist, do something."

3   The program exits if the file does not exist.

4   The `fopen()` function will open the file for reading and return a filehandle, assigned to `$fh`. From this point on, we will access the file through this handle.

5   The `while` loop is entered. The expression tests to see if the end of file (`feof()`) has *not* been reached. The loop will not end until we have reached the end of the file; that is, read in all the lines.

6   The `fgets()` function reads one line from the file using the newline character as the end of line marker. As soon as a line is read, the file pointer will move to the next line. Each time a line is read, it will be assigned to the variable `$line_of_text`. A line is printed to the browser after it is read and assigned to the variable `$line_of_text`. See Figure 11.4.

7   After all the lines have been read, and we are finished using the file, it will be closed.

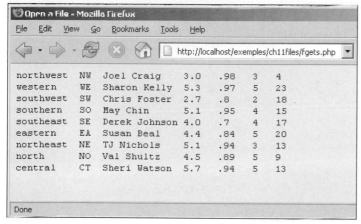

Figure 11.4 Viewing the contents of data.file. Output from Example 11.3.

The fgetss() Function—Stripping HTML Tags from a File. The fgetss() function is just like fgets() but strips out HTML and PHP tags from a file as it reads from the file. The optional third parameter can be used to specify tags that should not be stripped. (This is the same as strip_tags() except strip_tags removes tags from a string rather than a file.)

FORMAT

```
string fgetss ( resource handle [, int length [,
                string allowable_tags]] )
```

Example:
```
open($fh, "myfile.html");
$line = fgetss($fh);
```

EXAMPLE 11.4

```
      <html><head><title>Open a File</title></head>
      <body bgcolor="lavender">
      <pre>
      <?php
          $filename="getmethod.html";
1         $fh=fopen("$filename", "r");
          while(!feof($fh)){
2             $content=fgetss($fh);
              echo $content;
          }
          fclose($fh);
      ?>
      </pre>
      </body>
      </html>
```

EXAMPLE   11.4 (CONTINUED)

```
(The HTML File Before fgetss())
<head>
<title>First HTML Form</title>
</head>
<body bgcolor="lightblue"><font size="+1">
<form action="getmethod.php" method="GET">
<p>
Please enter your salary: <br />
<input type="text" size=30 name="salary" />
<p>
Please enter your age: <br />
<input type="text" size=10 name="age" />
<p>
<input type=submit value="submit" />
<input type=reset value="clear" />
</form>
<hr />
</body>
</html>
```

EXPLANATION

1   The file `getmethod.html` is opened for reading and it returns a filehandle, `$fh`.
2   The `fgetss()` function strips out all HTML and PHP tags from the file before storing each line in `$content`, as shown in Figure 11.5.

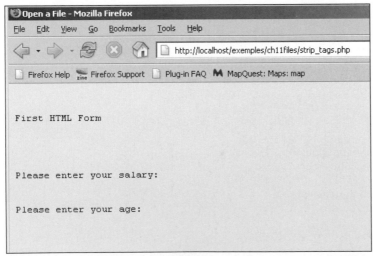

Figure 11.5   Stripping out HTML tags with `fgetss()`. Output from Example 11.4.

The fgetc() Function—Reading Characters from a File. The `fgetc()` function reads and returns one character at a time from an open file. It returns FALSE when the end of file is reached.

FORMAT

```
character = fgetc(filehandle);
```

Example:
```
$char = fgetc($fh);
```

EXAMPLE 11.5

```
      <html><head><title>Read a Character at a Time</title></head>
      <body bgcolor="lavender">
      <pre>
      <?php
1         $filename="$_SERVER[DOCUMENT_ROOT]/exemples/data.file";
2         if (!file_exists($filename)){
              print "No such file or directory";
              exit();
          }
3         $fh=fopen($filename,"r");
4         while( ! feof($fh)){
5             $char=fgetc($fh);
6             if ($char == "\n"){ $char="<br /><br />";}
              print $char;
          }
7         fclose($fh);
      ?>
      </pre>
      </body>
      </html>
```

EXPLANATION

1   The path and filename assigned to `$filename` are relative to the document root of the server.
2   If the specified file does not exist, the program will exit here.
3   The file is opened for reading and a filehandle is returned to `$fh`.
4   The expression in the `while` loop will continue to be true as long as the end of file has not been reached.
5   Each time the loop is entered, the `getc()` function reads one character from the file specified by `$fh`, and assigns that character to `$char`. The function will return false when the end of file has been reached.
6   If the character just read is a newline, it is assigned a string of two HTML line-breaks, which causes a blank line to appear between each printed line when displayed in the browser (see Figure 11.6).
7   The the filehandle is closed, no longer bound to `data.file`.

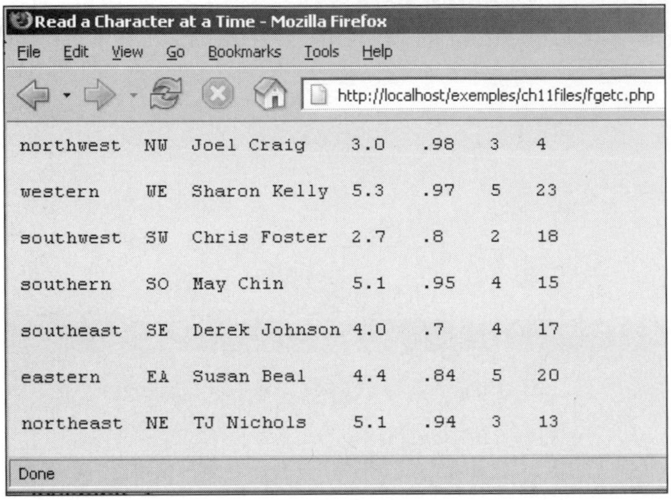

Figure 11.6 The getc() function reads one character at a time.

The fread() Function—Reading Chunks from a File.   The   fread()   function reads from a file a specified number of characters, treating the file as a simple binary file consisting of bytes without concern for end of line or other special characters. (On systems that differentiate between binary and text files [i.e., Windows], the file must be opened with 'b' mode by fopen()). If you are reading from the entire file, the filesize() function returns the number of bytes (characters) in the file.

In the following example, a chunk of text will be read from a file.

FORMAT

```
bytes_read= fread(filehandle, number_of_bytes);

Example:
$contents=fread("myfile", 4096);
```

EXAMPLE 11.6

```
    <html><head><title>Open a File</title></head>
    <body bgcolor="lavender">
    <?php
1      $filename="c:/wamp/www/exemples/data.file";
2      $filehandle=fopen($filename, "rt");
3      $contents=fread($filehandle, filesize($filename));
4      print "<pre>$contents</pre>";
5      fclose($filehandle);
    ?>
    </body>
    </html>
```

EXPLANATION

1   The full path to the file is assigned to `$filename`.
2   The `fopen()` function opens a text file for reading (Windows).
3   The `fread()` function reads the number of bytes from a file (`filesize()`) and stores the bytes in `$contents`. The `fread()` function reads the specified number of bytes, if it can, and does not concern itself with the end-of-line character. All characters are just bytes. It will stop reading when it reaches the specified file size or end of file, whichever come first.
4   The contents of the file are printed; that is, the number of bytes selected when the file was opened are printed, as shown in Figure 11.7.
5   The file is closed.

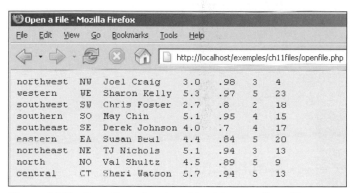

Figure 11.7   Reading chunks of text from a file with `fread()`.

In the following example a chunk of binary data is read from a file, in this example, an image file.

EXAMPLE 11.7

```
<?php
1   $filename = "c:\\wamp\\www\\exemplcs\\ch11files\\tulips.jpg";
    # $filename = "c:/wamp/www/exemples/ch11files/tulips.jpg";
2   $handle = fopen($filename, "rb");
3   $contents = fread($handle, filesize($filename));

4   header("Content-type: image/jpeg");
5   echo $contents;

    fclose($handle);
?>
```

EXPLANATION

1   The variable $filename is assigned the location of an image file, "tulips.jpg".
    If backslashes are used to separate Windows path elements, then they must be es-
    caped, but forward slashes can be used for both UNIX and Windows.

2   Because the file is an image file, it is a binary file and specified with the "b" mode.

3   The entire contents from the image file, specified by filesize(), are assigned to
    $contents. This data is binary and unreadable.

4   To see the image on the browser, the header() function sends the "Content-
    type: image/jpeg" as an HTTP header to the browser. Make sure the header()
    function is called before any other output is displayed to the browser or it will fail.

5   The image is displayed on the browser (see Figure 11.8) and the filehandle is
    closed.

Figure 11.8   Using fread() to retrieve a binary image file.

11.2.5 Positioning the File Pointer

If you have already read all the lines from a file, you are at the end of the file, meaning
the file pointer is at the end of the file. If you want to go back to the beginning of the
file, one way is to close the file and then reopen it. Another way is to use the fseek()
function. The fseek() function allows you to randomly access a file by moving to a

specified byte (not line) position within the file. On success, seek returns 0; otherwise, it returns −1. (Seeking past EOF is not considered an error.)

The fseek() Function.   The seek() function sets a postion in a file, where the first byte is 0. Positions are:

SEEK_SET = Beginning of the file, the default position.
SEEK_CUR = Current position in the file; use a negative or positive offset.
SEEK_END = End of the file; use a negative offset.

FORMAT

```
int fseek(filehandle, byteoffset, position);
```

Example:
```
fseek(fh, 0, SEEK_SET); // Start at the beginning of the file, byte 0
```

The offset is the number of bytes from the file position. A positive offset moves the position forward in the file; a negative offset moves the position backwards in the file for position 1 or 2, so if using a negative offset, you would not want to start at the beginning of the file, but somewhere in the middle or from the end of the file.

The rewind() Function.   The rewind() function moves the file back to the beginning of the file, the same as fseek(filehandle, 0, SEEK_SET). It takes a filehandle as its argument and returns true on success and false on failure.

FORMAT

```
bool rewind ( resource handle )
```

Example:
```
rewind($filehandle) ;   // Go back to the beginning of the file
```

EXAMPLE 11.8

```
      <html><head><title>Open a File</title></head>
      <body bgcolor="lavender">
      <?php
          $filename="$_SERVER[DOCUMENT_ROOT]/../mydir/data.file";
          $filehandle=fopen($filename, "r");
1         $total_bytes=filesize($filename);
2         $contents=fread($filehandle,$total_bytes);
3         fseek($filehandle, 0); // Go back to the beginning of the file
4         $contents=fread($filehandle, $total_bytes);
          echo "Reading from the beginning of the file:<br />
              <pre>$contents</pre>";
```

EXAMPLE 11.8 (CONTINUED)

```
5       fseek($filehandle, -40, SEEK_END );
6       $contents=fread($filehandle, $total_bytes);
        echo "Reading from the end of the file:<br />
7           <pre>$contents</pre>";
        fclose($filehandle);
    ?>
    </body>
    </html>
```

EXPLANATION

1   The filesize() function returns the number of bytes in the entire file.
2   The fread() function will read $total_bytes from the filehandle and return the data to $contents. After this read operation, the internal read pointer will be at the end of the file.
3   The fseek() positions the read pointer at the beginning of the file (the default position), at byte 0, the first character. (You can can also use the built-in rewind() function to start back at the beginning of the file.)
4   The fread() function will read in the whole file, specified by $total_bytes, and return the data and store it in $contents.
5   This time the fseek() function will go to the end of the file, SEEK_END, and back up 40 bytes. The next read operation will start at that position.
6   The fread() function will read until it reaches $total_bytes or end of file, starting at the position set by fseek() on line 5; that is, –40 bytes from the end of the file.
7   The contents of the file, after moving the file pointer back 40 bytes from the end of the file, are displayed in Figure 11.9.

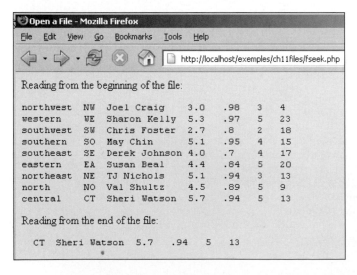

Figure 11.9
Using fseek() to reposition the read file pointer. Output from Example 11.8.

The ftell() Function—Finding the Current Position in a File. If you have read some data from a file and want to keep track of where you were in the file when you stopped reading, the `ftell()` function will return the current byte position, the number of bytes from the beginning of the file, and where the next read operation will start. This can be used in conjunction with the `seek()` function to return to the correct position in the file. (If you are using text mode, the carriage return and linefeed translation will be part of the byte count.)

FORMAT

```
int ftell ( resource handle )
```

Example.
```
$filehandle("myfile", "r");
$contents=fgets($filehandle, 1024);
echo ftell( $filehandle);   // Current read postion in bytes,
                            // starting at byte 1024
```

EXAMPLE 11.9

```
     <html><head><title>The ftell() Function</title></head>
     <body bgcolor="lavender">
     <h3>Marking a Position in a File</h3>
     <pre>
     <?php
         //$filename="c:/wamp/www/exemples/data.file";
         $filename="$_SERVER[DOCUMENT_ROOT]/exemples/data.file";
         if (!file_exists($filename)){
             print "No such file or directory";
             exit();
         }
1        $fh=fopen($filename,"r");
2        $substring="eastern";
         while( !feof($fh)){
             $line_of_text=fgets($fh);
             echo "$line_of_text";
3            if(substr_count($line_of_text, $substring)) {
4                $bytes=ftell($fh);
             }
         }
         if (! isset($bytes)){
             echo "$substring not found<br />";
             exit();
         }
5        fseek($fh, $bytes, SEEK_SET);
         echo "<hr />";
         echo "<b>Start reading again from byte position $bytes</b>
             <br />";
         while( !feof($fh)){
```

EXAMPLE 11.9 (CONTINUED)

```
6            $line_of_text=fgets($fh);
             echo "$line_of_text";
         }
         fclose($fh);
     ?>
     </pre>
     </body>
     </html>
```

EXPLANATION

1   A file is opened for reading.
2   The variable, $substring, is assigned the string "eastern", a string that will be searched for in the file that was just opened.
3   As each line is read from the file, the substr_count() function will search for the string "eastern" in a line and return the number of times it was found. The first time this function returns 1 or more, the next line will be entered.
4   The ftell() function will return the byte position of where the next read operation will take place. The line containing "eastern" has already been read. The byte position is the number of characters from the beginning of the file. This value is saved in $bytes, to be used later with the fseek() function.
5   The fseek() function will start at the beginning of the file, byte 0, and move to the position returned from ftell(), byte 291, in this example. See Figure 11.10.
6   When fgets() starts reading lines from the file it picks up right after the line where the substring "eastern" was found.

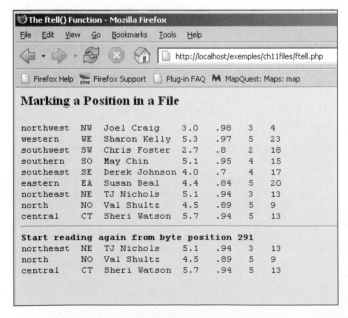

Figure 11.10
Marking a position with ftell().
Output from Example 11.9.

11.2.6 Opening a URL for Reading

You can open files with FTP or HTTP with the `fopen()` function. (Note: If opening the URL fails, check if the `allow_url_fopen` directive in the `php.ini` file is disabled.)

FORMAT

```
resource fopen ( string filename, string mode [,
                 bool use_include_path [, resource zcontext]] )
```

Example:
```
$filehandle=fopen('http://www.site.com/');
$filehandle=fopen('ftp://username:password@ftp.wherever.com/pub/index'
, 'r');
```

EXAMPLE 11.10

```
      <html><head><title>Open a File</title></head>
      <body bgcolor="lavender">
      <?php
1         $filename="http://www.ellieq.com/";
2         $fh=fopen("$filename", "r");
3         while( !feof($fh) ){
4             $contents=htmlspecialchars(fgets($fh, 1024));
              print "<pre>$contents</pre>";
          }
          fclose($fh);
      ?>
      </body>
      </html>
```

EXPLANATION

1 The file is the URL of a Web site.
2 The Web page is opened for reading and a filehandle is returned, called `$fh`.
3 The expression in the `while` loop uses the `feof()` function to check whether we are not yet at the end of the file.
4 The `fgets()` function reads 1024 bytes at a time from the page. The `htmlspecialchars()` function converts any special characters to HTML entities; for example, an `&` would become `&amp` and a `<` would become `&lt`, and so on. The output shown in Figure 11.11 is the actual source page (View Source) that was used to create the page.

Figure 11.11   Viewing the contents of a Web page opened as a URL.

11.2.7   Reading from Files Without a Filehandle

PHP provides functions that allow you to read the contents of a file without first opening a filehandle.

The file_get_contents() Function—Reading the Whole File into a String.   An easy way to read the contents of an entire file is with the `file_get_contents()` function. You do not even need to get a filehandle, just pass the name of the file to the function and it will get the contents of the whole file and store it in a string. You can also start reading from a specified offset in the file and specify how many bytes you want to read. The `file_get_contents()` function will return FALSE, if it fails. The PHP manual suggests this as the most efficient way to read a file into a string.

FORMAT

```
string file_get_contents ( string filename [, bool use_include_path [,
                           resource context [, int offset [,
                           int maxlen]]]] )
```

Example:
```
$contents=file_get_contents("datafile.txt");
```

The file() Function—Reading the Whole File into an Array. Without using a filehandle, you can read an entire file into an array with PHP's `file()` function. The filename can be a full path, relative path, or even a URL (if each element of the array corresponds to a line in the file, with the newline still attached. The function returns FALSE if it fails. If you do not want the end-of-line character at the end of each of the array elements, use the `rtrim()` function, described in Chapter 6, "Strings."[5] This function is identical to `file_get_contents()`, except that it returns the file in an array.

FORMAT

```
array file ( string filename [, int use_include_path [,
              resource context]] )
```

EXAMPLE 11.11

```
        <html><head><title>The file() Function</title></head>
        <body bgcolor="lightgreen">
        <font face="verdana">
        <h3>Assigning Lines of a File to an Array</h3>
        <?php
1          $filename="$_SERVER[DOCUMENT_ROOT]/../mydir/data.file";
2          $lines = file($filename); // Lines of file stored in an array
           // Loop through our array, show the file with line numbers
3          foreach ($lines as $line_num => $line) {
4              $line_num++;
5              echo "<b>" . $line_num  ."</b> : " . $line . "<br />\n";
           }
        ?>
        </font>
        </body>
        </html>
```

EXPLANATION

1 The variable, `$filename`, is assigned the path to a file called `data.file` one level above the document root of the server in a directory called `mydir`.

2 The built-in `file()` function takes the filename as its argument (not a filehandle) and returns an array where each line is an element of the array.

3 The `foreach` loop cycles over each element of the array of lines, extracting the index and the value of the line.

4 By adding one to the value of `$line_number`, the index in the array, we can start the count at 1. This value will be placed in front of each line every time the loop body is executed.

5 Each line and its line number are displayed as shown in Figure 11.12.

---

5. If PHP does not recognize the line endings (Macintosh), see the `php.ini` file to enable the `auto_detect_line_endings` runtime configuration option.

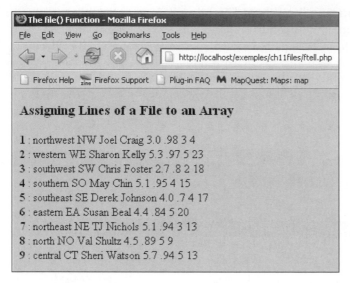

Figure 11.12
Using the `file()` function, creating line numbers.

Using explode() and implode().   After you have read in a line from a file or you get input from a file, you might want to break the lines into individual fields or create a string from an array of input items. This is where the array functions `explode()` and `implode()` can be useful, array functions discussed in Chapter 8, "Arrays."

Example 11.12 demonstrates how to use these functions. This example uses the text file called `datebook`.[6] Below are two lines from this file. Notice that the fields are separated by colons.

```
Steve Blenheim:238-923-7366:95 Latham Lane, Easton, PA 83755:11/12/56:20300
Betty Boop:245-836-8357:635 Cutesy Lane, Hollywood, CA 91464:6/23/23:14500
```

EXAMPLE   11.12

```
      <html><head><title>Parsing Lines</title></head>
      <body bgcolor="lightgreen">
      <font face=verdana" size="+2">
      <?php
         if( ! isset($_POST['submit'])){
1            show_form();
         }
         else{
2            process_file();
         }
3        function show_form(){
         ?>
            <h2>Exploding and Imploding</h2>
```

---

6. The datebook file can be found on the CD in the back of this book.

EXAMPLE 11.12 (CONTINUED)

```
                        <form method=POST
                            action="<?php echo $_SERVER['PHP_SELF'];?>">
                            <table cellspacing="0" cellpadding="2">
                            <tr>
                                <b> Select a first name from the file.</b>
                                <td><input type="text" size=30
                                            name="first_name" </td>
                            </tr>
                            <tr>
                                <td> </td>
                            </tr>
                            <tr>
                                <td><input type="submit"  name="submit"
                            </tr><br />
                            </table>
                        </form>
                    <?php
                    }
4                   function process_file(){
                    $filename="$_SERVER[DOCUMENT_ROOT]/../mydir/datebook";
5                   $lines = file($filename);     // Lines of file stored in an array
6                   $first_name=trim($_POST['first_name']);
7                   foreach ($lines as  $line_value) {
8                       $fields=explode(":", $line_value);
9                       $fullname=explode(" ", $fields[0]);
                        $phone=$fields[1];
                        $address=$fields[2];
                        $birthday=$fields[3];
                        $salary=$fields[4];
10                      if( strcasecmp($fullname[0],$first_name) == 0 ){
11                          $birth=explode("/",$birthday);
12                          $newstring=implode("<br />",array($fields[0],$phone,
                            $address,"19".$birth[2], '$'.number_format($salary,2)));
13                          echo "$newstring<br />";
14                          $count++;
                            echo "<hr />";
                        }
                    }
15                  if($count==0){
                        echo "$first_name is not in the file.<br />";
                    }
                }
                    ?>
                    </b>
                    </font>
                    </body>
                    </html>
```

EXPLANATION

1   If the form has not been submitted yet, the show_form() function will display it.

2   If the submit button was pressed, the form has already been filled out, and now it is time to process it. The process_file() function is called.

3   This is where the show_form() function is declared, which produces a very simple HTML form with one text box and a submit button. The user will type in the first name of someone from an external text file, called datebook. See Figure 11.13.

4   This is where the process_file() function is called. It will read a file into an array and break each line of the file into fields. If a line matches the first name of the input value typed into the form, that data for that person will be displayed.

5   The PHP file() function reads an entire file and assigns it to an array, where each line of the file is an element of the array.

6   The value of the variable called $first_name is what the user typed in the form and was sent via the POST method to this PHP program. Any whitespace is stripped out with the built-in trim() function.

7   The foreach loop iterates through each value in the array of lines that was created when the file() function read in the *datebook* file on line 5.

8   The explode() function splits up a string, $line, by a specified delimiter, in this case, by a colon. It creates an array where each of the elements represents the individual fields that were created.

9   The first element of the array called $fields[0] contains a first and last name. The explode() function will create a two-element array, called $fullname, consisting of a first and last name.

10 The strcasecmp() function compares two strings, case insensitive. If the value that came in from the form, $first_name, and the value of $fullname[0] are equal, then line 11 is entered.

11 The explode() function creates the $birth array by splitting $birthday; for example, 03/16/78, by slashes.

12, 13   The implode() function joins or "glues" the array elements together into one string, called "$newstring", displayed on line 13 and shown in Figure 11.14.

14 A variable called $count will be incremented each time through this loop to keep track of the number of lines found matching the name compared in line 10.

15 If the value of the $count is 0, there were no matches, and the program displays a message saying so.

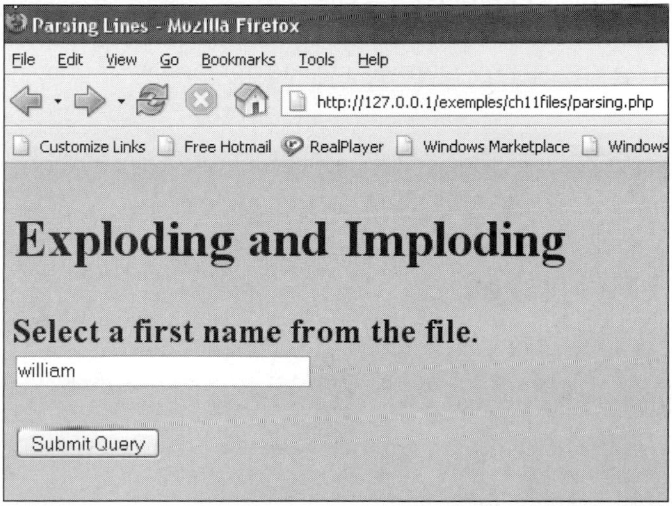

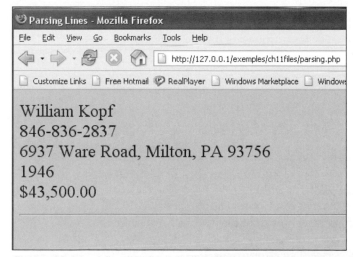

Figure 11.13   The HTML form.

Figure 11.14   After the lines in the file have been parsed. Output from Example 11.12.

The readfile() Function—Reading and Writing a File. The `readfile()` function reads from a file and writes it to the output buffer. It returns the number of bytes read from the file. If an error occurs, FALSE is returned and an error message is printed.

FORMAT

```
int readfile ( string filename [, bool use_include_path [,
               resource context]] )
```

Example:
```
readfile("myfile.txt");
```

EXAMPLE 11.13

```
    <html><head><title>Reading and Outputting a File</title></head>
    <body bgcolor="lightblue">
    <h3>Reading and Outputting a File</h3>
    <b>
1   <pre>

    <?php
2       $number_of_bytes=@readfile("data.file");
        echo "<br />Read $number_of_bytes bytes from the file.<br />";
    ?>

    </pre>
    </b>
    </body>
    </html>
```

EXPLANATION

1   The HTML <pre> tag is used here so that when the file is displayed, the newlines will be preserved, as shown in Figure 11.16.

2   The `readfile()` function will read in the contents of `data.file` and send the output to the the output stream; for example, browser or terminal. It returns the number of bytes read. The function was called as `@readfile()` to suppress the printing of an error message if an error occurred.

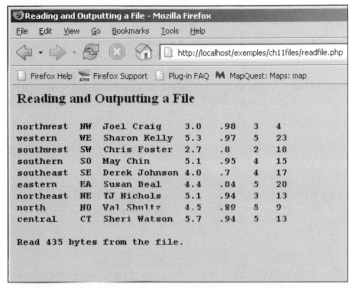

Figure 11.15 Reading a file and outputting its contents.

11.2.8 Opening a File for Writing and Appending

When you open a file for writing, the file is created if it does not exist, and truncated if it does. If you open a file for appending, the file will not be overwritten if it exists and the data will be appended to the bottom of the file. If it does not exist, opening for appending creates the file.

To open a file for writing, the fopen() function returns a filehandle to either a text or binary file. Although UNIX and MacOS do not distinguish between text and binary files, Windows does. If a file is to be shared by multiple operating systems, it is safer to open it in binary mode in conjunction with one of the other modes. (As of PHP 4.3.2, the default mode is set to binary for all platforms that distinguish between binary and text mode.)

UNIX and MacOS X represent the end-of-line character with \n, whereas Windows uses \r\n. If you use Windows, the "t" mode can be used with plain-text files to translate the \n to \r\n. Otherwise, the "b" mode should be used, which does not interpret data but treats it as just a series of bytes. If the file contents look weird when it is opened or you have a lot broken images, use the "b" mode.

```
$handle = fopen("/home/marko/file.txt", "wb");
$handle = fopen("http://www.ellieq.com/", "w");
$handle = fopen("ftp://user:password@ellieq.com/myfile.txt", "a");
```

The fwrite() and fputs() Functions.   The `fwrite()` function writes a string text to a file and returns the number of bytes written. An alias for the `fwrite()` function is `fputs()`. It takes two arguments: the filehandle returned by `fopen()` and an optional length argument, how many bytes to write to the file. If it fails, `fwrite()` returns `FALSE`.

The file_put_contents() Function.   The `file_put_contents()` also writes a string to a file and returns the number of bytes written, but does not require a filehandle. Otherwise it is the same as `fwrite()` and `fputs()`.

FORMAT

```
int fwrite ( filehandle, string, [ int length] )
```

Example:
```
$bytes=fwrite( $filehandle, "Peter Piper picked a peck of pickled
              peppers.\n");
$bytes=fwrite( $filehandle, "Jack in the Beanstalk", 4);
```

EXAMPLE 11.14

```
      <html><head><title>Open a File</title></head>
      <body bgcolor="lavender">
      <?php
1         $name="Joe Shmoe Jr.";
          $address="100 Main St.";
          $email="jshmoe@whatever.mil";
          $title="Major";
2         $outputstring="$name\t$address\t$email\t$title\n";
3         $filename="$_SERVER[DOCUMENT_ROOT]/../mydir/info.txt";
4         $filehandle=fopen($filename, "wb");
5         fwrite($filehandle, $outputstring, strlen($outputstring));
          fclose($filehandle);
      ?>
      </body>
      </html>
```

(Output: Contents of *info.txt*)
```
Joe Shmoe Jr.   100 Main St.    jshmoe@whatever.mil    Major
```

EXPLANATION

1   A set of scalar variables are defined, the information that will be written to a file.
2   A string is created with each word separated by a tab.
3   Because the file must be a writeable file, it is stored outside the server's root directory. It is located in the a directory called `mydir`, and the name of the file is `info.txt`.

4   The filehandle returned from `fopen()` is opened for writing. The `"b"` (binary) mode is recommended when using systems that differentiate between binary and text files; that is, Windows.

5   The `fwrite()` function writes the specified string, `$outputstring` to the filehandle, `$filehandle`. The number of bytes written are returned by the `strlen()` function.

Appending to a File.   When a file is opened for appending, the write will start at the end of the file. If the file does not exist, it will be created.

EXAMPLE 11.15

```
<html><head><title>Appending</title></head>
<body bgcolor="lightgreen">
<font face="verdana" size="+1">
<?php
    $name="John Doe";
    $address="1001 Logic Dr.";
    $email="johndoe@place.gov";
    $title="VP";
1   $outputstring="$name\t$address\t$email\t$title\n";
    $filename="$ SERVER[DOCUMENT_ROOT]/../mydir/info.txt";
2   $filehandle=fopen($filename, "ab");
3   if( fwrite($filehandle, $outputstring,
                   strlen($outputstring))==FALSE){
        echo "You cannot write to the $filename.<br />";
    }
    else{
4       $text= file_get_contents("$filename");
        echo "<pre>$text</pre>";
    }
    fclose($filehandle);
?>
</body>
</font>
</html>
```

EXPLANATION

1   The values of the variables are assigned to the variable, `$outputstring`. Each value is separated by a tab and the string ends with a newline.

2   The file `info.txt` is opened for appending, which means the internal file pointer will start writing at the end of the file, rather than the beginning.

3   If the `fwrite()` function fails, the program will produce an error. Otherwise, the string in `$outputstring` will be appended to the file. Output is shown in Figure 11.16. The line starting with `Joe Doe` has been appended.

4   The contents of the file are read and displayed.

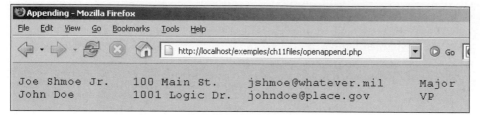

Figure 11.16 After writing and appending. Output from Example 11.15.

Locking Files with flock().   What if two or more customers are trying to write to a Web site at the same time? To prevent this, you can lock the file so that a user has exclusive access to it and then unlock it when he or she has finished using it. PHP supports a portable way of locking complete files with the `flock()` function. This is called *advisory locking* because all accessing programs have to use the same locking mechanism or it will not work. See Table 11.6 for a list of `flock()` operations.

The `flock()` function uses a filehandle returned from the `fopen()` function. The lock can be released by `fclose()`, which is also called automatically when the script finished. The function returns TRUE on success or FALSE on failure. Whether or not this function works properly is entirely dependent on your operating system; for example, it is not supported on older systems like Windows 98 or for networked file systems (NFS), and so on.

FORMAT

```
bool flock ( resource handle, int operation [, int &wouldblock] )
```

Table 11.6 `flock()` Operations

Operation	(Constant) Numeric Value	Operation It Peforms
LOCK_EX	2	Acquires an exclusive lock (writer).
LOCK_NB	4	Nonblocking (no waiting) while the lock is being acquired.
LOCK_SH	1	Acquires a shared lock (reader).
LOCK_UN	3	Releases a lock (shared or exclusive).

EXAMPLE 11.16

```
         <html><head><title>File Locking</title></head>
         <body bgcolor="lightgreen">
         <font face="verdana" size="+1">
         <?php
             $name="Jane Doe";
             $address="1 Sensible Ave.";
             $email="janedoe@school.edu";
             $title="Dean";
             $outputstring="$name:$address:$email:$title\n";
             $filename="$_SERVER[DOCUMENT_ROOT]/../mydir/info.txt";
1            $filehandle=fopen($filename, "ab");
2            if (flock($filehandle, LOCK_EX)) { // Acquire an exclusive lock
3                fwrite($filehandle, $outputstring, strlen($outputstring));
4                flock($filehandle, LOCK_UN); // Release the lock
             }
             else{
                 echo "Couldn't lock this file.<br />";
                 exit();
             }
             $text= file_get_contents("$filename");
             echo "<pre>$text</pre>";
5            fclose($filehandle); // This would also release the lock
         ?>
         </body>
         </font>
         </html>
```

EXPLANATION

1   A file is opened for appending.
2   The `flock()` function attempts to put an exclusive lock on the file; that is, the file cannot be shared while it is being written to.
3   If the lock is successfully set, the program can now write to the file.
4   Once the program has finished writing to the file, the exisiting lock is released with the `LOCK_UN` operation.
5   If the lock was not officially released with `flock()`, the `fclose()` function will cause the lock to be released when it closes the filehandle.

11.2.9 File Checks

Before performing operations on files or directories, it is a good practice to verify whether or not the file even exists, if it is readable, writable, executable, and so on. PHP provides a set of functions for testing the status of a file. See Table 11.7.

Table 11.7 File Testing Functions

Function	Description
file_exists()	Checks if the file or directory exists.
is_dir()	Checks if the filename is a directory.
is_file()	Checks if the filename is a file.
is_link()	Checks if the filename is a symbolic link.
is_readable()	Checks if the file is readable.
is_uploaded_file()	Checks if the file was uploaded by an HTTP host.
is_writable()	Checks if the file is writable.
is_writeable()	An alias for is_writable.
stat()	Gives information about a file.

The file_exists() Function.   The file_exists() function checks to see whether a file or directory exists. It returns TRUE if it does, and FALSE if it does not.

FORMAT

```
bool file_exists ( string filename );
```

Example:
```
if ( file_exists("filetest.php");
```

EXAMPLE 11.17

```
    <html><head><title>Appending</title></head>
    <body bgcolor="lightgreen">
    <font face="verdana" size="+1">
    <?php
1       $filename="c:\wamp\www\logo_i.gif";  // Windows
            if( file_exists("$filename")){
                echo "<img src='logo_i.gif'><br />";
        }
        else{
            echo "<em>$filename</em> doesn't exist.<br />";
            exit();
        }
    ?>
    </body>
    </font>
    </html>
```

EXPLANATION

1   The `file_exists()` function checks to see if the image file assigned to `$file-name` exists before displaying it.

The is_file() Function.   The `is_file()` function checks to see if a file exists and is a regular file; that is, not a directory. It takes the name of the file as its argument and returns TRUE if the file is a regular file, and FALSE if it is not.[7]

FORMAT

```
bool is_file ( string filename )
```

Example:
```
if ( is_file("myfile.php"){ print "True<br />"; }
```

EXAMPLE   11.18

```
<html><head><title>Is it a Regular File?</title></head>
<body bgcolor="lightgreen">
<font face="verdana" size="+1">
<?php
    $filename="c:\wamp\www";
1   if(is_file($filename)){
        echo "$filename exists and is a regular file.<br />";
    }
    else{
2       echo "<em>$filename</em> is not a regular file.<br />";
        exit();
    }
?>
</body>
</font>
</html>
```

EXPLANATION

1   The `is_file()` function not only checks to see if the file exists, but also if it is a regular file; that is, not a directory.
2   This line is displayed in Figure 11.17. The file `c:\wamp\www` is not a regular file.

---

7. Processing is faster if you use a relative path name rather than an absolute path.

Figure 11.17   The file exist, but it is not a plain file. Output from Example 11.18.

The is_readable() Function.   The `is_readable()` function checks to see if you can read from a file. It takes the filename as its argument and returns TRUE if the filename exists and is readable. If the PHP script is being executed by the server, the server's permissions (usually limited) determine whether or not the PHP program can read from the file, and if it is being executed at the shell prompt, the permissions of the user running the script are the deciding factor. Normally, the file should be readable by others.

FORMAT

```
bool is_readable ( string filename );
```

Example:
```
if ( is_readable("file.txt")) { echo "File is readable<br />";}
```

EXAMPLE 11.19

```
    <html><head><title>Is Readable?</title></head>
    <body bgcolor="lightgreen">
    <font face="verdana" size="+1">
    <?php
        $filename="testing.txt";
1       if( is_readable($filename)){
            echo "<em>$filename</em> is readable<br />";
        }
2       else{
            echo "Can't read from <em>$filename.</em><br />";
            exit();
        }
    ?>
    </body>
    </font>
    </html>
```

EXPLANATION

1   The `is_readable()` function returns true if `$filename` is readable by this PHP script.
2   If `is_readable()` returns false, the `else` block is executed, and the program exits.

The is_writable() Function.   When opening a file for writing, you might run into a problem with permissions if you are trying to put the file in a directory not accessible to the Web. Because the PHP script is executed on behalf of the server, it shares the same permissions. Normally, the server does not have world-write permissions turned on to prevent hackers from breaking into your site and causing havoc.

The `is_writable()` (or `is_writeable`) function returns true if a file exists and is writable, and false if it is not.

FORMAT

```
bool is_writable ( string filename )
```

Example:
```
if (is_writable($filename)) {echo "$filename is writable";}
```

EXAMPLE 11.20

```
        <html><head><title>Appending</title></head>
        <body bgcolor="lightgreen">
        <font face="verdana" size="+1">
        <?php
            $name="John Doe";
            $address="1001 Logic Dr.";
            $email="johndoe@place.gov";
            $title="VP";
1           $outputstring="$name\t$address\t$email\t$title\n";
2           $filename="testing.txt";
3           if( is_writable($filename)){
                $filehandle=fopen($filename, "wb");
                fwrite($filehandle, $outputstring, strlen($outputstring));
            }
            else{
4               echo "Can't write to <em>$filename.</em><br />";
                exit();
            }
            fclose($filehandle);
        ?>
        </font></body></html>
```

EXPLANATION

1   A string called `$outputstring` is created from the name, address, e-mail address, and title of John Doe. This string will be sent to the file listed on line 2.

2   The variable `$filename` is assigned the name of the file that will be written to. PHP must have permission to write to this file.

3   The `is_writable()` built-in function returns true if PHP can write to this file, and the `fopen()` function will attempt to open it.

4   If the `is_writeable()` function returns false, this line is executed and the program exits. See Figure 11.18.

Figure 11.18   This file is not writable. Output from Example 11.20.

EXAMPLE 11.21

```
<html><head><title>Handling Errors</title></head>
<body bgcolor="lavender">
<font face="verdana" size="+1">
<?php
    $name="Joe Shmoe Jr.";
    $address="100 Main St.";
    $email="jshmoe@whatever.mil";
    $title="Major";
    $outputstring="$name\t$address\t$email\t$title\n";
1   $filename="info.txt";
    // Suppress error message, if there is one
2   @ $fp=fopen($filename, "w");
3   if (! $fp ){
4       echo "Error: You don't have permission to open
            this file.<br />";
        exit();
    }
    fwrite($fp, $outputstring, strlen($outputstring));
    echo "Output was sent to $filename<br />";
    fclose($fp);
?>
</body>
</font>
</html>
```

EXPLANATION

1   This is the file that will be written to. If it already exists it will be overwritten; otherwise `fopen()` will try to create it.

2   If the `fopen()` function cannot create or open the file for writing, it is probably because it does not have write permission in the directory, in which case an error message would normally occur. By preceding the statement with the @ symbol, any errors will be suppressed.

3, 4   If the `fopen()` function on line 2 failed, a filehandle would not have been returned. This line tests to see if there is not a value for `$fp`, and if not goes to line 4, prints the error message, and exits. Output is shown in Figure 11.19.

Figure 11.19   Suppressing PHP errors and printing your own. Output from Example 11.21.

11.2.10   Creating, Copying, Renaming, and Deleting Files

Table 11.8 lists functions for creating, copying, renaming, and removing files. This section examines these functions.

Table 11.8   Functions to Manipulate Files

Function	Description
copy()	Copies a file.
rename()	Renames a file.
touch()	Updates its timestamp (modification and access times) or creates the file.
unlink()	Removes a file.

The copy() Function—Making a Copy of a File.   To make a copy of a file, the copy() function is used. The copy() function will return true if the file was correctly copied, or false if there was an error. To copy a file, you will need write permission on the directory where the new copy will be stored.

FORMAT

```
bool copy(string source_file,string destination_file)
```

EXAMPLE 11.22

```
        <html><head><title>Copy a File</title></head>
        <body bgcolor="lavender">
        <?php
1           $oldfilename="data.file";
2           $newfilename="data.file.bck";
3           if(! copy($oldfilename, $newfilename)){
                echo "Copy failed\n<br />";
                exit();
            }
            else { echo "Copy succeeded!\n<br />";}
        ?>
        </body>
        </html>
```

EXPLANATION

1   This is the name of the original file, the source. It must exist or the copy will fail.
2   This is the name of the destination file, the file that will be created.
3   If the copy fails, an error will be printed and the program will exit.

The rename() Function—Renaming and/or Moving a File.   The `rename()` function is used to give a file or directory another name. If the destination file is in another directory, then you are essentially moving the file. It returns true on success, and false if it fails.

FORMAT

```
bool rename(string old_file,string new_file)
```

Example:
```
rename("/tmp/tmpfile", "/home/ellie/exemples/data.txt");
```

The unlink() Function—Removing a File.   The `unlink()` function is used to remove a file. It returns true if it can remove the file and false if not.

FORMAT

```
bool unlink ( string filename [, resource context] )
```

Example:
```
unlink("datafile.txt");  // Deletes the file from the directory
```

11.3 Directories

PHP supports a number of functions to allow you to work with directories in the file system. From a PHP script, you can open a directory and read its contents (similar to the `ls` (UNIX) or `dir /b` (DOS). You can change to a new directory, list the current working directory, remove a directory, and so on. Table 11.9 lists functions that will be used in the following examples.

Table 11.9 PHP Directory Functions

Function	Description
chdir()	Changes the directory.
chroot()	Changes the root directory.
closedir()	Closes a directory handle previously opened with `opendir()`.
getcwd()	Gets the current working directory.
opendir()	Returns a directory handle that can be used with `readdir()`, `closedir()`, and `rewinddir()`.
readdir()	Reads the next file from a directory handle opened with `opendir()`.
rewinddir()	Rewinds directory handle pointer to the beginning of the directory.
rmdir()	Deletes a directory. It must be empty and have write permission.
scandir()	Returns an array of files and directories from a given path.
unlink()	Deletes a file from a directory.

11.3.1 Opening and Reading from a Directory

When you open a directory with the `opendir()` function, you create a directory handle to allow access to the directory as it is stored on the disk by the operating system regardless of its internal structure. Once it is opened, you can access the directory with the PHP functions listed in Table 11.9.

The opendir() Function. The `opendir()` function is used to open a directory, similar to the `fopen()` function for opening files. Once a handle to the directory is returned, the other directory functions, such as `readdir()`, `rewindir()`, and `closedir()`, can be applied to the directory filehandle. If the directory cannot be opened, false will be returned.

FORMAT

```
resource opendir ( string path [, resource context] )
```

Example:
```
// $dirhandle is a resource similar to a filehandle
$dirhandle=opendir("/home/john");
```

The readdir() Function.   A directory can be read by anyone who has read permission on the directory. When we speak of reading a directory, we are talking about looking at its contents with the `readdir()` function. `readdir()` reads an entry from a directory handle, given as its argument, and returns the name of a file from the directory. Each file appears in the order in which it is stored by the file system on the disk. You can use this function in a loop to list the contents of the entire directory, one file at at time. The `readdir()` function returns either a filename, or false if it fails. If it succeeds, it moves its internal pointer to the next file in the directory, until it reaches the end of the list.

FORMAT

```
string readdir ( resource dir_handle )
```

Example:
```
$dirhandle=opendir("/home");
// Gets one file from the directory. Use a loop to get them all
$one_file=readdir($dirhandle);
```

EXAMPLE 11.23

```
        <html><head><title><Directory Functions</title></head>
        <body bgcolor="aqua">
        <font face="verdana">
        <h3>Listing the Contents of a Directory</h3>
        <b>
        <?php
1           $dirhandle=opendir("c:/wamp/mysql");
            // List all files in the directory
2           while(false !== ($file=readdir($dirhandle))){
                echo $file,"<br />";
            }
            closedir($dirhandle);
        ?>
        </font>
        </b>
        </body>
        </html>
```

EXPLANATION

1   The `opendir()` function returns a directory handle to `c:/wamp/mysql`.
2   The format for this loop was advised as the correct method to loop through the directory in the PHP manual with this explanation: "We are explicitly testing whether the return value is identical to ... FALSE since otherwise, any directory entry whose name evaluates to FALSE will stop the loop (e.g., a directory named 0)." See *http://us3.php.net/manual/en/function.readdir.php*. Output is shown in Figure 11.20.

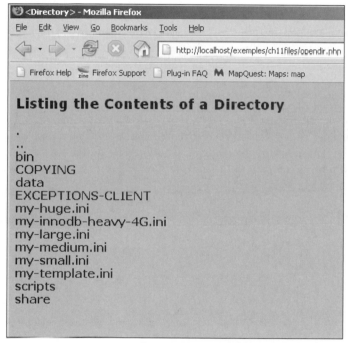

Figure 11.20   Open a directory and list its contents.

11.3.2   Getting Path Information

The `dirname()` function returns the name of the directory from a path name and the `basename()` function returns the name of a file without the directory component. A dot indicates the current working directory.

FORMAT

```
string dirname ( string path )
```

Example:
```
$path = "/home/etc/passwd";
$file = dirname($path); // $file is set to "/etc"
```

EXAMPLE 11.24

```
    <html><head><title>Copy a File</title></head>
    <body bgcolor="lavender">
    <?php
        $path="c:/wamp/www/exemples/first.php";
1       echo dirname($path),"\n<br />"; // Outputs: c:/wamp/www/exemples
2       echo basename($path), "\n<br />"; // Outputs: first.php
    ?>
    </body>
    </html>
```

EXPLANATION

1   The dirname() function returns the directory where the file is found.
2   The basename() function returns the filename portion of the path.

11.3.3   Changing and Getting the Current Directory

The chdir() function changes to a specified directory. You can use either relative or absolute path names. The function returns true on success, and false on failure.

The getcwd() function returns the path to the current working directory if successful, and false if not.

FORMAT

```
bool chdir ( string directory )
```

Example:
```
chdir("/usr/home/john");
```

EXAMPLE 11.25

```
    <html><head><title>Copy a File</title></head>
    <body bgcolor="lavender">
    <?php
1       echo getcwd(),"\n<br />"; // Get the current directory
2       chdir(".."); // Change directory; go up one level
        echo getcwd(),"\n<br />";
    ?>
    </body>
    </html>
```

EXPLANATION

1   The getcwd() function returns the current working directory.
2   The chdir() function changes the current directory to the one specified as its argument. In this example, the two dots represent a relative path to the parent directory. See the output in Figure 11.21.

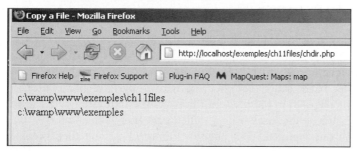

Figure 11.21 Changing directory and printing the current directory.

11.4 Managing Content with Include Files

As your site adds more pages, you will find it easier to maintain if you manage the content with template files, external files that separate the content, HTML client-side instructions, from the application, the PHP server-side programming instructions. Creating a structure for your site will not only make it more manageable for designers and programmers, but easier to navigate and debug. This section focuses on how to include simple files to help manage content. (There are many templating solutions available for PHP today easily found on the Web. See *http://smarty.php.net* to find about Smarty, a template engine designed for PHP.)

To include files in your PHP program, the PHP `include()` and `require()` functions are used. When a file is included, it is similar to a copy and paste operation. The contents of the included or required file are placed within the file in the same way. Often, a convention is to name the included file with an .inc extension and store it in a directory outside the document tree.

The `require()` and `include()` statements are identical in every way except how they handle failure. The `include()` produces only a warning if the file cannot be found, whereas `require()` results in a fatal error causing the program to die. (Be sure that the file you include or require can be located by updating the `include_path` directive in the `php.ini` configuration file.)

Examples:

```
// Replaces instances of require with the contents of file;
// fatal error if file is missing
require("copyright.inc");

// Replaces only first instance of require with contents of file
require_once("header.inc");

// Same as replace() but produces a warning if file is missing
include("disclaimer.inc");

// Happens only once during program execution
include_once("footer.inc");
```

11.4.1   A Real-World Example

In the following example, we create a file called `header.php` that contains the HTML design for the top of the Web page; next, the page that contains the body of the document, that is, the PHP instructions to open a database to retrieve and display information; and finally the footer page, called `footer.php` with copyright information to appear at the bottom of the page. If, in the body of the page, the requested data cannot be found, the user will be directed to another page called *page_not_found.html*.

Let's start by displaying the complete Web page in Figure 11.22 and then break it down into its separate components. All of the pages used to create the complete Web page will be stored in separate files as shown in Figure 11.23.

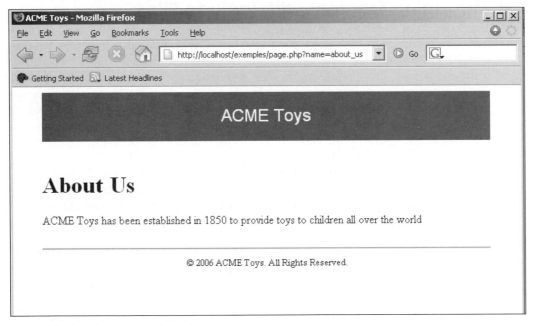

Figure 11.22   A complete Web page.

Web Page Components   MySQL Database

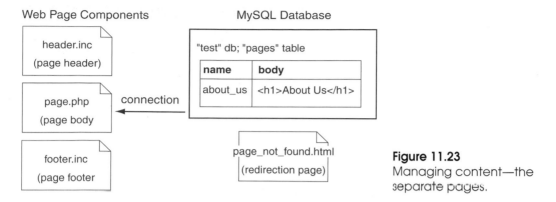

Figure 11.23
Managing content—the separate pages.

EXAMPLE 11.26

```
      (The header file: header.inc)
      <!DOCTYPE html PUBLIC "-//W3C//DTD XHTML 1.0 Strict//EN" "http://
      www.w3.org/TR/xhtml1/DTD/xhtml1-strict.dtd">
      <html>
      <head>
      <title>Acme Toys</title>
      </head>
          <!--   BODY -->
          <BODY text="#000000" BGCOLOR="#ffffff">
          <center>
          <!-- HEADER -->
1         <table width="90%" height="100%" cellspacing="0"
                  cellpadding="0" border="0">
            <tr bgcolor="green"><td align="center"><br />
          <font face="Arial" size="5" style="bold" color="white">ACME
          Toys<font><br /><br />
          </td></tr>
2         <tr><td valign="top"><br />
          <!-- Main Content-->
```

EXPLANATION

1, 2   This is the HTML page that creates the header of the Web page. You can see in the output in Figure 11.24 that it consists of a green table, with a white arial font, centered and vertically aligned at the top of the page.

ACME Toys

Figure 11.24 The page header.

EXAMPLE 11.27

```
        (The main page: page.php)
        <?php

1       $page_name = $_REQUEST['name'];
2       /*  http://localhost/exemples/page.php?name=about_us */

        // Get the body of the page
3       mysql_connect("localhost","root","") or die(mysql_error());
4       mysql_select_db("test") or die(mysql_error());
5       $sql = "SELECT * from pages WHERE name='$page_name'";
        /*
6       --------------What is being selected from the database--------------
+----------+--------------------------------------------------------------------+
| name     | body                                                               |
|          |                                                                    |
+----------+--------------------------------------------------------------------+
| about_us | <h1>About Us</h1> ACME Toys has been established in 1850 to provide toys
|          | to children all over the world                                     |
+----------+--------------------------------------------------------------------+
1 row in set (0.00 sec)
-------------------------------------------------------------------------------
        */
7       $result = mysql_query($sql) or die(mysql_error() );

        // If the page is not found, redirect to a static page
8       if(mysql_num_rows($result) == 0 ) {
9           header("Location: page_not_found.html");
        }
10      $row = mysql_fetch_assoc( $result );
11      $body = stripslashes( $row["body"] );

        // Include the header
12      include("header.inc");

        // Print the body of the page
13      echo $body;

        // Include the footer
14      include("footer.inc");
        ?>
```

EXPLANATION

1   The $_REQUEST['name'] value is sent via the GET method from the URL of this program where the user types a question mark and the name of the page he or she wants to visit (see the next commented line); in this case, the name of the page is about_us. The variable $page_name is assigned about_us.

2   This is the URL address to the server and the PHP script. The string appended to the question mark, "name=about_us", is sent to this script via the GET method and assigned to the $_REQUEST array.

EXPLANATION (CONTINUED)

3   Even though the MySQL database system is not discussed until Chapter 13, "Introduction to MySQL," we use it here to provide a more real-world example. All you really need to understand is that the the PHP script makes a connection to a database and fetches data from it that will be displayed in the browser. In this line, the PHP `mysql_connect()` function attempts to open a connection to the MySQL database server on this computer (localhost) with a user named `"root"` and no password. If the connection fails, the program will die.

4   If the connection is successful, the `"test"` database is selected and ready for use.

5   This is an SQL `select` statement that says, "Select all fields from the `"pages"` table where the `"name"` column is `$page_name`, that is, `"about_us"`. The variable `$sql` is assigned the query string.

6   This commented block is just to show you the actual `"pages"` table in the `"test"` database to help understand what will become the body of this page.

7   Once the query is executed on the `"test"` database, a result is returned, that is a reference to the rows that were retrieved.

8   If any rows were retrieved, line 10 is executed, otherwise line 9 is executed.

9   If no rows were retrieved from the `"pages"` table, the user is redirected to a new page, called `page_not_found.html`, letting him or her know that the request failed.

10   The `mysql_fetch_assoc()` function fetches a row from the database table and returns an associative array, called `$row`, consisting of the name of the table column and the value associated with it.

11   The variable, `$body`, is assigned the value that came from the database column called `"body"`.

12   The contents of `"header.inc"` are inserted into the file to replace the `include` line. It is just as if we had cut and pasted the `header.inc` file right at this point in the current file, `pages.php`.

13   This is where the body of the document is displayed. The value of `$body` in this example is what was retrieved from the `"body"` field of the `"test"` database. The value of `$body` is:

```
<h1>About Us</h1> ACME Toys has been established in 1850 to provide
toys to children all over the world
```

14   The contents of `"footer.inc"` are inserted into the file to replace the `include` line.

```
              (The redirection page: page_not_found.html)
              <!DOCTYPE html PUBLIC "-//W3C//DTD XHTML 1.0 Strict//EN" "http://
              www.w3.org/TR/xhtml1/DTD/xhtml1-strict.dtd">
              <html>
1             <head><title>ACME Toys</title></head>
              <!--  BODY -->
              <BODY text="#000000" BGCOLOR="#ffffff">
              <center>
              <!-- HEADER -->
              <table width="90%" height="100%" cellspacing="0" cellpadding="0"
                     border="0">
              <tr bgcolor="green"><td align="center"><br />
                 <font face="Arial" size="5" style="bold" color="white">ACME
                 Toys<font><br /><br />
              </td></tr>
              <tr><td valign="top"><br />
              <!-- Main Content-->
              <h1>Page Not Found</h1>
```

EXPLANATION

1   This is the redirection page, sent in the Location header, that is displayed if the number of rows selected from the database table was 0. See Figure 11.25.

Figure 11.25   The redirection page.

EXAMPLE 11.29

```
      (The footer Page)
      <br /><br /><hr></td></tr>
      <!-- FOOTER -->
      <tr><td align="center">
      <small>
1        &copy; <?= date("Y") ?> ACME Toys. All Rights Reserved.
      </small>
      </td></tr>
      </table>
      </body>
      </html>
```

EXPLANATION

1   This is the footer page, HTML, and an embedded PHP function to get the current year for the copyright. This page is displayed on the bottom of the page as shown in Figure 11.26.

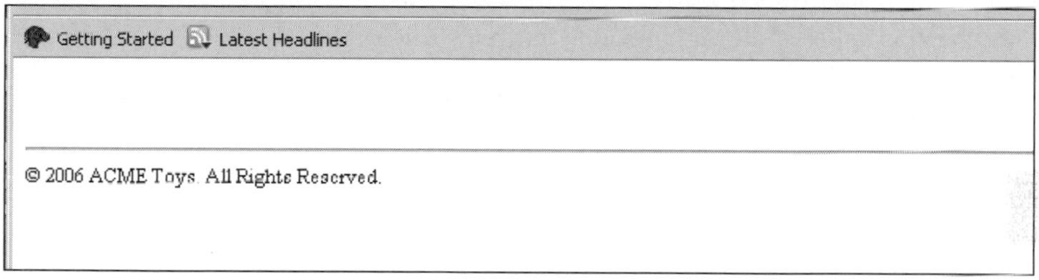

Figure 11.26   The footer page—`footer.inc`.

(These are the SQL statements used to create the table that is being accessed in the main program. This example is provided only to clarify what is going on in the `pages.php` file.)

EXAMPLE 11.30

```
1   use test;
2   CREATE TABLE 'test'.'pages' (
        'name' VARCHAR(50) NOT NULL,
        'body' TEXT DEFAULT ' '
    )

3   insert into pages (name, body) values ('about_us',
    '<h1>About Us</h1> ACME Toys has been established in 1850 to
    provide toys to children all over the world');
```

EXPLANATION

1   After connecting to the MySQL server, we switch to the database called `test`.
2   This is the way the table was created that contains the `'name'` and `'body'` fields.
3   This is where the data is inserted into the table. This is the data that will become the body of the Web page, called `pages.php`.

11.5 Chapter Summary

This chapter focused on how to open text and binary files for reading, writing, and appending from within a PHP script, how to deal with permissions and ownership, upload files, and navigate directories. The last part of the chapter discussed content management using external files.

11.5.1   What You Should Know

Now that you have finished this chapter you should be able to answer the following questions:

1. What is a filehandle and how do you create one?

2. What functions are used to open and close a file?

3. What function reads lines, characters, and blocks from a file? What is meant by the "mode"?

4. How do you write to a file?

5. How do you append data to the end of a file?

6. What is an advisory lock?

7. How do you reposition the file pointer?

8. What functions can you use to parse data in a file?

9. How do you test for file attributes, such as whether it is readable or writable?

10. What is meant by "uploading" a file? What encoding type is used by the browser for file uploads?

11. How do you copy and remove files?

12. How do you open a directory in a PHP script and list its contents?

13. How do you manage files with `include()` and `require()`?

11.5.2 What's Next?

In Chapter 12, "Regular Expressions and Pattern Matching," we discuss how to use regular expression metacharacters, and use regular expressions to validate form data.

chapter

12

Regular Expressions and Pattern Matching

/^[a-zA-Z][\w \.\-]+[a-zA-Z0-9]@([a-zA-Z0-9][a-zA-Z0-9\-]*\.)+[a-zA-Z]{2,4}$/
huh?

12.1 What Is a Regular Expression?

```
/^[a-zA-Z][\w\.\-]+[a-zA-Z0-9]@([a-zA-Z0-9][a-zA-Z0-9\-]*\.)+[a-zA-Z]{2,4}$/
```

is called a regular expression and might look like jibberish, but by the time you finish this chapter, you will understand what all these symbols mean and how to use them. We will break the expression into very small units, and when all of the pieces have been explained, we will use it to validate an HTML form. Let's start by defining a regular expression and what it is used for.

When a user fills out a form, you might want to verify that the format was correct before sending the data to a database. For example, did the user enter a valid birthdate, e-mail address, or credit card number? This is where regular expressions enter the picture. Their power is great and they are used by many other programming languages for handling text, for performing refined searches and replacements, capturing subpatterns in strings, testing input data for certain characters, and more.

So, what is a regular expression? A regular expression is really just a sequence or pattern of characters that is matched against a string of text when performing searches. When you create a regular expression, you test the regular expression against a string. The regular expression is enclosed in forward slashes. For example, the regular expression /green/ might be matched against the string "The green grass grows". If green is contained in the string, there is a successful match. Like Perl, PHP also provides a large variety of regular expression metacharacters to control the way a pattern is found; for example, the regular expression /^[Gg]reen/ consists of a caret and a set of square brackets. These metacharacters control the search so that the regular expression matches only strings starting with an upper- or lowercase letter g. The possibilities of fine-tuning your search with regular expressions and their metacharacters are endless.

PHP regular expressions are used primarily to verify data on the server side. When a user fills out a form and presses the submit button, the form is sent to a server, and then to a PHP script for further processing. Although it is more efficient to handle form validation on the client side with programs like Javascript or JScript, these programs might be disabled, or might not be programmed to verify form data. Checking the form on the client side allows for instant feedback, and less travelling back and forth between the browser and server, but to ensure that the data has been verified, PHP can recheck it. Once the user has filled out a form and submitted it, PHP can check to see if all the boxes have been filled out correctly, and if not, the user is told to reenter the data before the form data is processed. With the power provided by regular expressions, the ability to check for any type of input, such as e-mail addresses, passwords, social security numbers, birthdates, and so on, is greatly simplified. You can also use regular expressions to complete complex search and replace operations in text files, processes that would be difficult, if not impossible, with PHP's standard string functions.

PHP supports two types of regular expressions: POSIX and Perl style regular expressions. Each type has a set of functions to implement regular expressions. The first set of functions (POSIX style) are those prefixed with `ereg_`. They behave much like the traditional UNIX `egrep` command. The advantage of the `ereg` functions is that they are supported by the oldest versions of PHP. The disadvantages are that they tend to be slow, work only with text data, and be less flexible than the Perl style. The second set of regular expression functions (Perl style) start with `preg_`. These functions mimic Perl regular expressions and support the newer features, such as backreferences, capturing, lookahead, and lookbehind, as discussed later in this chapter. These functions are only available if your version of PHP was compiled with support for the PCRE (Perl Compatible Regular Expression) library, and the PCRE library is installed on your Web server. Check the `phpinfo()` output from your first test scripts to see if PCRE is enabled (see Figure 12.1).

pcre

PCRE (Perl Compatible Regular Expressions) Support	enabled
PCRE Library Version	4.5 01-December-2003

Figure 12.1 Ouput of the `phpinfo()` function.

Why Perl style regular expressions? Perl is a popular powerful scripting language known for its ability to manipulate and extract text. It supports regular expressions and regular expression metacharacters to make pattern matching relatively easy and quick. PHP has mimicked Perl by providing special functions to handle pattern matching (see Table 12.1) and included Perl's metacharacters for pattern matching. We discuss each of the pattern-matching functions before delving into regular expression metacharacters.

12.2 Pattern-Matching Functions

Table 12.1 lists the PHP built-in functions that will be used for performing searches with regular expressions, performing searches and replacements, splitting up strings based on a regular expression delimiter, and so on. Both the Perl style and POSIX style functions are listed in the following two tables, but this chapter focuses on the Perl style functions.

Table 12.1   Regular Expression Functions—Perl5 Compatible Functions

Function	What It Does
preg_grep() (PHP 4, PHP 5)	Returns an array of patterns that were matched.
preg_match()	Performs a regular expression pattern match.
preg_match_all()	Performs a global regular expression match.
preg_quote()	Puts a backslash in front of regular expression characters found within a string.
preg_replace()	Searches for a pattern and replaces it with another.
preg_replace_callback()	Like preg_replace(), but uses a function for the replacement argument.
preg_split()	Splits up a string into substrings using a regular expression as the delimiter.

Table 12.2   Regular Expression Functions—POSIX Style

Function	What It Does
ereg()	Performs a regular expression pattern match.
eregi()	Performs a case-insensitive regular expression pattern match.
ereg_replace()	Searches for a pattern and replaces it with another.
eregi_replace()	Searches for a pattern and replaces it with another, case insensitive.
split()	Splits a string into an array by using a regular expression as the delimiter.
spliti()	Splits a string into an array by a regular expression and is case insensitive.

12.2.1   Finding a Pattern

The `preg_match()` and `preg_match_all()` functions are both used to find a pattern (regular expression) within a string of text. The real difference between these two functions is that `preg_match()` stops searching after the first match, whereas `preg_match_all()` will continue searching until the end of the string, saving what it finds in an array.

The preg_match() Function.   The `preg_match()` function matches for the first pattern it finds in a string (called the subject). Because the `preg_match()` function stops searching after it finds the first match, the returned value will be 1 if the pattern was found, and 0 if it was not. The first argument is the regular expression search pattern, the second argument is the string being searched, and the third argument is an array. (The only flag that can be specified is `PREG_OFFSET_CAPTURE`, which causes the array returned to also list the offset in the string where the pattern was found.) If an offset value is specified as an argument, then `preg_match()` will start searching from that place in the string, rather than from the beginning.

The first matched pattern will be assigned to the first element of the array, and if capturing is done (capturing is discussed in "Remembering or Capturing" on page 545), then the next element of the array will contain the first captured pattern.

FORMAT

```
int n  =  preg_match('/regular expression/', 'subject_for_search'[,
                 array_of_matches[ flags [, offset]]]);
```

Example:
```
// $result is 1; $matches contains needle
$result  =  preg_match("/needle/", "looking for a needle in a
                    haystack", $matches);
```

EXAMPLE 12.1

```php
    <?php
1       $string="My gloves are worse for wear.";
        // Returns 1 if true
2       if( preg_match("/love/", $string, $matches)){
3           echo "Pattern /love/ was matched.<br />";
        }
        else{
4           echo "Pattern was not matched.<br />";
        }
        print_r($matches);
    ?>
```

1 The variable $string is assigned "My gloves are worse for wear."

2 Does $string contain the pattern /love/? The preg_match() function searches for the first occurrence of /love/ in $string and returns 1 if it matched, and 0 if it did not. preg_match() also creates an array, the third argument, called $matches, containing the pattern it found in the search string.

3 If love is found in gloves, the block of statements after the if is executed; otherwise, the else block is executed. See Figure 12.2.

4 This block is executed, if the pattern was not found in $string.

Figure 12.2 The preg_match() function. Output from Example 12.1.

Case Sensitivity

The i modifier turns off case sensitivity in the search pattern so that any combination of upper- or lowercase letters can be used and not affect the search.

EXAMPLE 12.2

```php
<?php
    $string="My lovely gloves are worse for wear, Love.";
    // Turn off case sensitivity
1   if (preg_match("/LOVE/i", $string, $matches)){
        echo "Pattern /LOVE/ was found.<br />";
    }
    else{
        echo "Match was not found.<br />";
    }
    print_r($matches);
?>
```

1 The i modifier turns off the case sensitivity in the pattern. Now when preg_match() searches for the pattern /LOVE/ in $string, it will find love in lovely, regardless of case. See Figure 12.3.

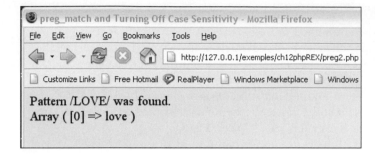

Figure 12.3
Case-insensitive search.
Output from Example 12.2.

Captured Patterns

If patterns within the regular expression are enclosed in parentheses, the `preg_match()` function saves these subpatterns as an array, the third argument. The first element of the array is the matched pattern, and each subsequent element, the subpatterns, in the order in which they were found.

EXAMPLE 12.3

```
<html><head><title>preg_match</title></head>
<body bgcolor="lavender">
<font size="+1">
<?php
1      $string="Looking for a fun and games";
2      $result=preg_match("/(fun) and (games)/", $string, $matches);
       if ( $result == 1){
           echo "Pattern was matched.<br />";
3          print_r($matches);
       }
       else{
           echo "Pattern was not matched.<br />";
       }
?>
</font></body></html>
```

EXPLANATION

1   This is the string that will be searched in line 2.
2   The regular expression is `/fun and games/`. The subpatterns `fun` and `games` are enclosed in parentheses. The `preg_match()` function saves each of the subpatterns in $matches as an array. If the first argument of the array, `$matches[0]`, contains the pattern, `$matches[1]` will contain the first subpattern, `fun`, and `$matches[2]` will contain `games`, the second subpattern.
3   The `print_r()` function prints the contents of $matches; the first element is the pattern or regular expression, and the rest of the elements are those parts of the regular expression enclosed in parentheses, called subpatterns. See the output in Figure 12.4.

Figure 12.4
Capturing subpatterns.
Output from Example 12.3.

The preg_match_all() Function. The `preg_match_all()` function is like the `preg_match()` function, but creates an array of all of the patterns matched in the string, not just the first one, and returns the number of times it matched the pattern.

FORMAT

```
int number_found =  preg_match_all(("/regular expression/", "string",
                                    $matches);
```

Example:
```
$num=preg_match_all("/ring/","Don't string me along, just bring me the
                    goods!", $matches);
```

EXAMPLE 12.4

```
    <?php
1       $string="My lovely gloves are lost in the clover, Love.";
2       $result=preg_match_all("/love/",$string, $matches);
        if( $result== true){
            print "Found $result matches";
        }
        else {print "Didn't find a match";}
3       print_r( $matches);
    ?>
```

EXPLANATION

1   The string `"My lovely gloves are lost in the clover, Love."` is assigned to `$string`.
2   The `preg_match_all` function searches for regular expression `/love/` in `$string` and returns an array of matches. The pattern `love` is case sensitive.
3   The PHP `print_r` function lists all elements of the `$matches` array. Three matches were found, as shown in Figure 12.5.

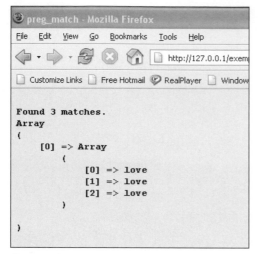

Figure 12.5 Matching all occurrences of a pattern. Output from Example 12.4.

EXAMPLE 12.5

```
    <?php
1       $string="My lovely gloves are lost in the clover, Love.";
2       if (preg_match_all("/love/i", $string, $matches,
                        PREG_OFFSET_CAPTURE)){
            echo "The pattern /love/ was matched $result times.<br />";
        }
        else{
            echo "Match was not found.<br />";
        }
        print "PREG_OFFSET_CAPTURE shows the offset position of each
            pattern found.<br />";
3       print_r($matches);
    ?>
```

EXPLANATION

1 The string contains the pattern love and Love, which preg_match() will search for in the next line.

2 The preg_match_all() function is performing a case-insensitive match using the regular expression /love/i in $string and will return an array, $matches, of all matches found. The PREG_OFFSET_CAPTURE flag shows the offset position where each pattern was found in the string.

3 The output of the print_r() function shows that the pattern /love/ was found four times, as shown in Figure 12.6.

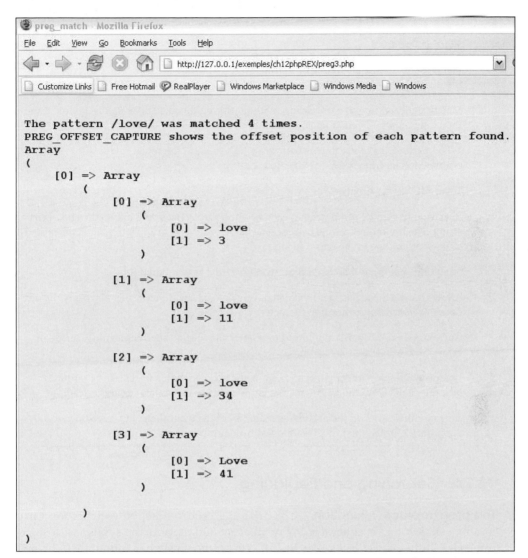

Figure 12.6 Finding the starting position of each matched pattern. Output from Example 12.5.

Pattern-Matching Modifiers.   A pattern modifier allows you to control the way a pattern match is handled. For example, if you want to search for a pattern and turn off the case sensitivity, you can use the i modifier: /pattern/i. Table 12.3 lists the possible pattern modifiers.

Table 12.3   Pattern-Matching Modifiers

Modifier	What It Does
A	Matches only to the beginning of a string even if newlines are embedded and the m modifier is used.
D	Matches only at the end of the string. Without this modifier, a dollar sign is ignored if the m modifier is set. (There is no equivalent to this modifier in Perl.)
e	When performing replacements with `preg_replace()`, the replacement side is evaluated as an expression. See Example 12.8.
i	Turns off case sensitivity.
m	If a string has embedded newlines, each newline within the string marks the end of that string. The beginning and end of line metacharacters (^ and $) apply to each of the nested strings rather than to the entire string.
S	Studying a pattern if it is used often to optimize the search time.
s	Allows the dot metacharacter to match on any newlines within a string. Normally the dot does not match on the newline character.
X	Any backslash in a pattern followed by a letter that has no special meaning causes an error.
x	Ignores whitespace in the pattern except when escaped with a backslash or within brackets; good for commenting regular expressions to make them easier to read.
U	This modifier turns off the default "greediness" of the quantifiers, but greediness can be temporarily turned on if the U is followed by a question mark.

12.2.2 Searching and Replacing

The preg_replace() Function.   The `preg_replace()` function searches for a pattern in a subject that is either a string or an array, and replaces the subject with something else. If the subject being searched is a string and a match is found, then the new subject string will be returned; otherwise the old string is returned. If the subject being searched is an array, then the search and replace is performed on every entry of the subject, and the returned value is an array. The first argument to `preg_replace()` is the regular expression used for the search, the second argument is the replacement value, and the third argument is the subject that is being searched and where the replacement will occur.

Capturing subpatterns and replacing the subpatterns with something else can also be performed. See "Remembering or Capturing" on page 545 for a complete discussion on capturing.

Using the e modifier causes `preg_replace()` to evaluate the replacement value as a valid PHP expression; for example, 4 + 3 becomes 7. See Example 12.8 for a demonstration on how the e modifier affects substitution.

The i modifier turns off case sensitivity in the search pattern.

The parameters used with `preg_replace` are listed in Table 12.4.

Table 12.4   The `preg_replace()` Parameters

Parameter	Description
count	The number of replacements that were performed.
limit	The limit of replacements for each pattern in each subject string. Defaults to –1 (no limit).
pattern	The regular expression or search pattern; that is, what is being searched for in a string or array.
replacement	The string or an array of strings to replace what was found in the string or array.
subject	The subject string where the search and replacement are being performed.

Examples 12.6 through 12.8 demonstrate use of the `preg_replace()` function.

FORMAT

```
mixed preg_replace ( mixed pattern, mixed replacement,
                     mixed subject [, int limit [, int &count]] )

Examples:
$new_string = preg_replace("/blue/", "upbeat", "I am feeling blue,
                            blue, blue.");
$new_string: "I am feeling upbeat, upbeat, upbeat."


$new_string = preg_replace("/blue/", "upbeat", "I am feeling blue,
                            blue, blue.",1);
$new_string: "I am feeling upbeat, blue, blue"


$new_string = preg_replace("/blue/i", "upbeat", "I am feeling BLue,
                            BLUE.");
$new_string: "I am feeling upbeat, upbeat.


$new_string=preg_replace("/(Peace) and (War)/i", "$2 and $1",
                         "Peace and War");
$new_string: "War and Peace"


$new_string=preg_replace("/5/e", "6*7", "He gave me 5 dollars.")e;
$new_string: "He gave me 42 dollars."
```

EXAMPLE 12.6

```php
   <?php
1      $old_string="I live in New Orleans.";
       print "Original string: <em>$old_string</em><br />";
2      $new_string=preg_replace("/New Orleans/", "Philadelphia",
                                "$old_string");
       print "New string: <em>$new_string</em><br />";
   ?>
```

EXPLANATION

1 This is the string that will be used for both searching and replacing.
2 The `preg_replace()` function takes a regular expression as its first argument.
   Note that the regular expression is enclosed in quotes. The second argument is
   the replacement string. The subject string, the one where the replacement will be
   made, is the original string, `$old_string`. If New Orleans is found in the subject
   string, it will be replaced with Philadelphia. The new string is now "I live in
   Philadelphia." as shown in Figure 12.7.

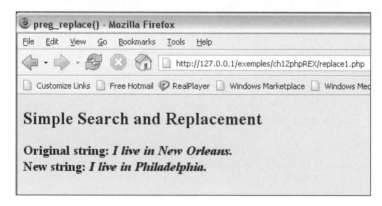

Figure 12.7
Search for a pattern and
replace it with another
string. Output from
Example 12.6.

EXAMPLE 12.7

```php
   <?php
1      $subject="The flag was <em>red, white, </em>and <em>blue</em>.";

2      $search=array('/red/','/white/','/blue/');

3      $replace=array('yellow','orange','green');

       echo "Before replacement: $subject<br />";
4      $subject=preg_replace($search,$replace,$subject);
       echo "After replacement: $subject";
   ?>
```

EXPLANATION

1 This is the subject string where the replacements will be performed.
2 The array $search contains an array of three regular expressions that will be used in the search.
3 The array $replace contains an array of strings that will be replaced in the subject string. If in the search, the pattern /red/ is found, it will be replaced with yellow; if /white/ is found, it will be replaced with orange; and if /blue/ is found, it will be replaced with green. If there are fewer items in the search string than in the replacement string, then the excess items are ignored. If, on the other hand, there are more items in the search string than in the replacement string, the extra elements will be replaced with the null string.
4 The preg_replace() function takes an array as its search string, and an array as its replacement string, and performs the operations on the subject string. Be careful not to quote either the variables, $search or $replace, or they will not be interpreted as arrays. See Figure 12.8 for the output.

Figure 12.8 Search an array and replace it with another array. Output from Example 12.7.

Evaluating the Replacement Side with the e Modifier. Normally, once a pattern is matched, the replacement value is a string. The search string is replaced with the replacement string. With the e modifier, the preg_replace() function treats the replacement side as an expression to evaluate, such as a function, arithmetic, or string operation.

EXAMPLE 12.8

```php
<?php
1    $subject_string="He ate 5 pies.";
2    echo preg_replace("/5 pies/e", "(5*3) . 'cupcakes'",
                        "$subject_string");
?>
```

EXPLANATION

1   This is the string where the replacements will be made.
2   The search string contains a regular expression and the e modifier. This tells PHP
    to evaluate the replacement argument as an expression and substitute the result
    of that evaluation into the subject string. If the pattern 5 pies is found in the sub-
    ject string, it will be replaced with the result of the evalutaion of "(5 * 3) .
    'cupcakes'"; that is, multiply 5 by 3 and concatenate the string 'cupcakes' re-
    sulting in the output shown in Figure 12.9.

Figure 12.9   Evaluating the replacement side with the e modifier. Output from
Example 12.8.

The preg_split() Function—Splitting Strings.   The preg_split() function splits
up a string by some delimiter that marks the separation between the words in the string,
such as a space or a colon or a combination of such characters. The function returns an
array of substrings. If a limit is specified, then only that many substrings are returned.
This function also has a number of flags that are described in Table 12.5. (Note: If you
are using a single character or simple string as the delimiter, the explode() function is
faster; see "The explode() Function" on page 276. The preg_split() function is useful
when you have more than one delimiter that can only be expressed as a regular expression, such as a string that is separated by a colon, tab, or space. See also the split() and
spliti() functions in Table 8.11 on page 330.

FORMAT

```
array preg_split ( string pattern, string subject [, int limit [,
                   int flags]] )
```

Example:
```
$array_of_animals = preg_split("/:/", "dogs:cats:birds:fish");
```

EXAMPLE 12.9

```php
<?php
1    $string="apples#oranges#peaches";
2    $array=preg_split("/#/", $string);    // Split by #
3    print_r($array);
?>
```

EXPLANATION

1   The words in this string are delimited by the # mark.
2   The `preg_split()` function will split up the string by the # delimiter and return an array of substrings.
3   The array returned from the `preg_split()` function is displayed in Figure 12.10.

Figure 12.10 Splitting up a string by a specified delimiter with `preg_split()`.

Table 12.5 Flags for `preg_split()`

Flag	What It Does
PREG_SPLIT_DELIM_CAPTURE	The captured pattern in the delimiter pattern will be saved and returned as well. (See "Remembering or Capturing" on page 545.)
PREG_SPLIT_NO_EMPTY	Returns only nonempty pieces.
PREG_SPLIT_OFFSET_CAPTURE	For every occurring match, an offset will be returned where the match occurred within the string.

Splitting on Multiple Alternative Delimiters. Because the delimiter is a regular expression, you can place a list of delimiters within square brackets to create a regular expression character set (see Table 12.8 on page 526), which means any one character within the set will be considered a valid delimiter in the string.

EXAMPLE 12.10

```php
    <?php
1       $colors="Primary:red,yellow,blue;Secondary:violet,orange,
            green";

2       $array=preg_split("/[:,;]/", $colors);

        echo "<h2>Splitting Colors</h2>";
3       print_r($array);
4       foreach ($array as $key=>$value){
            if ($value == "Primary" || $value == "Secondary"){
                print "$value<br />";
            }
            else{
                print "\t$key: $value<br />";
            }
        }
    ?>
```

EXPLANATION

1   The subject string is `$colors`. The words in this string are separated by colons, commas, and semicolons.

2   The PHP `preg_split()` function uses a regular expression, square brackets, to define the possible delimiters used for splitting up the string. The square brackets, called a character set, contain the list of possible delimiters. Any one character within the set is a delimiter, in this example the colon, comma, and semicolon.

3   The `print_r()` function displays the resulting array created by splitting up the subject string. See Figure 12.11 (top part of display).

4   The `foreach` loop is used to cycle through the array that was created by the `preg_split()` function, and print the key–value pairs in the array in a readable format, as shown in Figure 12.11 (bottom part of display).

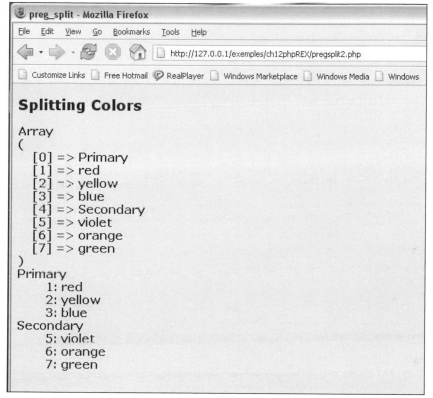

Figure 12.11 Splitting with multiple delimiters. Output from Example 12.10.

EXAMPLE 12.11

```php
<?php
1       $alpha="SAN FRANCISCO";
2       $array=preg_split("//", $alpha, -1, PREG_SPLIT_NO_EMPTY);
        echo "<h2>Splitting A Word into Letters</h2>";
3       print_r($array);
?>
```

EXPLANATION

1   This is the string that will be split up.
2   By using an empty delimiter, `preg_split()` will split up the string by its individ-
    ual characters. The `PREG_SPLIT_NO_EMPTY` flag causes the function to return an
    array without any empty elements.
3   The array of letters created by splitting on an empty delimiter is displayed as an
    array by the `print_r()` function, shown in Figure 12.12.

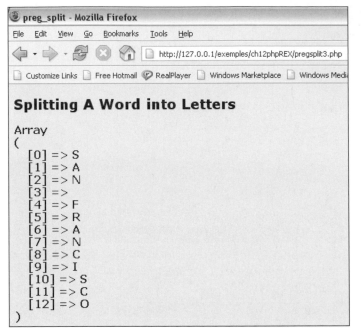

Figure 12.12 Splitting up a word with the `preg_split()` function. Output from Example 12.11.

EXAMPLE 12.12

```php
    <?php
1       $alpha="PORT OF SAN FRANCISCO";
2       $array=preg_split("/\s/", $alpha, -1,
                    PREG_SPLIT_OFFSET_CAPTURE);
        echo "<h2>Splitting A Word into Letters</h2>";
        print_r($array);
    ?>
```

EXPLANATION

1   This is the string we will be splitting on line 2.
2   The `preg_split()` function takes a number of arguments. In this example, the
    first argument is the delimiter. `\s` represents a whitespace character. The second
    argument is the string that is being split, `$alpha`. The third argument (normally
    omitted) is `-1`, stating that there is no limit to the number of array elements that
    can be created when splitting up this string. The `PREG_SPLIT_OFFSET_CAPTURE`
    flag says that for every array element created, the offset of where it occurred with-
    in the string will also be returned. You can see in the output of this example
    (Figure 12.13) that each substring is an array element, and its offset within the
    string is another array consisting of two elements, the array element (substring)
    and the offset position of where that substring was found in the original string.

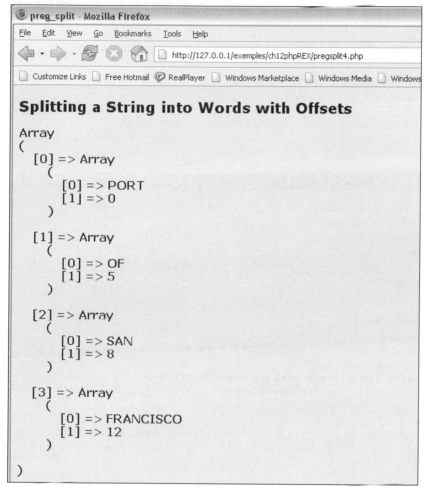

Figure 12.13 Splitting up a string with the `preg_split()` function. Output from Example 12.12.

Other related PHP functions are: `spliti()`, `split()`, `implode()`, and `explode()`. See Chapter 8, "Arrays," for more on these.

The preg_grep() Function. Similar to the UNIX `grep` command, the `preg_grep()` function returns an array of values that match a pattern found in an array instead of a search string. You can also invert the search and get an array of all elements that *do not* contain the pattern being searched for (like UNIX `grep -v`) by using the `PREG_GREP_INVERT` flag.

FORMAT

```
array preg_grep ( string pattern, array input [, int flags] )
```

Example:
```
$new_array = preg_grep("/ma/", array("normal", "mama", "man","plan"));
// $new_array contains: normal, mama, man

$new_array=preg_grep("/ma/",array("normal","mama","man",
                                "plan"),PREG_GREP_INVERT);
// $new_array contains: plan
```

EXAMPLE 12.13

```
     <html><head><title>The preg_grep() Function</title></head>
     <body bgcolor="lavender">
     <font face="verdana" >
     <b>
     <h2>The preg_grep() Function</h2>
     <font size="+1">
     <pre>
     <?php
1        $regex="/Pat/";
2        $search_array=array("Margaret","Patsy", "Patrick",
                           "Patricia", "Jim");
         sort($search_array);
3        $newarray=preg_grep( $regex, $search_array );
4        print "Found ". count($newarray). " matches\n";
5        print_r($newarray);

6        $newarray=preg_grep($regex,$search_array, PREG_GREP_INVERT);
         print "Found ". count($newarray). " that didn't match\n";
         print_r($newarray);
     ?>
     </b>
     </pre>
     </font>
     </body>
     </html>
```

EXPLANATION

1 The variable $regex is assigned the regular expression, /Pat/, that will be used later by preg_grep() as the search pattern.
2 This array will be used as the subject for the search with the preg_grep() function.
3 After the array has been sorted, the preg_grep() function will search for the pattern, /Pat/, in each element of the array, and return and assign the matched array elements to another array called $newarray.

4 The count() function returns the number of elements in the new array; that is, the number of elements where the pattern /Pat/ was found.

5 The found elements are displayed. Note that the index values have been preserved.

6 When the PREG_GREP_INVERT flag is specified, the preg_grep() function will match and return any elements not found in the original array, as shown in the output in Figure 12.14.

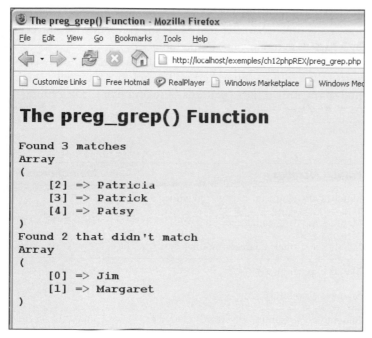

Figure 12.14 The preg_grep() function. Output from Example 12.13.

12.2.3 Getting Control—The RegEx Metacharacters

Regular expression metacharacters are characters that do not represent themselves. They are endowed with special powers to allow you to control the search pattern in some way (e.g., finding a pattern only at the beginning of the line, or at the end of the line, or if it starts with an upper- or lowercase letter). Metacharacters will lose their special meaning if preceded with a backslash. For example, the dot metacharacter represents any single character, but when preceded with a backslash is just a dot or period.

If you see a backslash preceding a metacharacter, the backslash turns off the meaning of the metacharacter, but if you see a backslash preceding an alphanumeric character in a regular expression, then the backslash is used to create a metasymbol. A metasymbol provides a simpler form to represent some of regular expression metacharacters. For example, [0-9] represents numbers in the range between 0 and 9, and \d represents the same thing. [0-9] uses the bracketed character class, whereas \d is a metasymbol (see Table 12.6).

The following regular expression contains metacharacters:

```
/^a...c/
```

The first metacharacter is a caret (^). The caret metacharacter matches for a string only if it is at the beginning of the line. The period (.) is used to match for any single character, including a space. This expression contains three periods, representing any three characters. To find a literal period or any other character that does not represent itself, the character must be preceded by a backslash to prevent interpretation.

The expression reads: Search at the beginning of the line for a letter a, followed by any three single characters, followed by a letter c. It will match, for example, abbbc, a123c, a   c, aAx3c, and so on, only if those patterns were found at the beginning of the line.

Table 12.6　Metacharacters

Character Class	What It Matches	Metacharacter
Single characters and digits (for more, see "Matching Single Characters and Digits" on page 524)	Matches any character except a newline.	.
	Matches any single character in a set.	[a-z0-9]
	Matches any single character not in a set.	[^a-z0-9]
Single characters and digits —Metasymbols (for more, see "Metasymbols" on page 530)	Matches one digit.	\d
	Matches a nondigit, same as [^0-9].	\D
	Matches an alphanumeric (word) character.	\w
	Matches a nonalphanumeric (nonword) character.	\W
Whitespace characters	Matches whitespace character, spaces, tabs, and newlines.	\s
	Matches a nonwhitespace character.	\S
	Matches a newline.	\n
	Matches a return.	\r
	Matches a tab.	\t
	Matches a form feed.	\f
	Matches a null character	\0

Table 12.6 Metacharacters (continued)

Character Class	What It Matches	Metacharacter
Anchored characters (for more see "Anchoring Metacharacters" on page 520)	Matches a word boundary.	\b
	Matches a nonword boundary.	\B
	Matches to beginning of line.	^
	Matches to end of line.	$
	Matches the beginning of the string only.	\A
	Matches the end of the string or line.	\D
Repeated characters (for more, see "Metacharacters to Repeat Pattern Matches" on page 533)	Matches 0 or 1 occurrences of the letter x.	x?
	Matches 0 or more occurrences of the letter x.	x*
	Matches 1 or more occurrences of the letter x.	x+
Grouped characters (for more, see "Grouping or Clustering." on page 544)	Matches one or more patterns of xyz (e.g., xyxxyzxyz).	(xyz)+
	Matches at least m occurrences of the letter x, and no more than n occurrences of the letter x.	x{m,n}
Alternative characters (for more, see "Metacharacters for Alternation" on page 513)	Matches one of was, were, or will.	was|were|will
Remembered characters (for more, see "Remembering or Capturing" on page 545)	Used for backreferencing.	(string)
	Matches first set of parentheses.	\1 or $1
	Matches second set of parentheses.	\2 or $2
	Matches third set of parentheses.	\3 or $3
Positive lookahead and lookbehind (for more, see "Positive Lookahead" on page 550 and "Positive Lookbehind" on page 552	Matches x but does not remember the match. These are called noncapturing parentheses.	(?:x)
	Matches x only if x is followed by y. For example, /Jack(?=Sprat)/ matches Jack only if it is followed by Sprat. /Jack(?=Sprat|Frost)/ matches Jack only if it is followed by Sprat or Frost. Neither Sprat nor Frost is kept as part of what was matched.	x(?=y)
	Matches x only if x is not followed by y. For example, /\d+(?!\.)/ matches one or more numbers only if they are not followed by a decimal point.	x(?!y)

In the following examples, we perform pattern matches, searches, and replacements based on the data from a text file called data.txt. In the PHP program, the file will be opened and, within a while loop, each line will be read. The functions discussed in the previous section will be used to find patterns within each line of the file. The regular expressions will contain metacharacters, described in Table 12.6.

Anchoring Metacharacters.   Often it is necessary to find a pattern only if it is found at the beginning or end of a line, word, or string. The "anchoring" metacharacters (see Table 12.7) are based on a position just to the left or to the right of the character that is being matched. Anchors are technically called zero-width assertions because they correspond to positions, not actual characters in a string; for example, /^abc/ means find abc at the beginning of the line, where the ^ represents a position, not an actual character.

Table 12.7   Anchors (Assertions)

Metacharacter	What It Matches
^	Matches to beginning of line or beginning of string.
$	Matches to end of line or end of string.
\A	Matches the beginning of a string.
\b	Matches a word boundary.
\B	Matches a nonword boundary.
\D	Matches the end of a string.

Beginning-of-Line Anchor

The ^ metacharacter is called the beginning-of-line anchor. It is the first character in the regular expression and matches a pattern found at the beginning of a line or string.

EXAMPLE 12.14

```
(The file data.txt Contents)
Mama Bear 702
Steve Blenheim 100
Betty Boop 200
Igor Chevsky 300
Norma Cord 400
Jon DeLoach 500
Karen Evich 600
BB Kingson 803
---------------------------------------------------------------
(The PHP Program)
    <?php
1       $fh=fopen("data.txt", "r");
2       while( ! feof($fh)){
3           $text = fgets($fh);
4           if (preg_match("/^B/", $text)){
5               echo "$text";
            }
        }
    ?>
---------------------------------------------------------------
(Output)
Betty Boop 200
BB Kingson 803
```

EXPLANATION

1 The file data.txt is opened for reading.
2 As long as the end of file has not been reached, the while loop will continue to execute.
3 For each iteration of the loop, the fgets() function reads in a line of text.
4 The preg_match() function will return TRUE if a pattern consisting of a string beginning with a B is matched.
5 The lines that matched are printed.

End-of-Line Anchor

The end-of-line anchor, a dollar sign, is used to indicate the ending position in a line. The dollar sign must be the last character in the pattern, just before the closing forward slash delimiter of the regular expression, or it no longer means "end-of-line anchor."[1]

EXAMPLE 12.15

```
(The File data.txt Contents)
Mama Bear 702
Steve Blenheim 100
Betty Boop 200
Igor Chevsky 300
Norma Cord 400
Jon DeLoach 500
Karen Evich 600
BB Kingson 803
--------------------------------------------------------------
(The PHP Program)
    <?php
1        $fh=fopen("data.txt", "r");
2        while( ! feof($fh)){
3            $text = fgets($fh);
4            if (preg_match("/0$/", $text)){
5                echo "$text";
            }
        }
    ?>
--------------------------------------------------------------
(Output)
Steve Blenheim 100
Betty Boop 200
Igor Chevsky 300
Norma Cord 400
Jon DeLoach 500
Karen Evich 600
```

EXPLANATION

1 The file `data.txt` is opened for reading.
2 As long as the end of file hasn't been reached, the `while` loop will continue to execute.
3 For each iteration of the loop, the `fgets()` function reads in a line of text.
4 The `preg_match()` function will return TRUE if a pattern consisting of a line ending with a `0` is matched. The `$` metacharacter indicates that 0 must be followed by a newline.
5 The lines that matched are printed.

---

1. If moving files between Windows and UNIX, the end-of-line anchor might not work. You can use programs such as dos2unix to address this problem.

Word Boundaries

A word boundary is represented in a regular expression by the metasymbol \b. You can search for the word that begins with a pattern, ends with a pattern, or both begins and ends with a pattern; for example, /\blove/ matches a word beginning with the pattern love, and would match lover, loveable, or lovely, but would not find glove. /love\b/ matches a word ending with the pattern love, and would match glove, clove, or love, but not clover. /\blove\b matches a word beginning and ending with the pattern love, and would match only the word love.

EXAMPLE 12.16

```
(The File data.txt Contents)
Mama Bear 702
Steve Blenheim 100
Betty Boop 200
Igor Chevsky 300
Norma Cord 400
Jon DeLoach 500
Karen Evich 600
BB Kingson 803
------------------    -------------------------------------
(The PHP Script)
    <?php
        $fh=fopen("data.txt", "r");
        while( ! feof($fh)){
            $text = fgets($fh);
1           if (preg_match("/\bbear\b/i", $text)){
2               echo "$text";
            }
        }
    ?>
-------------------------------------------------------------
(The Output)
Mama Bear 702
```

EXPLANATION

1   The preg_match() function will return TRUE if a pattern consisting of the word bear is matched, and it is insensitive to case. Because the regular expression is anchored on both ends of the word with the word boundary metasymbol, \b, only bear is matched in $test, not "unbearable," "beard," or "bears."

2   The lines that matched are printed.

Matching Single Characters and Digits.   There are metacharacters to match single characters or digits, and single noncharacters or nondigits, whether in or not in a set.

The Dot Metacharacter

The dot metacharacter matches for any single character with exception to the newline character. For example, the regular expression /a.b/ is matched if the string contains a letter a, followed by any one single character (except the \n), followed by a letter b, whereas the expression /.../ matches any string containing at least three characters. To match on a literal period, the dot metacharacter must be preceded by a backslash; for example, /love\./ matches on love. not lover.

EXAMPLE 12.17

```
(The File data.txt Contents)
Mama Bear 702
Steve Blenheim 100
Betty Boop 200
Igor Chevsky 300
Norma Cord 400
Jon DeLoach 500
Karen Evich 600
BB Kingson 803
-----------------------------------------------------------------
(The PHP Program)
    <?php
1       $fh=fopen("data.txt", "r");
2       while( ! feof($fh)){
3           $text = fgets($fh);
4           if( preg_match("/^... /", $text )){
                echo "$text";
            }
        }
    ?>
-----------------------------------------------------------------
(Output)
Jon DeLoach 500
```

EXPLANATION

1   The file data.txt is opened for reading.
2   As long as the end of file has not been reached, the while loop will continue to execute.
3   For each iteration of the loop, the fgets() function reads in a line of text.
4   The regular expression /^... / contains the dot metacharacter. The regular expression means: go to the beginning (^) of the line and find any three characters, followed by a space. (The dot metacharacter does not match the newline character.) The only line that matched the pattern starts with Jon. It begins with three characters followed by a space.

EXAMPLE 12.18

```
(The File data.txt Contents)
Mama Bear 702
Steve Blenheim 100
Betty Boop 200
Igor Chevsky 300
Norma Cord 400
Jon DeLoach 500
Karen Evich 600
BB Kingson 803
------------------------------------------------------------------
(The PHP Program)
    <?php
1       $fh=fopen("data.txt", "r");
2       while( ! feof($fh)){
            $text = fgets($fh);
3           $newtext=preg_replace("/J../", "Daniel", $text);
            echo "$newtext";
        }
    ?>
- ----------------------------------------------------------------
(Output)
Mama Bear 702
Steve Blenheim 100
Betty Boop 200
Igor Chevsky 300
Norma Cord 400
Daniel DeLoach 500
Karen Evich 600
BB Kingson 803
```

EXPLANATION

1   The text file `data.txt` is opened for reading.
2   Until the end of the file is reached, the `while` loop will continue looping, reading
    in one line at a time from the file.
3   The first argument to the `preg_replace()` function is a regular expression con-
    taining the dot metacharacter. If the regular expression (a capital J followed by at
    least two characters) is matched in `$text`, the found pattern will be replaced with
    `Daniel`.

The Character Class

A character class represents one character from a set of characters. For example, `[abc]`
matches either an a, b, or c; `[a-z]` matches one character from a set of characters in the
range from a to z; and `[0-9]` matches one character in the range of digits between 0 to
9. If the character class contains a leading caret ^, then the class represents any one character not in the set; for example, `[^a-zA-Z]` matches a single character not in the range
from a to z or A to Z, and `[^0-9]` matches a single digit not in the range between 0 and
9 (see Table 12.8).

PHP provides additional metasymbols to represent a character class. The symbols \d and \D represent a single digit and a single nondigit, respectively (the same as [0-9] and [^0-9]); \w and \W represent a single word character and a single nonword character, respectively (the same as [A-Za-z_0-9] and [^A-Za-z_0-9]).

If you are searching for a particular character within a regular expression, you can use the dot metacharacter to represent a single character, or a character class that matches on one character from a set of characters. In addition to the dot and character class, PHP supports some backslashed symbols (called metasymbols) to represent single characters.

Table 12.8 Character Classes

Metacharacter	What It Matches
[abc]	Matches an a or b or c.
[a-z0-9_]	Matches any single character in a set.
[^a-z0-9_]	Matches any single character not in a set.

Matching One Character from a Set

A regular expression character class represents one character out of a set of characters, as shown in Example 12.19.

EXAMPLE 12.19

```
(The File data.txt Contents)
Mama Bear 702
Steve Blenheim 100
Betty Boop 200
Igor Chevsky 300
Norma Cord 400
Jon DeLoach 500
Karen Evich 600
BB Kingson 803
-----------------------------------------------------------------
(The PHP Program)
    <?php
1       $fh=fopen("data.txt", "r");
2       while( ! feof($fh)){
3           $text = fgets($fh);
4           if(preg_match("/^[BKI]/",$text)){
5               echo "$text";
            }
        }
    ?>
-----------------------------------------------------------------
(Output)
Betty Boop 200
Igor Chevsky 300
Karen Evich 600
BB Kingson 803
```

1 The file `data.txt` is opened for reading.
2 As long as the end of file has not been reached, the `while` loop will continue to execute.
3 For each iteration of the loop, the `fgets()` function reads in a line of text.
4 The regular expression `/^[BKI]/` contains a character class matching a string that contains a single uppercase character from the set `[BKI]` meaning: a B or K or I. The `preg_match()` function will return TRUE if the pattern is matched.
5 These lines begin with one of the three characters B or K or I.

Matching One Character in a Range

A character class can also be represented as a range of characters by placing a dash between two characters, the first being the start of the range and the second the end of the range; for example, `[0-9]` represents one character in the range between 0 and 9 and `[A-Za-z0-9]` represents one alphanumeric character. If you want to represent a range between 10 and 13, the regular expression would be `/1[0-3]/`, not `/[10-13]/` because only one character can be matched in a character class.

```
(The File data.txt Contents)
Mama Bear 702
Steve Blenheim 100
Betty Boop 200
Igor Chevsky 300
Norma Cord 400
Jon DeLoach 500
Karen Evich 600
BB Kingson 803
------------------------------------------------------------
(The PHP Program)
    <?php
1       $fh=fopen("data.txt", "r");
2       while( ! feof($fh)){
3           $text = fgets($fh);
4           if(preg_match("/[E-M]/",$text)){
5               echo "$text";
            }
        }
    ?>
------------------------------------------------------------
(Output)
Mama Bear 702
Igor Chevsky 300
Jon DeLoach 500
Karen Evich 600
BB Kingson 803
```

EXPLANATION

1   The file `data.txt` is opened for reading.
2   As long as the end of file has not been reached, the `while` loop will continue to execute.
3   For each iteration of the loop, the `fgets()` function reads in a line of text.
4   The regular expression `/[E-M]/` contains a character class matching a string that contains a single character from the range of characters between `E` and `M`. The `preg_match()` function will return TRUE if the pattern is matched.
5   Each of these lines contain an uppercase letter in the range between `E` and `M`.

EXAMPLE 12.21

```
(The File data.txt Contents)
Mama Bear 702
Steve Blenheim 100
Betty Boop 200
Igor Chevsky 300
Norma Cord 400
Jon DeLoach 500
Karen Evich 600
BB Kingson 803
------------------------------------------------------------
(The PHP Program)
    <?php
1       $fh=fopen("data.txt", "r");
2       while( ! feof($fh)){
            $text = fgets($fh);
3           if(preg_match("/[a-z] [0-5]/",$text)){
                echo "$text";
            }
        }
    ?>
------------------------------------------------------------
(Output)
Steve Blenheim 100
Betty Boop 200
Igor Chevsky 300
Norma Cord 400
Jon DeLoach 500
```

EXPLANATION

1   The text file `data.txt` is opened for reading.
2   Until the end of the file is reached, the `while` loop will continue looping, reading in one line at a time from the file.
3   The first argument to the `preg_match()` function is a regular expression containing character classes using a range, `[a-z]` and `[0-9]`. The function will return TRUE if the pattern is matched in `$text`; that is, one lowercase letter in the range from `a` to `z`, a space, and a digit between `0` and `9`.

Matching One Character Not in a Set

When a character set contains a caret right after the opening square bracket, then the search is inversed; that is, the regular expression represents one character not in the set or in the range. For example, [^a-z] represents one character that is not in the range between a and z.

EXAMPLE 12.22

```
(The File data.txt Contents)
Mama Bear 702
Steve Blenheim 100
Betty Boop 200
Igor Chevsky 300
Norma Cord 400
Jon DeLoach 500
Karen Evich 600
BB Kingson 803
```

```
(The PHP Program)
    <?php
1       $fh=fopen("data.txt", "r");
2       while( ! feof($fh)){
            $text = fgets($fh);
3           if(preg_match("/^[^BKI]/",$text)){
                echo "$text";
            }
        }
    ?>
```

```
(Output)
Mama Bear 702
Steve Blenheim 100
Norma Cord 400
Jon DeLoach 500
```

EXPLANATION

1   The text file data.txt is opened for reading.
2   Until the end of the file is reached, the while loop will continue looping, reading in one line at a time from the file.
3   The first argument to the preg_match() function is a regular expression containing character classes using a range, [^BKI]]. The function will return TRUE if the pattern is matched in $text; that is, the line begins with one character that is not a B or K or I. The ^ means "not" when enclosed in square brackets as part of a character set.

Metasymbols.   Metasymbols offer an alternative way to represent a character class or whitespace characters (see Table 12.9). For example, instead of representing a number as [0-9], it can be represented as \d, and the alternative for representing a nonnumber [^0-9] is \D. Metasymbols are easier to use and and to type.

Table 12.9   Metasymbols

Symbol	What It Matches	Character Class
\d	One digit	[0-9]
\D	One nondigit	[^0-9]
\w	One word character	[A-Za-z0-9_]
\W	One nonword character	[^A-Za-z0-9]
\s	One whitespace character (tab, space, newline, carriage return, form feed, vertical tab)	
\S	One nonspace character	

Metasymbols Representing Digits and Spaces

The character class [0-9] represents one digit in the range between 0 and 9, as does the metasymbol \d. To create a regular expression that matches on three digits, you could write /[0-9][0-9][0-9]/ or simply /\d\d\d/. To represent a space, you can either insert a blank space, or use the metasymbol \s.

EXAMPLE 12.23

```
(The File data.txt Contents)
Mama Bear 702
Steve Blenheim 100
Betty Boop 200
Igor Chevsky 300
Norma Cord 400
Jon DeLoach 500
Karen Evich 600
BB Kingson 803
-----------------------------------------------------------------
(The PHP Program)
    <?php
1       $fh=fopen("data.txt", "r");
        while( ! feof($fh)){
2           $text = fgets($fh);
3           if(preg_match("/h\s\d\d\d/",$text)){
                echo "$text";
            }
        }
    ?>
```

EXAMPLE 12.23 (CONTINUED)

```
------------------------------------------------------------------
(Output)
Jon DeLoach 500
Karen Evich 600
```

EXPLANATION

1 The text file `data.txt` is opened for reading.
2 Until the end of the file is reached, the `while` loop will continue looping, reading in one line at a time from the file.
3 The first argument to the `preg_match()` function is a regular expression containing the metasymbol `\s` representing a space, and `\d` representing a digit. The function will return TRUE if the pattern is matched in `$text`; that is, the line contains an `h`, followed by a space, and three digits.

Metasymbols Representing Alphanumeric Word Characters

The metasymbol to represent one alphanumeric word character is `\w`, much easier to write than `[a-zA-Z0-9_]`. To represent not one alphanumeric character, you simply capitalize the metasymbol, `\W`, which is the same as `[^a-zA-Z0-9_]`.

EXAMPLE 12.24

```
(The File data.txt Contents)
Mama Bear 702
Steve Blenheim 100
Betty Boop 200
Igor Chevsky 300
Norma Cord 400
Jon DeLoach 500
Karen Evich 600
BB Kingson 803
------------------------------------------------------------------
(The PHP Program)
    <?php
1       $fh=fopen("data.txt", "r");
2       while( ! feof($fh)){
            $text = fgets($fh);
3           if(preg_match("/^\w\w\w\W/",$text)){
                echo "$text";
            }
        }
    ?>
------------------------------------------------------------------
(Output)
Jon DeLoach 500
```

EXPLANATION

1   The text file `data.txt` is opened for reading.

2   Until the end of the file is reached, the `while` loop will continue looping, reading in one line at a time from the file.

3   The first argument to the `preg_match()` function is a regular expression containing three alphanumeric word characters, `\w\w\w`. The `\w` represents the character class `[A-Za-z0-9_]`. The metasymbol `\W` represents the character class `[^A-Za-z0-9_]`. The function will return TRUE if the pattern is matched in `$text`; that is, the line begins with three alphanumeric word characters, followed by a character that is not an alphanumeric character.

EXAMPLE 12.25

```
(The File data.txt Contents)
Mama Bear 702
Steve Blenheim 100
Betty Boop 200
Igor Chevsky 300
Norma Cord 400
Jon DeLoach 500
Karen Evich 600
BB Kingson 803
----------------------------------------------------------------------
(The PHP Program)
    <?php
1       $fh=fopen("data.txt", "r");
2       while( ! feof($fh)){
            $text = fgets($fh);
3           $newtext=preg_replace("/\W\D/","XX",$text);
            echo "$newtext";
        }
    ?>

----------------------------------------------------------------------
(Output)
MamaXXear 702
SteveXXlenheim 100
BettyXXoop 200
IgorXXhevsky 300
NormaXXord 400
JonXXeLoach 500
KarenXXvich 600
BBXXingson 803
```

EXPLANATION

1 The text file `data.txt` is opened for reading.
2 Until the end of the file is reached, the `while` loop will continue looping, reading in one line at a time from the file.
3 The first argument to the `preg_replace()` function is the search value, a regular expression containing one nonalphanumeric `\W` (same as `[^A-Za-z0-9_]`) and one nondigit `\D` (same as `[^0-9_]`). The second argument `XX` is the replacement value. The function will replace `$text` with `XX` if the regular expression is matched.

Metacharacters to Repeat Pattern Matches. In the previous examples, the metacharacter matched on a single character. What if you want to match on more than one character? For example, let's say you are looking for all lines containing names and the first letter must be in uppercase, which can be represented as `[A-Z]`, but the following letters are lowercase and the number of letters varies in each name. `[a-z]` matches on a single lowercase letter. How can you match on one or more lowercase letters? Zero or more lowercase letters? To do this you can use what are called *quantifiers*. To match on one or more lowercase letters, the regular expression can be written: `/[a-z]+/` where the + sign means "one or more of the previous characters," in this case, one or more lowercase letters. PHP provides a number of quantifiers as shown in Table 12.10.

Table 12.10 The Greedy Metacharacters

Metacharacter	What It Matches
x?	Matches 0 or 1 occurrences of the letter x.
(xyz)?	Matches 0 or 1 pattern of xyz.
x*	Matches 0 or more occurrences of the letter x.
(xyz)*	Matches 0 or more patterns of xyz.
x+	Matches 1 or more occurrences of the letter x.
(xyz)+	Matches one or more patterns of xyz.
x{m}	Matches exactly m occurrences of the letter x.
x{m,n}	Matches at least m occurrences of the letter x and no more than n occurrences of the letter x.
x{m,}	Matches m or more occurrences of the letter x.

The Greed Factor

Normally quantifiers are greedy; that is, they match on the largest possible set of characters starting at the left side of the string and searching to the right, looking for the last possible character that would satisfy the condition. For example, given the string:

```
var string="ab1234567834455554437AB"
```

and the regular expression:

/ab[0-9]*/

if the `preg_replace()` function were to substitute what is matched with an `"X"`:

```
$new_string=preg_replace(/ab[0-9]/*, "X", "ab12345678445554437AB");
```

the resulting string would be:

```
"XAB"
```

The asterisk is a greedy metacharacter. It matches for zero or more of the preceding characters. In other words, it attaches itself to the character preceding it; in the preceding example, the asterisk attaches itself to the character class `[0-9]`. The matching starts on the left, searching for `ab` followed by zero or more numbers in the range between 0 and 9. It is called greedy because the matching continues until the last number is found, in this example the number `7`. The pattern `ab` and all of the numbers in the range between 0 and 9 are replaced with a single `X`.

Greediness can be turned off so that instead of matching on the maximum number of characters, the match is made on the minimal number of characters found. This is done by appending a question mark after the greedy metacharacter. See Example 12.26.

EXAMPLE   12.26

```
(The File data.txt Contents)
Mama Bear 702
Steve Blenheim 100
Betty Boop 200
Igor Chevsky 300
Norma Cord 400
Jon DeLoach 500
Karen Evich 600
BB Kingson 803
-------------------------------------------------------------------
(The PHP Program)
      <?php
1        $fh=fopen("data.txt", "r");
2        while( ! feof($fh)){
            $text = fgets($fh);
3           if(preg_match("/e\s?[A-Z]/",$text)){
                echo "$text";
            }
        }
      ?>
-------------------------------------------------------------------
(Output)
Steve Blenheim 100
Jon dELoach 500
```

EXPLANATION

1   The text file data.txt is opened for reading.
2   Until the end of the file is reached, the while loop will continue looping, reading in one line at a time from the file.
3   The first argument to the preg_match() function is a regular expression containing a greedy metacharacter. The function will return TRUE if the pattern is matched in $text; that is, a letter e followed by either a space or no space at all, and an uppercase letter. The question mark means "zero or one of the preceding character." Note that the letter e in DeLoach is not followed by a space (zero or more spaces).

The * Metacharacter and Greed

The * metacharacter is often misunderstood as being a wildcard to match on everything, but it only matches the character that precedes it. In the regular expression, /ab*c/, the asterisk is attached to the b, meaning that zero or more occurrences of the letter b will be matched. The strings abc, abbbbbbbc, and ac would all be matched.

EXAMPLE 12.27

```
(The File data.txt Contents)
Mama Bear 702
Steve Blenheim 100
Betty Boop 200
Igor Chevsky 300
Norma Cord 400
Jon DeLoach 500
Karen Evich 600
BB Kingson 803
-----------------------------------------------------------------
(The PHP Program)
    <?php
1       $fh=fopen("data.txt", "r");
2       while( ! feof($fh)){
            $text = fgets($fh);
3           if(preg_match("/B[a-z]*/",$text)){
                echo "$text";
            }
        }
    ?>
-----------------------------------------------------------------
(Output)
Mama Bear 702
Steve Blenheim 100
Betty Boop 200
BB Kingson 803
```

EXPLANATION

1   The text file *data.txt* is opened for reading.
2   Until the end of the file is reached, the while loop will continue looping, reading in one line at a time from the file.
3   The first argument to the preg_match() function is a regular expression containing a greedy metacharacter. The function will return TRUE if the pattern is matched in $text: that is, a pattern that begins with an uppercase B, followed by zero or more lowercase letters. The only character required to make a match is the first B. The starred character class represents zero or more letters ranging from a to z, which means there might not be any at all, as shown in BB Kingson.

EXAMPLE 12.28

```
(The File data.txt Contents)
Mama Bear 702
Steve Blenheim 100
Betty Boop 200
Igor Chevsky 300
Norma Cord 400
Jon DeLoach 500
Karen Evich 600
BB Kingson 803
-----------------------------------------------------------------
(The PHP Script)
     <?php
1        $fh=fopen("data.txt", "r");
2        while( ! feof($fh)){
             $text = fgets($fh);
3            if(preg_match("/^[A-Z][a-z]*\s[A-Z][a-z]*\s/",$text)){
                 echo "$text";
             }
         }
     ?>
-----------------------------------------------------------------
(Output)
Mama Bear 702
Steve Blenheim 100
Betty Boop 200
Igor Chevsky 300
Norma Cord 400
Karen Evich 600
```

EXPLANATION

1   The text file data.txt is opened for reading.
2   Until the end of the file is reached, the while loop will continue looping, reading in one line at a time from the file.
3   The first argument to the preg_match() function is a regular expression containing a greedy metacharacter. The function will return TRUE if the pattern is matched in $text: that is, a pattern that begins with an uppercase letter, followed by zero or more lowercase letters, a space, another uppercase letter, followed by zero or more lowercase letters (only lowercase), and a space. Because the last name DeLoach contains an uppercase letter D, followed by both upper- and lowercase letters, this line is not a match. The first name in BB Kingson is not a match because the first letter is not followed by a lowercase letter or a space.

EXAMPLE 12.29

```
(The File data.txt Contents)
Mama Bear 702
Steve Blenheim 100
Betty Boop 200
Igor Chevsky 300
Norma Cord 400
Jon DeLoach 500
Karen Evich 600
BB Kingson 803
------------------------------------------------------------------
(The PHP Script)
    <?php
1       $fh=fopen("data.txt", "r");
2       while( ! feof($fh)){
            $text = fgets($fh);
3           if(preg_match("/^[A-Z][a-z]*\s[A-Z][a-zA-Z]*\s/",$text)){
                echo "$text";
            }
        }
    ?>
------------------------------------------------------------------
(Output)
Mama Bear 702
Steve Blenheim 100
Betty Boop 200
Igor Chevsky 300
Norma Cord 400
Jon DeLoach 500
Karen Evich 600
```

EXPLANATION

1 The text file data.txt is opened for reading.
2 Until the end of the file is reached, the while loop will continue looping, reading in one line at a time from the file.
3 The first argument to the preg_match() function is a regular expression containing a greedy metacharacter. The function will return TRUE if the pattern is matched in $text: that is, a pattern that begins with an uppercase letter, followed by zero or more lowercase letters, a space, another uppercase letter, followed by zero or more upper- and lowercase letters. In the previous example, DeLoach did not match because the last name contained a mix of upper- and lowercase letters. That problem was addressed in this example, by including [a-zA-Z] in the expression, McDougal or MacDonald would also match, but what about O'Reilley?

The + Metacharacter and Greed

The + metacharacter attaches itself to the preceding character and matches on one or more of that character.

EXAMPLE 12.30

```
(The File data.txt Contents)
Mama Bear 702
Steve Blenheim 100
Betty Boop 200
Igor Chevsky 300
Norma Cord 400
Jon DeLoach 500
Karen Evich 600
BB Kingson 803
------------------------------------------------------------------
(The PHP Script)
    <?php
1       $fh=fopen("data.txt", "r");
2       while( ! feof($fh)){
            $text = fgets($fh);
3           if(preg_match("/B[a-z]+/", $text)){
                echo "$text";
            }
        }
    ?>
------------------------------------------------------------------
(Output)
Mama **Bear** 702
Steve **Blenheim** 100
**Betty** Boop 200
```

EXPLANATION

1   The text file data.txt is opened for reading.
2   Until the end of the file is reached, the while loop will continue looping, reading in one line at a time from the file.
3   The first argument to the preg_match() function is a regular expression containing a greedy metacharacter, the + sign. The function will return TRUE if the pattern is matched in $text; that is, a pattern consisting of an uppercase B, followed by one or more lowercase letters, [a-z]+.

Matching for Repeating Characters

To match for a character that is repeated a number of times, the character is followed by a set of curly braces containing a number to represent how many times the pattern should be repeated (see Table 12.11). A single number within the curly braces (e.g., {5}), represents an exact amount of occurrences; two numbers separated by a comma (e.g., {3,10}), represents an inclusive range; and a number followed by a comma (e.g., {4,}), represents a number of characters and any amount after that.

Table 12.11   Repeating Characters

Metacharacter	What It Does
a{10}	Matches exactly 10 occurrences of the letter a.
a{3,5}	Matches between 3 and 5 occurrences of the letter a.
a{6,}	Matches 6 or more occurrences of the letter a.

EXAMPLE 12.31

```
(The File data.txt Contents)
Mama Bear 702
Steve Blenheim 100
Betty Boop 200
Igor Chevsky 300
Norma Cord 400
Jon DeLoach 500
Karen Evich 600
BB Kingson 803
------------------------------------------------------------
(The PHP Script)
    <?php
1       $fh=fopen("data.txt", "r");
2       while( ! feof($fh)){
            $text = fgets($fh);
3           if(preg_match("/\s\d{3}$/",$text)){
                echo "$text";
            }
        }
    ?>
------------------------------------------------------------
(Output)
Mama Bear 702
Steve Blenheim 100
Betty Boop 200
Igor Chevsky 300
Norma Cord 400
Jon DeLoach 500
Karen Evich 600
BB Kingson 803
```

EXPLANATION

1 The text file `data.txt` is opened for reading.
2 Until the end of the file is reached, the `while` loop will continue looping, reading in one line at a time from the file.
3 The regular expression contains the curly brace `{}` metacharacters, representing the number of times the preceeding expression will be repeated. The expression matches for a space, followed by exactly 3 repeating digits, anchored at the end of the line (`$`).

Metacharacters That Turn Off Greediness

By placing a question mark after a greedy quantifier, the greed is turned off and the search ends after the first match, rather than the last one.

EXAMPLE 12.32

```
(The File data.txt Contents)
Mama Bear 702
Steve Blenheim 100
Betty Boop 200
Igor Chevsky 300
Norma Cord 400
Jon DeLoach 500
Karen Evich 600
BB Kingson 803
----------------------------------------------------------
(The PHP Script)
    <?php
1       $fh=fopen("data.txt", "r");
2       while( ! feof($fh)){
            $text = fgets($fh);
3           $newtext=preg_replace("/B.* /","John ",$text);
            echo "$newtext";
        }
        echo "--------------------\n";
4       rewind($fh);
5       while( ! feof($fh)){
            $text = fgets($fh);
6           $newtext=preg_replace("/B.*? /","John ",$text);
            echo "$newtext";
        }
    ?>
----------------------------------------------------------
```

EXAMPLE 12.32 (CONTINUED)

```
(Output)
        ---------------------Greed turned on
        Mama John 702
        Steve John 100
        John 200
        Igor Chevsky 300
        Norma Cord 400
        Jon DeLoach 500
        Karen Evich 600
        John 803
        --------------------Greed turned off
        Mama John 702
        Steve John 100
        John John 200
        Igor Chevsky 300
        Norma Cord 400
        Jon DeLoach 500
        Karen Evich 600
        John Kingson 803
```

EXPLANATION

1   The text file `data.txt` is opened for reading.
2   Until the end of the file is reached, the `while` loop will continue looping, reading in one line at a time from the file.
3   The regular expression contains a `B.*`. The `.*` means zero or more of any character. When a `B` is matched, it and all characters after it until the last space will be consumed and replaced with "John ". The `Bear` in the line `Mama Bear` will be replaced with `John`; `Blenheim` in the line `Steve Blenheim` is replaced with "`John` "; and `Betty Boop` is also replaced with "`John` ".
4   The `rewind()` function moves the file pointer back to the beginning of the file (`$fh`), so that we can loop through it again.
5   The `while` loop starts looping through the file, a line at a time until the end of the file is reached.
6   By placing a `?` after the `.*`, the greed factor of the asterisk is turned off; that is, find a `B`, followed by zero or more characters up until the first space and replace it with "`John` ".

Metacharacters for Alternation.   Alternation allows the regular expression to contain alternative patterns to be matched; for example, the regular expression /John|Karen|Steve/ will match a line containing John or Karen or Steve. If Karen, John, or Steve are all on different lines, all lines are matched. Each of the alternative expressions is separated by a vertical bar (pipe symbol) and the expressions can consist of any number of characters, unlike the character class that only matches for one character; that is, /a|b|c/ is the same as [abc], whereas /ab|de/ cannot be represented as [abde]. The pattern /ab|de/ is either ab or de, whereas the class [abcd] represents only one character in the set, a, b, c, or d.

EXAMPLE   12.33

```
(The File data.txt Contents)
Mama Bear 702
Steve Blenheim 100
Betty Boop 200
Igor Chevsky 300
Norma Cord 400
Jon DeLoach 500
Karen Evich 600
BB Kingson 803
---------------------------------------------------------------
(The PHP Script)
    <?php
1       $fh=fopen("data.txt", "r");
2       while( ! feof($fh)){
           $text = fgets($fh);
3          if(preg_match("/Steve|Betty|Jon/",$text)){
              echo "$text";
           }
        }
    ?>
---------------------------------------------------------------
(Output)
Steve Blenheim 100
Betty Boop 200
Jon DeLoach 500
```

EXPLANATION

1   The file data.txt is opened for reading.
2   As long as the end of file has not been reached, the while loop will continue to execute.
3   The pipe symbol, |, is used in the regular expression to match on a set of alternative string patterns. If any of the strings, Steve, Betty, or Jon, are found, the match is successful. The preg_match function will return true if the pattern contains either Steve, Betty, or Jon.

Grouping or Clustering.   If the regular expression pattern is enclosed in parentheses, a subpattern is created. Then, for example, instead of the greedy metacharacters matching on zero, one, or more of the previous single character, they can match on the previous subpattern. Alternation can also be controlled if the patterns are enclosed in parentheses. This process of grouping characters together is also called *clustering*.

EXAMPLE 12.34

```
(The File data.txt Contents)
Mama Bear 702
Steve Blenheim 100
Betty Boop 200
Igor Chevsky 300
Norma Cord 400
Jon DeLoach 500
Karen Evich 600
BB Kingson 803
------------------------------------------------------------
(The PHP Script)
    <?php
1       $fh=fopen("data.txt", "r");
2       while( ! feof($fh)){
            $text = fgets($fh);
3           if(preg_match("/(Steve|Alexander) Blenheim/",$text)){
                echo "$text";
            }
        }
    ?>
------------------------------------------------------------
(Output)
Steve Blenheim 100
```

EXPLANATION

1   The file data.txt is opened for reading.
2   As long as the end of file has not been reached, the while loop will continue to execute.
3   The regular expression contains the alternation character; the alternative patterns are Steve and Alexander? By enclosing this pattern in parentheses, it is treated as a grouped unit so that the regular expression matches either Steve Blenheim or Alexander Blenheim.

EXAMPLE 12.35

```
(The File data.txt Contents)
Mama Bear 702
Steve Blenheim 100
Betty Boop 200
Igor Chevsky 300
Norma Cord 400
Jon DeLoach 500
Karen Evich 600
BB Kingson 803

--------------------------------------------------------------

(The PHP Script)
    <?php
1       $fh=fopen("data.txt", "r");
2       while( ! feof($fh)){
            $text = fgets($fh);
3           if(preg_match("/(ma)+/",$text)){
                echo "$text";
            }
        }
    ?>

--------------------------------------------------------------

(Output)
Mama Bear 702
Norma Cord 400
```

EXPLANATION

1   The file data.txt is opened for reading.
2   As long as the end of file has not been reached, the while loop will continue to execute.
3   If one or more occurrences of the pattern ma are found, the preg_match() function will return TRUE. The + metacharacter is applied to the group of characters within the parentheses; that is, ma.

Remembering or Capturing.   If the regular expression pattern is enclosed in parentheses, a subpattern is created. The subpattern is found in the third argument to preg_match() as an array of subpatterns. With preg_replace(), parenthesized patterns can be backreferenced by using a backslash and the number of the pattern; for example, the first parenthesized pattern is referenced as \1, the second as \2, the third as \3, up to \9. If enclosed in double quotes, the backreferences are referenced as \\1, \\2, \\3, and so on. Newer versions of PHP use $1, $2, $3, and so on, rather than backslashes without limit on the number of subpatterns captured (see Example 12.37).

EXAMPLE 12.36

```
(The File data.txt Contents)
Mama Bear 702
Steve Blenheim 100
Betty Boop 200
Igor Chevsky 300
Norma Cord 400
Jon DeLoach 500
Karen Evich 600
BB Kingson 803
------------------------------------------------------------------
(The PHP Script)
    <?php
1       $fh=fopen("data.txt", "r");
2       while( ! feof($fh)){
            $text = fgets($fh);
3           if(preg_match("/(Steve)\s(Blenheim)/",$text, $matches)){
                echo "$matches[0]\n";
                echo "$matches[1]\n";
                echo "$matches[2]\n";
            }
        }
    ?>
------------------------------------------------------------------
(Output)
Steve Blenheim
Steve
Blenheim
```

EXPLANATION

1   The file `data.txt` is opened for reading.

2   As long as the end of file has not been reached, the `while` loop will continue to execute.

3   The regular expression contains two subpatterns, `Steve` and `Blenheim` both enclosed in parentheses. These patterns are captured and saved in the third argument to `preg_match()`, an array called `$matches` that contains the whole pattern in `$matches[0]`, the captured pattern, `Steve`, in `$matches[1]`, and the captured pattern, `Blenheim`, in `$matches[2]`.

EXAMPLE 12.37

```
(The File data.txt Contents)
Mama Bear 702
Steve Blenheim 100
Betty Boop 200
Igor Chevsky 300
Norma Cord 400
Jon DeLoach 500
Karen Evich 600
BB Kingson 803
------------------------------------------------------------------
(The PHP Script)
    <?php
1       $fh=fopen("data.txt", "r");
2       while( ! feof($fh)){
            $text = fgets($fh);
3           $new=preg_replace("/(Betty)\s(Boop)/",'$2, $1',$text);
4           echo "$new";
        }
    ?>
------------------------------------------------------------------
(Output)
Mama Bear 702
Steve Blenheim 100
Boop, Betty 200
Igor Chevsky 300
Norma Cord 400
Jon DeLoach 500
Karen Evich 600
BB Kingson 803
```

EXPLANATION

1   The file data.txt is opened for reading.
2   As long as the end of file has not been reached, the while loop will continue to execute.
3   The preg_replace() function will search the target string containing the regular expression with two parenthesized subpatterns. The first one, (Betty), will be captured in $1, the second one, (Boop), will be captured in $2. The second argument is the replacement string and contains the captured subpatterns. It causes the subpatterns to be reversed in the replacement string.
4   The return from pre_replace() contains the new string, $new, after replacement.

Searching, Capturing, and Replacing.   If the search pattern contains parenthesized (captured) strings, those subpatterns can be referenced in the replacement side by either backslashed numbers such as \1, \2, up to \9, or the preferred way since PHP 4.0.4, with $1, $2, up to $99. The number refers to the position where the parenthesized pattern is placed in the search pattern (left to right); for example, the first captured string is referenced in the replacement string as $1, the second as $2, and so on. $0 or \0 refers to the text matched by the entire pattern.

EXAMPLE   12.38

```
(The File data.txt Contents)
Mama Bear 702
Steve Blenheim 100
Betty Boop 200
Igor Chevsky 300
Norma Cord 400
Jon DeLoach 500
Karen Evich 600
BB Kingson 803
```

```
(The PHP Script)
    <?php
1       $fh=fopen("data.txt", "r");
2       while( ! feof($fh)){
            $text = fgets($fh);
3           $new_text=preg_replace("/(\w+)\s(\w+)\s(\w+)/",'$2, $1 $3',
                              $text);
4           echo "$new_text";
        }
    ?>
```

```
(Output)
Bear, Mama 702
Blenheim, Steve 100
Boop, Betty 200
Chevsky, Igor 300
Cord, Norma 400
DeLoach, Jon 500
Evich, Karen 600
Kingson, BB 803
```

EXPLANATION

1   The file data.txt is opened for reading.
2   As long as the end of file has not been reached, the while loop will continue to execute.

EXPLANATION (CONTINUED)

3   The `preg_replace()` function will search the target string containing the regular expression with three parenthesized subpatterns. The first one, (\w+), will be captured in $1, the second one (\w+) will be captured in $2, and everything after the last space will be captured in $3. The second argument is the replacement string and contains the captured subpatterns to be printed in the order in which they are placed.

4   The variable, $new_text, contains the result of the replacement; that is, reversing first and last names, separated by a comma.

EXAMPLE 12.39

```
(The File data.txt Contents)
Mama Bear 702
Steve Blenheim 100
Betty Boop 200
Igor Chevsky 300
Norma Cord 400
Jon DeLoach 500
Karen Evich 600
BB Kingson 803
------------------------------------------------------------------
(The PHP Script)
    <?php
1       $fh=fopen("data.txt", "r");
2       while( ! feof($fh)){
            $text = fgets($fh);
3           list($fname, $lname, $number)=preg_split("/\s+/",$text);
4           $new_number=preg_replace("/(\d{3})$/e",'$1 * 1.1',$number);
5           printf("%.2f\n", $new_number);
        }
    ?>
------------------------------------------------------------------
(Output)
772.20
110.00
220.00
330.00
440.00
550.00
660.00
883.30
```

EXPLANATION

1   The file data.txt is opened for reading.

2   As long as the end of file has not been reached, the while loop continues to execute.

3   The preg_split() function splits up the line by one or more spaces. The list() function creates variables from each of the items returned from the split() function.

4 The `preg_replace()` function will search for any number ending in three digits, capture and save those three digits in `$1`, and replace the number it saved with that number, `$1`, muliplied by `1.1`; that is, increase the number by 10 percent.

5 The `printf()` function formats and prints the number as a floating-point number with precision two places to the right of the decimal point.

Positive Lookahead.   A lookahead is used to help refine a search but is not part of the resulting pattern. The lookahead peeks ahead of a pattern in the regular expression to see if the text in the lookahead is there. The lookahead text is enclosed in parentheses and prepended with `?=`. The text in the lookahead is not captured as in the previous examples, but is only used as criteria for the search. For example, the regular expression `"/Bob (?= Black|Jones)/"` says search for `Bob` and look ahead to see if either `Black` or `Jones` are next, and if so, there is a match. The parentheses will not capture and create `$1`, and the values `Black` and `Jones` will not be altered in a replacement.

EXAMPLE 12.40

```
(The File moredata.txt Contents)
Mama Bear 702
Mama Bird 234
Steve Blenheim 100
Betty Boop 200
Igor Chevsky 300
Norma Cord 400
Jon DeLoach 500
Karen Evich 600
BB Kingson 803
Mama Monkey 900
------------------------------------------------------------------
(The PHP Script)
    <?php
1       $fh=fopen("moredata.txt", "r");
2       while(! feof($fh)){
            $text = fgets($fh);
3           $newstring=preg_replace("/mama (monkey|bird)/i",
                                    "Papa $1",$text) ;
            print $newstring;
        }
4       rewind($fh);
        # Forward lookahead
        print"-------lookahead---------\n";
        while(! feof($fh)){
            $text = fgets($fh);
5           $newstring=preg_replace("/mama (?=monkey|bird)/i",
                                    "Papa ",$text) ;
            print $newstring;
        }
    ?>
```

EXAMPLE 12.40 (CONTINUED)

```
(Output)
Mama Bear 702
Papa Bird 234
Steve Blenheim 100
Betty Boop 200
Igor Chevsky 300
Norma Cord 400
Jon DeLoach 500
Karen Evich 600
BB Kingson 803
Papa Monkey 900


-------lookahead---------
Mama Bear 702
Papa Bird 234
Steve Blenheim 100
Betty Boop 200
Igor Chevsky 300
Norma Cord 400
Jon DeLoach 500
Karen Evich 600
BB Kingson 803
Papa Monkey 900
```

EXPLANATION

1. The file `data.txt` is opened for reading.
2. As long as the end of file has not been reached, the `while` loop will continue to execute.
3. This example does not use a positive lookahead. Instead, it uses capturing. The `preg_replace()` function searches for either `Mama monkey` or `Mama bird`. If either `monkey` or `bird` are found, its value will be captured and placed in `$1`. The original string will be replaced with `Papa Bird` and/or `Papa Monkey`. If `$1` is not used in the replacement string, both `Mama monkey` and `Mama bird` will be replaced with simply `Papa`.
4. The `rewind()` function moves the internal file pointer to the start of the file.
5. The `preg_replace()` function searches for either `Mama monkey` or `Mama bird`, but uses what is called a lookahead, text preceded by `?=` and enclosed in parentheses. Capturing is *not* performed when using lookahead. Notice that the lookahead text is not included in the replacement string. It simply asserts that either `monkey` or `bird` must follow `Mama`, but are not considered part of what will be replaced. `Papa` replaces `Mama`. The rest of the string is left intact.

Positive Lookbehind.   Like a positive lookahead, a positive lookbehind is used to help refine a search but is not part of the resulting pattern. It looks to see if the text in the lookbehind precedes the pattern being searched or replaced. The lookbehind text is enclosed in parentheses and prepended with ?<=. The text is not captured as in the previous examples, but is only used as criteria for the search.

EXAMPLE 12.41

```
(The File moredata.txt Contents)
Mama Bear 702
Mama Bird 234
Steve Blenheim 100
Betty Boop 200
Igor Chevsky 300
Norma Cord 400
Jon DeLoach 500
Karen Evich 600
BB Kingson 803
Mama Monkey 900
-----------------------------------------------------------------
    <?php
1       $fh=fopen("moredata.txt", "r");
2       while(! feof($fh)){
            $text = fgets($fh);
3           $newstring=preg_replace("/(?<=ma )[MC][a-z]+/",
                                    "Goose",$text) ;
            print $newstring;
        }
    ?>
-----------------------------------------------------------------
(Output)
Mama Bear 702
Mama Bird 234
Steve Blenheim 100
Betty Boop 200
Igor Chevsky 300
Norma Goose 400
Jon DeLoach 500
Karen Evich 600
BB Kingson 803
Mama Goose 900
```

EXPLANATION

1   The file data.txt is opened for reading.
2   As long as the end of file has not been reached, the while loop will continue to execute.
3   The lookbehind is (?<=ma). The text in the lookbehind is ma. If that pattern precedes the pattern in the regular expression, "[BM][a-z]+", the string will be replaced by Goose; that is, Ma**ma** **B**ear and Nor**ma** **C**ord will be replaced with Mama Goose and Norma Goose.

Commenting Regular Expressions and the x Modifier. You can add whitespace and comments to a regular expression if you want to clarify how the regular expression is broken down and what each symbol means. This is very helpful in unraveling a long regular expression you might have inherited from another program and are not sure of what is taking place. To do this the closing delimiter is appended with the x modifier.

EXAMPLE 12.42

```
      <?php
1     # /^([A-Z][a-z]+)\s([A-Z][a-zA-Z]+)\s(\d{3})/
2     $regex =
      "/
      ^            # At the beginning of the line
      (            # start a new subpattern $1
      [A-Z]        # Find an uppercase letter
      [A-Za-z]     # find an upper or lowercase letter
      *            # match it zero or more times
      )            # close first subpattern
      \s           # find a whitespace character
      (            # start another subpattern $2
      [A-Z]        # match an uppercase letter
      [a-zA-Z]     # match an upper or lowercase letter
      +            # match for one or more of them
      )            # close the subpattern
      \s           # match a whitespace character
      (            # start subpattern $3
      \d           # match a digit
      {3}          # match it three times
      )            # close the subpattern
      $            # end of line
3     /x";
          $fh=fopen("data.txt", "r");
          while( ! feof($fh)){
              $text = fgets($fh);
              $new_text=preg_replace("$regex",'$2, $1 $3', $text);
              echo "$new_text";
          }
      ?>
```

```
(Output)
Bear, Mama 702
Blenheim, Steve 100
Boop, Betty 200
Chevsky, Igor 300
Cord, Norma 400
DeLoach, Jon 500
Evich, Karen 600
Kingson, BB 803
```

EXPLANATION

1   This is the regular expression that we will examine, from left to right.
2   The variable, $regex, is assigned a commented regular expression where each regular expression metacharacter is described. By breaking down the expression in this way, you can decipher what it is trying to do.
3   The x modifier and the end of the expression allows the regular expression to contain whitespace and comments without affecting the parsing of the regular expression at all.

12.2.4   Searching for Patterns in Text Files

You might be using text files, rather than a database, to store information. You can perform pattern matching with regular expressions to find specific data from a file using the PHP built-in functions such as preg_match(), preg_replace(), and so on. In the following example, a form is provided so that the user can select all names and phone numbers within a particular area code found in a text file.

EXAMPLE 12.43

```
      (The Form)
      <html><head><title>Searching for a Phone from a File</title><head>
      <body bgcolor="silver">
      <font face="verdana" size="+1">
      <form action="patterns.php" method="POST">
      <p>
      Please enter the area code
1     <input type="text" name="area_code" size=5>
      <p>
      <input type="submit">
      <input type="reset">
      </form>
      </body>
      </html>
      ------------------------------------------------------------------
      (The PHP File)
      <html><head><title>Finding Patterns</title></head>
      <body bgcolor="silver">
      <font face=verdana">
      <b>

      <?php
2         $filename="$_SERVER[DOCUMENT_ROOT]/../mydir/datebook";
3         $lines = file($filename);
4         $area_code=trim($_POST['area_code']);
          echo "<H2>Names and Phones in $area_code area code</h2>";
```

EXAMPLE 12.43 (CONTINUED)

```
5       foreach ($lines as $the_line) {
6           $fields=explode(":",$the_line);
            $name=$fields[0];
7           $phone=$fields[1];
            $address=$fields[2];
            $birthday=$fields[3];
            $salary=$fields[4];
8           if( preg_match("/^$area_code-/","$phone")){
9               echo "$name: $phone<br />";
10              $count++;
            }
        }
11      if ($count == 0 ){
            echo "The area code is not found.<br />";
        }

    ?>
    </b>
    </font>
    </body>
    </html>
```

EXPLANATION

1 In this HTML form, the user is asked to enter an area code into the text box, shown in Figure 12.15.

2 This is the path to the text file that will be opened for reading.

3 The PHP built-in `file()` function reads the entire file and assigns it to an array. Each element of the array is a line of the file.

4 The input data coming in from the form via the POST method is assigned to a variable called `$area_code`.

5 The `foreach` loop is used to cycle through the array; that is, each line of the file.

6 Each line is split up into fields where the colon designates the field separator.

7 The variable, `$phone`, contains the phone field that will be used in the search for the area code.

8 The `preg_match()` function searches in the `$phone` variable for the area code that was requested by the user in the form. The regular expression reads: go to the beginning of the `$phone` field, find the area code (value of `$area_code`), followed by a dash. If the requested area code is found, the `preg_match()` function returns true and the block starting on line 9 is entered.

9 The name and phone number are printed, as shown in Figure 12.16.

10 For every successful match, the counter, `$count`, is incremented by 1.

11 If the value of `$count` is 0, no matches were found, and the program outputs the next line.

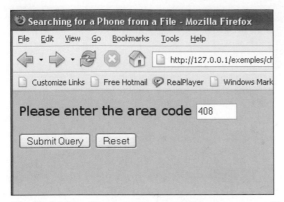

Figure 12.15   The user is searching for a specific area code.

Figure 12.16   The lines that matched the pattern are output. Output from Example 12.43.

12.2.5   Form Validation with PHP

If you are going to use PHP to validate data in a fillout form, you can use regular expressions to create sophisticated patterns for finding e-mail addresses, phone numbers, credit card data, and so on. But rather than create the pattern yourself, there are a number of Web sites that can help you. Table 12.12 provides regular expressions for input data that can be routinely checked and Example 12.44 shows you how to create a form and process the validation using a regular expression.

Table 12.12 Regular Expressions Used for Validating Form Input

Type of Input	Regular Expression[a]
Social Security number	`/^\d{3}-?\d\d-?\d{4}$/`
U.S. phone number	`/^\(?\d{3}\)?-?\s*\d{3}\s*-?\d{4}$/`
Zip code	`/^\d{5}((-|\s)?\d{4})?$/`
E-mail	`/^([0-9a-zA-Z]([-.\w]*[0-9a-zA-Z])*@([0-9a-zA-Z][-\w]*[0-9a-zA-Z]\.)+[a-zA-Z]{2,9})$/`
Credit card number	`/^((4\d{3})|(5[1-5]\d{2})|(6011))-?\d{4}-?\d{4}-?\d{4}|3[4,7]\d{13}$/`
URL	`/^((http|https|ftp).//)?([\w-]+(\.)(\w){2,4}([\w/+=%&_.~?-]*)$/`

a. See *regexlib.com* for authors of these regular expressions and for more variations.

Checking for a Valid E-Mail Address. In the following example, we validate an e-mail address, and once that is done, you can apply any of the regular expressions from Table 12.12 to create similar functions to add to the validation program.

When validating an e-mail address, you are looking for the typical format found in such addresses. There might be some domain names that are more than four characters, but it is not typical. Also, just because the user types what looks like a valid e-mail address, does not mean that it is; for example, the e-mail address *santa@northpole.org* uses a valid syntax, but does not check to see if *santa* is a real user.

E-mail addresses usually have the following format:

- An @ sign between the username and address (*lequig@aol.com*).
- At least one dot between the address and domain name (.com, .mil, .edu, .se).
- At least six characters (a@b.se).[2]

The following are examples of valid e-mail addresses:

username@mailserver.com
username@mailserver.info
username@mailserver.org.se
username.moretext@mailserver.mil
username@mailserver.co.uk
user-name.moretext.sometext.mailserver.se

---

2. As of this writing, domain names have at least two characters.

Breaking down the regular expression:

```
/^[a-zA-Z][\w\.\-]+[a-zA-Z0-9]@([a-zA-Z0-9][a-zA-Z0-9\-]*\.)+[a-zA-Z]{2,4}$/
 ❶    ❷      ❸         ❹      ❺              ❻                    ❼      ❽
```

❶ `^` Go to the beginning of the line.

❷ `[a-zA-Z]` The username must begin with a letter.

❸ `[\w \.\-]+` The username can consist of one or more word characters, dots, spaces, dashes; for example, *Joe.Shome_somebody*.

❹ `[a-zA-Z0-9]` The last character in the user's name must be an alphanumeric character.

❺ `@` A literal @ symbol is required in the e-mail addresses.

❻ `([a-zA-Z0-9][a-zA-Z0-9\-]*\.)+` The mail server's name is like the user's name, a group consisting of a word character, followed by zero or more word characters and a dash, and then a dot. Because the parentheses are followed by a +, the group can be repeated one or more times.

❼ `[a-zA-Z]{2,4}` The domain name follows the mail server's name. The domain name consists of between two and four alphabetic characters; for example, *savageman@IMEFDM.USMC.MIL* or *patricia.person@sweden.sun.com*

❽ `$` This the end-of-line anchor, where the pattern ends.

Example 12.44 uses a regular expression to check for a valid e-mail address.

EXAMPLE 12.44

```
      <html><head><title>Validate an Email Address</title>
      <body bgcolor="#ccffcc">
      <font size="+1" color="darkblue">
      <h1>Validating Email</h1>
      <?php
1       $errors=array();
2       if(isset($_REQUEST['submit'])){
3           validate_input();
4           if(count($errors) != 0){
5               show_form();
            }
6           else{ echo "<b>OK! Go ahead and Process the form</b><br />";
                echo "<em><b>$_REQUEST[email]</em></b> is a valid email
                address.<br />";
            }
        }
        else{
7           show_form();
        }
8       function validate_input(){
```

EXAMPLE   12.44 (CONTINUED)

```
 9          global $errors ;
            $email=stripslashes(trim( $_POST['email'] ));
10          if($email == ""){   // Did the user enter anything?
                $errors['email']="<b><font color='red'>***Email
                address?***</font><b>";
            }
            else{
11              $ok=validate_email($email);
                if ( ! $ok ){
12                  $errors['email']="<b><font color='red'>***Invalid
                    email address***</font></b>";
                }
            }
        }
13      function validate_email($email) {
14          $regex="/^[a-zA-Z][\w \.\-]+[a-zA-Z0-9]@([a-zA-Z0-9]
            [a-zA-Z0-9\-]*\.)+[a-zA-Z]{2,4}$/";
15          if ( preg_match($regex, $email)){
                return true;
            }
            else{
                return false;
            }
        }
16      function show_form(){
            global $errors;
            extract($_REQUEST);
        }
    ?>
17  <form method=POST action="<?php echo $_SERVER['PHP_SELF']?>">
    <table cellspacing="0" cellpadding="2">
        <tr>
            <b> Email address:</b>
            <td><input type="text" size=30
                name="email"
18                value="<?php echo $email;?>">
                <br />
19                <?php echo $errors['email'];?>
            </td>
            </td>
        </tr>
        <tr>
            <td> </td>
        </tr>
        <tr>
            <td><input type="submit"
                name="submit"
```

EXAMPLE   12.44 (CONTINUED)

```
        </tr>
        <br />
</table>
</form>
<?php
}
?>
</b>
</div>
</body>
</html>
```

EXPLANATION

1   An empty array is started.

2, 3   If the form has already been submitted, then the `validate_input()` function will be called.

4   If the `$errors` array has elements in it, then there are problems in the way the form was submitted.

5   If there are errors in the way the user filled out the form (the user did not enter an e-mail address or what he or she entered was invalid), the `show_form()` function will be called to redisplay the form with the appropriate error message.

6   If there were no errors in the submitted input (i.e., the user entered a valid e-mail address), then it is time to process the form. At this point the e-mail address is ready to be sent to a file, database, used to send a message to the user, and so on. See Figure 12.20.

7   If the form has not been submitted, the `show_form()` function will be called, and the form will appear in the browser, shown in Figure 12.17.

10   If the user did not enter anything at all, the `$errors['email']` array will be assigned a message that will appear in red under the input field in the browser.

14   The regular expression is assigned the variable `$regex`. The regular expression reads: Start at the beginning of the string ^, (the user's name) look for a beginning alphabetic character, followed by one or more alphanumeric characters, dashes, or periods, and ending with an alphanumeric character. This means that the pattern can be repeated one or more times; for example, `abc.xyz.ya-dy.y_dy.yady`. Next comes a literal @ symbol, required in all e-mail addresses. The mail server name comes right after the the @ sign. Like the username, it is represented by one or more alphanumeric characters or a dash, and ends with a single period. Now we have: *Joe.Blow@aol.* or *DanSav@ucbc.* This pattern, like the first pattern, can be repeated one or more times. The domain name part of the address comes next; a literal dot, and at least two and not more than four alphabetic characters, `[a-zA-Z]{2,4}`; for example, *JoeBlow@Chico.com, danny@.Stomford.edu, .se, .uk*, and so on. There are other varieties that could also be considered, such as *john@localhost*, but for most e-mail addresses, the regular expression used in this example should suffice.

EXPLANATION (CONTINUED)

17 The HTML form starts here. When the form is submitted this same script will be called to process it, referenced by $_SERVER['PHP_SELF'].

18 If this is the first time the form was submitted, $email will have no value. If the form has already been submitted and there were errors, the original value the user typed, stored in $email, will be replaced in the input text field box. PHP will echo its value and HTML will assign it to the text box.

18 The error message will now appear under the input box with the type of error letting the user know what he did wrong. See Figures 12.18 and 12.19.

Figure 12.17
The HTML form from
Example 12.44.

Figure 12.18
After the user submits an
invalid e-mail address, an
error is shown.

Figure 12.19   The user has submitted a valid e-mail address.

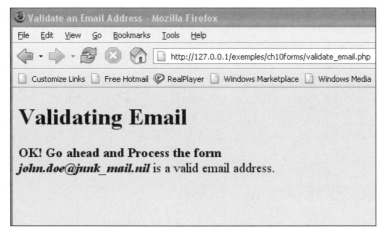

Figure 12.20   After successful validation with a regular expression.

12.2.6   Help on the Web

There are a number of regular expression validators on the Internet that can help you unravel regular expressions. The regular expression library at *http://regexlib.com* is an excellent resource for finding and testing regular expressions for e-mail, phone numbers, credit cards, Social Security numbers, and more (see Figure 12.21).

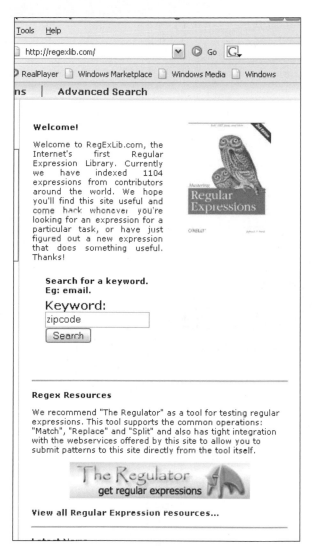

Figure 12.21 http://regexlib.com. The user has selected the keyword "zipcode." After pressing the Search button (see Figure 12.22), the page containing regular expressions representing a valid zip code is displayed in the browser.

Figure 12.22   Using a regular expression to find a zip code.

12.3 Chapter Summary

Because PHP is tightly integrated with HTML and receives input from forms, regular expressions provide an excellent tool for validating incoming data. They are also useful for finding patterns in data coming from files or databases. This chapter was designed to teach you how to use regular expressions and the PHP functions that handle them, and to provide short examples to show you how to use the often mysterious regular expression metacharacters.

12.3.1 What You Should Know

Now that you have finished this chapter you should be able to answer the following questions:

1. What is PCRE?

2. What is meant by POSIX style?

3. What is the difference between `preg_grep()` and `preg_match()`?

4. What are regular expression metacharacters used for?

5. What is meant by anchoring?

6. What is capturing?

7. What is greed (when talking about regular expressions)?

8. What are metasymbols? Why are they useful?

9. What is the function of the `e` modifier? Which function uses it?

10. What is a character class?

11. What is a delimiter?

12. What is a positive lookahead?

12.3.2 What's Next?

In the next chapter, we start our discussion of the MySQL relational database system and describe the client/server model, anatomy of a database, schema, and the MySQL privilege system, along with the strengths and weaknesses of MySQL.

CHAPTER 12 LAB

Open the `datebook` file (found on the CD) to perform the following exercises. Each exercise requires a separate open and close of the file.

1. a. Print all lines containing the pattern `Street` (case insensitive).
    b. Print firsts and last names in which the first name starts with letter B.
    c. Print last names that match `Ker`.
    d. Print phones in the 408 area code.
    e. Print Lori Gortz's name and address.
    f. Print Ephram's name in capital letters.
    g. Print lines that do not contain a number 4.
    h. Change William's name to Siegfried.
    i. Print Tommy Savage's birthday.
    j. Print lines that end in exactly five digits.
    k. Print the file with the first and last names reversed.

2. a. Print the city and state where Norma lives.
    b. Give everyone a $250.00 raise.
    c. Calculate Lori's age (just by year, not month and day).
    d. Print lines 2 through 6.
    e. Print names and phone numbers of those in the 408 area code.
    f. Print names and salaries in lines 3, 4, and 5.
    g. Print a row of asterisks after line 3.
    h. Change `CA` to `California`.
    i. Print the file with a row of asterisks after the last line.
    j. Print the names of the people born in March.
    k. Print all lines that don't contain `Karen`.
    l. Print all cities in California and the first names of those people who live there.

chapter
13

Introduction to MySQL

13.1 About Databases

Whether you are running a bank, a hospital, a gas station, or a Web store, good record keeping and organized data are crucial to the success of any business. One way to store data might be in a text file, but as the amount of data increases, a database might be a better choice for storing and managing your data. Different types of databases determine what kind of structure will be used to store and retrieve the data. The most basic type uses a flat file structure, storing the data in a big table, but this type is difficult to modify and really best suited for simple applications. Another type of database is one in which the data is organized in a hierarchy or network, much like the structure of a directory tree, a parent–child model, but these kinds of databases are hard for end users to grasp. Then in the 1980s relational databases became the "in" thing because the relational model made data manipulation easier and faster for the end user and easier to maintain by the administrator. At the core of this model is the concept of a *table* (also called a relation) in which all data is stored. Each table is made up of records consisting of horizontal rows and vertical columns or fields, like a two-dimensional array. Unlike the hierarchical model, the relational model made it easy for the user to retrieve, insert, update, and delete data without having to understand the underlying structure of the data in the database.

Due to the popularity of relational databases, known as relational database management systems (RDBMS), a number of relational databases are used today, among them, Oracle, Sybase, PostgreSQL Informix, DB2, SQL Server, and MySQL.

MySQL is the most commonly used database program for developing database-driven Web sites with PHP. As we mentioned in Chapter 1, "Introduction," MySQL is an open source database (it is free[1]) that runs on a majority of operating systems, such as UNIX, Linux, Macintosh, and Windows. PHP and MySQL fit very well together. They are both

---

1. Although maintained by MySQL AB, a commercial company, MySQL comes with a GPL (GNU Public License) open source license as well as a commercial license.

reasonably easy to use, fairly scalable and reliable and have a good set of features for small- and medium-sized Web applications. Although PHP can be used with any database through its set of ODBC functions, it comes loaded with MySQL specific functions. This set of specific functions makes for a tight integration between the PHP language and the MySQL database.

13.1.1 Client/Server Databases

If your Web site is to be up and available to customers around the world, and you are using a database management system to manage the data, the type of relational database best suited for the task is a client/server database, where the database server runs around the clock to handle client requests as they come in, no matter what the time zone. Today MySQL is one of the most popular client/server database systems in the open source community for serving Web pages.

Figure 13.1 shows the model for a client/server architecture. The user requests a page from the browser (e.g., Internet Explorer, Netscape, Firefox), and an HTTP connection is made to the Web server (Apache, ISS) where the request is received and handled. If the action is to start up a PHP program, the Web server starts up the PHP interpreter and PHP starts processing the script. If the PHP script contains an instruction to connect to a database, in this case MySQL, then once the connection is made and a database selected, the PHP program has access to the database through the MySQL server. The MySQL server receives requests, called *queries*, from the PHP program and sends back information collected from the database. Once PHP gets the information from the MySQL server, it can then format it into nice tables using HTML tags, and send it back to the Web server where it is then relayed to the browser where the whole process started. In this example, we have a client/server relationship between the browser and Web server and a client/server relationship between the PHP program and the MySQL database server.

Figure 13.1 The client/server architecture.

13.1.2 Talking to the Database

To communicate with the MySQL server, you will need a language, and SQL (Structured Query Language) is the language of choice for most modern multiuser, relational databases. SQL provides the syntax and language constructs needed to talk to relational databases in a standardized, cross-platform structured way. We discuss how to use the SQL language in the next chapter.

Like the English language with a variety of dialects (British, American, Australian, etc.), there are many different versions of the SQL language. The version of SQL used by MySQL follows the ANSI (American National Standards Institute) standard, meaning that it must support the major keywords (e.g., SELECT, UPDATE, DELETE, INSERT, WHERE, etc.) as defined in the standard. As you can see by the names of these keywords, SQL is the language that makes it possible to manipulate the data in a database.

13.1.3 MySQL Strengths and Weaknesses

From *www.mysq.com/why-mysql*:

> The MySQL® database has become the world's most popular open source database because of its consistent fast performance, high reliability, and ease of use. It's used in more than 8 million installations ranging from large corporations to specialized embedded applications on every continent in the world. (Yes, even Antarctica!)

> Not only is MySQL the world's most popular open source database, it's also become the database of choice for a new generation of applications built on the LAMP stack (Linux, Apache, MySQL, PHP/Perl/Python). MySQL runs on more than 20 platforms including Linux, Windows, OS/X, HP-UX, AIX, Netware, giving you the kind of flexibility that puts you in control.

Having said that, like any tool, MySQL is right for certain types of applications and not as suitable for others. Let's look at what the strengths and weaknesses of MySQL are.

Easy to Use. MySQL is a relatively easy to use and administer database system. Large database systems with all the bells and whistles often require a knowledgable database administrator (DBA) to set up and administer it. MySQL is a database built for programmers with very little overhead in terms of maintenance.

Large Community of Developers. What makes MySQL so appealing is the large community of other developers who are building applications around it. This makes it a relatively safe choice. If you ever need anything, chances are that someone already experienced that issue and has it resolved. You can often find the solutions with a little searching online.

Open Source License. MySQL is free to use as long as you do not bundle it with your commercial product. As an application provider, you can always tell your customers to download and set up their own MySQL database to which your application will connect. This is a fairly easy procedure and there is no license cost involved, making it an attractive choice for application developers.

Commercial License. When in fact you want to ship your application with a copy of the MySQL database server built into it, then you must purchase the license from MySQL AB. This might not be an attractive feature for true believers in open source and

General Public License models, but for most of us, obtaining a license will not be an issue. For Web applications, the database is rarely shipped as part of the application. Because customers who install server-side applications usually have sufficient skills to perform the tasks of downloading and setting up databases, it is sufficient to document the setup process with your application and leave the rest to them.

Scalability.   Scalability refers to how well an application can support larger or smaller volumes of data and more or fewer users without degrading performance and costing more. MySQL used to be regarded as a small database for small systems. Over time, MySQL has become a serious RDBMS with its own way of managing scalability, claiming that it can handle from small (a megabyte) to large (several terabytes) volumes of data with ultimate scalability. For example, there are currently some very large sites in production with multiclusters of MySQL database servers. Scalability is beyond the scope of this book but it is good to know that MySQL can handle your application as it grows in size.

13.2 The Anatomy of a Relational Database

What makes up a database? The main components of an RDBMS are:

- The database server
- The database
- Tables
- Records and fields
- Primary key
- Schema

We discuss each of these concepts in the next sections of this chapter. Figure 13.2 illustrates their relationship to each other.

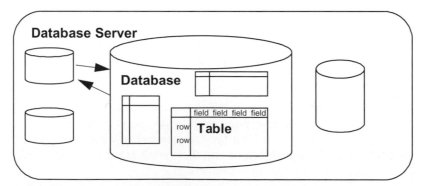

Figure 13.2   The database server, the database, and a table.

13.2.1   The Database Server

The database server is the actual server process running the databases. It controls the storage of the data, grants access to users, updates and deletes records, and communicates with other servers. The database server is normally on a dedicated host computer, serving and managing multiple clients over a network, but can also be used as a standalone server on the local host machine to serve a single client (e.g., you might be the single client using MySQL on your local machine, often referred to as "localhost" without any network connection at all). This is probably the best way to learn how to use MySQL.

If you are using MySQL, the server process is the MySQL service on Windows or the `mysqld` process on Linux/UNIX operating systems. The database server typically follows the client/server model where the front end is the client, a user sitting at his or her workstation making database requests and waiting for results, and the back end is the database server that grants access to users, stores and manipulates the data, performs backups, even talks to other servers. The requests to the database server can also be made from a program that acts on behalf of a user making requests from a Web page. In the following chapters, you will learn how to make requests from the MySQL command line first, and then to connect to the database server from a PHP program using PHP built-in functions to make requests to the MySQL database server.

13.2.2   The Database

A database is a collection of related data elements, usually corresponding to a specific application. A company might have one database for all its human resource needs, perhaps another one for its sales staff, a third one for e-commerce applications, and so on. Figure 13.3 lists the databases installed on a particular version of MySQL. The databases are listed as "mysql," "northwind," "phpmyadmin," and "test."

Figure 13.3   MySQL databases.

13.2.3   Tables

Each database consists of two-dimensional tables. In fact, a relational database stores all of its data in tables, and nothing more. All operations are performed on the table, which can then produce other tables, and so on.

One of the first decisions you will make when designing a database is what tables it will contain. A typical database for an organization might consist of tables for customers, orders, and products. All these tables are related to one another in some way. For example, customers have orders, and orders have items. Although each table exists on its own, collectively the tables comprise a database. Figure 13.4 lists the tables in the database called "northwind,"[2] a fictional database provided by Microsoft to serve as a model for learning how to manipulate a database. (This database is included on the CD provided with this book.)

```
+-----------------------+
| Tables_in_northwind   |
+-----------------------+
| categories            |
| customercustomerdemo  |
| customerdemographics  |
| customers             |
| employees             |
| employeeterritories   |
| order_details         |
| orders                |
| products              |
| region                |
| shippers              |
| suppliers             |
| territories           |
| usstates              |
+-----------------------+
```

Figure 13.4   Tables in the northwind database.

13.2.4   Records and Fields

A table has a name and consists of a set of rows and columns. It resembles a spreadsheet where each row, also called a *record*, is comprised of vertical columns, also called *fields*. All rows from the same table have the same set of columns. The "shippers" table from the "northwind" database has three columns and three rows, as shown in Figure 13.5.

```
+-----------+-------------------+----------------------+
| ShipperID | CompanyName       | Phone                |
+-----------+-------------------+----------------------+
|         1 | Speedy Express    | (503) 555-9831       |
|         2 | United Package    | (503) 555-3199       |
|         3 | Federal Shipping  | (503) 555-9931       |
+-----------+-------------------+----------------------+
```

Figure 13.5   The rows (records) and columns (fields) from the "shippers" table in the "northwind" database.

---

2. The Northwind Traders sample database typically comes as a free sample with Microsoft Access, but is available for MySQL at *http://www.flash-remoting.com/examples/*.

There are two basic operations you can perform on a relational table. You can retrieve a subset of its columns and you can retrieve a subset of its rows. Figures 13.6 and 13.7 are samples of the two operations.

```
mysql> select companyname from shippers;
+------------------+
| companyname      |
+------------------+
| Speedy Express   |
| United Package   |
| Federal Shipping |
+------------------+
```

Figure 13.6 Retrieving a subset of columns.

```
mysql> select * from shippers where companyname="Federal Shipping";
+----------+------------------+----------------+
| ShipperID | CompanyName     | Phone          |
+----------+------------------+----------------+
|        3 | Federal Shipping | (503) 555-9931 |
+----------+------------------+----------------+
```

Figure 13.7 Retrieving a subset of rows.

Remember, a relational database manipulates only tables and the result of all operations are also tables. The tables are sets, which are themselves sets of rows and columns. You can view the database itself as a set of tables.

You can also perform a number of other operations between two tables, treating them as sets: You can join information from two tables, make cartesian products of the tables, get the intersection between two tables, add one table to another, and so on. Later we show you how to perform operations on tables using the SQL language. SQL allows you to "talk" to a database. Figures 13.6 and 13.7 use SQL commands to retrieve data.

Columns/Fields.   When discussing tables, we must talk about columns because they are an integral part of the table. Columns are also known as fields or attributes. Fields describe the data. Each field has a name. For example, the "shippers" table has fields named "ShipperID," "CompanyName," and "Phone" (see Figure 13.7). The field also describes the type of data it contains. A data type can be a number, a character, a date, a time stamp, and so on. In Figure 13.8 "ShipperID" is the name of a field and the data type is an integer, and the shipper's ID will not exceed 11 numbers. There are many data types and sometimes they are specific to a particular database system; for example, MySQL might have different data types available than Oracle. We will learn more about the MySQL data types in the next chapter.

Field	Type	Null	Key	Default	Extra
ShipperID	int(11)		PRI	NULL	auto_increment
CompanyName	varchar(40)			NULL	
Phone	varchar(24)	YES		NULL	

Figure 13.8 Each field has a name and a description of the data that can be stored there.

Rows/Records.   A record is a row in the table. It could be a product in the product table, an employee record in the employee table, and so on. Each table in a database contains zero or more records. Figure 13.9 shows us that there are three records in the "shippers" table.

```
+------------+------------------+------------------+
| ShipperID  | CompanyName      | Phone            |
+------------+------------------+------------------+
|          1 | Speedy Express   | (503) 555-9831   |
|          2 | United Package   | (503) 555-3199   |
|          3 | Federal Shipping | (503) 555-9931   |
+------------+------------------+------------------+
3 rows in set (0.00 sec)
```

Figure 13.9   There are three records in the "shippers" table.

13.2.5   Primary Key and Indexes

A primary key is a unique identifier for each record. For example, every employee in the United States has a Social Security number, every driver has a driver's license, and every car has a license plate. These identifiers are unique. In the world of database tables, we call the unique identifier a primary key. Although it is a good idea to have a primary key, not every table has one. The primary key is determined when the table is created and is more in keeping with a discussion on database design. In Figure 13.10, the "ShipperID" is the primary key for the "shippers" table in the "northwest" database. It is a unique ID that consists of a number that will automatically be incremented every time a new company (record) is added to the list of shippers.

```
+-------------+-------------+------+-----+---------+----------------+
| Field       | Type        | Null | Key | Default | Extra          |
+-------------+-------------+------+-----+---------+----------------+
| ShipperID   | int(11)     |      | PRI | NULL    | auto_increment |
| CompanyName | varchar(40) |      |     |         |                |
| Phone       | varchar(24) | YES  |     | NULL    |                |
+-------------+-------------+------+-----+---------+----------------+
```

Figure 13.10   The "ShipperID" is the primary key in the "shippers" table.

In addition to a primary key, one or more indexes are often used to enhance performance for finding rows in tables that are frequently accessed. Indexes are like the indexes in the back of a book that help you find a specific topic more quickly than searching through the entire book. When searching for a particular record in a table, MySQL must load all the records before it can execute the query. An index, like the index of a book, is a reference to a particular record in a table.

13.2.6 The Database Schema

Designing a very small database is not difficult, but designing one for a large Web-based application can be daunting. Database design is both an art and a science and requires understanding how the relational model is implemented, a topic beyond the scope of this book. When discussing the design of the database, you will encounter the term *database schema*, which refers to the structure of the database. It describes the design of the database similar to a template or blueprint; it describes all the tables, and their layout, but does not contain the actual data in the database. Figure 13.11 describes the schema for the tables in the "northwind" database.

Figure 13.11
Database schema.

13.3 Connecting to the Database

Here we assume you have installed a database server and it is running. Downloading and installing MySQL is usually a straightforward process. For details, see Appendix E.

The MySQL database system uses the client/server model described in "Client/Server Databases" on page 568. There are a number of client applications available to connect to the database server, the most popular and most widely available being the `mysql` command-line client shown in Example 13.1.

EXAMPLE 13.1

```
$ mysql
Welcome to the MySQL monitor.  Commands end with ; or \g.
Your MySQL connection id is 3 to server version: 4.1.8-nt-log

Type 'help;' or '\h' for help. Type '\c' to clear the buffer.

mysql>
```

Regardless of the type of client you choose, you will always need to specify the username, and the host you are connecting to. Most configurations expect you to have a password, although if just working by yourself, it is not required. You have the option to specify the default database as well.

13.3.1 MySQL Command-Line Options

The `mysql` command-line client ships with the MySQL installation and is universally available. It is a `mysql.exe` program located in the `bin` folder of your MySQL installation.

To run this command-line application, you must start the command-line prompt. In Windows, you go to the Start menu and choose the Run... option, then type **cmd** in the Run window. In Mac OS X, go to the Applications folder in your Finder and then navigate to Utilities. You will find the Terminal application there. You should navigate to the location where you installed MySQL and find the `bin` folder. With UNIX, type commands at the shell prompt in a terminal window.

The `mysql` client executable is normally located in the `bin` folder.

To connect to a database using this client, you will enter information similar to the following line (see Figure 13.12):

```
mysql --user=root --password=my_password --host=localhost
```

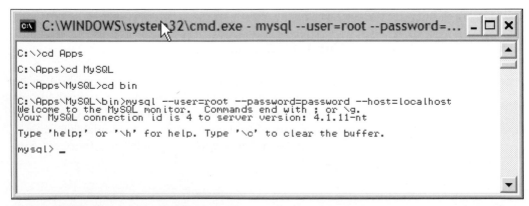

Figure 13.12 The `mysql` client.

Once you are successfully connected, you will get the `mysql>` prompt instead of your standard DOS/UNIX prompt. This means you are now sending commands to the MySQL database server and not to your local computer's operating system.

There are many command-line options for the MySQL client. The most common are shown in Table 13.1.

Table 13.1 MySQL Command-Line Options

Short Format	Long Format	Description
-?	--help	Display this help and exit.
-I	--help	Synonym for -?.
-B	--batch	Do not use history file. Disable interactive behavior. (Enables --silent.)
-C	--compress	Use compression in server/client protocol.
-#	--debug[=#]	This is a nondebug version. Catch this and exit.
-D	--database=name	Database to be used.
	--delimiter=name	Delimiter to be used.
-e	--execute=name	Execute command and quit. (Disables --force and history file.)
-E	--vertical	Print the output of a query (rows) vertically.
-f	--force	Continue even if we get an sql error.
-i	--ignore-spaces	Ignore space after function names.
	--local-infile	Enable or disable LOAD DATA LOCAL INFILE.
-b	--no-beep	Turn off beep on error.
-h	--host=name	Connect to host.
-H	--html	Produce HTML output.
-X	--xml	Produce XML output
	--line-numbers	Write line numbers for errors.
-L	--skip-line-numbers	Do not write line number for errors. WARNING: -L is deprecated, so use long version of this option instead.
	--no-tee	Disable outfile. See interactive help (\h) also. WARNING: Option deprecated; use --disable-tee instead.

Table 13.1   MySQL Command-Line Options (continued)

Short Format	Long Format	Description
-n	--unbuffered	Flush buffer after each query.
	--column-names	Write column names in results.
-N	--skip-column-names	Do not write column names in results. WARNING: -N is deprecated, use long version of this option instead.
-o	--one-database	Only update the default database. This is useful for skipping updates to other databases in the update log.
-p	--password[=name]	Password to use when connecting to server. If password is not given, it is asked from the tty.
-W	--pipe	Use named pipes to connect to server.
-P	--port=#	Port number to use for connection.
	--prompt=name	Set the mysql prompt to this value.
-q	--quick	Do not cache result, print it row by row. This might slow down the server if the output is suspended. Does not use history file.
-r	--raw	Write fields without conversion. Used with --batch.
	--reconnect	Reconnect if the connection is lost. Disable with --disable-reconnect. This option is enabled by default.
-s	--silent	Be more silent. Print results with a tab as separator, each row on a new line.
-t	--table	Output in table format.
-T	--debug-info	Print some debug info at exit.
	--tee=name	Append everything into outfile. See interactive help (\h) also. Does not work in batch mode.
-u	--user=name	User for login if not current user.
-U	--safe-updates	Only allow UPDATE and DELETE that uses keys.
-U	--i-am-a-dummy	Synonym for option --safe-updates.
-v	--verbose	Write more (-v -v -v gives the table output format).
-V	--version	Output version information and exit.

13.3.2 Graphical User Tools

The phpMyAdmin Tool.   The phpMyAdmin tool (see Figures 13.13 and 13.14) is written in PHP to handle the administration of MySQL over the Web. It is used to create and drop databases, manipulate tables and fields, execute SQL statements, manage keys on fields, manage privileges, and export data into various formats. See *http://www.php-myadmin.net/home_page/ index.php.*

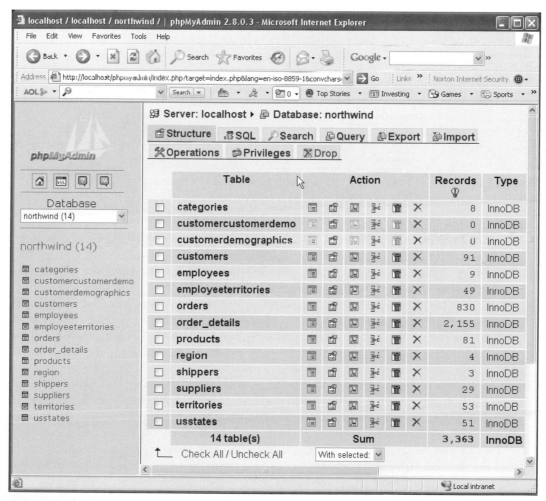

Figure 13.13   The phpMyAdmin tool.

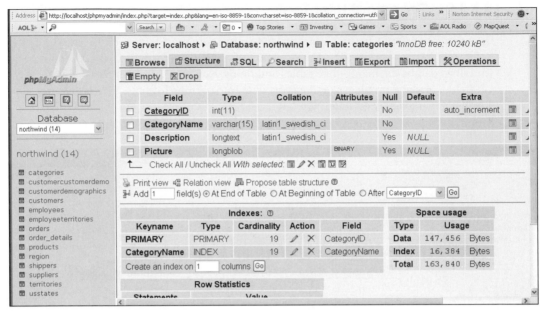

Figure 13.14   After checking the "categories" box in the left frame, the structure of that table is displayed in the phpMyAdmin main window.

The MySQL Query Browser.   The MySQL Query Browser is a graphical user interface (GUI) client available from *mysql.com* used to connect to the MySQL database server. Once you download it and follow the simple installation wizard, you can start the application from the Start menu under Windows.

The MySQL Query Browser then displays a connection dialog box. You must specify the MySQL server where you want to connect, the credentials needed for authorization on that server, which machine that server runs on (and which port it listens to), and the default database (called the "Schema") you will be using. There are also a number of additional options you can specify if necessary.

You must choose a default database to issue queries. Although it is possible to choose a default database after connecting to the server, setting the default from the connection dialog box can save time on subsequent connections.

The information to enter is very similar to the command-line client: username, password, and the server host where the database server is running. You can optionally enter the database name and port number (3306 is the default for MySQL) and save the connection information as a bookmark under the Stored Connection section (see Figure 13.15).

By using the familiar tree-like navigation structure on the right side of the application window, you can also navigate through the various databases in the MySQL Query Browser (see Figure 13.16).

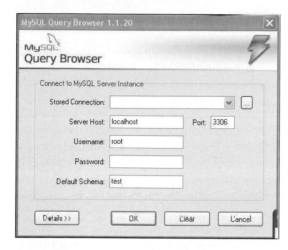

Figure 13.15
The MySQL Query Browser connection dialog box.

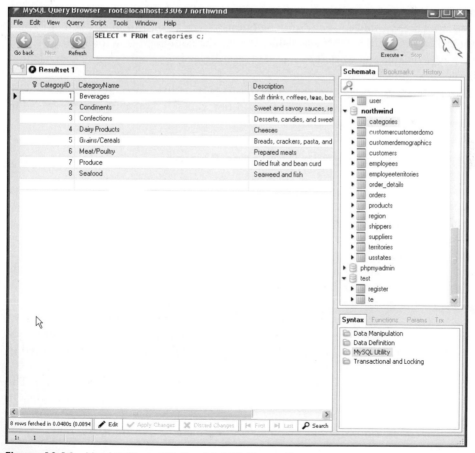

Figure 13.16 Navigating with the MySQL Query Browser.

13.4 The MySQL Privilege System

With a drivers' license, "authentication" means verifying that it is really you who owns the license by checking your picture and expiration date, and "authorization" means validating what type of vehicle you are authorized to drive, such as a car, a large truck, or a school bus.

Similarly, the primary purpose of the MySQL privilege system is to authenticate that the user and password are valid to connect to the specified host, as demonstrated in the previous examples in both the command-line and graphical client. The second purpose of the privilege system is to specify what the user, once connected to the database, is authorized to do. For example, some users might be authorized to only select and view the data from a specific database, but not make any changes to it. Some might be able to delete records, but not tables.

Once you have installed MySQL, it is time to understand some basic guidelines of how to administer a MySQL database server, such as setting up the users and the privileges they have on certain databases. You can use either the `mysql` command-line tool or the `mysqladmin` tool for performing administrative tasks. Although there are some graphical administrative tools avaialable, we use the command-line tools because they are always available and work the same way regardless of your operating system whether it is Windows, Macintosh, or Linux.

The next section assumes you have basic SQL skills, such as familiarity with INSERT/UPDATE/DELETE/SELECT statements. If not, the SQL language is summarized in Chapter 14, "SQL Language Tutorial."

13.4.1   Logging into the Database Server

When MySQL is installed, the mysql database is created with tables, called grant tables that define the initial user accounts and privileges. The first account is that of a user named "root," also called the superuser. The superuser can do anything, meaning anyone logging onto the database as root is granted all privileges. Initially the root account has no password, making it easy for anyone to log on as the superuser. The other type of accounts created are anonymous user accounts, also without a password. For both the root and anonymous accounts, Windows gets one each and UNIX gets two. Either way, to avoid security problems, the first thing you should do, once the MySQL server starts, is to set a password on the root account and the anonymous accounts.

MySQL keeps track of its own users and passwords separate from the operating system where it is running. All the privileges for the MySQL database server are stored in the "mysql" database (the database with name "mysql").

For administration purposes, you should have root access rights to your server. The `mysqladmin` utility is useful for creating passwords as well as performing other MySQL administrative tasks. In the next example it is used to set the password for the root user.

When working with MySQL, a number of like-name terms are used. Table 13.2 is provided to help clarify the use of these terms.

Table 13.2 MySQL Terminology

Term	Description
mySQL	The actual software for the database management system
mysqld	The mySQL daemon or server process
mysql monitor	The monitor where MySQL commands are issued (command-line interpreter)
mysql	The name of the database MySQL uses to manage access privileges
mysqladmin	A MySQL utility program for administering the database

EXAMPLE 13.2

```
1   $ mysqladmin -u root -h localhost password quigley1

2   $ mysql -uroot -hlocalhost -pquigley1
    Welcome to the MySQL monitor.  Commands end with ; or \g.
    Your MySQL connection id is 29 to server version:
    5.0.21-community-nt

    Type 'help;' or '\h' for help. Type '\c' to clear the buffer.
```

EXPLANATION

1   The `mysqladmin` program is used to set the password for root user on the local-host. The password is `quigley1`.
2   This logs the root user into the database server. The `-u` switch is followed by the user or login name (no spaces between `-u` and the username). This user is logging in as `root`. Similarly, the `-p` switch is followed by the actual password, in this case `quigley1`. If a password is not provided, you will be prompted to enter one.

13.4.2 Finding the Databases

The database server keeps a list of available databases that can be displayed as a table by issuing the `show` command at the `mysql` prompt, as shown in Example 13.3. Typically when you install MySQL it comes with two databases: "test" and "mysql". The "test" database is used for testing various features or creating sample databases. You normally do not need to have any special permissions to be able to do anything in that database. The "mysql" database is a special database where the MySQL server stores various access permissions. We look at the contents of the "mysql" database in the next section.

EXAMPLE 13.3

```
C:\>mysql -uroot -ppassword
Welcome to the MySQL monitor.  Commands end with ; or \g.
Your MySQL connection id is 5 to server version: 4.1.11-nt

Type 'help;' or '\h' for help. Type '\c' to clear the buffer.

mysql> show databases;
+--------------+
| Database     |
+--------------+
| authority    |
| best         |
| jsf          |
| marakana_cms |
| mysql        |
| northwind    |
| test         |
+--------------+
7 rows in set (0.69 sec)

mysql>
```

EXPLANATION

The show databases command gives us the list of all the databases on this server. Typically, when you install MySQL, you will be given the "mysql" database and the "test" database. The "test" database is just for testing purposes and is empty. The "mysql" database contains all the MySQL server privilege information.

EXAMPLE 13.4

```
1   mysql> use mysql
    Database changed
2   mysql> show tables;
+---------------------------+
| Tables_in_mysql           |
+---------------------------+
| columns_priv              |
| db                        |
| func                      |
| help_category             |
| help_keyword              |
| help_relation             |
| help_topic                |
```

EXAMPLE 13.4 (CONTINUED)

```
| host                         |
| tables_priv                  |
| time_zone                    |
| time_zone_leap_second        |
| time_zone_name               |
| time_zone_transition         |
| time_zone_transition_type    |
| user                         |
+------------------------------+
15 rows in set (0.19 sec)
```

EXPLANATION

1 The use `mysql` command tells the server to switch to the "mysql" database and make that the current database.

2 The `show tables` command displays all the database tables in the current "mysql" database. This database contains 15 tables. The tables we are concerned with now are "host," "user," and "db."

13.4.3 The "user" Table

The "user" table specifies the users who are allowed to log into the database server and from what host. It also holds their passwords and global access privileges.

Let's look at the fields of the "user" table:

```
mysql> describe user;
+--------------------------+-------------------------------------+
| Field                    | Type                                |
+--------------------------+-------------------------------------+
| Host                     | varchar(60)                         |
| User                     | varchar(16)                         |
| Password                 | varchar(41)                         |
| Select_priv              | enum('N','Y')                       |
| Insert_priv              | enum('N','Y')                       |
| Update_priv              | enum('N','Y')                       |
| Delete_priv              | enum('N','Y')                       |
| Create_priv              | enum('N','Y')                       |
| Drop_priv                | enum('N','Y')                       |
| Reload_priv              | enum('N','Y')                       |
| Shutdown_priv            | enum('N','Y')                       |
| Process_priv             | enum('N','Y')                       |
| File_priv                | enum('N','Y')                       |
| Grant_priv               | enum('N','Y')                       |
| References_priv          | enum('N','Y')                       |
| Index_priv               | enum('N','Y')                       |
| Alter_priv               | enum('N','Y')                       |
| Show_db_priv             | enum('N','Y')                       |
```

```
| Super_priv            | enum('N','Y')                        |
| Create_tmp_table_priv | enum('N','Y')                        |
| Lock_tables_priv      | enum('N','Y')                        |
| Execute_priv          | enum('N','Y')                        |
| Repl_slave_priv       | enum('N','Y')                        |
| Repl_client_priv      | enum('N','Y')                        |
| ssl_type              | enum('','ANY','X509','SPECIFIED')    |
| ssl_cipher            | blob                                 |
| x509_issuer           | blob                                 |
| x509_subject          | blob                                 |
| max_questions         | int(11) unsigned                     |
| max_updates           | int(11) unsigned                     |
| max_connections       | int(11) unsigned                     |
+-----------------------+--------------------------------------+
31 rows in set (0.00 sec)
```

The key fields are Host, User, and Password. All the other fields are used to fine-tune the privileges. To log in, the user and password must match and the user must be from the given host.

The password field should be encoded so that it is not easily readable by someone looking over your shoulder. MySQL provides a function called `password()` to do just that. We see how to use it in the next example.

13.4.4   The "db" Table

The "db" table determines which databases a user is permitted to read, edit, and delete, limiting access to a certain host and user. Its contents are described in the following table:

```
mysql> describe db;
+-----------------------+---------------+
| Field                 | Type          |
+-----------------------+---------------+
| Host                  | char(60)      |
| Db                    | char(64)      |
| User                  | char(16)      |
| Select_priv           | enum('N','Y') |
| Insert_priv           | enum('N','Y') |
| Update_priv           | enum('N','Y') |
| Delete_priv           | enum('N','Y') |
| Create_priv           | enum('N','Y') |
| Drop_priv             | enum('N','Y') |
| Grant_priv            | enum('N','Y') |
| References_priv       | enum('N','Y') |
| Index_priv            | enum('N','Y') |
| Alter_priv            | enum('N','Y') |
| Create_tmp_table_priv | enum('N','Y') |
| Lock_tables_priv      | enum('N','Y') |
+-----------------------+---------------+
```

The key fields are the Host, Db, and User fields. The other fields are used for fine-tuning the access rights. The default value is always "No" for the privileges, meaning that access rights must be explicitly granted. ('N' is no and 'Y' is yes.)

13.4.5 The "host" Table

The "host" table is an extension of the "db" table if the "db" table does not have a host entry. It contains the hosts (IP addresses), databases, and privileges that can connect to the MySQL database server. Typically, your PHP script is running on the same host computer as your database server. The host is called "localhost," which is simply an alias for the current host machine located at IP address 127.0.0.1. For example, if you are on the server myserver.com, you can refer to it to as the localhost. If later you change the name of the server to yourhost.com, your database connection will still be available because localhost always refers to the current host computer.

The fields in the "host" table are shown in the following table:

```
mysql> describe host;
+----------------------+----------------+------+-----+---------+-------+
| Field                | Type           | Null | Key | Default | Extra |
+----------------------+----------------+------+-----+---------+-------+
| Host                 | char(60)       |      | PRI |         |       |
| Db                   | char(64)       |      | PRI |         |       |
| Select_priv          | enum('N','Y')  |      |     | N       |       |
| Insert_priv          | enum('N','Y')  |      |     | N       |       |
| Update_priv          | enum('N','Y')  |      |     | N       |       |
| Delete_priv          | enum('N','Y')  |      |     | N       |       |
| Create_priv          | enum('N','Y')  |      |     | N       |       |
| Drop_priv            | enum('N','Y')  |      |     | N       |       |
| Grant_priv           | enum('N','Y')  |      |     | N       |       |
| References_priv      | enum('N','Y')  |      |     | N       |       |
| Index_priv           | enum('N','Y')  |      |     | N       |       |
| Alter_priv           | enum('N','Y')  |      |     | N       |       |
| Create_tmp_table_priv| enum('N','Y')  |      |     | N       |       |
| Lock_tables_priv     | enum('N','Y')  |      |     | N       |       |
+----------------------+----------------+------+-----+---------+-------+
14 rows in set (0.31 sec)
```

The Db field contains all the users, databases, and hostnames for this MySQL server. The other fields are switches with Yes/No options to grant or revoke certain privileges and specify the level of that access right.

EXAMPLE 13.5

```
mysql> insert into host (host, db, Select_priv, Insert_priv,
    ->          Update_priv, Delete_priv, Create_priv, Drop_priv)
    ->          values ('localhost',
'northwind','Y','Y','Y','Y','Y','Y');
Query OK, 1 row affected (0.53 sec)
```

EXPLANATION

The insert into host command grants Select/Insert/Update/Delete/Create/Drop access to the "northwind" database from the localhost, setting certain switches to Y for yes. The ones that are not set will default to no. See Figure 13.17 for actual command and output.

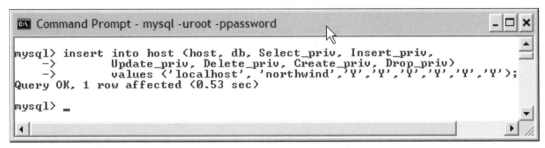

Figure 13.17 Output from the insert into host command.

13.4.6 A Real-World Example

The following steps set privileges so that user bob can log into a MySQL database called "northwind" from the localhost using the password guess. After entering the mysql database with the use mysql command, the steps are:

1. Create the host record:

   ```
   mysql> insert into host (host, db, Select_priv, Insert_priv,
       ->          Update_priv, Delete_priv, Create_priv, Drop_priv)
       ->          values ('localhost',
   'northwind','Y','Y','Y','Y','Y','Y');
   ```

2. Create the user:

   ```
   mysql> insert into user (host,user,password)
       ->          values('localhost','bob',password('guess'));
   ```

3. Update the "db" table:

```
mysql> insert into db
(host,db,user,Select_priv,Insert_priv,Update_priv,
    ->          Delete_priv,Create_priv,Drop_priv)
    ->          values
('localhost','northwind','bob','Y','Y','Y','Y','Y','Y');
```

4. Flush privileges:

```
mysql> flush privileges;
```

Flushing privileges makes the latest changes active.

5. Finally, to test whether everything is set up properly, you can log out of the mysql server and try to reconnect using the user bob, password guess, and host localhost to the database northwind:

```
C:\>mysql -ubob -pguess -hlocalhost northwind
Welcome to the MySQL monitor.  Commands end with ; or \g.
Your MySQL connection id is 8 to server version: 4.1.11-nt

Type 'help;' or '\h' for help. Type '\c' to clear the buffer.
```

13.4.7 The Grant and Revoke Commands

MySQL access control involves two stages when you try to connect to the mysql server. First the server checks to see if you are allowed to connect, and second, if you can connect, the server checks each statement you issue to determine whether or not you have sufficient privileges to execute the command. For example, if you try to create or drop a table in the database, or try to update a record, the server verifies that you have the correct privileges to execute those commands. To simplify all the steps required to set up the privileges on a database or a table, MySQL provides two commands: GRANT and REVOKE.

The best way to illustrate how to use them is to see the following examples.

EXAMPLE 13.6

```
1   GRANT ALL ON *.*
2   REVOKE ALL ON *.*
```

EXPLANATION

1   Grants all the privileges to all databases on the current server.
2   Revokes all the privileges to all databases on the current server.

EXAMPLE 13.7

```
1   GRANT ALL ON db_name.*
2   REVOKE ALL ON db_name.*
```

EXPLANATION

1   Grants all the privileges to all the tables in the database db_name.
2   Revokes all the privileges to all the tables of the database identified by db_name.

EXAMPLE 13.8

```
1   GRANT ALL ON db_name.tbl_name
2   REVOKE ALL ON db_name.tbl_name
```

EXPLANATION

1   Grants all the privileges to a specific table tbl_name in the database db_name.
2   Revokes the privileges of a table tbl_name in the database db_name.

You can also specify the user for which you are granting or revoking the privileges by adding the TO '*user*'@'*host*' and IDENTIFIED BY '*password*' statement.

EXAMPLE 13.9

```
GRANT ALL PRIVILEGES ON db_name.tbl_name TO 'bob'@'localhost'
IDENTIFIED BY 'guess'
```

EXPLANATION

This command will give user bob all the privileges when he logs in from the localhost and tries to access database db_name and table tbl_name.

13.4.8 Creating and Dropping a Database

Creating a database is simple. Designing it is another story and depends on your requirements and the model you will use to organize your data. With the smallest database, you will have to create at least one table. The next chapter discusses how to create and drop both databases and tables. Assuming you have been granted permission to create a database, you can do it at the mysql command line or with the mysqladmin tool as in Example 13.10.

EXAMPLE   13.10

```
1   mysql> create database my_sample_db;
    Query OK, 1 row affected (0.00 sec)

2   mysql> use my_sample_db;
    Database changed

3   mysql> show tables;
    Empty set (0.00 sec)

4   mysql> create table test(
    -> field1 INTEGER,
    -> field2 VARCHAR(50)
    -> );
    Query OK, 0 rows affected (0.36 sec)

5   mysql> show tables;
    +-------------------------+
    | Tables_in_my_sample_db  |
    +-------------------------+
    | test                    |
    +-------------------------+
    1 row in set (0.00 sec)

6   mysql> drop table test;
    Query OK, 0 rows affected (0.11 sec)

7   mysql> drop database my_sample_db;
    Query OK, 0 rows affected (0.01 sec)
```

EXPLANATION

1   This is how to create a database called my_sample_db.
2   Just because the database has been created does not mean you are in it. To enter the new database, the use command is executed.
3   The show command lists all the tables in the database.
4   To create a table, the table columns are defined with the data types for each column. In this table the two columns field1 and field2 are defined. The first field will be assigned integer values and the second field will be assigned up to 50 characters.
5   After creating the table, the show command displays the contents of the table.
6   The drop table command destroys a table test and its contents.
7   The drop database command destroys the my_sample_db database and its contents.

13.4.9   Some Useful MySQL Functions

MySQL comes with a number of built-in functions (see Table 13.3) that provide information about the server, the user, connection, version, how to encrypt and encode strings, display date and time, and so on. Examples follow the table.

Table 13.3   MySQL Functions

Function	What It Returns	Example
database()	Name of the current database	select database();
version()	Version of MySQL software	select version();
user()	Name of current MySQL user	select user();
password()	Encrypts a string passed as an argument	select password("mypassword");
now()	The current date and time	select now();
curdate()	The current year, month, day	select curdate();

```
mysql> use northwind;
Database changed

mysql> select database();
+------------+
| database() |
+------------+
| northwind  |
+------------+
1 row in set (0.00 sec)

mysql> select version();
+--------------------+
| version()          |
+--------------------+
| 5.0.21-community-nt |
+--------------------+
1 row in set (0.00 sec)

mysql> select user();
+----------------+
| user()         |
+----------------+
| root@localhost |
+----------------+
1 row in set (0.00 sec)
```

```
mysql> mysql> set password for root@localhost = password('ellieq');
Query OK, 0 rows affected (0.03 sec)


select password("ellieq");
+---------------------------------------------+
| password("ellieq")                          |
+---------------------------------------------+
| *5313CC84288581F3B15B0ECBBFA2E9AF6AE4FD5A   |
+---------------------------------------------+
1 row in set (0.00 sec)

mysql> select now();

+---------------------+
| now()               |
+---------------------+
| 2006-06-07 15:09:16 |
+---------------------+
1 row in set (0.02 sec)

mysql> select curdate();
+------------+
| curdate()  |
+------------+
| 2006-06-07 |
+------------+
1 row in set (0.00 sec)
```

13.5 Chapter Summary

This chapter discussed the basic components of a relational database management system, the client/server model, and how MySQL fits in. The basics of MySQL database administration were explained by issuing MySQL commands at the `mysql` command line. There are other tools for administration as well, such as the Windows application MySQL Administration, freely available from MySQL.com. If you understand everything in this chapter, using any of these tools should be very easy to you.

There are other areas of consideration when it comes to database administration, such as backup and restore, clustering, fault tolerance, security, replication, and so on. These topics are beyond the scope of this book and most programmers will not be concerned with them.

For more details on how the particulars of the privilege system work, look at the MySQL Access Privilege System set of documents at *http://mysql.com*.

13.5.1   What You Should Know

Now that you have finished this chapter you should be able to answer the following questions:

1. What are some advantages of using MySQL?

2. What are the components of a database system?

3. How do you connect to a database server using the command-line client?

4. How do you use a graphical application to connect to the database server?

5. What are some of the files used in administering MySQL and what are their purposes?

13.5.2   What's Next?

In the next chapter we look at SQL, known as "Sequel," in detail, which allows you to talk to a database. You will learn the basic SQL commands as well as how to manipulate the structure of the data in a database. Topics will include:

- Retrieving all the records from a database table.
- Retrieving select set of records or a single record from a table based on a specific criteria.
- Selecting and sorting records in a database.
- Selecting a range of rows from a database.
- Creating a database.
- Creating and droping database tables.
- Assigning a primary key to a field.
- Inserting records into the database table.
- Updating a record in a table.
- Deleting a record.

chapter
14

SQL Language Tutorial

```
> SELECT * FROM geeks WHERE
  style LIKE '%kewl%';
0 rows selected
```

14.1 What Is SQL?

When you go to Google and request information, that request is called a *query* and the search engine will collect any Web pages that match your query. To narrow down the search, you might have to refine your request with more descriptive keywords. The same process applies to database lookups. When you make requests to a database, the request follows a certain format and the database server will try to locate the information and return a result. The way in which you query the database is defined by the query language you are using. The standard language for communicating with relational databases is SQL, the Structured Query Language. SQL is an ANSI (American National Standards Institute) standard computer language, designed to be as close to the English language as possible, making it an easy language to learn. Popular database management systems such as Oracle, Sybase, and Microsoft SQL Server, all use SQL and, although some create their own proprietary extensions to the language, the standard basic commands for querying a database such as SELECT, INSERT, DELETE, UPDATE, CREATE, and DROP will handle most of the essential tasks you will need to perform database operations.

The SQL language can be traced back to E.F. "Ted" Codd, an IBM researcher who first published an article in June 1970 that laid the foundations for the theory of relational databases, an English-like language used to communicate with these databases. Cobb's article triggered a major research project at IBM to design a relational database system called System/R and a database language called SEQUEL (Structured English Query Language), which is known today as SQL (often pronounced "see-quell"). In the late 1970s two other companies were started to develop similar products, which became Oracle and Ingres. By 1985 Oracle claimed to have more than 1,000 installations, and by the early 1990s SQL had become the standard for database management in medium to large organizations, especially on UNIX and mainframes.

14.1.1   Standarizing SQL

Like the English language, with all its dialects, many flavors of SQL evolved. Today's SQL is based on IBM's original implementation, with a considerable number of additions. Standards are created to help specify what should be supported in a language. In 1986, the ANSI designated the SQL standard. It was then revised in 1989, 1992, and 1999. The most commonly used standard today is SQL92, representing the second revision of the original specification (SQL2). Most commercial databases (MySQL, Oracle, Sybase, Microsoft Access, and Microsoft SQL Server) support the full SQL and claim to be 100 percent compliant with the standard. However, the standard is quite complex, and as with different dialects of the English language, various vendors have added extensions to their version of SQL, making it difficult to guarantee that an application will run on all SQL server databases.

In this chapter we focus on the basic SQL language and examine such concepts as table creation, insertion, deletion, and selection of data.

14.1.2   Executing SQL Statements

Because the database management system discussed in this book is MySQL, the server being used in the following examples is the MySQL database server, and most of the SQL commands will be executed at the `mysql` command-line client, although you might prefer to use the MySQL Query Browser. Once connected to the database, you simply type the commands in the `mysql` console (command-line window, see Figure 14.1) as explained in the previous chapter.

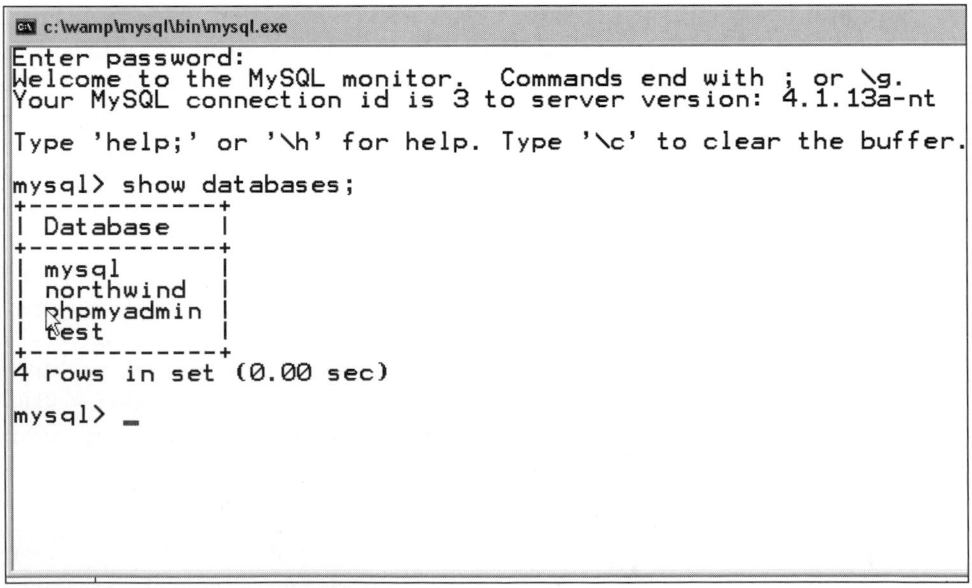

```
c:\wamp\mysql\bin\mysql.exe
Enter password:
Welcome to the MySQL monitor.  Commands end with ; or \g.
Your MySQL connection id is 3 to server version: 4.1.13a-nt

Type 'help;' or '\h' for help. Type '\c' to clear the buffer.

mysql> show databases;
+------------+
| Database   |
+------------+
| mysql      |
| northwind  |
| phpmyadmin |
| test       |
+------------+
4 rows in set (0.00 sec)

mysql> _
```

Figure 14.1   The `mysql` console.

The MySQL Query Browser.   To run SQL commands in the MySQL Query Browser, type them in the box in the top of the application window and click the Execute button.

Once you click the Execute button (the green button to the right of the query window), the result will be displayed in the center of the application as a Resultset tab (see Figure 14.2).

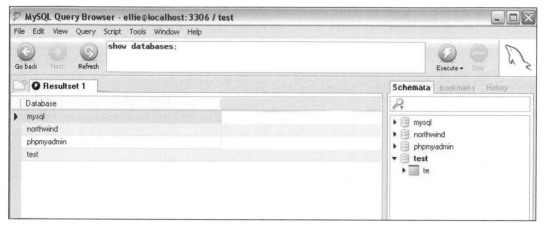

Figure 14.2   The MySQL Query Browser GUI.

14.1.3   About SQL Commands/Queries

SQL is a computer language, and like languages in general, SQL has its rules, grammar, and a set of special or reserved words. Different variants of the language have evolved over the years because different relational database vendors offer additional features to manipulate data in the name of competition. This section covers the basic SQL commands and syntax.

Because SQL has so many commands, they are divided into two major categories: the commands to manipulate data in tables, and the commands to manipulate the database itself. There are many excellent tutorials on the Web that cover all the SQL commands and how to use them. See *http://www.w3schools.com/sql/default.asp*.

English-Like Grammar.   When you create a SQL statement it makes a request or "queries" the database in the form of a statement, similar to the structure of an English imperative sentence, such as "Select your partner," "Show your stuff," or "Describe that bully." The first word in a SQL statement is an English verb, an action word called a command such as show, use, select, drop, and so on. The commands are followed by a list of noun-like words, such as show databases, use database, or create databases. The statement might contain prepositions such as in or from. For example:

```
show tables in database
```

or

```
select phones from customer_table
```

The language also lets you add conditional clauses to refine your query such as:

```
select companyname from suppliers where supplierid > 20;
```

When listing multiple items in a query, like English, the items are separated by commas; for example, in the following SQL statement each field in the list being selected is comma separated:

```
select companyname, phone, address from suppliers;
```

If the queries get very long and involved, you might want to type them into your favorite editor, because once you have executed a query, it is lost. By saving the query in an editor, you can cut and paste it back into the MySQL browser or command line without retyping it. Most important, make sure your query makes sense and will not cause havoc on an important database. MySQL provides a "test" database for practice.

Semicolons Terminate SQL Statements.   When searching with Google for "SQL query," one of the top results is a Web site called *thinkgeek.com*, which sells T-shirts and apparel, electronics, gadgets, and home office and computing items. Their ad for the "SQL query" T-shirt reads:

> Black tshirt with the following SQL query written in white on front "SELECT * FROM users WHERE clue > 0". Unfortunately, zero rows are then returned....uh oh. And hey! there is no freakin semi-colon at the end of this query because not everybody under the sun uses the same database with the same console/shell—and there is more than one way to skin a cat. Umkay? Umkay.

The semicolon is the standard way to terminate each query statement. Some database systems do not require the semicolon, but MySQL does (exceptions are the USE and QUIT commands), and if you forget it, you will see a secondary prompt and execution will go on hold until you add the semicolon, as shown in Figure 14.3.

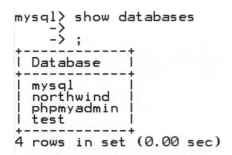

```
mysql> show databases
    ->
    -> ;
+------------+
| Database   |
+------------+
| mysql      |
| northwind  |
| phpmyadmin |
| test       |
+------------+
4 rows in set (0.00 sec)
```

Figure 14.3 Missing semicolon and the secondary prompt.

Naming Conventions. A database and its tables are easier to read when good naming conventions are used.

For example, it makes good sense to make table names plural and field/column names singular. Why? Because a table called "Shippers" normally holds more than one shipper, but the name of the field used to describe each shipper is a single value such as "Company_Name", "Phone", and so on. The first letter in a table or field name is usually capitalized.

Compound names, such as "Company_Name", are usually separated by the underscore, with the first letter of each word capitalized.

Spaces and dashes are not allowed in any name in the database.

Reserved Words. All languages have a list of reserved words that have special meaning to the language. Most of these words will be used in this chapter. The SQL reserved words are listed in Table 14.1. (See the MySQL documentation for a complete list of all reserved words.)

Table 14.1 SQL Reserved Words

ALTER	JOIN
AND	LEFT JOIN
AS	LIKE
CREATE	LIMIT
CROSS JOIN	ON
DELETE	OR
DROP	ORDER BY
FROM	RIGHT JOIN
FULL JOIN	SELECT
GROUP BY	SET
INSERT	UPDATE
INTO	WHERE

Case Senstivity. Database and table names are case sensitive if you are using UNIX, but not if you are using Windows. A convention is to always use lowercase names for databases and their tables.

SQL commands are not case sensitive. For example, the following SQL statements are equally valid:

```
show databases;
SHOW DATABASES;
```

Although SQL commands are not case sensitive, by convention, SQL keywords are capitalized for clarity while only first letter of the field, table, and database names is capitalized.

```
SELECT * FROM Persons WHERE FirstName='John'
```

If performing pattern matching with the `LIKE` and `NOT LIKE` commands, then the pattern being searched for is case sensitive when using MySQL.

The Result-Set. A result-set is just another table created to hold the results from a SQL query. Most database software systems even allow you to perform operations on the result-set with functions, such as `Move-To-First-Record`, `Get-Record-Content`, `Move-To-Next-Record`, and so on. In Figure 14.4, the result-set is the table created by asking `mysql` to show all the fields in the table called "shippers".

```
mysql> show fields in shippers;
+-------------+-------------+------+-----+---------+----------------+
| Field       | Type        | Null | Key | Default | Extra          |
+-------------+-------------+------+-----+---------+----------------+
| ShipperID   | int(11)     |      | PRI | NULL    | auto_increment |
| CompanyName | varchar(40) |      |     |         |                |
| Phone       | varchar(24) | YES  |     | NULL    |                |
+-------------+-------------+------+-----+---------+----------------+
3 rows in set (0.00 sec)
```

Figure 14.4 The result-set is just a table produced from a query.

14.1.4   SQL and the Database

A database server can support multiple databases. For example, an Oracle or MySQL database server might serve one database for accounting, a second for human resources, a third for an e-commerce application, and so on. To see the available databases, SQL provides the `show` command.

The Show Databases Command. To see what databases are available on your database server, use the `show databases` command. The list of databases might be different on your machine, but the "mysql" and "test" databases are provided when you install MySQL. The "mysql" database is required because it describes user access privileges and the "test" database, as the name suggests, is provided as a practice database for testing how things work.

FORMAT

```
SHOW DATABASES;
```

EXAMPLE 14.1

```
1   mysql> SHOW databases;
    +------------+
    | Database   |
    +------------+
    | mysql      |
    | northwind  |
    | phpmyadmin |
    | test       |
    +------------+
    4 rows in set (0.03 sec)show databases;
```

USE Command. The USE command makes the specified database your default database. From that point on, all SQL commands will be performed on the default database. This is one of the few commands that does not require a semicolon to terminate it.

FORMAT

```
USE database_name;
```

EXAMPLE 14.2

```
1   mysql> USE northwind;
    Database changed
```

EXPLANATION

1   The USE command changes the database to "northwind".[a] The command-line client will report that the database has been changed.

a. The "northwind" database is available for download from *http://www.microsoft.com/downloads/details.aspx?FamilyID=C6661372-8DBE-422B-8676-C632D66C529C&displaylang=EN*.

14.1.5 SQL Database Tables

A database usually contains one or more tables. Each table is identified by a name, such as "Customers" or "Orders." The SHOW TABLES IN command displays all the tables within a database, as shown in Figure 14.5. The SELECT * FROM command lists all the fields and rows in a specified table. Tables contain rows, called records, and columns called fields. The table in Figure 14.6 contains three records (one for each shipper) and three columns ("ShipperId", "CompanyName", and "Phone").

```
mysql> show tables in northwind;
+---------------------+
| Tables_in_northwind |
+---------------------+
| categories          |
| customercustomerdemo |
| customerdemographics |
| customers           |
| employees           |
| employeeterritories |
| order_details       |
| orders              |
| products            |
| region              |
| shippers            |
| suppliers           |
| territories         |
| usstates            |
+---------------------+
14 rows in set (0.03 sec)
```

Figure 14.5   Show all the tables in the "northwind" database.

```
mysql> select * from shippers;
+-----------+-----------------+----------------+
| ShipperID | CompanyName     | Phone          |
+-----------+-----------------+----------------+
|         1 | Speedy Express  | (503) 555-9831 |
|         2 | United Package  | (503) 555-3199 |
|         3 | Federal Shipping | (503) 555-9931 |
+-----------+-----------------+----------------+
3 rows in set (0.00 sec)
```

Figure 14.6   Display the contents of a particular table.

The Show and Describe Commands.   To see what type of data can be assigned to a table, use the DESCRIBE command, specific to MySQL, and SHOW FIELDS IN command, a standard SQL command. The output displayed is the name of each field, and the data types of the values that correspond to each field, as shown in Figure 14.7. The data type can be a variable string of characters, a date, a number, and so on. For example, the type varchar(40) means a field with up to 40 characters. Also displayed is the primary key that is used to uniquely identify the record.

FORMAT

```
SHOW FIELDS IN table_name;

or

DESCRIBE table_name;
```

```
mysql> show fields in customers;
+--------------+-------------+------+-----+---------+-------+
| Field        | Type        | Null | Key | Default | Extra |
+--------------+-------------+------+-----+---------+-------+
| CustomerID   | varchar(5)  |      | PRI |         |       |
| CompanyName  | varchar(40) |      | MUL |         |       |
| ContactName  | varchar(30) | YES  |     | NULL    |       |
| ContactTitle | varchar(30) | YES  |     | NULL    |       |
| Address      | varchar(60) | YES  |     | NULL    |       |
| City         | varchar(15) | YES  | MUL | NULL    |       |
| Region       | varchar(15) | YES  | MUL | NULL    |       |
| PostalCode   | varchar(10) | YES  | MUL | NULL    |       |
| Country      | varchar(15) | YES  |     | NULL    |       |
| Phone        | varchar(24) | YES  |     | NULL    |       |
| Fax          | varchar(24) | YES  |     | NULL    |       |
+--------------+-------------+------+-----+---------+-------+
11 rows in set (0.05 sec)
```

Figure 14.7   The SQL SHOW FIELDS IN command.

The shorter DESCRIBE version is shown in Figure 14.8.

```
mysql> describe shippers;
+-------------+-------------+------+-----+---------+----------------+
| Field       | Type        | Null | Key | Default | Extra          |
+-------------+-------------+------+-----+---------+----------------+
| ShipperID   | int(11)     |      | PRI | NULL    | auto_increment |
| CompanyName | varchar(40) |      |     |         |                |
| Phone       | varchar(24) | YES  |     | NULL    |                |
+-------------+-------------+------+-----+---------+----------------+
3 rows in set (0.00 sec)
```

Figure 14.8   The MySQL DESCRIBE command.

14.2 SQL Data Manipulation Language (DML)

SQL is a nonprocedural language providing a syntax for extracting data, including a syntax to update, insert, and delete records.

These query and update commands together form the Data Manipulation Language (DML) part of SQL. We cover the following SQL commands in this section:

- SELECT—Extracts data from a database table.
- UPDATE—Updates data in a database table.
- DELETE—Deletes data from a database table.
- INSERT INTO—Inserts new data into a database table.

14.2.1 The SELECT Command

One of the most commonly used SQL commands is SELECT, mandatory when performing a query. The SELECT command is used to retrieve data from a table based on some criteria. It specifies a comma-separated list of fields to be retrieved and the FROM clause specifies the table(s) to be accessed. The results are stored in a result table known as the result-set. The * symbol can be used to represent all of the fields.

FORMAT

```
SELECT column_name(s) FROM table_name
```

Example:
```
SELECT LastName, FirstName, Address FROM Students;
```

EXAMPLE 14.3

```
mysql> SELECT CompanyName FROM Shippers;
+------------------+
| CompanyName      |
+------------------+
| Speedy Express   |
| United Package   |
| Federal Shipping |
+------------------+
3 rows in set (0.05 sec)
```

EXPLANATION

The SELECT command will retrieve all items in the field "CompanyName" FROM the "Shippers" table. The result-set table is displayed in response to the query.

Select Specified Columns. To select the columns named "CompanyName" and "Phone" from the "Shippers" table, SELECT is followed by a comma-separated list of fields to be selected FROM the "Shippers" table. The resulting table is called the result-set as shown in Example 14.4.

EXAMPLE 14.4

```
mysql> SELECT CompanyName, Phone FROM Shippers;
+------------------+----------------+
| CompanyName      | Phone          |
+------------------+----------------+
| Speedy Express   | (503) 555-9831 |
| United Package   | (503) 555-3199 |
| Federal Shipping | (503) 555-9931 |
+------------------+----------------+
3 rows in set (0.09 sec)
```

Select All Columns.   To select all columns from the "Shippers" table, use a * symbol instead of column names, as shown in Example 14.5. The * is a wildcard character used to represent all of the fields (columns).

EXAMPLE 14.5

```
mysql> SELECT * FROM Shippers;
+-----------+------------------+------------------+
| ShipperID | CompanyName      | Phone            |
+-----------+------------------+------------------+
|         1 | Speedy Express   | (503) 555-9831   |
|         2 | United Package   | (503) 555-3199   |
|         3 | Federal Shipping | (503) 555-9931   |
+-----------+------------------+------------------+
3 rows in set (0.06 sec)
```

The SELECT DISTINCT Statement.   The DISTINCT keyword is used to return only distinct (unique) values from the table. If there are multiple values of a specified field, the DISTINCT result-set will display only one.

In the next example, ALL values from the column named "ShipName" are first selected and more than 800 records are displayed, but notice that with the DISTINCT keyword, fewer than 90 records are retrieved.

FORMAT

```
SELECT DISTINCT column_name(s) FROM table_name
```

EXAMPLE 14.6

```
SELECT ShipName from Orders
(Partial Output)
| North/South                    |
| Blauer See Delikatessen        |
| Ricardo Adocicados             |
| Franchi S.p.A.                 |
| Great Lakes Food Market        |
| Reggiani Caseifici             |
| Hungry Owl All-Night Grocers   |
| Save-a-lot Markets             |
| LILA-Supermercado              |
| White Clover Markets           |
| Drachenblut Delikatessen       |
| Queen Cozinha                  |
| Tortuga Restaurante            |
| Lehmanns Marktstand            |
| LILA-Supermercado              |
| Ernst Handel                   |
| Pericles Comidas clásicas      |
```

EXAMPLE 14.6 (CONTINUED)

```
| Simons bistro                      |
| Richter Supermarkt                 |
| Bon app'                           |
| Rattlesnake Canyon Grocery         |
+------------------------------------+
830 rows in set (0.00 sec)
```

With the DISTINCT keyword, fewer than 90 records are retrieved:

```
SELECT DISTINCT ShipName FROM Orders;
| Océano Atlántico Ltda.            |
| Franchi S.p.A.                    |
| Gourmet Lanchonetes               |
| Consolidated Holdings             |
| Rancho grande                     |
| Lazy K Kountry Store              |
| Laughing Bacchus Wine Cellars     |
| Blauer See Delikatessen           |
| North/South                       |
| Cactus Comidas para llevar        |
| Great Lakes Food Market           |
| Maison Dewey                      |
| Trail's Head Gourmet Provisioners |
| Let's Stop N Shop                 |
```

Limiting the Number of Lines in the Result-Set with LIMIT.   If you do not want to display a huge database, you can limit the number of lines to print by using LIMIT; for example, the tables in the "northwind" database contain thousands of records. In the previous examples, it would have been better to display a few lines to demonstrate that the query was successful. Because you are only getting a partial list, you might want to know the total number in the table. This can be done by using the SQL_CALC_FOUND_ROWS option and the SQL FOUND_ROWS() function. (We discuss functions in the next chapter.) SQL will calculate the total number of records and the FOUND_ROWS() function will let you display the results of that calculation.

EXAMPLE 14.7

```
mysql> select ShipName from Orders LIMIT 10;
+---------------------------+
| ShipName                  |
+---------------------------+
| Vins et alcools Chevalier |
| Toms Spezialitaten        |
| Hanari Carnes             |
| Victuailles en stock      |
| Suprêmes délices          |
| Hanari Carnes             |
| Chop-suey Chinese         |
| Richter Supermarkt        |
| Wellington Importadora    |
| HILARION-Abastos          |
+---------------------------+
10 rows in set (0.00 sec)
```

EXPLANATION

With one argument, in this case 10, LIMIT specifies the number of rows to return from the beginning of the result-set.

EXAMPLE 14.8

```
mysql> SELECT SQL_CALC_FOUND ROWS ShipName from Orders
    -> LIMIT 5;
+---------------------------+
| ShipName                  |
+---------------------------+
| Vins et alcools Chevalier |
| Toms Spezialitaten        |
| Hanari Carnes             |
| Victuailles en stock      |
| Suprêmes délices          |
+---------------------------+
5 rows in set (0.03 sec)

mysql> SELECT FOUND_ROWS();
+--------------+
| FOUND_ROWS() |
+--------------+
|          830 |
+--------------+
1 row in set (0.03 sec)
```

EXPLANATION

SQL will calculate the total number of records, limited to 5, and the FOUND_ROWS() function will let you display the results of that calculation.

The WHERE Clause.   What if you want to select fields only when a certain set of conditions is true? For example, you might want to list all the customers who come from Sweden and were paid more than $50,000 last year. The WHERE clause is optional and specifies which data values or rows will be selected, based on a condition described after the keyword WHERE. To create the conditions, called the selection criteria, SQL provides a set of operators to further qualify what criteria should be specified in the WHERE clause. See Table 14.2.

FORMAT

```
SELECT column FROM table WHERE column operator value
```

Example:
```
SELECT phone FROM shippers WHERE country like "Sw";
```

Table 14.2   SQL Operators

Operator	Description	Example
=	Equal to	`where country = 'Sweden'`
<>, !=	Not equal to[a]	`where country <> 'Sweden'`
>	Greater than	`where salary > 50000`
<	Less than	`where salary < 50000`
>=	Greater than or equal	`where salary >= 50000`
<=	Less than or equal	`where salary <= 50000`
IS [NOT] NULL	Is NULL (no value) or Not NULL	`where birth = NULL`
BETWEEN	Between an inclusive range	`where last_name BETWEEN 'Dobbins' AND 'Main'`
LIKE	Search for a value like a pattern	`where last_name LIKE 'D%'`
NOT LIKE	Search for a value not like a pattern	`where country NOT LIKE 'Sw%'`
!, NOT	Logical not for negation	`where age ! 10;`
||, OR	Logical OR	`where order_number > 10 || part_number = 80`
&&, AND	Logical AND	`where age > 12 && age < 21`
XOR	Exclusive OR	`where status XOR`

a.   In some versions of SQL the <> operator can be written as !=.

Using Quotes.   Quotes are always an issue in programming languages. Should you use a set of single quotes or double quotes and when should you use them?

SQL uses single quotes around text values (most database systems, including MySQL, also accept double quotes). Numeric values should not be enclosed in quotes.

For text values, this example is correct:

```
SELECT * FROM Students WHERE FirstName='Marco'
```

and this example is wrong:

```
SELECT * FROM Students WHERE FirstName=Marco      Marco should be
"Marco"
```

For numeric values, this example is correct:

```
SELECT * FROM Students WHERE Year>2004
```

and this example is wrong:

```
SELECT * FROM Students WHERE Year>'2004'      '2004' should be 2004
```

Using the = and <> Operators.   In Figure 14.9, the "CompanyName" and "Phone" are retrieved from the "Customers" table if the condition following the WHERE clause is true; that is, if the string values in the "Country" field are exactly equal to the string "Italy" (they must contain the same number and type of characters). The <> operator can be used to test for "not equal to."

```
mysql> select CompanyName, Phone FROM Customers
    -> WHERE Country='Italy';
+------------------------------+--------------+
| CompanyName                  | Phone        |
+------------------------------+--------------+
| Franchi S.p.A.               | 011-4988260  |
| Magazzini Alimentari Riuniti | 035-640230   |
| Reggiani Caseifici           | 0522-556721  |
+------------------------------+--------------+
3 rows in set (0.00 sec)
```

Figure 14.9   The WHERE clause with the = operator.

What Is NULL?   Null means that there is not a value in a field, or it is unknown, but does not mean a value of zero. If a field is NULL, it is empty, and if it is NOT NULL, it has data. Fields have NULL as a default unless they are specified by NOT NULL in the definition of the table.

EXAMPLE 14.9

```
mysql> SELECT region, country FROM suppliers
    -> WHERE region IS NULL;
+--------+-------------+
| region | country     |
+--------+-------------+
| NULL   | UK          |
| NULL   | Japan       |
| NULL   | Japan       |
| NULL   | UK          |
| NULL   | Sweden      |
| NULL   | Brazil      |
| NULL   | Germany     |
| NULL   | Germany     |
| NULL   | Germany     |
| NULL   | Italy       |
| NULL   | Norway      |
| NULL   | Sweden      |
| NULL   | France      |
| NULL   | Singapore   |
| NULL   | Denmark     |
| NULL   | Netherlands |
| NULL   | Finland     |
| NULL   | Italy       |
| NULL   | France      |
| NULL   | France      |
+--------+-------------+
20 rows in set (0.00 sec)
```

EXPLANATION

Displays the region and country from the "suppliers" database where the region IS NULL; that is, has no value.

EXAMPLE 14.10

```
mysql> SELECT region, country FROM suppliers
    -> WHERE region NOT NULL;
+----------+-----------+
| region   | country   |
+----------+-----------+
| LA       | USA       |
| MI       | USA       |
| Asturias | Spain     |
| Victoria | Australia |
```

EXAMPLE 14.10 (CONTINUED)

```
| OR       | USA       |
| MA       | USA       |
| NSW      | Australia |
| Québec   | Canada    |
| Québec   | Canada    |
+----------+-----------+
9 rows in set (0.00 sec)
```

EXPLANATION

Displays the "region" and "country" from the "suppliers" database where the region is NOT NULL; that is, has a value.

The > and < Operators. The > and < operators are used to select rows where the value of a field is greater or less than some value such as:

```
SELECT product, price FROM table WHERE price > 50;
```

```
SELECT product, price FROM table
WHERE price > 50 && price < 100;
```

You can also use the >= and <= to select rows that are greater than or equal to or less than or equal to some value:

```
SELECT product, price FROM table
WHERE price >=50;
```

EXAMPLE 14.11

```
mysql> SELECT UnitPrice, Quantity FROM Order_Details
    -> WHERE UnitPrice > 1 && UnitPrice < 3;
+-----------+----------+
| UnitPrice | Quantity |
+-----------+----------+
|    2.0000 |       25 |
|    2.0000 |       60 |
|    2.0000 |       24 |
|    2.0000 |       20 |
|    2.0000 |        8 |
|    2.0000 |       60 |
|    2.0000 |       49 |
|    2.0000 |       50 |
|    2.0000 |       20 |
```

EXAMPLE 14.12

```
mysql> SELECT CategoryName from categories WHERE CategoryName < 'D';
+---------------+
| CategoryName  |
+---------------+
| Beverages     |
| Condiments    |
| Confections   |
+---------------+
3 rows in set (0.00 sec)
```

The AND and OR Operators.   AND and OR operators are used in a WHERE clause to further qualify what data you want to select from a table. The AND operator tests one or more conditions to see if the all conditions are true; if so, SELECT displays the rows. The OR operator displays a row if only one of the conditions listed is true. The AND operator can be designated by the && symbol, and the OR operator can be designated as ||.

EXAMPLE 14.13

```
mysql> SELECT ContactName FROM Suppliers
    -> WHERE City = 'Montreal' AND Region = 'Quebec';
+------------------+
| contactname      |
+------------------+
| Jean-Guy Lauzon  |
+------------------+
1 row in set (0.03 sec)
```

EXPLANATION

When using the && (AND) operator both of the conditions being tested in the WHERE clause must be true; that is, both the City must be Montreal *and* the Region must be Quebec. If both conditions are true, then SELECT will print the "ContactName" from the "Suppliers" database.

EXAMPLE 14.14

```
mysql> SELECT CompanyName, City FROM Suppliers WHERE
    -> City = 'Montreal' OR City = 'Boston';
+------------------------------+----------+
| CompanyName                  | City     |
+------------------------------+----------+
| New England Seafood Cannery  | Boston   |
| Ma Maison                    | Montreal |
+------------------------------+----------+
2 rows in set (0.00 sec)
```

EXPLANATION

When using the || (OR) operator only one of the conditions being tested must be true; that is, if either the City is Montreal *or* the City is Boston, then SELECT will print the "CompanyName" and "City" from the "Suppliers" database.

The LIKE and NOT LIKE Condition. The LIKE pattern-matching operator is a powerful operator that can be used as a condition in the WHERE clause, allowing you to select only rows that are "like" or match a pattern.

A percent sign (%) can be used as a wildcard to match any possible character that might appear before and/or after the characters specified.

A _ is used to match a single character.

The LIKE condition can be used in any valid SQL statement, including SELECT, INSERT, UPDATE, or DELETE.

FORMAT

```
SELECT column FROM table WHERE column LIKE pattern
SELECT column FROM table WHERE column NOT LIKE pattern
```

Example:
```
SELECT column FROM customer WHERE last_name LIKE 'Mc%';
```

The next examples will demonstrate how the % and _ are used with LIKE and NOT LIKE as a wildcard in pattern matching.

Pattern Matching and the % Wildcard. The % wildcard is used to represent one or more of any character when performing pattern matching. For example, if you are looking for all phone numbers in the 408 area code, you could say 408% and the % will be replaced by any characters after 408.

EXAMPLE 14.15

```
mysql> SELECT CompanyName, Country FROM Customers
    -> WHERE country like 'Sw%';
+---------------------+-------------+
| CompanyName         | Country     |
+---------------------+-------------+
| Berglunds snabbköp  | Sweden      |
| Chop-suey Chinese   | Switzerland |
| Folk och fä HB      | Sweden      |
| Richter Supermarkt  | Switzerland |
+---------------------+-------------+
4 rows in set (0.00 sec)
```

EXPLANATION

The SELECT returns all the customers who are from countries that start with Sw.

EXAMPLE 14.16

```
mysql> SELECT City, Country FROM Suppliers WHERE City LIKE '%o';
+-----------+---------+
| City      | Country |
+-----------+---------+
| Tokyo     | Japan   |
| Oviedo    | Spain   |
| Sao Paulo | Brazil  |
| Salerno   | Italy   |
+-----------+---------+
4 rows in set (0.00 sec)
```

EXPLANATION

The SELECT returns all cities and countries where the % matches any city that ends with a letter o.

EXAMPLE 14.17

```
mysql> SELECT Companyname FROM customers
    ->       WHERE CompanyName LIKE '%Super%';
+---------------------+
| Companyname         |
+---------------------+
| LILA-Supermercado   |
| Richter Supermarkt  |
+---------------------+
2 rows in set (0.00 sec)
```

EXPLANATION

The SELECT returns all company names where the % matches any company name that contains the pattern Super.

The _ Wildcard.   The next example shows how the underscore (_) wildcard character works. Remember that the _ matches only one character.

EXAMPLE   14.18

```
mysql> SELECT extension, firstname FROM employees
    -> WHERE extension LIKE '4_ _';
+-----------+-----------+
| extension | firstname |
+-----------+-----------+
| 428       | Michael   |
| 465       | Robert    |
| 452       | Anne      |
+-----------+-----------+
3 rows in set (0.00 sec)
```

EXPLANATION

This SELECT returns all extensions and first names where the extension has three characters and the first character is a 4. The _ symbol is used to match a single character.

The BETWEEN Statement.   The BETWEEN keyword allows you select a field based on criteria that represents a range of values. The syntax for the BETWEEN clause is as follows:

FORMAT

```
SELECT column  FROM table
WHERE column BETWEEN 'value1' AND 'value2'
```

Example:
```
select age from person where age BETWEEN 10 && 20;
```

EXAMPLE   14.19

```
mysql> SELECT ProductName, ProductId
    -> FROM Products WHERE ProductId BETWEEN 30 AND 33;
+-----------------------+-----------+
| ProductName           | ProductId |
+-----------------------+-----------+
| Nord-Ost Matjeshering |        30 |
| Gorgonzola Telino     |        31 |
| Mascarpone Fabioli    |        32 |
| Geitost               |        33 |
+-----------------------+-----------+
4 rows in set (0.06 sec)
```

EXPLANATION

The SELECT returns product names and product IDs if the "ProductId" value is in the range between 30 and 33.

Sorting Results with ORDER BY.   You can display the output of a query in a particular order by using the ORDER BY clause. Rows can be sorted either in ascending (ASC, the default) or descending (DESC) order where the values being sorted are either strings or numbers.

FORMAT

```
SELECT column FROM table
[WHERE condition]
ORDER BY column [ASC, DESC]
```

Example:
```
SELECT Company, OrderNumber FROM Orders
ORDER BY Company
```

EXAMPLE 14.20

```
mysql> SELECT CompanyName, ContactName FROM suppliers
    -> ORDER BY CompanyName LIMIT 10;
+------------------------------------+----------------------------+
| CompanyName                        | ContactName                |
+------------------------------------+----------------------------+
| Aux joyeux ecclésiastiques         | Guylène Nodier             |
| Bigfoot Breweries                  | Cheryl Saylor              |
| Cooperativa de Quesos 'Las Cabras' | Antonio del Valle Saavedra |
| Escargots Nouveaux                 | Marie Delamare             |
| Exotic Liquids                     | Charlotte Cooper           |
| Forêts d'Trables                   | Chantal Goulet             |
| Formaggi Fortini s.r.l.            | Elio Rossi                 |
| G'day, Mate                        | Wendy Mackenzie            |
| Gai pâturage                       | Eliane Noz                 |
| Grandma Kelly's Homestead          | Regina Murphy              |
+------------------------------------+----------------------------+
10 rows in set (0.06 sec)
```

EXPLANATION

The "CompanyName" is sorted in ascending order, limited to 10 records.

EXAMPLE 14.21

```
mysql> SELECT CompanyName, ContactName FROM suppliers
    -> ORDER BY CompanyName DESC LIMIT 10;
+-------------------------------------+----------------------------+
| CompanyName                         | ContactName                |
+-------------------------------------+----------------------------+
| Zaanse Snoepfabriek                 | Dirk Luchte                |
| Tokyo Traders                       | Yoshi Nagase               |
| Svensk Sjöföda AB                   | Michael Björn              |
| Specialty Biscuits, Ltd.            | Peter Wilson               |
| Refrescos Americanas LTDA           | Carlos Diaz                |
| Plutzer Lebensmittelgro-markte AG   | Martin Bein                |
| PB Knackebröd AB                    | Lars Peterson              |
| Pavlova, Ltd.                       | Ian Devling                |
| Pasta Buttini s.r.l.                | Giovanni Giudici           |
| Norske Meierier                     | Beate Vileid               |
29 rows in set (0.00 sec)
```

EXPLANATION

The "CompanyName" is sorted in descending order, limited to 10 records.

14.2.2 The INSERT Command

The INSERT INTO statement is used to insert new rows into a table. After the VALUES keyword, a comma-separated list of column names follows.

FORMAT

```
INSERT INTO table_name VALUES (value1, value2,....)
```

You can also specify the columns for which you want to insert data:

```
INSERT INTO table_name (column1, column2,...)
VALUES (value1, value2,....)
```

EXAMPLE 14.22

```
INSERT INTO Shippers (CompanyName, Phone)
VALUES ('Canada Post', '416-555-1221');
+-----------+------------------+----------------+
| ShipperID | CompanyName      | Phone          |
+-----------+------------------+----------------+
|         1 | Speedy Express   | (503) 555-9831 |
|         2 | United Package   | (503) 555-3199 |
|         3 | Federal Shipping | (503) 555-9931 |
|         4 | Canada Post      | 416-555-1221   |
+-----------+------------------+----------------+
```

EXPLANATION

The INSERT INTO statement is inserting a new row into the "Shippers" table, first by listing the field name, and then the corresponding values after the VALUES keyword. The "ShipperID" value is not included because when the table was created, "ShipperID" was set as a PRMARY KEY to be auto-incremented by the database every time a new shipper record is added. (Letting the database increment the PRIMARY KEY ensures that the value is always unique.) To see how the table was originally set up, see the output from the DESCRIBE command here:

```
mysql> DESCRIBE shippers;
+-------------+-------------+------+-----+---------+----------------+
| Field       | Type        | Null | Key | Default | Extra          |
+-------------+-------------+------+-----+---------+----------------+
| ShipperID   | int(11)     |      | PRI | NULL    | auto_increment |
| CompanyName | varchar(40) |      |     |         |                |
| Phone       | varchar(24) | YES  |     | NULL    |                |
+-------------+-------------+------+-----+---------+----------------+
```

14.2.3 The UPDATE Command

The UPDATE statement is used to modify the data in a table. After the UPDATE command, you list the name of the table where the data will be changed, followed by the SET statement to indicate what field will be changed, and then the new value that will be assigned to the field. The WHERE clause further qualifies what data is to be modified, thereby limiting the scope of the update.

In Example 14.23, the key is the use of the WHERE statement to limit the scope of the update.

FORMAT

```
UPDATE table_name
SET column_name = new_value
WHERE column_name = some_value
```

Example:
```
UPDATE orders SET ShipCountry="Luxembourg" WHERE CustomerId='whitc';
```

EXAMPLE 14.23

```
1   mysql> select * from shippers;
    +-----------+-----------------+----------------+
    | ShipperID | CompanyName     | Phone          |
    +-----------+-----------------+----------------+
    |         1 | Speedy Express  | (503) 555-9831 |
    |         2 | United Package  | (503) 555-3199 |
    |         3 | Federal Shipping| (503) 555-9931 |
    +-----------+-----------------+----------------+
    3 rows in set (0.00 sec)

2   mysql> UPDATE shippers SET PHONE='(777) 444-1334'
        -> WHERE companyname = 'Federal Shipping';
    Query OK, 1 row affected (0.08 sec)
    Rows matched: 1  Changed: 1  Warnings: 0

3   mysql> select * from shippers;
    +-----------+-----------------+----------------+
    | ShipperID | CompanyName     | Phone          |
    +-----------+-----------------+----------------+
    |         1 | Speedy Express  | (503) 555-9831 |
    |         2 | United Package  | (503) 555-3199 |
    |         3 | Federal Shipping| (777) 444-1234 |
    +-----------+-----------------+----------------+
    3 rows in set (0.00 sec)
```

EXPLANATION

1   The SELECT command shows all the fields in the "Shippers" table.
2   The UPDATE command allows you to change an existing record. The phone number for Federal Shipping is being changed.
3   This SELECT command shows that the phone number for Federal Shipping was changed by the previous UPDATE command.

14.2.4 The DELETE Statement

The DELETE statement is used to delete rows in a table and returns the number of rows that were deleted. DELETE uses the FROM clause to specify the name of the table that contains the data you want to delete, and the WHERE clause specifies the criteria to identify what data should be removed.

Be careful! Without a WHERE clause, all rows are deleted.[1]

If the ORDER BY clause is specified, the rows are deleted in the order that is specified. The LIMIT clause places a limit on the number of rows that can be deleted.

---

1. You can set up MySQL so that if you use DELETE without a WHERE clause, the rows will not be deleted.

```
DELETE FROM table_name
WHERE column_name = some_value
```

The DELETE statement is very similar to the UPDATE statement. To delete the previous record, you would enter this query:

DELETE FROM Shippers WHERE CompanyName='Canada Post';

14.3 SQL Data Definition Language

The Data Definition Language (DDL) part of SQL permits database objects to be created or destroyed. You can also define indexes (keys), specify links between tables, and impose constraints between database tables. Often decisions to create and remove databases are handled by a database administrator and having permission to create and drop tables depends on what access rights are granted.

The most important data definition statements in SQL are:

- CREATE TABLE—Creates a new database table.
- ALTER TABLE—Alters (changes) a database table.
- DROP TABLE—Deletes a database table.
- CREATE INDEX—Creates an index (search key).
- DROP INDEX—Deletes an index.

14.3.1 Creating the Database

Creating the database is very simple. All you have to do is issue one command and the only parameter is the database name.

FORMAT

```
CREATE DATABASE database_name
```

In the earlier examples, we used the "northwind" database. Because we will be working on a complete Web application for an art gallery in Appendix A, now we will create the database for that application.

EXAMPLE 14.24

```
1   mysql> CREATE DATABASE gallerydb;
    Query OK, 1 row affected (0.03 sec)

2   mysql> show databases;
    +------------+
    | Database   |
    +------------+
    | gallerydb  |
    | mysql      |
    | northwind  |
    | phpmyadmin |
    | test       |
    +------------+
    5 rows in set (0.00 sec)
```

EXPLANATION

That's it. The database is now created. Note that just because we created the database, we are still not in that database. The USE command in the next example will make it the new database the current default database.

EXAMPLE 14.25

```
1   mysql> USE gallerydb;
    Database changed
```

EXPLANATION

We are now in the "gallerydb" database and all the SQL commands will be executed on that database.

14.3.2 SQL Data Types

After creating a database, you will add the tables that make up the database. Before creating a table, you have to decide what kind of data will be stored in it; for example, will you have rows of names, dates, part numbers, social security numbers, prices, and so on? The data type specifies what type of data the column can hold. The basic types are string, numeric, and date and time types. For a fully documented list, see *http://dev.mysql.com/doc/refman/5.0/en/data-types.html*.

Table 14.3 contains the most common data types in SQL.

Table 14.3 Most Common SQL Data Types

Data Type	Description
Numbers	
INTEGER	Holds a 4-byte whole number.
INT UNSIGNED	Holds a 4-byte nonnegative whole number.
SMALLINT	Holds a 2-byte whole number.
TINYINT	Holds a 1-byte whole number.
FLOAT(m,d)	A 4-byte fractional number. FLOAT(7,4) for value 999.00009 results in 999.0001. The maximum number of digits are specified in m. The maximum number of digits to the right of the decimal is specified in d.
DOUBLE(m,d)	An 8-byte fractional double precision number.
DECIMAL(m,d)	A real or fractional 8-byte number. The maximum number of digits is specified in m. The maximum number of digits to the right of the decimal is specified in d.
NUMERIC(m,d)	The DECIMAL and NUMERIC data types are used to store exact numeric data values with exact precision; e.g., monetary data. Hold numbers with fractions.
Strings	
CHAR(SIZE)	Holds a fixed-length string (can contain letters, numbers, and special characters) from 0 to 255 characters long. The fixed size is specified in the parentheses.
VARCHAR(SIZE)	A variable-length string (can contain letters, numbers, and special characters) from 0 to 65,535 in MySQL 5.0.3 and later versions. The maximum size is specified in the parentheses.
TINYTEXT	A string with a maximum length of 255 characters.
TEXT	A variable-length text string with a maximum length of 65,535 characters, used for storing large text files, documents, text areas, etc.
BLOB	Binary large object. A binary string with a maximum length of 65,535 characters, used for storing binary files, images, sounds, etc.
Date and Time	
DATE	(yyyy-mm-dd) year, month, day; e.g., 2006-10-30 (Note: MySQL also allows you to store 0000-00-00 as a "dummy date.")
DATETIME	(yyyy-mm-dd hh:mm:ss) date and time; e.g., 2006-10-30 22:59:59
TIMESTAMP	(yyyy-mm-dd hh:mm:ss) date and time; e.g., 1970-01-01 (date and time of last transaction on a row)
TIME	(hh:mm:ss) time; e.g., 10:30:58
YEAR	(yyyy | yy) year in four or two digits; e.g., 1978 or 78

14.3.3 Creating a Table

Creating a table is a little more complicated than creating the database. The CREATE TABLE statement is used to create a new table in the database. First you must name the new table and then specify all the fields that will be included in the table as well as the data types and any other attributes. A data type can be an integer, a floating-point (real) number such as 5.4, a string of characters, a date, a time, and so on. Not all databases will specify data types in the same way. To see what data types and attributes are available for MySQL, see Table 14.3 or the MySQL documentation.

Designing your tables correctly is important and a subject that merits further research if you have not worked with databases before. See *http://databases.about.com/od/specificproducts/a/normalization.htm* for an excellent beginner's tutorial on database design. For now, here are some rules to keep in mind when designing the table:

1. Choose the right data type for your fields; for example, use integer types for primary keys, use float and double types for large numbers, use decimal or numeric types for currency, use the correct date format for times and dates, and give yourself ample field width for strings containing variable numbers of characters, such as names and addresses. If you are saving binary data such as images and sounds, use a data type that supports such large amounts of data such as blob and text types. See Table 14.3.

2. Give columns sensible and concise names. Make them unique within the table. Do not have duplicate columns in the same table, as shown below. These should not be three columns all headed with phone.

First_Name	Last_Name	Phone1	Phone2	Phone3
Joe	Blow	415-444-3333	333-111-1233	652-345-1123

3. Store only one value under each column heading in each row; for example, if you have a "Phone" field, you should not have "cell, home, business" all in one table cell, as shown here:

First_Name	Last_Name	Phone
Joe	Blow	415-444-3333, 333-111-1233, 652-345-1123

4. Create separate tables for each group of related items and give each row a unique column or primary key, as shown here:

User Table:

Customer_Id	First_Name	Last_Name
1	Joe	Blow

Phone Table:

Customer_Id	Cell	Business	Home
1	415-444-3333	333-111-1233	652-345-1123

5. If you still have redundant data, put it in its own table and establish a relation between the tables with foreign keys.

FORMAT

```
CREATE TABLE table_name
(
column_name1 data_type,
column_name2 data_type,
column_name3 data_type    <-- no comma on the last entry
)
```

EXAMPLE 14.26

```
1   mysql> CREATE DATABASE pets;
    Query OK, 1 row affected (0.24 sec)
2   mysql> USE pets;
3   mysql> CREATE TABLE dog
    -> ( name varchar(20),
    ->   owner varchar(20),
    ->   breed varchar(20),
    ->   sex char(1),
    ->   birth date,
    ->   death date
    -> );
    Query OK, 0 rows affected (0.16 sec)
4   mysql> describe dog;
    +-------+-------------+------+-----+---------+-------+
    | Field | Type        | Null | Key | Default | Extra |
    +-------+-------------+------+-----+---------+-------+
    | name  | varchar(20) | YES  |     | NULL    |       |
    | owner | varchar(20) | YES  |     | NULL    |       |
    | breed | varchar(20) | YES  |     | NULL    |       |
    | sex   | char(1)     | YES  |     | NULL    |       |
    | birth | date        | YES  |     | NULL    |       |
    | death | date        | YES  |     | NULL    |       |
    +-------+-------------+------+-----+---------+-------+
    6 rows in set (0.00 sec)
```

EXPLANATION

1   A database called "pets" is created.
2   The "pets" database is selected and entered.
3   A table called "dogs" is created with fields and their data types. The "name", "owner", and "breed" will consist of a varying number of up to 20 characters. The "sex" is one character, either "f" or "m" for female or male. The "birth" and "death" columns are assigned `date` type.
4   The `DESCRIBE` command is like the `SHOW` command. It displays the layout of the new table.

Now we can insert some data into the new table.

EXAMPLE   14.27

```
mysql> INSERT INTO dog(name,owner,breed, sex, birth, death)
    -> VALUES('Fido','Mr. Jones', 'Mutt', 'M', '2004-11-12',
       '2006-04-02');
Query OK, 1 row affected (0.09 sec)
```

14.3.4   Creating a Key

In real life, people can be identified by Social Security numbers, driver's license numbers, and employee numbers; books can be identified by ISBN numbers; and a Web store order can be identified by a purchase order number. These identification numbers must be unique so that no two people have the same Social Security number, no two books have the same ISBN number, and so on. Keys are used to uniqely identify a record in a table. There are two types of keys: *primary* keys and *foreign* keys.

Primary Keys.   Each table typically has a primary key. Primary keys are used to uniquely identify a record in the database. They must be unique, never change, occur only once per table, and are normally numeric types.

You can choose to manually generate this unique number for each record or let the database do it for you. If you let the database generate the primary key, it will generate a unique number, given a starting value (e.g., 1) and then for each new record increment that number by one. Even if a record is deleted, that number is never recycled. The database increments its internal counter, guaranteeing that each record will be given a unique "key."

To set a field as a primay key, use the attribute `PRIMARY KEY (field_name)` and to tell the database to automatically create the unique number, use the `AUTO_INCREMENT` attribute following the field definition. The primary key cannot be null.

The following two examples describe a table called "categories" where the primary key is called "CategoryID". It will automatically be incremented each time a new category is added to the table.

EXAMPLE 14.28

```
mysql> USE northwind;
Database changed
mysql> DESCRIBE categories;
+--------------+-------------+------+-----+---------+----------------+
| Field        | Type        | Null | Key | Default | Extra          |
+--------------+-------------+------+-----+---------+----------------+
| CategoryID   | int(11)     |      | PRI | NULL    | auto_increment |
| CategoryName | varchar(15) |      | MUL |         |                |
| Description  | longtext    | YES  |     | NULL    |                |
| Picture      | longblob    | YES  |     | NULL    |                |
+--------------+-------------+------+-----+---------+----------------+
4 rows in set (0.09 sec)
```

EXPLANATION

The "CategoryID" is the primary key, an integer of up to 11 digits, which will be incremented by 1, initially set to NULL (no value). The first time a record is inserted into the database, the value will be 1.

EXAMPLE 14.29

```
mysql> SELECT CategoryID, CategoryName FROM categories;
+------------+----------------+
| CategoryID | CategoryName   |
+------------+----------------+
|          1 | Beverages      |
|          2 | Condiments     |
|          3 | Confections    |
|          4 | Dairy Products |
|          5 | Grains/Cereals |
|          6 | Meat/Poultry   |
|          7 | Produce        |
|          8 | Seafood        |
+------------+----------------+
8 rows in set (0.16 sec)
```

EXPLANATION

The primary key is called "CategoryID". It is used to uniquely identify the different categories in this table from the "northwind" database. When a new category is added to the table, the "CategoryID" will be automatically incremented by 1.

Foreign Keys.   If a primary key is referenced in another table, it is called a foreign key. Foreign keys are used to create relation between tables. In the following example, two tables are described, which both reference the "CategoryID" key, although it is primary in one and foreign in the other.

EXAMPLE 14.30

```
mysql> DESCRIBE categories;
+--------------+--------------+------+-----+---------+----------------+
| Field        | Type         | Null | Key | Default | Extra          |
+--------------+--------------+------+-----+---------+----------------+
| CategoryID   | int(11)      |      | PRI | NULL    | auto_increment |
| CategoryName | varchar(15)  |      | MUL |         |                |
| Description  | longtext     | YES  |     | NULL    |                |
| Picture      | longblob     | YES  |     | NULL    |                |
+--------------+--------------+------+-----+---------+----------------+
4 rows in set (0.00 sec)

mysql> DESCRIBE products;
+--------------+--------------+------+-----+---------+----------------+
| Field        | Type         | Null | Key | Default | Extra          |
+--------------+--------------+------+-----+---------+----------------+
| ProductID    | int(11)      |      | PRI | NULL    | auto_increment |
| ProductName  | varchar(40)  |      | MUL |         |                |
| SupplierID   | int(11)      | YES  | MUL | NULL    |                |
| CategoryID   | int(11)      | YES  | MUL | NULL    |                |
| QuantityPerUnit| varchar(20) | YES  |     | NULL    |                |
| UnitPrice    | decimal(19,4)| YES  |     | NULL    |                |
| UnitsInStock | smallint(6)  | YES  |     | NULL    |                |
| UnitsOnOrder | smallint(6)  | YES  |     | NULL    |                |
| ReorderLevel | smallint(6)  | YES  |     | NULL    |                |
| Discontinued | tinyint(4)   |      |     | 0       |                |
+--------------+--------------+------+-----+---------+----------------+
10 rows in set (0.00 sec)
```

EXPLANATION

1   The "categories" table has a primary key field called "CategoryID".
2   The "products" table has its own primary key ("ProductID") in addition to a foreign key called "CategoryID". If a primary key is referenced in another table, it is called a foreign key.

14.3.5   Relations

A major advantage of the relational database systems is the ability to create relations between tables. Simply put, a relation is a connection between a field of one table and a field of another. This relation allows you to look up related records in the database.

The operation of matching rows from one table to another using one or more column values is called a *join*. There are several types of join statements, such as *full joins*, *cross joins*, *left joins*, and so on, but let's start with a simple joining of two tables, called an *inner join*.

Tables can be related to each other with keys. As we discussed earlier, a primary key is a column with a unique value for each row. A matching key in a second table is called a foreign key. With these keys, you can bind data together across tables without repeating all of the data in every table where a certain condition is met.

Consider the the previous Example 14.30, in which two tables from the "northwind" database are described. One table is called "categories" and the other called "products". "CategoryId" is a primary key field in the "categories" table, and it is a foreign key in the "products" table. The "CategoryId" key is used to create a relationship between the two tables.

Two Tables with a Common Key.   As discussed previously, both the "categories" table and the "products" table have a "CategoryID" key with the same values, making it possible to create a relation between the two tables.

Let's create a relation in which all the product names are listed if they are in the "Seafood" category. Because every product in the "products" table falls into one of the eight categories in the "categories" table, the two tables can be bound by their common "CategoryID".

EXAMPLE 14.31

```
mysql> SELECT CategoryID, CategoryName FROM categories;
+------------+----------------+
| categoryID | categoryName   |
+------------+----------------+
|          1 | Beverages      |
|          2 | Condiments     |
|          3 | Confections    |
|          4 | Dairy Products |
|          5 | Grains/Cereals |
|          6 | Meat/Poultry   |
|          7 | Produce        |
|          8 | Seafood        |
+------------+----------------+
8 rows in set (0.00 sec)
```

EXAMPLE 14.31 (CONTINUED)

```
mysql> SELECT CategoryID, ProductName FROM products;
(Partial Output)
+------------+--------------------------------+
| CategoryID | ProductName                    |
+------------+--------------------------------+
|          1 | Chai                           |
|          1 | Chang                          |
|          2 | Aniseed Syrup                  |
|          2 | Chef Anton's Cajun Seasoning   |
|          2 | Chef Anton's Gumbo Mix         |
|          2 | Grandma's Boysenberry Spread   |
|          7 | Uncle Bob's Organic Dried Pears|
|          2 | Northwoods Cranberry Sauce     |
|          6 | Mishi Kobe Niku                |
|          8 | Ikura                          |
|          4 | Queso Cabrales                 |
|          4 | Queso Manchego La Pastora      |
|          8 | Konbu                          |
|          7 | Tofu                           |
|          2 | Genen Shouyu                   |
```

EXPLANATION

This example displays columns from both the "categories" table and the "products" table. In the "categories" table the "CategoryID" is the primary field and uniquely identifies all other fields in the table. In the "products" table, the "CategoryID" is a foreign key and is repeated many times for all the products.

Using a Fully Qualified Name and a Dot to Join the Tables. When querying more than one table, a dot is used to fully qualify the columns by their table name to avoid potential ambiguity if two tables have a field with the same name, as shown in Example 14.32.

EXAMPLE 14.32

```
mysql> SELECT CategoryName, ProductName FROM categories, products
    -> WHERE products.CategoryID = 8 AND categories.CategoryID = 8;
+--------------+--------------------------------+
| CategoryName | ProductName                    |
+--------------+--------------------------------+
| Seafood      | Ikura                          |
| Seafood      | Konbu                          |
| Seafood      | Carnarvon Tigers               |
| Seafood      | Nord-Ost Matjeshering          |
| Seafood      | Inlagd Sill                    |
| Seafood      | Gravad lax                     |
| Seafood      | Boston Crab Meat               |
```

EXAMPLE 14.32 (CONTINUED)

```
| Seafood        | Jack's New England Clam Chowder |
| Seafood        | Rogede sild                     |
| Seafood        | Spegesild                       |
| Seafood        | Escargots de Bourgogne          |
| Seafood        | Röd Kaviar                      |
+----------------+---------------------------------+
12 rows in set (0.00 sec)
```

EXPLANATION

In the SELECT, two tables (separated by commas) will be joined by the "CategoryID" field. Because the field name is the same in both tables, the table name is prepended to the field name with a dot, as products.CategoryId and categories.CategoryId. In the WHERE clause, the two tables are connected if the both tables have a "Category-ID" equal to 8.

Aliases.   To make things a little easier by typing less with complicated queries, SQL provides an aliasing mechanism that allows you to use symbolic names for columns and tables. The alias is defined with the AS keyword and the alias consists of a single character or an abbreviated string. When the alias is used in the WHERE clause to represent a table name, it is appended with a dot and the name of the field being selected from that table.

FORMAT

(Column Alias)
```
SELECT column_name AS column_alias_name
FROM table_name
```

(Table Alias)
```
SELECT column_name
FROM table_name AS table_alias_name
```

EXAMPLE 14.33

```
mysql> SELECT CategoryName as Foods FROM categories;
+----------------+
| Foods          |
+----------------+
| Beverages      |
| Condiments     |
| Confections    |
| Dairy Products |
| Grains/Cereals |
| Meat/Poultry   |
| Produce        |
| Seafood        |
+----------------+
8 rows in set (0.00 sec)
```

EXPLANATION

The column name from table "categories" was named "CategoryName". An alias called "Foods" is created by using the AS keyword after "CategoryName". Now when the SELECT returns a result-set, the output will show "Foods" as the name of the column.

EXAMPLE 14.34

```
mysql> SELECT ProductName FROM products AS p, categories AS c WHERE
    -> p.CategoryID = c.CategoryID AND c.CategoryName="SeaFood";
+---------------------------------+
| ProductName                     |
+---------------------------------+
| Ikura                           |
| Konbu                           |
| Carnarvon Tigers                |
| Nord-Ost Matjeshering           |
| Inlagd Sill                     |
| Gravad lax                      |
| Boston Crab Meat                |
| Jack's New England Clam Chowder |
| Rogede sild                     |
| Spegesild                       |
| Escargots de Bourgogne          |
| Röd Kaviar                      |
+---------------------------------+
12 rows in set (0.00 sec)
```

EXPLANATION

This example might look a little tricky at first. The table named "products" is given an alias called "p" and the table name "categories" is given the alias "c". These aliases are short names, making it easier to type the query when more than one table is involved; for example, instead of typing `products.CategoryID`, we can type `p.CategoryID`, and `categories.CategoryName` can be referenced as `c.CategoryName`.

14.3.6 Altering a Table

When you alter a table, you redefine its structure by adding or dropping a new columns, keys, indexes, and tables. You can also use the ALTER command to change column names, types, and the table name.

FORMAT

```
ALTER TABLE tablename
ADD column datatype
```

Example:
```
alter table artist add column ArtDate date;
alter table artist drop column "Address";
```

EXAMPLE 14.35

```
     use pets;
1    mysql> ALTER TABLE dog ADD pet_id int(11);
     Query OK, 0 rows affected (0.13 sec)
     Records: 0  Duplicates: 0  Warnings: 0
2    mysql> ALTER TABLE dog MODIFY column pet_id int(11)
     -->    auto_increment primary key;
     Query OK, 1 row affected (0.11 sec)
     Records: 1  Duplicates: 0  Warnings: 0
3    mysql> describe dog;
```

Field	Type	Null	Key	Default	Extra
name	varchar(20)	YES		NULL	
owner	varchar(20)	YES		NULL	
breed	varchar(20)	YES		NULL	
sex	char(1)	YES		NULL	
birth	date	YES		NULL	
death	date	YES		NULL	
pet_id	**int(11)**		**PRI**	**NULL**	**auto_increment**

```
     7 rows in set (0.00 sec)
     mysql> select * from dog;
```

name	owner	breed	sex	birth	death	pet_id
Fido	Mr. Jones	Mutt	M	2004-11-12	2006-04-02	1
Lassie	Tommy Rettig	Collie	F	2006-01-10	NULL	2

```
     2 rows in set (0.00 sec)
```

EXPLANATION

1   The ALTER command will change the table by adding a new field, called "pet_id", an integer of 11 digits.

2   Once the "pet_id" field has been created, the ALTER command is used again to make this a primary key that will automatically be incremented each time a record is added.

3   The DESCRIBE command shows the structure of the table after it was changed. A primary key has been added.

14.3.7 Dropping a Table

To drop a table is relatively simple. Just use the `drop` command and the name of the table:

```
mysql> drop table dog;
Query OK, 20 rows affected (0.11 sec)
```

14.3.8 Dropping a Database

To drop a database, use the `drop database` command:

```
mysql> drop database pets;
Query OK, 1 row affected (0.45 sec)
```

14.4 SQL Functions

The following functions are used to alter or format the output of a SQL query. Functions are provided for strings, numbers, dates, server and information, and so on. They return a result-set. Functions are vendor specific, meaning functions supported by MySQL might not be supported by Microsoft SQL Server. See the MySQL documenation for a list of all functions supported.

When using SELECT with a function, the function, as it was called, is displayed as the name of the column in the result-set as shown in Example 14.36.

EXAMPLE 14.36

```
1    mysql> SELECT avg(UnitPrice)
     FROM order_details;
     +----------------+
     | avg(UnitPrice) |
     +----------------+
     |    26.21851972 |
     +----------------+
     1 row in set (0.01 sec)

2    mysql> SELECT avg(UnitPrice) as 'Average Price'
     FROM order_details;
     +---------------+
     | Average Price |
     +---------------+
     |   26.21851972 |
     +---------------+
     1 row in set (0.00 sec)
```

EXPLANATION

1   The function is displayed as the name of the column.
2   You can use the AS keyword to create an alias or another name for the column where the function displays the result-set.

14.4.1   Numeric Functions

Suppose you want to get the sum of all the orders, or the average cost of a set of items, or to count all the rows in a table based on a certain condition. The aggragate functions will return a single value based on a set of other values. If used among many other expressions in the item list of a SELECT statement, the SELECT must have a GROUP BY clause. No GROUP BY clause is required if the aggregate function is the only value retrieved by the SELECT statement. The functions and their syntax are listed in Table 14.4.

Table 14.4   Aggregate Functions

Function	What It Does
AVG()	Computes and returns the average value of a column.
COUNT(*expression*)	Counts the rows defined by the expression.
COUNT()	Counts all rows in a table.
MIN()	Returns the minimum value in a column.
MAX()	Returns the maximum value in a column by the expression.
SUM()	Returns the sum of all the values in a column.

EXAMPLE   14.37

```
1   mysql> select count(*) from products;
    +----------+
    | count(*) |
    +----------+
    |       81 |
    +----------+
    1 row in set (0.00 sec)

    mysql> SELECT count(*) as 'Number of Rows' FROM products;
    +----------------+
    | Number of Rows |
    +----------------+
    |             81 |
    +----------------+
    1 row in set (0.00 sec)
```

EXPLANATION

1   The COUNT() function counts all rows in a table.

EXAMPLE 14.38

```
1   mysql> SELECT avg(UnitPrice)
    FROM order_details;
    +----------------+
    | avg(UnitPrice) |
    +----------------+
    |    26.21851972 |
    +----------------+
    1 row in set. (0.01 sec)

2   mysql> SELECT FORMAT(avg(UnitPrice),2) as 'Average Price'
    FROM  order_details;
    +----------------+
    | Average Price  |
    +----------------+
    | 26.22          |
    +----------------+
    1 row in set (0.00 sec)
```

EXPLANATION

1   The AVG() function computes and returns the average value of a column, called "UnitPrice".

2   The FORMAT function returns the result of the AVG() function with a precision of two decimal places.

Using GROUP BY. The GROUP BY clause can be used with a SELECT to collect all the data across multiple records and group the results by one or more columns. This is useful with the aggregate functions such as SUM, COUNT, MIN, or MAX. See the following two examples.

EXAMPLE 14.39

```
mysql> select CategoryID, SUM(UnitsInStock) as 'Total Units in Stock'
    -> FROM products
    -> GROUP BY CategoryID;
+------------+----------------------+
| CategoryID | Total Units in Stock |
+------------+----------------------+
|       NULL |                    0 |
|          1 |                  559 |
|          2 |                  507 |
|          3 |                  386 |
|          4 |                  393 |
|          5 |                  308 |
|          6 |                  165 |
|          7 |                  100 |
|          8 |                  701 |
+------------+----------------------+
9 rows in set (0.00 sec)
```

EXAMPLE 14.40

```
mysql> select C.CategoryName,
    -> SUM(P.unitsInsStock) AS Units
    -> FROM products as P
    -> join categories AS C ON C.CategoryID=
    -> P.CategoryID Group By C.CategoryName;
+-----------------+-------+
| CategoryName    | Units |
+-----------------+-------+
| Beverages       |   559 |
| Condiments      |   507 |
| Confections     |   386 |
| Dairy Products  |   393 |
| Grains/Cereals  |   308 |
| Meat/Poultry    |   165 |
| Produce         |   100 |
| Seafood         |   701 |
+-----------------+-------+
8 rows in set (0.00 sec)
```

14.4.2   String Functions

SQL provides a number of basic string functions, as listed in Table 14.5.

Table 14.5   MySQL String Functions

Function	What It Does
`CONCAT(string1,string2,...)`[a]	Combines column values, or variables together into one string.
`LOWER(string)`	Converts a string to all lowercase characters.
`SUBSTRING(string, position)`	Extracts a portion of a string (see Example 14.41).
`TRANSLATE`	Converts a string from one character set to another.
`TRIM(' string ');`	Removes leading characters, trailing characters, or both from a character string.
`UPPER(string)`	Converts a string to all uppercase characters (see Example 14.41).

a.   SQL99 defines a concatenation operator ($||$) to use with the `CONCATENATE()` function. MySQL uses the `concat()` function shown in Table 14.5.

EXAMPLE 14.41

```
mysql> select upper(CompanyName) as 'Company' from shippers;
+------------------+
| Company          |
+------------------+
| SPEEDY EXPRESS   |
| UNITED PACKAGE   |
| FEDERAL SHIPPING |
+------------------+
3 rows in set (0.00 sec)

mysql> select lower(CompanyName) as 'Company' FROM shippers;
+------------------+
| Company          |
+------------------+
| speedy express   |
| united package   |
| federal shipping |
+------------------+
3 rows in set (0.00 sec)
```

14.4.3   Date and Time Functions

To get the date and time, MySQL provides the functions shown in Table 14.6.

Table 14.6   MySQL Date and Time Functions

Function	*Example*

NOW()	`select NOW()`
	`--> 2006-03-23 20:52:58`
	(See Example 14.42.)

CURDATE()	`select CURDATE();`
	`--> '2006-12-15'`
	(See Example 14.42.)

CURTIME()	`select CURTIME();`
	`--> '23:50:26'`
	(See Example 14.42.)

DAYOFYEAR(date)	`select DAYOFYEAR('2006-12-15');` `--> 349`
DAYOFMONTH(date)	`select DAYOFMONTH('2006-12-15');` `--> 15`
DAYOFWEEK(date)	`select DAYOFWEEK('2006-12-15');` `--> 6`
WEEKDAY(date)	`select WEEKDAY('2006-12-15');` `--> 4`
MONTHNAME(date)	`select MONTHNAME('2006-12-15');` `--> December`
DAYNAME(date)	`select DAYNAME('2006-12-15');` `--> Friday`
YEAR(date)	`select YEAR('2006-12-15');` `--> 2006`
QUARTER(date)	`select QUARTER('2006-12-15');` `--> 4`

EXAMPLE 14.42

```
mysql> select NOW();
+---------------------+
| NOW()               |
+---------------------+
| 2006-03-21 00:32:37 |
+---------------------+
1 row in set (0.00 sec)

mysql> select CURDATE();
+----------------+
|    CURDATE()   |
+----------------+
| 2006-03-21     |
+----------------+
1 row in set (0.03 sec)

mysql> select CURTIME();
+----------------+
|    CURTIME()   |
+----------------+
| 00:12:46       |
+----------------+
1 row in set (0.01 sec)
```

Formatting the Date and Time. When retrieving dates and times from a table, you might find you want to format the output. For example, when selecting the dates of the orders from the orders table in the "northwind" database, the result-set is not user friendly. Date values in SQL are always saved in MM/DD/YY(YY) format. The DATE_FORMAT() and TIME_FORMAT() functions (see Example 14.43) are provided with a list of parameters (see Table 14.7) used to specify how the the output should be displayed.

EXAMPLE 14.43

```
mysql> select DATE_FORMAT('2006-03-23', '%W %M %d, %Y') as Today;
+-------------------------+
| Today                   |
+-------------------------+
| Thursday March 23, 2006 |
+-------------------------+
1 row in set (0.00 sec)
```

EXAMPLE 14.43 (CONTINUED)

```
mysql> select DATE_FORMAT(OrderDate,'%M %e, %Y - %l:%i %p')
            FROM orders LIMIT 5;

+--------------------------------------------------+
| DATE_FORMAT(OrderDate,'%M %e, %Y - %l:%i %p')    |
+--------------------------------------------------+
| July 4, 1996 - 12:00 AM                          |
| July 5, 1996 - 12:00 AM                          |
| July 8, 1996 - 12:00 AM                          |
| July 8, 1996 - 12:00 AM                          |
| July 9, 1996 - 12:00 AM                          |
+--------------------------------------------------+
5 rows in set (0.00 sec)
```

Table 14.7   DATE_FORMAT() and TIME_FORMAT()

Paramater	What It Means
%a	Weekday abbreviation (Sun, Mon, Tues, etc.)
%b	Month name abbreviation (Jan, Feb, Mar, etc.)
%c	Month (1–12)
%d	Two-digit day of the month (01–31)
%D	Day with a suffix (30th, 31st)
%e	Day of the month (1–31)
%f	Microseconds (000000..999999)
%H	Hour (00..23)
%h	Hour (01..12)
%i	Minutes, numeric (00..59)
%I	Hour (01–12)
%j	Day of year (001–366)
%k	Hour (0..23)
%l	Hour (1–12)
%m	Month with a leading 0 (01, 06, etc.)
%M	Month name (March, April, May, etc.)
%p	AM/PM

Table 14.7 `DATE_FORMAT()` and `TIME_FORMAT()` (continued)

Paramater	What It Means
%r	Time, 12-hour (hh:mm:ss followed by AM or PM)
%S	Seconds (00..59)
%s	Seconds (00..59)
%T	Time, 24-hour (hh:mm:ss)
%U	Week (00..53) starting with Sunday
%u	Week (00..53) starting with Monday
%v	Week (01..53) starting with Monday
%V	Week (01..53) starting with Sunday
%W	Weekday (Sunday, Monday, etc.)
%w	Day of the week (0 = Sunday..6 = Saturday)
%Y	Year (1999, 2007)
%y	Two-digit year (99, 07)
%%	A literal % character

The MySQL EXTRACT Command. The `EXTRACT` command is an example of a MySQL extension, not described in the SQL standard. It allows you to extract different parts of a date or time, as shown in Table 14.8.

Table 14.8 Date and Time Parts

Type	Format
SECOND	SECONDS
MINUTE	MINUTES
HOUR	HOURS
DAY	DAYS
MONTH	MONTHS
YEAR	YEARS (see Example 14.44)
MINUTE SECOND	"MINUTES:SECONDS"
HOUR_MINUTE	"HOURS:MINUTES"

Table 14.8   Date and Time Parts (continued)

Type	Format
DAY_HOUR	"DAYS HOURS"
YEAR_MONTH	"YEARS-MONTHS"
HOUR_SECOND	"HOURS:MINUTES:SECONDS"
DAY_MINUTE	"DAYS HOURS:MINUTES"
DAY_SECOND	"DAYS HOURS:MINUTES:SECONDS"

EXAMPLE 14.44

```
mysql> select EXTRACT(YEAR FROM NOW());
+--------------------------+
| EXTRACT(YEAR FROM NOW()) |
+--------------------------+
|                     2006 |
+--------------------------+
1 row in set (0.03 sec)
```

14.5 Chapter Summary

In this chapter you learned how to use the SQL language to create database schemas as well as how to insert, update, retrieve, alter, and delete records from a database.

14.5.1   What You Should Know

Now that you have finished this chapter you should be able to answer the following questions:

1. How do you retrieve all the records from a database table?

2. How do you retrieve a select set of records or a single record from a table based on specific criteria?

3. How do you select and sort records in a database?

4. How do you select a range of rows from a database?

5. How do you create a database?

6. How do you create database tables?

7. How do you assign a primary key to a field?

8. How are records inserted into the database table?

9. How are records updated in a table?

10. How do you delete a record?

14.5.2   What's Next?

Now that you have learned how to use the SQL language, you can talk to your database. In the next chapter, we learn how to use PHP functions to connect to the MySQL server and retrieve and display data from a database using the SQL statements.

CHAPTER 14 LAB

1. Go to the MySQL console and use the `show` command to list all the databases. Use the `mysql` database. Now display all of its tables.

2. Create a new database called `school`. Once you create the database, you need to be able to use it:

   ```
   use school;
   ```

3. Create a table called `student`. The table will consist of the following fields:

   ```
   FirstName
   LastName
   Email
   CellPhone
   Major
   GPA
   StartDate
   StudentId (the primary key)
   ```

   The following information is the type of data you will use to define your table. Go to the Web and look for a table similar to this to use as your guide.

Data Type	Description
integer(*size*)	
int(*size*)	
smallint(*size*)	
tinyint(*size*)	Holds integers only

   The maximum number of digits are specified by *size* in parentheses.

```
decimal(size,d)
numeric(size,d)
```     Holds numbers with fractions.

The maximum number of digits are specified in `size`. The maximum number of digits to the right of the decimal is specified in `d`.

-------------------------------------------------------------------------------------------

`char(size)`     Holds a fixed-length string (can contain letters, numbers, and special characters). The fixed size is specified by `size` in parentheses.

`varchar(size)`     Holds a variable-length string (can contain letters, numbers, and special characters). The maximum size is specified by `size` in parentheses.

-------------------------------------------------------------------------------------------

`date(yyyymmdd)`     Holds a date.

-------------------------------------------------------------------------------------------

4. Use the SQL `describe` statement to display the information you used to create the `school` database.

5. Insert three rows into the table:

    Row 1:     FirstName: John
               LastName: Doe
               Email: johndoe@smileyface.edu
               CellPhone: 408-333-3456
               Major: CIS
               GPA: 2.8
               StartDate: 09/22/2004  (use the correct date format!)
               StudentId: 1

    Row 2:     FirstName: Mary
               LastName: Chin
               Email: mchin@qmail.com
               CellPhone: 408-204-1234
               Major: Biology
               GPA: 3.3
               StartDate: 06/22/2003
               StudentId: 2

Row 3:     FirstName: Sadish
           LastName: Pamel
           Email: sadi@univ_ab.edu
           CellPhone: 415-204-1234
           Major: CIS
           GPA: 3.9
           StartDate: 06/22/2003
           StudentId: 2

6. Use the `show` commands to display all the fields.

7. Use `select` statements to display the following (write your query in the blank line):

   a. The data in all of the columns
   b. The first and last name of the students
   c. The student's first and last name and major
   d. The student's cellphone and e-mail addresses
   e. Any distinct majors
   f. Only 2 rows

8. a. Select all students who have a GPA over 3.0.
   b. Select all students who have a GPA between 3.0 and 4.0.
   c. Select students whose cell phones are in the 408 area code.
   d. Display rows for students who started in 2003.
   e. Select student first and last names who are majoring in CIS and have a GPA over 3.5.
   f. Select student first name and e-mail address if the e-mail address ends in `.com`.

9. a. Insert a new entry into the table.
   b. Sort the student table by last names.
   c. Sort the student table by GPA in descending order.

10. Change Mary's phone number to 650-123-4563.

The next three questions deal with SQL functions:

11. Find the average GPA for all the students.

12. Find the number of rows in the table.

13. Print today's date using a SQL function.

# chapter
# 15

# PHP and MySQL Integration

## 15.1 Introduction

The user has filled out a form and submitted it. It contains a list of items he or she wants to purchase. The information for that user is stored in a database table called "customers". You want to retrieve all the orders and product information for that customer from the database and display selected data on the Web page directly from your PHP script. Now you will learn how to integrate PHP and MySQL.

PHP provides built-in functions that allow all the necessary operations for opening and selecting the database, and for sending it SQL queries to create tables, update and delete them, retrieve records, and display the results. You can create your HTML form, process it, and connect to the MySQL database all in one PHP program!

At the beginning of this book, we described PHP and MySQL as a perfect marriage. In this chapter, we see how that marriage works.

### 15.1.1 Connecting to the Database Server

To establish a connection to the MySQL database server from your PHP script, use the PHP `mysql_connect()` function.

---

**FORMAT**

```
resource mysql_connect ( [string server [, string username [,
                         string password [, bool new_link [,
                         int client_flags]]]]] )
```

Example:
```
$link = mysql_connect("localhost", "root", "password");
```

The first argument is the host server where the MySQL server will be running. It can also include an IP address, port number, a path to a local socket, and so on. The second argument is the username, the default value for the name of the owner of the server process. The next argument is the password, if there is one.

If a second call is made to mysql_connect() with the same arguments, a new link will not be established, but instead, the link identifier of the already opened link will be returned. If you specify the new_link parameter, mysql_connect() will always open a new link.

If the connection is successful, mysql_connect() returns the connection link and if not, the function returns FALSE. The resource returned points to the database server and is used by all the other mysql functions in the script.

When a Web page or PHP script ends, the database is automatically closed and the resource that links to it is released, so that if you start another page you will have to reconnect to the database. If you want to close the database before the program ends, PHP provides the mysql_close() function. The mysql_close() function closes the connection to the MySQL server referenced by the link.

FORMAT

```
bool mysql_close ( [resource link_identifier]
```

Example:
```
mysql_close($link);
```

EXAMPLE 15.1

```
    <?php
        print "Opening the connection to the database server< br />";
1       $link = mysql_connect("localhost", "root", "password");
2       print "The connection worked. The link is: $link < br />";
        print "Closing the connection< br />";
3       mysql_close( $link );
    ?>
```

EXPLANATION

1   The PHP mysql_connect() function connects to a MySQL database server running on the localhost using root as username and password as the password.
2   In this line, the value of the resource is Resource id #2. If the connection failed, the result is FALSE. See Figure 15.1.
3   The mysql_close() function closes the connection to the database previously opened by mysql_connect(). mysql_close() is not necessary because the connection will automatically be closed once the script reaches the end of execution.

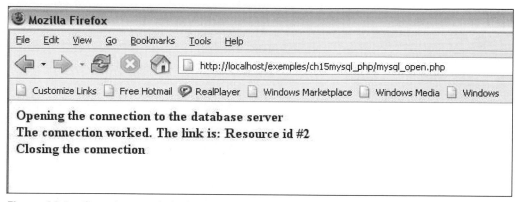

Figure 15.1 Opening and closing a connection to the database server. Output from Example 15.1

15.1.2 Choosing the Database

Once connected to the database server, the next step is to set the default database that you will be using. The mysql_select_database() function is used to select a MySQL database. (This is the equivalent to the use command when using mysql client.) The first argument is the name of the database. The second argument is the MySQL connection (the link) established when the mysql_connect() function was executed.

FORMAT

```
bool mysql_select_db ( string database_name [,
                       resource link_identifier] )
```

Example:
```
$link = mysql_connect('localhost', 'ellie', 'my_password');
$db_selected = mysql_select_db('northwind', $link);
```

EXAMPLE 15.2

```
      <?php
          print "Opening the connection to the database server< br />";
1         mysql_connect("localhost", "root", "password");
          print "Selecting a database< br />";
2         $result = mysql_select_db( "northwind" );
3         if ( $result ) {
             print "Database selected successfully< br />";
          } else {
             print "There was a problem with the database
                     selection< br />";
          }
      ?>
```

EXPLANATION

1   First, establish a connection to the MySQL database server; in this example the connection is made to `localhost` using `root` and `password` for authentication.

2   Using the `mysql_select_db()` function, the "test" database is set as the default database. From now on, all the queries executed assume this database. Because once the connection is closed, the default database is also closed, you might need to perform `mysql_connect()` and `mysql_select_db()` on every page needing this database connectivity.

3   If successful, `mysql_select_db()` returns boolean `TRUE`, otherwise it returns `FALSE`. See Figure 15.2.

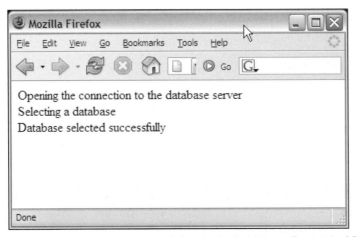

Figure 15.2   Selecting a database. Output from Example 15.2.

15.1.3 Executing SQL Statements (INSERT, UPDATE, DELETE)

Once connected to the database server, and having selected a database, it is time to start executing SQL commands. PHP provides the `mysql_query()` function to perform database queries. You must have adequate permissions to execute queries on a given database (see "The Grant and Revoke Commands" on page 589).

FORMAT

```
resource mysql_query ( string query [, resource link_identifier] )
```

Example:
```
$result = mysql_query("SELECT CompanyName, Phone FROM Shippers");
$result = mysql_query("DESCRIBE Shippers");
```

For the SELECT, SHOW, DESCRIBE, or EXPLAIN statements, mysql_query() returns a resource on success, or FALSE on error. For other types of SQL statements (UPDATE, DELETE, DROP, etc.), mysql_query() returns TRUE on success or FALSE on error.

PHP provides a number of functions to deal with the result, such as mysql_fetch_array(), mysql_num_rows(), mysql_affected_rows(), and so on. You can also use the built-in error-handling functions to find out where a query failed.

You can test that your SQL statement is valid by executing it in any other client, such as the mysql command line. For INSERT, UPDATE, and DELETE, this function will return TRUE if the operation was successful and FALSE otherwise.

EXAMPLE 15.3

```
<html><head><title>MySQL Query in PHP</title></head>
<body bgcolor="lightblue">
<font size='+1' face='arial'>
<?php

        print "Opening the connection to the database server< br />";
1       $link = mysql_connect("localhost", "ellie", "");
        print "Selecting the 'northwind' database< br />";
2       mysql_select_db("northwind");

3       $query="UPDATE Shippers SET phone='(777) 430-2346'
        WHERE CompanyName = 'Federal Shipping'";

4       $result= mysql_query($query);

5       $rows_affected=mysql_affected_rows($link);   /* numbers of rows
            affected by the most recently executed query */
        echo "You have updated $rows_affected rows.< br />";

        if ($result){
            print "Query successful!< br />";
        }
        else{
6           die("Query failed.". mysql_error());
        }

        print "Closing the connection< br />";

7       mysql_close( $link );

?>
</body>
</html>
```

EXPLANATION

1   First, connect to the database server.

2   Then, the "northwind" practice database is selected.

3   The SQL statement is created here. It is assigned to a variable, called $query. No-
    tice that the SQL string is just like any other SQL statement you would type in the
    MySQL Query Browser or at the mysql command line. It can also contain explicit
    values or variables evaluated by PHP before sending the query to the database.

4   The mysql_query() function is executed and will return true if the query is suc-
    cessful and false if not.

5   The mysql_affected_rows() function returns the number of affected rows from
    the previous MySQL query.

6   If the query is successful, the database will be updated. If not, the PHP script will
    die (exit) with the message: "Query failed: " followed by the reason for the error.
    The mysql_error() message will tell you what was wrong with your query, sim-
    ilar to the message you would receive at the MySQL console. In the output shown
    in Figure 15.3 the first one is successful. The second one failed because the quotes
    surrounding the phone number were removed.

7   The database is closed.

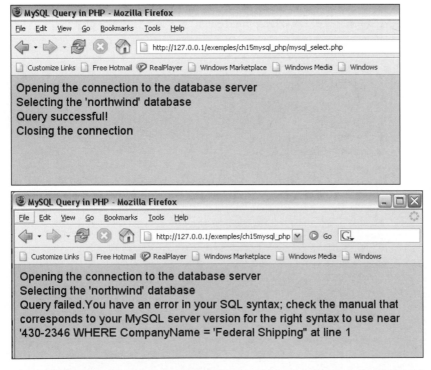

Figure 15.3   (top) A successful SQL query. (bottom) There was an error in the SQL
statement.

15.1.4 Retrieving the Query Results (SELECT)

The SQL commands INSERT, UPDATE, and DELETE do not return any data as shown in the previous examples, whereas the SELECT statement normally returns a set of data records, called the result-set. The format for the mysql_query() function does not change, but a result-set is returned rather than a true–false value or a resource, and false if the query fails.

FORMAT

```
resource mysql_query ( string query [, resource link_identifier] )
```

Example:
```
$result_set = mysql_query( "SELECT subject, body FROM messages" );
```

Many rows of data might be returned to the result-set as the result of the SQL execution. If this function fails to execute the SQL statement, it will return FALSE instead of the result-set.

To display the result-set, PHP has provided a number of functions including mysql_result(), mysql_fetch_array(), and mysql_fetch_row().

The mysql_fetch_row() Function. The mysql_fetch_row() function is used to extract one record of the data from the result-set.

FORMAT

```
array mysql_fetch_row ( resource result )
```

Example:
```
$result_set = mysql_query($query_string)
$record = mysql_fetch_row( $result_set );
```

The $result_set variable is assigned the value returned from mysql_query() function, a numeric array. Although the result-set might contain many records, the value returned from the mysql_fetch_row() function is only the first row. Each successive call to the mysql_fetch_row() function returns the next record (by moving an internal pointer) until there are no more records.

EXAMPLE 15.4

```
<html><head><title>MySQL Fetch a Row</title></head>
<body bgcolor="lightblue">
<font size='+1' face='arial'>
<?php

         print "Opening the connection to the database server< br />";
1        $link = mysql_connect("localhost", "ellie", "");
         print "Selecting the 'northwind' database< br />";
2        mysql_select_db("northwind");
         $query="SELECT CompanyName, Phone from Shippers";
3        $result_set= mysql_query($query);
             if ($result_set){
                 print "Fetch the first row of data.< br />";
4                $record= mysql_fetch_row($result_set);
                 // print_r($record);
5                foreach ($record as $value){
                     print "<em>$value </em>";  // print the row
                 }
                 print "< br />";
             }
             else{ die("Query failed.". mysql_error());
             }
             print "Closing the connection< br />";
             mysql_close( $link );

?>
</body>
</html>
```

EXPLANATION

1   A connection is made to the database server. Notice that we have to do this on every single page that needs the database connection because the connection is implicitly closed at the end of the script.

2   Next, the database is selected. Again, line 1 and 2 are required at the beginning of all database-enabled pages. Alternatively, you can put these statements in a script that will be loaded on every page using the `include()` function.

3   The SQL query executes the query and the result is assigned to the `$result_set` variable. There might be a lot of data returned.

4   One record is fetched from the result-set. The function keeps an internal counter of what records have been fetched so that the next call to `mysql_fetch_row()` returns the next record in the set, until there are no more.

5   The `foreach` loop is used to list the contents of the array that was returned by `mysql_fetch_row()`. The output is shown in Figure 15.4.

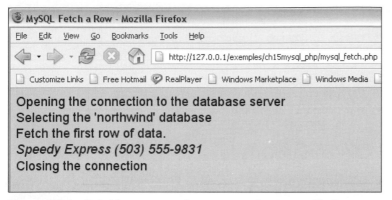

Figure 15.4 Fetching a record as a numeric array with the `mysql_fetch_row()` function. Output from Example 15.4.

The mysql_fetch_assoc() Function. In the previous example we fetched a record from the record set and the record returned was a numerically indexed array. However, PHP also supports associative arrays, which are sometimes much easier to use. (You can refresh your knowledge of associative arrays in Chapter 8, "Arrays.")

The `mysql_fetch_assoc()` function is very similar to `mysql_fetch_row()` except that the result returned is an associative array.

FORMAT

```
array mysql_fetch_assoc ( resource result )
```

Example:
```
$record = mysql_fetch_assoc( $record_set )
```

In this example, the `$record_set` variable contains what was returned from the `mysql_query()` function, and `$record` is the current row from that record set expressed as an associative array.

EXAMPLE 15.5

```
        <html><head><title>MySQL Fetch Associative Array</title></head>
        <body bgcolor="lightblue">
        <font size='+1' face='arial'>
        <?php
            print "Opening the connection to the database server< br />";
            $link = mysql_connect("localhost", "ellie", "");
    1       print "Selecting the 'northwind' database< br />";

    2       mysql_select_db("northwind");

    3       $query="SELECT CompanyName, Phone from Shippers";

    4       $result_set= mysql_query($query);

            if ($result_set){
                print "Fetch the first row of data.< br />< br />";
    5           $record= mysql_fetch_assoc($result_set);
    6           foreach ($record as $key=>$value){
                    print "<em>$key: $value </br></em>";   // Print the row
                }
                print "< br />";
            }
            else{ die("Query failed.". mysql_error());
            }

            print "Closing the connection< br />";

            mysql_close( $link );

        ?>
        </body>
        </html>
```

EXPLANATION

1, 2 The "northwind" database is opened and selected.
  3   The SQL SELECT statement string is assigned to the variable, $query.
  4   The result-set contains the results returned from the database query.
  5   Instead of using mysql_fetch_row() and getting an array indexed by numbers,
      the mysql_fetch_assoc() function returns an associative array with the index
      being the name of the field specified in the database, and its value what is found
      in that field. See Figure 15.5.
  6   The foreach loop is used to iterate through the associative array, to retrieve both
      the key (field name) and the value associated with it.

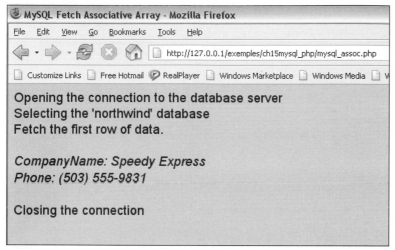

Figure 15.5 Fetching a record as an associative array with the `mysql_fetch_assoc()` function. Output from Example 15.5

15.1.5 Other Useful MySQL Functions

PHP comes with a few more built-in MySQL functions. In this section we look at some other commonly used ones.

Table 15.1 lists some of the MySQL functions you might find useful when integrating PHP and MySQL.

Table 15.1 MySQL Functions

Database Function	What It Does
`mysql_connect()`	Opens a connection to a MySQL server.
`mysql_pconnect()`	Opens a persistent connection.
`mysql_selectdb()`	Selects the default database.
`mysql_change_user()`	Changes the identity of the user logged on.
`mysql_list_dbs`	Lists databases for this MySQL server.
`mysql_list_tables`	Lists tables in the database.
Query Functions Affecting Rows	
`mysql_fetch_assoc()`	Returns one result row, as an associative array.
`mysql_fetch_row()`	Returns one result row, as an array.
`mysql_affected_rows()`	Returns number of rows affected by query.

Table 15.1 MySQL Functions (continued)

Database Function	What It Does
mysql_num_rows()	Returns number of rows selected.
mysql_fetch_object()	Returns a result row, as an object.
Query Functions Affecting Columns	
mysql_fetch_field()	Gets column information from a result and returns as an object.
mysql_field_name()	Gets the name of the specified field in a result.
mysql_list_fields()	Sets result pointer to a specified field offset.
mysql_num_fields()	Gets number of fields in a result.
mysql_field_seek()	Sets result pointer to a specified field offset.
mysql_field_type()	Gets the type of the specified field in a result.
mysql_field_len()	Returns the length of the specified field.
mysql_field_table()	Gets name of the table the specified field is in.
mysql_tablename()	Gets table name of field.
Functions for Error Handling	
mysql_errno()	Returns the numerical value of the error message from previous MySQL operation.
mysql_error()	Returns the text of the error message from previous MySQL operation.

The mysql_error() Function.   The execution of a database function might fail for a variety of reasons. Perhaps the database server is down, or the network connection is unavailable, or simply the username and password used to connect are not authorized to access the database.

The mysql_error() function returns the text of the error message generated by the MySQL server. If there were error messages generated by multiple MySQL calls, this function returns the most common error message.

FORMAT

```
$error_message mysql_error()
```

In the preceding format, the $error_message is the text of the error message returned from the database server. See Example 15.6.

EXAMPLE 15.6

```
<?php
    print "Opening the connection to the database server< br />";
1   mysql_connect("localhost", "root", "password");
    print "Selecting a database< br />";
2   $result = mysql_select_db( "addressbook" );
3   if ( $result ) {
        print "Database selected successfully< br />";
    } else {
4       $error_message = mysql_error();
        print "There was a problem with the database
               selection:< br />";
5       print $error_message;
    }
?>
```

EXPLANATION

1   The user root is attempting to connect to the database server.
2   The database we will work with, "addressbook," is selected. We assume that this database is available and that we have access to it.
3   We check the value of the $result variable. Most MySQL functions in PHP will return FALSE if the call to the database server failed.
4   To find out the reason for this failure, the mysql_error() function is called. It will return a text message from the database server explaining the problem. In this case the error states that the database "addressbook" does not exist.
5   This line prints out the error message. See Figure 15.6.

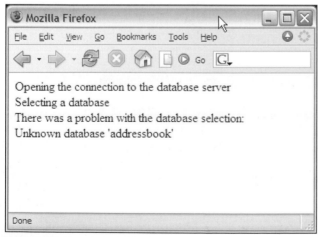

Figure 15.6   The text "Unknown database 'addressbook'" was generated by the MySQL server. Output from Example 15.6.

The mysql_num_rows() Function.   The `mysql_num_rows()` function returns the number of rows in the result-set.

FORMAT

```
int mysql_num_rows( resource result )
```

Example:
```
$number_of_rows = mysql_num_rows( $result_set )
```

In the preceding example, the `$result_set` is what you got back from executing the SELECT query, and `$number_of_rows` is the number of rows that were retrieved.

EXAMPLE 15.7

```
      <?php
         mysql_connect("localhost", "ellie", "");
         mysql_select_db( "northwind" );
         print "Executing SQL...< br />";
1        $result_set = mysql_query( "SELECT ShipName FROM orders");
2        $num_rows = mysql_num_rows( $result_set );
3        print "<b>There are a total of $num_rows ship names
            in the \"orders\" table.";
      ?>
```

EXPLANATION

1   After connecting to the database server and selecting the database, the SELECT statement is executed. The variable, `$result_set`, will contain all the rows selected from the "orders" table.
2   The `mysql_num_rows()` function will return the number of rows in the record set.
3   This displays the number of rows selected. See Figure 15.7.

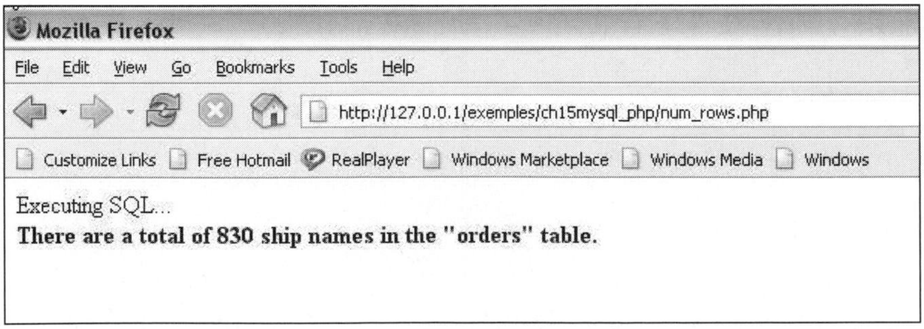

Figure 15.7   Finding the number of rows in a table. Output from Example 15.7.

The mysql_num_fields() Function. The `mysql_num_fields()` function returns the number of fields in a table and the `mysql_field_name()` function returns the name of a field.

FORMAT

```
int mysql_num_fields( resource result )
```

Example:
```
$number_of_fields = mysql_num_fields( $result_set )
```

In the preceding example, the `$result_set` variable contains the records retrieved with the SELECT query and `$number_of_fields` contains the total number of columns in that result set.

The mysql_field_name() Function. The `mysql_field_name()` function returns the name of a specific field.

FORMAT

```
string mysql_field_name( resource result, int field_offset )
```

Example:
```
$field_name = mysql_field_name( $result_set, $index )
```

In the preceding example, the variable `$result_set` is the result of executing a SELECT statement, and the variable `$index` is the index of a specific field in the current result set.

EXAMPLE 15.8

```php
    <?php

        mysql_connect("localhost", "root", "password");
1       mysql_select_db( "northwind" );

        print "Executing SQL...< br />";
2       $result_set = mysql_query( "SELECT * FROM customers");

3       print "<table>";

        // Print the headers
4       for( $c=0; $c<mysql_num_fields( $result_set ); $c++ ) {
5           print "<th>". mysql_field_name( $result_set,
                                            $c ) . "</th>";
        }
```

EXAMPLE 15.8 (CONTINUED)

```
        // Print all the rows
6       while( $record = mysql_fetch_row( $result_set ) ) {
7           print "<tr>";
8           for( $c=0; $c<mysql_num_fields( $result_set ); $c++ ) {
9               print "<td>". $record[$c] ."</td>";
            }
10          print "</tr>";
        }
11      print "</table>";

    ?>
```

EXPLANATION

1   The "northwind" database is selected as the default database.
2   All the records from the "customers" table are selected. The * is a wildcard char-
    acter for all the records, meaning all the fields will be returned.
3   Because a lot of data is expected, it is much better to use an HTML table to display
    the output than to simply print it to the screen. The HTML <table> tag starts the
    table.
4   In this loop we print out the headings for the table (the <TH> tags). The
    mysql_num_fields() function returns the number of fields or columns there are
    in the "customers" table. Rather than typing in a number, this function will return
    the number of fields for any table that needs to be tested.
5   The mysql_field_name() function is used get the name of a particular field in a
    table. The first argument is the result-set. The second one is the index of a partic-
    ular field. Because we are getting all the fields with the SELECT * clause, the order
    will correspond to that of the database. The HTML <TH> tags specify a table head-
    ing for the HTML table.
6   The while statement loops over all the available rows in the result-set.
7   <TR> is the HTML tag for a row. All the field values will be placed within this row,
    one row for each iteration of this while loop.
8   This is a nested for loop to loop over all the columns.
9   This inner loop is used to retrieve each column/field value from the current row.
    The HTML <TD> tags are used to separate the table cells.
10 Once the inner for loop has finished going through each of the fields in the cur-
    rent row, the loop exits, the HTML </tr> tag ends its table row, and control goes
    back to the while loop where another row from the database is fetched and then
    processed; then the next row, and so on, until there are no more rows to fetch.
11 Finally, the table is terminated. All the data has been retrieved and displayed. See
    Figure 15.8.

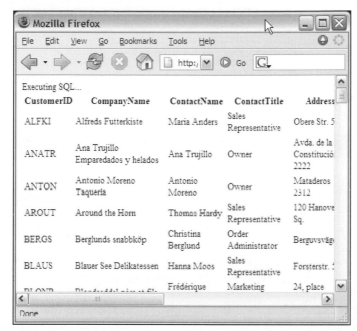

Figure 15.8 All the rows have been retrieved. Output from Example 15.8.

15.2 The Guest Book Example

The following sections guide you through an example of building a database-driven Web site. We will design a guest book application, where visitors to the Web site can add comments and those comments are visible to others.

Although this is a very simple example, the concepts illustrated here are found in almost all dynamic Web sites. You will create a Web form asking the user for some data, insert that data into the database, and then create another page to display all the data from the database.

15.2.1 Step 1: Designing the Database

As with most database-driven applications, we start by desiging the database schema. The design process can be a very complex process, but for this example, we use the MySQL "test" database, and design just one simple table to store messages entered by random Web site visitors.

The following example provides the SQL CREATE TABLE command to create the "messages" table.

EXAMPLE 15.9

```
1   mysql> create TABLE messages(
2       -> id INT NOT NULL AUTO_INCREMENT,
3       -> subject VARCHAR(150),
4       -> body TEXT,
5       -> PRIMARY KEY(id))
        -> ;
```

EXPLANATION

1   The CREATE TABLE statement creates a database table called "messages". (The current database is "test".)
2   The first field is the "id" field, called PRIMARY KEY, a unique identifier for each record in this table. It is an integer, meaning a whole number, and NOT NULL indicates that this field cannot be null, that is, it must have a value. To ensure that this number is unique, the AUTO_INCREMENT attribute tells MySQL to increment the "id" field by 1 for each new entry added to the database.
3   The field "subject" will be variable-length text with a maximum value of 150 characters that is by default not set (NULL).
4   The "body" field will be TEXT of unlimited size. Data type of varchars is limited to 255 characters and TEXT is not.
5   This line specifies that the "id" field is to be considered the PRIMARY KEY by the database server.

The table has been defined and created. The SQL DESCRIBE command will show you if the table has been created successfully. If not satisified, you can drop the table with the DROP TABLE 'messages' statement and define it again. Note: The DROP TABLE command will delete the entire table and all its data!

EXAMPLE 15.10

```
mysql> describe messages;
+---------+--------------+------+-----+---------+----------------+
| Field   | Type         | Null | Key | Default | Extra          |
+---------+--------------+------+-----+---------+----------------+
| id      | int(11)      | NO   | PRI | NULL    | auto_increment |
| subject | varchar(150) | YES  |     | NULL    |                |
| body    | text         | YES  |     | NULL    |                |
+---------+--------------+------+-----+---------+----------------+
3 rows in set (0.14 sec)
```

EXPLANATION

The SQL DESCRIBE command shows information about the table: the names of the fields, the data type for each field, whether it should have data, keys, and so on. You can also use the show command to see the same results.

15.2.2   Step 2: Posting a Message Page

Now that the table has been designed, the next step is to create the Web page containing the HTML form, and the PHP code that will process the form and enter the posted data into a MySQL database.

EXAMPLE   15.11

```php
<?php

1       extract($_REQUEST);

2       if ( isset($subject) && isset($body) ) {
            mysql_connect("localhost", "root", "password");
            mysql_select_db( "test" );

3           mysql_query( "INSERT INTO messages (subject, body) ".
                         "VALUES ('$subject', '$body' )" );

4           $status = "Message <i>$subject</i> has been
                        posted< br />< br />";
        }

?>
<html>
<body>

<h1>Post a Message</h1>

5   <string><?= $status ?></strong>

6   <form action="<?= $_SERVER['PHP_SELF'] ?>" >
        Subject <input type="text" name="subject" size="35">
        < br />< br />
        <textarea name="body" cols="40" rows="15"></textarea>
        < br />< br />
        <input type="submit" value="Post">
    </form>
</body>
</html>
```

EXPLANATION

1   The form data is extracted from the $_REQUEST array, and assigned to variables with the same names as the input devices.

2   This if statement is only executed if data has been entered. The first time the user visits this page, no data has been submitted, and the empty form is displayed.

3   After connecting to the database server and selecting the correct database, the SQL statement is executed to insert the new record into the database table.

EXPLANATION (CONTINUED)

4   Setting the $status variable is a nice way to communicate to the user that the database statement has been successfully executed.

5   This line prints the status statement. If the status is not set (like the first time the page is loaded), nothing will be printed.

6   This is a self-processing form. When the user presses the submit button, this page will be displayed again. Remember, $_SERVER['PHP_SELF'] always points to the current page. (Also, these pages are using short_tags defined in the php.ini file. If not using short_tags, this line would read: <?php echo $_SERVER['SELF'] ?>

Figure 15.9 shows the screen that appears first time we get to this page, before the message has been posted.

Figure 15.9   Posting a message.

Once the user clicks on the Post (submit) button, the message will be submitted to the database and the same page redisplayed, but with a status line (see Figure 15.10) indicating that the message was posted successfully.

Figure 15.10   The message was sent to the database. The status line is displayed.

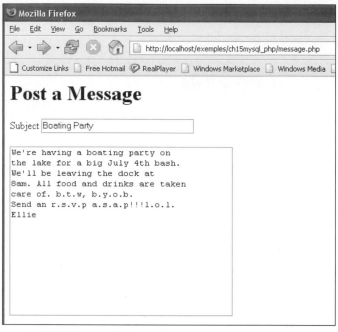

Figure 15.11
Posting another message. The message is typed in (top) and after the Post button is pressed, the message is submitted to the database (bottom).

15.2.3 Step 3: Listing All Messages

Once data has been sent to the database, a page is created to list all the postings in the "Guest Book". The MySQL database is opened and all the fields from the table called "messages" are selected and printed.

EXAMPLE 15.12

```php
<?php
    mysql_connect("localhost", "root", "ellieq");
    mysql_select_db( "test" );
1   $result_set = mysql_query( "SELECT * FROM messages" );
2   $num_messages = mysql_num_rows( $result_set );
?>


<html>
<body>
<h1>Guest Book</h1>

3   <i>There are a total of <?= $num_messages ?> posts on this
    website.</i>
< br /> < br /> <hr>

<?php

    // Loop over all the posts and print them out

4   while( $row = mysql_fetch_assoc( $result_set ) ) {
5       $subject = $row['subject'];
6       $body = $row['body'];
7       print "<strong>$subject</strong>< br />";
8       print "$body< br /> < br />";
    }

?>
```

EXPLANATION

1　The SQL statement selects all the fields from the "messages" table.
2　The `mysql_num_rows()` function gets the total number of messages in the database.
3　This line prints out the total number of messages obtained from line 2.
4　The `while` loop iterates through all the records of the record set. The `mysql_fetch_assoc()` function returns an associative array representing the current row of data.
5, 6　The "subject" field from the current row is assigned to a variable called `$subject`.
7, 8　The values in the "subject" and the "body" fields are displayed. See Figure 15.12.

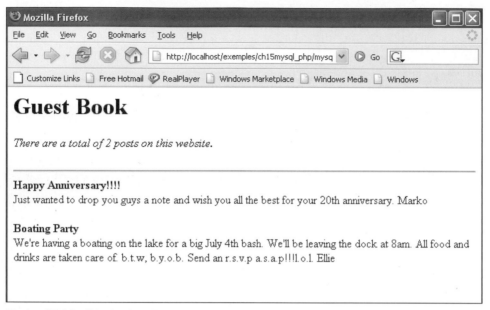

Figure 15.12 Displaying the contents of the MySQL table called "messages". Output from Example 15.12

15.2.4   Example Summary

The "Guest Book" example illustrates the main steps needed in creating most Web applications. Let's reexamine the steps involved:

1. We start by defining the database and its tables with one table called "messages" consisting of three fields: the unique ID, a subject, and the body of the message.
2. Once the database and its tables are defined, all the other pages are designed that will interact with with it.
3. The PHP script creates the HTML form where the user can post his or her message in a text area. After it is submitted, the PHP script calls itself, and the process of inserting the form data into the database is handled with MySQL functions.
4. In the final step, the database is opened and all of the fields from the "messages" table are displayed. A `while` loop iterates over all the records of the result-set returned by the `SELECT` query.

15.3 Chapter Summary

This chapter introduced you to the way PHP and MySQL work together. From the PHP program, you learned to connect to a MySQL database and use PHP built-in functions to perform SQL queries and get back results from the database. The final example was provided to illustrate a complete Web page with an HTML form, PHP script, and MySQL database all interacting with one another.

15.3.1   What You Should Know

Now that you have finished this chapter you should be able to answer the following questions:

1. How would you connect to the database server from a PHP script?

2. How could you use PHP MySQL functions to:

    a. Select a database?
    b. Execute SQL statements and iterate over the result-set?
    c. Check for errors generated by the database server?
    d. Keep track of the number of records retrieved?
    e. Send the output to the browser?

3. How would you disconnect from the database from a PHP script?

15.3.2   What's Next?

In the next chapter we discuss cookies and session management to keep track of visitors and their preferences. You will learn what cookies and sessions are, how they are used, how they differ, how handle data, their advantages, and their drawbacks.

CHAPTER 15 LAB

1. a. Write a PHP script that connects to your mySQL database. Use `localhost` as your machine name.
    b. Once connected, select the `school` database you created in the Chapter 14 Lab. Check to see if the database was opened. Use `mysql_error()`.
    c. Use a `SELECT` statement to display the first names, last names, and majors in the `student` table. Use the `mysql_query()` and `mysql_fetch_assoc()` functions.
    d. Find the number of rows in which the GPA was above 3.0.
    e. Display the whole student table with headers across the fields.

2. a. Create a form to ask for the information you will need to create a new record in the `student` table. Prompt the user for all the table information.

   b. In the PHP script, extract the information, check that all the fields were filled, remove backslashes from quoted text, make sure the e-mail address is valid, and so on. (Hint: See the end of Chapter 12, "Regular Expressions and Pattern Matching").

   c. Open up the `school` database and check that the connection was made. Create a query that will insert the data into the `student` table.

   d. Sort the table and display it, formatted.

   e. Close the database.

16

Cookies and Sessions

16.1 What Is Stateless?

The HTTP Web protocol was designed to be stateless to keep transactions between a browser and server brief and cut down on the overhead of keeping connections open. *Stateless* means that after a transaction takes place between the browser and server, the connection is lost and neither the browser nor server has any recollection of what transpired between one session and the next. Each request to the server is considered a brand new request. This works well for static documents, but not so well when we need to keep track of a Web site user. Imagine, for example, an online banking Web site. If each request were brand new, you would have to retype your username and password every time you clicked any link on that Web site. You would log in to see your balance, log in again to see a specific transaction, then log in again to make a transfer, and so on.

The shopping cart is used as the most obvious reason for saving state. As the Internet grew, people started filling up their virtual carts with groceries, music, books, prescription drugs, and even cars and homes. It became necessary for merchants to remember what their customers purchased, their preferences, registration numbers, IDs, and so on.

Cookies and sessions are used to let programs like PHP remember past requests. *Cookies* are used to store small amounts of information on the user's browser, whereas sessions can manage much larger amounts of data and store information on the server side. Because cookies and sessions often work together in saving state, this chapter discusses both methods and the advantages and disadvantages of both.

16.2 What Are Cookies?

Before we delve into using cookies with PHP, let's discuss what they are. In 1994 Netscape came up with the concept of a cookie. A cookie is a small packet of information stored on the browser, and it is persistent, meaning it is maintained between browser sessions and might persist even when the user shuts down his or her computer. The cookie idea became very popular and is now supported by all major browsers.

The term *cookie* comes from an old programming trick for debugging and testing routines in a program. A text file called a *magic cookie* was created. It contained text that was shared by two routines so that they could communicate with each other. The cookie feature started by Netscape[1] is also just a little piece of textual data that is stored in a file (often called the cookie jar) on the hard drive of the client (browser). It contains information about the viewer that can be retrieved and used at a later time. The HTTP server sends the cookie in a header to the browser when the browser connects for the first time and from then on, the browser returns a copy of the cookie to the server each time it connects. The information is passed back and forth between the server and browser via HTTP headers.

Cookies can make a Web page personal and friendly, and store important information about the user's language, reading, or music preferences; how many times he or she has visited your site; track items in a shopping cart, and so on. They can also be annoying, and some question the security of putting unknown data on their hard drive. Users do have a say about whether or not to use them.

Cookies can be turned off and removed from the hard drive. For example, under the Tools menu in Navigator, go to Cookie Manager, and from there you can block all cookies for a site. If you are using Internet Explorer you can delete cookies by going to the Tools menu and then to Internet Options. For Firefox, you can control cookies by selecting Options from the Tools menu.

Unlike Grandma's old-fashioned cookie jar packed full of sugar cookies, Web browser cookies are limited (although today those limits seem to be higher). Browsers usually cannot store more than 300 cookies and servers usually not more than 20. Storage is usually limited in length to only 4 kilobytes (4,000 characters) per cookie, so you cannot store a lot of information. The actual filename that holds the cookie data varies on different platforms. Netscape Navigator (on Windows) stores cookies in a file named `cookies.txt` in Navigator's system directory; Internet Explorer stores them in the *Window\Cookies* directory; and on the Mac, they are found in a file called `MagicCookie`. Note: When you are setting cookies, they are stored in the browser's memory and not written to the hard drive until you exit the browser.

16.2.1   Cookie Ingredients

Cookies consist of a string of text stored on the user's hard drive as a small text file. They are sent from a server-side program to the browser through the HTTP request and response headers. The cookie's default lifetime is the length of the current session (when the user exits his or her browser), after which it is destroyed. The expiration time for the end of a cookie's life can be set as an attribute of the Cookie header (see the "Expiration Date" section that follows) making it possible to extend the life of the cookie forever.

---

1. See *www.netscape.com/newsref/std/cookie_spec.html* for cookie specification.

Cookies are comprised of text in the form of key–value pairs, often nicknamed "crumbs," and up to 20 pairs can be stored in a single cookie string. The browser stores only one cookie per page.

When making cookies, the crumbs consist of `name=value` pairs, called attributes, terminated with a semicolon. Within the string, semicolons, commas, or whitespace characters are not allowed. The HTTP `Set-Cookie` header has the following format.

FORMAT

```
Set-Cookie: name=value; [expires=date};[ path=path];
            [domain=domainname]; [secure];
```

Example:
```
Set-Cookie: id="Bob";expires=Monday, 21-Oct-05 12:00:00 GMT;
            domain="bbb.com"; path="/"; secure;
```

16.2.2   The Attributes of a Cookie

When setting the cookie, it is important to understand its components. A cookie has a name, a value, and another set of optional attributes to determine the expiration date, the domain, path, and whether the cookie must be sent over a secure communications channel (HTTPS). All of these attributes are assigned as strings.

Name.   The actual cookie text consists of the name of the cookie and the value stored there. It can be a session ID, a username, or whatever you like.

FORMAT

```
nameofcookie=value;
```

Examples:
```
id=456;
email=joe@abc.com;
name=Bob;
```

The name of the cookie is on the left side of the = sign and the cookie text that gets stored is on the right side. The value assigned is a string. To add multiple values to the string, unique characters are used to separate the values, such as `Bill*Sanders*345`.

Expiration Date.   The cookie normally expires when the current browser session ends, which gives it little value, but you can specify an expiration date that will let it persist, by using the following format.

FORMAT

```
;expires=Weekday, DD-MON-YY  HH:MM::SS GMT
```

Example:
```
;expires=Friday, 15-Mar-07 12:00:00 GMT
```

The day of the week is specified by `Weekday`, the day of the month by `DD`, the first three letters of the month by `MON`, and the last two numbers of the year by `YY`. The hour, minutes, and seconds are specified in `HH:MM:SS` and the GMT time zone is always used. Some cookies last for days, but it is possible for them to even last for years. It is up to the designer to decide how long a cookie should live. Setting the expiration date also limits the amount of possible damage that could be done if the cookie is intercepted by some hacker. Once the cookie has expired it is called *stale* and is automatically destroyed.

Domain Name.   The domain name, not commonly used, specifies a general domain name to which the cookie should apply. It allows the cookie to be shared among multiple servers instead of just the one you are on. If you do not use the full `http://domain` syntax, then a leading dot must precede the domain name.

FORMAT

```
; domain=.domain_name
; domain=http://somedomain.com
```

Example:
```
; domain=.kajinsky.com
; domain=http://kajinksy.com
```

Path.   The path is used to specify where the cookie is valid for a particular server. Setting a path for the cookie allows other pages from the same domain to share a cookie.

FORMAT

```
; path=pathname
```

Example:
```
; path=/home
```

Security. If a cookie is secure, it must be sent over a secure communication channel (HTTPS server).

FORMAT

```
; secure
```

16.3 PHP and Cookies

Now that we have discussed HTTP cookies and their ingredients, it is time to use them with PHP. You will use the same ingredients to make, send, and delete cookies, but all of the underlying details shown in the previous section will be handled with PHP functions.

16.3.1   Creating Cookies with the setcookie() Function

Before creating a cookie, remember that the cookie is part of an HTTP header. Headers must be sent before anything else on the page. One echo statement, even a blank line or space preceding the header will cause an error (see Figure 16.1; see "Buffering and HTTP Headers" on page 689).

> **Warning:** Cannot modify header information - headers already sent by (output started at c:\wamp\www\exemples\sessions\message.php:4) in **c:\wamp\www\exemples\sessions\message.php** on line 5

Figure 16.1   Sending output before headers is an error.

A cookie is created with the PHP built-in setcookie() function, which takes at least one argument, the name of the cookie. (If only the name argument is present, the cookie by that name will be deleted from the remote client.) The second argument is the value that will be stored in the cookie such as a username, date, e-mail, and so on. It is not a good idea to put any kind of sensitive personal information in cookie files because cookie files are readable text files.

Other optional arguments include the expiration date of the cookie, and the path where the cookie is valid, and lastly, whether or not to make the cookie secure. If you do not set the expiration date, the cookie will be removed when the browser session ends. To skip an argument you can use the empty string (""), but you must use zero (0) to skip the expire and secure arguments because their values must be integers. The expire argument is an integer representing the time in seconds as returned by the time() or mktime() functions. The secure argument indicates that the cookie should only be transmitted over a secure

HTTPS SSL connection. You can check to see if the page is being sent over an SSL connection by checking the $_SERVER['HTTPS'] superglobal array, as follows:

```
if ($_SERVER['HTTPS'] == 'on') {  }
```

If necessary, you can send more than one cookie by using more setcookie() function calls, but remember that the protocol has a limit of 20 cookies from one site to a single user. (For storing more than one value in a cookie, you can use an array. See "Storing Multiple Values in One Cookie—Serialization" on page 681.)

FORMAT

```
boolean setcookie ( string name [, string value [, int expire [,
string path [, string domain [, int secure]]]]] )
```

Example:
```
setcookie("cookie_name", "value");
setcookie("uid", $uid, time() + 60 * 60 * 24 * 60, "/mydir",1);
```

When you name the cookie, follow the same conventions as you would when creating any PHP variable; that is, no spaces or odd characters. For example, you cannot use whitespace, semicolons, pipe symbols, or commas in the name of the cookie.

The cookies are stored in the PHP global $_COOKIE array. The server variable, $_SERVER['REQUEST_TIME'], gives the time when a request started.

The $_COOKIE Global Array.   Once the server has set a cookie, the browser sends it back to the server every time the page loads. When you start your browser, if there are cookies, they pertain to the current page. When a cookie is set, PHP assigns it to the global $_COOKIE associative array, consisting of key=value pairs where the keys are the names of all the cookies and the values are what is stored in the cookie, such as a session ID number, a user ID, e-mail, and so on. (You can only get those cookies that were written for the server you are on and belong to you. You cannot read and write cookies that belong to someone else or reside on a different server.)

To see all the cookies on a page, extract the contents of the $_COOKIE array. When you reload the page, the $_COOKIE array will contain all the cookie values saved for that page. When retrieving cookies, you can check to see if the cookie was set with the built-in isset() or empty() functions, as shown in Example 16.1.

EXAMPLE 16.1

```
  <?php
1     setcookie("usr","Ellie Quigley");
2     setcookie("color","blue");
  ?>
  <html><head><title>The Cookie Array</title></head>
  <body bgcolor="lavender">
  <font face="verdana" size='+1'>
  <h2>$_COOKIE[]</h2>
  <?php
3     if(! empty($_COOKIE['color'])){
          echo "<pre>";
4         print_r($_COOKIE);
          echo "</pre>";
      }
  ?>
  </font>
  </body>
  </html>
```

EXPLANATION

1 The first cookie key–value pair is set. The name of the cookie is `"usr"` and the corresponding value is `"Ellie Quigley"`.

2 The second cookie key–value pair is set. The name of the cookie is `"color"` and the corresponding value is `"blue"`. Normally, the user would provide the value from a form.

3 Because cookies will not become visible until the next loading of the page where the cookie should be visible, you can test if a cookie was successfully set before extracting its contents. See Figure 16.3.

4 The `print_r` function displays the contents of the cookie. If the cookie had not been set or had expired there would be no output (see Figure 16.2). All the other attributes set for the cookie, like expiration date, path, security, and so on, are not visible.

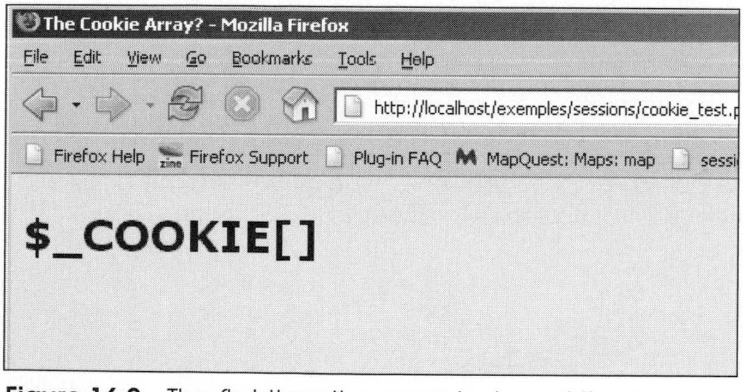

Figure 16.2 The first time the page is viewed the `$_COOKIE` array is empty.

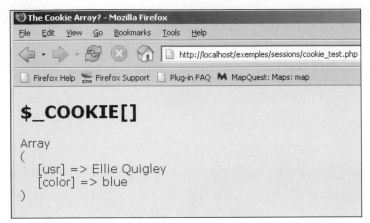

Figure 16.3 When the page is refreshed, the $_COOKIE array has cookie values.

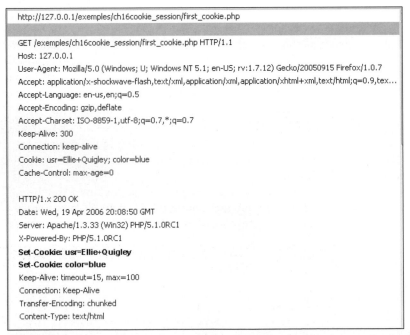

Figure 16.4 The browser sends the cookie back to the server; the server sets the cookie in a header. See Figure 16.5, a diagram illustrating server/browser/PHP interaction with cookies.

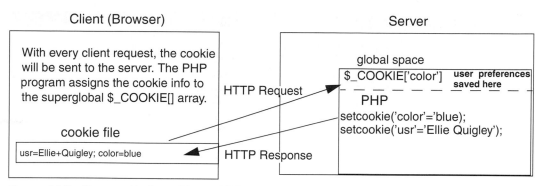

Figure 16.5 The cookie is sent in an HTTP header.

Storing Multiple Values in One Cookie—Serialization. The setcookie() function accepts one string as its value. In the previous example, the setcookie() function was called twice to register two cookie values. Because the number of cookies is limited to 20 per domain, you might want to assign multiple values to one cookie, for example, data coming in from a form. In the following example, one cookie will store three values. This example demonstrates how to serialize data. Serializing the data allows you to convert an array into a string that will be accepted by the cookie. After retrieving the cookie contents, you will have to unserialize it to convert the string back to an array.

The PHP serialize() function returns a string containing a byte-stream representation of the value, making the value acceptable for storage anywhere—in this example, a cookie, though serialization is also used for storing variables and objects in a file or database. (If you go to your browser and look at the actual data stored in the cookie, it has been URL-encoded.)

Use unserialize() to return the string to its orginal form.

EXAMPLE 16.2

```
      <?php
1         $info = array("ellie", "yellow",  22);
2         setcookie("usr", serialize($info));
      ?>
      <html><head><title>Multiple Cookie Values</title></head>
      <html><head><title>The Cookie Array?</title></head>
      <body bgcolor="lavender">
      <font face="verdana" size='+1'>
      <h2>$_COOKIE[]</h2>
      <pre>
      <b>
      <?php
```

EXAMPLE   16.2 (CONTINUED)

```
3        if(! empty($_COOKIE['usr'])){
4            $cookie_data= $_COOKIE['usr'];
5            $cookie_data=stripslashes($cookie_data);
6            $cookie_data=unserialize("$cookie_data");
             echo "What's in the cookie array< br />";
7            print_r($_COOKIE);
             echo "<pre>Unserialized data< br />";
8            print_r( $cookie_data);
         }
     ?>

     </b>
     </pre>
     </font>
     </body>
```

EXPLANATION

1   The array is assigned a list of values.

2   The setcookie() function is given the name of the cookie followed by the value. The value is an array that is serialized into one string. The new string will be in a format that is acceptable for any type of storage. It represents the data type and number of characters in the original data. a:3 means a three-element array, s:5 a 5-character string, and so on, as shown in the output of this program. By serializing the array into one string, we only need to call setcookie() once.

3   Check to see if the cookie has any value, that is, if it was set.

4   The cookie data is retrieved for the user and assigned to $cookie_data. It is a serialized string. See Figure 16.6.

5   The slashes are stripped from the string. If you do not remove the backslashes, the unserialize() function on the next line fails.

6   The unserialize() function returns the original array.

7   You can see in the value of the cookie the serialized array.

8   The unserialized array is printed. We now have the original values back. See Figure 16.6.

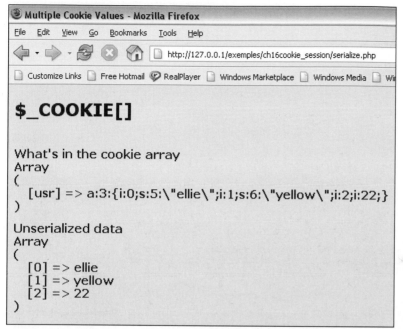

Figure 16.6 Storing an array in a single cookie.

16.3.2 Tracking Visitors with Cookies

The following examples demonstrate the use of cookies for tracking visitor activities, such as when the visitor last viewed the page and how many times he or she has been there, but they can also be used to check user preferences, user IDs, and so on. Cookies are useful for retaining small amounts of information, but not all browsers support cookies and if they are supported, a user can turn them off. To overcome these problems, a better solution is to use PHP sessions (discussed in "What Is a Session?" on page 694 of this chapter).

Visitor Count Example. The following example uses a cookie to count the number of times the user has visited this page. Once the cookie is set, its value will be increased by 1 each time the visitor comes back to the page.

EXAMPLE   16.3

```php
    <?php
1      $count = $_COOKIE['visits']; // Accessing the cookie value

2      if( $count == "" ){
3          $count = 1;    // Initialize the counter
       }
       else{
4          $count++;
       }
5      setcookie("visits",$count); // "visits" is the cookie name
    ?>
    <html><head><title>Setting Cookies</title></head>
    <body bgcolor="lavender">
    <font size=+1 face="arial">
    <h2>Visitor Count with Cookies</h2>
    You are visitor number <?php echo $count; ?>.<br />
    </font>
    </body>
    </html>
```

EXPLANATION

1   The value stored in the $_COOKIE array is extracted and assigned to $count. The
     value is just an integer that continues to be incremented by 1 each time the user
     reloads the page. If this is the first time the page has been loaded, the $_COOKIE
     array will be empty.

2, 3 If this is the first time the user has visited this page, $count will be empty, and it
      will be set to 1. See Figure 16.7.

4   For each subsequent visit to this page, the value of the counter will be increased
     by 1. See Figure 16.8.

5   The setcookie() function sets the cookie when the page is first loaded. The
     name of the cookie is visits and the value stored there will be incremented by 1
     each time the page is revisited. The cookie is stored on the user's browser and will
     be deleted when the browser is exited. What is important to note here is that the
     cookie is sent in a header, and headers must be sent before any other output from
     this page. The HTML output is placed after this line or PHP will send warnings to
     the screen.

Figure 16.7   Cookies used to count visitors.

Figure 16.8   The cookie value is incremented each time the page is reloaded.

Tracking the Visitor's Last Visit.   The following example keeps track of when a visitor last viewed the page. The cookie will store the current date, which will be retrieved the next time the page is refreshed.

EXAMPLE 16.4

```
(Page 1--The HTML page)

    <html><head><title>Setting Cookies</title></head>
    <body bgcolor="lavender">
    <font size=+1 face="arial">
    <h2>Tracking Visitors with Cookies</h2>
    <H1>Welcome to our Site!</H1>
    <p>
1   Check out our product line
        <a href="http://localhost/exemples/sessions/message.php">
        Click here</a>
    </font>
    </body>
    </html>
-------------------------------------------------------------------
(Page 2--The PHP Script--Set a Cookie)

    <?php
        // Filename: "message.php"
2       $date_str="l dS \of F Y h:i:s A";
        $last_visit="Your last visit was on ".  date("$date_str");
3       setcookie("message","$last_visit");
    ?>
    <html><head><title>Products</title>
    </head>
    <body bgcolor="lavender">
    <font face="verdana" size='+1'>
    <h2>Products Page</h2>
    <!--  Rest of page goes here  -->
    <?php
4       if(! empty($_COOKIE['message'])){  // Has the cookie been set?
5           $when="$_COOKIE[message]";
            echo $when,".< br />";
        }
    ?>
    </font></body></html>
```

EXPLANATION

1 When the user clicks on the link in this HTML form, he or she will be directed to
   the page (page 2) that contains the code for setting a cookie. The initial form is
   shown in Figure 16.9.

2 After clicking the link (Figure 16.9) in page 1, the user is directed to page 2, the
   "Products Page" (Figure 16.10). The variable is assigned a string of arguments
   that will be sent to the PHP date() function on the next line, the current date and
   time on the server. (Keep in mind that the date on the browser and server might
   not be in sync.)

EXPLANATION (CONTINUED)

3   The cookie is set with the setcookie() function. The first argument, "message", is the name of the cookie and the second argument, "$last_visit", is the value that will be stored in the cookie.

4   The first time this page is accessed the cookie is set. Its value will not be available until the next time the page is viewed. If the cookie has a value (i.e., is not empty), the message will contain the date string that was assigned to the cookie by the setcookie() function in the previous viewing of the page.

5   The value of the cookie is extracted. It is the date string that was assigned to the cookie the last time the visitor viewed this page. Every time the visitor refreshes this page, the value of the cookie will be the cookie value that was set on his or her last visit, that is, the date and time of the last visit.

Figure 16.9   The HTML initial form (page 1).

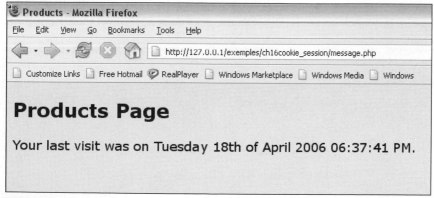

Figure 16.10   After returning to this page, the cookie value is displayed.

16.3.3   Extending the Life of a Cookie

How long will a cookie stay in the cookie jar? Normally a cookie expires when the browser is exited. However, the cookie's life span can be controlled by setting the expiration date in the cookie's `expire` attribute, the third argument in PHP's `setcookie()` function. The time the cookie expires is represented as a UNIX timestamp; that is, the number of seconds since January 1, 1970, 00:00:00 GMT, known as the epoch. The `time()` function will give you the current time in seconds, and by adding additional seconds, you can set the expiration date of a cookie to some time in the future. By subtracting from this value, the time will be past time, which will cause the cookie to be deleted. The time returned is expressed in GMT time, the required format for the `expire` attribute.

To get the time, two PHP functions are provided: `time()` and `mktime()`.

The time() Function.   The `time()` function returns the current time in UNIX time (UNIX timestamp). By adding the number of seconds to the output of the `time()` function, you can set the amount of time from now until some future time when the cookie is to expire.

Table 16.1   Units of Time in Seconds

Unit of Time	Seconds
Minute	60
Hour	60 * 60
Day	60 * 60 * 24
Week	60 * 60 * 24 * 7
Month	60 * 60 * 24 * 30

FORMAT

```
int time ( void )
```

Example:
```
$nextWeek = time() + (60 * 60 * 24 * 7);
             (60  seconds * 60 minutes * 24 hours * 7 days)
```

EXAMPLE 16.5

```
<?php
    $date_str="l dS \of F Y h:i:s A";
    $last_visit="Your last visit was on ".  date("$date_str");
1   $expire=60*60*24*30 + time();  // One month
2   setcookie("message","$last_visit", $expire);
?>
```

EXPLANATION

1   The variable is assigned the value of one month, 30 days, from now in milliseconds.
2   The setcookie() function is named message, it contains the date of the last visit, and it will expire in one month. The expire value is calculated by adding the number of seconds in a month to the current time (time()). After one month, if the visitor returns, the cookie will be reset.

The mktime() Function.   The mktime() function will also get the UNIX time. It has a different format. Arguments can be set to 0 (zero) from left to right if you want to use the default values. However, you can leave out arguments on the right side to get the defaults. (The year is either two or four digits.)

FORMAT

```
int mktime ( [int hour [, int minute [, int second [, int month [,
             int day [, int year [, int is_dst]]]]]]] )
```

Example:
```
$lastday = mktime(0, 0, 0, 6, 0, 2006);          // Last day of May
echo date("M-d-Y", mktime(0, 0, 0, 1, 1, 2006));  // "Jan-01-2006"
```

16.3.4   Buffering and HTTP Headers

Because cookies are sent in an HTTP header, you cannot execute any other output before sending the header or you will get a PHP warning. In the following example, the fact that there is a blank line at the top of the file caused the warning. The cookie headers must be set first unless you turn on buffering.

EXAMPLE 16.6

```
                        <-- this blank line caused a warning !!!
<?php
    setcookie("usr","Ellie Quigley");  // Headers must be sent first
    setcookie("color","blue");
?>
<html>
<head><title>The Cookie Array?</title></head>
    <body bgcolor="lavender">
     < Code continues here >
    </body>
</html>
```

EXPLANATION

The header information must be sent first, or a warning is issued, as in Figure 16.11. Even a blank line will cause a warning.

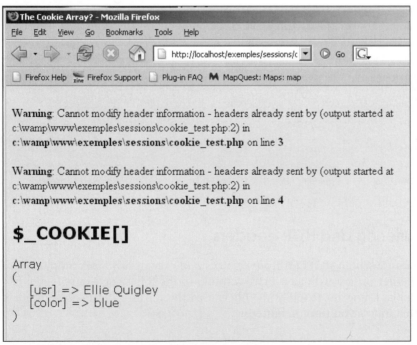

Figure 16.11   Header information should be sent first!

If you need to precede any HTTP headers (not just cookie headers) with other output, PHP provides a set of buffering functions that allow you to save all the script's output in a buffer until the script ends (starting with PHP 4.0). When the script ends, first the HTTP headers, and then the contents of the output buffer, are sent to the browser. The functions that help you control output buffering are shown in Table 16.2.

Table 16.2 Buffering Functions

Function	What It Does
ob_start()	Enables output buffering. No output is sent from the script (other than headers). It is saved in an internal buffer.
ob_end_flush()	Flushes the output buffer, and disables output buffering.
ob_end_clean()	Cleans the output buffer without sending it, and disables output buffering.
ob_get_clean()	Returns the contents of the output buffer and ends output buffering
ob_get_length()	Returns the length of the output buffer.
ob_get_contents()	Returns the current output buffer as a string. This allows you to process whatever output the script emitted.
ob_gzhandler()	A callback function for ob_start(). Useful for sending compressed data.

The ob_start() and ob_end_flush() Functions. The ob_start() function enables output buffering and the ob_end_flush() function flushes out the buffers and then turns buffering off. When your script ends, PHP will automatically flush the buffers, so you can omit ob_end_flush(). It is possible to call ob_start() multiple times; and if so, you would have to call ob_end_flush() for each level.

FORMAT

```
bool ob_start ( [callback output_callback [, int chunk_size [,
               bool erase]]] )
bool ob_end_flush ( void )
```

Example:
```
ob_start();
ob_end_flush();
```

EXAMPLE 16.7

```php
    <?php
1       ob_start();     // Turn on output buffering
    ?>

    <html><head><title>The Cookie Array?</title>
    </head>
        <body bgcolor="lavender">
        <font face="verdana" size='+1'>
        <h2>$_COOKIE[]</h2>

    <?php
2       setcookie("usr","Ellie Quigley");
        setcookie("color","blue");
    ?>

    <?php
        if(! empty($_COOKIE[color])){
            echo "<pre>";
            print_r($_COOKIE);
            echo "</pre>";
        }
    ?>

    </font>
    </body>
    </html>
    <?php
3       ob_end_flush();     // Flush the buffer and end output buffering
    ?>
```

EXPLANATION

1   The ob_start() function turns on output buffering. Now only HTTP headers will be sent and the rest of the program's output will be saved until the program ends, at which time it will be sent.

2   The setcookie() function can be placed below the other ouput without causing warnings. This output will be sent first due to the buffering set up on line 1.

3   The ob_end_flush() function is not necessary, but is used here to flush out the buffers and end the output buffering for this session.

Output Buffering and php.ini. If you want buffering set for all your PHP scripts, you can enable the `php.ini` directive `output_buffering`. If you do, every PHP script will behave as if it begins with a call to `ob_start()`.

From the `php.ini` file:

```
; Output buffering allows you to send header lines (including cookies) even
; after you send body content, at the price of slowing PHP's output layer a
; bit.  You can enable output buffering during runtime by calling the output
; buffering functions.  You can also enable output buffering for all files by
; setting this directive to On.  If you wish to limit the size of the buffer
; to a certain size -you can use a maximum number of bytes instead of 'On', as
; a value for this directive (e.g., output_buffering=4096).
output_buffering = Off
```

Output buffering is turned off by default. If you want to turn it on for all scripts, go to the `php.ini` initialization file and change the `output_buffering` directive to "On".

16.3.5   Deleting a Cookie

When cookies are created, they are, by default, deleted when the user closes his or her browser. You have seen how to expand the life of a cookie, but what if you want to delete the cookie right now, even before the user closes his or her browser? Instead of adding to the current time, you simply subtract from the current time to some earlier date. This will cause the cookie to be deleted right away.

Remember, deleting a cookie is the responsibility of the browser and the time settings there might be different from the time settings on the server. Even though technically setting the expiration time to −1 would be an earlier time, it might be better to set it to a bigger negative number to assure that it will be removed. Setting the expiration time to 0 has no effect.

EXAMPLE 16.8

```
<?php
    setcookie ("cookie_name", "", time( ) - 3600);   // One hour ago
?>
```

EXPLANATION

Because we are destroying the cookie, there is no point in giving it a value, thus the second argument is intentionally left empty.

Using the Browser to Remove Cookies. Another way to delete cookies is to go in your browser to the Tools menu in Navigator, then to the Cookie Manger, and then to Manage Stored Cookies. In Internet Explorer, go to the Tools menu and Internet Options. Then you can remove all or some cookies from the hard drive. Figure 16.12 shows you how the Firefox browser manages cookies by going to Tools, Options, Privacy.

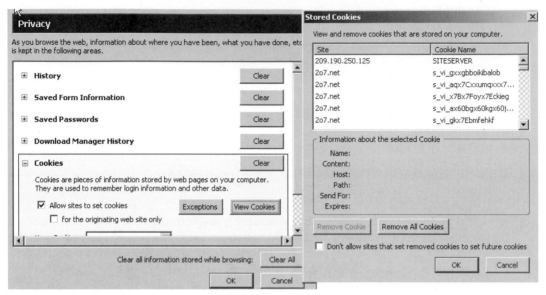

Figure 16.12   Cookie management on the Firefox browser.

16.4 What Is a Session?

Simply put, a session is the time that a user spends at a Web site. PHP provides us with a mechanism to manage sessions so that we can keep track of what a visitor is doing, what he or she likes, what he or she wants, and so on, even after the user logs off. Like cookies, the idea is to maintain state. Before delving into the details, let's use an analogy to give you an idea of how sessions work.

Imagine taking your favorite wool sweater to a dry cleaning establishment. You will drop off the sweater and be handed a claim ticket that will be used to identify the sweater when you return. The other half of the claim ticket is pinned to your sweater with the same number you have on your claim ticket. Later when you come back, you will give your claim ticket to the attendant and he or she will use it to identify your sweater in the long rack of clothes. A session works the same way.

A PHP session, like a cookie, is a way for the PHP to keep track of that Web site visitor even after he or she leaves or logs off. A visitor makes a request from his or her browser to retrieve a Web page as follows:

```
http://server/homepage.php
```

The server program, in this example, `homepage.php`, is a PHP program. PHP starts a session and sends a unique session ID number, similar to the claim ticket, back to the visitor's browser. This unique ID number is a long random hexadecimal number that is used to key into the user's data. It can be sent via a cookie or added to all URLs of the pages for the site. The actual user information is saved in a session file on the server, usually in a temporary directory (see Figure 16.13). The session filename contains the unique ID number for the session. The next time the visitor asks for the page, his or her browser hands the ID number back to the server, just as you hand the claim ticket to the dry cleaning attendant. The server uses the session ID number to locate the file with the name that corresponds to the same session ID number. The session file contains the actual session data; for example, username, preferences, or items in the shopping cart—information about the visitor that was stored the last time he or she visited the page. If this is the first time the user has visited the page, his or her preferences will be collected and stored into the session file, to be retrieved later on.

By default, the session ID is sent in a cookie and the cookie's name is `PHPSESSID`. Unlike the cookies we discussed in the first part of this chapter, where the user information was passed in a cookie, with sessions, the only data in the cookie is the session ID, not any other information about the user. The user information is saved in a session file on the server so that the size limitation of cookies is not a factor and sensitive information is not being passed back and forth across the network.

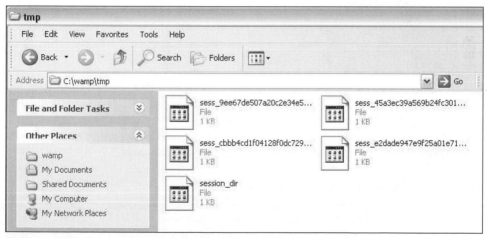

Figure 16.13 The session data is stored in a /tmp directory on the server.

This session file starts with "sess" followed by the session number (Apache/Windows). The text it contains is a serialized line representing the data, the data type, and the number of characters saved for a session.[2] This is a line from a session file:

```
book|s:7:"History";user|s:13:"Ellie Quigley";
```

Once the user's browser has a session ID, it passes that ID back to the server program on every subsequent request. The session ID is disposable, so after some time it will expire and the information associated with it will also be removed. A session might last for a few minutes or a few hours since the last request or it could last indefinitely. We look at various configuration options later in this chapter. Figure 16.14 illustrates the way the session ID is passed in a cookie.

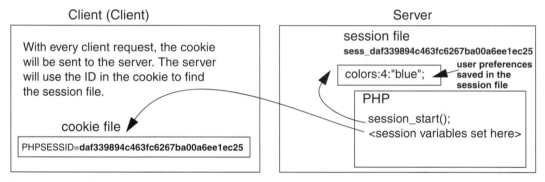

Figure 16.14   The cookie file and the session file have the session ID in common.

Although cookies are the default way to pass the session ID back and forth between browser and server, you can also pass the session ID as GET or POST data in the same way as when submitting a form. Recall that GET data is URL-encoded and attached with a ? to the URL, whereas the POST data is part of the page header information. It is also possible to send a session ID through a URL with a link within a page.

16.4.1   Where to Store Sessions

If your site is sharing a server, it is recommended that session files for users should be in their own user area under the server, but not in a world writable directory such as /tmp. If a site has a large number of users and session files, it is possible to store the session files in multiple levels of subdirectories. To find out where your sessions are stored, or to change the default path, see `session.save_path` in the `php.ini` file or use PHP's `session_save_path()` function.

---

2. Because the (session) library uses different storage modules, you can keep the data in plain-text files, shared memory, or databases. The exact location of data is not really important (as long the performance of the medium is sufficient). From Tobias Ratschiller, *http://www.zend.com/zend/tut/session.php*.

From the `php.ini` file:

```
; session.save_path = "N;/path"
;
; where N is an integer. Instead of storing all the session files in
; /path, what this will do is use subdirectories N-levels deep, and
; store the session data in those directories. This is useful if you
; or your OS have problems with lots of files in one directory, and is
; a more efficient layout for servers that handle lots of sessions.
;
```

The `session_save_path()` function returns the path of the current directory used to save session data. If a path is specified, the path to where data is saved will be changed for this session. If this page will be linked to other pages, then the function must be called before starting the session in all the pages involved. Of course, PHP will need read and write access to the new path to retrieve and save session data.

FORMAT

```
string session_save_path ( [string path] )
```

Example:
```
session_save_path("/newpath");
echo session_save_path();
```

EXAMPLE 16.9

```
<?php
    echo "Your session files are stored in <b>".
1       session_save_path(). ".</b>< br />";
2   if ($handle = opendir(session_save_path())) {
        echo "<b>Files:< br />\n";
        /* Loop over the directory. */
3       while (false !== ($file = readdir($handle))) {
            echo "$file< br />\n";
        }
        echo "</b>";
        closedir($handle);
    }
?>
```

EXPLANATION

1   The `session_save_path()` function returns the path location where the session files are stored.

2   The `opendir()` function opens the directory folder where the session data is stored and returns a handle to that directory, `$handle`.

3   The readdir() function retrieves the contents of the directory, and its output is displayed in Figure 16.15.

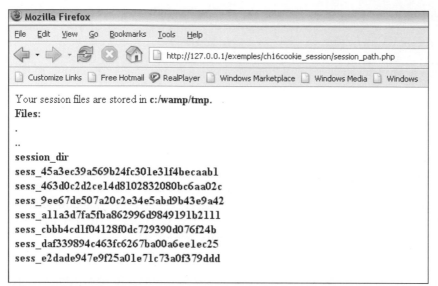

Figure 16.15 The session path and files. Output from Example 16.9.

16.4.2 Starting a Cookie-Based Session

A PHP session is started either explicitly with the `session_start()` function, or implicitly by registering a variable for the session with the `session_register()` function. Typically, `session_start()` is called on top of the page, and then session variables are registered in the superglobal `$_SESSION` array.

When PHP starts a session, it has to check first to see whether a valid session ID already exists for this user. If a valid session ID does exist, PHP will go to the session file that corresponds to the ID number, retrieve the data from the file, and assign it to the superglobal `$_SESSION` associative array. The values in this array are then made available to your program. If this is the first time the user has visited the page, PHP will create a new session ID, and the `$_SESSION` array will be empty.

The session_start() Function. The `session_start()` function creates a session or resumes one that has already started. The session ID is passed via a cookie, via GET/POST, or in a link (see a cookie-based session in Figure 16.16). Each page that uses a session must start the session with the `session_start()` function. If the session ID is being sent by a cookie, then as with all cookie headers, the `session_start()` function is called before any other statements that send output to the browser. This function always returns TRUE.

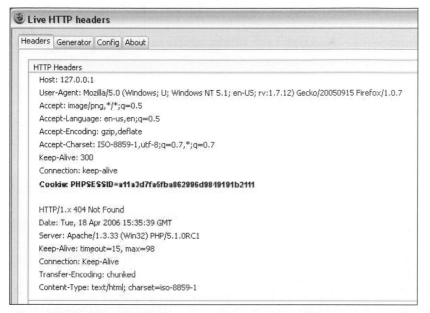

Figure 16.16 A cookie-based session. Note the session ID is sent as an HTTP `Cookie` header.

FORMAT

```
bool session_start ( void )
```

Example:
```
session_start();
```

16.4.3 Registering a Session

The data that is stored in the session file is created in a PHP script in the form of variables. The session variables can then be referenced across page requests during the life of a session. These variables might represent the items placed in a shopping cart, a user's login and password, a user's color preference, and so on.

Although `session_start()` starts a session, it does not register session variables. To create session variables, you must register the variables in the session library. This can be done in two ways. We address both methods next.

The $_SESSION Associative Array.   To register variables for the session, the preferred way is to assign values to the superglobal $_SESSION array. Superglobals are available everywhere in your script, even within functions. PHP automatically registers the $_SESSION variables for you. The global $_SESSION associative array is used to handle the session variables that will be saved on the server for the life of the session. The key for the $_SESSION associative array is the name of the variable, and the value is what you are assigning to it.

To access the values in the $_SESSION associative array, you must first start a session and then extract the array values as you would any other associative array.

To unset these variables, the unset() function is used; for example, unset($_SESSION['color']).

You must use session_start() before using the $_SESSION array.

FORMAT

Example:
```
$_SESSION['username'] = "john";
$_SESSION['password'] = $_POST['passwd'];
```

EXAMPLE 16.10

```
        <?php
1       session_start();
        ?>
        <html><head><title>Sessions</title></head>
        <body bgcolor="lavender">
        <font size=+1 face="arial">
        <h2>Tracking Visitors with Sessions</h2>
        <?php
2       if ( ! isset( $_SESSION)){
3           $_SESSION[visitor_count]=0;
        }
        else{
4           $_SESSION[visitor_count]++;
        }
5       echo "You are visitor number ",$_SESSION['visitor_count'],".
        <br />";
6       echo "The session id is: ",session_id();
        ?>
        </font>
        </body>
        </html>
```

EXPLANATION

1 The session is started here. All scripts using sessions start with the `session_start()` function.
2 If the session variable has not been set, this is the start of a brand new session. A session ID will be assigned and the `$_SESSION` array will be initialized on the next line.
3 The key in the `$_SESSION` associative array is `visitor_count`. The value assigned to it is `0`.
4 Once the user refreshes this page, the value of the `$_SESSION` is incremented by 1 (see Figure 16.17).
5 Every time the visitor returns to this page, the count is incremented by 1 and this line displays the output, as shown in Figure 16.18.
6 The `session_id()` function returns the value of the current session ID.

Figure 16.17 Using the `$_SESSION` array to save and retrieve a session. Initial output from Example 16.10.

Figure 16.18 Each time the user refreshes this page, the count is incremented by 1.

The session_register() Function.   The traditional way to register session variables was to use the PHP session_register() function, but to use this function you must set register_globals to "On" in the php.ini file, no longer the default setting. If, on the other hand, you are using the session_register() function, once registered in the session library, these global variables will be available until the session ends or until the session_unregister() function is called. Unlike registering session variables with the $_SESSION array, with the session_register() function it is not necessary to call session_start() first. After registering a variable, PHP will make an implicit call to session_start().

The arguments to session_register() can be strings containing the name of a variable or an array name. Note that this function takes the name of a variable as argument, not the variable itself.

The session_is_registered() function can be used to check if a session variable has been set and session_unregister() to remove variables from the session; for example, to remove a product item from the shopping cart. These functions should not be used if you are registering sessions with the $_SESSION array.

FORMAT

```
bool session_register ( mixed name [, mixed ...] )
```

Example:
```
session_start();
session_register('username');
session_register('password');
```

16.4.4   Saving Arrays in a Session

When using a shopping cart, you can add multiple items to your cart, browse around, come back, delete some items, and go on like this until you submit your order. A program that collects this data can store it in an array and save the data with a session. The $_SESSION array accepts simple scalar variables, but can also accept arrays. The following example demonstrates how to register multiple items in a session, list the saved values on another page, return to the selection page, and add more items to the array.

EXAMPLE   16.11

```
    (Page 1)
    <?php

1       session_start();
2       if ( ! isset($_SESSION['choices'])){
3           $_SESSION['choices']=array();
        }
```

EXAMPLE 16.11 (CONTINUED)

```
4          if ( is_array( $_POST['books'])){
5              $items=array_merge($_SESSION['choices'], $_POST['books']);
6              $_SESSION['choices'] = array_unique($items);
7              header("Location: listing_page.php");  // Redirect to this
                                                      // page now!
           }
       ?>

       <html>
       <head><title>Arrays and Sessions</title></head>
       <body bgcolor="#6666ff">
       <font face="verdana" >
       <div align="center">
8      <form action="<?php echo $_SERVER['PHP_SELF']?>" method="POST">
       <p>
       Book Categories< br />
9      <select name="books[]" multiple=multiple size="8">
           <option>Art</option>
           <option>Computer</option>
           <option>Engineering</option>
           <option>Fiction</option>
           <option>Language</option>
           <option>Non Fiction</option>
           <option>Poetry</option>
           <option>Travel</option>
       </select>
       </p>
       <input type=submit value="Select category"/>
       </p>
       </font>
       </body>
       </html>
```

EXPLANATION

1   A session for this page is started. All scripts that use sessions must call the `session_start()` function.

2, 3   If this is the first time the visitor has viewed this page, the session variables will not be set. In line 3 the `array()` function makes sure the `$_SESSION['choices']` array is created with no values.

4   If the form has been submitted, `$_POST['books']` will contain a list of the books selected from the menu in the form.

5   The `array_merge()` function joins the values in `$_SESSION['choices']` and the books that were listed in the form, `$_POST['books']`. If this is the first time the user has visited the page, the `$_SESSION[]` array will be empty, but it will exist because it was set to the empty array on line 3.

EXPLANATION (CONTINUED)

6   If this is not the first visit and the $\$\_SESSION['choices']$ array has values from a previous session, the `array_unique()` function will remove any duplicates that might occur after the merge on line 5.

7   The visitor is redirected to page 2, `listing_page.php`, to see his or her currently saved selection of books.

8   This is a self-processing form. Once the visitor has filled out the form, the PHP code on this page will process it and then redirect the user to page 2.

9   The HTML selection list is named `"books[]"` (shown in Figure 16.19), the name of the array PHP will use to collect the visitor's book choices.

Figure 16.19
Page 1: The visitor selects some books.

EXAMPLE 16.12

```
    (Page 2)
    <?php
1       session_start();
    ?>

    <html><head><title>Listing User's Book Categories</title></head>
    <body bgcolor="#6666FF">
    <font face="verdana">
    <table width="25%" border='1'>
    <caption><b>Selected Book Categories</b></caption>
    <col span="1" width="100"/>
    <?php
```

EXAMPLE 16.12 (CONTINUED)

```
2        if ( is_array($_SESSION['choices'])){
3           foreach($_SESSION['choices'] as $book){
    ?>
4       <tr bgcolor="#ffffff"><td ><?php echo $book ?></td></tr>
    <?php
            }   // End foreach block
        } // End if block
        else{ echo "<p>You have not selected any book categories
             yet</p>";}
    ?>
    </table>
    <p>
5   <a href="selections_page.php">Click here to return to category
             page</a>
    </p>
    </font>
    </body>
    </html>
```

EXPLANATION

1   A session is started for this page.
2   If `$_SESSION['choices']` has values, then the user has selected books in a pre-
    vious session, and the statements in the `if` block will be executed.
3   The `foreach` loop is used to iterate over the array and list each of the books in the
    `$_SESSION['choices']` associative array.
4   The books selected by the user are displayed in the table shown in Figure 16.20.
5   This link is used to send the user back to the first page, shown in Figure 16.21.
    After selecting another book item from the Book Categories in the original form,
    the new selection is saved by the session and redisplayed in Figure 16.22.

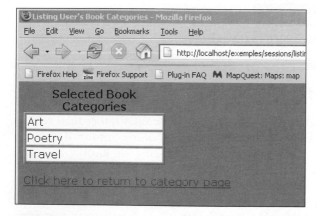

Figure 16.20
Page 2: This page lists the user
selections saved in the session.

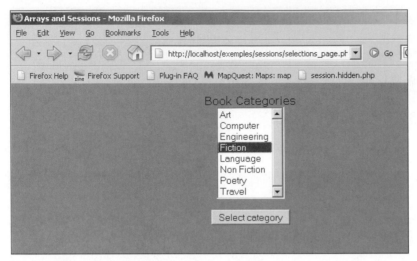

Figure 16.21   Page 1: User returns to selection page and adds another item.

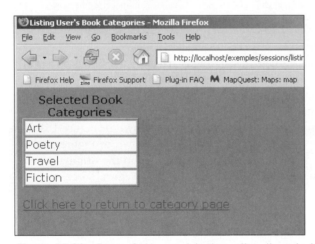

Figure 16.22   Page 2: User added another item to his or her list. Previous selections were saved in the session.

16.4.5   Session Cookie Functions and Configuration Options

Some developers feel that it is better to enforce the use of cookies rather than rely on passing sensitive session information through URLs (see "Passing Session IDs with a Link" on page 721), and because the default method of passing session IDs back and forth from browser to server is through cookies, PHP provides specific cookie functions to handle the cookie-based sessions.

To set the cookie parameters use the `session_set_cookie()` function, similar to the way we used the `setcookie()` function when working strictly with cookies, not sessions.

The effect of this function lasts only for the duration of the script. Thus, you need to call `session_set_cookie_params()` for every request and before `session_start()` is called.

FORMAT

```
void session_set_cookie_params ( int lifetime [, string path [,
                                  string domain [, bool secure]]] )
```

Example:
```
$expire=60*60*24*60 + time();   // Two months
session_set_cookie_params($expire, "/", "abc.com", 1);
```

Not only are there a number of functions to handle cookies, but you can also set specific directives in the `php.ini` file that affect the cookies for all of your scripts.

The `ini_set()` option can be used in a script to change the value of a configuration option just for the duration of the session; for example, the following header file enforces the use of cookies so that the user must have cookies enabled in his or her browser:

```
ini_set('session.use_cookies', 1);
ini_set('session.use_only_cookies', 1);
session_start();
```

Table 16.3   Cookie Configuration Directives (in the `php.ini` File)

Directive	What It Does
session.cookie_lifetime	Specifies the lifetime of the cookie, sent to the browser, in seconds . The value 0 means "until the browser is closed." Defaults to 0.
session.cookie_path	Specifies path to set in session_cookie. Defaults to /.
session.cookie_domain	Specifies the domain to set in session_cookie. Defaults to the host name of the server that generated the cookie.
session.cookie_secure	Specifies whether cookies should only be sent over secure connections. Defaults to off.
session.use_cookies	Specifies whether the module will use cookies to store the session ID on the client side. Defaults to 1 (enabled).
session.use_only_cookies	Specifies whether the module will only use cookies to store the session ID on the client side. Enabling this setting prevents attacks involved in passing session IDs in URLs.

16.4.6   Setting Preferences with Sessions

Consider the following example. One page lets the user select a favorite background color; using the session mechanism, when the user goes to another page, the color is displayed in the new page.

```
(Page 1)
<?php
1    if( isset($_REQUEST['color'] ) ) {
        // Start the new session
2        session_start();
        // Set the favorite color for this user
3        $_SESSION['favorite_color'] = $_REQUEST['color'];
    }
?>
<html>
<body>
<h1> Select Favorite Color</h1>
  <select name="color">
4 <form action="<?php echo ${_SERVER}['PHP_SELF']; ?>" method="GET">
 <select name="color" >
    <option value="" selected>Please select</option>
    <option value="white">White</option>
    <option value="blue">Blue</option>
    <option value="red">Red</option>
    <option value="yellow">Yellow</option>
    <option value="gray">Gray</option>
 </select>
 <input type="submit" value="Set color">
 </form>
 </body>
 </html>
```

EXPLANATION

1   Because this form is submitting to itself, first we check whether the request contains the color variable at all. If there is no color variable, there is no point in processing the form data. The first time the user visits the page, there will be no color variable set because the form has not yet been submitted.

2   Now that we do know that the color is set in the $_REQUEST, we can start the session. We use session_start() function to do so. This function will create a brand new session for this user, or reinstantiate an existing one if the session ID is present in the cookie or POST/GET data.

EXPLANATION (CONTINUED)

3   Next we extract the color the user selected from $_REQUEST and record it in the user's $_SESSION associate array. Notice that $_REQUEST is maintained for each request to PHP whereas $_SESSION is maintained for each user. The 'favorite_color' is an arbitrary key that we use to identify this variable in the $_SESSION array. The 'color' key corresponds to the input field in the form on the same page with the name "color".

4   Again, notice that the form action is submitting to itself. We use the property of the $_SERVER variable where the name of the current page is stored in this array under the key PHP_SELF.

Figure 16.23   Page 1: The color is set to "Yellow."

EXAMPLE   16.14

```
      (Page 2)
      <?php
1         session_start();
2         $favorite_color = $_SESSION['favorite_color'];
      ?>
      <html>
3     <body bgcolor="<?php echo $favorite_color; ?>">
      <h1>Your Favorite Color</h1>
4     Your favorite color is <b><?php echo $favorite_color; ?></b>.
      </body>
      </html>
```

EXPLANATION

1   This page will retrieve the user's favorite color from the session. The first step is to start the session using the `session_start()` function. In this case, `session_start()` will retrieve the `$_SESSION` array for this user based on the current session ID (created in the previous page).

2   Once the session starts, the global `$_SESSION` array corresponding to this user can be accessed. The key–value pair of the `$_SESSION` array consists of `favorite_color`, the key, and the color, `yellow`, that was selected from the previous page. If the previous page had not been viewed, `$_SESSION` would not have any session values.

3   The value of `$favorite_color` is assigned to the `<body>` of this page to customize the background color for this user.

4   This line prints the favorite color just to confirm that the selected color was passed to this session.

Figure 16.24   Page 2: The session is used to "remember" the user's preference.

Notice that in this example the only connection between the page that sets the color and the page that displays the color is the session. Unlike forms where one page collects the information and passes it to another page via a GET/POST request, the session pages need not be connected. In other words, we can set the color, then surf anywhere else and once we come back, the color should still be set.

Note that this "stickiness" is valid only as long as the session is valid. A typical session might expire within an hour or two, or never. This is configured in the `php.ini` file and is up to the server setting to manage it. Also, if the user restarts the computer or the Web browser, his or her session ID might be lost and the next visit to these pages will create a brand-new session.

Remembering Users and Preferences over Multiple Pages. The following example consists of three pages: the HTML form, a file that handles the form data and starts a session, and links to another page where the session variables are used. The example demonstrates a session using cookies to pass the form data from page to page.

EXAMPLE 16.15

```
(Page 1--The HTML Form)
<html><head><title>Sessions</title>
</head>
<body bgcolor="lavender">
<font face="verdana" size="+1" >
<H1>Book Categories</H1>
<form action="sessions.php" method="Post" >
    Your name:
    <br />
    <input type="text" name="user" size="50" />
    <p>
    Select a book category:
    <br />
    <input type="radio" name="book" value="Art">Art
    <br />
    <input type="radio" name="book" value="Computer">Computer
    <br />
    <input type="radio" name="book" value="Drama">Drama
    <br />
    <input type="radio" name="book" value="History">History
    <br />
    <input type="radio" name="book" value="Poetry">Poetry
    <br />
    <input type="radio" name="book" value="Sports">Sports
    <p>
    <br />
    <input type="radio" name="book" value="Sports">Sports
    <p>
    <input type="submit">
</form></body></html>
```

EXPLANATION

This is the first page, shown in Figure 16.25, of a series of three pages. Once this form is submitted, the file named `session.php` will be executed.

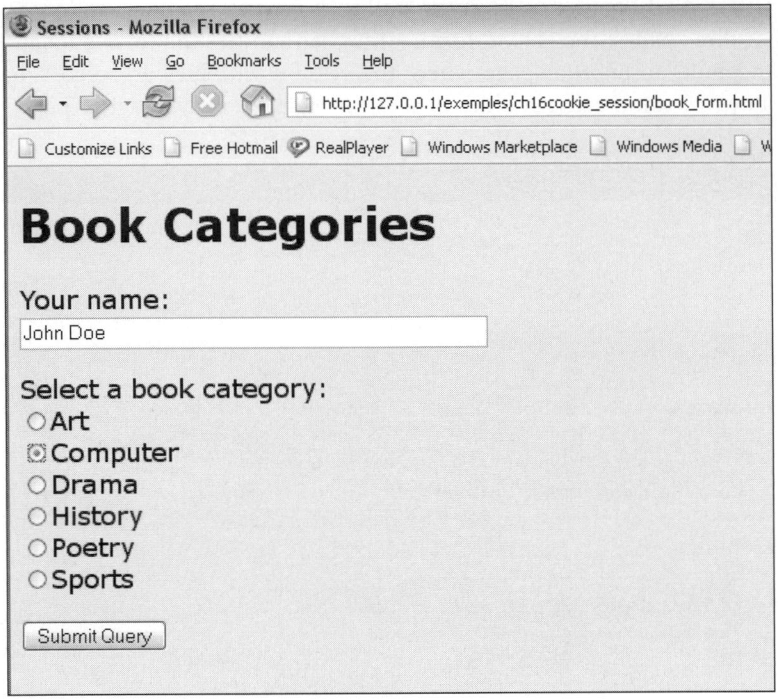

Figure 16.25 Page 1: The HTML form. The visitor selects a book category.

EXAMPLE 16.16

```
(Page 2--Starting the Session)
<?php
    session_start();
?>
<html><head><title>Sessions</title></head>
<body bgcolor="lavender">
<font face='arial' size="+1">
<?php
1    if ( ! (empty($_POST['book']) or empty($_POST['user']))){
2        // Create short variables
         $book=trim(stripslashes($_POST['book']));
         // Create short variables
         $user=trim(stripslashes($_POST['user']));
3        if( isset($_SESSION['user'])){
             echo "<H2>Welcome back, $_SESSION[user]!</H2>";
             echo "<H2>You recently visited our $_SESSION[book]
                   store.</h2>";
         }
```

EXAMPLE 16.16 (CONTINUED)

```
4          else{
5              $_SESSION['book']=$book;
               $_SESSION['user']=$user;
               echo "<H2>Welcome, $user!</H2>";
           }
       }
       else{ die ("Form incomplete< br />");
       }
       echo "The session id is: ",session_id(), "< br />";
       echo "You have chosen to enter the <b>$book</b>
          section.< br />";
6      $section=$book. "_page.php";   // Creating a variable
   ?>
   To browse the <?php echo $book; ?> Section:
7  <a href="<?php echo $section; ?>">Click here</a>
   < br />
   </body>
   </html>
```

EXPLANATION

1   If the user has filled out the form properly both the `'book'` and `'user'` fields will have values and the statements in the `if` block will be executed.

2   Any slashes or whitespace in the form data are removed. Variables are created from the `$POST_[]` array.

3   If the visitor has already been to this page, then the session variables will be available, and the statements in the `if` block will be executed. See Figure 16.28.

4   If this is the first time the user has visited this page, the statements in the `else` block will be executed. See Figure 16.26 for output.

5   The session variables are assigned the values that came from the form.

6   The name of the selected book and the string `"_page.php"` are concatenated together as a single string and assigned to the variable `$section`, which will be the next page where the user will be directed when he or she clicks the link on line 8. (Figure 16.27 displays the page that appears when the user clicks this link.)

7   This link will take the user to his or her book category page.

Figure 16.26   Page 2: The first time the visitor has entered this page. (Note that the session ID is remembered from session to session.)

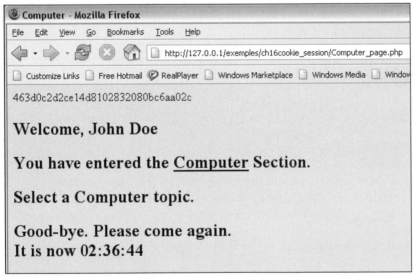

Figure 16.27   Page 3: After the visitor clicked on the link in the previous page, shown in Figure 16.26.

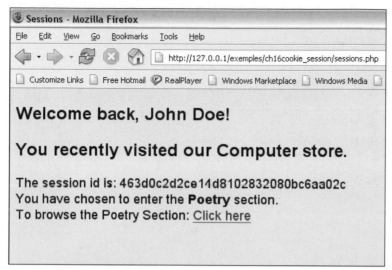

Figure 16.28 The visitor has returned to page 1, filled out the form, and is sent to page 2.

16.4.7 Naming Sessions

The session name refers to the session ID stored in both cookies and URLs. Instead of using the default name of your session, PHPSESSID, you can give your session a different name. However, remember that if you change the name of the session, every page that uses your application must call session_name() with the new name before calling session_start(). The session_name() function will return the current session name if given no arguments, or reset the session name when the first argument is a string. See also the session.name configuration directive in the php.ini file.

FORMAT

```
string session_name ( [string name] )
```

Example:
```
// Only alphanumeric characters are allowed in the name
// (at least one letter)
session_name("MyKewlSite");
session_start();
```

EXAMPLE 16.17

```
   (Start the session on this page)
   <?php
   obstart();
   if( isset($_REQUEST['color'] ) ) {
       // Start the new session with a new name
1      print "The previous session name was ". session_name() .
             ".< br />";
2      session_name("ColorSite");
       print "The new session name was ". session_name() . ".< br />";
3      session_start();

       // Set the favorite color for this user
       $_SESSION['favorite_color'] = $_REQUEST['color'];
   }
   ?>


   <html>
   <body>
   <h1> Select Favorite Color</h1>
4  <form action="<?php echo ${_SERVER}['PHP_SELF']; ?>" method="GET">
   <select name=color>
       <option value="" selected>Please select</option>
       <option value="white">White</option>
       <option value="blue">Blue</option>
       <option value="red">Red</option>
       <option value="yellow">Yellow</option>
       <option value="gray">Gray</option>
   </select>
   <input type="submit" value="Set color">
   </form></body></html>
   <?
-------------------------------------------------------------------
   (This page uses the new name)
   <?php
5      session_name('ColorSite');
6      session_start();
       $favorite_color = $_SESSION['favorite_color'];
       print_r($_SESSION);
   ?>
   <html>
   <body bgcolor="<?php echo $favorite_color; ?>">
   <h1>Your Favorite Color</h1>
   <font size='+2'>
   Your favorite color is <b><?php echo $favorite_color; ?></b>.
   </font></body></html>
   <?php
       ob_end_flush();  // Flush the buffer and end output buffering
   ?>
```

EXPLANATION

1   Before changing the name of the session, the `session_name()` function returns the name of the current session.

2   The `session_name()` function will change the name of the session to `ColorSite`. Now any page using this session will also need to call `session_name('Color-Site')` before starting a new session.

3   A session is started for this page. The session's name is `"ColorSite"`.

4   This is a self-processing PHP script. It will present the form and then process it.

5   To use the session ID from the previous session, this page needs to be able to refer to the correct session by its name.

6   A new session is started after the session name was changed. See the output in Figure 16.29.

Figure 16.29   Changing the session's name. Output from Example 16.17.

16.4.8   Sessions Without Cookies

As we have seen in the previous examples, a cookie is used to hold the session ID. This is the default and considered the most secure way to handle session data. The problem with cookies, however, is that the user can disable them for his or her browser or refuse to accept them. To overcome the obstacle of a cookieless client, the other way to send the session ID is in the URL or by using hidden fields with GET/POST.

When propagating the session ID with GET/POST, it must be done only when the URL resides on your local Web server and is not passed to an external URL.

Using a Hidden Form Element.   When working with HTML the session ID can be propagated through the use of a hidden form element. When assigning the name and value to the hidden input device, the name will be the name of the current session and the value, the session ID. You can use the `session_name()` and `session_id()` functions to get the those values. The SID constant can also be used to get the current session ID. For example:

```
<FORM ACTION="order.php" METHOD=GET>
<INPUT TYPE="hidden" NAME="<?php echo session_name(); ?>"
                     VALUE="<?php echo session_id(); ?>">
<!-- The remainder of the form HTML code //-->
</FORM>
```

EXAMPLE   16.18

```
    (Page 1)
    // Disable cookies for this session
1   ini_set('session.use_cookies', 0);
2   ob_start();

    /* start the session */
3   session_start();

4   if( isset($_REQUEST['mycolor'] ) ) {
5       $_SESSION['favorite_color'] = $_REQUEST['mycolor'];
6       $sess_name=session_name();
7       $sess_id=$_REQUEST[$sess_name];
8       header("Location:other_page.php?$sess_name=$sess_id");
    }
    ?>
    <html>
    <body>
    <h1> Select Favorite Color</h1>

9   <form action="<?php echo ${_SERVER}['PHP_SELF']; ?>" method="GET">
    <select name="mycolor">
    Please select</option>
        <option selected value="green">Green</option>
        <option value="white">White</option>
        <option value="blue">Blue</option>
        <option value="red">Red</option>
        <option value="yellow">Yellow</option>
        <option value="gray">Gray</option>
    </select>
10  <input type="hidden" name='PHPSESSID'
11      value="<?php echo session_id(); ?>">
    <input type="submit" value="Set color">
    </form>

    </body>
    </html>
    <?php
        ob_end_flush();
    ?>
```

EXPLANATION

1   The `ini_set()` function is used to change the configuration value for the duration of this script, in this case to temporarily disable the use cookies. The session will try to use them if they are not disabled. (Note: Make sure that your browser also has cookies disabled.)

2   The `ob_start()` function turns on output buffering.

3   The `session_start()` function creates a session or resumes the current one based on the current session ID that is being passed via a request, such as GET, POST, or a cookie.

4   If the HTML form has been submitted, the variable `$_REQUEST['mycolor']` has been set and the `if` block is executed.

5   A session variable called `$_SESSION['favorite_color']` is assigned the value of `$_REQUEST['mycolor']`.

6   The `session_name()` function returns the name of this session.

7   The value of the session ID is stored in the hidden field in the form. `$_REQUEST[$sess_name]` is an associative array where the key is the session name, `PHPSESSID`, and the value is the session ID number, the number visible in the URL when this file is viewed in the browser.

8   The `header()` function sends an HTTP header—in this example, a redirection header to send the user to the location `other_page.php`—and passes, as part of the URL, the session ID listed after the `?`.

9   The self-processing form starts here; the method is GET. See Figure 16.30.

10, 11   The name and value of the session ID are assigned to a hidden field in the form.

Figure 16.30   The HTML form and self-processing PHP page.

EXAMPLE 16.19

```
        (Page 2)
        <?php
1           session_start();
2           if ( isset($_SESSION['favorite_color'])){
                print "favorite_color is registered< br />";
3               $color = $_SESSION['favorite_color'];
            }
        ?>
        <html>
        <body bgcolor="<?php echo $color; ?>">
        <h1>Your Favorite Color</h1>
        Your favorite color is <b><?php echo $color; ?></b>.
        <?php
4           unset( $_SESSION['favorite_color']);
5           session_destroy();
        ?>
        </body>
        </html>
```

EXPLANATION

1   The session is started for this redirection page. It gets the session ID from the URL that pointed to this page.
2   The favorite color of the user is passed in the session variable.
3   The favorite color of the user is assigned as the background color of the page, as shown in Figure 16.31.
4   The unset() function destroys a single session variable.
5   The session_destroy() function removes the entire session.

Figure 16.31   The user is redirected to this page with a location header.

16.4.9 Passing Session IDs with a Link

If cookies are not available because the user has disabled them, another alternative is to pass session IDs via a link. There are two ways to do this: manually or automatically. The manual way requires that for every relevant page in your site, you attach the session ID to the link and PHP will send it to the linked page. The automatic method requires changing the `session.use_trans_sid` setting in the `php.ini` file.

The SID Constant.   If you have disabled cookies, the SID constant holds the value of the session ID. If cookies are enabled, this constant is empty.

   The SID constant can be concatenated to the URL in a hyperlink to pass it to another page as shown here:

```
$sid=SID;
<a href="phpscript.php?<?=echo $sid"> Order now!</a>

echo '<a href="checkout.php?' SID . '">Checkout<a/>';
```

If there are a lot of links in your Web site, automatic URL rewriting is a PHP feature that adds the session ID automatically to all the links within linked the pages. To enable this feature, you need to edit the PHP `php.ini` configuration file. Look for the line

```
session.use_trans_sid
```

and set it to 1, save the changes, and restart your Web server. Then the session ID will be added to all relative links within your PHP pages. Notice that by default this feature is turned off for security reasons, so proceed with caution. There is also a performance cost because PHP has to add the session ID to every page where the link is relative, whereas a cookie is only set once.

   From the `php.ini` file:

```
; trans sid support is disabled by default.
; Use of trans sid may risk your users security.
; Use this option with caution.
; - User may send URL contains active session ID
;   to other person via. email/irc/etc.
; - URL that contains active session ID may be stored
;   in publically accessible computer.
; - User may access your site with the same session ID
;   always using URL stored in browser's history or bookmarks.
session.use_trans_sid = 1
```

To summarize, when automatically passing a session ID via a URL, the following should be considered:

1. The browser does not accept cookies.
2. The `session.use_trans_sid` directive in the `php.ini` file is set to 1. You will need to restart your Web server for this directive to take effect.
3. The URL in the PHP script must be a relative path name.
4. If using the constant, SID, use `striptags()`. Remember the SID is not available unless cookies are disabled.

EXAMPLE 16.20

```
    (Page 1)
    <?php
1       ob_start();   // Turn on output buffering
2       ini_set('session.use_cookies', 0);  // Don't accept cookies
    ?>
    <html><head><title>Sessions and Links</title>
    </head>
    <body bgcolor="lavender">
    <font face="verdana" size='+1'>
    <h2>Sessions and Links</h2>

    <?php
3       session_start();
4       $_SESSION['user']="John Doe";
        $_SESSION['color']="aqua";
    ?>

    <?php
5       if(! empty($_SESSION['color'])){
            echo "<pre>";
            print_r($_SESSION);
            echo "</pre>";
6           $sid = session_id();
            echo "SessionID is ", $sid, "< br />";
        }
    ?>
7   <a href="/exemples/sessions/link2file1.php"> Click here</a>
    </font>
    </body>
    </html>
```

EXPLANATION

1   The `ob_start()` function turns on output buffering, so that any PHP headers will be sent before the rest of the program's output is sent. Without this function, the program will produce a warning when the program tries to ouput header information:

Warning: session_start() [function.session-start]: Cannot send session cache limiter - headers already sent (output started at c:\wamp\www\exemples\ sessions\session_url.php:11) in c:\wamp\www\exemples\sessions\session_url.php on line 12

2   This directive states that cookies will not be turned on for this session. You can also turn off cookies in your browser, but then they will be turned off until you enable them again.

3   The `session_start()` function starts a new session and generates a new session ID.

4   The session variables are registered and assigned to the global `$_SESSION` array.

5   This line checks to see if a session variable has been set.

6   Once the session is started, PHP generates a session ID, shown in Figure 16.32.

7   This link will take the user to the next page. Along with the link, PHP will automatically send the session ID to the file `link2file1.php`.

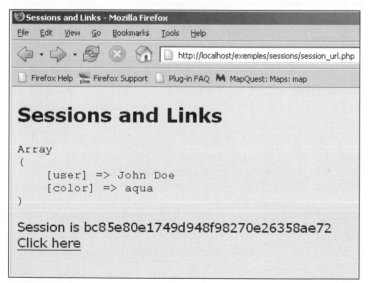

Figure 16.32   Page 1: Passing the session ID in a link. Output from Example 16.20.

EXAMPLE 16.21

```
    (Page 2)
    <?php
1       ini_set('session.use_cookies', 0); // Turn cookies off
2       session_start();  // Start a session
    ?>
    <html>
3   <body bgcolor="<?php echo ${_SESSION}[color]; ?>">
    <h3>
    <?php
4       print_r($_GET);
5       echo "< br />The session id is " , session_id(), "< br />";
6       echo "The session name is " , session_name(), "< br />";
7       echo "SID is ", SID;
    ?>
    </h3>
    <h2>
    Hi <?php echo $_SESSION['user']; ?>. You like <b>
        <?php echo $_SESSION['color']; ?></b>.
8   <a href="/exemples/sessions/link2file2.php">
    Click here</a>
    </h3>
    </body>
    </html>
```

EXPLANATION

1   For this session, cookies are turned off.

2   The session starts.

3   The session ID was passed in from the link on page 1. The background color of the page is set to the value of the $_SESSION['color'] assigned and registered on page 1.

4, 5   The $_GET[] array contains information coming in from the link; that is, the session name and the session ID. See the first line of output for page 2.

5, 6   The session_id() function returns the value of the session ID that came in from the link on page 1 and the session_name() function returns the name of the session.

7   The constant SID contains the name and ID for the session. This constant is not set if cookies are turned on.

8   Now we link to yet another file. The session ID will be passed through this link. For output of this example, see Figure 16.33.

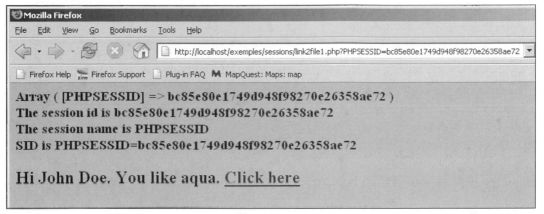

Figure 16.33 Page 2: The session ID and data passed in from a link in page 1. Output from Example 16.21.

EXAMPLE 16.22

```
     (Page 3)
     <?php
1        session_start();
2        extract($_SESSION);
3        printf("%s",SID);  // Print the session ID
4        echo "The session id is " , session_id(), "< br />";
     ?>
     <html>
     <body bgcolor="<?php echo $color?; >">
     <h2>
5    Hi again <?php echo $user; ?>. You still like <b>
               <?php echo $color; ?></b>.
     </h2>
     </body>
     </html>
```

EXPLANATION

1   Start the session for this page.
2   The session data is extracted from the $_SESSION[] array and assigned to variables.
3   The value of the constant SID is printed, the same values as in the previous page.
4   The session values are still available, all passed through the links. Because the value of the session ID is visible in the URL, it can easily be hijacked by someone else, which is not a secure situation.
5   The session data values are displayed in Figure 16.34.

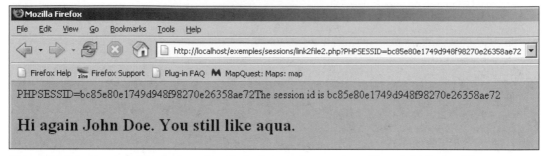

Figure 16.34 Page 3: Passing session data to another page with a link. Output from Example 16.22

16.4.10   Changing the Session ID

Using the URL to pass session IDs can lead to security problems, as they are plainly visible in the URL, bookmarkable, and accessible in HTTP_REFERER entries. To deal with the possibility of "leaking" the session ID, you should make sure that sessions are cleared frequently either by destroying them or by giving them a probable lifetime. (See the gc_probability directive in the php.ini file.)

Another technique is to change the session ID number with the session_regenerate_id() function. This function will change the ID number and leave the data intact so that if a session ID has been "hijacked," the data will no longer be available to the hijacker, but you will still have access to to it through the new session ID.

The only argument to this function is a boolean value, which determines whether or not to delete the old session file associated with the session ID being changed. The default is false.

FORMAT

```
bool session_regenerate_id ( [bool delete_old_session] )
```

Example:
```
session_regenerate_id();
session_regenerate_id(TRUE);
```

EXAMPLE 16.23

```php
    <?php
1       session_start();
2       $current_sessionid = session_id();
3       session_regenerate_id();
4       $new_session_id = session_id();
        echo "Session id was: $current_sessionid< br />";
        echo "Regenerated session id is: $new_session_id< br />";
    ?>
```

> **EXPLANATION**
>
> 1 A session is started. A session ID will be generated for this session if this is a new session.
> 2 The `session_id()` function returns the session ID number.
> 3 The `session_regenerate_id()` function will change the session ID number and leave the data intact that was associated with the session ID number just changed.
> 4 The new session ID is printed, as shown in Figure 16.35.

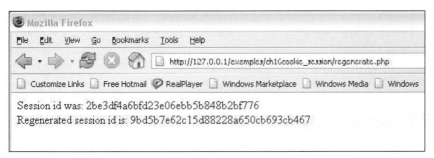

Figure 16.35 Regenerating a new session ID. Output from Example 16.23.

16.4.11 Ending a Session

PHP really has no way to know when the user has left a session, so it provides several functions to help you control when to end a session. The following sections describe how to unset session variables and how to destroy the session files associated with them.

Deleting Session Variables.   If you are sending the session ID via cookies, the cookie by default is deleted when the user closes his or her browser, but the session data still remains in the session file on the server. To destroy the session data, you can unset all the values in the `$_SESSION` array and then use the `setcookie()` function to remove the cookie by changing the expiration time of the cookie to an earlier date. Finally, you can force the session to end with the `session_destroy()` function, which deletes the session and the session file.

   The PHP manual suggests that the nice way check for the existence of cookies is by simply calling `print_r($_COOKIE)`.

   Here are some examples:

```
// Unset a single session variable
unset($_SESSION['color']);

// Unset all of the session variables
$_SESSION = array();
```

```
// Delete the session cookie
if (isset($_COOKIE[session_name()])) {
    setcookie(session_name(), '', time() - 32000, '/');
}
```

The session_write_close() Function.   If more than one script is using a session at any time, for example, two or three frames are loading one by one, PHP locks the session until each page has finished loading. This feature prevents two pages from writing out session data concurrently to the $_SESSION array and thereby corrupting the data. However, if the pages are primarily reading session data, then this locking feature can be worked around with the session_write_close() function. After the session data has been written, this function ends the current session and makes sure the session data is stored as soon as all changes have been made (see Example 16.26 at the end of this chapter). Normally, you will not need to use this function, as PHP takes care of storing session data and ending the session.

FORMAT

```
void session_write_close ( void )
```

Example:
```
session_write_close();
```

The session_destroy() Function.   The session_destroy() function deletes the session file and all of its data for the current session, but it does not unset a cookie or any global variables such as the $_COOKIE or $_SESSION arrays currently cached for the current session.

FORMAT

```
bool session_destroy ( void )
```

Example:
```
session_destroy();
```

EXAMPLE   16.24

```
    (Page 3)
    <?php
1       session_start();
2       extract($_SESSION);
        printf("%s",SID);  // Print the session ID
        echo "The session id is " , session_id(), "< br />";
    ?>
    <html>
    <body bgcolor="<?=$color?>">
    <h2>
    Hi again <?= $user?>, You still like <b><?= $color ?></b>.
    <?php
        // Individually remove session variables
3        unset($_SESSION["user"]);
         unset($_SESSION["color"]);
4       //$_SESSION = array();    // Remove all session variables
5       session_destroy();
        exit();
    ?>
    </h2>
    </body>
    </html>
```

EXPLANATION

1   A session is started for this page that was called from another page where form information was gathered.
2   The session data is extracted and assigned to variables.
3   The unset() function removes individual session variables.
4   The array() function without arguments causes the $_SESSION array to be emptied. All session variables are removed.
5   The session_destroy() function removes the session and all its data.

Cleaning up Session Files and Garbage Collection.   If you look in the directory or folder where your sessions are stored, you will see that the number of session files builds up quickly. Garbage collection is the process of cleaning up old sessions, a task left to PHP. If cookies are being used, the server does not know whether or not the cookie file still exists on the user's browser. Also, session files have a default lifetime of 24 minutes and then they will be cleaned up by the PHP garbage collector unless you extend their lifetime. The gc_maxlifetime configuration directive is used to determine how long PHP should wait (in seconds) before destroying a session based on how long the session has been idle since the last time was it was accessed.

   For example:

```
$garbage_timeout = 3600; // 3600 seconds = 60 minutes = 1 hour
ini_set('session.gc_maxlifetime', $garbage_timeout);
```

The garbage collector does not just jump up and start removing files every time a session is invoked. It collects garbage based on a probability factor set in the `session.gc_probability` directive in the `php.ini` file. This directive specifies with what probability the files identified as garbage should be removed. If `gc_probability` is 100, the cleanup is performed on every request (i.e., with a probability of 100 percent); if it is 1, as it is by default, old sessions will be removed with a probability of 1 percent every time a session starts.

After setting these two configuration directives, the last bit of advice is to move the timed session files into their own directory. Otherwise, the garbage collector will not be able to differentiate between timeouts on a per-file basis.

For a complete and very readable explanation on PHP garbage collection, see *http://www.captain.at/howto-php-sessions.php*.

16.4.12   Session Runtime Configuration

PHP session management has many configuration options for us to choose from.

PHP Session Functions.   PHP provides the functions shown in Table 16.4 to handle sessions, many of which we have covered in this chapter. Each of these functions is documented in the PHP manual at *http://us3.php.net/session*.

Table 16.4   PHP Session Functions

Function	*Definition*
`session_cache_expire()`	Returns the current setting of `session.cache_expire`, default 180 minutes.
`session_cache_limiter()`	Returns the name of the current cache limiter that defines the cache control HTTP headers sent to the client and what rules determine how the page content can be cached.
`session_commit()`	An alias for `session_write_close()`.
`session_decode()`	Decodes the session data.
`session_destroy()`	Destroys all of the data associated with the current session, but does not unset any of the global variables associated with the session, or unset the session cookie.
`session_encode()`	Encodes the current session data as a string.
`session_get_cookie_params()`	Returns an array with the current session cookie information, including `lifetime`, `path`, `domain`, and `secure`.
`session_id()`	Returns the session ID for the current session.
`session_is_registered()`	Returns `TRUE` if there is a global variable if its name is registered in the current session.

Table 16.4 PHP Session Functions (continued)

Function	Definition
session_module_name()	Returns the name of the current session module. If module is specified, that module will be used instead.
session_name()	Returns the name of the current session or if a name is specified, changes the name of the current session.
session_regenerate_id()	Replaces the current session ID with a new one, and keeps the current session date.
session_register()	Registers one or more global variables with the current session
session_save_path()	Returns the path of the current directory used to save session data or sets a new path.
session_set_cookie_params()	Sets cookie parameters defined in the php.ini file. The effect of this function lasts only for the duration of the script.
session_set_save_handler()	Sets the user-level session storage functions that are used for storing and retrieving data associated with a session; for example, for file and database storage.
session_start()	Starts a session.
session_unregister()	Unregistered a global session variable.
session_unset()	Unsets all session data currently registered.
session_write_close()	Stores the session data and closes the session.

16.4.13 Implementing a Login System with Sessions

The following example consists of three separate files.

1. The first file is a simple HTML form, the login page, where the user enters a username and password.
2. The second file, the authentication page, is a PHP script that will verify the username and password, and establish a "logged in state" if the username and password are valid. This file will also be used for logging out the user. The action to log in depends on the parameter (login) provided by the POST method from the HTML form (hidden input element). The action to log out is performed after the user has logged on, been redirected to the third page with protected content, and clicks on the logout link.
3. The third file is a PHP script that will show protected content only if the user is logged in. This file also describes a simple way to conditionally display a whole HTML block.

Sessions are used to remember users who are logged in and their password. In a real-world situation, you will probably use a database to store the username and password, and the protected content could be stored in a text file or database.

EXAMPLE 16.25

```
(Page 1)
##### begin #####
##### login.html #####
<html>
<head>
    <title>Simple login page</title>
</head>
<body>
    <p>
1       <a href="protected.php">Protected content</a>
    </p>
    <p> Type phpbee for both username and password </p>
2       <form action="auth.php" method="post">
        Username< br />
3       <input type="text" name="username">< br />
        Password< br />
4       <input type="password" name="password">< br />
5       <input type="hidden" name="login">< br />
        <input type="submit">
        <input type="reset">
    </form>
</body>
</html>


##### login.html #####
##### end #####
```

EXPLANATION

1   This is a link to the protected page (page 3) where special content can be read only if the visitor has typed in a valid username and password.
2   After the form has been submitted, the PHP script (page 2), `auth.php`, will be executed. This page will determine whether or not the visitor is authorized to log in.
3   The visitor is asked to type in the username here. See Figures 16.36 and 16.37.
4   This is where the user types in the password.
5   To submit information that is not entered by the visitor, a hidden field is used and assigned the value `"login"`.

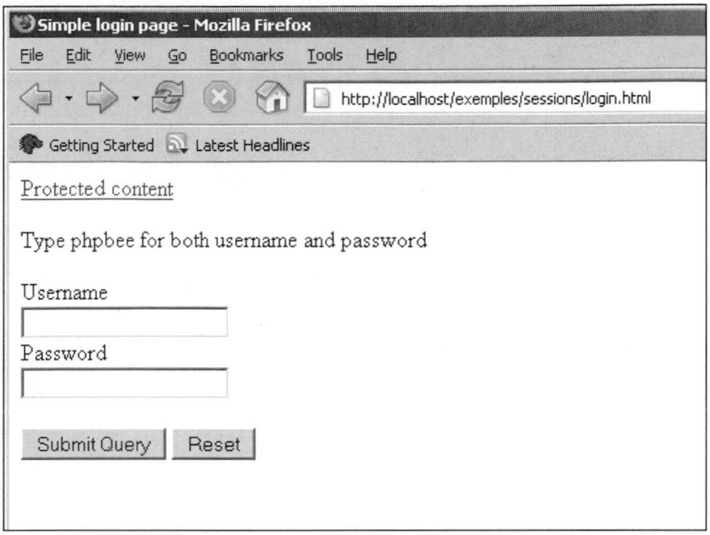

Figure 16.36 Page 1: The `login.html` file.

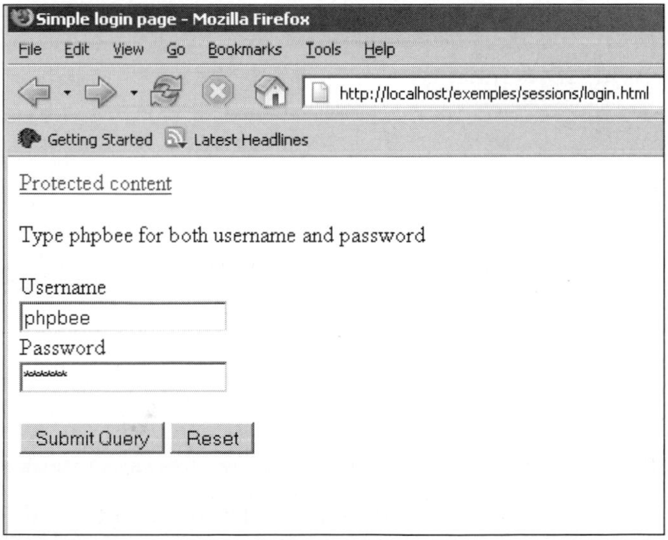

Figure 16.37 Page 1: The visitor fills out the form.

EXAMPLE 16.26

```
(Page 2)
##### begin #####
##### auth.php #####

<?php
1       session_start();
        // User is logging in
2       if (isset($_POST["login"])){
3           if (isset($_POST["username"]) && ($_POST["username"]
                == "phpbee")
            &&  isset($_POST["password"]) && ($_POST["password"]
                == "phpbee"){
4               $_SESSION["Authenticated"] = 1;
            }
            else{
5               $_SESSION["Authenticated"] = 0;
            }
6           session_write_close();
7           header("Location: protected.php");
        }
        // User is logging out
8       if (isset($_GET["logout"])){
9           session_destroy();
10          header("Location: login.html");
        }
?>

##### auth.php #####
##### end ####
```

EXPLANATION

1   The session for this page starts here for auth.php (page 2).
2   If the user has filled out the login form in login.html (page 1), then the
    $_POST["login"] variable will be set, and the statements in the if block will be
    executed.
3   If the username is set and has a value "phpbee", and the password is set and also
    has the value "phpbee", the statement in line 4 is executed.
4   The session variable is set to 1. The value of 1 will be used later to determine that
    the user is logged in.
5   If either a valid username or password were not entered, the session variable is set
    to 0. A value of 0 will be used to determine that the user is not logged in.
6   The session_write_close() function stores the session data now and closes the
    session.

EXPLANATION (CONTINUED)

7   The user is directed to `protected.php` (page 3). This is the page that is not accessible to anyone who is not logged in.

8   If the user entered the protected page and clicked the link to log out, the variable `$_GET["logout"]` will be set, and the statements in the `if` block will be executed.

9   The session and all its data are destroyed.

10 The user is redirected back to the login page. Because the session was destroyed, he or she is no longer authenticated to go to the protected page.

EXAMPLE 16.27

```
    (Page 3)
    ##### begin #####
    ##### protected.php #####

    <?php
1       session_start();
    ?>
        <html><head><title>Protected page</title></head>
        <body>
    <?php
2       if (isset($_SESSION["Authenticated"])
            && ($_SESSION["Authenticated"] == 1)){
    ?>
3       <h2>Protected content</h2>
        <p>Hello. Since you are logged in, you can view protected
            content</p>
4       <p>You can also <a href="auth.php?logout">log out</a></p>
    <?php
        }
        else{
    ?>
        <h2>You are not logged in</h2>
        <p>Hello. Since you are not logged in, you cannot view
            protected content</p>
5       <p>But you can <a href="login.html">log in</a></p>
    <?php
        }
    ?>
    </body>
    </html>

    ##### protected.php #####
    ##### end #####
```

EXPLANATION

1   The session starts for page 3. See Figure 16.38.
2   If, on page 2, the session variables were set and `$SESSION["Authenticated"]` was set to 1, the visitor is logged in and will be able to read whatever is on line 3.
3   This is where the content would be added for this page, the content only viewable if the user successfully logged in.
4   This link will send the user back to page 2, `auth.php`. The word `logout` appended to the question mark, will be passed via the `GET` method and assigned to the `$_GET[]` array.
5   This link returns the visitor back to the login page, page 1.

Figure 16.38   Page 3: The visitor is logged in.

16.5 Chapter Summary

In this chapter we discussed how PHP uses cookies and sessions to maintain state; that is, save information between different accesses to a Web page, allowing you to customize your applications based on user preferences, manage logging in and out of your site, use links and hidden fields to pass session information back and forth, and so on.

What are the pros and cons of cookies versus sessions and vice versa? The cookie stores the visitor information on the user's computer even if a session has ended. The the lifetime of a cookie can be a long period of time or it can end when the user closes his or her browser. A user can go to a Web site, browse around and come back, even log out and the cookie can persist on his or her hard drive, keeping track of the user's preferences, shopping cart information, number of times he or she visited the site, and so on. But if the cookie has important information such as a password or user ID, it is easy to read that information unless it is encrypted, and some people feel that cookies are a security threat because they are passed back and forth across the network and are stored in a text-based readable files. Because a user can disable cookies for his or her particular browser, you have no guarantee that they are being accepted.

PHP sessions are safer because they do not send any sensitive data over the network. They store the user information in variables on the server. As you have seen in this chapter, even sessions rely on cookies because the session ID is encrypted and normally passed in a cookie, but there are alternative ways to handle users who have disabled cookies for their browser, such as passing the data in hidden form fields or URLs. Although this is considered insecure, you can regenerate the session ID after using it or destroy all the session variables. The lifespan of sessions is normally the length of a session, and after 24 minutes, the session files are deleted, but this can also be controlled in the `php.ini` file. What if you have a cluster of servers? How will the session files be managed? At least with a cookie, only one browser is necessary, no matter how many servers are involved. Which is best?

It has been said that over 90 percent of sessions use cookies, so perhaps a symbiotic relationship between the two is a reasonable approach. Ultimately, you must weigh the pros and cons and decide what works best for you. (See *http://www.thescripts.com/forum/thread433783.html* for further discussion.)

16.5.1 What You Should Know

Now that you have finished this chapter you should be able to answer the following questions:

1. What is meant by *stateless*?

2. What are cookies used for and where do they reside?

3. What is the life span of a cookie?

4. How are cookies sent from the server to the browser?

5. How does PHP store cookies?

6. What is serialization?

7. What is the advantage of using PHP sessions?

8. What is meant by a cookie-based session?

9. What is a session ID number and where is it stored?

10. What are the PHP buffering functions?

11. How are sessions registered?

12. How are sessions deleted?

13. What is the purpose of the PHP `session_write_close()` function?

14. What is garbage collection?

15. What are the disadvantages of using cookies? What are the disadvantages of using sessions?

16.5.2 What's Next?

The next and last chapter introduces object-oriented programming with PHP. You will learn how to create classes to encapsulate data and functions. You will create instances of a class, called objects, and assign properties to describe the object. You will design methods, special functions, to manipulate the object and learn how to keep the object's data protected from outside access. You will see how one class inherits from another.

CHAPTER 16 LAB

1. Create a login page that asks the user for a username and password. Trim the username and password to remove any unwanted whitespace. The `action` attribute of the from will redirect you to a new page, called `verify.php`.

2. The `verify.php` page will start a session and check that the username and password fields are not empty and also that they are correct. If not, the user will be informed, and redirected back to the login page. If correct, the user will be directed to your home page (you may want to use the database form from the last exercise).

3. When the user is ready to log out, end the session.

4. Create a drop-down menu that allows the user to select from a list of vacation spots. Save his choices in a cookie.

5. Link to another page that will print images of the vacation spots that the user selected.

6. When the user returns to the menu, he or she will see the list selected the last time he or she was on this page.

chapter
17
Objects

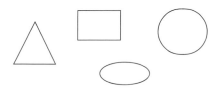

17.1 What Are Objects?

Objects are things we deal with every day. PHP deals with objects, as do most programming languages, and these languages are called object-oriented programming (OOP). OOP is a way of trying to solve a problem in terms of real-world objects. Some people are apprehensive at the thought of tackling this kind of programming, and are perfectly happy to stick with top-down, procedural programs. Just as the everyday objects we use are not switchblades and hacksaws, neither are programming objects. They are just a way of representing data.

As PHP has evolved from a tool for building simple home pages to a language for serious Web development, so has its support for OOP. Once programs start to get larger and more complex, planning and design become more important. Think of a simple home page put together with some family photos, links, and blogs. Then think of a Web site like Amazon or eBay where there are thousands of forms, links, and transactions taking place all the time, all over the world—the thought of putting something like that together is staggering. OOP is best suited to manage the complexity of such large Web sites. Even if you do not program using objects, if you are reading and using PHP programs written by other programmers, you are bound to run into this style of programming. This chapter gently introduces you to PHP objects and some of the features that have been added to the language in PHP 5.

When talking about PHP data types in Chapter 4, "The Building Blocks," we discussed two types: primitive types and composite types. Like arrays, objects are composite types. They provide a way to organize a collection of data into a single unit. Object-oriented languages, such as C++ and Java, bundle up data into a variable and call it an object. So does PHP. Each object-oriented language you encounter is based on the same principles, but often the terminology is not exactly the same when describing the concepts. You could say that PHP is like Java and C++, but has its own way of dealing with objects.

When you learn about objects, they are usually compared to real-world things, like a black cat, a modern painting, or a green pillow. Using the English language to describe an object, the object itself would be like a noun: a person, place, or thing.

Nouns are described with adjectives. For the cat it might be described as fat and furry with green eyes, four legs, and a tail; the painting is a British frigate, oil on canvas, and sells for $52,000; and the pillow is green silk, square, with dimensions of 18" × 18". The adjectives that collectively describe these objects are called the *properties* (or *attributes*) of the object. The object is made up of a collection of these properties.

In English, verbs are used to describe what the object can do or what can be done to it. The cat eats and sleeps, and its tail twitches; the painting can be framed, sold, or purchased; the pillow's dimensions can be increased or decreased, its fabric and color changed, and so on. These verbs are functions called *methods* in object-oriented languages.

17.1.1 Objects and Classes

Objects are defined in a *class*. A class is a template or a blueprint that defines what an object should look like and what it can do. A class represents a group of similar objects, such as a class of employees, a class of hotels, or a class of cars. The object in a class is a concrete person, place, or thing. Like a cookie cutter, a class gives an object its form, and as with a cookie cutter, you can build many objects of the same class. The employee object might be described to have a name, address, and phone number. Although the object can later change its values, it still belongs to the same class. You can change Bob's phone number, but he is still in the employee class. You can change the color of the car, but it is still in the car class.

A class contains a collection of variables (properties) and functions (methods). Like a blueprint, by itself the class does nothing. It defines an object and its properties and methods. Properties describe the object. Methods are functions that determine the behavior of the object; that is, what kind of actions can be performed on or by the object. As you can see in Figure 17.1, a class is a unit consisting of a name for the class, in this case `House`, the variables that describe the house, and the methods that describe the behaviors of the object, or what it can do. A class is an aggregate or composite data type. Like an array that contains a collection of key–value pairs, the class represents a collection of properties and methods.

```
class House
```

```
(variables/properties)

    var $owner;
    var $color;
```

```
(functions/methods)

function showHouse()
{

}
```

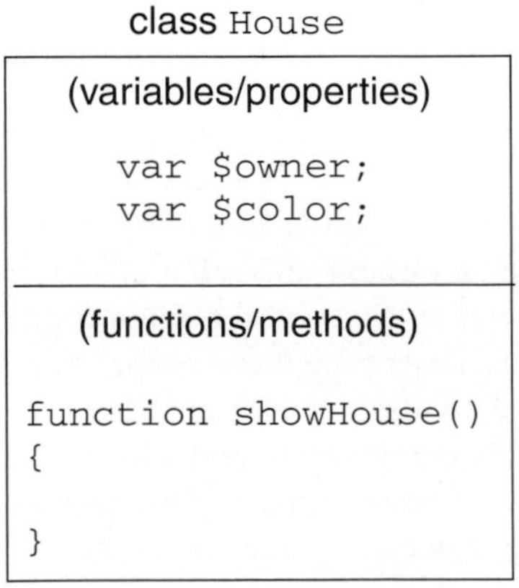

Figure 17.1 A `House` class.

17.2 Working with Classes

17.2.1 Defining the Class

To create a class you use the `class` keyword followed by the name of the class. The class definition, like a function definition, is enclosed in a set of curly braces. The name of a class follows the same naming conventions as normal variables (minus the dollar sign) and the class name, by convention, starts with a capital letter. For example:

```php
<?php
   class House
   {
      <definition goes here>
   }
?>
```

The class `House` might have variables (called attributes) such as `$owner`, `$address`, `$color`, or `$number_of_rooms`, as well as functions (called methods), such a `showHouse()`, `cleanHouse()`, or `paintHouse()`, for example.

Once the class is defined, it is used to create specific objects. Just as when you design a blueprint for a house, the real house does not yet exist. You must build it from the blueprint. The class is analogous to the blueprint and the object to the actual house. We could build many houses from the same blueprint and we can build many objects from a class. Just as a house is located at an address, each object has its own memory address. PHP provides the address and cleans up the memory when the object is no longer needed, when the program ends.

Once we have the basic stuff of which houses are made, we can extend the blueprint to add new features to the house, such as a new family room or a fireplace. Classes can also be extended to create more refined objects. Extending a class is called *inheritance*. Inheritance allows the programmer to create a new class without writing a brand new one. He or she can reuse an existing class and add some new features and functionality. Inheritance is one of the benefits of OOP that we discuss later in this chapter.

17.2.2 Instantiating the Class

Once the class is declared, the object needs to be created. In the real world you would build a new house; in the object-oriented world, you would instantiate a new `House` class or create a new instance of the `House` class. To make a new object, we use the reserved keyword `new`. To reference the object, we use the special variable called `$this`. Each instance of a class has the same property, but different copies, so that the values can be different; for example, if you have two house objects of the same class, and each house object has a property called `$owner`, the values assigned to `$owner` can differ from house object to house object, just like in the real world.

What's "new"?   The difference between an object and a class is that a class is conceptual and an object is real. The object is the actual variable that you manipulate. You can assign and retrieve its values, pass it to functions, delete it, copy it, and so forth. It holds a specific set of data. The new keyword is used to create a PHP object that is an "instance" of a class.

```
$myhouse = new House;
```

The new keyword causes PHP to look for a class named House, create a new copy, and assign it to the variable $myhouse. A new House object has been instantiated, which is like saying "We just built a new house and called it $myhouse," and to make another object from the House blueprint, you could say:

```
$yourhouse = new House;
```

Now we have two instances of the House class, two house objects, $myhouse and $yourhouse (see Figure 17.2).

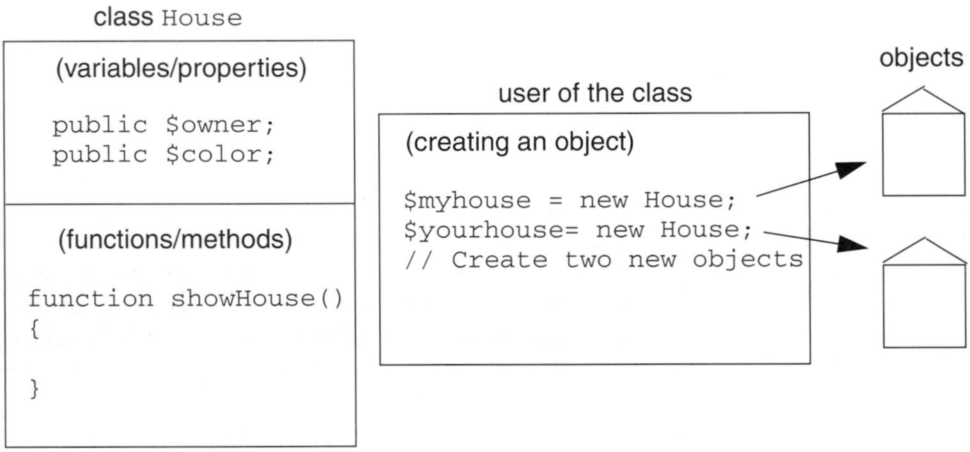

class House

Figure 17.2   Instantiating the House class.

The Properties and Methods.   Properties (variables) and methods (functions) together are called class "members." The properties of a class are defined as variables. Before PHP 5, the keyword var was used to define a public property of the class; that is, a property variable that is visible throughout the current PHP script. The var keyword has been deprecated as of PHP 5; you now declare public properties with the public keyword. Methods (class functions) default to public so you do not need to specify them as public:

(PHP 4)
```
var $owner = "John Doe:;
var $address;
```

(PHP 5)
```
$owner = "John Doe";   // Default is public
public $address;
```

You can assign initial values to the variables, but they must be string or numeric constants, not expressions like 5*6. New properties can be added at any time.

A method is a function defined within the class. It describes the behaviors of the class. It looks like any other function in structure:

```
function showHouse(){
   < statements go here>
}
```

The one major difference between methods and ordinary PHP functions is the $this keyword used to reference the current object, and in the way the methods are invoked.

What's $this?   When a class is defined, the object is created later, making it impossible for the class writer to know what the user of the class will name his or her objects. To reference an object, PHP provides a pseudo-variable, called $this, which references the current object. If the class built the two house objects as shown in the last section, then it would be able to keep track of which house was being used, because $this always references the current object. For example, if myhouse is the current object, then all the properties and methods of the class apply to myhouse. If the class has defined a cleanHouse() method for each house object, $this references the house object currently being used and $this>cleanHouse() applies to that object. In real-world terms, when I am in my house, I am not going to be cleaning your house. Notice that each property is preceded with the $this variable and an arrow operator. If you have many house objects, then $this will keep track of which house you are currently using, both its properties and methods.

```
function cleanHouse(){
   echo $this->owner;
   echo $this->address;
}
```

As we go further on, you will see how useful $this is.

The -> Operator.   After a class has been defined, it can be instantiated; that is, we create objects of that class. As you will see next, to assign properties and call methods, an arrow operator is used to get or set the value of the property; for example, if an object called $myhouse is created, to assign a value for the address property, the statement might look like this:

```
$myhouse->address="14 Main St.";
```

To call the method showHouse(), it might look like this:

```
$myhouse->showHouse();
```

The name of the object precedes the arrow and the property or method so that PHP knows to which object the property and method apply.

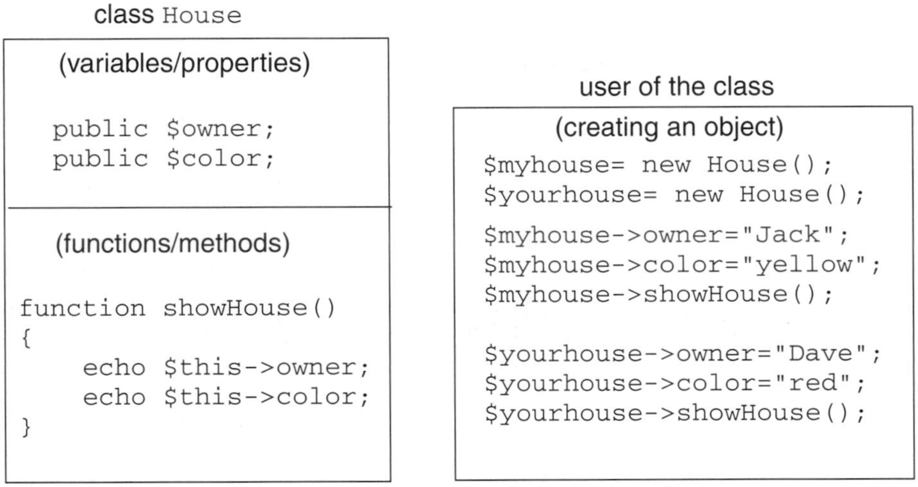

class House

(variables/properties)
public $owner; public $color;

(functions/methods)

function showHouse()
{
    echo $this->owner;
    echo $this->color;
}

user of the class

(creating an object)
$myhouse= new House(); $yourhouse= new House(); $myhouse->owner="Jack"; $myhouse->color="yellow"; $myhouse->showHouse(); $yourhouse->owner="Dave"; $yourhouse->color="red"; $yourhouse->showHouse();

Figure 17.3 A House class and creating a house object and accessing it.

The gettype() and get_class() Functions. PHP provides a number of built-in functions that return information about classes and objects. Table 17.1 gives you a complete list. Two functions that will be helpful as you start learning about objects are the gettype() and the get_class() functions. As you might remember (see Chapter 4, "The Building Blocks") from when we discussed data types, the gettype() function takes a variable as its argument and returns its data type, such as string, boolean, array, and so on. It will return "object" if the argument represents an object that was created using the new keyword. The get_class() function will tell you the name of the class from which the object was created.

EXAMPLE 17.1

```
  <?php
  # PHP5 Simple class
1 class House{    // Declare a class
2    public $owner="John";  // Create class variables/properties
     public $address="Anywhere, USA";
3    function displayHouse(){
4       echo "This house if of type ", gettype($this),".<br>\n";
5       echo "It belongs to the ", get_class($this),
             " class.<br>\n";
6       echo "This house is owned by $this->owner. ";
        echo "It's address is $this->address.\n<br>";
     }
  }
  // Using the class
7    $myHouse= new House();  // Create an ojbect
8    $myHouse->displayHouse();
  ?>
```

EXPLANATION

1. A `House` class is declared.
2. The variables for the `House` class, called properties, are `$owner` and `$address`. Both properties have been assigned inital string values.
3. A function for the `House` class is declared. Functions within classes are called methods.
4. The `gettype()` built-in function returns the data type of `$this`. Because `$this` represents the current object, the type returned is "object." See the output in Figure 17.4.
5. The `get_class()` function returns the name of the class to which the object represented by `$this` belongs.
6. The value of the object's property `$owner` is displayed.
7. A new object is created with its own properties defined in the class.
8. After creating the new object, the `displayHouse()` method displays its properties.

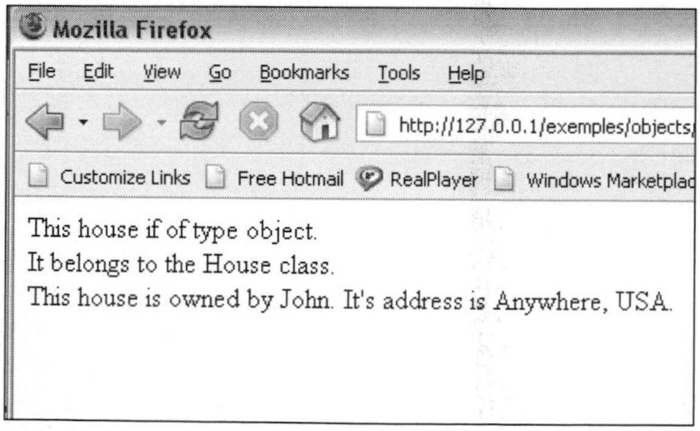

Figure 17.4 A simple class.

17.2.3   Creating a Complete Class

Now that we have defined some of the pieces involved in creating a class, we will build one from scratch. The following example defines an `Employee` class and then creates some objects of that class. To see a diagram of the class, see Figure 17.5.

EXAMPLE 17.2

```php
    <?php
    // Defining the Class
1   class Employee {  // Define the class

2       public $name;          // The properties/attributes
3       public $address;
4       public $phone;

5       function printPersonInfo()  // The methods
        {
            echo "<hr><b>Employee Info</b><br>";
            echo $this->name . "<br>\n";
            echo $this->address . "<br>\n";
            echo $this->phone . "<br>\n";
        }
    }
    // User of the class
6   $Heidi = new Employee();      // Create a new object
7   $Heidi->name = "Heidi Clum"; // Assign properties
8   $Heidi->address = "1234 Somewhere Blvd ";
9   $Heidi->phone = "123-456-7890";

10  $Brad = new Employee();       // Create another object
11  $Brad->name = "Brad Bit";
12  $Brad->address = "4321 Sunset Blvd ";
13  $Brad->phone = "987-654-3210";

14  $Heidi->printPersonInfo();   // Access the object with the method
15  $Brad->printPersonInfo();

    ?>
```

EXPLANATION

1   A class called `Employee` is declared. The class definition is enclosed within curly braces.

2–4   The variables, called properties, belonging to this class are defined. These properties are declared `public` meaning they are visible throughout your script. The `var` keyword is used for backward compatibility with PHP 4, but both `public` and `var` are now acceptable.

EXPLANATION (CONTINUED)

5   This is a function, called a method, defined for the class.

6   A new object is created for the class `Employee` and assigned to a variable called `$Heidi`. The `$Heidi` object is allocated its own copies of the properties defined within the `Employee` class.

7–9   To assign values to the properties of the object, the object is followed by an arrow and the property name. `$Heidi` is an object of class `Employee` and thus has variables `name`, `address`, and `phone`.

10   We declare another object of type `Employee` and this time assign it to variable `$Brad`. Although `$Heidi` and `$Brad` are both of class `Employee`, they have different values for the properties `name`, `address`, and `phone`.

11–13   Values are assigned to the properties of object `$Brad`.

14   The method, `printPersonInfo()`, applies to the object, `$Heidi`. The object is the noun, the method is the verb. It is the action that is taking place on the object. The method is called by appending the object with the arrow operator and the name of the method. By doing this PHP knows which object in the class this method applies to. The method's function is to print out the properties for the current object, in this case `$Heidi`. Because it is accessing the data for the object, an instance of the class, the method is called an "access" method or an "instance" method.

15   Similarly, for the object `$Brad`, the `printPersonInfo()` method is called and it will print values specific to the `$Brad` object.

17.2.4   Displaying an Object

In Chapter 8, "Arrays," we used the PHP built-in function `print_r()` to see the contents of an array. Now you can use it to view the contents of an object. In the previous example the output of `print_r()` would be:

```
Employee Object
(
    [name] => Heidi Clum
    [address] => 1234 Somewhere Blvd
    [phone] => 123-456-7890
)
Employee Object
(
    [name] => Brad Bit
    [address] => 4321 Sunset Blvd
    [phone] => 987-654-3210
)
```

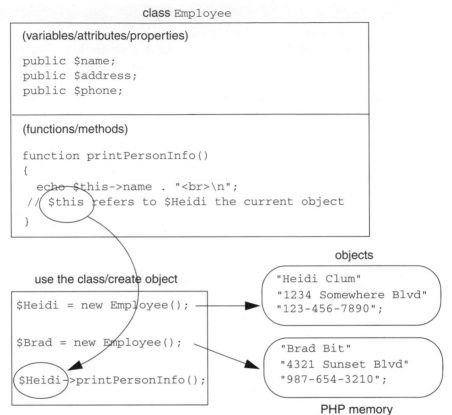

Figure 17.5   The Employee class and how it is used.

17.2.5   Functions for Getting Class Information

PHP provides a set of built-in functions that will return information about your class and its objects. Table 17.1 provides a list of these functions. For a complete list and examples of how these methods are used, see *http://us3.php.net/manual/en/ref.classobj.php*.

Table 17.1   PHP Built-In Class Functions

Function	*What It Does*	*Example*
get_class()	Returns the name of the class of an object.	string get_class([object obj])
get_class_vars()	Returns an associative array of public properties.	arrayget_class_vars(string class_name)
get_declared_classes()	Returns an array of classes defined in the current script.	array get_declared_classes(void)

Table 17.1 PHP Built-In Class Functions (continued)

Function	What It Does	Example
get_object_vars()	Returns an array of properties for an object.	array get_object_vars(object obj)
get_parent_class()	Returns the name of the parent class for the class or object.	string get_parent_class([mixed obj])
gettype()	Returns the data type of a variable; if an object is given, returns "object."	string gettype(mixed var)
instanceof (PHP 5)	A type operator that has replaced is_a().	instanceof classname

interface_exists()	Returns true if an interface has been defined.	bool interface_exists(
		    string interface_name [,
		    bool autoload])

is_a()	Returns true if the object is of this class or this class is its parent.	bool is_a(object object, string class_name)

is_subclass_of()	Returns true if object has this class as one of its parents.	bool is_subclass_of(
		    mixed object,
		    string class_name)

method_exists()	Returns true if this method exists.	bool method_exists(
		    object object,
		    string method_name)

property_exists()	Returns true if property exists in the class and is accessible.	bool property_exists(
		    mixed class,
		    string property)

17.2.6 Encapsulation and Information Hiding

Encapsulation and information hiding are closely related terms you will hear often in the object-oriented world. We use encapsulation when combining the properties and methods to make a class. By encapsulating the data in the class, the details of the class can be hidden from the user. When we created ordinary functions, the instructions were encapsulated within the function definition. When you call a function, you do not know all the details of how it works, you just need to know how to call it, what arguments to pass, and what it returns. When you create an object, you must know how to use its methods to access it. The details of the object are encapsulated within the class.

Information hiding is obscuring the details of the class from the user. In the previous example, the Employee class gave Heidi her own name, phone, and address. However, Heidi's information was "public" in scope. It could be directly accessed from outside the class. The user of the class could change Heidi's address and phone number. What if you do not want anyone to change Heidi's address or phone number? Often you have objects in which you do not want to allow direct access to the object's variables. For example, a bank account object might have a variable representing the account balance. This data should not be available to anyone outside the class, and to access it, the user should use methods provided specifically for that purpose. Methods such as `makeDeposit()`, `makeWithdrawal()`, and `getBalance()` should be the only way to manipulate the account balance, similar in the real world to using an ATM machine. In the object-oriented world, you will often hear the phrase, "Access private data with public functions."

Key principles of OOP are encapsulation and information hiding; that is, combining methods and properties into a class and keeping the class variables hidden from direct access by the class user. Data hiding helps to protect the object's data from being corrupted, and if the class implementation is modified, this should not affect the way the class is used; just as when you have the oil changed in your car, you do not change the way you see the car or how you drive it.

17.2.7   Class Members and Scope

The term *members* refers to the properties and methods of a class, and the term *scope* refers to where the members can be accessed within the program. Properties and methods are prefaced with a scope descriptor, such as `public`, `private`, or `protected`. If a member is not prefaced by a scope descriptor, it is considered to be public. You should always specify a scope descriptor for properties.

Public Scope.   Public scope is the default scope for all properties and methods of an object. Public means that class members can be accessed from everywhere in the script and are not restricted to the class. In Example 17.2 the name, address, and phone properties were public. From anywhere within the script, the value of those properties could be changed. As stated earlier in this chapter, prior to PHP 5, the descriptor was `var`; now you would use `public`. Methods themselves do not require the descriptor and are public by default.

Private Scope.   Private members are visible or accessible only in the class that defines them. They are not directly accessible outside the class or to subclasses (classes derived from the current class; see "Inheritance" on page 763). If you create private variables, then public methods are used to manipulate the data. In the following example, the three variables of the `Employee` class are declared private. It is not possible for some part of the program outside the class to change or manipulate the values of these variables—a good thing. In Example 17.2 if the properties had been declared `private`, the only way that the object's properties could have been changed would be through its methods.

```
class Employee{
   private $name;
   private $phone;
   private $address;
}
```

The methods used to manipulate this data would be publicly available.

Protected Scope. If you create a new class from an existing class, the private members will not be available to the new class. Protected members are available to the class where they are created and to any subclasses (see "Inheritance" on page 763).

Example Using Private Scope. The following example includes a `BankAccount` class. The only property is the balance that is marked `private`. The only way this balance can be changed from a user from outside the class is through its public methods. This example hides the balance from the user. The properties and methods are encapsulated within the `BankAccount` class.

EXAMPLE 17.3

```
    <?php

1   class BankAccount {

2       private $balance=0;

        function makeDeposit( $amount ) {
3           $this->balance += $amount;  // Add to the current balance
4           echo '<br>Deposited: $' . number_format( $amount, 2);
        }

        function makeWithdrawal( $amount ) {
            // Subtract from the current balance
5           $this->balance -= $amount;
6           echo '<br>Withdrew: $' . number_format( $amount, 2);
        }

        function getBalance() {
7           echo '<br>Current Balance: $' . number_format(
                $this->balance, 2);
        }
    }

8   $myAccount = new BankAccount();
9   $myAccount->makeDeposit( 100.00 );
10  $myAccount->makeWithdrawal( 40.00 );
11  $myAccount->getBalance();

    ?>
```

EXPLANATION

1 A class called `BankAccount` is defined.
2 This class has only one variable, `$balance`, initially set to zero. The keyword `private` tells PHP that this variable can be accessed only from within the class and not from outside. Thus, `$myAccount->balance=100000` will fail if that statement is issued from outside the class.

EXPLANATION (CONTINUED)

3 The only way to alter the balance is through the class methods. Method `makeDeposit()` will add the `$amount` to `$this->balance`. Remember, the pseudo-variable `$this` refers to the object currently being used.

4 This line prints the amout that was deposited. (The function `number_format()` is used to format the dollars with two decimal spaces.)

5–6 Similarly, the function `makeWithdrawal()` will deduct `$amount` from `$this->balance`.

7 The `getBalance()` method returns the value of the current balance. Although the user can view the balance, he or she does not have access to it and cannot change it directly.

8 A new object called `$myAccount` is created.

9 The `makeDeposit()` method is called and adds $100 to the account object, `$myaccount`.

10 The `makeWithdrawal()` method withdraws $40 from the account object, `$myaccount`.

11 A call to `getBalance()` for the object `$myAccount` will print the balance of $60, the correct amount. The output is shown in Figure 17.6.

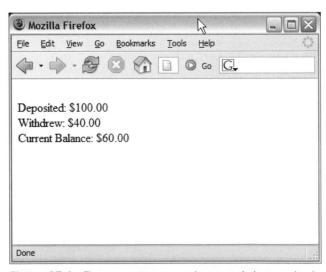

Figure 17.6 The `BankAccount` class contains a private variable to hold the balance, accessed only by public methods to deposit, withdraw, and get the balance. Output from Example 17.3.

17.2.8 Magic Methods

PHP provides special methods that are invoked automatically based on what the program is doing—creating an object, setting a property value, retrieving a value, or destroying an object. A constructor is a magic method that is invoked when you call `new` to create a new object, a `get` or `set` method is invoked when you access the object, and a destructor method is invoked when your program ends. These special methods have names starting with two underscores: `__construct()`, `__destruct()`, `__set()`, and `__get()`. We discuss each of the "magic" methods in the following sections. (See the PHP manual for a complete list of magic methods.)

Constructors.   A constructor, as the term implies, is a builder or creator. When you assign values to properties in a class, PHP will automatically build or construct a new object when `new` is called by the user of the class. When we created a new house, new employee, and new bank account, we did not explicitly call a constructor. We let PHP create the object and assign the properties to it. If you want to customize the initialization of an object, PHP lets you define a constructor method of your own. Once the object has been created with `new`, PHP will check to see if you have defined a constructor, and if so, it will automatically be called. This magic method is called right after `new` has created the object. For example, to set the initial bank account balance to zero for a new bank account, a constructor could be defined to perform this initial task.

Although functionally the same, PHP 4 and PHP 5 use a different syntax for creating constructor methods. PHP 4 constructor methods are named with the same name as the class. So, if you have a class named `MyClass`, the constructor is a function named `MyClass`.

PHP 5 provides the constructor, a magic method called `__construct()`. This method is not normally called directly by the user, but is automatically invoked when the `new` keyword is used. PHP 5 is backward compatible, so if a function named `__construct()` is missing in the class declaration, the old-style constructor will be used if there is one; if neither are declared, then PHP creates the object and assigns it values provided in the class, just as demonstrated in all of the examples thus far.

FORMAT

PHP 4 Format: `void class_name([mixed args[, ...])`

Example:
```
function MyClass(){
    $this->balance = 0;
}
```

PHP 5 Format: `void __construct ( [mixed args [, ...]] )`

Example:
```
function __construct()  {
    $this->balance = 0;
}
```

EXAMPLE 17.4

```php
    <?php
    # PHP 5
1   class House{
2       function __construct(){    // Constructor
            print "Constructor initializing a new house.\n";
        }
    }  /* End class definition */

3       $my_house= new House;
4       $your_house=new House;
    ?>
```

EXPLANATION

1   A House class is defined.
2   The __construct method acts as a class constructor and is called when the object is being created (PHP 5).
3   The new keyword is used to create a House object. The "magic" function on line 2 is automatically invoked at this time.
4   Another House object is created, causing the __construct() function to be invoked again. See Figure 17.7 (left).

EXAMPLE 17.5

```php
    <?php
    # PHP 4
1   class House{
2       function House(){    // Constructor PHP 4
            print "Constructor initializing a new house.\n";
        }
    }  /* End class definition */

3       $my_house= new House;  // Create object
4       $your_house=new House;
    ?>
```

EXPLANATION

1   A House class is defined.
2   When the function has the same name as the class, it is a constructor and will be invoked when a new House object is created.
3, 4 Two new House objects are created with the new keyword. The constructor on line 2, named after the class, is automatically invoked at this time. Prior to PHP 5, this was the only way to create a constructor method.

Figure 17.7 (left) Using the PHP 5 "magic" constructor method; (right) Using a constructor method named after the class. Output from Examples 17.4 and 17.5.

EXAMPLE 17.6

```php
   <?php
   # PHP 5
1  class House{

2     private $owner;
3     public $address;

4     function __construct($owner, $address){
          if (! empty($owner)&& ! empty($address)){
5            $this->owner=$owner;
             $this->address=$address;
6            print "Constructor initializing a new house.\n";
          }
       }

7     function displayHouse(){
          echo "This house is owned by $this->owner. ";
          echo "It's address is $this->address.\n<br>";
       }
   }

       // Using the class to create objects
8   $myHouse= new House("Joe","13 River Road");
9   $yourHouse = new House("Brad","1 Roundabout Drive");
10  $myHouse->displayHouse();
    $yourHouse->displayHouse();
   ?>
```

EXPLANATION

1 The House class is declared.

2 The $owner property is declared private. It cannot be directly accessed from outside the class. In this example, declaring this variable private is not really necessary; it is done just to illustrate the scope designator.

3   The `$address` property is publicly available throughout the script.

4   PHP's constructor is defined here. A class automatically calls this method for each new object that is created. The constructor method accepts arguments of varied types and number.

5   This is where the initial values are being set for the new object.

6   Each time the contstructor is called, that is, each time a new House object is created, this line is printed, as shown in Figure 17.8.

7   The class method `displayHouse()` is a getter method. It retrieves and displays the properties for the object that called it.

8   A new `House` object is created with `new`. Two arguments are passed to the constructor of the class, the name `Joe`, and the address `13 River Road`. The constructor is called automatically and will assign these values to the object's properties. This instance is called `$myHouse`.

9   Another `House` object is created. The constructor will automatically be called for this object and assign values to its properties. We now have two house objects in the program's memory, both at different memory addresses and both with their own properties.

10   To display the properties of the objects, each object calls `displayHouse()`, a user-defined function that retrieves and prints the properties of the object that is named on the left side of the `->` operator. See Figure 17.8.

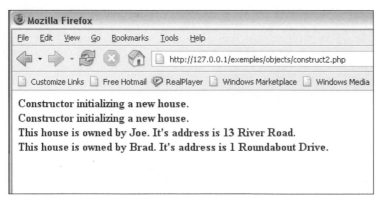

Figure 17.8   Calling the constructor in PHP 5. Output from Example 17.6.

Destructors.   A destructor, as the name implies, is used to destroy an object. A destructor method is called right before the object is released. Releasing an object means that all references to the object have been unset or the object has gone out of scope. The destructor would be used to perform any final actions you want to perform such as deleting old files, releasing resources, and so on. Typically, PHP releases the objects at the end of each script.

Being able to use a destructor is a PHP 5 feature. PHP 4 does not have destructors at all. In PHP 4 you created a function that simulated a destructor or you could use the PHP unset() function to force the removal of an object, but PHP 5 provides a specific destructor function named __destruct(). This method takes no parameters, and it cannot be called directly. It will be called implicitly when you release your object.

FORMAT

```
void __destruct ( void )
```

Example:
```
function _ _destruct();
```

EXAMPLE 17.7

```
# PHP 5
<?php
1   class House{

private $owner;
public $address;

    function __construct($owner, $address){
        if (! empty($owner) && ! empty($address)){
            $this->owner=$owner;
            $this->address=$address;
            echo "Constructor initializing a new house ";
            echo "in the ", get_class($this)," class.\n";
        }
    }
    function displayHouse(){
        echo "This house is owned by $this->owner. ";
        echo "Its address is $this->address.\n<br>";
    }
2   function __destruct(){
        echo "Evacuate now! $this being destroyed\n";
    }
}

    // Using the class to create objects
3   $myHouse= new House("Joe","13 River Road");
    $yourHouse = new House("Brad","1 Roundabout Drive");
4   $myHouse->displayHouse();
    $yourHouse->displayHouse();
?>
```

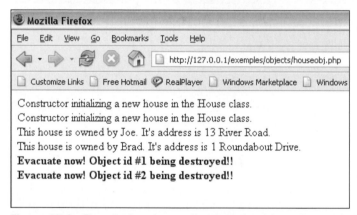

Figure 17.9   The destructor method. Output from Example 17.7.

Accessor Methods—Setters and Getters.   You do not have access to a real house or bank account until it has been created. Likewise you cannot access an object until you have created it, and then you can manipulate it, give it values, extract values, and so on. Functions that give you access to an object are called accessor or instance methods, often termed *setters* and *getters*. A setter is a method used to assign a value to a class variable, and a getter is a method used to retrieve the value of a class variable. Simply said, "Put something in, set it; take something out, get it."

PHP's Setter and Getter Access Methods

PHP provides two magic methods, `__set` and `__get`, to protect public variables from direct access outside a class. These special functions are called automatically whenever the user tries to access an object's property either by assigning (setting) a value to it or by retrieving (getting) a value. The `__set` method takes exactly two arguments, the object's property variable and the value being assigned to it. The `__get` method takes one argument, the property of the object. These functions do not work with private variables and each function can only be defined once within the class.

Let's look at an example to see how this works.

EXAMPLE 17.8

```php
<?php
// The class
1   class Employee {
2       public $name;    // Properties
        public $address;
        public $phone;
    // Public magic methods
3       function __set($property,$value)  // setter
        {
4           $this->property = $value;
        }
5       function __get($property)       // getter
        {
6           return $this->property;
        }
    };

    // User of the class
7   $Heidi = new Employee();
8   $Heidi->name="Heidi Clum";
9   echo $Heidi->name, "\n<br>";
    $Heidi->address="1234 Somewhere Blvd ";
    echo $Heidi->address, "\n<br>";
    $Heidi->phone="123-456-7890";
    echo $Heidi->phone,"\n<br>";
    echo "<hr>";
    $Brad = new Employee();
    $Brad->name="Brad Bit";
    echo $Brad->name, "\n<br>";
    $Brad->address="4321 Sunset Blvd ";
    echo $Brad->address, "\n<br>";
    $Brad->phone="987-654-3210";
    echo $Brad->phone, "\n<br>";
?>
```

EXPLANATION

1   The `Employee` class is declared.

2   The `Employee` class consists of three public properties, `$name`, `$phone`, and `$address`.

3   This magic method called `__set` takes two parameters: one to represent the incoming class property for the object, in this example called `$property`; and the second to represent the value that will be assigned to that property. When the user of the class makes a statement such as `$Heidi->phone="123-456-7890"`, PHP automatically invokes this `__set` method and assigns properties to the current object, referenced by the pseudo variable, `$this`.

4   This is where a value (in this example, a phone number) is assigned to the `$Heidi` object.

5   The magic method called `__get` takes one parameter to represent the incoming class property, in this example called `$property`. Its purpose is to automatically retrieve the value of the object's property when the user of the class makes a statement such as `echo $Heidi->phone;`. See Figure 17.10.

6   The object's property value is retrieved and returned by the `__get` method.

7   A new instance of the `Employee` class is created, an object named `$Heidi`.

8   When this line is executed, PHP automatically calls the magic `__set` method to assign a value to the object.

9   When the value of the object's property is retrieved, the `__get` method is automatically called.

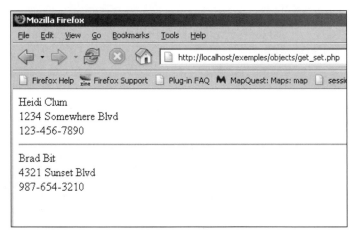

Figure 17.10   The magic `__set` and `__get` methods. Output from Example 17.8.

User-Defined Setters and Getters

When you design a class, you are not required to use PHP's built-in methods; you can write your own customized getters and setters. The properties can be declared as `private` and the only way they can be accessed is through the `public` setter and getter methods provided by the class, just another way to implement data hiding. The disadvantage of having a setter and getter for every property is that the program grows larger very quickly and thus more unwieldy and harder to maintain.

EXAMPLE 17.9

```php
<?php
// The class
class Employee {
    // private variables
    private $name;
    private $address;
    private $phone;
    // public methods
    function setName($name)  //  setter
    {
        $this->name = $name;
    }
    function getName()   // getter
    {
        return $this->name;
    }
    function setAddress($address)
    {
        $this->address = $address;
    }
    function getAddress()
    {
        return $this->address;
    }

    function setPhone($phone)
    {
        $this->phone = $phone;
    }

    function getPhone()
    {
        return $this->phone;
    }

    function printPersonInfo()
    {
        echo "<hr><b>Employee Info</b><br>";
        echo $this->name . "<br>\n";
        echo $this->address . "<br>\n";
        echo $this->phone . "<br>\n";
    }
};
    // User of the class
    $Heidi = new Employee();
    $Heidi->setName("Heidi Clum");
    $Heidi->setAddress("1234 Somewhere Blvd ");
    $Heidi->setPhone("123-456-7890");
```

The line numbers in the left margin are: 1, 2, 3 (for the private variables), 4, 5, 6, 7, 8, 9, 10 (for the functions), and 11, 12 (for the user of the class).

EXAMPLE 17.9 (CONTINUED)

```
13      $Brad = new Employee();
14      $Brad->setName("Brad Bit");
        $Brad->setAddress("4321 Sunset Blvd ");
        $Brad->setPhone("987-654-3210");

15      $Heidi->printPersonInfo();
16      $Brad->printPersonInfo();
    ?>
```

EXPLANATION

1–3 The class variables are declared as private.

4   This is a setter method for the $name property of the class. This method is the only way the name can be updated from outside the class. In this implementation, the method simply assigns a new value to class property $name.

5   This is the getter method for the $name property. It simply returns its value.

6–7 These are the setter and getter methods for the address property.

8–9 These are the setter and getter methods for the $phone property.

10 The method getPersonInfo() displays all of the properties for the two objects. Because the method is part of the class, it has access to the private properties. This method does not attempt to change the object's properties; it simply displays them.

11 A new instance of the Employee class is created, an object called $Heidi.

12 The next three statements illustrate how the setter and getter methods are called for setting and retrieving the object's properties.

13 Another instance of the Employee class is created, an object called $Brad.

14–16 The setter and getter methods are now applied to the $Brad object. See Figure 17.11 for the output.

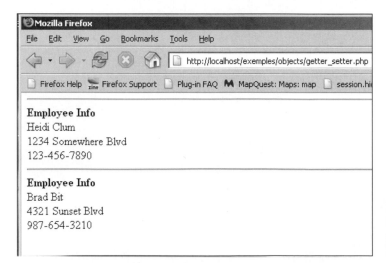

Figure 17.11
User-defined setters and getters. Output from Example 17.9.

17.2.9 Inheritance

The son inherited his father's title and estate. PHP classes can also inherit from a parent class. Inheritance is a mechanism of extending an existing class. By inheriting a class, we create a new class with all the functionality of an existing class, plus we can add new variables and methods to the new class. In this way, the existing class can be extended without modifying its code.

When one class inherits from another, the inherited class is called a subclass or a child. The class from which the subclass inherits is called the parent class, the super class, or the base class. A subclass is said to be derived from a parent class. In our examples we use terms subclass or child and parent class. Figure 17.12 shows a simple diagram of the parent–child relationship, each circle representing a class.

Inheritance requires that at least one class already exists. This class will be the parent class. A new subclass is declared by using the keyword `extends`. In the following example, the `Person` class contains properties for a generic person: a name, an address, and a phone number. Later we design a more specific type of person, a person who is employed. However, because employed people are still "persons" we can create another class called `EmployedPerson` that will inherit all the functionality of the `Person` class and then extend that functionality by adding new members. New members will be added, specific to employed persons. The body of the `printPersonInfo` method must be changed because now there is more information to display.

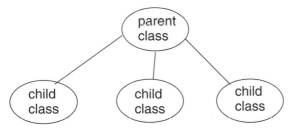

Figure 17.12 The parent–child class relationship.

Constructors and Inheritance.   When you create an inherited class, its constructor will be automatically executed, but its parent's constructor does not get called. To execute the parent constructor, you have to call it explicitly within a subclass constructor with

```
parent::ClassName()
```

or

```
parent::__construct()
```

EXAMPLE 17.10

```php
    <?php
1   class Computer {   // Parent/base/super class
2       private $password; // Is visible in this class
3       protected $userId; // Is visible in this class and subclass
4       public $printer;   // Is visible everywhere in the script

5       function __construct(){
            echo "Parent constructor just called.\n<br>";
            $this->userId="willie";
            $this->password="UrOKhi5";
        }
    }
    // Extend the computer class
6   class Laptop extends Computer{    // Child/derived/subclass
7       public $brand;
        public $weight;
8       private $password="LetMeIn2";

9       function __construct($brand,$weight){  // Subclass constructor
10          parent::__construct();  // Call to parent constructor
            echo "Child constructor just called.\n<br>";
11          $this->brand=$brand;       // New properties for the child
            $this->weight=$weight;
        }
    }

    // User of the class
12  $pc=new Computer();
13  $portable = new Laptop("Sonie","3.5");
14  $pc->printer="LazerBeam"; //direct access ok
    $portable->printer="Daisy";
15  // echo "$portable->password<br>"; // Fatal error
    //  echo "$pc->password<br>";    // Fatal error
    echo "<pre>";
    // Get publicly available properties
16  print_r(get_object_vars($pc));
    print_r(get_object_vars($portable));
    echo "</pre>";
    ?>
```

EXPLANATION

1   The Computer class is declared. It represents the parent class.
2   The first property in this class is marked private. The $password variable will not and should not be available outside the class. A new computer object will have its own private password.

EXPLANATION (CONTINUED)

3 The `$userId` property is declared `protected`. It is visible and accessible within this class and if this class has any subclasses, they will inherit this property, but the subclass will not be able to use it anywhere outside its class and it will not be able to use its own methods to manipulate the `$userId`. The subclass can only access the protected variable through the public methods of the parent `Computer` class. (However, the subclass can define its own property called `$userId` that is not related to this one. See "Overriding Methods" on page 766.)

4 The public property, `$printer`, is available anywhere within the script.

5 The contructor is defined for this class. The user ID and password are initialized.

6 Now the `Computer` class is going to be "extended" to include a child or subclass, called `Laptop`. The new class is just an extension of its parent. It can add more features to the parent. For example, a laptop might be more concerned with weight and portability issues, it is priced differently, it needs a carrying case, and so on. The user might not change, but the laptop will have its own private password.

7 New property variables are created for the laptop computer.

8 The `$password` variable is marked `private`. It is not the same `$password` as in the parent, but a separate and private property of the laptop.

9 The laptop defines its own constructor.

10 The `Laptop` class calls its parent's constructor. Otherwise, any variables set in the parent's constructor will not be made part of this class.

11 The new properties for the laptop are initialized.

12 The user of the `Computer` class creates a new object, called `$pc`.

13 The user then creates a new object called `$portable` from the `Laptop` class that inherits from the `Computer` class. The user does not really know this. He or she creates the objects for the `Laptop` class the same way he or she creates them from the `Computer` class.

14 A printer is assigned to the object's `printer` property. Because the property was declared `public`, this is okay, because public properties are available outside the class.

15 These lines were commented out because they produced a fatal error. You cannot access private variables from outside either parent or child class, or you get a fatal error:

Fatal error: **Cannot access private property laptop::$password** in C:\wamp\www\exeplee\obbectt\inner..hp on line 36
Fatal error: **Cannot access private property computer::$password** in C:\wamp\www\emppes\\bjeets\\nhee.phh onnlinn 37

16 The `get_object_vars()` function returns a list of public properties for each class. The `print_r` function displays these properties, as shown in Figure 17.13.

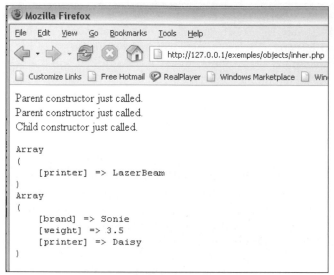

Figure 17.13
Display public properties for the parent and child class.

17.2.10   Overriding Methods

Overriding is when you give the a member of a subclass the same name as its corresponding property or method in the parent class. If, for example, you have a value for a serial number property in the parent class, in the subclass, you might want a different serial number for the new product that was derived from its parent. You might also want to create your own "display" method in the child rather than use the one in the parent class providing a different functionality. By using the same name for the members of the inherited class that you used in the parent class, you are overriding the operations in the parent class.

EXAMPLE 17.11

```php
      <?php
      // Define the parent or super class
1     class Person {
          public $name;
          public $address;
          public $phone;
          // Define the methods
          function printPersonInfo(){
              echo "<hr><b>Person Info</b><br>";
              echo $this->name . "<br>\n";
              echo $this->address . "<br>\n";
              echo $this->phone . "<br>\n";
          }
      }
```

EXAMPLE 17.11 (CONTINUED)

```
2    class EmployedPerson extends Person {
3        public $occupation;
4        public $company_name;
5        public $business_phone;

6        function printPersonInfo()   // overriding
         {
7            parent::printPersonInfo();
8            echo $this->occupation . "<br>\n";
9            echo $this->company_name . "<br>\n";
10           echo $this->business_phone . "<br>\n";
         }
     }

11   $kid = new Person();
     $kid->name = "Jimmy";
     $kid->address = "12 Elm Street";
     $kid->phone = "555-5555";
12   $adult = new EmployedPerson();
13   $adult->name = "Jimmy's Father";
14   $adult->address = "12 Elm Street";
15   $adult->phone = "555-5555";
16   $adult->occupation = "Programmer";
17   $adult->company_name = "Software Developer, Ltd.";
18   $adult->business_phone = "444-4444";

19   $kid->printPersonInfo();
20   $adult->printPersonInfo();

     ?>
```

EXPLANATION

1   First we declare the class Person. In this example, we extend the class. By doing so, Person will become the parent or super class.

2   Class EmployedPerson will contain all the members of the class Person. EmployedPerson is the child or subclass of the Person class, its parent. The PHP keyword extends defines this relationship.

3–5   These are the new variables specific to EmployedPerson. Note the name, phone, and address properties are available to the EmployedPerson. They were inherited from the Person class.

6   The EmployedPerson also inherits the function printPersonInfo() from the Person class. However, now we want to redefine the behavior of this child class to include added functionality. This process is called overriding the method.

EXPLANATION (CONTINUED)

7   In this line we call the parent's function `printPersonInfo()`. The keyword `parent` in PHP refers to the class that is the parent to the current class, in this case `Person`. In other words, we are overriding the original implementation of the parent's method by first calling it and then adding some new statements.

8–10   This is where the new variables specific to the child class are added to the `printPersonInfo()` method.

11   A new object, called `$kid`, of class `Person` is created.

12   Next, another object, called `$adult`, of class `EmployedPerson` is created.

13–18   The properties for the `$adult` object are set.

19   We call `Person`'s `printPersonInfo()` function.

20   We call `EmployedPerson`'s `printPersonInfo()` function. This function will print differently then the `Person` function because there is more data to print out.

17.2.11   Protected Access

When a class member is preceded with the `private` access modifier, it is visible only within the class where it was created. If you try to access it directly from outside the class, you will receive an error message such as:

> Fatal error: Cannot access **private** property computer::$password in . . .

If you call a class method from a class with private data, its private data will be visible, but if you call a method defined in a derived child class, the private data is not visible. If a private property is declared in a child class with the same name as a private property in its parent, it is unrelated to the parent's property. It is a separate variable in its own right.

If a class member is protected, then it is visible within a subclass; that is, it is inherited by the subclass and treated in the subclass like a private member but cannot be accessed outside the subclass. It can be accessed in the child class through the public methods defined in the parent and for methods defined within the child.

> Fatal error: Cannot access **protected** property computer::$userId

If the class member is public, it is visible throughout the entire script and can be accessed directly from anywhere. In the object-oriented world you normally access private and protected data through public methods. It is, however, also possible to create private and protected methods.

Note that when you try to get or set the value of the private property of a parent class from within the subclass, instead of getting an error message, you get nothing. You are simply ignored.

EXAMPLE 17.12

```
      <html><head><title>Private, Protected, Public</title>
      </head>
      <body bgcolor="lavender">
      <font face="ariel" size=+1>
      <h1>Private, Protected, Public</h1>
      <?php
1     class computer {
2         private $password;  // Visible only within this class
3         protected $userId;  // Visible within this class and subclass
4         public $printer;    // Visible anywhere in the script

5         function __construct() {  // Parent's constructor
              print "In the parent constructor.\n<br>";
              $this->userId = "willie";     // protected
              $this->password = "urAok5";   // private
          }
6         function setUserId($userId){
              $this->userId=$userId;
          }
7         function getUserId() {
              return $this->userId;
          }
8         private function setPassword($password){   // private method
              $this->password=$password;
          }
9         private function getPassword(){
              return $this->password;
          }
      }

10    class Laptop extends Computer{

11        public $model;
          public $weight;
12        private $password;

13        function __construct() { // Laptop's constructor
              echo "In the child's constructor\n<br>";
14            parent::__construct();
              // Inherited
15            echo "Inherited user name? ". $this->userId, "\n<br>";
              // Not inherited
              echo "Inherited password? ". $this->password, "\n<br>";
16            $this->brand=$brand;
              $this->weight=$weight;
          }
```

EXAMPLE **17.12** (CONTINUED)

```
17        function setPassword($password){
              $this->password=$password;
          }
18        function getPassword(){
              return $this->password;
          }
      }


      // Class user
19    $pc=new Computer();   // Create two new objects
20    $portable = new Laptop();

21    $portable->setPassword("letmein2");
22    $pc->printer="Lazerboy"; // Direct access okay
      $portable->printer="Daisy";
      //   echo $pc->userId;    // Error: Can't access directly
23    echo "<br>My Laptop username is ", $portable->getUserId(),
          "\n<br>";
24    echo "My pc username is ", $pc->getUserId(), "\n<br>";
      // echo "My pc password is ", $pc->getPassword(), "\n<br>";
25    echo "My Laptop password is ", $portable->getPassword(),
          "<br>";
26    echo "My pc printer is ", $pc->printer, "\n<br>";
      echo "My Laptop printer is ", $portable->printer, "<br>";
?>
</body>
</font>
</html>
```

EXPLANATION

1   A class called `computer` is declared.
2   The access designator `private` makes the `$password` property visible only within this class.
3   The `protected` access designator makes the `$userId` property available in this class and any subclasses; that is, it is inherited.
4   `public` scope makes the `$printer` property available anywhere in the script. This is the default scope.
5   The parent's constructor function is called when the object is created. Properties are assigned to the object.
6–7   These are the setter and getter functions typically used to provide access to class members.
10   The `laptop` class is a subclass of the `computer` class.
13   A constructor method for the `laptop` class is defined.
14   Because the parent's constructor is not automatically called, we are calling it here. The keyword `parent` is followed by the scope resolution operator, `::`, and the method that will be called, `__construct()`.

EXPLANATION (CONTINUED)

15 The variable $userId was designated `protected` in the parent class. It is visible within this inherited class. The `password` property was designated as `private` in the parent class and is not visible here in the inherited class. You can only access this variable through public methods provided in the parent.

16 New properties are defined for the `laptop` class. It "extends" the `computer` class.

19 Now we are outside the boundaries of both the parent and the subclass. A new instance of the `computer` class is created, an object named $pc.

20 An instance of the `laptop` class is created, an object name $portable.

22 Public properties are directly accessible throughout the script. A value is being assigned to the laptop object's `printer` property.

23 The `userId` is a protected property. It is visible in both the parent and the subclass.

24 The object of the parent class, `computer`, can get its private property as long as it accesses it through its public method.

25 The object of the inherited class, `laptop`, cannot get the private property of its parent even with the getter method.

26 Both objects can access their printers because the `printer` property is public.

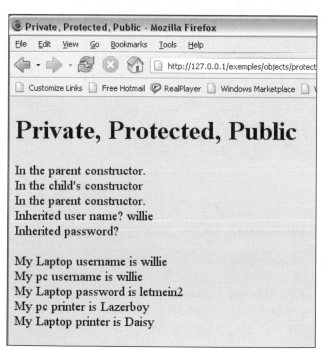

Figure 17.14 Inheritance and visibility with private, protected, and public variables.

17.3 Some PHP 5 Object Features

PHP 5 provided a number of new features for object-oriented programmers, some of which are discussed here and some of which are beyond the scope of this chapter. Not included are some of the magic methods, cloning, abstraction, iterators, and interfaces.

17.3.1 final Classes and Methods

A class that has been declared final cannot be inherited. Methods that have been declared as final can be used within subclasses, but they cannot be overridden. Let's consider an example next.

EXAMPLE 17.13

```php
    <?php
1   class Computer{
2       private $serial_number;
3       final function setSerialNumber($serial_number) {
            $this->serial_number=$serial_number;
        }
    }

4   class Laptop extends Computer {
5       private $new_serial_number;
6       function setSerialNumber() {
7           $this->new_serial_number=$new_serial_number;
        }
    }

8   $portable->new Laptop();
    $portable -> setSerialNumber("abc!@$#");

    ?>
```

(Output)
Fatal error: Cannot override final method computer::setSerialNumber()
in C:\wamp\www\exemples\objects\...

EXPLANATION

1   The Computer class is declared. It will be the parent class in this example.
2   A private property member called $serial_number is declared for this class.
3   The setSerialNumber() method has been declared final, meaning that a child class cannot redefine or override it. This prevents a subclass from changing the serial number.
4   The Laptop class is a subclass of the Computer class.
5   The child class declares a private property called $new_serial_number.

6   The child class declares a method name `setSerialNumber`.
7   The purpose of this class is to override the parent method of the same name and provide a new private serial number.
8   A fatal error occurs when the method `setSerialNumber()` in the child class is called. A method that is declared `final` cannot be overridden.

17.3.2 Static Members

Static members are new with PHP 5. They are properties or methods that do not require an instance of an object to be used. Static members are also called class members because they are created by and for the class as a whole. They are like global variables in any other PHP script in that they are available throughout the class. You can access a static property or method with the name of the class or the special class keyword `self`.

EXAMPLE 17.14

```php
<?php
class House{
    static $houseCount;
    private $owner;
    public $address;

    function __construct($owner,$address){
        self::$houseCount++;
        $this->owner=$owner;
        $this->address=$address;
        echo "Constructor initializing a new house ";
        echo "in the ", get_class($this)," class.\n<br>";
        echo "So far, we have built ", self::$houseCount,
            " houses.<br>";
    }

}
    // Using the class to create objects
    $myHouse= new House("Joe","13 River Road");
    $yourHouse = new House("Brad","1 Roundabout Drive");
    $theirHouse=new House("Mary", "5 Outthere Street");
?>
```

1
2

3

4

EXPLANATION

1   In the `House` class, a static property is declared with the `static` keyword.
2   The static variable is not associated with a specific object, only the class, which can be referenced with `self` and two colons. Each time the constructor method is called, the value of the static variable will be incremented by 1. We are keeping track of the number of objects that are created.

3   The value of the static variable is retrieved.

4   The next three lines create three new houses. Each time the constructor for a new house is invoked, the static variable will be incremented, as shown in the output of this program in Figure 17.15.

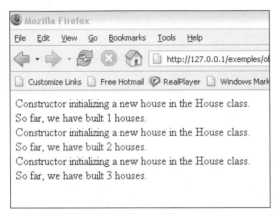

Figure 17.15 Static property.

17.3.3 Class Constants

Rising gas prices, taxes, and death are constants. You can create global constants by using PHP's `define()` function (see Chapter 4, "The Building Blocks"). PHP 5 allows you to encapsulate constants within a class. They are not objects and cannot be referenced with `$this`. Constants represent values that are not expected to change and can be used by the class as a whole. Such values might be the document root of this server, the database host and password, and so on. Once declared, constants cannot be changed by the program. They are declared with the `const` keyword and are referenced with the class name or `self` and the scope resolution operator followed by the name of the constant.

EXAMPLE 17.15

```
    <?php
    class House{
1       const TAX_COLLECTOR="Dick Scrooge";
2       const COUNTY="Butte";
        private $owner;
        public $address;
```

EXAMPLE   17.15 (CONTINUED)

```
        function __construct($owner,$address){
            $this->owner=$owner;
            $this->address=$address;
            echo "Constructor initializing a new house ";
            echo "in the ", get_class($this)," class.\n<br>";
        }
3       function Tax_info(){
4           echo "The tax collector for ", self::COUNTY,
                " is ",self::TAX_COLLECTOR,".<br>";
            // could use House::County or House::TAX_COLLECTOR
        }
    }
        // Using the class to create objects
        $myHouse= new House("Joe","13 River Road");
        $yourHouse = new House("Brad","1 Roundabout Drive");
        $theirHouse=new House("Mary", "5 Outthere Street");
5       House::Tax_info();
    ?>
```

EXPLANATION

1, 2   Two constants for this class are defined. These are values that are not expected to change for any instance of the class. These are called class constants. Outside the class constants are declared with the `define()` function (see Chapter 4, "The Building Blocks").

3   A class function called `Tax_info()` is declared.

4   The `self::` syntax refers to the name of the current class. You also say `House::County` to mean the same thing. The value of the constants `COUNTY` and `TAX_COLLECTOR` are retrieved and printed. They are the same no matter how many house objects you create. See the output in Figure 17.16.

5   The `Tax_info()` function is called. It does not require an instance of the class. It behaves the same for all objects. The `House::` syntax tells PHP to go to the `House` class and call the function `Tax_info()`.

Figure 17.16
Class constants in a class.

17.3.4   Reusing a Class

The following example starts with a class that will be used to create a guest book. The
class is stored in a separate file that will be included in a PHP self-processing form file.
The information for the guest book will come from an HTML form. After the user fills
out the fields in the HTML form, PHP will extract the form data. A new `GuestBook`
object is created and the input from the form is assigned as properties to the object. After
all the information is assigned to the object, the class methods will display the data in
the guest book and send it to a text file. This is a very simple form (see Figure 17.17)
and a very simple class. The form consists of text fields and a submit button. The class
consists of private property variables and setter and getter access methods. You could
create a constructor and destructor for the class, later extend the class to include e-mail
and cell phone data, save the information in a database rather than a text file, and certainly add error checking, form validation with regular expressions. The basic class can
be used and reused, the class details can be changed, but the user should not be concerned about internal changes to the class as long as the interface remains the same.

EXAMPLE 17.16

```
      (The Class File)
      <?php
1     class GuestBook{
2         protected $name;
          protected $address;
          protected $phone;
          protected birthday;
          private $file;
          // Setters
3         function setName($name){
              $this->name=$name;
          }
          function setAddress($address){
              $this->address=$address;
          }
          function setPhone($phone){
              $this->phone=$phone;
          }
          function setBirthday($birthday){
              $this->birthday=$birthday;
          }
          function setFile($file){
              $this->file=$file;
          }
          // Getters
4         function getName($name){
              return $this->name;
          }
```

EXAMPLE 17.16 (CONTINUED)

```php
        function getAddress($address){
            return $this->address;
        }
        function getPhone($phone){
            return $this->phone;
        }
        function getBirthday($birthday){
            return $this->birthday;
        }

        function getFile($file){
            return $this->file;
        }
5       function showGuest(){
            echo "$this->name<br>";
            echo "$this->address<br>";
            echo "$this->phone<br>";
            echo "$this->birthday<br>";
        }
6       function saveGuest(){
7           $outputstring=$this->name . ":" .$this->address.":"
                .$this->phone.":". $this->birthday. "\n";
8           $path="$_SERVER[DOCUMENT_ROOT]/../guests/$this->file";
9           @ $fh = fopen("$path", "ab");
10          if (! $fh){
                $fh = fopen("$path", "wb");
            }
11          fwrite($fh, $outputstring, strlen($outputstring));
            fclose($fh);
            echo "Data saved in $path<br>";
        }
    }
?>
```

EXPLANATION

1   The class called GuestBook is declared in a file called guest_book.class.
2   The class variables (members) are defined. They are made protected members, meaning they are available to the class where they are created and to any subclasses.
3   This is where the setter methods are defined for the class—object-oriented functions that will assign values to the properties of the class.
4   This is where the getter methods are defined for the class—methods used to retrieve values from the properties of the class.
5   The method called showGuest() is used to display all the properties of the class.
6   The method called saveGuest() is declared. This method will open the guest book file and save a string of guest information to the file.

EXPLANATION (CONTINUED)

7 The properties for a new guest entry are concatenated into a string called $outputstring.

8 The $path variable is assigned the full path to guestbook.txt, the file in this example, where the guest information is stored. The file is located in a directory or folder outside the server's document root to prevent outsiders from accessing it.

9 The file is opened for appending and a handle to it returned to $fh. If there is a problem in opening the file (e.g., it does not exist), the error message is suppressed by prepending the statement with an @ sign.

10 If the file did not exist, it will be created and opened for writing.

11 This is where the guest data is sent to the guestbook.txt file.

EXAMPLE 17.17

```
--------------------------------------------------------------------
(The HTML Form and Class User)
    include("header.inc");
1   include("guest_book.class");
    if ( isset($_POST['submit'])){       // Was the form submitted?
2       extract($_POST);                 // Get the form data
        /* Use the AddressBook Class */
3       $entry= new GuestBook();         // Instantiate the class
4       $entry->setName($your_name);     // Assign the properties
        $entry->setAddress($your_address);
        $entry->setPhone($your_phone);
        $entry->setBirthday($your_bd);
        $entry->setFile($your_file);
5       $entry->showGuest();             // Call the class methods
6       $entry->saveGuest();
    }
    else{   ?>
7       <form action="<?php echo $_SERVER['PHP_SELF']; ?>"
                    method="POST">
        <div align="center">
        <font face="arial" size=+1>
        <table cellspacing="1" cellpadding="1" border="0">
8           <tr><td>Enter your name:</td>
                <td><input type="text" size=50 name="your_name"></td>
            <tr>
            <tr><td>Enter your address:</td>
                <td><input type="text" size=50 name="your_address"></td>
            </tr>
            <tr><td> Enter your phone:</td>
                <td><input type="text" size=20 name="your_phone"></td>
            </tr>
            <tr><td>Enter your birthday:</td>
                <td><input type="text" size=12 name="your_bd"></td>
            </tr>
```

EXAMPLE   17.17 (CONTINUED)

```
9              <tr><td><input type=hidden name="your_file"
                          value="guestbook.txt">
                </td>
                <td><input type="submit" name="submit"
                          value="Submit Entry"></td>
            </tr>
            <tr><td></td>
                <td><input type=reset value="Clear"></td>
            </tr>
        <table>
        </form>
        </div>
        </html>
        <?php
        }
10      include("footer.inc");
    ?>
```

EXPLANATION

1   The header file (an HTML file to produce a centered block of text at the top of the page) and the class file (containing the GuestBook class) are "included," that is, made part of this script. (The header file was shown in Chapter 10, "More on PHP Forms.")

2   If the form has already been submitted by the user, PHP extracts the form data and assigns it to variables of the same name.

3   A new GuestBook object is created and a reference to it is assigned to $entry.

4   The name of the new guest is set here. The information that came in from the form was assigned to $your_name.

5   The showGuest() method retrieves and displays the data that was collected from the form.

6   The saveGuest() method is called. It saves the guest information in the file guest_book.txt.

7   If the form has not been submitted, the PHP else block is executed including the HTML form starting here. It is a self-processing form.

8   The user input devices are set up within an HTML table.

9   This hidden field contains the name of the file where the guest information is stored.

10 The footer.inc file is included here. It is an HTML file that produces copyright information and "Personal Guest Book" at the bottom of the page.

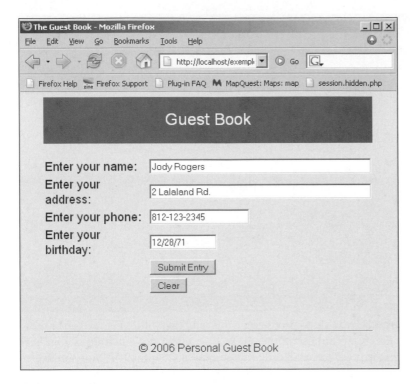

Figure 17.17
The HTML form.

17.4 Chapter Summary

This chapter introduced you to OOP using PHP. Its purpose was to familiarize you with common terms used in OOP and how to apply basic concepts. Because this type of programming tries to emulate real-world situations, the examples were to help you visualize OOP by providing real-world types of objects, such as computers, houses, bank accounts, and people. OOP is a way of thinking about a program. Knowing the basic concepts is just the beginning. Like any art, it takes time to create good design, error handling, modularity, and mastery, but the goal is to be able to write elegant code to solve complex problems.

17.4.1   What You Should Know

Now that you have finished this chapter you should be able to answer the following questions, and know how to put together all the elements discussed into a working application:

1. How would you define a class and its members?

2. How would you create an object from a class?

3. Define private, public, and protected properties.

4. How would you implement inheritance?

5. What is encapsulation?

6. How could you use magic methods?

7. What are constructors and destructors?

8. How would you override a property or method?

9. How would you provide information hiding using setters and getters?

10. How do you create static properties and methods?

11. How do you create `final` methods?

12. How do you create class constants?

CHAPTER 17 LAB

1. a. Create a `clock` object. It will have three properties: `seconds`, `minutes`, and `hours`.
   b. Write two methods, `setTime()` to set the current time, and `displayTime()` to display the time in the browser (like a digital clock).

2. Create a `circle` object and a method that will calculate its circumference.

3. a. In the Chapter 14 Lab, you created a `student` table for the MySQL `school` database. Write a PHP program that will add, delete, and update entries in the `student` table in the `school` database. You will create (use `__construct()`) a `student` object using the field names from the database table as properties. The methods will be `add_Student()`, `drop_Student()`, `update_Student()`, and `displayStudent()`. Use MySQL functions to retrieve the records for a student from the database.
   b. Create an HTML form to provide the user with a selection of functions from which to choose. If, for example, he or she selects "Add a new student", the PHP script will create another form to ask for the student information; and after the form information is completed, the PHP script will validate all the fields, and then use a MySQL function to add the new student to the `student` table in the database. The user should be able to add, delete, update, or display any number of students. Use a session to maintain state between operations.

Building an Art Gallery

A.1 Project Overview

To build a complete PHP/MySQL Web page, we summarize the concepts covered in *PHP and MySQL by Example* with a real-world example, called the Canvas Gallery. The Canvas Gallery is an actual art gallery in San Francisco. It is a large space featuring some of the most progressive artists of the West Coast as well as several artists from other parts of the world. The Canvas presents a new art show every month with new artists and often hundreds of pieces of art. Over the years, the Canvas has sponsored numerous art shows, resulting in a large inventory of art offered for sale or rent during and after the showings.

In this section, we will build a complete dynamic Web site to support the online presence of the Canvas Gallery.

A.2 The Public and the Private

Most Web applications consist of several major components: the public pages that are accessible by the users, and the private pages accessible to those who administer the site and update the pages. A site might have login and authentication pages; an index page with links to various areas of the site; pages that add, change, or delete data; a page for contact information, and e-mail; and header and footer files to include titles, copyright, or trademark information. The Canvas Gallery Web site is organized similarly with the files shown in Table A.1.

Table A.1 The Files That Make Up the Canvas Gallery Web Site

File Name	Description
admin_art_edit.php	Administration screen to add and edit an art record.
admin_art_list.php	Administration screen to display a list of the art in the inventory.
admin_artist_edit.php	Administration screen to edit an existing artist.
admin_artist_insert.php	Administration screen to add a new artist.
admin_artist_list.php	Administration screen with the list of all the artists.
admin_footer.php	Footer for all the administration pages.
admin_header.php	Header included on all the administraion pages to provide a connection to the database, to check if the administrator has logged in or not, and to provide the administration menu.
admin_login.php	A login screen to verify the username and password entered and to update the session so that the user can freely use the administration pages.
artist_detail.php	A public page to display all the information for a specific artist.
contact.php	A simple form to request contact with the staff. This form sends an e-mail when submitted.
db.sql	A SQL script to create the database tables for the art and artist.
footer.php	The footer that is included at the bottom of every public page.
gallerydb.sql	SQL commands to create the Art and Artist tables and populate them with demo data.
header.php	A header file included at the top of every public page to provide the navigation bar, dabatase connectivity, some PHP-specific functions, and the logo.
index.php	The initial page to display the list of all the artists and one piece of art for each artist.
style.css	A cascading style sheet, used to specify fonts, colors, and so on.

A.3   Creating the Web Site

There are a number of steps involved in creating the Web site. We will need a page to:

1. Create the database to hold the data for the art gallery.
2. Build administration pages to create a screen where new inventory can be added to the gallery.
3. List all the art and the artists in the database.
4. List the details of an art piece such as its price, artist name, and so on.

After these pages have been created, we have a working system. However, to make the site more functional and secure, we will include:

5. A login screen to protect the access to the administrative part of the site.
6. A contact form for users to request additional infromation about the art or the artist.

A.3.1   Creating the Database

The first step in this project is to set up the database schema.[1] To see the complete schema for this database, see the files `gallerydb.sql` and `db.sql`. The `db.sql` script is used to create and populate the database with some artists and art, whereas `gallerydb.sql` will contain no initial data and you will add all the artists and their art.

Because we are dealing with artists and their art, two database tables are created, one for the artist and one for the art:

```
CREATE TABLE artist (
  id int(10) unsigned NOT NULL auto_increment,
  name varchar(100) NOT NULL default '',
  bio text NOT NULL,
  phone varchar(50) NOT NULL default '',
  email varchar(100) NOT NULL default '',
  PRIMARY KEY  (id)
)

CREATE TABLE art (
  id int(10) unsigned NOT NULL auto_increment,
  artist_id int(10) unsigned NOT NULL default '0',
  title varchar(120) NOT NULL default '',
  description text NOT NULL,
  price decimal(10,0) NOT NULL default '0',
  PRIMARY KEY  (id)
)
```

---

1. In this example, the MySQL "test" database is used.

Both tables have their own unique ID, the primary key, that will be auto incremented by the database. Additionally, the art table has a foreign key called the `artist_id`. This key will be used to create a relation between the two tables; that is, a link from the artist table to the art table. The rest of the data consists primarily of either `text` for large fields such as the artist's biography or `varchar` for shorter fields such as the name or e-mail address. None of the fields are set to `NULL`.

A.3.2 Administration Pages

After designing the database and creating the tables, the next step is to build the administrative pages where the data is entered and updated in the Web site. All the administrative pages in this project are named with the `admin_` prefix. To enter these pages, the user must log in as the administrator.

Listing All the Artists from the Database (admin_artlist.php).   The initial administrative page, called `admin_artist_list.php`, displays all the names of the artists in the database as hyperlinks. Also included are the phone numbers and e-mail addresses of the respective artists. The second hyperlink under "Action" is used to delete an artist.

 If the user clicks an artist's name, the ID of the artist is passed in the hyperlink (line 4) to another file called `admin_art_edit.php`. If the user clicks the Delete hyperlink, the `action` value from the link will be set to `delete`, and the `id` of that artist will be used in the SQL `DELETE` statement (line 2) to determine which artist should be removed from the database.

The records are retrieved in sorted order (line 3) and displayed in an HTML table.

EXAMPLE A.1

```
(The admin_artist_list.php file)
    <?php
    // Connect to the database and insert the new artist
    mysql_connect("localhost", "root", "password") or
        die(mysql_error());
    mysql_select_db("test") or die(mysql_error());

    extract($_REQUEST);
1   if( isset($action) && $action="delete" ) {
2       $sql = "DELETE FROM Artist WHERE id='$id'";
        mysql_query( $sql ) or die(mysql_error());
    }
```

EXAMPLE A.1 (CONTINUED)

```
3    $sql = "SELECT * FROM Artist ORDER BY name";
     $recordset = mysql_query( $sql )or die(mysql_error());
     ?>
     <? include("admin_header.php") ?>

     <h1>Artist List</h1>
     <table cellpadding="5">
        <th>Artist</th><th>Phone</th><th>Email</th><th>Action</th>

     <?
     while( $row=mysql_fetch_assoc($recordset) ) {
4        print '<tr><td><a href="admin_artist_edit.php?id='
           . $row["id"]. '">'
           . $row["name"] .'</a></td>' .
           "<td>". $row["phone"] ."</td><td>". $row["email"] ."</td>".
5          '<td><a href="admin_artist_list.php?action=delete&id='
           . $row["id"]."\">Delete</a></td></tr>\n";
     }
     ?>

     </table>

     <? include("admin_footer.php") ?>
```

EXPLANATION

1 If the user clicked the Delete hyperlink in the form shown in Figure A.1, line 2 will be executed.
2 This is the SQL statement that will delete an artist from the "Artist" table, based on his or her ID.
3 This SQL selects all rows from the "Artist" table, sorted by the artist's name.
4 After extracting the records with the `mysql_fetch_assoc()` function, a table is displayed with links to each artist, his or her phone number and e-mail address, and a Delete hyperlink. If the user clicks the hyperlink with the artist's name, the artist's id will be passed to the `admin_artist_edit.php` script via a URL. (The value of the id is appended to the ? after the link.)
5 The Delete link, when clicked, passes the `action` value and the `id` of the artist to the PHP script (line 1).

Figure A.1 The admin_artlist.php page.

Updating an Artist in the Gallery (admin_artist_edit.php). To get to the admin_artist_edit.php page, the user clicked the hyperlink of an artist listed in the previous Figure A.1. Line 4 of Example A.1 shows that the hyperlink is sending the id for that artist via a URL. The admin_artist_edit.php page (Example A.2) uses the id to determine which artist to update. (You can see the value of the id in the URL because the GET method is being used). The id for the artist is stored in a hidden field (see line 6 in Example A.2). If this is the first time the page is displayed, a SQL SELECT statement (see line 5) is executed to retrieve all the data for that artist from the database. The user is presented with a self-processing HTML form containing the artist information, such as the name, e-mail address, phone, and so on, for the particular artist he or she selected for update. Once the user has updated the information in the form, it is passed into the PHP portion of the page and extracted from the $_REQUEST superglobal array (see line 1), The variables resulting from the extract() function are used to "SET" the new values for the artist in the SQL UPDATE command on line 3. (Be sure when you test this script that you update line 2 and provide the correct server, username, and password to connect to your version of MySQL.)

EXAMPLE A.2

```php
    <?php
1   extract($_REQUEST);
2   mysql_connect("localhost", "root", "password")
        or die(mysql_error());
    mysql_select_db("test")
        or die(mysql_error());
    if( isset($submit) ) {  // If the form has been submitted
        $status = "";
        if( $name=="" ) {    // If the user left the name field blank
            $status = "Please enter the artist's name.<br>";
        } else {
            // Connect to the database and insert the new artist
3           $sql = "UPDATE Artist SET name='$name', " .
            "email='$email', phone='$phone', bio='$bio'" .
            "WHERE id='$id'";
            mysql_query( $sql )
                or die(mysql_error());
4           $status = "SUCCESSFULLY updated $name";
        }
    } else {
5       $sql = "SELECT * from Artist WHERE id='$id'";
        $resultset = mysql_query( $sql )or die(mysql_error());
        $row = mysql_fetch_assoc( $resultset );
        extract( $row );  // Retrieve/extract all info on artist by ID
    }
    ?>


    <? include("admin_header.php") ?>
    <h1>Artist Update Screen</h1>
    <form action="<?=$_SERVER['PHP_SELF']?>" method="GET">
6       <input type="hidden" name="id" value="<?=$id?>">
        <table>
        <? if (isset($status)) {?>
            <tr><td colspan="2"><b><?=$status?></b><br><br></td></tr>
        <? } ?>
            <tr><td>Name</td><td><input type="text"
                name="name" value="<?=$name?>" /></td></tr>
            <tr><td>Email</td><td><input type="text"
                name="email" value="<?=$email?>" /></td></tr>
            <tr><td>Phone</td><td><input type="text"
                name="phone" value="<?=$phone?>" /></td></tr>
            <tr><td>Bio</td><td><textarea rows="15" cols="60"
                name="bio" value="<?=$bio?>" ><?=$bio?>
                </textarea></td></tr>
            <tr><td> </td><td><input type="submit"
                name="submit" value="Submit"/></td></tr>
        </table>
    </form>
    <? include("admin_footer.php") ?>
```

EXPLANATION

1 After the link with the artist's name (in Figure A.1) is clicked, PHP will extract the user input.

2 The MySQL connection is made to the localhost and the "test" database is opened.

3 If the form shown in Figure A.2 has been submitted, this SQL statement will update the "Artist" table for an artist selected by his or her `id` passed in the URL (Example A.1, line 4).

4 If the update was successful, the `$status` variable is assigned to the string `"SUC-CESSFULLY updated $name"`.

5 If the form hasn't been submitted, all rows are retrieved from the MySQL "Artist" table based on the `id` of the artist selected by the user in Figure A.1. The `extract()` function will create named variables for each column in the row for the selected artist, such as `$name`, `$email`, and so on, used as values for the form's input devices. The hidden field assigns the value of the artist's `id` (passed in the URL) to its `name` attribute, also called `id`.

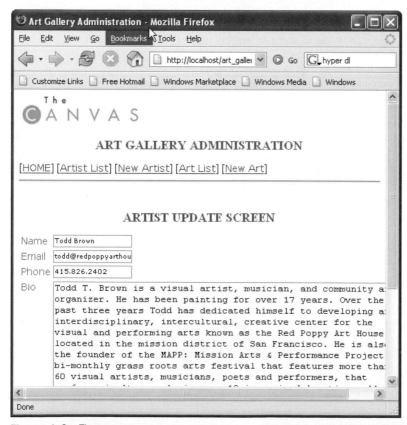

Figure A.2 The `admin_artlist_edit.php` page updates the information on a particular artist.

Adding a New Artist to the Gallery (admin_artist_insert.php).   The page for adding a new artist to the database, admin_artist_insert.php, is basically the same as the admin_artist_edit.php page except that it performs a SQL INSERT statement (see line 1 in Example A.3) instead of an UPDATE and does not require an ID to be passed into the page via a URL. The user will enter the name of the new artist and all the requested information in a simple HTML form presented as a table (see line 5). An ID, primary key, will automatically be generated by the database for each new artist that is added. (When testing this page, make sure to enter the correct information when connecting to the database; that is, host, username, and password are supplied for the mysql_connect() function on line 2.)

EXAMPLE   A.3

```
       <?php
       extract($_REQUEST);
       if( isset($submit) ) {
           $status = "";
           if( $name=="" ) {
               $status = "Please enter the artist's name.<br>";
           } else {
               // Connect to the database and insert the new artist
1              $sql = "INSERT INTO Artist (name, email, phone, bio)" .
               "VALUES ('$name', '$email', '$phone', '$bio')";
2              mysql_connect("localhost", "root", "password")
                   or die(mysql_error());
               mysql_select_db("test")
                   or die(mysql_error());
3              mysql_query( $sql )
                   or die(mysql_error());
               $status = "SUCCESSFULLY inserted $name";
           }
       }
       ?>


       <? include("admin_header.php") ?>

       <h1>Artist Insert Screen</h1>
4      <form action="<?=$_SERVER['PHP_SELF']?>" method="GET">
5          <table>
           <? if (isset($status)) {?>
               <tr><td colspan="2"><b><?=$status?></b><br><br></td></tr>
           <? } ?>
               <tr><td>Name</td><td><input type="text"
                   name="name"/></td></tr>
               <tr><td>Email</td><td><input type="text"
                   name="email"/></td></tr>
               <tr><td>Phone</td><td><input type="text"
                   name="phone"/></td></tr>
```

EXAMPLE A.3 (CONTINUED)

```
            <tr><td>Bio</td><td><textarea rows="15" cols="60"
                name="bio"></textarea></td></tr>
            <tr><td colspan="2"><input type="submit"
                name="submit" value="Submit"/></td></tr>
        </table>
    </form>
    <? include("admin_footer.php") ?>
```

EXPLANATION

1 This SQL statement is used to insert a new artist into the "Artist" table.
2 Make sure the host, username, and password are supplied for the `mysql_connect()` function.
3 The `mysql_query()` function sends the SQL statement to the database, and if it fails, displays the MySQL error and dies. Otherwise, the new record has been inserted.
4 Figure A.3 displays the `admin_artist_insert.php` form.

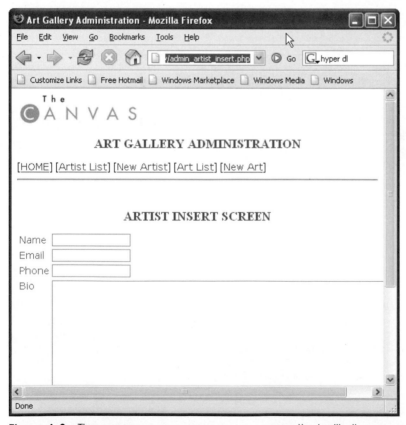

Figure A.3 The `admin_artist_insert.php` page that will allow a new artist to be added to the Gallery.

Adding and/or Editing a Piece of Art (admin_art_edit.php).   The page for adding a new art piece is slightly different from the pages previously shown where one page added a new artist and another page updated an existing artist. The process of inserting and updating a new piece of art is handled on a single page. A drop-down menu will present the user with a list of artists from which to choose. The art is linked to the artist who owns it by the artist's ID, id in the "Artist" table and a foreign key in the "Art" table, artist_id, a one-to-many relationship in which one artist can have multiple pieces of art. The drop-down menu displays a list of artists by name and the value of the option is the artist's ID (see Example A.4).

EXAMPLE A.4

(Section of the page source to view the drop-down menu after an artist, Laura Blair, was checked)

```
<table>
    <tr><td colspan="2"><b>Please enter the art
        title.<br></b><br><br></td></tr>
    <tr><td>Title</td><td><input type="text" name="title"
        value="" /></td></tr>
    <tr><td>Artist</td>
        <td><select name="artist_id">
        <option value="">Please Select</option>
        <option value="10"  >Todd Brown</option>
        <option value="11"  >stuART Sheldon</option>
        <option value="12"  >Elliott Easterling</option>
        <option value="13"  selected="SELECTED"  >Laura Blair</option>
        </select></td>
    </tr>
```

After selecting an artist from the drop-down list (line 5 in Example A.5), the page simply checks whether the art ID has been set. If it has, the matching art record is selected for update (line 1). Otherwise, the script inserts a new record (line 2) into the database and the database determines the new ID.

EXAMPLE A.5

(The admin_art_edit.php page)

```
<?php
extract($_REQUEST);

mysql_connect("localhost", "root", "password")
    or die(mysql_error());
mysql_select_db("test")
    or die(mysql_error());
```

EXAMPLE A.5 (CONTINUED)

```
      if( isset($submit) ) {    // If form has been submitted
         $status = "";
         if( $title=="" ) {    // Must provide an art title
            $status = "Please enter the art title.<br>";
         } else {
            // Connect to the database and insert the new art
            if( isset( $id) && $id!="" ) {    // Update art for artist
1              $sql = "UPDATE Art SET title='$title', " .
               "price='$price',
               description='$description',
               image='$image', artist_id='$artist_id'" .
               "WHERE id='$id'";
            } else {    // Insert new art for artist
2              $sql = "INSERT INTO Art (title, price,
                  description, image, artist_id ) ".
                  "VALUES ('$title', '$price', '$description',
                  '$image', '$artist_id' )";
            }

            mysql_query( $sql )
               or die(mysql_error());
            $status = "SUCCESSFULLY updated $title";
         }
      } elseif ( isset($id) ) {    // If id is set, but form has not
                                   // been submitted

         $sql = "SELECT Art.title, Art.description, Art.price,
            Art.image, Art.artist_id
3           FROM Art, Artist WHERE Art.artist_id=Artist.id
            AND Art.id='$id'";
         $resultset = mysql_query( $sql )  // Get all art for an artist
            or die(mysql_error());
         $row = mysql_fetch_assoc( $resultset );
         extract( $row );

      } else {
         $id=""; $title=""; $description=""; $price=""; $image="";
            $artist_id=0;
      }

      ?>
      <? include("admin_header.php") ?>

      <h1>Art Update Screen</h1>

4     <form action="<?=$_SERVER['PHP_SELF']?>" method="get">
      <input type="hidden" name="id" value="<?=$id?>">
      <table>
```

EXAMPLE A.5 (CONTINUED)

```
<? if (isset($status)) {?>
    <tr><td colspan="2"><b><?=$status?></b><br><br></td></tr>
<? } ?>
    <tr><td>Title</td><td><input type="text" name="title"
        value="<?=$title?>" /></td></tr>
    <tr><td>Artist</td>
5       <td><select name="artist_id">
    <option value="">Please Select</option>
<?php
6   $sql = "SELECT * FROM Artist";
    $resultset = mysql_query( $sql )or die(mysql_error());
    while( $artist = mysql_fetch_assoc( $resultset ) ) {
7       if ( $artist['id'] == $artist_id )
            $check=" selected=\"SELECTED\" ";
        else $check="";
        print '<option value="' . $artist['id'] .
            "\" $check >" . $artist['name']
            . "</option>\n";
    }
?>
</select></td>
</tr>
8   <tr><td>Description</td><td><textarea rows="10" cols="60"
    name="description"
    value="<?=$description?>"
    ><?=$description?></textarea></td></tr>
    <tr><td>Price</td><td><input type="text" name="price"
        value="<?=$price?>" /></td></tr>
    <tr><td>Image</td><td><input type="text" name="image"
        value="<?=$image?>" />
    <small>(Path to the file relative to the root of the
        Web site)</small></td></tr>
    <tr><td colspan="2"><input type="submit" name="submit"
9       value="Submit"/></td></tr>

</table>
</form>
<? include("admin_footer.php") ?>
```

EXPLANATION

1   If a title for the art piece was provided (see Figure A.4) by clicking a link in the
    admin_art_list.php file, a SQL UPDATE statement is prepared for an artist based
    on his or her id.

2   If a new title has been provided directly into the form, a new art piece for an artist
    can be inserted into the "Art" table.

3   The art for an artist is retrieved from the "Art" table where the id in both the "Art"
    and "Artist" tables are the same as the ID selected by the user.

EXPLANATION (CONTINUED)

4   The form for this page starts here. The `id` for the artist is stored in a hidden field.

5   A drop-down select menu starts here.

6   A table is created, as shown in Figure A.4, that contains a drop-down menu with each of the artist's names. See source in Example A.4. The value of the option is the artist's `id`. After the user selects an artist, the checked option value will contain the `id` of the artist.

7   When fetching the fields for a particular artist from the MySQL result-set, the artist `id` from the database is matched against the artist ID selected by the user.

8   This part of the table is where the description, price, and image location are filled in either for update or for inserting a new piece of art.

9   The form will be submitted here.

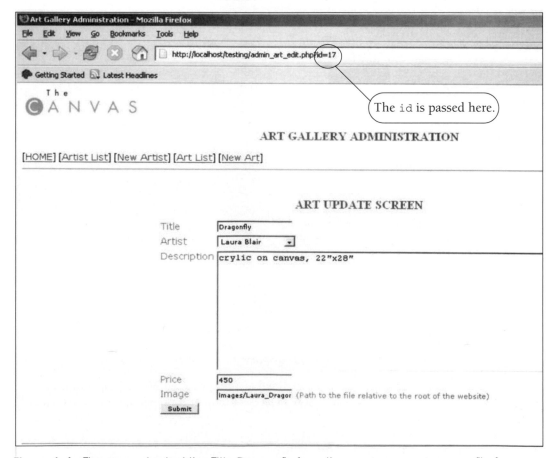

Figure A.4   The user selected the Title Dragonfly from the `admin_art_list.php` file for update. (Note the `id` is passed in the URL.)

A.3.3   Public Pages

The public pages are the pages a user can view without being required to log in. The public pages for the Art Gallery are are `index.php`, `artist_detail.php`, and `contact.php`. All these pages include `header.php` and `footer.php` at the beginning and at the end of the page.

The Header Page (header.php).   The `header.php` page is an HTML page included to provide the navigation menu, consisting of links to the other pages for the site (see Example A.6 and Figure A.5). Typically, the links to the administration section would not be included for security reasons, but we include them here for this demo Web site to make it easier to navigate between the private and public pages. Session data verifies whether or not the user has successfully logged in, and if not, redirects him or her to a login page called `admin_login.php`, discussed in detail in Chapter 16, "Cookies and Sessions."

EXAMPLE   A.6

```
<html>
<head>
<title>The Canvas Gallery, San Francisco Art Gallery, Music Club,
    Bar, and Restaurant, Open Mic, Poetry, Film</title>
<meta http-equiv="Content-Type" content="text/html;
    charset="iso-8859-1">
<link href="style.css" rel="stylesheet" type="text/css">
</head>

<body bgcolor="#FFFFFF" leftmargin="0" topmargin="0"
    marginwidth="0" marginheight="0"

<table cellSpacing=0 cellPadding=0 align=center border=0
    borderColor="#CCCCCC" width="563"
    <tr>
        <td><br><IMG src="header.jpg" border="0"
        <div align="left">
        [<a href="index.php">HOME</a>]
        [<a href="contact.php">Contact Us</a>]
        [<a href="admin_artist_list.php">Administration</a>]
        </div>
        </td>
    </tr>
    <tr>
        <td width="100%"><font face="Verdana, Arial, Helvetica,
                                sans-serif"><br>
```

Figure A.5   The `header.php` page.

The Index Page (index.php).   The initial public page is `index.php` (see Figure A.6). This page will be opened by default when the user comes to the Canvas Gallery Web site. The SQL `SELECT` statement (see line 1 in Example A.7) retrieves all the information for each artist by name, in sorted order, from the database. A function called `art_for_artist` is called for each record and is passed the `id` of the artist. Art for each artist is selected (line 3) and limited to one piece of art for each artist. That piece of art is returned by the function and used as the image to display with the artist's information.

If the user clicks the artist's name, the hyperlink will pass along the `id` of the artist and send it to another page called by `artist_detail.php` (line 5). If the user clicks the link with the artist's e-mail address, a "mailto" box will appear where an e-mail message can be composed and sent to the artist (line 6).

EXAMPLE A.7

```php
    <?php
1   $sql = "SELECT * FROM Artist ORDER BY name";
    mysql_connect("localhost", "root", "password")
        or die(mysql_error());
    mysql_select_db("test") or die(mysql_error());
    $recordset = mysql_query( $sql ) or die(mysql_error());
2   function art_for_artist( $artist_id ) {
3       $sql = "SELECT * FROM Art WHERE artist_id='$artist_id'
            LIMIT 1;";
        $recordset = mysql_query( $sql ) or die(mysql_error());
        $row = mysql_fetch_assoc( $recordset);
        return $row['image'];
    }
    ?>
    <? include("header.php") ?>
    <h1>Welcome To The Canvas Gallery</h1>
    <p> Welcome to The Canvas Gallery. Please choose an artist from
    the list below to view the details. </p>
    <table cellpadding="15">
    <?
    while( $row=mysql_fetch_assoc($recordset) ) {
4       $image = art_for_artist( $row["id"] );
```

EXAMPLE A.7 (CONTINUED)

```
5       print '<tr><td><a href="artist_detail.php?id='. $row['id'].
            '"><img src="'.$image.'" width="150"
            border="0"><br></td>';
        print '<td><strong><a href="artist_detail.php?id='
            . $row["id"]. '">'
            .$row["name"] .'</a></strong><br>' .
6           $row["phone"] ."<br><a href=\"mailto:\"".
            $row["email"] ."\">". $row["email"] ."</a>\n";
        print "</td></tr>\n";
    }
    ?>
    </table>
    <? include("footer.php") ?>
```

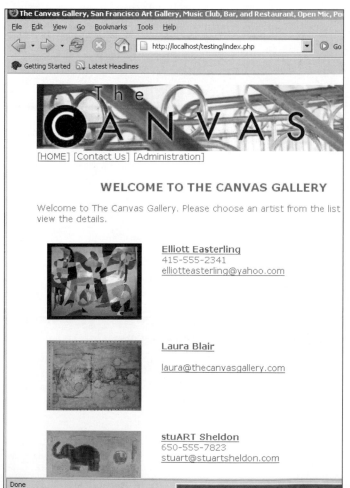

Figure A.6
The `index.php` page
(default page).

The Detail Page (artist_detail.php). The link to the atist's detail page (see Figure A.7) contains the ID of the particular artist so that page can determine what artist was requested. The first SQL statement (see line 1 in Example A.8) selects all the information about the selected artist by his or her `id` number to be displayed on the page (line 2) with the artist's name centered over the text area containing his or her bio information, and under that his or her e-mail address as a link, and his phone number. The next SQL statement (line 2) links the art to the artist and retrieves all the art information for the selected artist by joining the two tables based on the artist's `id`. If the art has an image(s) associated with it, the image(s) (line 6) will be displayed below the other information about the art, such as the name or price (line 7). All of the artwork for the artist is displayed at the bottom of the page.

EXAMPLE A.8

```php
    <?php
    extract($_REQUEST);
    mysql_connect("localhost", "root", "password")
        or die(mysql_error());
    mysql_select_db("test")
        or die(mysql_error());

1   $sql = "SELECT * from Artist WHERE id='$id'";
    $resultset = mysql_query( $sql )or die(mysql_error());
    $row = mysql_fetch_assoc( $resultset );
    extract( $row );

    ?>
    <? include("header.php") ?>
    <h1><?=$name?></h1>

2   <table width="100%">
        <tr><td colspan="2"><?=$bio?><br><br></td></tr>
        <tr><td>Email <a href="mailto:<?=$email?>">
            <?=$email?></a></td></tr>
        <tr><td>Phone <?=$phone?></td></tr>
        <tr><td colspan="2"><hr><br></td></tr>
    <?
3   $sql = "SELECT Art.id, Art.title, Art.price, Art.image,
        Art.description, Artist.name ". "FROM Art Art,
        Artist Artist " . "WHERE Artist.id='$id' AND
        Artist.id=Art.artist_id";
    $recordset = mysql_query( $sql ) or die(mysql_error());
    ?>
    <?
4   while( $row=mysql_fetch_assoc($recordset) ) {
5       print "<tr><td><h2>".$row['title']."</h2>\$"
            .number_format($row['price'],2);
        print "<br>" .$row['description'];
```

EXAMPLE A.8 (CONTINUED)

```
        // Display the image if one exists
6       if ( isset($row['image']) && $row['image'] != "" ) {
            print '<br><br><img src="'. $row['image']
                . '" align="center">';
        }
        print "<br><br><hr></td></tr>\n";
    }
    ?>
</table>
<? include("footer.php") ?>
```

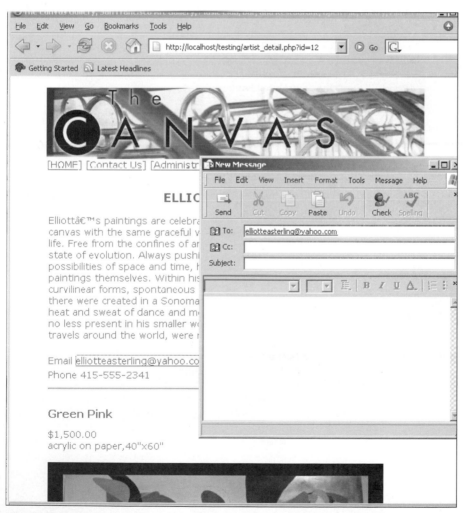

Figure A.7 The `artist_detail.php` page. (The ID of this artist is 12, as shown in the URL.)

The Contact Us Page (contact.php).   Finally, the Contact Us page (see Figure A.8), `contact.php`, asks the user to enter the contact information in a form and submit it. After the user clicks the submit button, the data is formatted and e-mailed to the administrator of the Web site, *manager@The CanvasGallery.com* (see line 1 in Example A.9), as well as a copy to the user to confirm that the e-mail was sent (line 2). This page also displays the status information confirming that the e-mail has been sent (line 3).

EXAMPLE A.9

```php
      <?php
      extract($_REQUEST);

      if(isset($submit)) {
          $body = "\r\nContact Requested:\r\n\r\n $Name\r\n ".
                  "$Phone\r\n $Email\r\n $Message\r\n";
1         mail( "manager@TheCanvasGallery.com", "Contact Form",
              $body, "From: form@TheCanvasGallery.com" );
2         mail( $Email, "Contact Form", $body,
              "From: form@TheCanvasGallery.com" );
3         $status = '<br><strong><font color="red">'.
              'Your message has been sent. Thank you!</font><br><br>';
      }

      ?>
      <? include("header.php") ?>

      <h1>Contact Us</h1>

      <?=$status?>

      <p> Please fill out your contact information and we will contact
      you within 24 hours. </p>

      <form>
      <table cellpadding="5">
          <tr><td>Name</td><td><input type="text" name="Name"></td></tr>
          <tr><td>Phone</td><td><input type="text"
              name="Phone"></td></tr>
          <tr><td>Email</td><td><input type="text"
              name="Email"></td></tr>
          <tr><td>Message</td><td><textarea name="Message"
              rows="5"></textarea></td></tr>
          <tr><td> </td><td><input type="submit" name="submit"
              value="Send"></td></tr>
      </table>
      </form>

      <? include("footer.php") ?>
```

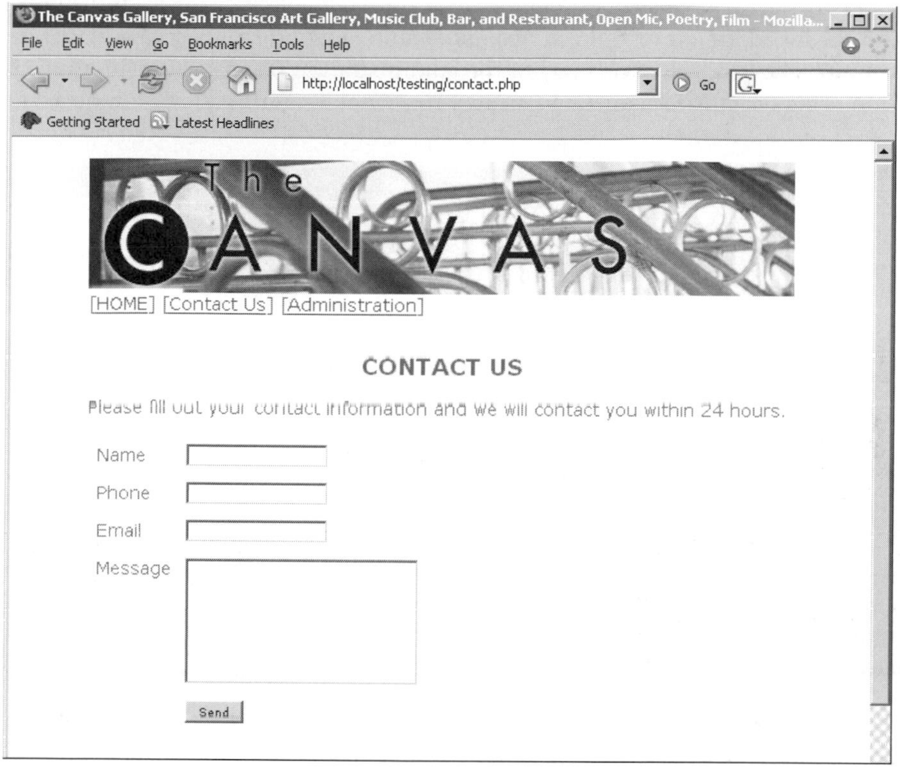

Figure A.8 The `contact.php` page.

A.3.4 Securing Pages with Login

To secure the administration pages from unauthorized access, we require the user to log in. Because every administration page will include the `admin_header.php`, this is a good place to check if the user has already logged in.

The following example script is taken from `admin_header.php`, which starts the session and gets the value of the variable `'authorized'`. If this value is not `'yes'`, the script redirects the user to the `admin_login.php` page.

```
EXAMPLE  A.10
        <?php
        session_start();
        // Check if the user is logged in
        if( !isset($_SESSION['authorized']) || $_SESSION['authorized']
            != 'yes' ) {
            header( "Location: admin_login.php" );
            exit();
        }
        ?>
```

The `admin_login.php` page (see Figure A.9) prompts the user to log in. If the user-name and password are correct, the script puts value `'yes'` for the variable `'autho-rized'` so that the user can access any of the administration pages for the duration of the session. This script is explained in Chapter 16, "Cookies and Sessions," in detail.

EXAMPLE A.11

```php
<?php
extract($_REQUEST);
if( isset($login) && $login=="admin" &&
        isset($password) && $password="guess" ) {
    session_start();
    $_SESSION['authorized'] = 'yes';
    header( "Location: admin_artist_list.php" );
    exit();
}
?>

<html>
<head><title>Art Gallery Administration</title>
<link href="style.css" rel="stylesheet" type="text/css">
</head>
<body align="center">
<img src="images/CanvasLogo-plain.gif"><br>
<h1>Art Gallery Administration</h1>
<center>
<h1>Please Login</h1>
<small>(Use 'admin' and 'guess' for login and password)<br>
    <br></small>
<form>
<table>
    <tr><td>Login:</td><td><input type="text"
        name="login"></td></tr>
    <tr><td>Password:</td><td><input type="password"
        name="password"></td></tr>
    <tr><td> </td><td><input type="submit"
        value="Login"></td></tr>
</table>
</form>
</center>
</html>
```

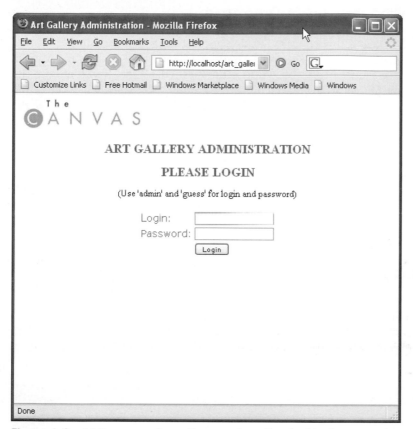

Figure A.9 At the same time, the user is redirected to the page to administer the list of artists.

A.4 Installing the Art Gallery

To install the art gallery on your computer, you must have successfully installed and configured PHP and MySQL.

A.4.1 Where to Find the Files for the Canvas Gallery Site

To install the PHP files on your computer, unzip and copy the entire art gallery directory into your Web root—the default directory that is opened when you go to *http://localhost/* on your computer. The files can all be found on the CD.

A.4.2 Installing the MySQL Database

Next, you need to install the database. To do this, log into MySQL using either the `mysql.exe` command prompt (as shown in Figure A.10) or a GUI such as the MySQL Query Browser (see Figure A.11). We will use the "test" database. If you choose the `gallerydb.sql` script to populate the database (see Figure A.12), there will be no initial data, and you will be responsible for adding the artists and their art work. If you use the `db.sql` script, you will be provided with some demo art and artists.

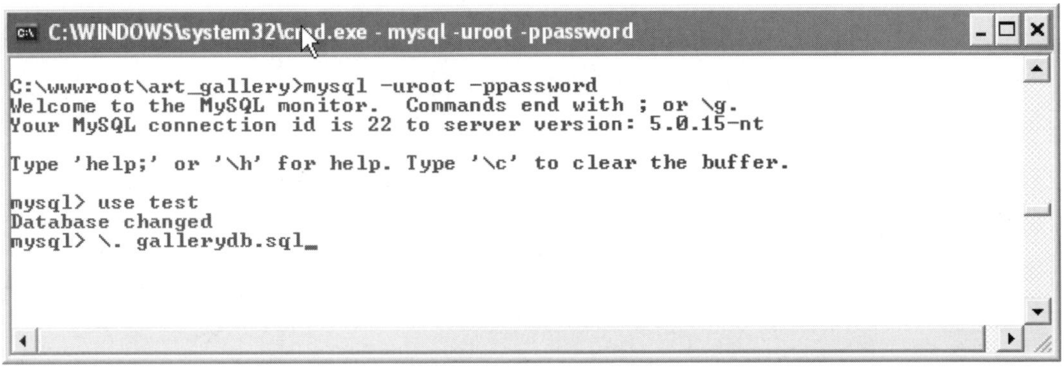

```
C:\WINDOWS\system32\cmd.exe - mysql -uroot -ppassword          _ □ ×

C:\wwwroot\art_gallery>mysql -uroot -ppassword
Welcome to the MySQL monitor.  Commands end with ; or \g.
Your MySQL connection id is 22 to server version: 5.0.15-nt

Type 'help;' or '\h' for help. Type '\c' to clear the buffer.

mysql> use test
Database changed
mysql> \. gallerydb.sql_
```

Figure A.10 Logging into the MySQL "test" database.

EXAMPLE A.12

```
1   mysql> use test;
    Database changed
    mysql> \. db.sql
    Query OK, 0 rows affected, 1 warning (0.00 sec)
    Query OK, 0 rows affected (0.02 sec)
    Query OK, 0 rows affected, 1 warning (0.00 sec)
    Query OK, 0 rows affected (0.00 sec)
    Query OK, 17 rows affected (0.03 sec)
    Records: 17  Duplicates: 0  Warnings: 0

    Query OK, 0 rows affected (0.00 sec)
    Query OK, 0 rows affected, 1 warning (0.02 sec)
    Query OK, 0 rows affected, 1 warning (0.00 sec)
    Query OK, 0 rows affected (0.00 sec)
    Query OK, 0 rows affected, 1 warning (0.00 sec)
    Query OK, 0 rows affected (0.00 sec)
    Query OK, 4 rows affected (0.00 sec)
    Records: 4  Duplicates: 0  Warnings: 0

    Query OK, 0 rows affected (0.00 sec)
    Query OK, 0 rows affected, 1 warning (0.00 sec)
```

EXAMPLE   A.12 (CONTINUED)

```
mysql> show tables in test;
+----------------+
| Tables_in_test |
+----------------+
| art            |
| artist         |
| messages       |
| register       |
| te             |
+----------------+
5 rows in set (0.00 sec)
mysql>
```

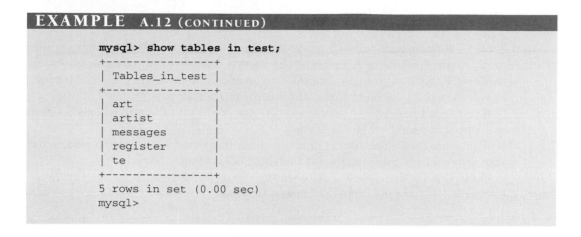

Figure A.11
Using the Query Browser, rather than
the `mysql.exe` command prompt.

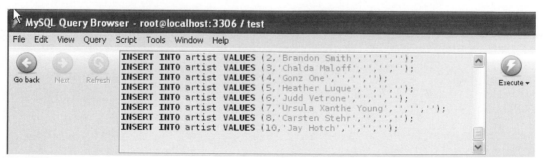

Figure A.12   Once you log in, you could simply copy and paste the contents of the
`gallerydb.sql` file into the SQL field and click the Execute button.

A.4.3   Editing the PHP Pages

The art gallery application assumes that the data is stored in the MySQL database called "test", that the username is root, and the password is password root running on the localhost. If this is not the case, you will have to update all the pages presented here and change the `mysql_connect()` parameters at the top of each page.

If you do not have `short_tabs` set to "On" in the `php.ini` file, you will need to start each php script with: `<?php`

If your images are not loading properly, check that they are located in a place where your server recognizes them, usually under the document root directory.

Once this is done, you can open up your browser and go to *http://localhost/art_gallery/* and the list of the artists will appear.

A.5   Conclusion

The purpose of presenting the Canvas Gallery Web project was to give you a chance to see the features of both PHP and MySQL working together as a team as described in Chapter 15, "PHP and MySQL Integration." Although there is much that could be added to this site, it serves as an example to demonstrate how to organize the pages and to use what you have learned to build a working, viable Web site.

appendix

B

PHP and E-Mail

B.1 The Mail Server

For a PHP script to be able to send e-mail, it must be able to talk to a *mail server* that is willing to accept its request and deliver the e-mail to the Internet.

A mail server, sometimes referred to as the Simple Mail Transfer Protocol (SMTP) server, is a software process that takes an e-mail message for delivery and forwards it to other mail servers on the Internet until the message reaches its final destination.

To set up PHP to talk to your mail server, first you must know the IP or the Internet address of your mail server. Typically, your local Internet Service Provider (ISP) will provide this information to you. The mail server for SBC DSL, for example, is *mail.sbcglobal.net*. Next, you need to update the SMTP property in the `php.ini` file to point to this server. The default value of this property is `localhost` because all UNIX-based machines already have a mail server installed locally at IP address 127.0.0.1. Windows, on the other hand, does not have a local mail server set up by default.

In the past, any mail server would accept a request to deliver any message by anyone to anyone. However, because spammers abused this loophole, almost all mail servers are protected now, the most common protection being a mail server, provided by an ISP, that will only accept messages originating from its own network.

Some ISPs require that the mail server request a login and password. If this is the case, you can use the mail function provided by PHP Extension and Application Library (PEAR). PEAR's Mail package defines an interface and functions for sending e-mail. See *http://pear.php.net/package/Mail*. You always have the option of setting up your own mail server to take delivery requests, a topic outside the scope of this book.

B.2   MIME (Multipurpose Internet Mail Extensions)

MIME, as the name implies was an extension to the e-mail standard protocol for sending e-mail messages. In the early days of the Internet, e-mail messages consisted of plain text. The extension allowed e-mail content to contain HTML tags embedded in the message text, images, links, graphics, and logos, as well as e-mail attachments. Most e-mail messages sent today use MIME.

An e-mail containing different types of content, such as HTML text and images, is called a *multipart* MIME message. When setting up this type of e-mail, the content type and encoding type is sent in MIME headers as you will see in the following examples.

B.3   Runtime Configuration Options

The following list describes all e-mail–related properties in the `php.ini` configuration file.

SMTP (Simple Mail Transfer Protocol)
This is the main property for e-mail. It specifies where the server is that will accept and deliver the messages sent from a PHP program. By default it is set to `localhost`, which will work on most UNIX-based systems, but can be configured to point to your local ISP's mail server.

smtp_port
The SMTP port is, in most cases, port 25, the default value. The SMTP standard specifies that all SMTP servers must use port 25 for incoming mail. In most situations, you should not change this property or you might not be able to receive incoming mail from the Internet.

sendmail_from
If you are relying on sendmail, a local program on UNIX-based systems to deliver e-mail, you can specify your default "From" value for your messages in this field. By default it is empty.

sendmail_path
This property is used to set up the path to the local sendmail program. It is typically a path such as */usr/sbin/sendmail* or */usr/lib/sendmail* on UNIX systems.

B.4   The mail() Function

The built-in PHP mail function makes sending e-mail quite simple. It uses the following format.

FORMAT

```
bool mail ( string to, string subject, string message [,
string additional_headers [, string additional_parameters]] )
```

Example:
```
mail ( "joe@joesite.com", "Contact Us Form", "This is an email from
your site", "From: marko@markosite.com" )
```

The mail() function returns TRUE if the message was delivered to the mail server successfully, FALSE otherwise.

The arguments can be broken down as follows:

to:	The reciever(s). If multiple, then comma-separated. Must be in format such as: user@example.com user@example.com, anotheruser@example.com User <user@example.com> User <user@example.com>, Another User <anotheruser@example.com>
subject:	Subject of the message.
message:	The actual text of the message.
additional_headers (optional):	If specified, it will be passed in the header of the message. Might alter the behavior of the reader when rendering the message (such as when using HTML in the message).
additional_parameters (optional):	Used to pass additional parameters to the mail server. The use of this feature heavily depends on the particular mail server version.

B.5   Sending a Simple E-Mail Message

In the following example, PHP sends a simple e-mail message. In this example, the data is supplied, but you might want to use an HTML form to submit the information from a Web page, validate the form fields, and then send e-mail based on user input.

EXAMPLE B.1

```php
        <?php

1       $Recipient = "marko@marakana.com";
2       $MsgSubject = "Message subject";

        // You must set sender through message header
3       $MsgHeader = "From: Joe Smith <joe@yahoo.com>\r\n";
4       $MsgBody = "Message body.";
5       mail($Recipient, $MsgSubject, $MsgBody, $MsgHeader);
        ?>
```

EXPLANATION

1   First a standard e-mail address specifies where the mail is to be sent.
2   This is the subject of the e-mail message.
3   The From part of the e-mail specifies the complete name as an e-mail header. E-mail messages have headers just like Web pages. The format of this line is redefined by the e-mail standard (RFC 822), so you must use that format. You can change the sender name and the e-mail address. The \r (carriage return) is required by most e-mail servers for legacy reasons.
4   The message body is just text with no real size limit.
5   This line causes the e-mail to be sent. For this to work, you must have an SMTP server available to you and have the php.ini file properly configured. See "The Mail Server" on page 809.

The e-mail message will look like that shown in Figure B.1. Notice that the Subject, From, and To fields correspond to the values entered in the PHP script. (This script does not output any HTML data to the browser—you will get a black page on running it.)

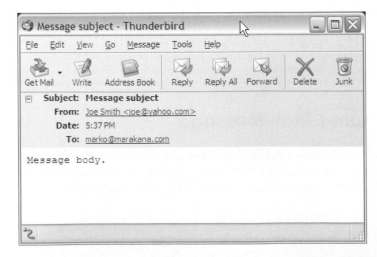

Figure B.1
Sending an e-mail.

B.6   Example: Sending an HTML Message

Sending an HTML message is very similar to sending a plain text message. The advantage of sending an HTML e-mail message is that you can gain greater control over the presentation of the message by including hyperlinks, images, tables, colors, fonts, and so on.

The important difference between sending plain text and HMTL text is in the message header. Headers are meta-information passed to the mail server to tell it how to treat the message; for example, what type of content is being sent, or which encoding is used. These headers are similar to the HTML headers used to redirect the user to another Web site. Because this e-mail includes HTML text and or images, sound, and so on, it is formatted using the MIME format. This type of e-mail includes three extra headers:

1. MIME-Version
2. Content-Type
3. Content-Transfer-Encoding

The message body consists of plain text and HTML tags, images, links, and so on.

EXAMPLE B.2

```php
    <?php
1   $Recipient = "marko@marakana.com";
2   $MsgSubject = "Message subject";

    // You must set a sender through message header
3   $MsgHeader = "From: Joe Smith <joe@yahoo.com>\r\n";

    // These two lines are required
4   $MsgHeader .= "MIME-Version: 1.0\n";
5   $MsgHeader .= "Content-type: text/html; charset=us-ascii\n";

    // Message body is HTML
6   $MsgBody = "
    <html>
        <head>
            <title>HTML message</title>
        </head>
        <body>
            <h2>Congratulations!</h2>
            <p>You have just learned how to send an HTML message</p>
        </body>
    </html>";

7   mail($Recipient, $MsgSubject, $MsgBody, $MsgHeader);
    ?>
```

1   The recipient or receiver of the e-mail is set up as a standard e-mail address.
2   This text is the subject of the message.
3   The message header specifies who the message is coming from. The format is specified by a standard (RFC 822).
4   This line adds some more header information. It specifies that the message is using MIME types.
5   This line specifies that the MIME type of this e-mail is HTML and that the encoding is in the U.S. ASCII standard. Lines 4 and 5 state that the content of the message is HTML and should be rendered as such.
6   The message body is specified here and is just text and plain HTML.
7   The `mail()` function sends the e-mail to the mail server, and the message is sent.

The e-mail message will look like that shown in Figure B.2. Notice that the content of the message is HTML this time and not just the plain text.

Figure B.2
An HTML e-mail.

B.6.1   Sending a Message with an Attachment

An e-mail message sent with an attachment consists of different types of content, called a multipart MIME message. The message is divided into at least two parts, one for the message and one for the attachment. To allow this type of e-mail to be sent, the MIME Content-Type header must be specified as multipart/mixed to identify the different parts, called *chunks*, of the e-mail message. This allows the e-mail program to read the separate parts correctly. Each part has its own type of content and will need its own headers to identify that content. The different parts are separated by a boundary parameter, a user-defined unique word enclosed in two hyphens.

In the following example, an HTML message will be sent with an attachment included. The content of the attachment is read from a file, and converted to an encoding format that allows it to be transferred by the mail program. The HTML message and the attachment text are divided into two parts and sent as multipart/mixed content separated by a boundary and each containing its own MIME headers.

EXAMPLE B.3

```php
    <?php
    // Reading file content
1   $FilePathName = "/tmp/golden_gate.gif"; // e.g. /tmp/myapp/file.gz
2   $FileName = "golden_gate.gif"; // just file.gz
3   $FileHandle = fopen($FilePathName, "rb");
4   $FileContent = fread($FileHandle, filesize($FilePathName));
5   fclose($FileHandle);


    // Encode file content
6   $AttachmentData = chunk_split(base64_encode($FileContent));


    // Message text
7   $MsgHTMLPart = "
    <html>
        <head>
            <title>HTML message with attachment</title>
        </head>
        <body>
            <h2>Congratulations!</h2>
            <p>You have just learned how to send an HTML message
            with attachment</p>
        </body>
    </html>
    ";


    // Forming message
    $Recipient = "marko@marakana.com";
    $MsgSubject = "Golden Gate Bridge";


    // You must set sender through message header
    $MsgHeader = "From: Joe Smith <joe@yahoo.com>\n";


    // These two lines mark message as multipart
8   $MsgHeader .= "MIME-Version: 1.0\n";
9   $MsgHeader .= "Content-Type: multipart/mixed; boundary=\"
        --NSD35F65YGsgrg3--\"";
```

EXAMPLE   B.3 (CONTINUED)

```
        // First part begins
        $MsgBody = "
10  --NSD35F65YGsgrg3--
11  Content-Type: text/html; charset=us-ascii
12  Content-Transfer-Encoding: 8bit\n";

13  $MsgBody .= $MsgHTMLPart;


        // Second part begins
        $MsgBody .= "
14  --NSD35F65YGsgrg3--
15  Content-Type: application/octet-stream; name=\"" . $FileName . "\"
16  Content-Transfer-Encoding: base64
17  Content-Disposition: attachment; filename=\"" . $FileName
        . "\"\n\n";

18  $MsgBody .= $AttachmentData;

        // Message ends
19  $MsgBody .= "\n--NSD35F65YGsgrg3--\n";

        // Sending message
20  mail($Recipient, $MsgSubject, $MsgBody, $MsgHeader);


    ?>
```

EXPLANATION

1   This line defines the full path to the file on the local file system that will be sent as an e-mail attachment. You can open the file from the local file system or upload it, but in either case the file is read and later encoded for e-mail transfer.

2   This is the name of the file that will be attached. It is an image file.

3   The `fopen()` function, as you recall, returns a handle to the file and opens it for reading in binary mode (`rb`).

4   The `fread()` function reads in the content of the image file and stores it in a variable.

5   The filehandle is closed.

6   After converting the file to base64_encoded text (to match the RFC 2045 formatting standard), the file data is split into smaller chunks. The `chunk_split()` function inserts end (defaults to `\r\n`) every 76 characters. It returns the new string, leaving the original string untouched.

7   The e-mail message is created.

8   This message will be using MIME data encoding as part of the header.

9   This message has multiple parts. One part will be the message itself, and the other will be the attachment. The required boundary used to separate the two parts of the e-mail is specified as: `--NSD35F65YGsgrg3--`. Two dashes are required on either side of the boundary.

10   The e-mail reader on the user end uses this boundary to determine what part of the message is the attachment and what part is plain text.

11   The first part of the message is HTML.

12   The encoding used is the standard 8-bit U.S. ASCII encoding.

13   Next, the HTML part is appended to the message body. We are basically assembling a valid multipart message one part at a time.

14   The boundary is sent as output again, this time for the attachment.

15   The binary data (attachment files) is of content type application/octet-stream, a binary file, that cannot be viewed in a text-based client, such as an image, spreadsheet, or Microsoft Word document. The name of the file is also specified.

16   Typical binary encoding is base64.

17   This line tells the e-mail reader that this part of the e-mail is the attachment.

18   After the headers are set for the attachment part of the mail, all that remains is adding the e-mail message.

19   We end the message with the same boundary we used to indicate the start and stop of each multipart.

20   Finally, the message is sent using the built-in PHP `mail()` function.

The e-mail sent by this script follows in Figure B.3. Notice that there is an attachment in this e-mail. Some e-mail programs might display the attachment directly in the message. This depends on the configuration in the user's e-mail program.

Figure B.3   The e-mail message is sent.

appendix

PHP and Date/Time

Working with dates and time is reasonably easy, but can be quite complex when dealing with different time zones, Daylight Saving Time, and so on. PHP offers a range of functions to handle date and time, and many of these functions use the UNIX timestamp, the number of seconds since July 1, 1970, 00:00:00 GMT, also called *the epoch*.

We cover some of the functions that deal with the timestamps and those that are used to format the date and time. If you are just interested in formatting the date and time, the easiest way to get formatted date strings is with the date() and the strftime() functions.

C.1 Formatting Dates and Times

C.1.1 The date() Function

The date() function is used to format a local time, date, or both. It returns a formatted string based on formatting options. The time is the timestamp on your computer and defaults to the value of time(), a function that returns the number of seconds since January 1, 1970, GMT. The options for date() are shown in Table C.1.

FORMAT

```
string date ( string format [, int timestamp] )
```

Example:
```
date("M d, Y"); Outputs:  July 04, 2006
```

Table C.1 Date and Time Formatting Options

Option	Description
a	am or pm
A	AM or PM
B	Swatch Internet time
d	Day of the month, two digits with leading zeros (i.e., 01 to 31)
D	Day of the week in text, three letters (e.g., Mon for Monday)
F	Month in text (e.g., January)
g	Hour, 12-hour format without leading zeros (i.e., 1 to 12)
G	Hour, 24-hour format without leading zeros (i.e., 0 to 23)
h	Hour, 12-hour format with leading zeros (i.e., 01 to 12)
H	Hour, 24-hour format (i.e., 00 to 23)
i	Minutes with leading zeros (e.g., 00 to 59)
I	1 if Daylight Savings Time, 0 if not
j	Day of the month without leading zeros (i.e., 1 to 31)
l	Day of the week in text (e.g., Friday)
L	1 if it is a leap year, 0 if not
m	Month with leading zeros (i.e., 04 to 11)
M	Month in text, three letters (e.g., Jul)
n	Month without leading zeros (e.g., 1 to 12)
r	RFC 822 formatted date (i.e., Thu, 21 Dec 2000 16:01:07 +0200)
s	Seconds with leading zeros (e.g., 00 to 59)
S	English ordinal suffix, textual, two characters (e.g., th, nd)
t	Number of days in the given month (i.e., 28 to 31)
T	Time zone setting of this machine (i.e., MDT)
U	Seconds since the epoch, January 1 1970 00:00:00 GMT
w	Day of the week, numeric (i.e., 0 [Sunday] to 6 [Saturday])
Y	Year, four digits (i.e., 2007)
y	Year, two digits (i.e., 07)
z	Day of the year (i.e., 0 to 365)
Z	Time zone offset in seconds (i.e., -43200 to 43200). The offset for time zones west of UTC is always negative, and for those east of UTC is always positive.

EXAMPLE C.1

```
<html><head><title>Using the date() Function</title></head>
<body bgcolor="lavender">
<font size="+1" face="verdana">
<?php
// Output for this example is displayed in Figure C.1
echo '1. <b>date("d-M-Y")</b> returns <em>',
    date("d-M-Y"),"</em><br>";

echo '2. <b>date("M/d/Y")</b> returns <em>',
    date("M/d/Y"),"</em><br>";

echo '3. <b>date("D dS M, Y h:i a")</b> returns <em>',
    date("D dS M, Y h:i a"),"</em><br>";

echo '4. <b>date("\T\h\e \\t\i\m\e \i\s: h:m a")</b> returns<em> ',
    date("\T\h\e \\t\i\m\e \i\s: h:m a"),"</em><br>";

echo '5. <b>date("\T\o\d\a\y \i\s: l")</b> returns <em>',
    date("\T\o\d\a\y \i\s: l"), "</em><br>";

?>
</font>
</body>
</html>
```

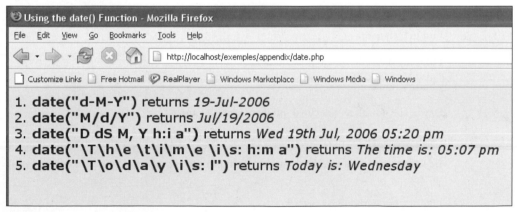

Figure C.1   Output of the `date()` function.

C.1.2 The strftime() Function

The `strftime()` function is also used to format the date and time (based on the locale settings), similar to the `date()` function but with different options. To get information on how to see the locale settings see *http://www.phpfreaks.com/phpmanual/page/function.setlocale.html*.

FORMAT

```
string strftime ( string format [, int timestamp] )
```

Example:
```
echo "Today is ", strftime("%A"),".\n";   // Today is Friday.
```

The conversion specifiers shown in Table C.2 are based on the current locale; for example, France, Japan, and so on.

Table C.2 Arguments for the `strftime()` Function

Format Character	What It Means
%a	Abbreviated weekday name
%A	Full weekday name
%b	Abbreviated month name
%B	Full month name
%c	Preferred date and time representation
%C	Century number
%d	Day of the month as a decimal number (range 01 to 31)
%D	Same as %m/%d/%y
%e	Day of the month as a decimal number, a single digit is preceded by a space (range " 1" to "31")
%g	Like %G, but without the century
%G	The four-digit year corresponding to the ISO week number (see %V)
%h	Same as %b
%H	Hour as a decimal number using a 24-hour clock (range 00 to 23)
%I	Hour as a decimal number using a 12-hour clock (range 01 to 12)

Table C.2 Arguments for the `strftime()` Function (continued)

Format Character	*What It Means*
`%j`	Day of the year as a decimal number (range `001` to `366`)
`%m`	Month as a decimal number (range `01` to `12`)
`%M`	Minute as a decimal number
`%n`	Newline character
`%p`	Either `am` or `pm` according to the current locale
`%r`	Time in a.m. and p.m. notation
`%R`	Time in 24-hour notation
`%S`	Second as a decimal number
`%t`	Tab character
`%T`	Current time, equal to `%H:%M:%S`
`%u`	Weekday as a decimal number (`1` to `7`), with `1` representing Monday
`%U`	Week number of the current year as a decimal number, starting with the first Sunday as the first day of the first week
`%V`	The ISO 8601:1988 week number of the current year as a decimal number (range `01` to `53`), where week 1 is the first week that has at least four days in the current year, and with Monday as the first day of the week
`%W`	Week number of the current year as a decimal number, starting with the first Monday as the first day of the first week
`%w`	Day of the week as a decimal, Sunday being `0`
`%x`	Preferred date representation for the current locale without the time
`%X`	Preferred time representation for the current locale without the date
`%y`	Year as a decimal number without a century (range `00` to `99`)
`%Y`	Year as a decimal number including the century
`%Z` or `%z`	Time zone or name or abbreviation
`%%`	A literal `%` character

EXAMPLE C.2

```
<?php
echo "Today in San Francisco it is ", strftime("%A, %x"),",
    " and the time is ", strftime("%X"),".\n";
/* Set locale to Sweden */
setlocale(LC_ALL, 'sw');

echo "In Stockholm the current date: ",
    strftime("%A %d %B %Y" ) ,"\n";

/* Set locale to France */
setlocale(LC_ALL, 'fr');
echo "In Paris the current date: ",
    strftime("%A %d %B %Y") ,"\n";
?>
```

(Output)
Today in San Francisco it is Friday, 07/21/06 and the time is
14:48:22.
In Stockholm the current date: fredag 21 juli 2006
In Paris the current date: vendredi 21 juillet 2006

C.2 Getting the Timestamp

How many days until Christmas? How long ago was your last birthday? When will the mortgage be paid off? You can use the timestamp functions to get the date and time for now, next month, last month, yesterday, and so on, and then convert the output (seconds) to a readable format with the `date()` and `strftime()` functions.

C.2.1 The time() Function

The `time()` function returns the current timestamp in seconds. (For a more accurate time you can use the `microtime()` function.) By adding or subtracting the number of seconds from the output of the `time()` function, you find the amount of time from now until some future or past time. The formulas in Table C.3 are used to convert seconds to minutes, hours, days, and so on.

Table C.3 Units of Time in Seconds

Unit of Time	Seconds
Minute	60
Hour	60 * 60

Table C.3 Units of Time in Seconds (continued)

Unit of Time	Seconds
Day	60 * 60 * 24
Week	60 * 60 * 24 * 7
Month	60 * 60 * 24 * 30
Year	60 * 60 * 24 * 365

FORMAT

```
Format:
int time ( void )
```

Example:
```
echo time(),"\n";
1153267124
```

EXAMPLE C.3

```php
<?php

echo time(),"\n";       // Now in seconds
print time() + (7 * 24 * 60 * 60);   // Next week in seconds
echo date("M-d-Y", time()),"\n";  // Today
echo date("M-d-Y", time() + (7 * 24 * 60 * 60)),"\n";  // Next week
echo date("M-d-Y", time() - (7 * 24 * 60 * 60)),"\n";  // Last week

?>

Output:
1153267504
1153872304
Jul-19-2006
Jul-26-2006
Jul-12-2006
```

C.2.2 The mktime() Function

This function returns the timestamp for a particular date. This timestamp is an integer containing the number of seconds between the UNIX epoch (January 1 1970 00:00:00 GMT) and the time specified in the argument list. This function is useful for calculating future and past dates and will automatically calculate the correct value for dates given to it that are out of range; for example, 7, 32, 2006 will be converted to 08, 01, 2006.

FORMAT

```
int mktime ( [int hour [, int minute [, int second [, int month [,
int day [, int year [, int is_dst]]]]]]] )
```

Example:
```php
<?php
    $seconds=mktime(0, 0, 0, 7, 19, 2007);
    print "$seconds\n"; //    1184828400
    echo date("M-d-Y", $seconds), "\n";   // Jul-19-2007
?>
```

The arguments can be omitted in any order from right to left, and the ones that are left out will be set to the value of the local date and time for that setting. The arguments are shown in Table C.4.

Table C.4   Arguments for the `mktime()` Function

Argument	Meaning
hour	Number of the hour
minute	Number of the minute
second	Number of seconds past the minute
month	Number of the month
day	Number of the day
year	Number of the year, can be a two- or four-digit value
is_dst	Daylight Saving Time; 0 if it is; 1 if not; –1 is the default

EXAMPLE C.4

```php
<?php
    echo date("M-d-Y", mktime(0, 0, 0, 7, 18, 2007)), "\n";
    echo date("M-d-Y", mktime(0, 0, 0, 1, 1, 07)), "\n";
    echo date("M-d-Y", mktime(0, 0, 0, 7, 32, 7 )), "\n";
?>

(Output)
Jul-18-2007
Jan-01-2007
Aug-01-2007
```

EXAMPLE C.4 (CONTINUED)

```
<html><head><title>Using the date() Function</title></head>
<body bgcolor="lavender">
<font size="+2" face="verdana">

<?php
    // See Figure C.2 for output of this example
    $today=mktime(0,0,0, date("m"),date("d"),date("Y"));
    echo strftime("Today is %m/%d/%Y",$today),".<br>";
    $tomorrow = mktime(0, 0, 0, date("m"),date("d")+1, date("Y"));
    echo strftime("Tomorrow is %A", $tomorrow),".<br>";
    $yesterday = mktime(0, 0, 0, date("m")   , date("d")-1, date("Y"));
    echo strftime("Yesterday was %A", $yesterday),".<br>";
    $nextmonth = mktime(0, 0, 0, date("m")+1, date("d"), date("Y"));
    echo strftime("Next month is  %B", $nextmonth),".<br>";
    $lastmonth = mktime(0, 0, 0, date("m")-1, date("d"), date("Y"));
    echo strftime("Last month was %B", $lastmonth),".<br>";
    $nextyear = mktime(0, 0, 0, date("m"), date("d"), date("Y")+1);
    echo strftime("Next year is  %Y", $nextyear),".<br>";
    $lastyear = mktime(0, 0, 0, date("m"), date("d"), date("Y")-1);
    echo strftime("Last year was  %Y", $lastyear),".<br>";
?>

</font>
</body>
</html>
```

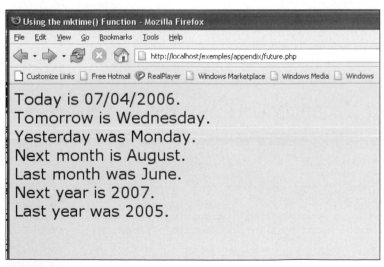

Figure C.2   Output from Example C.4.

C.2.3   Creating a UNIX Timestamp from a String

The `strtotime()` function returns a timestamp from a string consisting of any U.S. English-style date and time description. With an argument, it returns the timestamp relative to that time, and without an argument, it returns the timestamp for the current date and time. You can format the timestamp value returned from `strtotime()` with other PHP date functions such as `getdate()`, `strftime()`, and `date()`. (If the number of the year is specified in a two-digit format, values between 0 and 69 will become 2000 to 2069, and 80 to100 will become 1980 to 2000.)

FORMAT

```
int strtotime ( string time [, int now] )
```

Example:
```
echo strtotime("now"), "\n";
echo strtotime("10 September 2006"), "\n";
echo strtotime("+1 day"), "\n";
```

EXAMPLE C.5

```php
<?php
// Getting the timestamp from strings
echo strtotime("last month"), "\n";
echo strtotime("02 September 2006"), "\n";
echo strtotime("+2 days"), "\n";
echo strtotime("+1 week"), "\n";
echo strtotime("+1 week 2 days 4 hours 2 seconds"), "\n";
echo strtotime("next Thursday"), "\n";

// Using getdate() and strtotime()
$tomorrow=strtotime("+1 day"); // Convert string to timestamp
$tomorrow=getdate($tomorrow);  // Use timestamp to get readable date
echo "Tomorrow is $tomorrow[month]
$tomorrow[mday],$tomorrow[year].\n";

$next_week= strtotime("next week");
$next_week=getdate($next_week);
echo "I go on vacation next $next_week[weekday].\n";

// Using strftime() and strtotime()
echo "Last Monday was ", strftime("%m/%d/%y", strtotime(
   "last Monday")), ".\n";
echo "Last month was ", strftime("%B", strtotime("last month")),".\n";
echo "Next month is ", strftime("%B", strtotime("+1 month")),".\n";
?>
```

EXAMPLE   C.3 (CONTINUED)

```
(Output)
1150925115
1157180400
1153689915
1154121915
1154309117
1154588400
Tomorrow is July 22,2006.
I go on vacation next Friday.
Last Monday was 07/17/06.
Last month was June.
Next month is August.
```

C.3   Getting the Date and Time

The getdate() function (see Table C.5) returns an associative array containing date and time values for the local time, and if a timestamp is given as an argument, the date and time for that timestamp. The key or index of the associative array is a string representing the time and date value. This function can be used with mktime() or date() to retrieve dates and times.

FORMAT

```
array getdate ( [int timestamp] )
```

Example:
```
$now = getdate();  // Returns an associative array of date/time values
```

Table C.5   The getdate() Function Key-Value Pairs

Key	Value
seconds	Seconds, range 0 to 59
minutes	Minutes, range 0 to 59
hours	Hours, range 0 to 23
mday	Day of the month, range 1 to 31
wday	Day of the the week, range 0 (Sunday), through 6 (Saturday)
mon	A month, range 1 through 12

Table C.5 The `getdate()` Function Key–Value Pairs (continued)

Key	Value
year	A year in four-digit format, such as 1999 or 2006
yday	Day of the year, range 0 through 365
weekday	The day of the week, range Sunday through Saturday
month	The month, such as January or December
0	Seconds since the UNIX epoch, similar to the values returned by `time()` and used by `date()`

EXAMPLE C.6

```php
<?php
    $now = getdate();
    echo "<pre>";
    print_r($now);
    echo "</pre>";
?>

(Output)
Array
(
    [seconds] => 30
    [minutes] => 35
    [hours] => 6
    [mday] => 20
    [wday] => 4
    [mon] => 7
    [year] => 2006
    [yday] => 200
    [weekday] => Thursday
    [month] => July
    [0] => 1153402530
)
```

EXAMPLE C.7

```php
<?php
$date=mktime(0, 0, 0, 12, 25, 2006);  // Christmas 2006
$holiday=getdate($date);
print_r($holiday);
echo "$holiday[month] $holiday[mday], $holiday[year] is on a ",
    $holiday["weekday"], ".\n<br>";
?>
```

```
(Output)
Array
(
    [seconds] => 0
    [minutes] => 0
    [hours] => 0
    [mday] => 25
    [wday] => 1
    [mon] => 12
    [year] => 2006
    [yday] => 358
    [weekday] => Monday
    [month] => December
    [0] => 1167033600
)
December 25, 2006 is on a Monday.
```

C.3.1 Validating Dates

The checkdate() function checks whether the arguments it receives are valid date values. It returns TRUE if the date is valid, and FALSE if not. Valid date values are:

- The month must be between 1 and 12 inclusive.
- The day must be within the allowed number of days for the given month, and leap years are allowed.
- The year must be between 1 and 32767 inclusive.

FORMAT

```
bool checkdate ( int month, int day, int year )
```

Example:
```php
<?php
var_dump(checkdate(12, 31, 2000));  // Retuns true
var_dump(checkdate(2, 30, 2001));   // Returns false
?>
```

EXAMPLE C.8

```php
<?php
    echo "\nIs 12/31/2006 a valid date? ";
    var_dump(checkdate(12, 31, 2006));

    echo "\nIs 12/32/2006 a valid date? ";
    var_dump(checkdate(12,32, 2006));
    echo "Is this better? ";

    // Let mktime() adjust the date to the correct date
    echo date('m/d/Y', mktime(0,0,0, 12,32,2006)),"\n";

    echo "\nIs 2/29/2008 a leap year? ";
    var_dump(checkdate(2, 29, 2008));

    echo "\nIs 2/29/2006 a leap year? ";
    var_dump(checkdate(2, 29, 2006));
?>

(Output)
Is 12/31/2006 a valid date? bool(true)

Is 12/32/2006 a valid date? bool(false)
Is this better? 01/01/2007

Is 2/29/2008 a leap year? bool(true)

Is 2/29/2006 a leap year? bool(false)
```

appendix

D

Security and Debugging

D.1 About Security

Security is a set of measures applied to a Web application to meet the security requirements of the Web site. A site will never be 100 percent secure—there is always a way in. Just as there is always a thief who can break into bank vault, there is always a hacker who can break into your site.

To be secure, you must define your security requirements and how much you are willing to spend to meet them. In defining the security requirements of your site, there are several issues to consider: The security of your network, the operating system, the file system, the Web server your Web applications are running on, and, finally, the Web application itself and the database it is using. Because the focus of this book is on PHP and MySQL, we discuss the security of PHP scripts and the MySQL database as they relate to one another. The security of the network, operating system, file system, and Web server depend on specific vendors and are typically managed by your ISP or system administrator.

D.1.1 Network Security and SSL

Network security refers to securing the physical communication between the user of a Web application and the application itself. For example, you may go to a local Internet coffee shop while traveling and want to pay your bills online, so you go to your bank's Web site and type in your username and password. This information is highly sensitive, yet it travels over public lines that cannot be trusted. Most Web applications solve this problem by using an inexpensive system called Secure Sockets Layer (SSL). SSL is an encryption system that automatically creates a secure channel between the client's Web browser and Web server. For example, when you go to your online banking site, you will be redirected to a secure server shown in the address bar of your browser as an address starting with *https*, the protocol for SSL. The client and server do a hand-shake in which they generate a key to be used for encryption. This key is good for only this one session and it is disposable. Even if a hacker could break it, chances are it would take much longer than the time needed to pay your bills and log out!

To prepare a Web server for accepting HTTPS connections, the administrator must create a public key certificate for the Web server. You will need to purchase an SSL certificate from a trusted party. This certificate, usually good for one year at a time, certifies that you are who you say you are. There are a number of companies who sell SSL certificates, among them VeriSign, Thawte, and GoDaddy. Installing SSL is also dependent on the Web server you are using. Contact your ISP or your system administrator for help with setting up SSL. Once set up, there is nothing you need to change in your PHP/MySQL application. You just want ensure that all the links use the HTTPS protocol rather than the HTTP protocol.

D.1.2   Operating System, Web Server, and File System Security

Even before a hacker attacks your PHP application, he or she might try to exploit the weaknesses of your underlying infrastructure. Web servers are a common target for the attackers. Commonly used servers are Apache and Microsoft Internet Information Server. These Web servers are available to everyone and security holes are constantly being discovered and patched. Make sure you stay on top of security updates for your Web server. The same rule applies to the security of the operating system, regardless of whether you are using Windows, Linux, or Mac OS X. Additionally, it is good practice to run the Web server under its own system user. Then, even if someone breaks into your Web server, he or she cannot easily exploit the rest of your operating system. Create a user specific to the Web server. (On UNIX systems, this is already done and is commonly given a username of http or nobody.) Make sure that this new user has read/write access only to the file system directories where your PHP files are stored and not to the directories where you have system files (such as */etc/* on UNIX or *C:\Windows* on Windows). Also, make sure this user does not have access to your database files. The database server, MySQL, should also run under its own system username and have access only to its own files. By separating the Web server and the database server into their own system user accounts, you are creating multiple levels of safety. If one level is breached, the damage is limited to that component, not spread through the entire infrastructure.

D.2   Securing PHP and MySQL

Whereas the infrastructure components such as the operating system, Web server, and the network are created by someone else, the Web application itself is something that you wrote, so you have much more say in how secure it is. In this section we discuss securing PHP and MySQL scripts.

D.2.1 Basic PHP Security Principles

Validate Form Fields.   To ensure basic security in a PHP script that uses HTML forms, all the user input fields should be validated. For example, an application might have many forms consisting of fields to be filled in with contact information. If the fields are not validated before being processed, a smart hacker can inject unwanted information into those fields, causing unwanted behavior in the script. For example, if an e-mail address is not validated first, then instead of an e-mail address, an entire e-mail message could be inserted and later sent from your site as spam.

Validating user input is discussed in Chapter 12, "Regular Expressions and Pattern Matching."

About register_globals.   The `register_globals` directive in the `php.ini` file, if set to "On," converts all the data submitted from a form to PHP global variables. Because global variables might represent a major security risk, `register_globals` has been disabled, by default, since PHP 4.2.0. and it is recommended to keep it set to "Off" as shown in the following section from the `php.ini` file:

```
; You should do your best to write your scripts so that they do
 not require
; register_globals to be on;  Using form variables as globals could
an easily lead
; to possible security problems, if the code is not very well thought of.
register_globals = Off
```

The following example demonstrates how security can be undermined when `register_globals` is set to "On."

EXAMPLE D.1

```php
    <?php

1   if( $user_name=="admin" && $password=="guess" ) {
       $authorized=true;
    }

2   if ($authorized) {
       include ( "secret.php" );
    }

    ?>
```

EXPLANATION

1   The program checks to see if the user has entered a valid username and password. If so, `true` is assigned to the variable `$authorized`.

2   If the value of `$authorized` is set to `true`, the `secret.php` page is included.

   If the hacker knows how this program is written, he or she can bypass the authentication test by passing the value of the `$authorized` variable directly into the script via the URL line. Assuming this script is called `login.php`, a `?` is appended to to the address and `authorized` is set to 1:

```
http://localhost/login.php?authorized=1
```

   Then PHP would create a global variable called `$authorized` in the script with a value of 1, making the expression in line 2 always evaluate to `true` and include the file `secret.php` even if the user has not logged in.

If the `register_globals` directive in the `php.ini` file had been set to "Off," the values of `$user_name` and `$password` could then be explicitly tested as index values for the `$_REQUEST`/`$GET`/`$POST` superglobals, a small inconvenience to pay for security.

The next example demonstrates how to use the `$_REQUEST[]` superglobal array for checking user input.

EXAMPLE D.2

```php
    <?php

1   if( $_REQUEST['user_name']=="admin" &&
        $_REQUEST['password']=="guess" ) {
            $authorized=true;
    } else {
2       $authorized=false;
    }

    if ($authorized) {
        include ( "secret.php" );
    }

    ?>
```

EXPLANATION

1   The `$_REQUEST` array is used to retrieve the data from the form. If the `register_globals` directive is off, the user cannot directly set `$authorized` from the URL.

2   An added security precaution is to set the variable to `false` if the username and password do not match. Then even if `register_globals` is set to on and the culprit user specifies `$authorized=true`, the script resets it to `false` because the login information is incorrect.

In summary, with `register_globals` turned on, a user can overwrite and inject unwanted variables into your PHP script. From a security standpoint, it is much better to set register globals to off, and explicitly retrieve and validate everything passed into the script from a form. It is also good practice to initialize all variables (see line 2 in Example D.2) and then check the error logs for the use of uninitialized variables. We discuss error logs more at the end of this section.

SQL Injections.   A SQL injection is a technique that allows unwanted text to be placed into a SQL statement that will then be executed on the database server. In the following example, the culprit user fills a form field with unwanted parentheses, quotes, and text, which will then be used as part of a SQL INSERT statement and sent to the database.

EXAMPLE D.3

```php
<?php
$sql = "INSERT INTO users (username, password)
        "VALUES ('{$_REQUEST[username]}', '{$_REQUEST[password]}')";
?>
```

EXPLANATION

The username and password are coming in from a form and will be added to the SQL INSERT statement and entered into the "user" table of the database. The user can inject unwanted information into the database by entering a username such as:

```
mikey','secret'),('bob
```

and then entering a password for user "bob", such as "hello". So the final SQL will be:

```
INSERT INTO users (username, password)
VALUES ('mikey','secret'),('bob','hello')
```

Now the username and password for `mikey/secret` have been injected into the database.

SQL injection is a simple process, but requires that the culprit have some knowledge of the code within the Web application. This knowledge is easy to obtain if the application is open sourced (free for anyone to download and examine), or if your application is using third-party software.

The solution to inhibiting a SQL injection is to escape all quotes in the user input. This can be done automatically by enabling magic quotes in the `php.ini` file or explicitly by using the PHP built-in function `addslashes()`. See *http://www.spidynamics.com/papers/SQLInjectionWhitePaper.pdf* for a thorough discussion.

EXAMPLE D.4

```php
<?php
$username = addslashes( $_REQUEST[username] );
$password  = addslashes( $_REQUEST[password] );

$sql = "INSERT INTO users (username, password)
        "VALUES ('$username', '$password')";
?>
```

EXPLANATION

In this code, even if the user inputs:

```
mikey','secret'),('bob
```

for the username, the quotes will be escaped and the final SQL will look like:

```
INSERT INTO users (username, password)
VALUES ('mikey\',\'secret\'),(\'bob','hello')
```

In other words, the username will just be one long piece of text:

```
mikey\',\'secret\'),(\'bob
```

File Names.   Most Web sites use include files to include headers, footers, or database connection information for each page. The following example uses a `global.inc` file included at the beginning of every script requiring database connectivity.

EXAMPLE D.5

```php
<?php
    // This is the database_connect.inc file
    $db = mysql_connect( "localhost", "root", "secret" );
?>
```

The problem with naming a file with the .inc extension is that the Web server might not process .inc files as PHP scripts. In other words, if someone knew the name of this file, he or she could view the source code just by typing the address of the file in the URL. For example,

```
http://localhost/global.inc
```

would return, in most cases, the actual source code, thus revealing the username and password.

Although you can set your server to process .inc files as PHP files, it is better to add the .php extension to your include files; for example, `global.inc` would become `global.inc.php`. By doing this, even if you install your Web application on another server, the source code of the include file cannot be viewed in the browser.

Safe Mode. PHP offers a configuration directive called `safe_mode` to help secure your PHP environment. However, you will quickly realize that many things that should be allowed for your application to function properly are disabled with this directive. As a better alternative you should consider exactly which features should be allowed and which should not. To do this, look at the directives `disabled_functions` and `disabled_classes` in the `php.ini` file. The functions your script should never be able to execute can be listed here.

For example, the following line denies access to the underlying operating system, a good idea:

```
disable_functions = exec, passthru, proc_open, shell_exec, system
```

The File System. Another useful directive in the `php.ini` file is `open_basedir`. When set, it limits what directories and subdirectories PHP can access. For example, you might have a folder called *C:\Webroot* that contains all your public PHP scripts. If you set

```
open_basedir=C:\Webroot\
```

PHP could open files only within this folder. If you had another folder where you keep all your database files, such as *C:\MySQL\Data*, PHP would not have direct access to that folder, preventing the files from being exploited by a potential hacker, and any raw data files residing outside the `open_basedir` directory could not be downloaded either.

Log Everything. A good rule of thumb is to log everything. There will always be security holes you did not think about, and if someone exploited them, the log files will give you clues as to what happened. PHP 5 offers configuration directives you can set to ensure everything you want logged is logged. You can set these directives either in the `php.ini` file or by using the `ini_set()` function in your script.

error_reporting

This directive specifies what is going to be logged. There are multiple settings you can use (see Table D.1). You can combine the settings with the & character or exclude certain options with the ~ character.

Table D.1 Error Reporting Settings

Setting	What It Reports
E_ALL	All errors and warnings (does not include E_STRICT).
E_ERROR	Fatal runtime errors.
E_WARNING	Runtime warnings (nonfatal errors).
E_PARSE	Compile-time parse errors.

Table D.1 Error Reporting Settings (continued)

Setting	What It Reports
E_NOTICE	Runtime notices. These are warnings that often result from a bug in your code, but it is possible that it was intentional; for example, using an uninitialized variable and relying on the fact it is automatically initialized to an empty string.
E_STRICT	Runtime notices. Enable to have PHP suggest changes to your code that will ensure the best interoperability and forward compatibility of your code.
E_CORE_ERROR	Fatal errors that occur during PHP's initial startup.
E_CORE_WARNING	Warnings (nonfatal errors) that occur during PHP's initial startup.
E_COMPILE_ERROR	Fatal compile-time errors.
E_COMPILE_WARNING	Compile-time warnings (nonfatal errors).
E_USER_ERROR	User-generated error message.
E_USER_WARNING	User-generated warning message.
E_USER_NOTICE	User-generated notice message.

Here are some examples:

```
- Show all errors, except for notices and coding standards warnings
error_reporting = E_ALL & ~E_NOTICE & ~E_STRICT

- Show all errors, except for notices
error_reporting = E_ALL & ~E_NOTICE
```

If you set error reporting to E_ALL, you will get all the errors, warning, notices, and so on—often an overwhelming amount of data. Try to fine-tune this directive to meet your particular needs. The data will be logged into the Web server specified log file.

display_errors

This directive is either on or off. If set to on, errors will be displayed in the browser as well as logged. This is what you want while you are developing the application. Once you are happy with how it is working, you can turn this feature off so that your users and potential hackers do not see the error messages.

log_errors and error_log

These two directives set whether the errors are to be logged and where the log file is located. You want errors logged and you want to know where this file is to locate any suspicious activity and debugging clues. This file should be monitored in the early stages of application development as it can quickly become quite large.

Where to Get More Security Information.   Security is a huge topic and requires being educated and staying on top of the trends. The PHP Security Consortium states:

> Founded in January 2005, the PHP Security Consortium (PHPSC) is an international group of PHP experts dedicated to promoting secure programming practices within the PHP community. Members of the PHPSC seek to educate PHP developers about security through a variety of resources, including documentation, tools, and standards.

Visit their Web site at *http://phpsec.org/*.

D.3   Debugging

No program is ever perfect and you will probably be fixing bugs more than writing the original code. Debugging code is part art and part science. Over time, you will get much better at spotting errors and fixing them. The key is to not get frustrated with errors. There will always be stress-producing bugs in your programs. This section outlines some helpful techniques proven successful in the real world for debugging PHP and MySQL code.

D.3.1   Turn on the Error Reporting

How can we know what the problem is if we cannot see the actual error message? To turn on all the error reporting, set `display_error` to `On` and `error_reporting` to `E_ALL` in the `php.ini` initialization file.

```
display_errors = On
```

and

```
error_reporting  =  E_ALL
```

When your application goes to production, the bugs should have been worked out, at which time you should turn error reporting off.

D.3.2   Fix the Parse Errors First

Parse errors are the most common and easiest errors to fix. They are caused when the PHP scans over your program code, and you have broken the PHP grammar rules, called the syntax. Common causes are unescaped quotes (using the operator), missing semicolons (every instruction of PHP code, with few exceptions, must end with a semicolon), and missing parentheses and curly brackets. Breaking these syntax rules will cause your program to terminate with a message, which is sometimes hard to understand, but like anything else, after you have made the same error enough times, you will know what you did wrong.

The PHP interpreter will report parse errors during the execution. It attempts to tell us what to look for and where.

EXAMPLE D.6

```
     <?php
1        $welcome_message = "Hello there, what a nice day!';
2        print $welcome_message;
     ?>
```

EXPLANATION

When this program is executed (assume this is saved in file called `welcome.php`), PHP produces the following error message:

`Parse error: syntax error, unexpected $end in welcome.php on line 7`

Although the error messages look strange at first glance, they are very informative and relatively simple to understand. This error is basically telling us that there is a problem on line 7 or above in our code and that it reached the unexpected end.

So you would want to look at this line 7 first. But what if there is no line 7; there are only six lines in the code? PHP was expecting a certain type of syntax and reached the end of the script without finding it. In a case like this, it is best to look at the lines preceding line 7 and try to find the error, such as unmatched brackets, unclosed quotes, or a missing semicolon. Because this is a very simple script, the problem is found on line 1, where the string has not been properly terminated. We started the string `$welcome_message` with a double quote but have terminated it with a single quote. (As you might recall, a single quote is matched with another single quote, and a double quote is matched with another double quote.)

In general, the parse error is a hint as to where PHP noticed that something was wrong with the syntax, and after some time, you will be able to pinpoint the errors more quickly. To help you, you can use a color-coding editor when writing PHP scripts. The code will show up in different colors depending on what you are doing. For example, if my strings are in red and commands in green, and I have forgotten to close a string, all the rest of my code will be in red. This color coding provided by the editors makes it much easier to spot errors. For some free editors, see *http://codepunk.hardwar.org.uk/editors.htm*.

D.3.3 Diagnostic Print Statements

Parse errors are errors that can be determined before the program even runs because they are caused by syntactically invalid code. On the other hand, there are errors that can happen only at runtime. This is because these errors depend on the data fed into the application and cannot be easily predetermined.

Say, for example, we wrote the program shown in Example D.7 to print out all the Fibonacci numbers smaller than 1,000. (Recall that the Fibonacci numbers are 0, 1, 1, 2, 3, 5, 8, 13, ... in which the last two numbers are added to get the next.)

EXAMPLE D.7

```php
<?php

    $a=0;
    $b=1;
    print "$a - $b - ";
    while( $fib<1000 ) {
        $fib=$a+$b;
        print "$fib  -  ";
        $a=$b;
        $b=$fib;

    }
?>
```

With this program, we get the following output:

```
0 - 1 - 1 - 2 - 3 - 5 - 8 - 13 - 21 - 34 - 55 - 89 - 144 - 233 - 377 -
610 - 987 - 1597 -
```

However, we are not convinced this is working well and not sure how the calculation went. We could add a diagnostic print statement to see what is going on.

EXAMPLE D.8

```php
<?php
    $a=0;
    $b=1;
    print "$a - $b - ";
    while( $fib<1000 ) {
        $fib=$a+$b;
        print "$fib  -  ";
    print "[$b + $a = $fib]<br>";
        $a=$b;
        $b=$fib;

    }
?>
```

Notice that the diagnostic print statement is in bold text and is not indented with the rest of the code. This makes it make it easier to find and remove the line later when it is no longer needed. By adding the print statement, it is easier to see how the numbers were calculated and to validate that the script is working properly. The following output is produced:

```
0 - 1 - 1 - [1 + 0 = 1]
2 - [1 + 1 = 2]
3 - [2 + 1 = 3]
5 - [3 + 2 = 5]
8 - [5 + 3 = 8]
13 - [8 + 5 = 13]
21 - [13 + 8 = 21]
34 - [21 + 13 = 34]
55 - [34 + 21 = 55]
89 - [55 + 34 = 89]
144 - [89 + 55 = 144]
233 - [144 + 89 = 233]
377 - [233 + 144 = 377]
610 - [377 + 233 = 610]
987 - [610 + 377 = 987]
1597 - [987 + 610 = 1597]
```

Here is another example of how to find some hard-to-spot errors.

EXAMPLE D.9

```php
<?php
    $dice1 = rand(1,6);
    $dice2 = rand(1,6);
    $total = $dice1 + $dice2;

    if( $total=7 || $total=11 ) {
        print "You win!";
    } else {
        print "Better luck next time!";
    }
?>
```

Example D.9 is a craps game script. It simulates the rolling of two dice. The game is won if the sum of the two dice rolls is 7 or 11.

The way this script is written, there is always a winning roll of the dice. There is obviously a problem with the script. To figure out what is going on, create a diagnostic print statement to demonstrate what is going on, as shown in Example D.10.

EXAMPLE D.10

```php
<?php
    $dice1 = rand(1,6);
    $dice2 = rand(1,6);
    $total = $dice1 + $dice2;

print "[You rolled $dice1 and $dice2 for total of $total]<br>";

    if( $total=7 || $total=11 ) {
       print "You win!";
    } else {
       print "Better luck next time!";
    }
?>


(Output)
[You rolled 4 and 5 for total of 9]
You win!
```

The diagnostic print line will print out the actual dice rolls. It is obvious that rolling 4 and 5 produces the total of 9, but that should not cause the program to print "You win!". There is a problem in the code.

Because the sum of the two die is correct, the next place to look for a problem is in the conditional `if` statement. Our strategy here is to go top-to-bottom and validate the execution of the code by printing out what is going on internally. By checking the expression in the `if` statement, a classic problem should come to light, and that is the improper use of the equal sign. Instead of a single sign, the expression should use the double equal sign, `==`. Remember, the single equal sign is used to assign a value, whereas the double equal sign is use to compare the equality of two values. The conditional expression should be:

```php
if( $total==7 || $total==11 ) {
```

The script now works properly. Sometimes we win and more often we lose. Now the diagnostic print statement can be removed.

D.3.4 Fixing SQL Errors

SQL errors are also quite common. They are reported by the MySQL database. Although your PHP code might be fine, the query you are sending to the database might not be properly formatted. Let's look at Example D.11.

EXAMPLE D.11

```php
<?php
    mysql_connect( "localhost", "test", "" );

    mysql_query("INSERT INTO users (username, password, email)".
                "VALUES ('marko','password')";
?>
```

This is program has valid PHP code, but it is making some assumptions. The first one is that the database connection is going to work. This might fail for many of the reasons in and outside of our control: The database is offline, the server is unreachable, someone might have changed the login and password for the database, and so on. However, we never check this in the program.

The second assumption is that the SQL query is valid. Let's look at it:

```
INSERT INTO users (username, password, email)
VALUES ('marko','password');
```

If you look at it carefully, you will notice that the number of parameters (three) does not match the number of values (two). This error might be hard to find. One way to deal with SQL errors is to always keep SQL statements in a separate variable, and print out the error message in case things go wrong.

EXAMPLE D.12

```php
<?php
    mysql_connect( "localhost", "test", "" ) or die( mysql_error() );

    $sql = "INSERT INTO users (username, password, email)".
           "VALUES ('marko','password')";
    print $sql;

    mysql_query( $sql ) or die( mysql_error() );
?>
```

First, notice the use of the `die()` statement in Example D.12. This is a PHP error-handling mechanism. When an error occurs in the statement to its immediate left, the `die` statement prints out its string argument and the program exits. In this example the argument is the return value of the `mysql_error()` function, a function that sends the last error generated by the MySQL database server. By combining PHP's `die` statement and the returned error message from the MySQL database, the MySQL error is displayed when the program dies.

The next diagnostic tool is to create a separate variable to hold the SQL statement that will be sent to the database. In that way, you can print the value of the variable, in this case $sql, and see what will be sent to the database before actually sending it. If the SQL statement is very complex, you can copy and paste it from the failing script directly into the MySQL client and debug it there. Often, it is easier to debug SQL statements using the MySQL client rather then doing it from the PHP script because you are working directly with the database and the MySQL libraries rather than going to it indirectly through PHP first where some of the error messages might get lost in translation. Once you fix the SQL error, you can then update the PHP script.

D.3.5 More on Debugging

There are a number of excellent resources where you can find more information on how to debug PHP programs. If you find yourself consuming hours trying to debug your program, you might get additional insight from the following Web sites:

http://www.developer.com/lang/php/article.php/1472701

http://www-128.ibm.com/developerworks/library/os-debug/

http://www.webmasterstop.com/19.html

http://www.phpbuilder.com/columns/oier20010406.php3

appendix

E

Installation Procedures

E.1 About Web Servers

Before you set up PHP and MySQL, make sure you have a Web server available on your computer. Most modern operating systems ship with a built-in Web server. Windows comes with either Internet Information Services (IIS) or Personal Web Server, depending on the version. Mac OS X and other UNIX platforms ship with the Apache Web server.

To test that your computer is set up with a Web server and that it is running, point your browser to *http://localhost/*. You should get a welcome page or a list of files. If you get an error message that the server cannot be found, your computer either does not have a Web server or it is not running.

In Windows, you can start IIS by locating it in Control Panel -> Administrative Tools -> Servers. It is usually the very last service in the list: Worldwide Web Publishing Service. Make sure it is started.

In Mac OS X, go to the System Properties and choose Sharing. Make sure that Personal Web Sharing is turned on.

If you do not have a Web server, you can always download Apache, the world's most popular Web server, from *http://apache.org/*. The rest of this document focuses on Apache Web server.

E.2 Installing Apache on Windows

Download the Apache Web server from *http://httpd.apache.org/download.cgi*. Choose the Win32 Binary with MSI Installer. This installer will guide you through the installation process and, for the most part, you should accept the default options.

Once Apache is installed, you can configure it by opening the `httpd.conf` file located in the *conf* directory where you installed Apache.

The first thing you might want to change in this file is where the Web server looks for the Web documents on your file system. To update this, look up the `DocumentRoot` parameter in the `httpd.conf` file and change it to your desired location, for example:

```
DocumentRoot "C:/wwwroot"
```

Notice that Apache uses the forward slashes even on Windows. Next, you need to give Apache permissions to view the files in that directory. To do that, modify the `<Directory>` directive to point from the old `DocumentRoot` to the new one. Once finished, you should have something like this:

```
<Directory "C:/wwwroot">
    Options Indexes FollowSymLinks
    AllowOverride None
    Order allow,deny
    Allow from all
</Directory>
```

Any time you make a change to the configuration file, you must restart Apache for the changes to take effect because Apache reads its configuration file only at startup. To restart Apache, go to the Start menu and open Control Panel. In Control Panel, go to Administrative Tools and choose Services. Apache is most likely set up as a service on Windows. Locate it in the list of services, select it, and choose Restart.

If everything starts fine, you should be able to now point your browser to *http://localhost/* and get a list of files in that directory.

If Apache fails to start, you probably have a syntax error in the `httpd.conf` configuration file. To get a hint about what is wrong, open up the Event Viewer from Control Panel -> Administrative Tools. You should be able to view the error messages in this screen and get a hint about what went wrong.

E.3 Installing PHP on Windows

PHP can be downloaded from *www.php.net* and it typically comes in two different packages: the installer application and a ZIP file. Although the installer is much easier to use and a smaller file to download, it typically does not provide most of the extensions that are needed.

In this section, we go over the manual installation on Windows. Go to *http://www.php.net/downloads.php* and download the ZIP package under the Windows Binaries section. Once you download this, extract the ZIP archive into the folder *C:\php*, and follow these instructions:

1. Copy the file *C:\php\php5ts.dll* into the *C:\Windows\System32* directory.
2. Copy the file *C:\php\php5apache2.dll* into the *C:\Windows\System32* directory.
3. Copy *C:\php\ext\php_mysql.dll* into the *C:\Windows\System32* directory.

4. Copy *C:\php\libmysql.dll* into the *C:\Windows\System32* directory.
5. Copy *C:\php\php.ini-dist* into the *C:\Windows* directory and rename it into `php.ini`.

This will ensure that the libraries necessary for PHP to work are where Windows can find them.

For detailed information, visit *http://www.php.net/manual/en/install.windows.php*.

E.4   Installing PHP on Linux/UNIX

Linux and UNIX systems differ greatly from distribution to distribution. These are the general installation instructions, but you might have to modify them for your particular system.

For the manual installation, download the latest source file from *http://php.net/downloads/*. PHP for Linux is downloaded in source format and needs to be compiled. To do so, you will need certain tools, commonly available on all UNIX/Linux platforms. You will also need root access to set up PHP and Apache to work with each other.

For detailed information, visit *http://www.php.net/manual/en/install.unix.php*.

E.5   Installing PHP on Mac OS X

Mac OS X comes preconfigured with the Apache Web server. Download the PHP 5 binary for Apache 1.3, which is the version that ships with OS X. Follow the installation instructions, and PHP will be installed. You will have to restart your Apache Web server. To do this, open System Preferences, and under Sharing, turn on the Personal Web Sharing.

You can now put your files in the Sites folder under your Home folder and access them by going to *http://localhost/~your_user_name/*.

For more details see *http://www.entropy.ch/software/macosx/php/* and *http://www.php.net/manual/en/install.macosx.php*.

E.6   Configuring Apache to use PHP Module (All Platforms)

PHP can be installed both as a CGI script and as an Apache module. It is preferred that you install it as a module as it will run much faster and require less memory.

To install the PHP module for Apache, you need to insert the following two lines in the Apache `httpd.conf` configuration file. The `httpd.conf` file is under the the *conf* directory where you installed Apache on Windows, or in the */etc/* directory on Mac OS X.

```
# For PHP 5 do something like this:
LoadModule php5_module "c:/php/php5apache2.dll"
```

```
AddType application/x-httpd-php .php

# configure the path to php.ini
PHPIniDir "C:/Windows"
```

Make sure you have the paths set up properly for your setup.

E.6.1   Testing PHP and Apache Installation

To see if everything is working properly, create a simple PHP script that will call the phpinfo() function:

```
<?php
phpinfo();
?>
```

When you open this page in the browser, it should display all the variables from the php.ini file and the system information, as shown in Figure E.1.

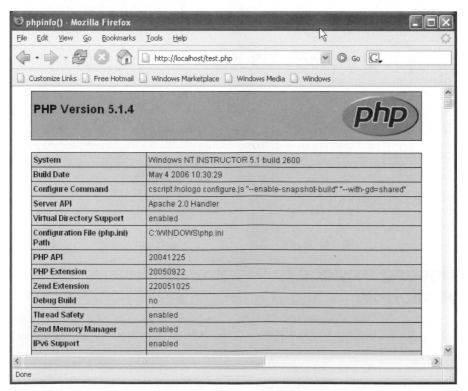

Figure E.1   The php.ini settings and system information.

E.7 Configuring php.ini (All Platforms)

Everything about the behavior of your PHP environment is set up in the file `php.ini`. On the Windows system, this file is usually located in the *C:\Windows* directory. On Mac OS X and other UNIX-based platforms, this file is in the */etc/* directory.

You can edit this file directly with an editor such as Notepad on Windows or TextEdit on Mac OS X and `vi` or `emacs` on most UNIX platforms.

If you modify the `php.ini` file with an editor, you will notice that it is just a text file consisting of `name=value` lines, also known as name–value pairs. Lines that start with a semicolon are comments and are ignored by the system.

To change the behavior of your PHP environment, simply change the appropriate value in the `php.ini` file. Table E.1 lists some of the more common configuration options.

Note that MySQL extensions are disabled in PHP 5 by default. To enable them, you must uncomment the line `extension=php_mysql.dll` in the `php.ini` file by removing the leading semicolon.

Table E.1 `php.ini` Configuration Options

Option	Explanation
`short_open_tag`	If this is on, you can use a short tag to indicate the beginning of a PHP code `<?` instead of a default open tag `<?php`. This feature is usually on.
`asp_tags`	It this is on, you can use ASP-style tags `<%` and `%>`. Unless you just cannot change your habits from ASP, it is recommend you not use this feature as it just generates confusion.
`error_reporting`	Specifies the level of error reporting on this server. There are various options: `E_ALL` means all errors are reported, `E_ERROR` is just for the fatal errors, and `E_NOTICE` is for runtime notices. You can combine and negate certain errors. For example, `E_ALL & ~E_NOTICE` means report all errors and do not report runtime notices. This is the default setting. For other options, see the `php.ini` file.
`display_errors`	This option lets you turn error reporting on or off. For example, while you are developing your Web site, you typically want to see all the errors but once your Web site is live, you do not want your customers to see the error messages.
`register_globals`	PHP can optionally create variables for all the form data that was submitted. This is a nice time-saving feature of the language and many programmers love it. However, there are certain security issues with this feature and newer versions of PHP ship with this option turned off by default. You should try to write your code so it does not depend on `register_globals` being on.
`magic_quotes_gpc`	Another security feature of PHP to prevent users from submitting code that attacks your database, PHP can "escape" dangerous characters and sanitize the user input. This feature is on by default.

Table E.1   `php.ini` Configuration Options (continued)

Option	Explanation
`extension_dir`	Sometimes you might have to update this setting, but basically it points to the place where your PHP extensions are located.
`SMTP`	Specifies the SMTP server that PHP uses to send e-mail out. Default is localhost and it will work on most UNIX systems. For Windows systems, you might have to contact your ISP to find out what SMTP you can use.

E.8   Installing MySQL on Windows

For the most part, MySQL installation is a straightforward process. You need to download the latest MySQL server binary by going to *http://dev.mysql.com/downloads/mysql/5.0.html* and selecting the Windows (x86) version for Windows, or Standard version for Mac OS X.

Both of these installations will guide you through the setup process. For the most part, you simply need to agree to the default settings. When prompted to specify a password for the superuser, aslo known as root user, select the word "password" because our art gallery example assumes that root's password is the word "password".

E.9   Installing MySQL on Linux/UNIX

For Linux platforms, the MySQL Server is provided as an RPM package. Most Linux platforms will have an RPM package manager provided for installation of this package.

Detailed Linux installation instructions can be found at *http://dev.mysql.com/doc/refman/5.0/en/linux-rpm.html*.

E.10 Installing MySQL on Mac OS X

To install MySQL Server on Mac OS X, please visit *http://dev.mysql.com/doc/refman/5.0/en/mac-os-x-installation.html*.

E.11 Read the Manual

The installation instructions change from version to version. If you run into problems, please read the manual that comes with the download archive. Configuration settings that were turned on in the past, might now be turned off, and although the directory structure might change, the manual is usually up to date.

Look for a file called README or INSTALL. They are usually text files and contain all the installation details.

Index

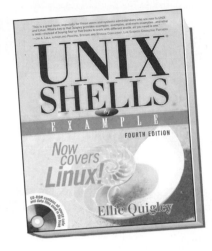

informIT

Safari
BOOKS ONLINE
ENABLED

THIS BOOK IS SAFARI ENABLED

INCLUDES FREE 45-DAY ACCESS TO THE ONLINE EDITION

The Safari® Enabled icon on the cover of your favorite technology book means the book is available through Safari Bookshelf. When you buy this book, you get free access to the online edition for 45 days.

Safari Bookshelf is an electronic reference library that lets you easily search thousands of technical books, find code samples, download chapters, and access technical information whenever and wherever you need it.

TO GAIN 45-DAY SAFARI ENABLED ACCESS TO THIS BOOK:

- Go to **http://www.prenhallprofessional.com/safarienabled**

- Complete the brief registration form

- Enter the coupon code found in the front of this book on the "Copyright" page

If you have difficulty registering on Safari Bookshelf or accessing the online edition, please e-mail customer-service@safaribooksonline.com.

PRENTICE
HALL

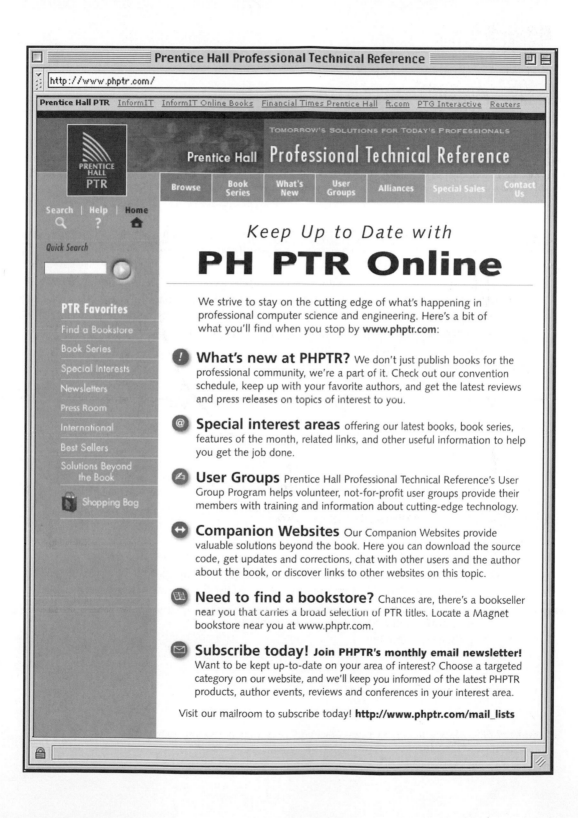

CD-ROM Warranty

Prentice Hall PTR warrants the enclosed CD-ROM to be free of defects in materials and faulty workmanship under normal use for a period of ninety days after purchase (when purchased new). If a defect is discovered in the CD-ROM during this warranty period, a replacement CD-ROM can be obtained at no charge by sending the defective CD-ROM, postage prepaid, with proof of purchase to:

Disc Exchange
Pearson Technology Group
75 Arlington Street, Suite 300
Boston, MA 02116
Email: AWPro@aw.com

Prentice Hall PTR makes no warranty or representation, either expressed or implied, with respect to this software, its quality, performance, merchantability, or fitness for a particular purpose. In no event will Prentice Hall, its distributors, or dealers be liable for direct, indirect, special, incidental, or consequential damages arising out of the use or inability to use the software. The exclusion of implied warranties is not permitted in some states. Therefore, the above exclusion may not apply to you. This warranty provides you with specific legal rights. There may be other rights that you may have that vary from state to state. The contents of this CD-ROM are intended for personal use only.

More information and updates are available at:
http://www.phptr.com/